4/21/04
5/12/04

ALSO BY BRENDA WINEAPPLE

Genêt: A Biography of Janet Flanner

Sister Brother: Gertrude and Leo Stein

Hawthorne

HAWTHORNE

A LIFE

———

Brenda Wineapple

Alfred A. Knopf NEW YORK

2003

THIS IS A BORZOI BOOK
PUBLISHED BY ALFRED A. KNOPF

Grateful acknowledgment is made to Farrar, Straus and Giroux, LLC
for permission to reprint an excerpt from the poem
"Question of Travel" from *The Complete Poems:
1927–1979* by Elizabeth Bishop. Copyright © 1979, 1983
by Alice Helen Methfessel. Reprinted by permission of Farrar,
Straus and Giroux, LLC.

Library of Congress Cataloging-in-Publication Data

Wineapple, Brenda.
Hawthorne : a life / Brenda Wineapple.—1st ed.
p.   cm.
ISBN 0-375-40044-3 (alk. paper)
1. Hawthorne, Nathaniel, 1804–1864.   2. Novelists, American—
19th century—Biography.   I. Title.

PS1881 .W53 2003
813'.3—dc21

[B]   2002192485

Manufactured in the United States of America
First Edition

For Michael Dellaira

Contents

Illustrations

Hawthorne

CHAPTER ONE

The Prison Door—Introductory

*The wrong-doing of one generation lives into the successive ones,
and, divesting itself of every temporary advantage, becomes a
pure and uncontrollable mischief.*

Nathaniel Hawthorne, *The House of the Seven Gables*

*And to make an end is to make a beginning.
The end is where we start from.*

T. S. Eliot, "Little Gidding"

But the past was not dead.

Nathaniel Hawthorne, "The Custom-House"

G UILTY. He heard the verdict and flinched. The second-born child of
the very famous author had been convicted of defrauding the public,
a violation of section 215 of the United States Criminal Code, in the matter of the Hawthorne Silver and Iron Mines, Ltd., Julian Hawthorne, president. Julian's father had written obsessively of crime and punishment and
the sins of fathers visited on sons, and here he was, the son, sixty-six years
old, hair white as sugar, well known, respected, and guilty—guilty—sitting
in a New York City courtroom, sporting a scarlet tie.

Judge Mayer banged his gavel. Staring straight ahead, Julian frowned
slightly as befitted a man of his stature and his shame. He, Nathaniel
Hawthorne's son, would be imprisoned a year and a day in the United
States federal penitentiary in Atlanta, his term set to run from November
25, 1912, the day the public trial began.

Likely his personal trials began much earlier. The great name of
Nathaniel Hawthorne will "always handicap you more or less," poet James

3

Russell Lowell had warned. "To be the son of a man of genius is at best to be born to a heritage of invidious comparisons," Henry James Jr. had acknowledged—and placed the Atlantic Ocean between himself and his philosopher father. At least the younger James wrote fiction, which the elder James did not; comparisons are especially invidious when the son plies the father's trade, as Julian did.

But it was even more than that. Nathaniel and Sophia Hawthorne's children seemed to spring from one of Hawthorne's tales, incarnating their father's paradoxes writ large. "To plant a family!" Hawthorne had written. "This idea is at the bottom of most of the wrong and mischief which men do." It was as if the past always lay in wait, just around the bend. The fortunes of each Hawthorne child uncannily bore out what Hawthorne considered a curse of guilt and grief, of somberness and what we today call depression, as well as talent, penury, pluck, and fortitude, all stitched together in a bright pattern, like Hester Prynne's letter "A."

Hawthorne's firstborn, a daughter, descended directly from literature. Christened Una after Spenser's heroine in *The Faerie Queene,* she served as the model for Pearl, the precocious child in *The Scarlet Letter,* and many observers noticed her resemblance to her literary father. Like him, she was handsome, tall, exacting, and remote. "The more I feel the more it seems a necessity to be reserved," said Una at fifteen. Una had worshipped sorrow, said her mother, since the age of six. "It was impossible she should ever be happy," remarked a friend. The sky was too blue, the sun too blazing, her own feelings too hard to bear. She died mysteriously at the age of thirty-three.

Rose Hawthorne, the youngest Hawthorne child, fared better—eventually. After the death of both her parents, a horrible marriage, a feud with her siblings, and the early loss of her only child to diphtheria, Rose fulfilled the unspoken mission of one of the characters in Hawthorne's novel *The Marble Faun:* she takes communion. As a self-ordained Sister of Mercy, Rose consecrated herself to the poor and the sick, and at the age of forty-four, in 1896, established the charitable organization Sister Rose's Free Home (after St. Rose of Lima) to care for indigent cancer patients. In 1899 she received the Holy Habit of the Third Order of St. Dominic, and two years later, in 1901, the home was incorporated as the Servants of Relief for Incurable Cancer, still extant today in Hawthorne, New York.

Then there was Julian, in the middle. On Easter Sunday, 1913, he was transported to the federal penitentiary in Atlanta. The formal charge against him and his cronies was misuse of the United States Postal Service, a catchall complaint designed to nail the defendants, whose real offense, according to Judge Mayer, wasn't selling shares in a worthless silver and iron mine so much as the exploitation of their recognizable names. "Theirs is the greater crime," spat the New York district attorney, "for they have prostituted them." The general counsel for the Hawthorne mines, former mayor of Boston Josiah Quincy, was cleared of the one conspiracy count against him, but the neurologist Dr. William J. Morton, whose father had discovered ether just before the Civil War, went to jail with Julian.

Julian held his head up high. His conviction disgraced neither him nor his name, he said, just the sleazy people who wished to see him—for some inexplicable reason—go to prison. What else could he say? After his sentencing, he briskly strode from the courtroom into the marshal's office and with remarkable sangfroid pulled out a small cigarette case, which he pushed toward Morton and the fourth accomplice, Alfred Freeman, a petty swindler without a fancy name. Morton stood paralyzed. Freeman circled the room. Hawthorne pocketed his case and shook the hand of a sympathetic well-wisher. "In such extremities," he later noted, "a man's manhood and dignity come to his support."

But when the deputy marshal clicked a pair of steel handcuffs round his wrist, Julian blinked in disbelief and with some confusion walked through the slanting rain to the city jail, a place familiarly known, à la Hawthorne, as the Tombs. "I was sure we should be acquitted," he muttered.

Yet by and large the only son of America's most esteemed novelist maintained a transcendental faith in his own innocence, a trait that linked him more to his tender, doting mother than to his morally particular father, who spent a lifetime probing motives, his own most of all. An epicure of intent, Hawthorne knew what the heart held in thrall. "It is a very common thing," he wrote near the end of his life, "—this fact of a man's being caught and made prisoner by himself." But Julian knew what he was doing when he exploited the Hawthorne name, which he plainly saw as false. *Nathaniel Hawthorne:* to the public it conjured American probity and success; to Julian it was fraudulent, overblown, hollow at the core.

Dissimulation was the keystone of Julian's career. And inadvertent parody of his father. Nathaniel Hawthorne's writing life was short and well crafted; Julian's, an interminable flood: hundreds of second-rate novels and poems, stories, histories, travel books, reminiscences, essays, even a two-volume biography of his parents, all capitalizing on the eminent patronymic. (With spooky foresight, his father once said of Julian that "his tendencies . . . seem to be rather towards breadth than elevation.") In

1908, when Julian abandoned literature for geology, as the president of the Hawthorne Silver and Iron Mines, Ltd., he managed to write hundreds of promotional letters as well as several promotional books. His energy was amazing.

If his father obeyed the Muse, Julian served Mammon. On selling his first short story, he thought, "Why not go on adding to my income in this way from time to time?" It seemed easy enough. "I think we take ourselves too seriously," he said of his fellow novelists, and at his death was credited as one of the first American writers to make literature "a bread-and-butter calling." When Henry James published his incisive study of Hawthorne, Julian confided to his diary that James deserved success "better than I do, not only because his work is better than mine, but because he takes more pains to make it so." In public, however, Julian protected himself from James and, more importantly, from his father's literary scruples. "I cannot sufficiently admire the pains we are at to make our work . . . immaculate in form," he declared. Aesthetic niceties are effeminate. Success is a racket.

Broad-chested and handsome—like his father—and with the same high coloring and dark wavy hair, Julian was born "to have ample means," declared his adoring mother. Friends thought she overpraised him, and that his father hadn't praised him enough. Whatever had happened, Julian combined his father's cynicism with his mother's ebullience. He loved women (though he was no feminist), tailored clothes, abundance, and a good scam. Hawthorne dryly assessed his son's character; he ought to join a ministry, he said.

Julian floundered at Harvard, quitting just months after his father's death, his interests inclining more to sport than study. He floundered at the Lawrence Scientific School and at the Realschule in Dresden, where he proposed to study civil engineering with a view toward knocking together a huge fortune in the American West. This plan also went awry. Unlike his father, who had delayed his marriage to Sophia, Julian married at the age of twenty-four and sired ten children, eight of whom survived. But he never had enough, kept enough, saved enough, planned enough.

His insouciance exasperated Rose. That he wouldn't accept a pardon unless William Morton also received one was yet another instance of his irresponsibility, she told his family. "But he is he, so to speak," she said, throwing her hands up. Still, Rose mounted a loyal defense. "I know that he really believed in the mines," she reportedly told Joseph P. Tumulty, Woodrow Wilson's secretary. To Julian, however, she starchily observed, "I am consoled about your personal trials by knowing that you have always adapted yourself to deprivations with the unconcern—or, rather, the manly vigor of one of your remote ancestors."

Coming from Rose, it was an equivocal compliment. She knew their Puritan ancestors whipped, scorched, hanged, and banished women such as herself for views far less heretical than hers. Julian too had disapproved of her vocation, though more amiably than their ancestors would have. After her death, he remembered Rose as a headstrong girl prone to egregious errors of judgment. Her errand in Washington, D.C., on his behalf, was one of these. On April 3, 1913, Mother Alphonsa, as Rose was known, traveled by train to the nation's capital to ask President Wilson to pardon her brother.

"What had I to do with 'pardons'?" Julian was furious. "Pardon for what?" But Rose was determined to restore luster to the Hawthorne name. A band of white cloth pleated across her forehead and stern black robes sweeping about her ample figure, she was every bit as fierce as Hester Prynne and probably just as nervous when she boarded a humid trolley for the White House. Tumulty received her. Strangely affected by the pink-cheeked woman in black and white, he ignored protocol and sent her request directly to the president.

Or said he had. Nothing happened. Public opinion was against Julian. Parole was denied. Not until the following fall, on October 15, 1913, was Julian Hawthorne released from prison. Again, he wore the scarlet tie.

Rose Hawthorne was born when her father was forty-seven. "She is to be the daughter of my age," he remarked, "—the comfort (at least so it is to be hoped) of my declining years." Hawthorne died, however, just before his sixtieth birthday and the day before her thirteenth.

He had called her Pessima. She was mercurial, fastidious, self-critical, and impatient. Explained Sophia in the double-edged terms she perfected, "I think you inherited from Papa this immitigable demand for beauty and order and right, & though, in the course of your development, it has made you sometimes pettish and unreasonable, I always was glad you had it."

Rose wanted to write, but her father's interdiction against the literary life put an end to that. In fact, both parents were wildly ambivalent about the practice of literature, declining to teach their children to read until they reached the ripe age of seven. Sophia was adamant about this. "I have not the smallest ambition about early learning in my children," she declared. And though her two sisters were educators of note and her brother-in-law, Horace Mann, once the secretary of the Massachusetts Board of Education, Sophia refused to hand her children over to schoolmistresses of dubious intent. Hawthorne deferred to her. "The men of our family are compliant husbands," his own sister later scoffed.

Encouraged to paint by her artistic mother, Rose dutifully studied art until Sophia's death in 1871, and then she cut loose, sort of. Barely twenty, she quickly married George Parsons Lathrop, a twenty-year-old aspiring writer. But if Rose believed she was replacing her parents by replicating their wonderful marriage—artist to writer—she was utterly mistaken. "Love is different from what I supposed and I don't like it," admits a character in one of her short stories. She did write after all.

George Lathrop got a job as assistant editor at the *Atlantic Monthly,* the showcase for much of his father-in-law's work, and when he lost the post he and Rose drifted to New York, where they nibbled at the edge of the literary set. Often dressed in yellow, her favorite color, Rose was soon known as a passable if gloomy poet and indifferent author of short stories, her best production fittingly called "Prisoners." George, a conventional and reasonably prolific writer, was known as a drunk.

The Lathrops converted to Catholicism, but religion didn't help their failing marriage, and after much soul-searching, Rose separated from her husband in 1895. Una suspected abuse. Then, in a volte-face that Julian found "abrupt and strange," Rose chose to rededicate her life to "usefulness." To Rose, however, it was her father's fine-grained appreciation of suffering that motivated her. "He was as earnest as a priest," she said, "for he cared that the world was full of sorrow & sin." Certainly Hawthorne's last illness had cast a pall over his youngest child; and in 1887 she was devastated yet again by the premature death of poet Emma Lazarus, a cherished friend.

This stiffened her purpose once and for all. On May 19, 1898, the thirty-fifth anniversary of her father's death, she clipped her auburn hair and stowed the leftover tufts under a linen cap. Henceforth she dressed in an austere monkish gown. "I gave up the world," she said, "as if I were dead." She swore off men and earthly things, and for the rest of her life lived productively in a community of faithful women. "From close observation I have learned something about the true courage of women," she had written years earlier.

Her choice reflecting a condition of her parents' lives—intimate friendships with members of the same sex—Rose started one of the first hospices in America in a tenement house on Scammel Street on the Lower East Side of Manhattan where she nursed the dying poor. Proceeds from a memoir of her father, published in 1897, supported her in this, and with Alice Huber, a "life-helper" (her word), she opened Sister Rose's Free Home in a three-story red brick building at 426 Cherry Street. Unlike her siblings, Rose managed to remake Nathaniel Hawthorne's legacy into something of her own. "The ice in the blood which he feared," observed Flannery O'Connor, "and which this very fear preserved him from, was turned by her into a warmth which initiated action. If he observed, fearfully but truthfully; if he acted, reluctantly but firmly, she charged ahead, secure in the path his truthfulness had outlined for her."

In 1926, just three months after receiving the Gold Medal of the New York Rotary Club, Mother Mary Alphonsa Lathrop, the former Rose Hawthorne, died. It was her parents' wedding anniversary.

Una Hawthorne installed her father's walnut writing table in her bedroom, and after her mother's death slipped Sophia's wedding ring onto her finger. "I do indeed love them better than myself," she said of her parents. They were her compass and her doom.

Of the three children, Una was said to be most like her father. She thought so herself. "Sometimes I wish there had never been anything done or written in the world!" she once exclaimed. "My father and I seem to feel in this way more than the rest." A perfectionist, she battered herself with her own yardstick. And she seemed inspired not by realities but by fiction—again, like her father.

As a child, she'd been rambunctious, moody, and smart. "Her natural bent is towards the passionate and tragic," wrote Hawthorne. He watched Una with absorption and loved her deeply, though with characteristic ambivalence about her strength, willfulness, pride, and intellect—qualities he both admired and censured in his stunning female characters. "If there were not so many strong objections," he confided to his journal, "it would be an excellent thing to send her to school; we should see no more of this premature ennui—her mind would be filled . . . and—what I greatly desire—she would have a much happier childhood."

She was educated in desultory fashion but her brain matured too rapidly anyway, warned one physician, who prescribed vegetables. A few years later, another doctor suggested she terminate all instruction, including her dancing lessons. She protested, though not for long. To vanquish the vanquishers, she participated in her own imprisonment, smothering emotion with self-sacrifice and self-reprisal. Then, as if to crown her achievement, Una contracted malaria during the winter of 1858, when the Hawthornes lived in Rome. She lay in bed, face to the wall.

The brush with mortality provided an explanation for Una's increasingly drab temperament. But occasionally she chucked her good-girl manners and kicked and screamed until her terrified parents rigged her up to a galvanic battery and jolted her with electricity. Calm again when an aunt visited in the fall of 1861, Una rowed her and her father to the middle of Walden Pond and blithely announced it was a most dangerous place.

Engaged to be married shortly after her father's death, Una abruptly severed relations with her fiancé when he disappointed her in some unforgivable way. Besides, her parents' sublime marriage couldn't be reproduced in this vulgar world by mere men and women. So she stayed near her mother in London and participated in the new family enterprise, the publication of all of Hawthorne's journals and unfinished tales. When Sophia died, she simmered in misery, a strange light in her eye.

Six months later, at Rose's marriage, the lid flew completely off. Una alleged that Lathrop had jilted her for Rose. There was no truth to the charge, except of course the truth of Una's feelings. Descending into a pit of "insanity," Una spent great sums of money, and an uncle reported that she "nearly took the lives of three persons"—evidently her own, her sister's, and Lathrop's—while she denounced Rose for having betrayed her. Placed in restraints, she was hauled off to an anonymous asylum, where she was confined until Rose and George Lathrop could escape to America without her.

The sisters reconciled but crossed swords again when Lathrop, using family documents in Rose's possession, dared to write a book about Nathaniel Hawthorne. Allies since childhood, Una and Julian closed ranks, and Julian took the battle public, writing scurrilous pieces in newspapers—much to the public's chagrin, for Hawthorne was a national monument which it hated to see debased by anything as crude as family squabbling. Canonization had already begun.

The family injunction notwithstanding, all three Hawthorne children had wanted to be writers. Only Julian succeeded, after his fashion, though it wasn't until the death of both parents that he pursued the literary career they had inveighed against.

When Una declared she would compose romances, her mother ignored her. "She will fulfil her destiny doubtless," she'd said, "but I do not intend it shall be hastened one hour." As an adult, Una tried her hand at a novel, and she wrote at least one poem, ominously entitled "Dead Sunshine." Mostly, however, she involved herself in charity work, donating her time and small income to the Industrial Orphanage Home and School in London. When the effort grew too exhausting, she took refuge in Julian's home nearby and on occasion among the nearby Anglican Sisters of Clewer, where many women of her kind—"invalid ladies in reduced circumstances," as they were known—sought rest and moral refreshment.

She'd become engaged again, this time to a tubercular writer, Albert Webster. It was a ridiculous match, damned from the start. Webster immediately sailed to Hawaii, as far away from Una as he could. Meantime, at Julian's, Una sewed her wedding dress without, one suspects, much hope. On February 3, 1877, while Una was out, Julian noticed on the front table a white envelope postmarked Honolulu. It was addressed to Una, but the handwriting wasn't Webster's. Una returned at teatime, opened the letter, and slowly read the contents aloud, word by scalding word. Webster had died before his ship reached Hawaii. She lowered her head and sobbed.

Julian clenched his teeth. "Has Una had so happy and self-indulgent a life as to need this desolating blow at last?" he cried. For five months she corresponded with Webster's sister and in August envisioned a heavenly reunion between her and her sickly sweetheart. "The idea that you suggest that he wants me even where he is, never occurred to me. Oh I wonder if he does!"

A little more than a month later, on September 10, the unhappy Una died in her retreat at Clewer. Julian and his family were vacationing in Hastings in a house loaned by a fan of Nathaniel Hawthorne's, and though they'd urged Una to come with them, she'd gone to Clewer instead. But something was terribly wrong. She seemed ill. She wrote Rose, who received the letter "almost at the time—if not the hour—of her death, and was appalled at the agitation that beset me as I read it." Frantic, the Clewer Sisters contacted Julian, who told them if there was no improvement in Una's condition, they should telegraph him right away. Una seemed better. Then she fainted. She couldn't see. Another telegram brought Julian to Clewer too late.

From afar, Rose learned that the doctor diagnosed exhaustion and pyrosis, a stomach inflammation she blamed for her father's death. More romantic, Julian decided his sister had died of a broken heart.

No one contradicted him. Whatever records may have existed can no longer be found.

The Hawthorne children idealized their father, although, as Julian's career attests, their relation to him was neither uncomplicated nor untroubled. How not? In his own lifetime—and under his own roof—he was venerated as a model father, husband, and genius. Partly as a consequence, he was a man deeply isolated, unable to forget himself, and his children were unable to forget him.

With an insight so fine it bordered on the voluptuous, he crafted a style of exquisite ambiguity, of uncompromising passion and stubborn skepticism. Yet his characters are often curiously static, poised between self-knowledge and indifference and, like Hawthorne himself, confounded by what and who they are. For Hawthorne was a man of dignity, of mordant wit, of malicious anger; a man of depression and control; a forthright and candid man aching to confess but too proud, too obstinate, too ashamed to do so; a man of disclosure and disguise, both at once, keen, cynical, intelligent, who digs into his imagination to write of American men and women: isolated in their communities, burdened by their history, riven by their sense of crime and their perpetual, befuddled innocence; people ambitious and vain and displaced and willing, or perhaps forced, to live a double life, a secret life, an exemplary life, haunted and imprisoned, even as his children were—or, in Hawthorne's terms, as are we all.

CHAPTER TWO

———

Home

This long connection of a family with one spot, as its place of birth and burial, creates a kindred between the human being and the locality, quite independent of any charm in the scenery or moral circumstances that surround him. It is not love, but instinct.

Nathaniel Hawthorne, "The Custom-House"

SALEM IS A TOWN obsessed with itself.

The time is 1804; the place, a New England port city. Bright-colored sails snap and rustle in the wind. A scent of nutmeg, clove, and ginger fills the air—that and the acrid fragrance of red wine spilled from Spanish casks. Blowsy men in gold earrings lean on huge kegs of molasses, indifferent to the friendly pastor, the Reverend Dr. Bentley, who saunters beyond the docks to watch for returning vessels. Head bent, the Reverend Bentley wears his broad-brimmed hat, he usually does, and raises his skirts as if to dodge temptation, passing whorehouses and warehouses hunkered near the water's edge. He nods at the grizzled ship's captain, official papers stuffed in his seaman's tin box, and at the wizened merchant who, with pencil in his Yankee hand, is tallying barrels of sugar, fifty thousand pounds from the schooner *Speed*. Church bells clang. Horses tied to the drays flick their tails, and the wheeling gulls scream with irreverent glee.

Salem: pompous, pious, exotic, and rich.

Called Naumkeag by the local Pawtucket Indians who fished there, Salem—*salaam:* peace—is a gateway to America, with fifty-four ships, eighteen barks, seventy-two brigs, and eighty-six schooners to its far-flung name. Its seal bears a palm tree, a Parsee, a ship, and the Latin motto *Divitis Indiae usque ad ultimum sinum:* To the endmost port of the East sail the

13

tall ships. Bandanna handkerchiefs, Sumatran pepper, tea, china, silk, nuts, raisins, figs, olive oil, Indian cotton, and Arabian coffee enter America through Salem, which stocks an international market with tables, saddlery, chaises, and dried codfish, to say nothing of the oak planks, shoes, pickled bacon—and, from the South, tobacco and rice—lugged there for transport on an outbound ship.

Cod-merchant as Midas, a Salem trader tacks a carved gilt fish on every step of the staircase in his mansion.

But the city boasts more than cargo and piles of money, for the salty smell of conscience helps preserve such busy commerce. Generals, jurists, senators, and a secretary of state hail from mighty Salem, their families residing slightly to the north of the waterfront though never far from the creaking windlass. Naturally, the town's latter-day Puritans disdain outward display. Gilded cod notwithstanding, they live in the well-proportioned houses designed by Samuel McIntire, graceful structures supported by simple pilasters. Their daughters marry well; their sons go to Harvard.

One Salem daughter said no one new ever came there, for Salem had no need of outsiders. Slightly xenophobic, its citizens subsist on one another and their relations, now and in foregoing generations. Pedigree counts as much as money, frequently more; history furnishes a hierarchy of descent not to be gainsaid: who had come to America when and, of course, with whom, which mattered almost as much as what these ancestors did and whose interests—besides the Almighty's—they served.

Nathaniel Hathorne, as the name was then spelled, belonged to one of Salem's first families, which meant he was a sixth-generation Hathorne who prayed for redemption at the Congregationalist First Church, where his Puritan great-great-grandfather, William Hathorne, had occupied the first pew. This was important. Said the Reverend Dr. Bentley, Salem's connoisseur of kinship, "No family had more pride of descent" than the Hathornes. Accordingly, they claimed to bear the coat of arms described in the story "The White Old Maid": "Azure, a lion's head erased, between three flower de luces."

William Hathorne was a man of persecution although—perhaps because—he himself had fled it, Sidney's *Arcadia* tucked under his arm, sailing from England to America, some say on the *Arbella,* with fifty servants in tow. Or so his descendants heard. Hathorne settled in Dorchester, Massachusetts, and arrived in Salem in 1636, induced to relocate in part by the promise of a 200-acre land grant provided he quit the church of Dorchester. He did. A man of sundry and stubborn talents, Selectman Hathorne was a prize. He voted to banish the individualist Reverend Roger Williams from the colony, and soon became Massachusetts Bay delegate to the New England Confederation of colonies, captain in the militia, then major, surveyor, magistrate, and garrulous contributor to the General Court—the very first Speaker in the House of Representatives, said Nathaniel.

The adjudication of crime, particularly illegal fornication, was Hathorne's forte; heresy, his genius. He pursued Quakers with the inventive zeal of the true paranoid, hunting them "like a blood-hound," or so it was alleged. He ordered Ann Coleman dragged half naked through town while being lashed with a whip of knotted cords, and under his watch, another poor blasphemer was flogged until his back turned to jelly. For his own pains, William Hathorne received several more grants of land, 240 acres in 1648, 400 in 1654, 640 in 1675. "Let us thank God for having given us such ancestors," his descendant Nathaniel wryly observed, "and let each successive generation thank him, not less fervently, for being one step further from them in the march of ages."

William Hathorne earned the approval of his heirs when he defied Charles II's edict to return to England for a royal reprimand. He'd dressed down the king's commissioners, insulting the monarch by implication and fomenting a little insurrection to boot. The king took notice and recalled him. A thoroughgoing Massachusetts man though no democrat, Hathorne would not bow and scrape before a temporal sovereign, even one who might revoke the colony's charter. "I cannot remember the time when I had not heard that the King sent for our forefather . . . to come to England, and that he refused to go," said Nathaniel's sister Elizabeth. An evasive letter was dispatched to the king, who was occupied with other business by the time it arrived, and forever after Hathorne's heirs invested the Major with a "dim and dusky grandeur," Nathaniel would write, ". . . present to my boyish imagination as far back as I can remember."

For Salem—for Nathaniel—the past was never dead.

How could it be? Salem was where women had dangled from the gallows, and Hawthorne's great-grandfather had all but tied the rope. If William Hathorne crossed an angry sea, planted crops, catechized infidels, and laid the cornerstone for a new generation, his son, Colonel John Hathorne, outdid his father. As Salem magistrate during the witchcraft delusion of 1692, this flinty chip off a flinty block heard pleas from more than one hundred accused witches, each of whom he presumed guilty. Swift in judgment—hadn't the "black man" whispered obscenities to village women?—Colonel John mounted his steed and rode out to the stony

promontory later known as Gallows Hill, where, unyielding, he surveyed
what his ironclad piety had wrought. According to his family, he also
brought down a curse on subsequent Hathornes, hurled at him by one of
the dying witches.

John Hathorne's slate gravestone lies in Salem's oldest cemetery, the
Burying Point at Charter Street, where as a boy Nathaniel Hathorne saw it
canting slightly forward, still unbowed, even by time. And he listened to
what he called "chimney-corner" stories about the deeds, nefarious and
otherwise, of militant forefathers, which fascinated him so much that his
own published tales, when first collected, were aptly called "twice-told."
What he did not pick up, chimney-fashion, about his Hathorne relatives,
he eventually gleaned in the local antiquarian associations or libraries established to conserve—and create—a history of the new republic. (The
Boston Athenaeum, eighteen miles from Salem, opened in 1805; the Salem
Athenaeum in 1810; and in 1821, when Nathaniel was seventeen, Salem's
Essex Institute began to round up and preserve all the records of the
county.)

Inscriptions on family gravestones, fireside yarns, shipping records,
quarto-sized logbooks bound in marbled boards: none of these could supply
what he sought from his father, whom he barely knew. A seafaring man,
Captain Nathaniel Hathorne had died of yellow fever in Surinam in 1808.
Gone forever, buried without a Salem marker, he left his four-year-old son
as beguiled by genealogy as Salem itself.

Salem was a contentious town. Federalists and Republicans read different
newspapers, attended different churches, and for the most part docked their
ships at competing wharves. In 1796 Elias Hasket Derby, called "King
Derby" by detractors, sued the upstart George Crowninshield because
Crowninshield's wharf jutted out twelve feet too far—farther, that is, than
Derby's.

The dispute wasn't about size alone. Derby was a Federalist, Crowninshield a Republican. And so Salem citizenry split down party lines. "The
jealousy & envy which prevails among merchants, especially in this Town, is
fully equal to that supposed to exist among literary men," remarked the
Reverend Bentley, a vocal Jeffersonian, which is to say a Crowninshield man
and a liberal.

In 1804 the Federalists staged an Independence Day procession. The
plumes on their headgear swayed in the summer breeze, and their bayonets

Hawthorne's birthplace, 27 Union Street, Salem

glinted, brazen in the sun. Not to be outdone, the Republicans assembled at the courthouse to march down Essex Street, their own banners flying, to the East Church, which displayed, among the July flowers, portraits of Governor Endicott, Minister Higginson, and Salem's first merchant, Captain George Corwin. The congregation then prayed for God and Jefferson, and the cannons smoked until sundown.

From 27 Union Street one could hear the guns roaring on the Common if one listened carefully. Likely no one did. There, in the upstairs bedroom, two families celebrated deliverance of a more personal sort: Nathaniel Hathorne was born to the raven-haired beauty Elizabeth Clarke Manning Hathorne and her seagoing husband Nathaniel.

The Manning pastor, the Reverend Bentley, had married the child's parents three years earlier, on August 2, 1801. The bride, Betsy Manning, was then twenty-one years old and two months pregnant, a fact that raises eyebrows among literary detectives nosing after the origins of Hester Prynne, since her pregnancy forced to consummation a courtship that had stretched out for six or more years.

Her future husband's prospects may have caused the delay. Though

Hathorne was a good enough sailor, his maritime rise was neither meteoric nor lucrative. At the time of his marriage, Hathorne at twenty-six still hadn't been promoted to captain, meaning he didn't command his own ship or enough money to buy a house of his own; he was no cod-prince. So the newlyweds settled in the smallish Hathorne home on Union Street, where Hathorne's widowed mother Rachel, his unmarried brother, and his three unmarried sisters all lived.

Old even by Salem standards, the gambrel house had been built sometime before 1700 by Benjamin Pickman and had sheltered Hathornes since 1756, when Daniel Hathorne (the writer's grandfather) had married Rachel Phelps. Betsy Hathorne was familiar with it. The Hathorne place sat directly behind the newer Manning residence on Herbert Street, one separated from the other by a large patch of garden. Not surprisingly, the Mannings and the Hathornes saw one another often; they rode out together to Essex, Massachusetts, for the ordination of the local minister, and two of Betsy's brothers, William and Robert, occasionally bought shares in various sailing vessels. Robert Manning put over one hundred dollars into the voyage of the brig *Nabby* from which his brother-in-law Nathaniel Hathorne never returned.

Yet the families differed in crucial respects. Betsy's parents, Richard and Miriam Lord Manning, had come to Salem from nearby Ipswich and Essex, and though they traced their lineage back to the early settlers of Massachusetts, they dealt mainly in metals and horseflesh, not witches and General Courts. A former gunsmith and blacksmith, Richard Manning was far more prosperous than the Widow Rachel Hathorne of Union Street. In fact, by the year of his daughter's marriage to Hathorne, Manning had bought all available property, except the Widow Hathorne's, on Union Street and the adjacent Herbert Street, where he had built a three-story, commodious, and nondescript family mansion (as the place was known) right next to his stables. He was also hitching horses to his own stagecoach line, the Salem and Boston, which had the best team in New England.

Betsy sang in the choir at the Reverend Bentley's East Church, which tilted not just toward Jefferson but toward Unitarianism, though once married, she worshipped at her husband's church, where she was baptized in 1806 along with her children. Endowed by temperament with a sense of depravity better suited to the Congregationalists, Betsy Hathorne forbade her children to read any but religious books on the Sabbath. She was a bashful, inhibited woman averse to exuberance. Or so her son indicated, noting the "strange reserve, in regard to matters of feeling, that has always existed among us." Nonetheless, she wielded considerable power, and during periods of stress, indecision, or calamity, wrapped herself in illness, which she wore like a shroud, frightening the children, who may have feared she'd vanish like their father had.

But she was literate and intelligent and lovely, with exquisite manners, an aristocratic deportment, and according to one of her daughters, the same "capacity for placid enjoyment" as Nathaniel. An observer remarked she "looked as if she had walked out of an old picture," her large gray eyes "full of sensibility and expression." Nathaniel, her son, apparently resembled her, especially his sensitive (some called it weak) mouth.

Five years older than Betsy, the writer's father, Nathaniel Hathorne, was born on May 19, 1775. He followed the sea, as his father and brother had. If not as striking as the persecutors, the nautical Hathornes weren't a colorless crew. Hathorne's father, "Bold Daniel," had fought the British in 1776 from

Captain Nathaniel Hathorne, Hawthorne's father, engraving by S. A. Schoff

the deck of his privateer the *True American,* and when the old salt died twenty years after that, in 1796, the flags in the port of Salem flew at half-mast. By then his son Mate Hathorne was walking the decks of ships like King Derby's *America,* famous for lugging from India the first elephant ever seen in the United States. But Mate Hathorne was focused on treasures of a different kind: "In Storms when clouds obscure the Sky/And thunders roll and lightning fly/In the midst of all these dire allarms/I'll think dear Betsey on thy Charms." Charming Betsy was fifteen.

On learning of Betsy's engagement, Old Captain Knight had reputedly said to her father, "I hear your darter is going to marry the son of Captain Hawthorne [*sic*]. I knowed him: he was the sternest man that ever walked a deck!" Yet when compared with Salem's stern sailors and wily merchants, Mate Hathorne himself seems fairly undistinguished, even in looks: five feet, ten and a half inches tall, slightly built, and supposedly "inclined to melancholy, and of a reticent disposition." His son, the writer, traced his tendency toward seclusion to his father. Granite, he said, was his legacy.

Obviously Nathaniel wanted some connection with a father who left little. Hathorne had brought home blue crockery from China, monogrammed with "NH" painted in gold and passed down to his son; a punch bowl from Calcutta, some scattered meteorological observations, and a verse or two in his logbooks, which young Nathaniel saved, fantasizing over his father's few exploits, such as a near battle, when first mate on the *Herald,* with a French privateer. From these books he learned not much more, just that his father had seen creatures of land and sea, silver birds and Cape pigeons, and that Hathorne had kept a leaf from a cabbage tree and two shoots of a three-needle pine.

Having shipped for Sumatra, Hathorne was at sea when his first child, Elizabeth (nicknamed Ebe), was born on March 7, 1802. Nor was he at Union Street two years later when Nathaniel was born on the Fourth of July; and he would never see his third child, Maria Louisa, born on January 9, 1808. He had to sail. The sea was his livelihood, his calling, his future, and the future of his family.

In 1804, after the birth of his son, Hathorne came back to Salem a captain at last and soon earned a coveted membership in Salem's East India Marine Society for having navigated his ship round Cape Horn. But in Salem the tides were turning. In 1807 sixty-one ships left for the West Indies and South America, sixty-three for Europe, ten for India and China; later that year President Jefferson levied the embargo that would bleed the town. In 1808 no ships sailed from Salem. Docks stood idle, planks soggy with disuse, and soup kitchens soon fed over a thousand of the unemployed.

On December 28, 1807, just days before the embargo took effect, Captain Hathorne shipped out on the 154-ton brig *Nabby.* Now the father of three, he no longer circumnavigated the globe. The gesture didn't save him. Sometime between the birth of Louisa (as Maria Louisa was known) and

March 1808, he took ill in Surinam with the dreaded yellow jack. He didn't last a fortnight. On April 10, Betsy's father, Richard Manning, asked the Reverend Bentley to say a prayer for his son-in-law. A few invoices aboard the *Nabby* were all that remained of Hathorne, age thirty-two. His son had not turned four.

"I remember very well that one morning my mother called my brother into her room, next to the one where we slept, and told him that his father was dead," Ebe would recall. Nathaniel seldom spoke about his father or his death. Years later, though, Sophia Hawthorne insisted that the captain had "died in India very suddenly from being detained late in the country in the evening in a linen dress. On which account he took violent cold and the Indian fever. His funeral was gorgeous."

It's difficult to know whether she fabricated the story or whether Hawthorne himself had embroidered the truth for her benefit and his, the reality of his father's death having been so harsh. And hard financially. Captain Hathorne had died intestate, leaving his widow with the 4 percent owed from the *Nabby*'s voyage, amounting to $427.02 and from which she paid more than $200 to cover such sundry expenses as the minister's eulogy and the digging of a grave.

"He left very little property," remarked Ebe of her feckless father, "and my grandfather Manning took us home."

In later years, Nathaniel remarked that he should have been a sailor; and until the age of sixteen he'd actually hoped to become one, much to his mother's horror.

His earliest compositions were said to have been sea stories about bronzed pirates and hardy privateers, perhaps modeled on Byron's *Corsair*, and in two youthful poems he did marshal his fledgling talent to extol the ocean's awful strength: "The billowy Ocean rolls its wave/Above the ship-wreck'd Sailor's Grave." Those missing at sea, he wrote in another poem, are "those for whom we weep,/The young, the bright, the fair."

Such stuff might be standard for an adolescent who loped along the shore on a spring afternoon, but Hawthorne had lost his father to the water and spoke of the sea as a place of comfort, destruction, and wonder, of adventure and male bonding, a place salutary but ultimately unknowable, unreachable. "Of what mysteries is it telling?" he would ask in a sketch, "Foot-prints on the Sea-shore." "Of sunken ships, and whereabouts they lie?" Ebe recalled two lines of a song in one of her brother's earliest stories, possibly about pirates: "The rovers of the Sea, they were a fearful Race," and in copying one of his father's logbook entries, he rewrote his father's observations in what seems the first sentence of an adventure tale: "The weather not looking prudent to run over the shoals tonight, we are determined to wait for good weather and fair wind."

A friend recalled that Hawthorne's love for the sea "amounted to a passionate worship," and another said that as an adult he resembled the wharf rats of his youth and "looked like a boned pirate." Hawthorne said of himself that his breath "came fresh from the wilderness of ocean." Several of Hawthorne's closest friends had lost their own fathers to the sea or made their livings from it at one time or another. He returned to it as often as he could.

Richard Manning drove his horse hard. It was necessary for such a man, who frequently traveled between Salem and a small settlement, Raymond, in the district of Maine. In early winter, roads the color of tobacco juice filled with drifts of snow, making them impassable. Spring was no better. Mud, ankle deep, sucked horses' hooves into slimy ruts.

Manning pushed on. As far as he was concerned, Raymond might well have been a suburb of Salem, which in a way it was. Promised in 1690 to Captain William Raymond and other residents of Beverly, Massachusetts, for services rendered in a (failed) expedition to Quebec, the Maine property lay twenty miles northwest of Portland and bordered the great, gleaming Sebago Pond, which, like Maine itself, was part of Massachusetts. Maine was not a separate state.

Mean in winter, gorgeous in summer, its ponds teeming with fish and its forests with game, trees hung heavy with sugar pear, fields awash in berries, Raymond was the Land of Promise. That's what the Mannings called it. Speculators from Beverly and Salem had purchased large tracts of land there, though few of them wanted to relocate. Instead they discussed their holdings over spiked punch at Salem's Sun Tavern and in 1795 appointed Richard Manning their tax collector. It was a profitable post. From it, Manning acquired huge parcels of real estate at rock-bottom prices.

So he rode hard. He wanted to do "everything," as he said, "in my powre for my Children." He and his wife, Miriam, had raised nine children at 12 Herbert Street, and the family was still growing. For the summer after Captain Hathorne's death, Betsy had crossed the garden with her three children to join her parents, eight unmarried siblings, a great-aunt, a servant, and a passel of scampering cats who lived there. "There were four Uncles and four Aunts, all, for many years, unmarried, so that we were welcome in the family," Ebe reminisced.

According to relatives, the atmosphere in the Manning house resembled that of a noisy tavern, family members taking sides in the civil and religious controversies riling the rest of Salem. Betsy's sister Mary and her brother Samuel joined her at the Hathornes' Congregationalist First Church. Betsy's two other siblings, Priscilla and Maria, considered the First Church a little lax, so they worshipped with the more orthodox Trinitarians at the Tabernacle. The Manning parents stayed at Bentley's East Church. It was a singular case, marveled the Reverend Dr. Bentley, of a family internally divided. Brother Robert usually sided with Priscilla; Richard, yet another brother, spent much of his time in the rustic wilds of Maine, where he hoped to erect his own church—Congregationalist.

Doctrinal distinctions aside, the Mannings, like their fellow citizens, knit religion into the fabric of their enterprising lives, their ambition to get ahead, to own more land or stagecoaches or horses or fruit trees than any one else, to prove themselves equal to Salem's snobbish upper crust, to rise on the social ladder and yet make themselves of use, to disseminate the Bible and remind one another in perpetuity of their fallen nature, their need for redemption. "All have something to repent of," Mary Manning, the eldest sibling, pertly told her brother Richard.

None of this was lost on young Nathaniel, who complained about the hard wooden pews at the First Church and the ugly bust of John Wesley at home. Reputedly he removed the bust from its pedestal in the dead of winter and filled it with water through a hole in its bottom. He waited for the water to freeze, assuming Wesley would burst like a pitcher. Wesley stayed intact. But Nathaniel drank in the lilting cadence of Scripture and stored up its parables, repeated often at Herbert Street, which he prized for the fine stories they were. At the idea of damnation, however, he squirmed; though protest was unavailing.

The outward particulars of Nathaniel's early life seem unexceptional: he fought with a chum at school; he liked parades and fires; he teased the household cats and his younger sister. At one time he owned a pet monkey, which, when it died, he buried in the garden. He played in the Manning stables with a younger cousin, bouncing on the chaises, and supposedly plagued his family with theological questions: Who made God? Did Adam and Eve eat baked beans? Was John Calvin a Christian?

He was especially good-looking, said Ebe, "the finest boy, many strangers observed, whom they had ever seen": dark brown curly hair, flushed cheeks, long-lashed eyes the color of slate or water, depending on his mood. For the rest of his life his appearance attracted attention, embarrassing and pleasing him. And he was proud. Nathaniel once offended Simon Forrester, one of the richest men in Salem and an uncle by marriage on the Hathorne side, by refusing to accept a large coin Forrester had offered him on the street, in public. Forrester angrily informed the Mannings of the boy's bad manners, and they, obsequious but proud themselves, explained that his mother did not allow the child such large sums of spending money.

In later life, Nathaniel teased his mother about spoiling her three children; Betsy replied it was impossible to spoil such children as him and Ebe. (Louisa was more compliant than the other two.) But Nathaniel obeyed the instructions of his uncle Robert, which shed a little light on the boy's youth: "Study the hard lessons," Uncle Robert directed, "learn all you can at school, mind your mother, don't look cross, hold up your head like a man, and keep your cloths clean."

On Saturday, April 17, 1813, Grandfather Manning left Herbert Street for Maine, riding by way of Newbury, Massachusetts, where he stopped at a local inn to spend the night. Before sunrise he fell into an apoplectic fit, smacking his head as he hit the hard wooden floor. His family rushed to Newbury in their coaches, but there was nothing to be done. Aged fifty-eight, Richard Manning died the following Monday at noon. The funeral took place the next day, coffin draped in black, at Herbert Street.

Just days before, Rachel Hathorne, Nathaniel's paternal grandmother, had died. No more would the eight-year-old boy visit her house on Sundays, sit near the chimney, or read *Pilgrim's Progress* in a large chair in the corner of the room. "The heart never breaks on the first grave," he would write; "and, after many graves, it gets so obtuse that nothing can break it."

Yet Grandfather Manning had at least left his family fairly comfortable, as he'd hoped. The Salem portion of his estate was sizable: the mansion on Herbert Street, an attached store, a plot of land, several carriage houses, three lots on Derby Street near the wharf, and the Union Street stables and business. The Maine holdings consisted of over ten thousand acres of unimproved land "down east," along with a 150-acre farm in Bridgton, near Raymond, and a house and two lots in Portland. William, the eldest son, would continue to manage the stage business, and Richard Manning III, the second oldest, would oversee the property in Maine at least temporarily. Robert, two years younger than Richard, had opened a broker's office near the wharves, where he speculated in guns and trading ships. The next in line, John, took to the sea, perhaps hoping to fight in the war against the British. The youngest son, Samuel, worked in the Salem family stables.

But the Manning legacy caused a fault line in the family, imperceptible at first. "Uncle Richard he can grow his own tobacco here, & make his own segars," Uncle Robert wrote to his nephew from Maine, "and he can sail twenty five miles from Standish to the head of long pond in one direction." It was decided. Uncle Richard would stay in Maine to manage and expand the family holdings, and Robert would follow suit.

Partially crippled, Uncle Richard had damaged his leg or spine in a carriage accident that occurred sometime around 1810. "I do not forget to complain of my hard fortune, and very often, curse the day in which I was born," he wrote in his typically half-humorous vein to his sister Betsy. Dyspeptic, kind, scrupulously honest, fond of reading, tobacco, fishing, and freedom, Richard grew increasingly infirm as he aged. But always he loved the deep-sea green of the forest in summer, its white solitude in winter, and its distance from Salem, where everything was ranked—name, church, school, residence, clothes, achievements: no place for a lame eccentric such as he.

Uncle Robert liked Salem, and sure, he said he'd leave it. "I should rather live in the Woods poor than in the City rich," he protested—far too much. A man of striving, he was uncomfortable with his own ambitions yet unable to renounce them as the more ascetic Richard had, or seemed to have. Besides, he wanted to stay close to their mother and earn her approval, not an easy thing to do. So he put off moving to Raymond, and in the end never did except for extended visits and vacations.

Sitting before his own fire, poking at it with his cane, Richard felt he'd been betrayed. As did Nathaniel; when Uncle Richard left Salem, the loss was as devastating to him as any other he had suffered.

"My Lord, stand back, and let the coffin pass." As a young boy, recalled Nathaniel's sister Ebe, her brother frequently recited this line from *Richard III*. It seems a strange choice—except that for him the procession of coffins had become a terrible commonplace. In one of his early Salem sketches, he describes a busy waterfront, a military parade, and a funeral cortege, the psychological axis of his youth.

Actually, the whole of *Richard III* resonated with the boy. After the death of Grandfather Manning (officially Richard Manning Jr.), lame Uncle Richard—Richard Manning III—competed for the Manning throne and won, but only by making Maine his kingdom. Shakespeare's Richard III: malformed, robbed by nature, a villain to be sure; and crippled Uncle Richard: *paterfamilias absconditus,* a kind of hero and, for having abandoned his nephew, a kind of villain too.

Less than six weeks after Uncle Richard left Salem for good, Nathaniel injured his foot at school while playing, Ebe said, with a bat and ball. He took to crutches for the next fourteen months—that is, when he walked at all, which he often refused to do. It was an early rebellion, self-punitive and vindictive, in protest against the loss of his male guardians. No one had heard from his uncle John in quite some time, though he'd reportedly been spotted in New York City, bound for the Great Lakes to "work at his Trade." That was all. With Grandfather Manning dead and Uncle Richard gone and John feared lost, Nathaniel himself threatened to run away forever, recalled his sister. Unable to do this, he did the opposite. Like Uncle Richard, he committed himself to immobility.

Paralysis and aggression, twin handmaidens of a conflicted psyche: in his early stories, they appear as relatives and doubles, as in "The Gentle Boy," where patriarchal Puritans resembling William Hathorne harass the gentle Ilbrahim, an orphaned Quaker child. Paternal persecutors will invariably crop up in Hawthorne's work and so will characters like Ilbrahim's malicious friend, who cunningly breaks Ilbrahim's spirit. "Like a lame man of low stature and gravely appareled, with a dark and twisted countenance, and a bright, downcast eye," this satanic trickster—himself lame—destroys his double, the gentle child, with an aggression so deadly, it engenders the very passivity it loathes.

Affording him a certain guilty pleasure, the injury kept Nathaniel the center of attention. "Nathaniel was particularly petted," Ebe remarked almost sixty years later, "the more because his health was then delicate and he had frequent illnesses." Fearing an incurable deformity in Betsy's darling son and the sole grandson of the Mannings, they consulted a series of doctors. "Everybody thought that, if he lived, he would always be lame," Ebe recalled. Under the guidance of Dr. Smith of Hanover, New Hampshire, the family tried to invigorate his leg by dousing his foot with cold water.

Legend says they poured water from a window on the second story onto the foot, which they then encased in a specially fitted boot.

All treatments failed.

The embargo hadn't prevented war with Great Britain, and the war dragged on. There was talk of an armistice, but in April 1814 horses from Uncle William's stable conveyed men and women to the gunhouse on Salem Neck as the United States frigate *Constitution* retreated into Marblehead Harbor. In June, the British burned an American ship in Beverly. Then came news of the destruction of vessels off Cape Ann and Scituate. Hotly contested in Salem—Federalists and Republicans madder than ever—war-talk distracted the town, which nervously awaited a British invasion. Nathaniel unheroically limped about the garden both despising and relishing his helplessness. On his tenth birthday he stayed home, a child apart, listening, downcast, to the martial Independence Day celebration nearby, where boys toting bayonets turned into little men.

Robert and Priscilla Manning, in particular, respected education and sent all three Hathorne children to school, but after Nathaniel's injury, his teacher, Joseph Worcester, the future lexicographer, went to the Manning house to hear him recite his lessons privately. "One of the peculiarities of my boyhood was a grievous disinclination to go to school," Nathaniel later said, "and (Providence favoring me in this natural repugnance) I never did go half as much as other boys, partly owing to delicate health (which I made the most of for the purpose)." Delicate health, other boys: Nathaniel regarded himself as peculiar, even bizarre—entitled, and diminished by the entitlement.

In subsequent years he also spoke of a humiliating boyhood incident. During school recess he'd climbed onto a stage in the classroom to make a little speech, and a group of bigger boys had pulled him down. Whether apocryphal or not, the story suggests that Hawthorne had been mortified when he wanted to excel—or show off. From then on, unless forced, he refused to stand and declaim.

Taking refuge, then, from the activities he feared in an infirmity he loathed, the boy unconsciously identified not just with the men but with the women of his household, particularly his mother and two sisters. Thus Nathaniel's handicap became his fortunate fall into literature, according to his sister Ebe. Instead of pursuing the ragtag parade of schoolboys with muskets, Nathaniel could study Milton and Pope and James Thomson, lying at home on the carpet, where he built a house of books for the cats. He read Rousseau, deemed improper, or Byron, and he dreamed of faraway places. "If he had been educated for a genius," said Ebe of her brother, "it would have injured him excessively. He developed himself."

Doubtless Ebe had a point. Nathaniel compensated for his deprivations by constructing an imaginary counterworld over which he exercised supreme control. "He used to invent some long stories wild and fanciful, and to tell us where he was going when he grew up," recalled Ebe, "and of wonderful adventures he was to meet with." Though lame, he determined to travel far from home like the men in his family, his father, grandfather, his uncle John, even uncle Richard—and to die young. Such fantasies of liberation, as well as of malice and of revenge, sustained him. And not surprisingly, he writes of journeys frequently in later life, although escape is unrealized, truncated, or punished.

By the winter of 1815, Nathaniel's condition miraculously improved after his mother decided to decamp to Maine with her children and her sister Mary. Thrilled by the news, Uncle Richard—in a weird, proto-Freudian burst of weapons and lameness and limbs—promised that as soon as Nathaniel arrived, he'd give him the gun that had once belonged to Captain Hathorne.

CHAPTER THREE

The Forest of Arden

There is no use of life, but just to find out what is fit for us to do.

Nathaniel Hawthorne, "Septimius Felton"

O F THE THREE Hathorne children, Ebe was the dazzler. Certainly her brother thought so, recounting stories about her precocity, the way, for instance, she walked and talked at a mere nine months. Regardless, Ebe remains somewhat of a cipher in the Hawthorne chronicles, relegated to the back rooms of literary history, where she lingers, an American hamadryad of untapped potential inhibited by family, environment, and her own sardonic self.

She loved nature and books, particularly Shakespeare, whom she read assiduously at the age of twelve, and by adolescence her wit was dry, her humor pungent. She usually cut straight to the marrow, telling the truth and damning the Devil. (Of Emerson and Thoreau, she said: "I have a better opinion of their taste than to suppose that they really do think as they profess to.") And though she affected to do little, she excelled in most everything she did. She studied languages with ease, Spanish, French, and German. "You are learning astronomy, a learned little Lady studying the stars," exclaimed Uncle Robert with pleasure, prodding his niece forward—he called her a "female Newton"—even while holding her back. "Remember two [*sic*] much Learning is a Dangerous thing, but I know you will learn that only which is usefull for you."

Ebe spent a lifetime rebelling against the "usefull." Uncle Richard observed that "Elizabeth in particular cannot bear to think of doing any kind of Work," and an early teacher who praised her exactness scolded her sloth. "Useful knowledge, unless for immediate practical application, is the most useless of all," Ebe declared; on another occasion she warned a cousin that "if you ever write a book, take care that it be with no intention to be useful." Over the years, little changed. Sophia Hawthorne took notable offense. "Elizabeth is not available for every-day purposes of pot-hooks and trammels, spits and flat-irons," she once complained.

Ebe rose late. She avoided obligatory social calls. "People can talk about nothing tolerable but their neighbor's faults," she grimaced at fourteen. She considered letter writing demoralizing as well as ruinous to the style, and she abhorred cant, superstition, and organized religion. "The only argument for the inspiration of the Bible that has any weight with me is that it is readable," she announced, "which other religious books are not." Instead she liked newspapers. "The very best way to forget our own peculiar vexations is to consider those of other people," she proclaimed, "and other people's affairs in general, and especially the course of public events."

Although in youth she enjoyed a bracing sleigh ride or an unhurried sojourn in Newburyport with her cousins, in later life she withdrew from society, devoting herself to a translation of Cervantes, never finished, and to walking alone in the forest collecting flowers and ferns. "I am something of a wild creature," she admitted, "and it would suit me just as well to die alone, as wild creatures do." She did. She never married, by choice it seems; certainly her rich good looks—jet hair, gray eyes, skin the color of an eggshell—must have attracted many suitors. "I should not like to feel as if much depended upon me," she acknowledged on the eve of her brother's wedding.

A faint whiff of disappointed romance rises at Ebe's name, although no concrete evidence links her to any broken engagement. There is, however, the predictable supposition that "it was a love disappointment, as it [Ebe's seclusion] began after a visit she had made of three weeks in Newburyport, where she had met an interesting gentleman, who, she expected, would come to see her in Salem." He never did. Several family letters loosely connect her to a well-off widower, Captain Jeremiah Briggs, a keen-witted cohort of Uncle Robert, more his age than hers; so does some of Hawthorne's earliest writing. "The beautiful Miss E. M. Hathorne," he remarks in the family newspaper he printed, "formerly of this place [Maine], had consented to enter the holy state of Matrimony, in company with Capt. Jeremiah Briggs, a young gentleman of rank and accomplishments." Nathaniel may have been ribbing her, but Briggs married another in 1831.

As her nephew Julian would say, there was simply no foothold in life for one such as she.

She adored her only brother. He adored her. "She is the most sensible woman I ever knew in my life, much superior to me in general talent," he wrote in adulthood, trying to land her a job. But he was awed by her, even jealous. "I suppose she would not have the ghost of a chance in literature," he remarked, as if he secretly hoped she wouldn't. To him, Ebe was brilliant and dangerous. "The only thing I fear is the ridicule of Elizabeth," he reportedly said. And that he transformed her into a fabulous being, capricious and ephemeral, reveals how deeply she entered his imagination: "You must never expect to see my sister E. in the day-time, unless by previous appointment, or when she goes to walk," he would warn his fiancée. "So unaccustomed am I to daylight interviews, that I never imagine her in sunshine; and I really doubt whether her faculties of life and intellect begin to be exercised till dusk."

As children, the two siblings read each other's literary efforts with genuine interest, sending secret messages in a basket rigged between their two

"Moderate Views," poem written at thirteen years

rooms on Herbert Street, his on the third floor and hers on the second. But she was a severe critic, he later said, unamiable in her tastes.

Doubtless, too, Nathaniel envied the privileges Ebe enjoyed or that he imagined she did, both as elder sibling and the particular prize of her uncles, especially Uncle Robert, whom he grew to resent. For Uncle Robert would never wrench Ebe, a girl, from her beloved mother, as he would Nathaniel.

Betsy Hathorne was a languishing widow bonded to the memory of her dead husband. Or so testified Elizabeth Palmer Peabody, Nathaniel's sister-in-law, in later years. Believing the rumors spread by Salem busybodies, Peabody insisted the Widow Hathorne "made it the habit of her life never to sit down at a table but always eat her meals above in the chamber she never left. For this, she was constantly criticized & (blamed) condemned by the neighbours, including connections of the family." A Manning descendant rebutted her claim. If the Hathornes took their meals upstairs, they did so for reasons of economy—as well as privacy, rare in a household so large.

This last reason seems truer. And the Widow Hathorne did dream of escaping the hullabaloo of Herbert Street by "improving property of our own." She was referring to their property in Maine. To her, the future lay in its rugged wilderness, where, as a missionary of the backwoods, on Sundays she might teach Scripture to the local residents.

But with the move postponed, indefinitely it seemed, Nathaniel relapsed. Out came the crutches, pieces of wood added to lengthen them, since the boy was growing tall. "You say he is worse than I am," Uncle Richard wrote to Robert. Richard had recently fractured his collarbone. Linked once again, Nathaniel and his uncle convalesced at the same rate, both of them on the mend in the spring of 1815, when the move was back on track, and a jubilant Nathaniel, mounted on one of the Manning nags, galloped around town.

But the trip was again postponed. Richard decided the Hathornes ought to wait until the following spring, when his new house would be ready. Having married Susan Dingley, daughter of one of Raymond's first white settlers, he was building a mansion of his own, thirty-six feet long and thirty feet wide, with four rooms to a floor, so big by Raymond standards that it earned the sobriquet "Manning's Folly" from startled neighbors, who claimed the glass for its windows came all the way from Belgium.

Another year passed before the Hathornes finally arrived in Maine in 1816 along with Aunt Mary and Grandmother Manning, who consented to spend the summer. Betsy, however, planned to run the farm Richard had bought in nearby Bridgton—the roads between were passable. The children were ecstatic. There were sheep and hens and sweet country air, completely

Manning's Folly, Raymond, Maine

unlike the smoky fumes of Salem. "Stay here one summer," Ebe rhapsodized, "& you will not be reconciled to live in any other place."

Bent on domesticating the sacred wood, Betsy Hathorne defended her decision to go to Raymond to Priscilla Manning, the bossy sister who hated change. "It is true we are deprived of many privileges that you enjoy," Betsy explained, "it is much to be lamented that their is no settled Minister in this place we endeavour to compensate for the loss of public worship by studying our Bibles and other good books we are favored with I regret more every day the loss of the society of my friends yet I trust we shall be contented and I hope usefull." To that end, she asked that Priscilla send her furniture and china, Spenser's *Faerie Queene,* an edition of Shakespeare, and a dozen silk buttons.

Her nerve didn't last. The Mannings, especially Priscilla, pressured Betsy at least to send Nathaniel back to Salem to go to school, which she did reluctantly in the fall of 1816. Winter darkened on the lonely horizon. She coughed. Consumption? She ought to go to Salem too, if only for the winter. Richard didn't object; the idea of her running the farm had struck him as impracticable anyway. The Hathornes packed their belongings but promised to return as soon as possible.

In anticipation, Richard built another house across the brook from his. Plain, symmetrical, and large, it cost an immense sum, twenty-three hundred dollars, barn and outbuildings included, no expense spared for the Hathornes. The investment was worth the trouble, for just after Richard lit the fireplaces to take the chill from the boards, Robert arrived in Raymond with Betsy and Nathaniel and Ebe and Louisa. A year and a half had passed; it was now the fall of 1818.

"I do not feel at all surprised that people think it strange we should remove from Salem," Ebe primly informed her aunt Priscilla, "but I assure you we are extremely well contented here, and that nothing could induce us to return." Especially Nathaniel. He tracked bears in the rubbery bush, angled for black-spotted trout at Thomas Pond, and shot partridge with his father's gun, which Aunt Mary warned him against using so much. In the dry season, he rambled the Sebago's low-lying shores; that winter he walked for miles on its crunchy surface. And though his residence in Raymond, all told, amounted to less than a year, it swiftly assumed for him, as for his sister, the aura of myth. One could live best out-of-doors in the woods, she would say, just as one had dwelled in the Forest of Arden.

"I ran quite wild, and would, I doubt not, have willingly run wild till this time, fishing all day long, or shooting with an old fowling-piece; but reading

Hathorne house, Raymond, Maine

a good deal, too, on the rainy days, especially in Shakspeare and 'The Pilgrim's Progress,' and any poetry or light books within my reach," he would recall. "Those were delightful days; for that part of the country was wild then, with only scattered clearings, and nine tenths of it primeval woods."

According to Ebe, Maine toughened a once delicate brother. "It did him a great deal of good, in many ways," she remarked in retrospect. "It was a new place, with few inhabitants, *far away* 'from churches and schools,' so of course [he] was taught nothing; but he became a good shot, and an excellent fisherman, and grew tall and strong. His imagination was stimulated, too, by the scenery and by the strangeness of the people; and by the absolute freedom he enjoyed."

Some say that Nathaniel kept a record of his Maine escapades in a diary, the first he ever owned and a present from his uncle Richard, who, in his inscription, urged him to write out his thoughts, some every day, in words as good as he could find, "upon any and all subjects, as it is one of the best means of securing for mature years, command of thought and language." Several years after Hawthorne's death, copied selections from this putative diary were sent to Samuel T. Pickard, nephew of John Greenleaf Whittier and part owner of the *Portland Transcript* in Maine. The packet came from someone who called himself "W.S.," subsequently discovered to be William Simms or Symmes, a mulatto who lived in nearby Otisfield and an acquaintance of Nathaniel's.

Pickard began to publish these excerpts in 1871. Julian, quick to discredit whatever his family did not control, cried fraud and dismissed the excerpts as a "clumsy and leaky fabrication"; even if discovered to be genuine, they were, he said, "singularly destitute of biographical value." Ebe was not so sure. She remembered some of the incidents recounted in the diary, as did a number of Cumberland County old-timers, and Uncle Robert Manning's son discovered that Susan Dingley Manning had mentioned Richard's giving it to Nathaniel.

Unfortunately, the original diary never surfaced. Symmes assured Pickard he'd bring it to Portland. He didn't. Pickard, who printed one thousand copies of the diary in 1897, began to have misgivings. Corroborating much of the diary's information with "old-timers" in Maine, he also learned that the diarist recounted an event that took place in 1828, long after Hawthorne had left there. But the diary did seem written in Hawthorne's style. Confused, he stopped trying to locate the original and concluded that the whole thing was at the very least "a literary curiosity of the first water, whether Hawthorne's or the negro's work."

Indeed it is, although most scholars consider the diary a hoax. Admittedly, its prose seems polished, especially Richard Manning's inscription. Yet we, like Ebe, can't discard it out of hand. If not by Hawthorne himself, the passages were written by someone who knew him and his family. "I have made this account of the expedition to please uncle Richard, who is an invalid," comments the diarist, "and cannot get out to enjoy such support, and wished me to write and describe everything just as it happened, whether witty or silly, and give my own impressions."

The diarist is knowledgeable about persons and places in or near Raymond, and though this proves nothing, he's also a whimsical figure, a down east Huck Finn gifted in the rudiments of storytelling. He imagines a conversation between himself and a tired old workhorse: "This morning I saw at the grist-mill a solemn-faced old horse, hitched to a trough. He had brought for his owner some bags of corn to be ground, who, after carrying them into the mill, walked up to uncle Richard's store, leaving his half-starved animal in the cold wind, with nothing to eat, while the corn was being turned to meal. I felt sorry, and nobody being near, thought it best to have a talk with the old nag, and said, 'Good-morning, Mr. Horse, how are you to-day?' "

The shadow of Betsy Hathorne darts through these passages too. She's a solicitous woman capable of laughing at her son's naïveté and vigilant about his welfare. "Since the loss of my father, she dreads to have any one belonging to her go upon the water," the diarist remarks. Then Uncle Richard comes to the rescue, finagling her consent for Nathaniel to go on a fishing trip. "I was almost sorry," admits the diarist, "knowing that my day's pleasure would cost her one of anxiety."

This son, whoever he is, doesn't quite know how to leave his mother.

We glimpse Robert Manning fleetingly. Someone preserved a strand of his hair, the color of chestnuts in fall, in a small locket portrait made of him circa 1818. At thirty-four he looks both exhausted and adamant. He stands in front of a flowering tree and holds a leaf in his hand.

Like his siblings Richard and Betsy, Robert wanted to live close to the earth, to produce something, harvest something, claim something in the world as his own. He was no mere stagecoach manager. A man who required order and regulation, he was inventive and, in his own way, extraordinary, for he hoped to convert the wilderness, quite literally, into a garden—an orchard, actually—and he would take whatever time he needed to do it. He started by importing various types of fruit trees to Raymond. And when he

Robert Manning [circa 1818]

realized he'd be staying in Salem more or less permanently, he resigned as director of the family stage business to become its silent partner. Then he turned his attention to the wonderful varieties of pear.

Over the next twenty-five years, Robert Manning would also improve an assortment of cherry, apple, plum, and peach trees in an undertaking that demanded persistence, patience, and dedication as well as the long view. He helped establish the Massachusetts Horticultural Society, and as one of America's leading pomologists, a veritable prince among them, he dispensed his choicest fruit and seeds to anyone knowledgeable or curious. "An orchard has a relation to mankind," Nathaniel would write in veiled tribute to Uncle Robert, "and readily connects itself with matters of the heart."

In 1838 Manning published *The Book of Fruits: Being a Descriptive Catalogue of the Most Valuable Varieties of the Pear, Apple, Peach, Plum & Cherry, for New England Culture,* fully illustrated. In it, Manning praises the Hawthorndean apple as a medium-size fruit, remarkably handsome, flesh white and very juicy but not highly flavored: perhaps his perspective on Nathaniel. For try as he might, Robert Manning could not cultivate his nephew as he might an apple or a peach.

In an early story, Hawthorne invents a comic character, Parson Thumpcushion, the guardian of an orphan boy: "Though he had an upright heart," says the story's narrator, "and some called it a warm one, he was invariably stern and severe, on principle, to me." Robert could be similarly insufferable. He corrected the grammar and spelling of his siblings and shouldered the responsibility—he liked to believe—for the betterment of his entire family. Yet he loved Nathaniel. "The older 'dear uncle' grows, the more he will love you," he once told his nephew, and meant it. To this love, however, he attached various strings, which annoyed the fourteen-year-old rocketing toward independence, gun slung on his back, in the woodlands of Maine.

To Robert, Maine was no place for a boy in need of an education and, though Robert didn't say it, refinement. Uncle Richard didn't exactly object to education—he himself loved books of travel, history, and fiction—but he was leery of Salem pretensions. Betsy was caught between the brothers. The idea of a rural retreat in Maine, a farm, even a meetinghouse where she could hold her Bible class and comfort the unchurched—all this appealed to her. Wanting Nathaniel close by, she helped effect a compromise: Richard's young brother-in-law Jacob Dingley was being sent to school in Stroudwater, outside Portland, and Nathaniel would go with him.

The two boys boarded with the Reverend Caleb Bradley, an upright Congregationalist and descendant of the notorious female Indian-slayer Hannah Duston (about whom Hawthorne would later write). Bradley was an eccentric, parsimonious man who liked to knit and sermonize. Needless to say, the boys were unhappy. Richard went to Portland and found them threatening to run away; soon Nathaniel was back in Raymond. But Robert, who poked fun at Nathaniel's "dolefull complaints no mamma to take care of him," saw his chance. Mama's boy must become a man and go back to Herbert Street, this time for good.

Richard bristled at Robert's peremptory demand. "I have no chance to send Nathaniel nor is he willing to come to Salem," he answered. The Mannings ignored him, and Priscilla reserved a place in Salem for Nathaniel at Samuel Archer's school. He was slated to begin classes after his fifteenth birthday, in the summer of 1819.

This was a fate even worse than Stroudwater. Nathaniel fired off a salvo to the Salem Mannings, hoping to stave off the inevitable, if only for a little while. He had caught eighteen large brook trout and shot a partridge and a hen hawk, he told Uncle Robert, as if to impress him. "I am sorry you intend to send me to school again," he added. "Mother says she can hardly spare me."

Alas. The woods are no longer exempt from public haunt.

"He sighs for the woods of Raymond, and yet he seems to be convinced of the necessity of preparing to do something," Mary Manning reassured Betsy. Nathaniel was back on Herbert Street, where the Mannings cared less about his homesickness than his future. "I have no employment ready for him," Uncle Robert jested, "however as a last resort we can bind him for 7 years to turn a Cutters Wheel & perhaps better."

The adjustment was difficult. "Aunt Mary is continually scolding at me," Nathaniel complained to his mother. "Grandmaam hardly ever speaks a pleasant word to me." He was chided, he was rebuked. "If I ever try to speak a word in my defense, they cry out against my impudence," he protested. And none of the men backed him up. Uncles William and Samuel, having disgraced themselves in a failed business venture, were without much clout. Uncle Robert still spent long periods in Raymond. Hurry back, his nephew pleaded. "It seems very lonesome here," he said. "There is a pot of excellent guaver jelly now in the house and one of preserved limes and I am afraid they will mould if you do not come soon for it's esteemed sacrilege by Grandmother to eat any of them now because she is keeping them against somebody is sick and I suppose she would be very much disappointed if everybody was to continue well and they were to spoil."

"How often do I long for my gun, and wish that I could again savagize with you," he wrote his sister Louisa. "But I shall never again run wild in Raymond, and I shall never be so happy as when I did." His happiness, his gun, his sovereignty, his sisters, his mother: paradise lost in Raymond. "Oh how I wish I was again with you with nothing to do but to go a gunning," a forlorn Nathaniel lamented, this time to his mother. "But the happiest days of my life are gone. Why was I not a girl that I might have been pinned all my life to my Mother's apron."

Rising at six in the morning to study, he managed to satisfy his Salem teachers and his family, but when he wrote his mother and sisters, he insisted, "I shall never be contented here I am sure." Raymond was the measure of all he held dear. "I dreamed the other night, that I was walking by the Sebago, and when I awoke was so angry at finding it all a delusion, that I gave Uncle Robert (who sleeps with me) a most horrible kick."

It seems appropriate to mention here biographer James Mellow's speculation, based on this letter, that, "pressed to explain the nature of Hawthorne's critical experience [of sin], I would suggest that he may have been subjected to some homosexual assault or seduction, perhaps by his Uncle

Robert, during the period when the two were sleeping together." A responsible critic, Mellow knew his conjecture derived not from evidence but from the shaky attempt to pin a meaning on a single remark, one that has more significance today, when uncles and nephews do not normally sleep together, than in 1821, when the Mannings crowded into fewer rooms, having rented part of the house to boarders. Plus, the richly ambivalent relationship between Hawthorne and his uncle Robert Manning resists simple assumptions. And without evidence—we don't even know what Hawthorne was dreaming—we can as easily assume Nathaniel made a sexual overture toward his uncle rather than the reverse.

Nor can a single, flat interpretation untangle the imagery of guns and virility—or aggression, comfort, and escape—encircling Nathaniel's relation to more than one uncle and, later, to other men.

Whether in Raymond or Salem, Nathaniel was a voracious reader. A young man of his time, he consumed Walter Scott, Ann Radcliffe, the *Arabian Nights,* Tobias Smollett, William Godwin, Rousseau's *La Nouvelle Héloïse,* the poet James Greenland, Samuel Johnson, James Hogg, Oliver Goldsmith, Byron, Southey, Burns, and Henry Fielding, his taste running to Gothicism, poetry, and social comment. If he had friends, he doesn't mention them; he rationalized in later years that, "having spent so much of my boyhood and youth away from my native place, I had very few acquaintances in Salem."

And there was Ebe. With her he could share his reading and with her aspire to great verse. Or, if not great, at least publishable. "Tell Ebe she's not the only one of the family whose works have appeared in the papers," he bragged. Alas, if Ebe's or Nathaniel's work was in fact printed, no one knows what or where.

But some of Nathaniel's early poems have escaped oblivion, especially those mailed to Louisa in Raymond. A "Departed Genius" molders in his "lowly grave"; a lover mourns his beloved's death; and with less sanctimoniousness, the poet memorializes his favorite cat. In one didactic poem, a young man leaves home to go to war and finds himself lamenting "that lone cottage, where/The early hours of life flew by,/On wings of youthful ecstasy." Too late the callow warrior discovers "that Glory's ray,/Could never bring one happy day."

The themes of these productions anticipate motifs in his early fiction: displacement, homesickness, and the vanity of earthly things. In the story

"My Kinsman, Major Molineux," for instance, Robin longs for some prelapsarian spot far from the bustle—and temptations—of urban life. At the same time, Robin, like Nathaniel, has been hoping to profit from the good graces of his uncle, a city dweller of some stature, he assumes. He travels to town to earn his favor and "rise in the world," but, increasingly disillusioned, yearns for the rustic family he left behind in the woods. He imagines them gathering at sunset just before going indoors, "and when Robin would have entered also, the latch tinkled into its place, and he was excluded from his home. 'Am I here, or there?' cried Robin, starting; for all at once, when his thoughts had become visible and audible in a dream, the long, wide, solitary street shone out before him."

Robin can't go home again. Like it or not, he's a town boy now. And the town promises success—or failure. "Oh earthly pomp is but a dream," Nathaniel as poet waxes philosophic, repudiating it; yet he's no fool. "Those may be my rhymes," he tells Louisa, "yet they are not exactly my thoughts." Earthly pomp is gratifying, whatever the commandments of his Bible-thumping relatives, including his mother, who time and again warn against the vanity and uncertainty of the riches of this world. "One thing only is needfull," she reiterated, "an interest in Jesus Christ, secure that and you will have treasure in Heaven, where neither moth nor rust can corrupt, nor thieves break through and steal."

Estranged from two worlds—Raymond, Salem—Nathaniel inhabited both. ("Am I here, or there?" Robin asks.) Wishing to please his Manning relatives, especially Uncle Robert—I am almost as tall as he, Nathaniel strutted—he understood he'd have to succeed on Robert's terms. Was that so bad? Salem offered Mr. Boisseaux's dancing school; Edmund Kean in *King Lear;* nearby Boston; and even the satisfactions of Latin, which he liked. None of this existed in Raymond.

So Nathaniel brought Salem and Raymond together in *The Spectator,* a homemade newspaper he composed for his family, detailing their goings-on in both places. Using the format of the Salem papers, particularly the *Gazette,* he provided gossip as well as humorous and homiletic essays on topics like benevolence, wealth, courage, and industry—although he didn't know too much about the latter topic, he said, "it not being one of the attributes of literary men."

As Nathaniel's declaration of independence and his passport into literature, *The Spectator* presents Nathaniel in a new guise. Writing without the veil he adopted in later life—the veil of fiction—Nathaniel introduces himself as the gentleman scribbler, blue-blooded, aloof and indolent, a spectator of the roiling world but not of it, and a success of sorts, though not of the Thumpcushion kind.

But if the literary man is a cultured idler—the posture was then in vogue—he's also a wastrel, vain and decadent. This is America after all, not the England of Addison and Steele, and despite his chafing, Nathaniel at bottom accepted the Manning credo of practicality and hard work. "How far preferable is the sweet consciousness that we have diligently performed our Duty," he observes, "to the self reproaches which continually invade us, when we feel that we have idly neglected what should have been performed. . . . And although the exertions of an industrious man may be fruitless, yet he will have the reflection to console him in Adversity, that no fault of his own rendered him unsuccessful. The idle man will have no such comfort," he continued, "the many advantages that he has neglected, and the time that he has mis-spent will rise up in judgement against him, and poverty will be embittered by the reproaches of his own conscience."

At sixteen Nathaniel was articulating his psychological dilemma. The illicit pleasures of indolence, wildness, and autonomy drew him to Maine, associated with his mother and his uncle Richard, that place where he could safely rebel against regulation, usefulness, and enterprise, and even could sport his father's gun, untoppled by cackling schoolboys who might push him off the podium. But there's a hitch. As he writes in his *Spectator* essay, indolence avails nothing but poverty and dependence; it's the refuge of the lame.

Following his essay on idleness is a companion piece, "On Ambition," in which he admits that striving "raises man above the brutes, and places him in a station next to that of the Angels." Naked ambition may be odious and crass, the stuff of pride and Satan's fall, but Milton's Satan is not to be ignored or belittled. And Nathaniel was eager for laurels, even if they'd been dipped in sulfur. The problem was that he associated ambition with the materialistic, hard-driving city of Salem.

Idle, ambitious, and damned either way.

"What do you think of my becoming an Author, and relying for support upon my pen," he would soon query his mother. It was a perfect compromise. Then he paused. "But authors are always poor Devils, and therefore Satan may take them."

CHAPTER FOUR

The Era of Good Feelings

Our court shall be a little academy.

William Shakespeare, *Love's Labour's Lost,*
quoted by Nathaniel Hawthorne in *Fanshawe*

I HAVE ALMOST given up writing Poetry," Nathaniel postured in the fall of 1820. "No Man can be a Poet & a Book-Keeper at the same time." This was the plaint of the Romantic poet, who claimed that art and business didn't mix—meaning Nathaniel needed someplace far from the hubbub of Salem, like the Maine woods, to sing his stirring song.

The Mannings, however, were focused on more prosaic matters, like that of Nathaniel's future. "We must not have our expectations too much raised about him," Mary Manning cautioned Betsy with obvious delight, "but his Master speaks very encouragingly respecting his talents &c and is solicitous to have him go to Colleg." Mary backed the plan, she added, because it promised to make her nephew "worthy & usefull." With business in Salem slow and nothing for Nathaniel to do, Robert also approved, provided he had the money. Mary did. She supplied one hundred dollars, and Robert raised the rest, leaning on his brother Samuel and sister Priscilla's husband, John Dike. "So you are in danger of having one learned man in your family," boasted Nathaniel to his mother.

Within the month he was trudging through glossy snow early each morning to recite his Latin and Greek lessons at the home of Benjamin Lynde Oliver Jr., a literary-minded lawyer who may have considered Nathaniel a future apprentice. Afternoons, Nathaniel left Oliver's to clerk at the stagecoach office and keep the books for his uncle William. In his free time, he wrote *The Spectator* and prepared for the dancing school ball with

Louisa, now in Salem too. "Much time & money lost to no good purpose I fear," griped Uncle Robert, doubtless pleased.

Though he enjoyed his various employments, Nathaniel found himself unaccountably depressed. He was chewing tobacco "with all my might, which I think raises my spirits," he wrote to Ebe in Maine. He chafed under Uncle Robert's harness. But without him, what would he do? And how could he prove himself? At college? And supposing he was admitted, would he be found wanting once there? "Do not you regret the time when I was a little boy," he asked his mother. "I do almost."

He'd have to choose a profession. "Shall you want me to be a Minister, Doctor or Lawyer?" he again queried his mother, sounding anxious. "A Minister I will not be," he declared, as if guessing her answer; and he rejected law and medicine. "I should not like to live by the diseases and Infirmities of my fellow Creatures." It was then that he broached the idea of becoming a writer, angling for Betsy's approval. "How proud you would feel to see my works praised by the reviewers, as equal to proudest productions of the scribbling sons of John Bull," he wrote to his mother, trying to sweeten her with a bit of swagger.

Whatever his mother replied, his aunts and uncles in Salem were likely horror-struck. "An angel would fail to obtain their approbation," Ebe grimaced, "unless he came attired in a linsey-woolsey gown & checked apron, and assumed an *honourable* and *dignified station* at the washing tub." Pampered, insecure, and talented, she and Nathaniel aspired to the higher things the Mannings would never countenance, making failure all the more ignominious; it would prove the Mannings right, which Nathaniel and Ebe may have believed they were.

There were many reasons Nathaniel went to a "country college," as Henry James would later disparage Bowdoin. Partly there was the matter of money. At Harvard a student paid approximately $600 for his first year, whereas at Bowdoin the estimated annual tuition and room cost a more frugal $34, with board averaging $1.75 a week, and sundry expenses only three or so more dollars for two terms. And there was the matter of religion. Bowdoin had not succumbed to that weightless Unitarianism practiced at Harvard. Chartered in 1794, with its first class of seven graduated in 1806, Bowdoin stoutly embraced an unflappable Congregationalism, particularly during the tenure of Jesse Appleton, the current president (though not for long), who demanded piety as well as Virgil from prospective collegians.

There were other reasons still. The Mannings, even Robert, continued to regard Maine as their spiritual home, and with Bowdoin located in Brunswick, just thirty miles north of Portland—five hours in a bumpy stage—it was close to Betsy Hathorne. "I am quite reconciled to going," Nathaniel told his mother in the late winter of 1821, "since I am to spend the Vacations with you," and by spring he was picturing their reunions, "shut out from the world, and nothing to disturb us. It will be a second Garden of Eden."

But less than a year later, with Nathaniel in college, the Widow Hathorne boarded up her house in Raymond and headed back to Herbert Street, leaving her son to his own devices in the Promised Land.

All the way to Brunswick, Nathaniel fidgeted, so sure he'd fail the college entrance examination that he told Uncle Robert to be ready to take him home. "I encouraged him as much as possible," Robert reported to the Mannings.

They had departed Salem on the last Friday of September 1822 and

Bowdoin College, 1823, oil by John G. Brown

reached Bowdoin, via Raymond, on the following Tuesday. Located on a sandy plain near the falls of the Androscoggin River, the college quadrangle consisted of two brick Georgian-style structures, a white belfry at the crown of one of them, and an unpainted—and, as it turned out, unheated— wooden chapel that served as a library for an hour a day. In the background stood a forest of deep-needled pine.

Robert and Nathaniel called on Ebenezer Everett, one of Bowdoin's trustees, and presented Benjamin Oliver's letter of introduction. Everett read it, was satisfied, and sent the new student and his uncle to the president's house. After Appleton's sudden death, the Reverend William Allen had come to Bowdoin, fresh from the political controversies at Dartmouth University, where he'd briefly been president. The trustees of Dartmouth having dismissed Allen's father-in-law as president for religious lassitude, the Republicans in the New Hampshire state legislature in turn dismissed the trustees, replacing them with a board of overseers and Allen. A legal battle then ripped throughout the college and the state, with Daniel Webster, crack Federalist attorney and graduate of Dartmouth, successfully arguing before the United States Supreme Court that the New Hampshire legislature had no right to override the original charter of Dartmouth as a private institution. It was time for Allen, a Republican, to get out. He landed at Bowdoin, where he enforced the rules with pharisaical precision and meted out fire and brimstone to the students, who didn't like him. Nathaniel called Allen "a short, thick little lump of a man." But the little lump strengthened the faculty and started the medical school. Nathaniel was in capable hands.

At two o'clock Nathaniel appeared before the college authorities, passed his entrance examination, and was assigned to share a room with Albert Mason in a private home near the college. With a freshman class of thirty-eight—Bowdoin's largest thus far—the dormitory was temporarily full. Uncle Robert hunted for Nathaniel's trunk, sent to the wrong address, while Nathaniel looked around the village and purchased in the shops the items he needed for his room. Robert paid the bill, regretting he hadn't brought more money; tuition and board cost what he'd expected, but the outlay for books and furniture left just enough for firewood and some candles. Fortunately, Uncle William had given the boy an extra five dollars, a good thing, especially since his roommate was the son of the Honorable Jeremiah Mason and "has money enough," Nathaniel observed, "which is perhaps unfortunate for me, as it is absolutely necessary that I should make as good an appearance as he does."

Never intimate with Mason, Nathaniel rapidly made other friends. "I am very well contented with my situation," he wrote to Ebe, "and like a College Life much better than I expected"—all the more since his studies allowed plenty of time for wine, cards, and other "unlawful occupations, which are made more pleasant by the fines attached to them if discovered." By spring President Allen had to contact Mrs. Hathorne to ask her "to induce your Son faithfully to observe the laws of this Institution." Cushioning the blow, he suggested Nathaniel may have been unduly influenced by a wayward friend, recently dismissed from the college. Nathaniel took immediate umbrage. He alone was the author of his deeds, thank you very much.

He constantly broke the rules. He resented regulations stipulating how far one could walk on the Sabbath and that forbade smoking a "seegar" on the street or consuming alcohol. For if nothing else, the bone-chilling cold of a long Maine winter provided sufficient incentive to drink. Students smuggled alcohol into their rooms, loading extra lamp-fillers with liquor instead of oil. In 1826, the year after Hawthorne's graduation, twelve thousand gallons of liquor were drunk in the small village of Brunswick, population about two thousand, including women and children; one assumes the figures weren't altogether different during his residence.

Nathaniel was a charter member of the secret Pot-8-O Club, dedicated to weekly poems and the eating of tubers, or so their constitution alleged; they held meetings in Ward's Tavern, and refreshments included roasted potatoes and cider polished off, no doubt, with ale, wine, or hard liquor. Similarly, he helped found the Androscoggin Club, another informal organization dedicated to card playing and drinking. Nathaniel and a crony dragged a keg of wine into the forest for a hilarious weekend.

Nathaniel was adjusting to college life, or his version of it. He neglected his recitations and ducked all forms of public worship, including evening and Sunday prayers. Compulsory Bible lessons irritated him. "Meeting for this day is over," he joked to Ebe, poking fun at the red-hot Calvinism of the place. "We have had a Minister from the Andover mill, and he 'dealt damnation round' with an unsparing hand, and finished by consigning us all to the Devil."

Many of the men in Nathaniel's class were headed toward careers in government, and the college itself was subject to the political winds blowing outside academe. In 1819 the Era of Good Feelings, as the years of James Madison's administration had been called, was about to end. Missouri's application for admission to the Union had ignited an acrimonious political debate about whether Missouri would become a free or a slave state, and as everyone knew, the Missouri decision would shift the balance of power in the Senate, exposing yet again the moral contradiction at the heart of the Republic: slavery. The issue, as Jefferson famously said, rang a firebell in the night.

The clang had been heard from Missouri to Maine, particularly since the province of Maine, wishing to separate from Massachusetts, had applied for statehood. In 1820, Maine was admitted to the Union on Missouri's coattails in the famous Compromise that temporarily banked the fire; Maine entered a free state, Missouri a slave state, and slavery was forbidden above 36° 30′ north latitude, Missouri excepted, and permitted below.

The country's political divisions were reflected at Bowdoin in its rivalrous literary societies. Several of the professors as well as the more conservative, Federalist, and respectable undergraduates joined the Peucinian, which boasted a library of twelve hundred volumes. The Peucinians included Alfred Mason and the young Henry Wadsworth Longfellow, whose father was a college trustee. Longfellow's more dissolute brother Stephen joined the rowdier, newer, more dissident Athenaean Society (their smaller library, though founded first, contained about eight hundred books), a pack of "Young Bowdoin" Jeffersonians who in 1824 backed Andrew Jackson for president. Nathaniel Hathorne, an Athenaean, served on the society's standing committee.

His closest friends were three other Athenaeans, each of whom entered public service as Jacksonian Democrats. One of them, Franklin Pierce, became the fourteenth president of the United States—either the worst or the weakest president, said Ralph Waldo Emerson, ever elected. Hawthorne and Pierce were friends for a lifetime.

At college Nathaniel liked the ambitious men of action who hoped to dedicate their lives to principle by serving their country and, in the case of Pierce, by following in the footsteps of their fathers. Pierce's father Benjamin, a staunch Republican, was a Bunker Hill veteran and New Hampshire governor known to his Federalist detractors as a "noisy, foul-mouthed, hard-drinking tavern keeper." The elder Pierce was probably an alcoholic, and his son resembled him in this, minus the noisy, foul mouth.

Pierce started his career young. Born and raised in Hillsborough, New Hampshire, he entered Bowdoin at just sixteen in 1820, the year before Nathaniel. Dreaming of glory on the battlefield, he drilled Bowdoin undergraduates, Hawthorne included, among the pines. With a fair complexion, blue eyes, and light brown hair that sometimes fell forward in a raffish way, he was a handsome and popular man, his carriage erect, his personality warm, his sympathy real and affecting. Even his enemies in later years—and there were many—commented on his compassion. Not the abolitionists; they despised him.

He was honest, too—no small feat in a man headed for the presidency. Or honestly obtuse. A Bowdoin tutor, seeing Pierce's slate during an algebra quiz, asked him how he'd gotten his answer. "I got it from Stowe's slate," Pierce replied. He frittered away the first two years of his academic career, and in his third year ranked at the absolute bottom of his class. Bucking for more failure, he disappeared from recitation. His friends begged him to return, and for some reason college authorities ignored his delinquency. Touched by all the solicitude, Pierce vowed to mend his ways and from then on burned the midnight oil—not alcohol—every night, waking before dawn to study some more. He graduated fourth in his class.

Another Athenaean was Jonathan Cilley, the grandson of a Revolutionary War patriot who worked his way through college, his father having died in 1808. Nathaniel considered Cilley's mind practical—perhaps to a fault—and after Cilley's death recalled the innate oratorical skills that "seemed always to accomplish precisely the result on which he had calculated." President of the Athenaeans, Cilley was slim and sharp-featured and crafty, his geniality generous and well-managed. Yet, insisted Nathaniel, his real talent lay, like Pierce's, in his "power of sympathy." Only two years his senior, Cilley acted as an "elder brother" to Nathaniel, who would idealize him as possessing the "simplicity of one who had dwelt remote from cities, holding free companionship with the yeoman of the land." But Cilley was no rube, and Nathaniel knew it.

Nathaniel and his friends competed in all areas, from class standing to appearance, placing friendly wagers on their future. "If Nathaniel Hathorne is neither a married man nor a widower on the fourteenth day of November, One Thousand Eight Hundred and Thirty-six," Cilley bet, "I bind myself upon my honor to pay the said Hathorne a barrel of the best old Madeira wine." He lost, shrugged, and delayed paying his debt as long as he could: he had the makings of a stellar political career.

Like Pierce, Cilley quickly rose through the Democratic Party, as the Jeffersonian Republicans were called since Jackson's election. After college Cilley studied law in Thomaston, Maine, and then headed straight to the legislature. Known as a popular and conniving Democrat, he entered the

United States Congress in 1836. But he was also steering toward an early and violent death by dueling, "stretched in his own blood," Nathaniel would write, "—slain for an almost impalpable punctilio!"

Julian Hawthorne, preparing to write his father's biography, noted that when Nathaniel went to college, he was muscular and handsome, insubordinate toward the faculty, and condescending toward fellow students. In fact, remarked Julian, his father dominated men like Franklin Pierce, with whom he drank, but never got drunk himself.

Julian's observations ring with some small truth. Students who did not know him well remember Nathaniel as a taciturn young fellow, the most diffident member of the class, said one, "shrinking almost like a girl from all general intercourse either in the sports or meetings of his fellow students." His closest confidant, Horatio Bridge, conjured a somewhat different image, that of Nathaniel strolling by his side through the thick pine-sweet forest, two friends sharing the confidences of undergraduates no longer boys, not quite men.

Hawthorne too hailed these salad days of early friendship, honoring Bridge in the 1851 dedication to *The Snow-Image and Other Stories*. It was Bridge who encouraged him, then and later, as a writer when he needed it most. "I know not whence your faith came," he wrote in loving tribute; ". . . still it was your prognostic of your friend's destiny, that he was to be a writer of fiction."

Two years younger than Nathaniel, Horatio Bridge was the son of Hannah and James Bridge, the latter a mighty financier as well as trustee of Bowdoin College. Born in Augusta, Maine, and educated there at Hallowell Academy, Bridge was a self-effacing man so tall, said Longfellow, that he "stands and looks plumb-down onto the top of my head." Clear-eyed and confident, he regarded the world as a safe place if managed in correct, courteous fashion. "Polished, yet natural, frank, open, and straightforward, yet with a delicate feeling for the sensitiveness of his companion," Hawthorne would describe him, "never varying from a code of honor and principle, which is really nice and rigid in its way."

Bridge long remembered his first glimpse of the undergraduate from Salem: a youth with wavy dark hair who cocked his head slightly to the side, his eyes blinking under an awning of heavy eyebrows. With those he didn't know well, Nathaniel kept his opinions to himself, Bridge recalled, and didn't put himself forward in any way. On Saturdays when the two of them hired a wagon or a chaise for a drive, Nathaniel never wanted to hold the reins.

When he chose, however, Nathaniel could rear himself up and intimidate anyone who crossed or mocked him. One ribald evening at the tavern, when he became the butt of a silly joke, Nathaniel coolly accosted the most pugnacious of the group with "so much of danger in his eye," recalled Bridge, "that no one afterwards alluded to the offensive subject in his presence."

Bridge and Nathaniel roamed the woods together, shot pigeon and gray squirrel, or reeled in speckled trout fished from the cold forest stream, "two idle lads, in short (as we need not fear to acknowledge now)," said Nathaniel, "doing a hundred things that the Faculty never heard of, or else it had been the worse for us." On the road to Topsham they recited poetry in the moonlight, Nathaniel sharing his early verse with Bridge while the water from the falls rippled and roared. Such romantic scenes were an essential of college life: young men, secure with one another, far from the anxieties roused by women. When the two young men graduated from Bowdoin, they pledged their loyalty. Nathaniel gave Bridge his father's gold watch seal, and later, with no diminishment of devotion, would call him "the best friend I ever had or shall have (of the male sex)." Though his junior, Horatio Bridge was something of a father to Nathaniel and always a friend.

Each morning of the academic year, the students huddled in the chapel before breakfast to praise their Creator while bed-makers cleaned their rooms. Then, after they ate, at nine o'clock they returned to their dormitories to plow into Xenophon, Herodotus, Thucydides, Isocrates, Demosthenes, Livy, and extracts from Pliny's letters, along with algebra, geometry, and English grammar. Before noon they went to another recitation, and then a third before sundown, and finally evening prayers, all in the icy chapel. On Sunday evenings they recited from the Bible.

By their senior year they had digested Locke's *Essay Concerning Human Understanding*, Dugald Stewart's *Elements of the Philosophy of the Human Mind*, William Paley's *Evidences of Christianity*, and Joseph Butler's *Analogy of Religion*. They also read the celebrated *Mineralogy* of Bowdoin's own Professor Nehemiah Cleaveland. They studied no modern languages or history.

On Wednesdays students declaimed their lessons in the chapel. Nathaniel did not. One college acquaintance recalled that Nathaniel's "timidity prevented him from appearing well as a recitation Scholar; and besides he had but little love for the College curriculum as a whole." Bridge thought so too. "He stood hardly above mediocrity," Bridge recalled, "in declamation he was literally *nowhere*." Latin was the exception. "In Latin and Greek, when he got his lessons, his translations were elegant; and as a writer both of Latin and English he stood at the head of the class, his themes always receiving the highest marks." Benjamin Oliver had taught his pupil well, and Nathaniel performed whenever he knew he could excel. Otherwise he shirked his schoolwork or, in the case of French, studied on his own with a private tutor.

Most of his peers knew that he intended to write fiction. Nathaniel, who would soon write short profiles of historical figures, may have profited somewhat from President Allen, who had compiled the first dictionary of American biography, a huge, albeit conventional, tome. Allen also wrote poetry, hymns, and sermons, and taught Dr. Johnson and Thomas Gray, among Nathaniel's preferred authors. Other influential teachers may have been the friendly Thomas Cogswell Upham, a favorite among undergraduates, who arrived at Bowdoin Nathaniel's senior year. Though Upham's specialty was commonsense philosophy, in 1819 he had published a volume of poems, *American Sketches,* about New England—"enchanting topicks," he explained in the preface, "for the pencil."

The brilliant professor of rhetoric, oratory, and political economy Samuel P. Newman (said to be a closet Unitarian) remembered Nathaniel's essays. They were so good, he asked Nathaniel to read aloud. Years after Nathaniel left Bowdoin, Newman could recall a young man of "reluctant step and averted look" who approached his door with "girlish diffidence." The author of a standard book on rhetoric—still used today—Newman probably helped Nathaniel shape his polished, almost classical style; himself a modest man, Newman took no credit for Hawthorne's later success.

But except for Bridge's, most of the recollections about Nathaniel at Bowdoin resemble Jonathan Cilley's: "I love Hawthorne, I admire him; but I do not know him. He lives in a mysterious world of thought and imagination which he never permits me to enter."

For vacation during his freshman year, Nathaniel returned to Raymond and put out the issue of *The Spectator* that praised idleness and ambition. This was also the season of Ebe's reputed engagement and of his mother's decision to forsake Maine.

In the spring of 1822, Betsy packed clothes, kitchenware, and bedding into trunks that were lifted onto sturdy wagons, leaving her furniture and of course the house that Richard himself now called "Manning's Folly." She didn't care. She was in a hurry, though the reasons aren't clear. Likely her mother, Nathaniel's grandmother, expected her to come home; her health was failing. But Betsy's children thought she should stay in Raymond. "I *know* that in one week after your return [to Salem] you will regret your present peaceful home," Ebe warned.

Betsy's defection seems to have adversely affected Nathaniel. Gambling again, he flirted with suspension until he scared himself—or realized that Robert might actually yank him out of college. He curbed his drinking, or said he did. "As steady as a Sign post, and as sober as a Deacon," he described himself to Ebe, who suspected he was lying. She was right. The fines mounted. By the spring of the following year, 1823, he owed the college almost half his tuition for broken windowpanes, damage to his room, and for tavern-hopping on Saturday night. So egregious were his crimes that in July of that year the executive government of the college again alerted Nathaniel's family.

His braggadocio, like his mischief, was mostly boyish, trivial, and forgettable, and though the college authorities were annoyed, Nathaniel did not have to forfeit his place in an exhibition planned for the fall of his senior year, where he read his Latin exercise, "De Patris Conscriptus Romanorum," in which he argued that the Roman senate is like a father, responsible for his children. In turn, the children bow to their father's rule. But times and fortune change: fathers overstep their authority, and the sons mutiny. In retaliation, the fathers repress the sons' rebellion until foreign armies, threatening to destroy Rome, unite all Romans in a common cause.

The enemy repulsed, fathers and sons set to bickering again. And though Augustus salvages some of the senate's former reputation, truth be told, the fathers are nothing but a diminished race of insignificant men.

This seems Nathaniel's parable of the present.

During his first year at Bowdoin, a fire wrecked much of Maine Hall, his dormitory, at which time he moved into Mrs. Adams's house on Maine Street, across from the campus. During his second year, he returned to the dormitory, now repaired, but for his last two years at college Nathaniel stayed in the Dunning house on Federal Street at the corner of Cross, where

Bridge ate his meals. He reached his room, on the second floor, by an outside staircase. He often stopped at the top step to toss down a few blueberries to the town boys below, and from his window watched for the pretty girl across the street to answer the door.

But neither high jinks nor the Latin exercises he enjoyed nor the girl across the street warded off periodic bouts of gloom. "I verily beleive [*sic*] that all the blue devils in Hell, or wherever else they reside, have been let loose upon me," he wrote Ebe in the fall of his senior year. This time he wasn't posing, at least not completely. "I am tired of college, and all its amusements and occupations. I am tired of my friends and acquaintances, and finally I am heartily tired of myself."

Bridge remembered that though Nathaniel "rarely sought or accepted the acquaintance of the young ladies of the village, he had a high appreciation of the sex." But Nathaniel's pockets were so empty that he despaired of ever having female company. "My term bills remain unpaid for more than a year past," he declared. "I do not ask for money, but I thought it best that you should know how delightful are my prospects."

Prospects, the future: Uncle Robert's upcoming marriage was another blue devil. No more could Nathaniel count on Robert's purse, which, despite strings, had stayed open. Even his spanking new cane and shiny gold watch chain, worn to impress the rural freshmen, didn't chase away the blues. He avoided his classes. He wrote a few lines of poetry—four in all, he said—and then said he burned them. Raymond was no fun at vacation. "Uncle Richard seemed to care nothing about us," Nathaniel reported to Ebe in the summer of 1825, "and Mrs. Manning was as cold and freezing as a December morning."

In July of his senior year, Nathaniel, who had just celebrated his twenty-first birthday, was summoned to President Allen's office. Despite Nathaniel's class ranking, Allen explained, his repeated absences would cost him a speaking part at commencement. "I am perfectly satisfied with this arrangement," Nathaniel blustered, "as it is a sufficient testimonial of my scholarship, while it saves me the mortification of making my appearance in public at commencement." Then he nervously added, "Perhaps the family may not be so well pleased with it," and asked Ebe to tell him what they thought.

If the idea of going to college had daunted him, the idea of leaving it was just as bad, particularly since he'd sabotaged his own place at commencement. "The family had before conceived much too high an opinion of my talents," he told Ebe, "and had probably formed expectations, which

I shall never realize. I have thought much upon the subject, and have finally come to the conclusion, that I shall never make a distinguished figure in the world, and all I hope or wish is to plod along with the multitude."

Lest anyone mistake his meaning and offer consoling compliments, he added that he did not "say this for the purpose of drawing any flattery from you, but merely to set Mother and the rest of you right, upon a point where your partiality has led you astray." If disingenuous, he was genuinely demoralized. And he struck out at his most important benefactor. "I did hope that Uncle Robert's opinion of me was nearer to the truth, as his deportment toward me never expressed a very high estimation of my abilities."

Angry with his family for their lofty expectations, angry with Uncle Robert for his supposed low ones, Nathaniel was angriest with himself. He fell far short of what he thought himself capable; he had disappointed his family and betrayed their trust. Plus, he had fulfilled his own worst fears about his abilities.

Bridge declined to contribute a senior class silhouette to what Nathaniel called the Class Golgotha, and said that Nathaniel refused to too—even though one does exist in the class annals. He wasn't the renegade Bridge made him out to be. Bridge was probably right, though, when he recalled that he and several other friends, also forbidden to speak at commencement, formed a band of premium misfits called the Navy Club for reasons Bridge didn't recall. They met at the tavern, drowned their sorrows, and assigned titles to each other. Nathaniel was Commander.

The graduation took place on September 7, 1825, a bright day, with one or two clouds brushing the sky. A large crowd poured into Brunswick in coaches, phaetons, and chaises, all parked on Maine Street, where vendors set up stands to sell fruit pies, gingerbread, and root beer. Thirty-seven members of the class of 1825 dressed themselves in black silk robes borrowed from neighboring clergy and marched to the platform erected near a grove of pine and fir. Each youth likely scanned the audience, looking for a familiar face. Was Uncle Robert there? It's doubtful he would have missed the great event, unless to punish his nephew for having lost his part in the program. And if Robert didn't attend, Betsy Hathorne couldn't, for Robert would have provided her transportation. Uncle Richard was housebound.

Had she deigned to come, Ebe would have laughed at President Allen's depressing sermon, "Humility," designed to remind the graduates of their worthlessness. Maybe the class of 1825 didn't care. They were a remarkable

*College silhouettes [1825]: Hawthorne upper left; Longfellow, to his right;
Jonathan Cilley below. Included in Jonathan Cilley's set of silhouettes,
Bowdoin College class of 1825.*

group, then and later: their number included three future congressmen, a
renowned clergyman, the African-American governor of Liberia, and a
United States president. And along with Hawthorne, there was Longfellow,
unassuming and kind, whose heart, as he'd himself admitted, had a southern exposure.

Longfellow delivered the commencement address, "Our Native Writers," a last-minute substitution for a talk about the impostor poet Thomas
Chatterton.

"Already has a voice been lifted up in this land," Longfellow intoned; "—already a spirit and a love of literature are springing up in the shadow of our free political institutions."

Seated nearby, Nat Hathorne must have listened carefully as Longfellow spoke of the secret ambition lodged like a thorn in his own heart.

CHAPTER FIVE

That Dream of Undying Fame

*"Old and young, we dream of graves and monuments," mur-
mured the stranger-youth. "I wonder how mariners feel, when
the ship is sinking, and they, unknown and undistinguished, are
to be buried together in the ocean—that wide and nameless
sepulchre!"*

Nathaniel Hawthorne, "The Ambitious Guest"

HAWTHORNE HAD a taste for drama. He burned his first manuscripts,
he said, whole quires of them, "without mercy or remorse, (and moreover, without subsequent regret)." He was a man of high standards, rigorous
and stern, and like the protagonists in his stories who torch the tales that no
one reads, Hawthorne didn't separate anger from anguish, vengeance from
self-punishment, when he felt he had failed. Nor need he have. He was creating a compounded image—artist as pyromaniac, artist as self-hater—to
express the complex, incendiary truth of his feelings.

"I am as tractable an author as you ever knew," he once told an editor,
"so far as putting my articles into the fire goes; though I cannot abide alter-
ations or omissions."

He also portrayed himself as obliging and agreeable, a gentle Nathaniel
Hawthorne who, like those charred papers, remains passionately unavailable.

"He always puts himself in his books," his sister-in-law Mary Mann
later declared; "he cannot help it."

After graduation Nathaniel headed to Salem still vague about a career. He
had attended lectures at the Maine Medical School during his senior year,

perhaps considering medicine, but Horatio Bridge recalled that Nathaniel had "formed several plans," unable to settle on any one of them for very long.

In Salem the Manning stagecoaches rattled profitably over New England roads—Robert was active in the business again—and Nathaniel determined to join "Uncle Manning's counting-house," as Bridge called the family company. But even before graduating from college, he'd been writing droopy lyrics about the ocean and moonlight (to "cheer the hearts of those that grieve/And wipe the tear drop dry"), and once back on Herbert Street, he stayed in his sunny third-floor chamber all day to write stories unless the afternoon weather was good. Then he'd walk down Essex Street in trim attire, wrapped in his long dark cloak with velvet collar. Or he'd hike along the beach and watch the water crash against the rocks.

He showed Ebe his work and she liked what she saw, the rudiments of a volume to be called *Seven Tales of My Native Land,* with an epigraph from Wordsworth's "We Are Seven," a poem about siblings and separations. Ebe recalled that one of the stories, "Alice Doane," was about witchcraft, and there was another one, possibly about the sea; the identity of the rest and their dates of composition aren't certain although Nathaniel had scrawled "The Truant Boy" in his copy of the undergraduate manual the *Laws of Bowdoin College,* as if auditioning a title for a story. But from what remains, it's clear that *Seven Tales,* partly inspired by Washington Irving's *Sketch Book,* also bore the stamp of John Neal, whose books Nathaniel had devoured in college. "That wild fellow, John Neal," Nathaniel later described him, "who almost turned my boyish brain with his romances."

A Maine native, Neal loudly banged the drum for American literature without frills, a literature of democratic spunk, and he practiced what he preached in a spate of sensationalistic novels intended to shock the complacent Anglophile bourgeoisie. (He was also the first to praise Edgar Allan Poe.) "It is American books that are wanted of America; not English books;—nor books made in America, by Englishmen, or by writers, who are a sort of bastard English," Neal had proclaimed, reeling from Sydney Smith's gibe in the pages of the *Edinburgh Review,* "Who reads an American book?"

Like Longfellow and Cooper, Nathaniel was responding to the clarion call for native writers, at least in terms of subject matter, by making stories out of local history and legend. However, in his earliest stories, plots amble nowhere and the settings, all American, drip with Gothic gloom. Regardless, he was acquiring a grammar of primary images: paired women, fair and foul; fallen trees aglow with green slime; voices wailing in the night; and apparitions that march in ghoulish pageants.

Two of the stories likely intended for *Seven Tales*, "The Hollow of the Three Hills" and "An Old Woman's Tale," also demonstrate his early proficiency in creating mood. In "The Hollow of the Three Hills," for instance, a young woman meets with an old crone in the woods to ask about the fate of loved ones she apparently deserted, and in just a few paragraphs Hawthorne draws on his feelings about abandonment and death, producing a sustained, unremitting study in tone, the fixed mood of the story emanating from repeated auditory images, feet sounding upon the floor and ears measuring the length of a funeral procession: "Then came a measured tread, passing slowly, slowly on, as of mourners with a coffin, their garments trailing on the ground, so that the ear could measure the length of their melancholy array."

The other story, "An Old Woman's Tale," is a rudimentary excavation of the past in which the past is so psychologically and historically immediate it gives the present meaning and depth. The nature of that meaning, however, is not yet plain, even to Hawthorne. As a young couple cuddle in the moonlight, a parade of strange characters suddenly comes into view. One of them, an old woman wearing spangled shoes, begins to dig in the ground with an iron shovel. Then, just as suddenly, the couple wake from what turns out to be their shared dream—for what else was the parade? They discover the shovel. Seizing it, the young man plunges it into the earth. "Oho!—What have we here!" he cries. And here the story abruptly ends, as if its author, himself digging up the past, did not know what he sought or, seeking, might find.

Nathaniel rummaged among the dusty wills and papers carefully preserved in Salem, initiating genealogical and antiquarian investigations that lasted a lifetime. Identifying with the ancient Hathornes, in his imaginative life he began to underplay his connection to the Mannings; if he didn't much like his father's side of the family—reputedly he told a friend he wanted no connection to them—he begrudgingly admired their self-regarding vanity, so different from the secular strivings of blacksmiths and bookkeepers.

As a consequence, he relentlessly perused old documents in pursuit of something more personal than source material: patrimony, the kind taken for granted by his college friends. With a self-assurance he did not share, men like Frank Pierce or Stephen Longfellow—and they were not exceptional—could lean on or rebel against living fathers of distinction and marked descent. Hathorne had the descent, not the distinction. His own father had died without rejuvenating the ancestral name. Yet a shabby gentility was better than none, and so Nathaniel carried himself with the melancholy éclat of a young lord burdened by inconsolable loss.

For this he needed a usable past. He consumed public records, travel books, biography, and poetry, as well as great gobs of history. "All really educated men," he would soon write, "whether they have studied in the halls of a University, or in a cottage or a work-shop, are essentially self-educated." His reading was prodigious: Edward Clarendon on England, Thomas Hutchinson and Alden Bradford on Massachusetts, John Campbell on Virginia, Daniel Neal on the Puritans, William Allen's biographical encyclopedia, Jean Froissart's *Chronicles,* Cotton Mather's *Magnalia,* William Sewell's *History of the Quakers,* tattered copies of the *Salem Gazette,* Francis Bacon, Edward Gibbon, Jeremy Belknap, and the proceedings of the General Court of Massachusetts Bay. He relished old cookbooks, savoring the Yankee dishes of his childhood, and at the Salem courthouse he fondled the pins said to be used by witches, who jabbed them into the flesh of their victims.

Refusing to visit the Salem Athenaeum himself, so Ebe said, he sent her to the library instead. They used Aunt Mary Manning's borrowing privileges, transferred to him in 1828. "I am sure nobody else would have got half so much out of such a dreary old library as I did," Ebe declared. "There were some valuable works; *The Gentleman's Magazine,* from the beginning of its publication, containing many curious things, and 6 vols. folio of Howell's *State Trials,* he preferred to any others. There was also much related to the early History of New England, with which I think he become pretty well acquainted, aided, no doubt, by the Puritan instinct that was in him."

This Puritan instinct may have influenced the aesthetic credo he started to hammer together and which, though clarified over time, never substantially changed. All his stories, he insists, combine fancy and fact, even when he himself invented the facts. The dreamscape of "The Hollow of the Three Hills," for example, is one where "fantastic dreams and madmen's reveries were realized among the actual circumstances of life." More famously, in *The Scarlet Letter,* Hawthorne pretends to stumble on the old red "A" that gives rise to the story.

Aspiring to be a creative writer, not an antiquarian, Hawthorne implicitly justifies the writing of fiction. It may not serve the useful function of biography or history—works of fact—but without it biography and history are dull, dead, removed, unreadable. "The knowledge, communicated by the historian and biographer," he explains in his 1830 sketch of Sir William Phips, "is analogous to that which we acquire of a country by the map,— minute, perhaps, and accurate, and available for all necessary purposes,— but cold and naked." The solution: "Fancy must throw her reviving light on the faded incidents that indicate character, whence a ray will be reflected, more or less vividly, on the person to be described."

Readers familiar with Hawthorne will recognize his Coleridgean terms: the accurate, if faded, incidents represented by the detailed map, on the one hand, and the illumination of this map by imagination on the other. Almost twenty years later, in the "Custom-House" essay that introduces *The Scarlet Letter*, Hawthorne calls these two spheres "the real world and fairy-land," or "the Actual and the Imaginary"—implicitly warring factions of experience coaxed into a "neutral territory" by an author sensitive both to inner vision and to outer exigencies.

Yet in all these are "musts"—"A license must be assumed," "Fancy must throw her reviving light"—one hears a young, conscience-stricken writer plead not just for an audience but for its blessing. Of course, the audience hardest to please was internal. He was never content. Hence comes the story of the burned manuscript.

Devastated by the rejections of the several publishers to whom he'd sent his collection of short stories—one didn't even bother to read it—he claimed to set fire to *Seven Tales*. (Although Bridge wasn't with Nathaniel at the time, he recalled him reacting in "a mood half savage, half despairing.") In another version of events, Nathaniel hands over the stories to the printer Ferdinand Andrews, owner of the *Salem Gazette,* expecting to see them in print right away. But when Andrews hesitated, Nathaniel impatiently demanded his manuscript back. Then he torched it. Bridge called him "inexorable."

He did destroy all early drafts of his prose, obliterating clues to the work's inception or development. "He did not wish his struggles, his anxieties, the sweat of his brow to be visible," said Julian. Presumably he put the manuscript of *The Scarlet Letter* up the chimney as soon as the book was printed, and he may have scrapped early notebooks, since only those dated from 1835—the early Maine diary notwithstanding—have come to light. Similarly, he burned early correspondence and urged friends to do the same. Acutely aware of the power of history, he wanted to control it.

"Knowing the impossibility of satisfying myself, even should the world be satisfied," he wrote in one of his early stories, "I . . . investigated the causes of every defect, and strove, with patient stubbornness, to remove them in the next attempt." Whatever happened to the *Seven Tales,* whether he burned them or, in all likelihood, incorporated them into his subsequent work, he definitely began again, more determined than ever to earn recognition.

To this end, he changed his name and wrote a novel about fame.

On March 30, 1826, Nathaniel scratched his name onto a glass windowpane at Herbert Street—Nathaniel Hathorne—but for at least a year he'd been playing with his patronymic. In 1825 he practiced signing his name by adding the *w* over and over again in, of all places, his father's logbook, to imitate and differentiate himself from the Captain at the same time. Sometime in 1827 he again used the changed spelling, writing out his name, "Nath. Hawthorne, February 28, 1827," on a copy of the *American Bookkeeper.* Eventually Louisa and Ebe adopted the new spelling too. "We were in those days about as absurdly obedient to him," Ebe said.

Horace Conolly, a fellow Salemite, met Hawthorne in New Haven in the fall of 1829. Hawthorne had accompanied his roustabout uncle Samuel to Connecticut to buy horses for the stagecoaches, and at the New Haven inn where they stopped, Conolly recognized Samuel Manning's name on the register. When Samuel introduced Nathaniel, Conolly observed that he didn't look like the Salem Hathornes, who were descended from a great-uncle and with whom his family had very little to do. Hawthorne was five-foot-ten, with eyes like lit candles, and when he walked, recalled Conolly, he swung his right arm and tilted his head a little to the left, as if balancing himself aboard a rolling ship—a kind of seaman's gait. (College acquaintances also remembered the peculiar walk, no doubt developed when he was lame.) "I am glad to hear you say that," Conolly remembered Nathaniel replying, "for I don't wish to look like any Hathorne."

"Perhaps that is one reason why you have expanded your name to Hawthorne," Conolly surmised. Hawthorne didn't correct him. Whatever the reason—to revise an old spelling, as Conolly also guessed, or to dissociate himself from his family—he didn't use "Hawthorne" when he published his first major work, *Fanshawe: A Tale.*

The book appeared anonymously—in spite of the new name.

Two undergraduate men compete for the attentions of a pretty young woman. One of them is a decent and intelligent fellow, Edward Walcott, tall and good-looking, completely respectable as a scholar, polite, groomed by family and money, and the class poet. The other youth is known only as Fanshawe (a name that suggests the new spelling of Hawthorne). A natural-born aristocrat, Fanshawe is comely, proud, pale, and self-possessed. And he cares less for the stuff of this world than for matters more supernal, for during long meditative nights Fanshawe the scholar sits by his flickering lamp and converses with the dead, who speak to him from the pages of old books.

Harley College, where these undergraduates meet, resembles Bowdoin, and *Fanshawe* is a college novel about vocation, with its two romantic heroes, Walcott and Fanshawe, representing the choices available to a young man, or a young man as torn as Hawthorne was. Made for and by the world, like Franklin Pierce, Walcott is easy prey to its temptations. He jumps to conclusions. He is jealous, gallant, sensual. He drinks too much, fights too easily. Fanshawe, on the other hand, is the loner hungry for recognition and ashamed of that ravening "dream of undying fame, which, dream as it is, is more powerful than a thousand realities."

But Fanshawe is distracted from his goals by Ellen Langton, whom Walcott is courting. The daughter of a wealthy merchant who lives abroad, Ellen is presently the ward of the president of Harley College and his wife, two stock characters whose name—the Melmoths—derives from Charles Maturin's classic of gothic horror, *Melmoth the Wanderer*. In fact, the plot of the novel depends on a good deal of derivative paraphernalia: an abyss, an abduction, a villainous seducer, a virtuous rescuer, and the requisite denouement at novel's end, a marriage that restores property to those who already have it. Character, not plot, is Hawthorne's métier.

So is alliteration, almost to a fault: "The road, at all times, rough, was now broken into deep gullies, through which streams went murmuring down, to mingle with the river. The pale moonlight combined with the gray of the morning to give a ghastly and unsubstantial appearance to every object." As literary apprentice, Hawthorne employed his classical education and the English prose masters—Addison, Steele, Johnson, Burke, and Gibbon—to forge a style that owed less to Neal's cheek than to modulation, balance, and subdued antithesis. Phrase next to phrase, separated by commas, build a complex of meaning that at worst seems halting, artificial, and prim. "She knew not what to dread," Hawthorne writes of Ellen Langton's abduction; "but she was well aware that danger was at hand, and that, in the deep wilderness, there was none to help her, except that Being, with whose inscrutable purposes it might consist, to allow the wicked to triumph for a season, and the innocent to be brought low." The author is still green, and his showy epigraphs—Shakespeare, Scott, Thomson, Southey—as well as the novel's creaky wooden characters threaten to send the whole business, well-constructed sentences and all, over the cliff with the novel's villain.

To return to the plot: by helping to dispatch the villain, Fanshawe wins the hand of Ellen Langton, which he rejects, refusing to knot the "tie that shall connect" him to the "common occupation of the world." And so the ambitious narcissist dies before he turns twenty, appropriately punished for his solitary existence.

An equivocal hero of renunciation, Fanshawe leaps forward into the novels of Henry James. And he anticipates Hawthorne's ethereal loners, the passive clergyman Dimmesdale in *The Scarlet Letter* and the half-baked poet Miles Coverdale in *The Blithedale Romance,* to name just two. With tragic or pathetic consequences, these repressed men transform sexual curiosity into a desire for knowledge. Yet though Hawthorne damns Fanshawe's maniacal quest, albeit halfheartedly, he patronizes Walcott, whose marriage to Ellen "drew her husband away from the passions and pursuits that would have interfered with domestic felicity; and he never regretted the worldly distinction of which she thus deprived him."

"Theirs was a long life of calm and quiet bliss," Hawthorne concludes, mischievously wondering, "—and what matters it, that, except in these pages, they have left no name behind them?"

It matters a great deal. Hawthorne's novel, after all, bears Fanshawe's name.

Grandmother Manning died in December of 1826, and her heirs slowly divided the large holdings, five thousand acres in Raymond and the property and stables in Salem, that had helped to support Betsy Hathorne and her children. From this estate Hawthorne earned a small annuity. "It was my fortune or misfortune, just as you please," he reminisced some years later, "to have some slender means of supporting myself." In 1828, with his share of the estate, he doubtless paid the Boston publishers Marsh and Capen one hundred dollars to publish his first novel, *Fanshawe: A Tale.*

But the question of a career—a lucrative career—hung fire.

That may have been the reason he applied for and received an advanced degree from Bowdoin College just after the publication of *Fanshawe*. Reportedly given to almost anyone making a request three years after graduation, the master of arts degree was conferred on "Nathanaelem Hawthorne" in September 1828. But though he felt he needed the degree, he didn't know how to make use of it. Horace Conolly remembered Hawthorne's irritation when asked what he intended to do with himself. "I wish to God I could find out," he vehemently replied. To Ebe he said he'd been berated by an old Salem woman for "not going to work as other people did," and Manning descendants calculated "as so much had been done for 'Nat,' that it should now be thought time for him to do something for himself." The Mannings had paid for an education, and something better than writing stories ought to come of it.

Uncertain about the future, he cursed his own obsession with fame as harshly as some members of his family might have. Take the early tale "The Ambitious Guest." Here, Hawthorne concocts an avalanche to crush, quite literally, a young man's understandable desire "not to be forgotten in the grave."

On a chill September night, the young man arrives at the welcoming inn of a rural family, where he eats his supper and then chats with his unpretentious hosts as they gather about a warm hearth. Ambitious and somewhat haughty—"reserved among the rich and great; but ever ready to stoop his head to the lowly cottage door"—the youth is a solitary fellow like Fanshawe. "He could have borne to live an undistinguished life," Hawthorne writes, "but not to be forgotten in the grave."

The stranger and the family engage in friendly talk, the stranger insisting that "it is our nature to desire a monument, be it slate, or marble, or a pillar of granite, or a glorious memory in the universal heart of man," a view not completely shared by his hosts, who nonetheless begin to reveal their own secret wishes. That very night, however, an avalanche obliterates the lot of them, both the simple family and their ambitious guest, and since their bodies are never found, not even a rough tombstone marks their graves with a scrap of remembrance. A mound of snow is their marker, which, like all markers, will eventually disappear.

But their terrible end ironically supplies them with a different kind of memorial: "The story had been told far and wide, and will forever be a legend in these mountains."

"Who has not heard their name?" Hawthorne asks again, as he did in *Fanshawe*.

Hawthorne writes of the quest for fame, more obsession than wish, that converts a boyish desire to be appreciated—you will miss me when I am gone—into the youthful fantasies of the ambitious guest. Hawthorne trounces these fiercely, as if he needed to purge himself of his own grandiose ambitions and in so doing protect himself from the shame of failure. The solitary dreamer meets defeat: That'll show him for aiming so high. Or he's misunderstood by a cloddish multitude, their incomprehension another form of defeat, though more palatable. Genius is always misunderstood.

"Fame—some very humble persons in a town may be said to possess it:—as the penny-post, the town-crier, the constable &c; and they are known to every body," Hawthorne comments in an early notebook, "while many richer, more intellectual, worthier persons are unknown by the majority of their fellow citizens." That Hawthorne already feels neglected and unrecognized—or nullified by scorn—suggests his own expectations were sky high. Little satisfied him. And though the community would not in fact appreciate him fully, Hawthorne collaborated in his own obscurity.

Hawthorne reproaches Fanshawe and the ambitious guest for a yearning he knows too well. Yet reproach is only half the story. Ambition may come before a fall, but anonymity is a fate far scarier, and anyway, as he said of the little group in the mountains crushed by the falling rocks, "Who has not heard their name?"

When Hawthorne visited Uncle Richard in Maine in the fall of 1826, accounts of the Willey disaster froze New England hearts. As a landslide began to crash down the mountainside, the family ran out of the house seeking shelter nearby. They were all killed; their house was unharmed.

Like the Willey family tragedy, which inspired "The Ambitious Guest," tales of Maine transfixed the young author, who incorporated another Maine legend into "Roger Malvin's Burial," a story likely conceived as early as 1825, the year Hawthorne graduated from Bowdoin. That spring was the centennial of the battle at Lovewell's Pond, an event of such importance that Bowdoin seniors drove from Brunswick to Fryeburg to take part in the celebration. The ignominious battle had already been aggrandized by Bowdoin's Professor Upham in his nationalistic verse "Lovellspond," with Henry Longfellow scribbling his own version, "The Battle of Lovell's Pond," for the *Portland Gazette* of 1820:

> *The warriors that fought for their country—and bled,*
> *Have sunk to their rest; the damp earth is their bed;*

No stone tells the place where their ashes repose,
Nor points out the spot from the graves of their foes.

The battle at Lovewell's Pond was not in fact a valiant affair. In the spring of 1725, Captain John Lovewell and forty-six men slaughtered ten Pequawket warriors as they slept. The massacre, which occurred on the Sabbath, was meant to avenge the death of Lovewell's family; not coincidentally, Lovewell also intended to bring a satchel full of Pequawket scalps to Boston to collect a considerable bounty, but before he and his little army could even think about the reward, they were ambushed by a large group of Indians. Routed, the troops decamped in a rush, leaving behind three of their wounded for dead. The men survived, however, and told the tale of their abandonment.

Hawthorne visited Raymond the summer following the Lovewell centennial, complaining about Uncle Richard's indifference. Probably soon after, he began to write a story, set in Maine, about a young man's desertion of the surrogate father who, by dying, has rejected him. The surrogate father's initials happen to be those of Richard and Robert Manning.

And Hawthorne was evidently intrigued by another aspect of Lovewell's battle, that of the story of men left to die alone in the wilderness with no stone to commemorate them. One of these men became the story's title character, Roger Malvin. Malvin, mortally wounded, tries to convince his young companion, Reuben Bourne, to save himself from certain death should Reuben, also injured, remain with Malvin in the woods. "I have loved you like a father, Reuben," Malvin tells him, "and, at a time like this, I should have something of a father's authority."

Reuben at first refuses to leave his friend, but then with "no merely selfish motive," as Hawthorne informs us—subtly directing our attention to the adverb "merely"—Reuben lets Malvin persuade him to go. Rationalizing that he might encounter a party of men who could help, Reuben promises to return to the woods, either to save Malvin's life or to bury him with a prayer over his bones.

He does neither. Once back in town, Reuben is nursed to health by Malvin's daughter Dorcas, whom he marries. He doesn't tell her of her father's fate nor does he return to the forest to dig the man's grave. Instead he becomes one of Hawthorne's incorrigible concealers, hiding the truth of his speckled heart, first from himself and then from those who love him. But the price is high. Reuben sinks into a maelstrom of "mental horrors, which punish the perpetrator of undiscovered crime."

Forecasting another leitmotif of his later work, that of transformation, Hawthorne focuses on how Reuben's "one secret thought" changes him to "a sad and downcast, yet irritable man." His lands lay fallow, his neighbors quarrel with him, his debts mount. His only solace is his son Cyrus, in whom he sees a reflection of himself as he once had been.

When Cyrus is fifteen, Reuben and Dorcas decide to pull up stakes. Inadvertently they travel to the wooded spot where, eighteen years before, Roger Malvin was left for dead. Father and son explore the region, and Dorcus sets up camp. Soon Reuben hears a sound in the underbrush, picks up his rifle, and shoots, aiming toward a spot "not unlike a gigantic gravestone" where Malvin once lay. But it's not an animal that howls in pain; Reuben has accidentally killed his own son. "The vow that the wounded youth had made," says the story's narrator, "the blighted man had come to redeem."

Fusing psychological obsession with the historical circumstance of something like Lovewell's battle, Hawthorne in his earliest stories frequently wrote with a pen dipped in the bloody history to which he brought his personal angst. Frontiersman and Indian fighter, Roger Malvin veers into Richard Manning and Grandfather Manning and Robert Manning, kindly men and authoritarians who inevitably fail the boy they try to protect. As for the boy, he betrays his fathers by abandoning them, and in so doing must destroy his younger self.

That said, the strangest part of the story is Dorcas. Daughter, wife, and mother, she is Reuben's symbolic sister, herself deprived of the fruit of her unholy union with "brother" Reuben. Of course, she is literally innocent of any crime, though not in Reuben's psyche. And so Reuben's killing of Cyrus punishes Dorcas as much as Reuben. Pointing to their dead son, Reuben gestures toward the broad rock that is the grave of Roger Malvin and of Cyrus. "Your tears," he cruelly tells Dorcas, "will fall at once over your father and your son." She collapses with "one wild shriek." If Reuben's "sin was expiated," it was ransomed by the broken heart of a woman.

Hawthorne was a master of concealment. "Your father kept his very existence a secret, as far as possible," Ebe told Una. He doled out information when and where he saw fit, never telling his wife, for example, that he'd once written poetry, never mind *Fanshawe*. And so it's not surprising to learn that he revealed little about his relation to various women.

As far as his family knew, or wanted to know, no woman in Salem had struck his fancy. To them, he appeared solitary, his habits regular. In the evening, after a walk, he ate a pint bowl of thick chocolate full of crumbled bread, and in the summer substituted fruit for the chocolate. A stalwart Democrat, he argued politics with Ebe at night, or he read, or he played a rubber of whist with Louisa and friends. The family did not venture far from Salem nor from one another.

In the broiling months of summer, however, Hawthorne or his sisters often visited relatives in Newburyport, or they ambled over the hard sand at Nahant, where the fashionable rented spacious rooms ventilated by sea breezes. Hawthorne flirted. The "mermaid" shopkeeper of his tale "The Village Uncle" captured his heart for a time. He met her in the seaside village of Swampscott one summer and talked of her incessantly. "At that time," Ebe dismissively recollected, "he had *fancies* like that whenever he went from home." An early model for Phoebe Pyncheon of *The House of the Seven Gables,* the shopgirl gave Hawthorne a sugar heart, said his sister, but he kept her identity a secret, assuring his family that she came from the local gentry.

"I should have feared that he was really in love with her, if he had not talked so much about her," said Ebe on another occasion, divulging more about herself than about Hawthorne. Proprietary over the brother she adored, she patrolled his affections like a wary sentinel. Hawthorne returned the compliment. His intense feelings toward Elizabeth—the sister never at a loss for a tart riposte, the sister he aimed to please, his intimate and mentor—may have drawn him to the tacky claptrap of his early guilt-driven fiction. Children of the night, sisters and brothers merge into husbands and wives ("Roger Malvin's Burial") or they mingle with the undead in a hodge-podge fable of fratricide, patricide, and incest like "Alice Doane's Appeal."

The core of "Alice Doane's Appeal" was evidently one of the original *Seven Tales* that Hawthorne revised into a longer story about authorship, and though he didn't integrate the two sections, the jagged result reveals his frustration with the earlier manuscript. In the revised "Alice Doane's Appeal," a narrator recounts Alice's story one mild June afternoon, having accompanied two female companions to Gallows Hill. These days, he notes, the bloody spot is something of a tourist attraction. Times have certainly changed since 1692. In fact, young boys, heedless of the savage history of the place, come there yearly to honor "they know not what" with a bonfire.

The narrator pulls a manuscript from his pocket. He'd written other such stories, he piteously explains, but he'd tossed them into a bonfire of his own. "Thoughts meant to delight the world and endure for ages," he observes, "had perished in a moment, and stirred not a single heart but mine." But he does save one manuscript from the flames, which he then proceeds to read to his companions. It's the story of "Alice Doane."

Actually, the story is Leonard Doane's first-person account of his crimes. Leonard, Alice's brother, guiltily admits that he killed Walter Brome ("my very counterpart," says Leonard), a blackguard who taunted the jealous Leonard "with indisputable proofs of the shame of Alice." What was the chivalrous brother to do? But Leonard killed Walter only to learn that Walter was Leonard's twin brother. And if that weren't bad enough, when Leonard looked into his slain brother's face, he saw the image of his own haplessly murdered father. Yet fratricide and patricide don't satisfy Leonard's need for violence and revenge. Still tortured by the idea of his sister's disgrace—now incest—he feels "as if a fiend were whispering him to meditate violence against the life of Alice."

At this juncture, the narrator hastily summarizes the rest of the story. Alice and Leonard go to a haunted graveyard where Alice asks the dead Walter to exonerate her. Walter obliges, and there Alice's story ends.

Not quite: the "appeal" in "Alice Doane's Appeal" refers to Alice's plea that Walter attest to her innocence—and it refers to the sexual appeal that drives her brother to murder. But the narrator's two female companions ("timid maids," he calls them) don't get it. They're too chaste. As a matter of fact, they are bored silly. The narrator's overheated tale is "grotesque and extravagant," they say; as grotesque and extravagant, the narrator retorts, as the witchcraft delusion, another instance of erotic madness? The women don't understand the connection—it isn't altogether clear—but to the narrator their bafflement is just another example of obtuseness like that of publishers who reject his stories. "We are a people of the present and have no heartfelt interest in the olden time," he groans in disgust.

The narrator is the misunderstood artist par excellence, and he appears in one form or another in stories as dissimilar as Hawthorne's "The Christmas Banquet" or "The Artist of the Beautiful," both written a decade after "Alice Doane's Appeal." But the structure is similar: an artist brings one of his own creations, usually a manuscript, to someone he admires, and if he reads it aloud, the audience grows drowsy. In the case of "The Artist of the Beautiful," a baffled public inadvertently helps wreck his creation—much to the artist's relief. Its destruction ironically confirms what the artist knew all along: he is different from all the rest.

Besides, the artifact (in this case, a mechanical butterfly) deserved to be destroyed. The act of creation is, after all, an act of hubris.

But the artist is angry. And like so many of Hawthorne's future protagonists, he ritually conjures images of fire, bonfires and furnaces and, later, limestone kilns, as well as lunatics, bloodthirsty magistrates, and the trace of unnameable crimes—whatever it takes—to wake up his sleepy audience with the sneaking suspicion that writing, like sex, is taboo.

CHAPTER SIX

Storyteller

By some fatality, we all seemed to be brought back to Salem, in spite of our intentions, and even resolutions.

Elizabeth Hawthorne

I T WAS A MEAN season. Snow piled high on the narrow streets. The gutters were caked with ice, and at night the wind blew so cold it chilled the floorboards under the carpet. Uncle Samuel coughed a hollow, hacking cough. Betsy Hawthorne complained of exhaustion.

But Robert Manning, now a father, seemed spry and optimistic. His marriage had taken him to the dappled groves of North Salem, where he pruned his trees, imported new varieties of fruit, and built two houses, one for himself and a small gambrel cottage next door, at 31 Dearborn Street, for the Hawthornes. They moved in December of 1828, and Mrs. Hawthorne again fell ill.

"When sorrow is as selfish as hers was, there is no end to its inflictions," said Mary Mann, who didn't know her; doubtless this is the period in Betsy Hawthorne's life that inspired such summary judgment. For Betsy's years in Maine had taken effort and spunk, as did her Sabbath school of thirty students, and until coming back to Salem, she had not withdrawn from her children, her family, or her church. It was her return to Herbert Street in 1822 that sapped her strength; and the death of her mother seemed to break her spirit.

By 1829 the Widow Hawthorne was still mired in the lethargy her son would remember as indifference to his writings, though not to him. But he's an unreliable witness, so sensitive was he to what he considered his short-comings: three years after college, and this strapping young man still had no discernible vocation. "I, being heir to a moderate competence," he

73

explained in one of his autobiographical stories, "had avowed my purpose of keeping aloof from the regular business of life. This would have been a dangerous resolution, any where in the world; it was fatal, in New-England."

And nowhere more so than in Salem.

By that spring Uncle Sam had recovered, and in the late summer Hawthorne joined him on that trip to Connecticut where he met Horace Conolly, who pointed out several of New Haven's historical monuments to Hawthorne, in the market for good material. Spurred by some friendly reviews of *Fanshawe*—John Neal himself thought its author promised "a fair prospect of future success"—Hawthorne intended to write fiction steeped, as he said, in "the superstitions of this part of the country."

He mailed a few of these stories to Samuel Griswold Goodrich, a self-made publishing entrepreneur eager to print native authors like novelist Charles Brockden Brown. Brown was considered by many to be the first professional author in America; he died penniless, not an auspicious beginning for American literature. Goodrich, however, was determined to make something out of—or from—American authors. It was slow going. So he also juggled several more lucrative projects, such as the popular series of children's books, many ghostwritten, that he churned out under the name Peter Parley. By 1829 he was devoting most of his time to the Parley books and to another moneymaking venture, *The Token,* a gift book timed to appear each year just before the Christmas and New Year's holidays.

A feral man with a stout heart and a nose for good writing, Goodrich claimed to have initiated the meeting with Hawthorne. He'd read an anonymous publication—*Fanshawe?*—"which seemed to me to indicate extraordinary powers," he said. More likely is that Hawthorne's Bowdoin classmate the Reverend George B. Cheever, himself a Salem writer, encouraged Hawthorne to approach Goodrich after Hawthorne had complained that no one wanted to publish his book. Goodrich remembered Hawthorne as "unsettled as to his views; he had tried his hand in literature, and considered himself to have met with a fatal rebuff from the reading world. His mind vacillated between various projects, verging, I think, toward a mercantile profession."

Looking over "Roger Malvin's Burial," which Hawthorne had given him, Goodrich cautiously offered to help find a publisher for his new collection of stories, called *Provincial Tales of My Native Land.* "You do not anticipate much success," Hawthorne wrote, acknowledging Goodrich's offer—and his hesitancy. Undaunted, though, Hawthorne sent Goodrich three more stories in December, all finished, he said, "a considerable time" ago, except for the titles. These were "Alice Doane," "The Gentle Boy," and "My Uncle Molineux," undoubtedly each of them a version of stories originally intended for *Seven Tales*. (Other stories slated for *Provincial Tales* may have included "The Wives of the Dead," "Young Goodman Brown," "The May-Pole of Merry Mount," "The Gray Champion," and "The Minister's Black Veil.")

Representing American history as a series of victories and betrayals, confused motives and ambiguous ends, these early stories, especially "Roger Malvin's Burial" and "My Uncle Molineux" (published as "My Kinsman, Major Molineux"), rate among Hawthorne's best. Thematically, they set historical fiction within a psychological theater, suggesting that one creates and develops character in time, real time and internal time. And they showcase what rapidly became a signature style: phrases and clauses well-calibrated and modulated into sentences, sentences expanded into paragraphs, each grammatical component—and ultimately the whole tale—having accrued a meaning far beyond the literal. "It was near nine o'clock of a moonlight evening, when a boat crossed the ferry with a single passenger, who had obtained his conveyance, at that unusual hour, by the promise of an extra fare," Hawthorne writes at the opening of "My Kinsman, Major Molineux," his classical allusions half hidden in a story about the initiation of a young man into history, his own and the country's.

"Deep as Dante," Melville would write of Hawthorne's layered work, and he wasn't wrong.

Set against the backdrop of colonial-period politics in the 1730s, 1760s, and 1770s, "My Kinsman, Major Molineux," as we saw, tells of Robin Molineux's benighted search for the rich uncle who he hopes will help him rise in the world. But the quest for patrimony is over, it seems, when Robin discovers the uncle is a loyalist about to be tarred and feathered. In Hawthorne's hands, uncles inevitably disappoint nephews, especially nephews who rely too heavily on them.

Naturally, Hawthorne understood Robin's dilemma, that attachment to and animosity toward an ancestral name (Hathorne) and a living inheritance (Manning); they provide status, a sense of belonging, and an income while depriving the bearer of autonomy, the ability to make one's way alone "without the help of your kinsman," as Hawthorne writes at his story's end. Thus it's with slow steps that Robin lurches toward a self-reliant manhood free from aristocratic privilege, like the nation which he partly represents; to be a man, Robin must shuck his patrimony, just as the country must shake off England. But America's coming of age, like Robin's, is no uncomplicated assertion of independence. To throw off monarchy in the name of freedom or democracy is to subject oneself to an ugly crowd of rabble-rousers, called patriots, who tar and feather the major.

When the uproarious mob jeers at Robin's uncle in the story's climactic scene, Robin joins in the brutal merriment, his shout "the loudest there." Illusions punctured, particularly about himself, Robin finds that he, like the cruel merrymakers, is capable of trampling an old man's heart.

"Had 'Fanshawe' been in the hands of more extensive dealers,' Goodrich baited Hawthorne, "I do believe it would have paid you a profit." He rejected "Alice Doane," and assuming Hawthorne wanted to keep the other two for *Provincial Tales,* Goodrich offered him thirty-five dollars to print "The Gentle Boy" in *The Token,* promising Hawthorne that he could afterward reprint it in *Provincial Tales.*

Though Hawthorne wasn't sure he'd take the offer, in May he sent two shorter stories, as Goodrich had requested. Presumably they were better suited to *The Token,* especially the sketch "Sights from a Steeple," a depiction of Salem from the vantage point of a "spiritualized Paul Pry," or one who stands atop a church, the image of the spectator revived.

That Goodrich both championed Hawthorne and exploited him, there can be no doubt. Writers in America had to finance their own books—even Washington Irving had—with publishers operating mainly as booksellers or distributors, themselves dependent on regional outlets. And publishers undertook American books reluctantly. Since there were no international copyright laws, cheap editions of British books flooded the market. As a consequence, a man like Goodrich didn't worry too much about taking advantage of his authors since he also took the publishing risk. Of course, the author viewed the matter differently. Hawthorne would characterize Goodrich as an unscrupulous opportunist growing fat on someone else's labor, "born to do what he did, as maggots to feed on rich cheese."

For his part, Goodrich would remember Hawthorne as sturdy, dark, distrustful, with steel-gray eyes, a stony complexion, and a sarcastic mouth. Both men probably judged one another correctly—after the fact, of course—and Hawthorne was justifiably suspicious. Goodrich paid him poorly, between fifty-two and seventy-two dollars for the ten stories that appeared in the 1831, 1832, and 1833 *Tokens.* And since the stories were published anonymously, Goodrich could easily stuff his *Token* with more than one story by the same writer, "particularly," he rationalized, "as they are as good, if not better, than anything else I can get."

If Goodrich was able to capitalize on Hawthorne's obscurity, Hawthorne acceded to the arrangement, as if afraid of the recognition he desperately sought. No one associated him with stories trickling into periodicals and newspapers. Historical sketches like the "The Battle Omen," "Sir William Phips," and "Dr. Bullivant" appeared in the 1830 *Salem Gazette* unsigned, presumably at his own behest, and although he was reaching out to other publishers, more confident now since his work was appearing in *The Token,* he continued to say he "should not wish to be mentioned" as the author of his tales.

"He never liked to have his writings spoken of," said Ebe; "he knew their merit, and was weary of obscurity, but yet he shrank from observation." Hawthorne's son Julian also meditated on his father's enforced anonymity. His father, he intuited, "was resolved not to declare himself until the curiosity and enthusiasm aroused by his anonymous writings had reached such a pitch, as to render concealment no longer possible." This way he'd save himself embarrassment by bounding, as it were, onto the literary scene, without an audience for his work having been established. It was a calculation, savvy and self-protective and fully in keeping with the pose of author as the gentleman on the steepletop who didn't write for money.

Hawthorne wasn't successful. He'd planned to bring out *Fanshawe,* said Ebe, to whet the public's appetite for *Seven Tales,* but the novel had not sold and the tales went uncollected.

So too the manuscript of *Provincial Tales,* which probably languished in Goodrich's drawer, especially since he could make use of individual stories in *The Token.* Of course, Hawthorne consented to carving it up: what choice did he have? he must have wondered. He gave Goodrich "The Gentle Boy," "My Kinsman, Major Molineux," "Roger Malvin's Burial," and "The Wives of the Dead" for the 1832 *Token,* published at the end of 1831. And perhaps he justified the decision. The antiquarian Joseph B. Felt had brought out the very popular *Annals of Salem* in 1827, and in 1831 both John Greenleaf Whittier's *Legends of New England* and Delia Bacon's *Tales of the Puritans* appeared. The field was small and crowded.

But with Goodrich still eager for more material, Hawthorne was launched after a fashion, and none too soon. In 1831 he turned twenty-seven. Ebe said he had not expected to live to be twenty-five. "I nourished a regretful desire to be summoned early from the scene," he wrote in mock retrospect, explaining that "he who has a part in the serious business of life, though it be only as a shoemaker, feels himself equally respectable in youth and age, and therefore is content to live. . . . [I]t is far otherwise with the busy idlers of the world."

Yet not three years after the publication of *Fanshawe,* Hawthorne wanted to expunge it from his past. It mortified him. So he got hold of Ebe's copy, which she never saw again, and at Hawthorne's request Horatio Bridge destroyed his. Hawthorne's wife would never even learn of *Fanshawe*'s existence until after his death.

An avid reader, Hawthorne carefully assessed the work of his competitors— Ebe recalled him studying a great many novels—and, in particular, works by women writers, those "ink-stained Amazons" who, he feared, could bump their male rivals right out of the field, petticoats triumphant.

The terms are Hawthorne's, and they appear in the introductory paragraph of his historical sketch "Mrs. Hutchinson," published in the *Salem Gazette* in December 1830. Hawthorne was using "Mrs. Hutchinson" to some extent to inveigh against women writers and the troubling question of "feminine ambition."

His argument goes like this: at present there are no women quite like the brave Anne Hutchinson, an Antinomian banished from the Massachusetts Bay Colony for preaching, especially at her trial, that God communicated by direct revelation; she needed no priestly interlocutors, or patriarchs, to parcel out God's word. These days, says Hawthorne, contemporary women exploit the popular press, not an apostate church, as the "medium through which feminine ambition chiefly manifests itself." The phenomenon, however, isn't entirely positive. To be any good as a writer, a woman must sacrifice "a part of the loveliness of her sex," Hawthorne declares; and she is obliged to expose her "naked mind to the gaze of the world, with indications by which its inmost secrets may be searched out." Authorship, then, implies public exposure, unbecoming, improper, and shameful. Or, from another point of view, why should women have to endure the various trials that authors undergo, Hawthorne wonders with facetious gallantry. The condescension is obvious.

But the issue is personal. Hawthorne is reflecting on the choices he's made, or has felt compelled to make, having taken up a profession—storytelling—fraught with insecurity, vanity, and humiliation, a profession regarded as irresponsible and disreputable and likely to become even more so if women successfully enter it. That would prove that fiction is a kind of women's work, decorative and useless, an idler's trade, not a manly one. "It is one of my few sources of pride," Hawthorne defended himself in another context, "that, ridiculous as the object was, I followed it up with the firmness and energy of a man."

If the writer is a pariah, he is also a hero of sorts—ironically like Anne Hutchinson, who emerges in Hawthorne's sketch as pilloried and yet grand, intelligent, standing unafraid before her judges with "a flash of carnal pride half hidden in her eye." However, he has to make sure that she, as his signal female—courageous, smart, and sexy—does not best him. For she is not only complex but composite: a version of Ebe; a version of his mother, the widow who for a time ventured a different life; and something of himself as author, surmounting inhibitions and "relinquishing the immunities of a private character," as he admits elsewhere, "and giving every man, and for money, too, the right . . . of treating me with open scorn."

But "Mrs. Hutchinson" excepted, in most of Hawthorne's early tales and sketches women function largely as cardboard props in which Hawthorne is not invested: the damsel in distress (*Fanshawe*); the anguished wife (in "Roger Malvin's Burial"); innocence wronged ("Alice Doane's Appeal"); and, inevitably, temptation (the woman with a scarlet petticoat in "My Kinsman, Major Molineux"). Though peopled with stock women, these stories nonetheless shiver with a phantom sexuality, fearsome and inappropriate. Funeral bells toll at marriages, strange old spinsters interrupt wedding ceremonies, loving husbands intend to kill their loving wives, and a young minister dons a black veil for no apparent reason.

In the particularly fine "Young Goodman Brown," marital bliss sours after the newlywed Brown deserts his wife, Faith, for a night's frolic in the woods, losing his moral virginity and, one infers, his sexual innocence. But unable to confront his own desires, more subversive than he knew, Young Goodman Brown cannot endure anyone else's, and he returns to the village a harried man, condemned for his squeamishness to a lonely, desperate death.

It will not be the first time that the Hawthorne character comes home trapped, confused, and lonely.

"I very often say with Job," Richard Manning wrote to his family, "cursed be the day in which it was said there is a Manchild brought forth, and with Burns, Oh death the poor Mans dearest friend . . . and Oh that Mother had let me have burnt up in the Cradle, then I was sinless, and Oh that I was now prepared." At forty-eight, hands numb and body palsied, Richard Manning was mortally ill. He died just before the spring of 1831.

Old-time Calvinism, even if on the wane, and Richard's death, after that of so many others, helped shape Hawthorne's sense that the world is banked in sorrow. Uncle Robert was shattered. "The loss of Brother Richard will be like loosing the head of the family a second time, for he has truly been the head of the family since father's death," he told Mary Manning. She in turn warned the surviving men of the family, "Brother William and Robert and Samuel and Brother John and Nathaniel . . . [to] all improve this loud call, to improve the present time, to attend to the one thing need-full, to secure their best interest, a Treasure in Heaven wich faileth not."

Hawthorne decided to "improve the present time," though not quite the way Aunt Mary imagined. Again accompanying his uncle Sam, this time through New Hampshire in the summer of 1831, he envisioned writing yet another collection of tales, *The Story Teller,* based loosely on their travels. It would be a sketchbook of sorts, like Washington Irving's, replete with motley comrades and harmless summer escapades. That summer he didn't get as far as Canada, which he'd hoped to do, so the next year he set off again; he wanted to see Niagara, then Montreal and Quebec, and then go home through Vermont and New Hampshire, as he explained to Franklin Pierce, "on account of a book by which I intend to acquire an (undoubt-edly) immense literary reputation."

With two hundred dollars, part of the Manning legacy, Hawthorne evi-dently sped through the rugged White Mountains, and by the fall of 1832 was climbing Mount Washington in a snowstorm, traipsing to Burlington, Vermont, and voyaging west toward the watery turnpike, the Erie Canal. He cruised to Niagara Falls in a dirty canal boat pulled by three moth-colored horses. To judge from his stories and sketches, he was home by December.

Although *The Story Teller* was never published as a complete book, the various sections that were printed, once reassembled, do suggest a frame-work for the group. Hawthorne evidently planned to organize the stories around the first-person adventures of an itinerant novelist who peddles his own "extemporaneous fictions to such audiences as I could collect," or so the storyteller explains in "The Seven Vagabonds," probably one of the first tales. Spontaneous, lighthearted, and without responsibility, the picaresque rambler meanders through life, nomadic, easy, and liberated from that "dull race of money-getting drudges" who couldn't begin to comprehend a creature like him. "I had not of that foolish wisdom, which reproves every occupation that is not useful in this world of vanities." Instead, he says, "I manufactured a great variety of plots and skeletons of tales, and kept them ready for use, leaving the filling up to the inspiration of the moment."

Pretty maids with smiling eyes cavort with him (nothing happens); pretty women from the West take off their clothes on the canal boat, right before his prurient eyes (nothing happens). He flirts with an irresistible person of "doubtful sex" (nothing happens), and he joins forces with a preacher, Eliakim Abbot, a fellow outcast dressed in rusty black carrying a Bible in his pocket. "We kept together," says the storyteller, "day after day, till our union appeared permanent." This unlikely pair—the poet and his scruples—plan to entertain and edify the populace, one with a tale and the other with a sermon, as if each made up for the deficiencies of the other. And so Hawthorne salved his conscience, revealing the split within it.

According to his sister-in-law, Hawthorne submitted *The Story Teller,* which had grown to two volumes, to Goodrich, who refused to take it whole. Keeping "The Canterbury Pilgrims" and "The Seven Vagabonds" for himself, Goodrich passed the manuscript on to the *New-England Magazine,* which printed "Sketches from Memory by a Pedestrian" in the November and December 1834 issues. (These sketches included a related story, later known as "Mr. Higginbotham's Catastrophe.") In 1835 Park Benjamin, a mediocre poet and the new editor of the *New-England Magazine,* ripped out a few more of the tales and then took the remainder of *The Story Teller* to New York, where the *New-England Magazine* merged in early 1836 with *American Monthly.* "So they tore up the book," said Hawthorne's sister-in-law Elizabeth Peabody, "and Hawthorne said he cared little for the stories afterwards, which had in their original place in the 'Storyteller' a greater degree of significance."

And Hawthorne was probably paid a dollar a page, when, that is, Benjamin had the money.

But disillusion was stalking the storyteller long before the book's dismemberment. In a fragment called "My Home Return," the itinerant narrator comes home. He is sick. "It had been long enough for me to wander away and return again, with my fate accomplished, and little more hope in this world." Something terrible had happened.

Thirteen years older than Hawthorne and the youngest of his uncles, Samuel Manning was a good-natured man who had failed in business and in farming and these days, working for Robert, found his health to be failing too. For seven years he had battled the tubercular cough that kept him from the travel and horse trading he liked to do. He died on November 17, 1833, one month before his forty-third birthday.

Hawthorne's breezy storyteller, having hoped to wander the world untroubled, headed home to Salem, chastened and depressed.

"It was only after his return to Salem," recalled Ebe, "and when he felt as if he could not get away from there, and yet was conscious of being utterly unlike every one else in the place, that he began to withdraw into himself."

The last installment of *The Story Teller,* which Hawthorne never reprinted, appears in a sequence called "Fragments from the Journal of a Solitary Man," published in July 1837 in the *American Monthly Magazine.* It features a cadaverous character, Oberon, named for the figure in *A Midsummer Night's Dream* or perhaps in Ben Jonson's masque *Oberon;* Oberon is also the sobriquet Hawthorne sometimes used when writing to Horatio Bridge.

Hawthorne's Oberon is mortally ill, but before coughing his last, he begs a friend to burn all the papers in his escritoire. Obliging, the friend saves one journal, which he then reproduces for the reader. It's a pinched tale of defeat. Damning himself and his journey, Oberon delivers advice that one might have expected from Parson Thumpcushion or Uncle Robert:

> Adopt some great and serious aim, such as manhood will cling to, that he may not feel himself, too late, a cumberer of this overladen earth, but a man among men. I will beseech him not to follow an eccentric path, nor by stepping aside from the highway of human affairs, to relinquish his claim upon human sympathy. And often, as a text of deep and varied meaning, I will remind him that he is an American.

The disgruntled character of Oberon also crops up in a sentimental revenge fantasy, "The Devil in Manuscript," possibly another fragment from *The Story Teller,* in which he peevishly despairs, "I have become ambitious of a bubble, and careless of solid reputation." What is writing or the writer's life? An existence surrounded by shadows, drawing one away from "the beaten path of the world" into "a strange sort of solitude—a solitude in the midst of men—where nobody wishes for what I do, nor thinks nor feels as I do. The tales have done this."

Collecting his manuscripts "like a father taking a deformed infant into his arms," Oberon edges toward the hearth. "Would you have me a damned author?" he hysterically demands of his friend, who vainly protests as Oberon gleefully tosses them onto the logs. The papers curl and sputter in the fire, embers popping and sparking and flying up the chimney to spread over the town, which bursts into flame.

Oberon is vindicated. At last the town is ablaze, so to speak, with his work.

If anything, Oberon's theatrics keep Hawthorne in print, albeit anonymously. He signs "The Devil in Manuscript" as Ashley A. Royce, possibly in comic homage to Edgar A. Poe, and he contributed three stories to the 1836 *Token*, "The Wedding-Knell," "The Minister's Black Veil," and "The May-Pole of Merry Mount," unsigned; ditto contributions to the *New-England Magazine*, published monthly and which contained at least one of his stories and sometimes as many as three.

Yet a curtain seems temporarily to fall over Hawthorne. Clustered together in Salem since the death of Richard, the Mannings had no occasion to write about themselves in letters, and so very few family documents illumine this period of Hawthorne's life. The documents that do survive—even the portrait of Hawthorne by Henry Inman—don't reveal why, for instance, the Hawthornes left their Dearborn Street house to move back to Herbert Street shortly before Samuel's death. All we know is that Ebe was translating Cervantes's tales, Louisa making her seasonal visits to Newburyport, and that Hawthorne, thirty-one years old and—to judge by his portrait—intense, continued to live in a diminished household increasingly dominated by women: his two sisters, his mother, his aunt Mary.

He also complained about Salem, took his summer vacations in the country, and later referred to himself with some bitterness as "the obscurest man of letters in America." He hadn't achieved much success; in fact, his failed ventures in the book trade left him prey to the wags of "public opinion," as Hawthorne noted in one of the *Story Teller* tales, "and felt as if it ranked me with tavern-haunters and town-paupers,—with the drunken poet who hawked his own fourth of July odes, and the broken soldier who had been good for nothing since [*sic*] last war."

In stories recently published, like "The Haunted Mind," he dropped the image of the open road for the metaphor of small spaces. Like Fanshawe, the artist burrows within himself, remote and watchful and sepa-

Hawthorne, portrait by Henry Inman [1835]

rated for better or worse from ordinary people and events. "In the depths of every heart, there is a tomb and a dungeon."

A sodden sky hangs over Hawthorne's eeriest tales like the visor of guilt and remorse dimming the features of so many of his characters—or the blanket of anonymity covering the name of their author. And with a psychological insight that reveals even as it conceals—much like Hawthorne's fictional method—his stories delineate human character with a truly awful power of insight, as William Henry Channing would call it, into the unnameable strangeness of the everyday. Nowhere is this more true than in "The Minister's Black Veil," when, for some unexplained reason, Parson Hooper, a bachelor about thirty years old, arrives one Sunday at the meetinghouse, his face wrapped in a black veil of "two folds of crape." Hiding his features except his mouth and chin, the veil "probably did not intercept his sight, farther than to give a darkened aspect to all living and inanimate things."

"He has changed himself into something awful, only by hiding his face," a parishioner mumbles. With a gesture made more frightful by its inexplicable simplicity, Parson Hooper is a walking symbol—of what, no one can decide. Nor will he enlighten anyone as to why he wears his strange veil. Elizabeth, his fiancée, begs him to lift it just once. He refuses, and she leaves him. After a while the townspeople become so spooked they begin to doubt his very existence. "I can't really feel as if good Mr. Hooper's face was behind that piece of crape," says the sexton. How odd, comments one prescient woman, "that a simple black veil, such as any woman might wear on her bonnet, should become such a terrible thing on Mr. Hooper's face!"

Separating himself from everyone in a performance that draws attention to himself, Parson Hooper, veiled as a woman is veiled, is a parable of the artist: Hawthorne the storyteller embarks on a solitary journey that takes him, again and again, back home, where he burns his manuscripts and, tortoiselike, wears anonymity like a shell. "Have I dreaded scorn like death, and yearned for fame as others pant for vital air," the storyteller cries, "only to find myself in a middle state between obscurity and infamy?"

Obscurity and infamy, the Scylla and Charybdis of his temper, motivate the storyteller's journey, and because Hawthorne himself experienced writing as a kind of exhibitionism—the gist of "Mrs. Hutchinson"—he made much of hiding, or pretending to hide. "So far as I am a man of really individual attributes, I veil my face," he would write in subsequent years; "nor am I, nor have ever been, one of those supremely hospitable people, who serve up their own hearts delicately fried, with brain-sauce, as a tidbit for their beloved public." Dreading obscurity but half ashamed of his ambition and his profession, he wraps anonymity about him like a dark cloak, itself a kind of monastic identity that protects him from—terrifying to consider—nothing at all.

CHAPTER SEVEN

Mr. Wakefield

So! I have climbed high, and my reward is small.

Nathaniel Hawthorne, "Sights from a Steeple"

I
N THE OCTOBER twilight, an ordinary Englishman named Wakefield
bids his wife a brief farewell, pretending to go on a short trip, but instead
rents rooms in a neighboring street and stays there, by himself, for twenty
years. His wife slowly accommodates herself to widowhood, never aware
that her husband lives around the block or that he spies on her from time
to time. "Crafty nincompoop," Hawthorne calls the man who lives for two
decades in limbo, thinking all the while that he'll soon go home. Then, one
day, he does. He walks over to his house, the door opens . . . and there we
leave him.

Published in the *New-England Magazine* in May 1835, "Wakefield" is
more than another creepy story about a man who leaves his wife like Young
Goodman Brown, bound for a tryst in the woods. Wakefield is a drab,
undistinguished, and unexceptional man—except of course for the twenty-
year hiatus in his life, if that's what one calls it. But to Hawthorne, Wakefield is also an artist—the artist as crafty nincompoop—severed from the
world, having abandoned "his place and privileges with living men, without
being admitted among the dead."

For even as he castigates Wakefield, Hawthorne colludes with him, relishing an ordinary man's extraordinary caprice.

Hawthorne's best stories penetrate the secret horrors of ordinary life,
those interstices in the general routine where suddenly something or someone shifts out of place, changing everything. Parson Hooper puts on his
veil, Wakefield takes a little walk, Reuben Bourne tells himself a small lie. At
the same time, Hawthorne writes and rewrites a fable of the artist, story-

teller extraordinaire and crafty nincompoop alienated from his duller contemporaries by sensibility and vocation, an estranged, filmy figure who gropes with abashed ardor through the twilight, insecure himself but discerning and astute.

Wakefield and Hawthorne's storyteller are the truncated travelers obliged to return home; too much weirdness is a bad thing. "Amid the seeming confusion of our mysterious world, individuals are so nicely adjusted to a system, and systems to one another, and to a whole, that," as Hawthorne writes, "by stepping aside for a moment, a man exposes himself to a fearful risk of losing his place forever."

In the frozen January of 1836, Hawthorne was not the outcast of the universe but a denizen of Boston, a clanking metropolis where hammers banged out prosperity from the waterfront up to Charles Bulfinch's new State House, winking in gold-domed splendor. Houses were sold, torn down, rebuilt, replaced; soil was carted away, hills razed, and warehouses put up near the harbor. Textile investors discussed railroad stock while wagons of green produce clattered toward the wooden stalls at Quincy Market. And Boston women were pretty, their morals good: an unusual combination, said Franklin Pierce.

Hawthorne rambled over the wintry streets. He'd come to town to edit a monthly called the *American Magazine of Useful and Entertaining Knowledge,* published by the Bewick Company. Goodrich, who was affiliated with Bewick, had arranged the job. Elated, Bridge congratulated Hawthorne. "It is no small point gained to get you out of Salem," he shrewdly observed.

For a salary of five hundred dollars a year, Hawthorne was to collect all the droll or useful knowledge he could find and blend it into short pithy articles to be accompanied, on occasion, by engravings supplied by the publisher. The articles consisted of short biographies of statesmen like George Washington, Alexander Hamilton, and John C. Calhoun or short squibs about people, places, and odd phenomena, like the notice about a gardener who amputed his own arm with his clipping shears, and the mathematics professor said to self-combust—without consuming too much alcohol. He specialized in the absurd: an account of a nose, studied for phrenological purposes, or the report of stylish New England settlers wearing wigs made from the scalps of Indians, "a truly Yankee idea," he joked, "—to keep their ears comfortably warm with the trophies of their valour."

Other than himself, the only other writer was his sister Ebe, whose contributions resemble his, though one can detect her less polished prose style and more federalist politics, as in the profile of Alexander Hamilton, which Hawthorne finished. "I approve of your life," he told her, "but have been obliged to correct some of your naughty notions about arbitrary government." Often, though, her work and his merge seamlessly, except in certain cases like his account of the gravestones, a pet obsession, at Martha's Vineyard, or in his version of Hannah Duston's captivity and her killing of ten Indians, six of whom were children. "There was little safety for a red skin," Hawthorne writes, "where Hannah Duston's blood is up."

"You should not make quotations," he instructed Ebe, "but put other people's thoughts into your own words, and amalgamate the whole into a mass." Both of them excerpted bizarre tidbits from *Blackwood's*, the *Westminster Review*, or William Dunlap's *History of the Rise and Progress of the Arts of Design in the United States*. "You may extract every thing good that you come across—provided always it be not too good," Nathaniel wryly wrote to Ebe; "and even if it should be, perhaps it will not quite ruin the Magazine; my own selections being bad enough to satisfy any body."

Ebe borrowed books from the Salem Athenaeum, distilled the facts she needed, and then sent a packet to Boston. Hawthorne was having a more difficult time because his publishers had neglected to purchase him a share at the Boston Athenaeum so he could use its library. "The Bewick Co. are a damned sneaking set," he exploded. He asked Uncle Robert to get him books. There never seemed to be enough material. "Ebe should have sent me some original poetry—and other original concoctions," he complained to Louisa, in charge of his clean collars and shirts. The job was a family affair.

Hawthorne took room and board at Thomas Green Fessenden's house at 53 Hancock Street, one of the tight, sloping thoroughfares in leafy Beacon Hill, back of the State House. The connection to Fessenden was probably Uncle Robert, who doubtless knew the occasional poet through the *New England Farmer*, which Fessenden founded and where Manning published his pomology. A dabbler in poetry and politics, the affable Fessenden retired to his jumbled study each evening and invited Hawthorne to comment on the new sections of his interminably long poem, *Terrible Tractoration*. Hawthorne was fond of the man.

But within the month he was agitated, homesick, and disgusted with the job. "I am ashamed of the whole concern," he wrote Louisa. Goodrich owed him money, and without it Hawthorne had no cash for the smallest entertainment—a glass of wine and cigar cost nine cents—nor fare for the

Salem stagecoach to take him home. "For the Devil's sake, if you have any money send me a little," he begged his younger sister. "It is now a month since I left Salem, and not a damned cent have I had, except five dollars that I borrowed from Uncle Robert."

Meantime, he canvassed for something else, applying to the *New-York Mirror,* edited by George Pope Morris (famous for the justly forgotten verse "Woodman, Spare That Tree!"). Pierce supplied an introduction to Frank Blair, editor of the *Washington Globe,* the unofficial newspaper of Andrew Jackson's administration. Nothing materialized, which left Hawthorne at the mercy of Goodrich, "a good-natured sort of man enough," Hawthorne said, "but rather an unscrupulous one in money matters, and not particularly trustworthy in anything."

Life in Boston continued not to go well. By spring Hawthorne had received only twenty dollars of his salary. Regardless, he consented to take another job from Goodrich, this time to ghostwrite one of the Peter Parley books, a two-volume *Universal History on the Basis of Geography.* Again he turned to Ebe. "If you are willing to write any part of it (which I should think you might, now that it is warm weather) I shall do it." Hawthorne said he'd give her the one hundred dollars Goodrich offered. "It is a poor compensation," he admitted, "yet better than the Token; because the kind of writing is so much less difficult." For eight contributions in the upcoming (1837) *Token,* published at the end of 1836 and containing "Monsieur du Miroir," "Mrs. Bullfrog," "Sunday at Home," "The Man of Adamant: An Apologue," "David Swan: A Fantasy," "The Great Carbuncle: A Mystery of the White Mountains," "Fancy's Show Box: A Morality," and "The Prophetic Pictures," he was to receive only $108.

The Bewick Company went bankrupt in June. There was no reason— and no money—for Hawthorne to stay in Boston. The August issue of the *American Magazine* carried his farewell. "The brevity of our continuance in the Chair Editorial will excuse us from any lengthened ceremony in resigning it. In truth," he testily added, "there is very little to be said on the occasion."

The surface of the water was as opaque as iron. Dark clouds closed the sky like a fist. Occasionally the sun pried it open, lighting the promontory, and islands, half visible, floated into view. This is how Hawthorne saw the shore when he walked along the beach near Salem, casting small stones into the sea.

Accustomed to Hawthorne's low moods, Bridge tried his best to cheer him. "Brighter days will come," Bridge insisted, "and that within six months."

Hawthorne wasn't convinced. Nonetheless, after packing the *Universal History* off to Goodrich, he considered collecting his tales and publishing them as a book. The time seemed right. His audience was expanding. His stories had been reprinted from *The Token* in papers like Salem's *Essex Register,* and when the prestigious *Athenaeum* reviewed the 1836 *Token,* it singled out "The Wedding-Knell" and "The Minister's Black Veil." "My worshipful self is a very famous man in London," he proudly informed Ebe.

"What is the plan of operations?" Bridge jubilantly responded to word of Hawthorne's projected book. "Who [are] the publishers, and when the time that you will be known by name as well as your writings are?"

Exasperated by Hawthorne's deliberate anonymity, Bridge had decided to review the new (1837) *Token* for the *Boston Post* and unmask the author of eight of its tales—the finest in the book—as Hawthorne. "It is a singular fact that, of the few American writers by profession, one of the very best is a gentleman whose name has never yet been made public, though his writings are extensively and favorably known," wrote Bridge. "We refer to Nathaniel Hawthorne, Esq., of Salem, the author of the 'Gentle Boy,' the 'Gray Champion,' etc. etc."

Park Benjamin, in his magazine the *American Monthly,* did likewise. "How few have heard the name of Nathaniel Hawthorne!" Benjamin exclaimed in the fall of 1836. "He does not even cover himself with the same anonymous shield at all times; but liberally gives to several unknowns the praise which concentrated on one would be great, to several unknowns. If Mr. Hawthorne would but collect his various tales and essays into one volume, we can assure him that their success would be brilliant—certainly in England, perhaps in this country."

The veil was lifted. And yet Hawthorne reacted with a certain sourness. "In this dismal and squalid chamber, fame was won," he scribbled from his room in Herbert Street, as if contemptuous of the prize he sought or the way he felt forced to seek it. It wouldn't be the last time that he wrote of the artist's sacrifice—in love, life, or human warmth.

"I fear you are too good a subject for suicide, and that some day you will end your mortal woes on your own responsibility," Bridge worried. Negotiations for the book weren't going well. "You have the blues again," Bridge wrote Hawthorne in October, and begged him not to "give up to them, for God's sake and your own and mine and everybody's." A few days later,

Horatio Bridge, portrait by Eastman Johnson

Bridge wrote again, nervous about the "desperate coolness" of Hawthorne's last letter. Bridge would come to Boston. He had a plan.

Hawthorne didn't know that Bridge had contacted Goodrich about underwriting the book. "It will cost about $450 to print 1000 vols in good style," Goodrich had answered Bridge's query about the expense. "I have seen a publisher, & he agrees to publish, if he can be guaranteed $250—as an ultimate resort against loss. If you will give that guarantee, the thing shall be but immediately in hand." Delighted, Bridge boarded the Boston stage with the appointed sum and didn't tell Hawthorne.

Hawthorne himself could no longer pay for his own publication, as he'd done with *Fanshawe;* the Manning reserves were dwindling. Since Richard's death, the family had been selling off most of the Maine property, and in Salem business was terrible. The railroad whistled a death knell to the Manning stagecoach line. Anxious, Hawthorne tried to get his position back with the *American Magazine,* under new management, to no avail.

"You will have more time for your book," Bridge soothed; "there is more honor and emolument in store for you, from your writings, than you imagine. The bane of your life has been self-distrust."

"I expect, next summer, to be full of money," he informed Hawthorne with optimism, "a part of which shall be heartily at your service, if it comes." Bridge had left the practice of law to build a dam across the Kennebec River, for which he anticipated abundant reward. But a flood would wash out the entire project and destroy the Bridge family mansion, and Bridge would join the United States Navy as a purser, a future he couldn't of course have predicted in the fall of 1836.

With charming ignorance, Bridge did predict that the publication of Hawthorne's book would deluge Hawthorne with offers of "an editorship in any magazine in the country if you wish it." Perhaps Hawthorne, believing him, refused Goodrich's most recent offer to ghost another of the Peter Parley books. Or he didn't trust that Goodrich would pay the three hundred dollars he promised. In either case, Bridge was thrilled. "I rejoice that you have determined to leave Goodrich to his fate. I do not like him."

Bound in dark crimson leather, Nathaniel Hawthorne's first collection of eighteen stories was published by the American Stationers' Company on March 6, 1837. The stories included some of his finest forays into the macabre, like "The Minister's Black Veil" and "Wakefield"; historical tales like "The Gentle Boy," "The Gray Champion," and "The May-Pole of Merry Mount"; meditative sketches and stories like "Sights from a Steeple" or "Fancy's Show Box"; and some of the more humorous ones, "A Rill from the Town-Pump" and "Little Annie's Ramble." The volume also contained "Sunday at Home," "The Wedding-Knell," "Mr. Higginbotham's Catastrophe," "The Great Carbuncle," "The Prophetic Pictures," "David Swan," "The Hollow of the Three Hills," "The Vision of the Fountain," and "The Fountain of Youth" (later published as "Dr. Heidegger's Experiment"). Hawthorne excluded "My Kinsman, Major Molineux," "Roger Malvin's Burial," "Young Goodman Brown," and "Alice Doane's Appeal," which he may have considered too revealing, too early, or too autobiographically painful.

The volume cost a dollar and was called *Twice-told Tales,* after the lines from Shakespeare's *King John,* "Life is as tedious as a twice-told tale,/Vexing the dull ear of a drowsy man." All eighteen had been published before and selected, said Hawthorne, as "best worth offering to the public a second time."

By June about six or seven hundred copies of the one thousand printed had sold, and then these "awful times"—the ghastly depression that followed the Panic of 1837—virtually halted all sales. By the next year the American Stationers' Company was bankrupt and Hawthorne's book was remaindered.

The book was, however, a succès d'estime, "spoken of in the highest terms by discriminating gentlemen here and at Cambridge," said the publisher. Hawthorne's friend Caleb Foote wrote in the *Salem Gazette* that he admired Hawthorne's "fine moral tone," and Thomas Green Fessenden commended Hawthorne's "sedate, quiet dignity displayed in his diction" in the *New England Farmer.* The *Boston Daily Advertiser* enjoyed the lighter stories, such as "Little Annie's Ramble" or "A Rill from the Town-Pump," and recommended "The Minister's Black Veil" for its "more fearful interest." Most readers liked "The Gentle Boy," and even Bridge said he felt as though he'd never read it before: "It had the credit of making me blubber a dozen times at least during the two readings which I have given it." Bridge himself wrote a piece for the Augusta (Maine) *Age* differentiating Hawthorne's style from that of John Neal: "There is little or none of what is often termed powerful writing, i.e. ranting, and foaming at the mouth—lacerating the reader's nerves, and as it were, taking his sympathies by storm."

Uniformly, reviewers approved Hawthorne's style as graceful, his humor as gentle, and his fancy as "aerial," even too aerial, Bridge had criticized, though he added that "this very fault is, to a delicate taste, one of the greatest beauties." Park Benjamin went so far as to characterize "the soul of Nathaniel Hawthorne" as "a rose bathed and baptized in dew," a maddening, insulting phrase with an innuendo that Hawthorne caught. Admiring his penchant for American subjects, none of the reviewers mentioned the satire embedded in stories like "The Gray Champion," where Hawthorne speaks of "the veterans of King Philip's war, who had burnt villages and slaughtered young and old with pious fierceness, while the godly souls through the land were helping them with prayer." Similarly, they ignored the way Hawthorne yoked verbs or participles to nouns for jarring effect, as in the case of the "Quakers, esteeming persecution as a divine call to the post of danger" in "The Gentle Boy," or the recurrent dark forests, dusky mantles, and guilt-stained hearts in which Hawthorne transforms a troubled consciousness into concrete emblems difficult to interpret, the case of the minister's black veil being the most obvious. And though reviewers compared Hawthorne to Charles Lamb and Joseph Addison, they did not invoke Mandeville, Voltaire, Bacon, Swift, or Montaigne—moralists and satirists who obviously influenced Hawthorne and whose frequently harsh view of human nature matched his own.

Henry Wadsworth Longfellow,
daguerreotype by Southworth and Hawes

To help promote the book, Hawthorne sent a presentation copy of *Twice-told Tales* to his former classmate Henry Wadsworth Longfellow, along with a flattering letter. "We were not, it is true, so well acquainted at college, that I can plead an absolute right to inflict my 'twice-told' tedious-ness upon you," Hawthorne wrote; "but I have often regretted that we were not better known to each other, and have been glad of your success in litera-ture." Longfellow replied immediately and with typical largesse. "Though something more than ten years have elapsed since we met face to face," the poet said, "I have had occasional glimpses of you in the *Token*, and the *New England Magazine;* and in all good faith be it said, these glimpses have always given me very great delight." Longfellow then promised to review the book in the *North American Review,* an eminent publication for the lit-erary gentry.

Although the review didn't appear until July, its extravagant praise hurled Hawthorne ("a new star") into the company of angels ("the heaven of poetry") on syrupy wings of equivocal esteem (*Twice-told Tales* was a "sweet, sweet book"). Hawthorne's spirits flagged. The newspapers had been tepid, he thought, and many puffs had come from friends. Some buyers refused to purchase a collection of "twice-told" tales still available elsewhere. And Bridge had been wrong. No one handed Hawthorne any editorial post on the basis of his wonderful new book. In fact, money was tighter than ever, his prospects grimmer.

Franklin Pierce, his own star rising, decided Hawthorne needed a change of air. Recently elected to the United States Senate from New Hamp-shire, Pierce knew of the South Sea expedition recently authorized by Con-gress, a kind of scientific, navigational, and commercial junket set to circumnavigate the globe as early as the spring. This was Hawthorne's chance, at last, to explore the sea, not as a sailor but as the expedition's histo-rian. Pierce contacted Bridge, who promised to deliver "the whole Maine delegation" on Hawthorne's behalf, and Bridge mailed a copy of *Twice-told Tales* to Jonathan Cilley, now representing Maine in Congress. He also approached Jeremiah Reynolds, who he supposed would run the expedition, describing Hawthorne as modest and diffident, decidedly "not subject to any of those whims and eccentricities which are supposed to characterize men of genius."

Bridge's Hawthorne was a tame soul, eager for the political appointment and too honorable to maneuver for himself: a gentleman and a scholar.

Hawthorne was overjoyed. Bridge, concerned that he may have raised Hawthorne's hopes too high, cautioned him not to "set your heart wholly upon this cast" and reminded him that even if he didn't receive the appoint-ment, "you will be much better; for having made interest among many of the high officers and high privates in the land, your reputation will be of course extended, and the same men will feel bound to help you again, if called upon."

Besides, he added, Frank Pierce will never rest until he does something for you.

Dreaming of Orange Harbor, near the coast of Tierra del Fuego, Hawthorne also dreamed of marriage. That the South Sea expedition would lead him far from any prospective bride didn't faze him. Hawthorne was adept at linking marriage to flight: witness the careers of Goodman Brown and Wakefield or the fact that the Reverend Mr. Hooper dodges his betrothed with a veil. In "The May-Pole of Merry Mount," newlyweds encounter a somber John Endicott, who casts a shadow over their happiness, and the couple in "The Wedding-Knell" marry at the door of a tomb.

Hawthorne was thirty-two, robust, good-looking, and eligible. And despite his disappointment over *Twice-told Tales,* its publication ultimately boosted his morale. Having unveiled himself, and with his own hopes about the future rising, Hawthorne turned his attention to love.

Bridge had not married and wouldn't until 1845. Pierce had. In 1834 he wed Jane Appleton, the daughter of Bowdoin's second president. And Jonathan Cilley, who married Deborah Prince in 1829, congratulated the bachelor Hawthorne on the publication of *Twice-told Tales* with a gibe. "What! suffer twelve years to pass away, and no wife, no children, to soothe your care, make you happy, and call you blessed." Hawthorne may have agreed, or thought he did. Perhaps the time had come for more changes, he hinted to Bridge. Bridge shuddered. "Why should you 'borrow trouble'?"

The tone of Hawthorne's correspondence provides a tentative answer. Too long a seclusion, he confided to Longfellow, had made him a prisoner of himself. "For the last ten years, I have not lived, but only dreamed about living," he wrote his cosmopolitan classmate, now a Harvard professor as well as a linguist and a poet of balmy, accomplished verse. But he, Hawthorne, had seen so little of the world that "I have nothing but thin air to concoct my stories of, and it is not easy to give a lifelike semblance to such shadowy stuff. Sometimes, through a peep-hole, I have caught a glimpse of the real world; and the two or three articles, in which I have portrayed such glimpses, please me better than the others."

The self-dramatization presents Hawthorne's biography in miniature as he no doubt believed it to be: a man alone, unappreciated, timorous, an owl afraid of the light, rarely venturing forth until dusk, withdrawn from society into the nocturnal world of fantasy. "I have made a captive of myself and put me into a dungeon," Hawthorne continues his letter to Longfellow; "and now I cannot find the key to let myself out—and if the door were open, I should be almost afraid to come out."

It's a masterpiece of hyperbole. Yet the emotion is real.

As Hawthorne acknowledged, the door had opened, or at least it stood ajar. "I have now, or soon shall have, one sharp spur to exertion, which I lacked at an earlier period; for I see little prospect but that I must scribble for a living." Was the spur entirely financial? Not really. Aware that time was passing, that spring he confided to Bridge that he had decided to marry.

Astounded, Bridge sent no congratulations. "I confess that, personally, I have a strong desire to see you attain a high rank in literature," he stuffily replied. "Hence my preference would be that you should take the voyage if you can. And after taking a turn round the world, and establishing a name that will be worth working for, if you choose to marry you can do it with more advantage than now."

The fatherly, brotherly, and jealous advice fell on deaf ears. Hawthorne was enamored of a Salem belle.

At fourteen Nathaniel Silsbee weighed anchor as captain's clerk and became everything denied to Captain Hathorne, his contemporary. By nineteen he was steering a small sloop of forty tons, and by 1795 he owned a share in the vessels at his command. He married Mary Crowninshield, daughter of a Salem cod-prince, and he entered politics, serving eighteen years in the United States Congress, first as a representative from Massachusetts and then as its senator. He retired in 1835.

Named for his wife, Silsbee's daughter Mary, born in 1809, was a glamorous flirt whose wit shone bright in Washington and Boston, where she was known as "the Star of Salem." Her "intellectual style of beauty," mooned Longfellow, "leads one captive." Another acquaintance, Sarah Clarke, thought Mary "a grave & beautiful Greek in contour & expression. Her hair is done up like that of a statue & her smile reveals depths of internal beauty." But Mary Silsbee had her critics, one of them highly incensed that Silsbee, vamping for attention, would willingly forgo "much that is lovely and beautiful in a woman's character."

After the death of her mother, Mary Silsbee began to write plaintive, lachrymose poems to relieve the sorrow that gnawed at her for the rest of

Mary Crowninshield Silsbee Sparks, portrait by Francis Alexander

her busy, active life. Doubtless, many people continued to be offended by her beautiful hauteur—they probably didn't know the poetry—although just as many continued to flatter her. Others did both, like the historian and minister Jared Sparks, her former beau, who jilted Silsbee but, after his wife died, came courting again. The eventual marriage of the future Harvard president and the former Star of Salem proved long and happy.

Unfortunately, most information—or gossip—about Mary Silsbee comes from Elizabeth Peabody, Hawthorne's future sister-in-law. "She was a handsome girl, a great coquette, a mischief-maker, a fearful liar," Peabody told Julian Hawthorne. Peabody's appreciable resentment makes sense: she was at one time devoted to Jared Sparks and then to Nathaniel Hawthorne, whose heart, according to Peabody, Silsbee nearly crushed.

It was Mary Silsbee whom Hawthorne had been hoping to marry. With her father out of the Senate and her mother dead, the bereft Silsbee evidently unburdened her heart to the bashful bachelor with the deep-set eyes who, she later said, had published one of her poems, "Take Back the

Flower," in a tale of his. What's more, the title of another of Silsbee's early poems, "The Maniac Mother," appears in Hawthorne's notebooks.

But their romance is difficult to reconstruct. Hawthorne did plan to talk over the idea of marriage with Bridge when he visited him in Maine that summer, 1837, a last communion of bachelors in the promised land. "My circumstances, at least, cannot long continue as they are and have been," he wrote in his journal, reiterating what he'd told Longfellow and doubtless thinking about the need to secure a steady income or how difficult it would be to wed an heiress who, again according to Peabody, insisted that he first raise three thousand dollars.

The South Sea expedition having gone to Charles Wilkes, not Jeremiah Reynolds, a landlocked Hawthorne celebrated his thirty-third birthday with Bridge in July, staying with him in Augusta along with Bridge's French tutor, Monsieur Schaeffer, a talkative and cheery man with the unfortunate task of teaching French to blockheads. "Then here is myself, who am likewise a queer character in my way," Hawthorne wrote in his journal, "and have come to spend a week or two with my friend of half-a life-time;—the longest space, probably, that we are ever destined to spend together; for fate seems to be preparing changes for both of us." Boyhood regained, he fished for trout in the ice-blue brooks near Augusta and inhaled the sweet green of pine. He practiced his French with Monsieur Schaeffer and in the evenings ate bread slathered with cheese and eggs or cold mutton and ham and smoked beef, the three men "so independent, and untroubled by the forms and restrictions of society."

"Of female society I see nothing," Hawthorne noted with pleasure and relief. The men talked of Hawthorne's stories—of "The Minister's Black Veil" in particular, which Monsieur Schaeffer had translated—and of sex. Monsieur Schaeffer, observed Hawthorne with some surprise, "has never yet sinned with woman." (Had Hawthorne? The "yet" sounds as though he had.) "We live in great harmony and brotherhood—as queer a life as any body leads, and as queer a set as may be found anywhere."

In August, after a short visit to Cilley in Thomaston, Hawthorne returned to Salem without any mention of a paramour in his journals.

And he seems to have put the marriage plan on hold. Perhaps Bridge convinced him to wait, or he realized he wasn't ready to run with the common herd. Perching himself on a cliff by the shore, he again tossed pebbles at the shadows below, and in a journal entry, possibly written a few months later, he sounds eerily like Wakefield: "A man tries to be happy in love; he cannot sincerely give his heart, and the affair seems like a dream;—in domestic life, the same;—in politics, a seeming patriot; but still he is sincere, and all seems like theatre."

Exile and voyeur, not terribly sure of himself, between two worlds, Wakefield is Hawthorne's ghost, his semblable, his brother, pausing at the threshold. And yet he was the author of *Twice-told Tales,* no longer anonymous, and poised for some kind of change.

CHAPTER EIGHT

The Wedding Knell

Jollity and gloom were contending for an empire.

Nathaniel Hawthorne, "The May-Pole of Merry Mount"

H ER CHARITY began at home and ended nowhere, her credulity out-ran her charity, and by the end of her long life she knew less about people's motives than her traffic in them might suggest: so Henry James characterized Elizabeth Palmer Peabody in his 1886 novel *The Bostonians,* calling her Miss Birdseye and giving her a squint. One could see Peabody in those days, riding a Boston streetcar, hair disheveled, spectacles crooked, bonnet cockeyed, and her beaming face upturned. A garrulous commitment to what she called "the joy of the Ideal" made her insufferable to many—this she readily admitted—but she never yielded her principles or her self-respect. At eighty-two she was the sole survivor of her family, its oldest chronicler, and still the benevolent booster of causes, one of which happened to be her brother-in-law, Nathaniel Hawthorne.

Hawthorne presented Peabody with a copy of *Twice-told Tales* shortly after its publication. That much is certain. But how Peabody and Hawthorne met and when and where are matters of speculation. Sarah Clarke, a friend of Peabody's, thought they were introduced in Salem at Judge Daniel White's. It's a plausible suggestion, for White was the father-in-law of Hawthorne's friend Caleb Foote, editor of the *Salem Gazette.*

There is also reason to suppose Elizabeth Peabody had met Hawthorne sometime earlier, if not in Judge White's drawing room, then at the Washington Square mansion of Mary Silsbee, whom Peabody knew. In fact, Hawthorne and Mary Silsbee were likely flirting when Peabody first met the author, and Peabody's interference—meddling, some would call it—may have hastened the end of that affair. As Ebe Hawthorne once said, Elizabeth Peabody's philanthropy sowed dissension between husbands and wives and lovers once affianced. "Miss Peabody," she crisply remarked, "certainly has a propensity for doing mischief remarkable in a woman of so much benevolence."

Peabody told her own tale. She "discovered" Hawthorne. That is, having admired his anonymously published stories in *The Token,* she set about learning the author's identity, and after she did, the author himself sent her *Twice-told Tales* "with his respects." Then he came to call, a hooded sister on each arm, his wonderful eyes "like mountain lakes seeming to reflect the heavens." (Peabody's gifts did not include metaphor.) In near delirium, she ran upstairs to her sister Sophia's bedroom. "He is handsomer than Lord Byron!" cried Peabody. "You must get up and dress and come down." Sophia, an invalid, laughed. "If he has come once he will come again," she said.

There is some truth—Peabody-style—to the story. For as she herself once observed, she always spoke the truth as it appeared to her, "and with no regard to consistency," she added, a creed articulated best by her friend Ralph Emerson, who'd tutored her in Greek: "A foolish consistency is the hobgoblin of little minds," Emerson would write in his essay "Self-Reliance." With Emerson as moral touchstone and William Ellery Channing, the apostle of Unitarianism in Boston, as her spiritual guide, Peabody gladly dissembled whenever the unvarnished truth did not meet her higher standard. "I think she is benevolent," Ebe Hawthorne commented in later life, "and a well wisher of every human being, but I suspect no one who knows her relies upon her word."

It wouldn't have been hard to find the identity of the anonymous writer since Park Benjamin, Hawthorne's editor at the *American Monthly,* had married a Peabody cousin. But Peabody probably told the truth when she said that on learning the writer was Hawthorne, she assumed it had to be the astonishing Ebe, whom she'd remembered from childhood when her mother had taught both girls. According to Peabody, she then marched over to Herbert Street to renew her acquaintance. "Presently Louisa came in," Peabody reminisced, "and I soon learned from her that it was not Elizabeth but Nathaniel who was the author."

Louisa invited Peabody to call again, which she didn't, but she did receive a presentation copy of *Twice-told Tales,* which she read with delight. By then she'd heard, probably from Mary Silsbee, that Hawthorne had been invited to contribute to a new monthly, the *United States Magazine and Democratic Review,* edited by John O'Sullivan, a Washington friend of Silsbee's, so she wrote to Herbert Street asking for information on how to publish there, and, she added, why not put aside ceremony and come over to her family's home on nearby Charter Street that very night.

On Saturday evening, November 12, 1837, Nathaniel and the astonishing Ebe rang the Peabody bell. "He has a temple of a head (not a tower) and an eye full of sparkle, glisten, & intelligence," Peabody's other sister, Mary, described Hawthorne to their brother George. "He has lived the life of a perfect recluse till very lately—so diffident that he suffers inexpressibly in the presence of his fellow-mortals." Mary seemed smitten too. "He has promised to come again and if we can get fairly acquainted I think we shall find much pleasure in him."

To explain what the fuss was about, Mary mailed George the treasured presentation copy of *Twice-told Tales*—and was told to mail it back.

And so Hawthorne entered the Peabody circle. Since he liked to dramatize his favorite subject, himself, for Peabody he painted a picture similar to the one concocted for Longfellow. "We do not live at our house, we only vegetate," he enthralled her, portraying himself as friendless and forsaken. He ate alone, he said, his meals were left outside the door to his room, which he kept locked. He had not even seen his sister Ebe in three months, she being even more reclusive than he.

False in particulars, Hawthorne's self-portrait was faithful to his sense of alienation—he was like a man talking to himself in a dark place, he told Peabody—and it explained to contemporaries like Longfellow or Peabody, men and women already active in the world, why he had not yet made his mark. Your brother has no right to be idle, Peabody remembers telling Louisa, inadvertently touching the quick of Hawthorne's dilemma: here he was, able and more educated than his family—or his ancestors—and contributing less to society than they did.

Hawthorne could repair the damage with a tale of solitude that melted hearts, and Peabody, hers dripping, disseminated the Hawthorne fable. "An extreme shyness of disposition—and a passionate love of nature—together with some peculiar circumstances have made him live a life of extraordinary seclusion," she characterized Hawthorne to the educator Horace Mann. To William Wordsworth, with whom she had an occasional correspondence, she depicted Hawthorne as a pastoral person with a character beyond reproach. "His early & his college years were passed in the country. He is almost the only young American of any ability that I have known, who has hidden himself during his nonage and kept his own secret," she continued. "—A fineness of stature and holiness of spirit—which have nothing in common with effeminacy, seem to have borne him quite above the career of vulgar ambition, so that he has not encountered that current which sweeps everything into publicity & common stock."

Moreover, all her friends and acquaintances should read him. "He is a man of first rate genius," she wrote, pushing Hawthorne's stories on a dour Horace Mann and a daft Jones Very, another Peabody protégé. To Hawthorne's own family she called him one of nature's ordained priests, an Ariel breathing moral ambrosia, a second Homer. "I see that you both think me rather enthusiastic," she conceded.

A born publicist, Peabody was a loyal believer in Hawthorne's talent who remained true to him to the end. Fidelity of purpose, she later said, was her most prominent trait, perseverance her greatest virtue.

Early in February 1838, almost a year after the publication of *Twice-told Tales,* Hawthorne invited Bridge to meet him in Boston. He was planning to go to Washington and hoped to see Bridge before he left. "Not that you can do me the least good," Hawthorne enigmatically remarked. With even more mystery he added, "And, there may be cause for regret on your part, should we fail of a meeting. But I repeat that you cannot exercise the slightest favorable influence on my affairs—they being beyond your control, and hardly within my own."

Hawthorne's intended trip to Washington has been the subject of some biographical debate because Elizabeth Peabody later alleged that Mary Silsbee had precipitated a quarrel between Hawthorne and his new friend John O'Sullivan. According to Peabody, Silsbee pretended that O'Sullivan had compromised her integrity in some way. To defend her honor, Hawthorne challenged O'Sullivan to a duel, but O'Sullivan declined the invitation in a conciliatory letter that revealed Miss Silsbee's duplicities and bound the two men forever after.

The story of Hawthorne's near duel seems a Peabodyesque fantasia hatched out of "Alice Doane." Hawthorne had actually condemned the habit of dueling as early as *Fanshawe.* Edward Walcott foolishly accepts a challenge from the story's villain only to be wittily chided by a tavern keeper: "And you, Master Edward, with what sort of a face will you walk into the chapel, to morning prayers, after putting a ball through this man's head, or receiving one through your own?—Though in this last case, you will be past praying for, or praying, either." At age eighty, when Peabody recalled the dueling incident to Julian Hawthorne, she may have been remembering *Fanshawe*. What lends the story the pall of credibility is the death of Jonathan Cilley, who decided to accept a challenge himself.

Cilley was a radical Democrat who proudly expected to occupy his seat in Congress among men of "real heart felt & active benevolence, mutual simplicity, unaffected humility, manly strength of mind, & everlasting truth." But the muddy streets of the nation's capital, the taverns, boarding-houses, and smoky hotels promptly reminded him that politics was no tidy playground of well-behaved boys. "My labors here are arduous, & the opposition is as relentless & persecuting as can be," he said. "A man, if he think free & boldly, must take his life in his hand."

Cilley wasn't exaggerating. Writing to his wife on February 22, 1838, he'd already tangled himself in the affair that in two days' time would leave him bleeding to death on the Marlboro Pike, just outside Washington.

The ostensible reason for the duel makes no sense. On the congressional floor Cilley had questioned the ethics of the newspaper, the *New York Courier and Inquirer*, edited by General James Watson Webb—the very paper at the center of the recently formed Whig Party, a coalition of former Federalists, like Daniel Webster, who endorsed a strong federal government, and of those men who deplored Jackson's autocratic brand of Jeffersonian-ism. General Webb, believing his name had been sullied, deputized an intermediary, William Graves, to deliver a formal note to Cilley requesting that Cilley retract his statements. Cilley replied that he meant Graves no disrespect, but he couldn't comment one way or another about Webb; nor could he receive any communication from him. Graves persisted, Cilley was intransigent. Graves then frostily inquired "whether you declined to receive his communication on the ground of any personal exception to him as a gentleman or a man of honour?" When Cilley declined to answer, Graves challenged him to a duel, and Cilley accepted the challenge.

The two men, their seconds, and a surgeon met at about noon. Exchang-ing civilities, Cilley and Graves acknowledged one another and then, having opened their pistol cases, separated, counted paces, turned, raised their pis-tols, and fired. Each of them missed. Cilley again insisted that he meant no disrespect toward Graves. Yet he would say nothing more, certainly nothing about Webb, and Graves, unsatisfied, demanded another round. Again the two men raised their guns, shot, and missed. Their representatives conferred, pleading with the two men to quit. For a third time they counted paces, aimed, and fired. The smoke hadn't cleared when Cilley moaned, "I am shot," and thudded to the ground.

Congress exploded. Bloody accounts of the Washington murder spattered the newspapers. Cilley's friends cried foul, and several Democrats alleged Henry Clay had fomented the quarrel to get rid of Cilley, a firebrand willing to stand up to southerners; it was also rumored that Graves had been urged forward by Henry Wise of Virginia, another Whig. Franklin Pierce joined a committee set up by the House of Representatives to investigate the barbarous affair, and for another six years censures, dismissals, inquiries, and partisan denunciations racked all of Congress. More than fifty years later, Horatio Bridge was still enraged about the conspiracy "to put the brilliant young Democrat out of the way."

The uproar didn't console Cilley's family or make sense of the affair to Hawthorne, who believed Cilley had yielded his very life to a grotesque—and southern—form of chivalry.

John O'Sullivan remembered Cilley urging him to get a contribution from Hawthorne for the *Democratic Review,* O'Sullivan's new literary and political periodical that, he bragged, would publish the country's best. An excellent editor, O'Sullivan did attract to his magazine a band of choice writers that over time included William Ellery Channing, John Greenleaf Whittier, the young Walter Whitman, Poe, Longfellow, Catharine Maria Sedgwick, William Gilmore Simms, George Bancroft, and Orestes Brownson. Even Elizabeth Peabody contributed an unsigned review of Emerson's 1836 book, *Nature,* to the magazine's early pages, probably with Hawthorne's help.

Hawthorne supplied a small sketch, "The Toll-Gatherer's Day," to the magazine's first number in October 1837, and over the next eight years he contributed twenty new short stories in addition to a memorial of Jonathan Cilley. Impetuous and warmhearted, O'Sullivan was just the kind of man to engage Hawthorne, for despite his skeptical edge, he shared O'Sullivan's democratic vision, at least in theory, and he quickly came to consider O'Sullivan, nine years his junior, "one of the truest and best men in the world." Said Hawthorne, "The Devil has a smaller share in O'Sullivan than in other bipeds who wear breeches."

Born on a British ship off Gibraltar during the War of 1812, O'Sullivan devoted himself to the care of his mother after his father, a ship's captain, died when his ship went down in 1824. He graduated from Columbia College at nineteen, received a master of arts degree three years later, was admitted to the bar, and then, as a journalist in Washington, founded the *Democratic Review* with his brother-in-law, Samuel Langtree. The money came from his having successfully settled a suit against the United States government, which had impounded one of his father's ships for alleged piracy.

Hawthorne and O'Sullivan were contradictory men, and each recognized something of the other in himself. Like Hawthorne, O'Sullivan held on to the romantic story of his lineage, in this case Irish nobility, in lieu of a father, but he also bristled at the undemocratic privileges vested in class or rank. He condemned capital punishment, considered insanity a disease, and supported American expansion and imperialism, coining the phrase "manifest destiny." He believed in popular sovereignty and the working classes; he abominated lawyers, corporations, and bankers. He served in the New York legislature, was a nationalist, a pacifist, a spiritualist, and a racist. During the Civil War he backed the Confederacy. But in 1837 his loyalty to Martin Van Buren earned him the endorsement of Attorney General Benjamin F. Brown, and with it, the *Democratic Review* became a respected party organ. "The Best Government Is That Which Governs Least," its masthead blared.

Hoping to integrate literature into the political life of the country, O'Sullivan adapted Emerson's exhortatory style to political journalism. "The eye of man looks naturally *forward*," O'Sullivan proclaimed, and in the first number of his magazine posted the Democratic credo: "Democracy is the cause of Humanity. It has faith in human nature. It believes in its essential equality & fundamental goodness. . . . Its object is to emancipate the mind of the mass of men from the degrading, & disheartening fetters of social distinctions & advantages. . . ."

Poe considered O'Sullivan an ass. Whitman thought him handsome and generous, and Longfellow regarded the slender young man as nervous, dainty, and refined; "I cannot believe he is at heart a *radical*." Yet he was. And he soon became the first of Hawthorne's great editor friends, bolstering the author with the confidence—and the audience—he had not corralled on his own. O'Sullivan loved Hawthorne, whom he regarded "as gentle as a girl, as shy as a deer, with, at the same time, the highest attributes of the man of principle, honor, and heart."

According to O'Sullivan, Jonathan Cilley had been working hard to find Hawthorne a place at the Salem post office, and there had been talk of a position in Washington. It's likely, then, that Hawthorne invited Bridge to a rendezvous in Boston not because he was heading to Washington to duel but because he wanted to talk over the possibility of his taking a government job.

"We would not yoke Pegasus to the dray-car of utility," a horrified Elizabeth Peabody quaked with distaste. "I too would have him help govern this great people; but I would have him go to the fountains of greatness and power"—by which she meant art and literature. Voicing her objections to Ebe since Ebe exercised considerable influence over her brother, she produced an alternative: Hawthorne should be convinced to take "such a view of a literary life as will fill his desire of action, and connect him with society more widely than any particular office under Government could do." She relented only to acknowledge that if "he has been so long uneasy—however, perhaps he had better go; only, may he not bind himself long, only be free to return to freedom."

In later years, Peabody conveniently forgot about Hawthorne's government commission. To her, Washington was a death sentence, a sentiment that might explain her mixing up Hawthorne with the fateful Cilley duel. At the time of Cilley's death, however, she didn't even want Hawthorne to write a biographical sketch of Cilley, as O'Sullivan had requested, in the *Democratic Review*. His hands should be kept clean.

Unfortunately, Julian Hawthorne took a fancy to Peabody's story and trimmed it with a flourish of his own. When Hawthorne learned of Cilley's death, wrote Julian, "he felt as if he were almost as much responsible for his friend's death as with the man who shot him." Of course, neither Peabody nor Julian Hawthorne would want to recall that, at the time, Hawthorne wanted to marry Mary Silsbee and needed to provide concretely for his future. That meant writing less and earning more. The rewards of *Twice-told Tales* had not been as remunerative as Hawthorne had hoped—quite the opposite—and though no announcement of an engagement had been made public, Hawthorne himself supposed Silsbee's father "knew something of the affair, and sanctioned it."

With Cilley dead, Hawthorne had to busy himself with writing projects, much to Peabody's delight. In March he was hoping to collaborate with Longfellow on a book of fairy tales "provided I have time—which seems more probable now than it did a few months since," he wrote the poet. Their book might earn a "pleasant and peculiar kind of reputation," he surmised—and "put money in our purses." Henry Longfellow took a stage to "Sunday-looking" Salem and passed a friendly afternoon with

Hawthorne at a local coffeehouse; and though their book never materialized, Longfellow noted that his new friend was not the reclusive owl he said he was. Hawthorne played rubbers of whist with Horace Conolly, his sister Louisa, Susanna Ingersoll (a second cousin), and the attorney David Roberts. At Roberts's law office on Essex Street, he picked up the gossip, and when in Boston had researched family history with another cousin, Charles Andrew. At night he downed a glass of champagne with friends. "He is much of a lion here," Longfellow commented in his journal, "sought after, fed, and expected to roar."

Hawthorne had entered Elizabeth Peabody's life at a fortuitous time. The last few years had been difficult. As Bronson Alcott's assistant in Boston at his progressive Temple School, she had worked tirelessly for no pay, and when she published a book about the unconventional school in 1835, a warehouse fire destroyed all the unsold copies, consuming her scant profits and leaving her in debt since an author was responsible for all unsold books. Then she argued with Alcott, and when her sister Sophia took Alcott's side, she felt doubly betrayed, all the more so when Alcott, despite her objection, subsequently published the controversial *Conversations with Children on the Gospels,* which scandalized proper Bostonians with its allusions to sex and birth. But Peabody was loyal, always, and sacrificed her own pedagogical capital to defend Alcott. Meantime, though, she spent the rest of her emotional reserves worrying about two ill friends—one of them was Emerson's brother Charles; both friends died.

The appearance of handsome Nathaniel Hawthorne—his spirit unsoiled, his work fresh—rekindled Peabody's considerable zest for uncommon projects and unusual people. And that he now wanted to write a children's book was nothing she'd like better. (It must have seemed he was following her advice about a literary life actively connected to society.) So she immediately applied to Horace Mann, now secretary of Massachusetts's new state board of education. If Mann wanted a series of library books for children, Hawthorne was the person for the job, for Hawthorne hoped to accomplish, as she told Mann, "one great moral enterprise as I think it & you will agree—to make an attempt at creating a new literature for the young." But the author possessed no talent for negotiation, she sighed, hoping Mann might put in a word with the publisher Nahum Capen.

"He [Hawthorne] says that were he embarked in this undertaking he should feel as if he had a right to live—he desired no higher vocation, he considered it the highest," Peabody concluded her sales pitch. A right to live? Peabody's hyperbole hits a mark; she knew that Hawthorne's nagging sense of guilt partly derived from a sense of inadequacy. *Twice-told Tales* had not fulfilled any practical purpose; it hadn't made any money.

Lacking purpose—in the sense of moral purpose—is how Horace Mann read Hawthorne's stories. Although Mann liked the style well enough, he found Hawthorne's content pretty thin: "We want something graver and sterner even than those,—a development of *duties* in all the relation of life," he condescended. "Such a story as the 'Wedding Knell,' wherefore is it and to what does it tend?"

The gossips of Salem started to link Hawthorne to Elizabeth Peabody as well as to Mary Silsbee.

No one knows for sure what Hawthorne felt for Peabody in these early days of their acquaintanceship. He was definitely gratified by her unalloyed enthusiasm for his writing, and the two of them did spend a good deal of time together. Beyond that, there is little information. It isn't even known how Peabody looked as a young woman. Scattered correspondence indicates her sisters may have been prettier but not that she was unattractive or clumsy. A family silhouette supplies her with a cinched waist, a cap, and a book—nothing extraordinary—and a former student would remember her as slight and lovely, with fair hair and a glowing face. Of course, no silhouetted profile can peel away the dowdiness heaped upon her by years of caricature: Lizzie Peabody, the ungainly woman in a fuzzy cap who unwittingly crushes a litter of kittens when she sits upon them unawares.

Boston scuttlebutt about Peabody and Hawthorne persisted for decades. Sarah Sturgis Shaw, a contemporary, was said to dislike Hawthorne "on acct of his engagement to Miss E. P. his sister in law." Another woman vowed that "Sophia never knew of her sister's engagement to N.H. but Hawthorne lived in terror lest E.P.P. should tell her." But for many years male scholars recoiled in horror at such preposterous claims or the very idea that Hawthorne might have inclined in Peabody's direction. "An engagement with Elizabeth there almost certainly was not," Norman Holmes Pearson snarls, his syntax twisted by asperity.

Peabody's own romantic history is vague. She had suffered the affection of at least one suitor, whom she rejected, and she may have been infatuated with Horace Mann before she recognized that her sister Mary loved him. ("Everybody thought Miss Elizabeth Peabody was dead set on Hor-

The Peabody family, 1835. Left to right, top row: Mrs. Elizabeth Peabody,
Dr. Nathaniel Peabody, Elizabeth and Nathaniel Peabody;
lower row: George, Sophia, Mary, and Wellington Peabody.

ace Mann," reminisced Rebecca Clark, their boardinghouse proprietress.)
Before Mann entered her life, she'd seemed interested in Jared Sparks, but
then Mary Silsbee caught his eye. And now Mary Silsbee was studying German with Hawthorne—Peabody herself had suggested he study the language—borrowing Peabody's books to do so.

There was an even more ominous development. Peabody's brother, also
named Nathaniel, having failed in several business ventures, recently lost
the teaching post Peabody had arranged for him in Maine, where, poor and
cold, he had to sell his furniture to keep his wife and child supplied with
firewood. He looked to his parents for help, and they relied on their
redoubtable daughter Elizabeth, regardless of the cost to her. For Elizabeth
Peabody shouldered obligations. She agreed to help her brother set up a

school in West Newton, Massachusetts, ten miles west of Boston. "Circum-stances are such that there is no alternative," sighed her sister Mary. In the spring of 1838, Peabody left Salem.

Hawthorne and Peabody promised to write one another while apart on the condition that she burn his letters after reading them. But when Peabody rode out of Salem in the middle of April, she understood she'd sac-rificed a very special tactical advantage—and not to Mary Silsbee. Many years later, Peabody still could see Hawthorne's face the night he met her sis-ter Sophia. "And afterwards," said Peabody, "as we went on talking, she would interpose frequently a remark in her low sweet voice. Every time she did so, he looked at her with the same intentness of interest. I was struck with it, and painfully."

The languishing Sophia took morphine every morning, and though she might come downstairs when Mr. Hawthorne rang the bell, she declared she never meant to have a husband. "Rather, I should say," she pertly added, "I never intend any one shall have me for a wife."

CHAPTER NINE

The Sister Years

*I have several bundles of love-letters, eloquently breathing an
eternity of burning passion, which grew cold and perished,
almost before the ink was dry.*

Nathaniel Hawthorne, "The Sister Years"

THEY WERE AN evangelical lot, those Peabodys, especially the women.
Poor in worldly goods, they suffered the New England addiction to
pride and pedigree. Elizabeth Peabody's mother, a woman of clear principle, conducted her life—and that of the family—as a narrative of vanished
grandeur compensated by other, more spiritual wares.

She never forgot girlhood days passed at her grandfather's home,
Friendship Hall, an American palace of three stories with fireplaces big as
bedrooms, solid mahogany floors, and banisters richly carved on both the
front and back stairs. It stood far back from the road, and one approached it
with reverence—as her youngest daughter Sophia later did—passing under
a canopy of oak and elm. Like the orchard to the side of the house, these
trees had been planted by Sophia's grandfather Palmer, General Joseph
Palmer. But the general had also cultivated the enmity of John Hancock,
who confiscated Friendship Hall after the Revolution and sent the Palmers
packing.

His daughter, Elizabeth Palmer, preferred not to recall being cast out of
Friendship Hall, and the days that followed, scrubbing floors, keeping
school, or selling dry goods to contribute whatever she could to line the
family purse. When she married Nathaniel Peabody, the son of an unlet-
tered New England farmer, she took refuge in his ancestry, his forebears
having touched American soil in 1635. Better yet, the "Peabodie Race,"

claimed daughter Sophia, reached directly to the ancient British monarch, Queen Boadicea.

The couple's first child, Elizabeth, named for her mother, was born in 1804, the same year as Hawthorne. Mary Peabody arrived two years later, in 1806, and Sophia three years after that, on September 21, 1809. Then came the boys: Nathaniel in 1811, George in 1813, and in 1815 Wellington, so called after the English victor at Waterloo. In 1819 Mrs. Peabody bore her last child, Catherine, who lived only seven weeks.

A benevolent despot, Mrs. Peabody was a believer in high thinking, good breeding, and her own holy self, which readied her for the Unitarians and, later, the transcendentalists. Men, however, were something of a trial. Peabody males had no luck. When Mrs. Peabody met her gentle husband, he was an innocuous teacher of Latin at Phillips Andover Academy. Shortly thereafter he switched careers, studying medicine in Cambridgeport, presumably at his wife's insistence, and subsequently practiced the savage art of dentistry in Salem and Lynn, Massachusetts, until 1820, when the family headed to rural Lancaster. Dr. Peabody turned farmer, also without success. The Peabodys went back to Salem in 1823, and Dr. Peabody returned to teeth.

In like fashion, the Peabody boys never secured a spot in the world. The youngest, Wellington, was smart and handsome and like his elder brothers troubled, though he managed at least to leave Harvard with a certificate of creditable standing. Debt-ridden, he signed on to a New Bedford whaler—some say that Mrs. Peabody made him go—but jumped ship in Peru, beaten and starved. "It is dreadful not to be loved," observed Sophia, obliquely referring to Wellington, who died from yellow fever, contracted at a New Orleans hospital where he'd been nursing the sick. He was twenty-one. Next in line, George Peabody had sallied far and wide seeking he knew not what—escape, probably—until spinal meningitis sent him home in agony. It killed him in 1839. He was twenty-four. That left Nathaniel Peabody, never successful at much of anything: a failure and the heir of failure, as one chronicler bluntly said.

Not so Mrs. Peabody, and not her daughters. A former preceptress at the North Andover Academy for Girls, Mrs. Peabody continued to teach in Lancaster, where she pressed the sixteen-year-old Elizabeth into service, assigning her the instruction of Sophia, which, in a sense, was like giving her a child of her own. Elizabeth diligently played surrogate mother. A bookish and watery-eyed teenager in need of spectacles, approval, and a crusade, she ministered to Sophia's mental improvement even after moving to the grand city of Boston in 1822 to rustle up money for her brothers' education.

Opening her own school in Boston, Elizabeth blossomed. She was attending lectures and sermons, dancing, reading French and German, and studying Greek with Ralph Waldo Emerson. And she continued to harangue Sophia with interminable advice. "I wish you now to read only those poets with whom no one has found fault & which are perfectly moral," she counseled, warning against the likes of Byron until impressionable Sophia's mind was "more fully stor'd than yours is, with classical recollections."

Sophia fended Elizabeth off by pleading a chronic headache. Her head began to pound sometime between the infant Catherine's death, when Sophia was ten, and the onset of her menstruation, when she was about twelve or thirteen. The throbbing increased when Elizabeth, teaching in Maine in 1823, asked the fourteen-year-old Sophia to be her assistant. Sophia demurred. "They would think perhaps 'Surely she must be a prodigy—if she sends for her so young' and then they will find out to the contrary," she cried, her head an anvil of pain. She was free.

Sophia worshipped Elizabeth, or thought she did. "I thank you very much my dearest Sister for you [*sic*] excellent advice and the kindness and

Sophia Peabody, etching by S. A. Schoff

anxiety you manifest for my happiness," she fawned. "—I am sure I shall improve and answer your highest expectations." She obediently checked off her literary progress—Walter Scott, Maria Edgeworth, Gibbon, and Johnson—as well as her studies in astronomy, Latin, and chemistry. But soon she slid a murderous fantasy or two within the treacle. "I have often told you I believe that I never felt as if I could wish to live a moment after you were dead," she wrote, "—I have thought of this so much that I have dreamed of your death an hundred times with every particular circumstance."

Sophia was willful and insecure, and she resented both her elder sisters. Mary was pretty, Elizabeth smart. "Your loveliness all through our growing up together never one moment made me feel the contrast of my plainness," Sophia would confide to Mary. "But to your confidence, I never aspired," she continued, "—Elizabeth was the intimate friend, I felt, & that seemed right & fitting—I never contrasted myself with her any more than my face with yours." However, Sophia staked out a territory of her own: goodness. "Surely there never could have been a purer—more unselfish love than mine for you," she informed Mary with a tinge of sanctimony. "I did not even think whether you loved me in return."

Trim and tasteful, brows arched, face round, and brown hair flecked with a jovial red, Sophia Peabody walked across Boston Common boldly carrying a broom; she didn't care who saw her. She rather hoped they did. Unlike Elizabeth or Mary, who battled social injustice, Sophia rebelled on a smaller scale: she was a defiant conformist who questioned not the conditions of society, as her sisters did, but their right to do so. And she considered herself one of the less fortunate about whom Mary and Elizabeth should care. They did. They doused her with leeches, ether, mercury, and carbonate of iron and colchicum. Dr. Peabody blistered her. When the clank of knives and forks sent Sophia rushing upstairs, she ate alone and unperturbed, and when the family moved back to Boston in 1828, to spare her further discomfort they applied to the governor of Massachusetts to forbid the firing of cannons on the Common on the Fourth of July. The cannons boomed, but the governor aimed them toward the river.

The physician, Walter Channing, cousin to the famous minister, prescribed arsenic, extending a long career of addiction, according to Elizabeth, which first started when her father administered narcotics to relieve Sophia (and her mother) from the screech of teething. The addiction ended, or was curtailed, when the Peabodys switched to homeopathy to purge themselves of poison. But to Mrs. Peabody, her husband and his elixirs were superfluous. "I only fear he does not sufficiently realize her trials, or the danger of her complaint," she told Mary. Only she grasped Sophia's condition, and as a consequence could not bear to let her baby daughter out of her sight. "Home is best," declared Mrs. Peabody.

Thus stultified, Sophia took to the couch like a female Job. She struck visitors as perfectly well unless they stayed too long, and then she'd fall back onto the sofa, explaining how much her charade had cost her. "I still keep just above, so that every one says 'How well you look!' and while I can keep up the struggle successfully I care not—I feel that every separate [*sic*] pain is an instrument for good." Suffering was morally magnificent.

And her headaches had provided her with a vocation. She began to draw. Elizabeth—always generous, always meddlesome—suggested Sophia try oils and offered to supply both paints and lessons. Since art relieved her headaches without diverting too much attention from them, Sophia studied with the illustrator Francis Graeter and then with Thomas Doughty and Chester Harding, who painted her portrait in 1830. Elizabeth also introduced Sophia to the renowned Washington Allston, who deigned to inspect Sophia's work. "Superior to what I expected," he judged it. He proffered good advice: copy nature, not the work of other artists. Sophia demurred, calculating her talent and her personality in far different—but equally observant—terms. "I am rather a planet that shines by borrowed light," she said.

Painting and pain vied for Sophia's attention, and after 1830, when her doctor pronounced her free of any illness but the habit of being sick, her family decided to ship her off to Cuba, hoping to cure her there. Elizabeth and Mary had convinced their mother that Sophia would bloom in citrus groves, and as a matter of fact, with Elizabeth pushing her to churn out some lithographs for a book of "Grecian Theology and Mythology," Sophia was glad to go.

On December 4, 1833, Sophia and Mary leaned over the cold iron rail of the brig *Newcastle* waving goodbye to their family. Delegated Sophia's chaperone, Mary was to tend the children of La Recompensa, a pastoral hacienda, while Sophia sketched the coffee planter's family. And it worked; Mary minded the children as Sophia's cheeks flushed with health, and soon she was sending home long letters full of golden sunrises and lemon groves, which she preferred to the less picturesque aspects of Cuba, like the economic structure of slavery that made her visit—and the hacienda—possible.

"Her nature was eminently religious, her taste severe, and her dislike to contemplate or discuss repellant subjects was very great," reminisced her brother Nathaniel. Slavery sickened Mary. Not Sophia. "I do not allow myself to dwell upon slavery for two reasons," she reported to her family. "One is, it would certainly counteract the beneficent influences, which I have left home and country to court, and another is, that my faith in God makes me sure that he makes up to every being the measure of happiness which he loses thro' the instrumentality of others."

She galloped about on horseback by day and waltzed and flirted by night, much to everyone's shock. By the time she sailed back to Massachusetts in the spring of 1835, she seemed not just restored but resplendent. Recovery, however, was short-lived. Sophia claimed it had been nothing more than a performance enacted for the benefit of her Cuban hosts.

Returning to Salem, where the peripatetic family now lived, Sophia came home to a different, duller life on Charter Street, next to the ancient graveyard. The house was three stories high and low-studded, its rooms squat. "It gives queer ideas, to think how convenient to Dr. Peabody's fam-

Peabody home, 53 Charter Street, adjacent to Salem's old burial ground

ily this burial-ground is, the monuments standing almost within arm's reach of the side windows of the parlor," Hawthorne would remark. And the main characteristic of the place, he noted with some sarcasm, was "a decent respectability, not sinking below the boundary of the genteel."

To comfort herself, Sophia converted her bedroom into a palace of art. She displayed her pictures in the best light and arranged everything else with a discerning eye: the fragment of a bas-relief, a cast of Apollo's head, a flower, or a bunch of dried grass. Herself a painter, Sarah Clarke surveyed the room with solemn approval. Only Sophia could find beauty where no one else would think to look.

Sophia was innately reverent and saw all glasses as half full, fervently so. Her paintings, too, reflect the roseate view. In them, one sees a serenity, heartless or calm, depending on one's perspective. In either case, Sophia squelched feeling. A tireless journalizer and letter writer, she crams into her long, prolix sentences a surfeit of cloud, silver-tipped, and dewdrop pink, along with a pell-mell of noble steeds and glorious sunsets or sunrises (it makes little difference), strangling all the fiercer emotions, her own and her reader's. "Mr. Hawthorne endeavored to discipline my style of expression into his own statuesque and immaculate beauty," she later noted with calm assurance. The effort was fruitless. Sophia remained a rhapsodist who celebrated nature, God, and eventually her husband—each of whom she substituted readily for the other, for she knew all three on intimate terms.

By the spring of 1838, Hawthorne was fully installed in Elizabeth Peabody's social and intellectual world. The Peabodys offered culture without too much affectation: genuine enthusiasm, for instance, over John Flaxman's illustrations or Spenser, whose tale of St. George in *The Faerie Queene* Mrs. Peabody had published as a children's book. And the families drew close. Mrs. Peabody and Mary walked the Salem countryside with Ebe or Louisa Hawthorne and collected anemones, violets, and columbines. The Hawthorne sisters brought books and baskets of peaches to Charter Street for George. Still, Elizabeth Peabody was the linchpin. But she was in West Newton.

"Mary told Louisa Hawthorne yesterday that she thought they [the Hawthornes] could better appreciate our daily loss than anyone else," Sophia wrote Elizabeth, "though everybody regretted your departure sincerely." As compensation, Sophia sent Elizabeth a series of journal-like letters to keep her apprised of family business and the doings of precious Mr. Hawthorne, in whose affairs she slowly began to participate.

At first she had stood shyly behind her bedroom door when he came to call. "I opened my door, and tried to hear what he said," she confessed to Elizabeth. Soon she was tiptoeing downstairs to catch a better glimpse of the beautiful face. "He has a celestial expression," she beamed.

Of course he missed Elizabeth. "He had taken your letter out of the post office, and thought it was from New York, but upon opening it, found it was from you. 'It is from Elizabeth,' he exclaimed. When I went down, he told me of it, and said he knew it could be from no one else, because it was so full," Sophia consoled her sister but, unable to control herself, added, "He looked very brilliant. What a beautiful smile he has!"

Within weeks she was shy no more. She regaled Mr. Hawthorne with her adventures in Cuba, and when he said he might make a story from them, she fluttered with joy. "To be the means in any way of calling forth one of his divine creations, is no small happiness, is it?" she brightly asked Elizabeth, heedless of the answer.

On and on, she chattered. On and on, she documented Hawthorne's comings and goings for Elizabeth. He intended to rise every morning at dawn in the beginning of May, Sophia recounted, but the weather was cold and he wasn't sleeping well. He walked out to South Salem. As for herself, she valiantly battled her headaches, or so she told Mr. Hawthorne the evening he complained about one of his own. But he'd written Elizabeth in spite of it, and it was no small thing for him to do so. "I had a delightful night," she concluded, "and this morning I feel quite lark-like."

Hawthorne intended to go to Boston the following week and maybe to West Newton. When he did, Sophia withdrew to her room, unaware of what ailed her.

No fool, Elizabeth trembled with fear. "I like to hear the little items about H—" she answered Sophia, "but I am afraid you two girls will cut me out. I delight to have him like you & go to see you—but I am afraid he will forget me—'Out of sight—out of mind.' " Sophia answered placidly. "I am diverted at the idea of our cutting you out, of all things. Mr. H coming there is one sure way of keeping you in mind, & it must be extremely tame after the experience of your society & conversation so that I think you will shine more by contrast."

When Elizabeth accidentally ran into Hawthorne at the Tremont House in Boston, Sophia rocked with suppressed anger. "He thought it 'providential' that he should meet you as he did," Sophia sharply wrote her sister. "I told him that you were a most fortunate person—always accomplishing what you wished somehow or other." Elizabeth retaliated, suggesting that Sophia come to West Newton to assist at the school. "It makes me faint to think of it," Sophia retorted. "Do not suggest any plans to me, dear, for mercy's sake. . . . I do not want to have anything upon my mind to be done. You can have no idea how it wearies me. . . . I do not want anything expected of me."

Sometimes Sophia soothed Elizabeth, reminding her of Hawthorne's affection: he'd come to dinner just to see Elizabeth, and when he learned she was still stuck in West Newton he cried "too bad," "insufferable," "not fair." Just as often, though, she taunted her sister with a chronicle of Hawthorne's laughter, his wit, his warmth, his inimitable courtesy. Sophia showed him the letters to her family she'd written from Cuba; he called her the Queen of Journalizers. She gave him a forget-me-not, which he set in a brooch of block crystal, protesting it too fine to wear. He himself told Elizabeth that Sophia was "a flower to be worn in no man's bosom." Cold comfort.

The dance continued, each sister gifted in the art of denial. Insofar as Elizabeth hid her desires from herself, she sublimated them into the very real urge to do good, promote worthy causes, and succor anyone needier or more talented than she—like Hawthorne. She arranged to have Mrs. Hawthorne's copy of *Twice-told Tales* rebound, and she conspired with Ebe about a second volume of her brother's stories. She informed Sophia that she had talked to Nahum Capen, the bookseller, about Hawthorne's writing a children's book. "He has him in his mind—& I hope it will be to some good purposes for the public & I guess it will." To Emerson, she gave a copy of Hawthorne's recent sketch "Foot-prints on the Sea-shore," and in the pages of the *New-Yorker* defended him against Park Benjamin's review of *Twice-told Tales* where he'd suggested Hawthorne ("a rose bathed and baptized in dew") was not the manly writer required by a new nation. What did Benjamin know? Hawthorne was the American Wordsworth.

She also persisted in assuming Mary Silsbee her sole rival for Hawthorne's affections. In fact, she and Hawthorne discussed Silsbee while Sophia eavesdropped on the stairs. "I was astonished to find she did not admire you," Sophia jabbed; and Mr. Hawthorne "seemed very much inclined to be her defender."

But if Hawthorne seemed distraught, Elizabeth laid the cause at Silsbee's feet. She accused her of "coquetting" and even risked Hawthorne's friendship by saying so.

It was a messy, three-sided affair, and Hawthorne understandably left no account of it. But that spring, 1838, images of bright green vegetation and pungent honeysuckle steal into his notebooks along with excerpts copied from Sophia's Cuban letters. And noting his plan to take a secret trip to western Massachusetts and New York, he recalled a poem by Robert Southey, *The Curse of Kehama*. "On visiting a certain celestial region, the fire in his heart and brain died away for a season," he observed of its main character, "but was rekindled again on returning to earth. So may it be with me, in my projected three months seclusion from old associations."

No one knew where he was headed except his friend David Roberts. He informed the Peabodys that he hadn't even told his mother. He'd receive no letters nor write any—this, Sophia understood, was directed at Elizabeth. He wouldn't even visit Elizabeth before he left. And he'd change his name, so no one could find his grave should he die.

The romantic storyteller sallies forth, insisting he be left alone, far from the confusions of desire.

"A story to show how we are all wronged and wrongers, and avenge one another; as a man is jilted by a rich girl, and jilts a poor one," Hawthorne wrote in his notebook. After his return to Salem in the fall of 1838, Mary Silsbee announced that she was engaged to Jared Sparks and officially put an end to her romance with Hawthorne. Careful not to wound his pride, she declared she must "break off all intercourse" with him. Hawthorne asked her to burn his letters. She said she would.

He closed the door of her house, heart jangling, with the "sense that all had been a mistake—that I never really loved—that there was no real sympathy between us—and that a union could only insure the misery of both," he confided to John O'Sullivan. She meant honorably by me, he said, not quite sure what went wrong with him, with her, with them.

For solace he walked over to the Peabody house at Charter Street where Sophia reigned, convalescent and serene, a woman of great weakness and equal strength. Much like Hawthorne's own invalid mother but more urbane and sensual—and far more talkative—she sketched Hawthorne's likeness one December evening in 1838, the fire flickering warmly in the parlor. He tried to sit motionless, joking that in time his face might change so much she wouldn't recognize him. Even in heaven. But Sophia's saw the world—topaz, shimmering, immutable—with her inner eye. She smiled. "See if I don't!" she replied.

The "*fervor scribendi*" had been upon Mr. Hawthorne, said Sophia, and he was furnishing sketches and stories to the *Democratic Review* at a fairly regular rate. In 1838 the January and March numbers of the magazine had contained two sketches, "Foot-prints on the Sea-shore" and "Snow-flakes," and in May the first of four "Tales of the Province-House" appeared, followed by a second installment that July. In the September issue O'Sullivan published Hawthorne's portrait of Cilley along with his story "Chippings with a Chisel," and then the last two of the Province-House quartet, written after his secret trip, came out in December 1838 and January 1839.

Written during Hawthorne's imbroglio with Silsbee and the Peabodys, the four Province-House tales reflect his changing sense of himself as an author and a man. The husk of the story is historical, although that too mirrors an internal drama expressed best in the image of the Province-House, the former mansion of the royal governors, currently a tavern, where past and present commingle. It's an image—that of the house—to which Hawthorne will often return.

At the Province-House bar, his narrator, a citizen of Boston, hears a series of stories about several early inhabitants of the house, their defeats, self-deceptions, vanities, or small acts of heroism. In "Howe's Masquerade," the first and weakest of the tales recounted by the narrator, a ghostly pageant interrupts Sir William Howe's masked ball to foretell the end of British rule. Inspired by Sophia's account of cleaning a painting by Murillo, the second story, "Edward Randolph's Portrait," takes place after the fateful decision of the British to quarter troops in Boston. The third tale, "Lady Eleanore's Mantle," is the story of the arrogant Lady Eleanore Rochcliffe, supposedly the cause of a smallpox epidemic in America after her arrival, and finally "Old Esther Dudley" tells of the last royalist to dwell in the old house.

The three strongest stories also chronicle Hawthorne's recent emotional turmoil. Take "Lady Eleanore's Mantle," composed after his romance with Silsbee ended. Hawthorne introduces a pale young suitor called Gervase Helwyse, the name of Major William Hathorne's grandson and the man to whom the major bequeathed half his estate. This ersatz Hawthorne prostrates himself before the queenly Lady Eleanore, who responds with mirthful derision, placing her dainty foot on his craven form: "Never, surely, was there an apter emblem of aristocracy and hereditary pride," writes Hawthorne, "trampling on human sympathies and the kindred of nature." Yet Helwyse—hell-wise—somehow knows that proud Lady Eleanore's mantle carries the scourge of smallpox within its ruffles and that the highborn woman will be brought low, though not before she contaminates everyone in her reach.

Love is a contagious disease, its carrier woman. Beloved and deplored, she is inevitably damned—except when she appears in the kinder, more ineffectual guise of Alice Vane in "Edward Randolph's Portrait." Alice is a "pale, ethereal creature," childlike and wayward, with an "enthusiasm for sculpture and painting" much like Sophia. Gazing on the dingy portrait of Edward Randolph, the tyrant who revoked the first provincial charter, she understands that years of grime—and crime—have dulled his image. And so she advises her uncle, Lieutenant Governor Hutchinson, to heed the painting's symbolic meaning. If Uncle Hutchinson quarters British royal troops in Boston, his image will likewise be tarnished. But Alice Vane warns in vain—Hawthorne doesn't mind the pun—and Hutchinson, himself a writer of history, cannot see it when it's staring him straight in the face. He is a good man but remiss, like Alice, who lives in a world of black and white, dark pictures and spotless ones.

If these Province-House legends speak of Hawthorne's divided heart—his attraction to the arrogance of a Mary Silsbee and to the more playful, less fearsome charm of Sophia Peabody—they also reveal his allegiance to mistresses of another sort: the shadowy past and the sunlit present. Like the old Province-House, or Hawthorne's image of it, the past is rich, provocative, dark, and deep, an imagined place where the writer can lose himself for days and years. But he hates it too. The past is musty and bottomless, and his researches into its nooks and crannies deprive him, so he feels, of contact with the living, breathing world. "We are no longer children of the Past!" shouts a character in "Old Esther Dudley"; the outburst ricochets through Hawthorne's work. For Hawthorne wants to live in the present, to love in the present, to find inspiration in the buzzing, grimy, sensual world of female and male that is the present. And this is the world he gives up when locked in his squalid chamber.

There is also a political component in Hawthorne's conflict. A Democrat since college, Hawthorne deliberately shared, or tried to share, the democrat's vision of a better, more equal society, one not dominated by a privilege, caste, or group but welcoming to white workers, republicans and patriots all; it's a vision of a world where nothing is predetermined, everything possible. And it is O'Sullivan's seductive, sunshiny republicanism, dismissive of original sin and a wicked human nature. Yet however attractive, progressive, and presumably benign the vision, for Hawthorne contemporary life is loud, vulgar, and tobacco-stained, crammed with faceless warehouses, smarmy politicians, and shabby oyster shops. It's even taken over the Province-House.

The terrible conflict between past and present—the nostalgic pull of one, despite its darkness and doom, and the noisy, liberating tug of the other—is Hawthorne's great subject.

Mary Silsbee and the Peabodys—both Elizabeth and Sophia—helped yank Hawthorne out of the cloistered world of Herbert Street, where his two sisters and his mother regressed into the primitive habits of childhood, the past, the touchy sense of family pride propped up by chimney-corner legends. In "Old Esther Dudley," the fourth story of the Province-House quartet, Hawthorne writes as if to them:

> Your life has been prolonged until the world has changed around you. You have treasured up all that time has rendered worthless—the principles, feelings, manners, modes of being and acting, which another generation has flung aside—and you are a symbol of the past. And I, and these around me—we represent a new race of men, living no longer in the past, scarcely in the present—but projecting our lives forward into the future.

When Governor Hancock upbraids the poor deluded royalist Esther Dudley, we cannot help hearing Hawthorne chastise both his family and himself. Esther Dudley is a woman born of his own anxiety. Unable to embrace wholeheartedly the radical slogan of the Democrat, with its ecstatic sense of progress, Hawthorne pauses on the threshold of the present, loyal to the Esthers he loves: his mother Elizabeth, his sister Ebe, himself and his own fondness for grandees of a lost generation. But he also condemns the silly aristocrat Esther Dudley for her myopic allegiance to the old order.

At the end of this story, Hawthorne's narrator tremulously says goodbye to his Province-House guide, an old codger named Bela Tiffany—beautiful fancy—deciding "not to show my face in the Province-House for a good while hence, if ever." The clock of the Old South Church tolls the passing of the hours, but the modern democrat will no longer hide under the eaves of the old house, daydreaming about the past. What choice does he have? Renouncing Bela Tiffany and the Province-House, the narrator steps into the light.

For now.

CHAPTER TEN

Romance of the Revenue Service

But Adam, being of a calm and cautious character, was loath to relinquish the advantages which a single man possesses for raising himself in the world. Year after year, therefore, their marriage had been deferred.

Nathaniel Hawthorne, "The Shaker Bridal"

Now that Mary Silsbee was engaged, more than ever friends assumed a romantic connection between Elizabeth Peabody and Nathaniel Hawthorne. Sophia too. "I rejoice with my whole heart in H's sentiments towards you," Sophia informed Elizabeth. The glorious Hawthorne was nothing more to her, she said, than a "thousand brothers in one." But she'd fallen in love.

And Hawthorne had become a Peabody family staple. "I wish you could see him now he [has] grown so easy," Mary wrote a friend, "and he talks more & comes out of his den every day." Susan Burley, a wealthy friend of the Peabodys, was financing an edition of Hawthorne's story "The Gentle Boy," which would be published by George Palmer Putnam, a Peabody cousin; and the text would be accompanied by an engraving based on a sketch by Sophia.

Hawthorne's sacred "Word," she exulted, uttered "through my fingers in the face of Ilbrahim!"

Despite her headaches, Sophia was attending Miss Burley's Saturday night salons on the strong arm of her handsome squire, who protested he couldn't do without the Burley ritual. And back on Charter Street he met the eccentric poet Jones Very, a sensitive young man on the verge of madness. "No two could be more different," observed Mary, "but they take great interest in each other." Hawthorne asked Very if he found much sympathy for his work among the public. Very smiled. "Does the earth always speak to her children?" Elizabeth Peabody noticed that in Very's presence, Hawthorne wasn't petulant. She was relieved.

In December of 1838, *The Gentle Boy: A Thrice-told Tale* appeared. Sophia winced. The engraver had botched her design. Hawthorne mollified her somewhat, inscribing her copy of the publication with typical gallantry. What he called "her kindred art" doubled the value of his little tale; he was so kind, so self-effacing. And the small book contained a dedication to her—in print, no less—in which he said that Washington Allston, "the first

Sophia Peabody's illustration of The Gentle Boy, *1838*

painter in America," had praised Sophia's original sketch. The author tipped his hat to the artist: "If, after so high a meed," Hawthorne wrote, "the Author might add his own humble praise, he would say that whatever of beauty and of pathos he had conceived, but could not shadow forth in language, has been caught and embodied in the few and simple lines of this sketch." Though a rueful, stilted pose, it was at least flattering.

And it tickled Sophia. She let him read the last installment of her Cuban adventures and coyly scribbled a note. His commendation and regard had given her journals significance, she teased. "Now does that not equal your Dedication? And surpass it in being overshadowed by seclusion from the world—a private testimony of friendship & deference from me to you for which the public is none the wise."

Deference, seclusion, friendship in which no one is the wise: Sophia Peabody and Nathaniel Hawthorne understood one another.

"I am afraid he never will be happy here," Elizabeth Peabody declared. Still fearing Hawthorne might abscond to Washington, she tried to snag a government sinecure for him in Boston with "little time & work—& having abundant leisure & liberty." Of course, the spoils system was despicable, she admitted, "but for the life of me, whatever is the illiberal apostasy of it, I cannot help being glad. It would be better off for him to be in Boston than here." She hoped to make Ebe her ally. "Besides—he can come & see us on the Railroad," she said, "—& we will make him enter into some engagements to that effect—will we not?"

Without hesitation, Peabody wrote to Orestes Brownson, a feisty Unitarian minister recently appointed the steward of the Chelsea Marine Hospital, and asked him to plead Hawthorne's case to George Bancroft, collector of the Port of Boston and Massachusetts Democratic boss on the lookout for party loyalists. Brownson did what Peabody requested, and Bancroft replied he'd gladly supply Hawthorne with an office—would have done so already, he implied, but supposed Hawthorne the "sort of a man who would by no means accept one." Such was Hawthorne's reputation: aloof.

Himself a historian of note and shrewd party operator, Bancroft doubtless knew Hawthorne's credentials, not just as a teller of tales but as a Democrat who, if not active in local caucuses, hadn't traveled too far from their reach. Not only did Hawthorne have the support of O'Sullivan and his powerful *Democratic Review,* but good friends in Salem like David Roberts, years later a Salem mayor, supported Hawthorne. And the appointment of a writer was good politics.

So Bancroft made an offer, the inspectorship at the Boston Custom House. Hawthorne stalled. Afraid his ambivalence would spoil her plans and offend Bancroft, Peabody rushed forward to reassure him. Perhaps she'd painted Hawthorne as too reclusive; but it was she, not Hawthorne, who regretted his leaving "the quiet of nature which has done so much for his genius," or so she explained to Bancroft's wife, Elizabeth Bliss Bancroft, an old friend. Nor had she meant to imply that Hawthorne refused to act "an ordinary part in life." Not at all: Hawthorne himself "spoke with much earnestness of the necessity of action among men—as a means of healthiness." As for party politics, she frankly didn't think him interested, but "as a matter of Sentiment as well as habit," he supported the Democrats in the Van Buren administration.

In January, Bancroft appointed Hawthorne measurer of coal and salt at the Boston Custom House at fifteen hundred dollars a year, three more hundred than he'd have received as inspector. Hawthorne cringed.

It may not have been the job itself that bothered him; he may have simply been waiting for O'Sullivan, hoping he could wangle something for him at the Salem post office so that he could stay near Sophia. Sitting in the square parlor with Elizabeth, Hawthorne jumped to his feet when her sister Mary entered the room. "And how is Sophie?" he instantly asked, extending his hand. For he'd been walking over to Charter Street almost nightly, pulling the little bell. Sophia was in Boston for a few weeks to stay with friends and study sculpture with Shobal Clevenger. He wrote Bancroft and accepted the job. He'd go to Boston the very next week.

He called on her frequently. Beautiful calls they were, she sighed. "He wants to come every day," she wrote to Elizabeth, "etiquette alone prevents him." The only invitation he turned down—and not for the first or last time— was her invitation to hear Emerson lecture. But he refused so gallantly; he'd much rather hear Sophia describe it than sit through it himself.

Late one nippy winter afternoon, the couple strolled through the Commons on their way to visit a friend of Sophia's as the last ribbons of light played on the snow. Hawthorne confessed he'd just as soon continue walking with her, the two of them alone. Perhaps he took her hand then, warm and small in her wintry glove.

"January Fourth 1839," Hawthorne had scrawled in his journal in huge letters. The lovers had spoken.

Hawthorne stayed in Boston and Sophia jogged back to Salem on a bumpy stage or in the newer railway cars. Living in different cities, the couple met infrequently, or so it seemed, seeing one another when Hawthorne went to Herbert Street. "I had a parting glimpse of you, Monday forenoon, at your window," he wrote to Sophia in March, "—and that image abides by me, looking pale, and not so quiet as is your wont." Sitting alone in his room at Somerset Place, where he was boarding—rooms evidently found by relatives—Hawthorne wrote to his beloved, his snow-white Dove, his inspiration and spiritual sustenance. "My surest hope of being a good man," he wrote the Dove, "and my only hope of being a happy man, depends on the permanence of our union."

The courtship was epistolary. In his letters Hawthorne soared at the thought of their last or future meeting, marveled at his newfound joy, and just as often crashed to earth, certain that Sophia couldn't really love his poor stupid self. He strutted, he careened, he pranced. "How did I live before I knew you—before I possessed your affection!" He flexed his newfound authority. "It is I who have the charge of you," he reminded her, "and that my Dove is to follow my guidance and do my bidding. Am I not very bold to say this?" In midsummer he wrote to her that he and she were married, rhetorically that is. "I felt it long ago; and sometimes, when I was seeking for some fondest work, it has been on my lips to call you—'Wife'!" The divine Dove metamorphosed into "naughty Sophie Hawthorne," whom he yearned to hold in his arms. "I would not give up the hope of loving and cherishing you by a fireside of our own, not for any unimaginable bliss of higher spheres," Hawthorne wrote to her, "swollen," he said, "with pent-up love." One assumes she knew what he meant.

Over and over, Hawthorne pit his newfound lusty wife against his angelic Dove, but the divide lay in him, not in her, and would not be easily bridged. He approached; he backed off. There was no talk of an immediate marriage. They would wait. In fact, they wouldn't even tell anyone of their feelings; quite the reverse: they took pains to conceal the affair, particularly from his family. They wrote one another every two weeks, his letters arriving on alternate Saturdays, so that no one would suspect anything more than a casual friendship, and Sophia sent her letters to the Custom House, handwriting disguised so that Hawthorne's "brother measurers" wouldn't guess the author was a woman.

Such elaborate chicanery seems odd unless one imagines that all of them—Peabodys, Hawthornes, Elizabeth, Nathaniel, Sophia—assumed that Elizabeth had some prior stake in Nathaniel, or that she supposed, as all of them did, that she and Nathaniel were engaged. Moreover, Sophia and Hawthorne were both complicit in the deception, as if they had something to hide. "I have great comfort in such thoughts as those you suggest," Hawthorne responded to one of Sophia's letters, ". . . that we have not cultivated our friendship, but let it grow." They had not sought their "friendship"; it sought them. Was this a sop to an overfine conscience, to the sense they'd betrayed Elizabeth? We don't know. Hawthorne burned Sophia's letters to him, hundreds of them, before sailing to England in 1853; and if he hadn't already destroyed Elizabeth's, he surely did so then. "What a trustful guardian of secret matters fire is!" he breathed in relief. "What should we do without Fire and Death?"

To male friends, Hawthorne dissembled far less. Mary Silsbee's upcoming marriage prompted him to tell O'Sullivan he had neither resentment nor regrets, "having fallen in love," he put it, "with somebody else." She wasn't Elizabeth Peabody; that he made clear. "She is a good old soul," he patronized Peabody to O'Sullivan, "and would give away the only petticoat, I do believe, to anybody that she thought needed it more than herself."

That summer, when Elizabeth failed to find Hawthorne at an exhibition at the Athenaeum—"a thing I had set my heart upon—not a little"— Sophia consoled her with a clipped sentence, remarkable for its restraint. "I am very sorry that you were disappointed in not meeting Mr. H. at the galleries," she had replied.

Weary of teaching, Elizabeth had decided to spend a few weeks near her friend Emerson's house in Concord, Massachusetts, to recuperate, and afterwards she said she intended "to enjoy such elements of enjoyment as have never before been within my reach—you know what I mean." Today, her intention is unclear: what enjoyments did she anticipate? Did she think she would soon be reunited with Hawthorne? And if so, she must immediately be told about his engagement to Sophia.

She was. She took the news gamely, assuring Sophia she didn't see marriage in her own future anyway, a prophecy as it turns out. Reassured, Sophia answered, "I have often doubted whether you considered your destiny as the proper one— . . . & I am thankful to have you say that you think it is." As for her own destiny, she couldn't resist crooning. "*Now* I am indeed made deeply conscious of what it is to be loved."

Still, Hawthorne and Sophia continued to keep their romance hidden. "We will wait patiently and quietly," Hawthorne wrote to his sweetheart, "and He will lead us onward hand in hand (as He has done all along) like little children, and will guide us to our perfect happiness—and will teach us when our union is to be revealed to the world." If she balked, he stayed resolute. "The world might, as yet, misjudge us," he counseled; "and therefore we will not speak to the world."

Elizabeth Peabody too stayed mum, even in later life when she contrived an official version of events, plausible from her vantage point. "It is true that for the first three years after Hawthorne became known to and a visitor in our family, it was *rumoured* that there was *probably* an engagement between him and me for we were manifestly very intimate friends, and Sophia was considered so much of an invalid as not to be marriageable by any of us, including *herself* and Hawthorne." By the time of the actual marriage, she continued, the gossip had stopped—which seems to have been the plan.

As for Elizabeth, her good heart—as well as her flair for rationalization—lifted her above selfishness like a magical petticoat, although if need be, she'd give that away too—Hawthorne was right—without a second thought.

Hawthorne had accepted his government appointment "with as much confidence in my suitableness for it, as Sancho Panza had in his gubernatorial qualifications." Tongue in cheek, he enumerated for Longfellow a list of the Custom House sketches he'd write: "Nibblings of a Wharf-Rat," "Trials of a Tide-water," "Romance of the Revenue Service." But he was still hoping to write a compendium of historical sketches for Nahum Capen's series of children's books.

Actually, though, he produced very little. His only story was a minor effort, "John Inglefield's Thanksgiving," for O'Sullivan's *Democratic Review,* and though he hoped to publish the expanded volume of *Twice-told Tales,* spurred on by Elizabeth Peabody, he dallied. When he wrote at all, he wrote love letters to Sophia. "Uncle Sam is rather despotic as to the disposal of my time," Hawthorne justified himself to Longfellow. Though his tasks demanded attentiveness, they didn't consume him day and night. Mornings, he walked over narrow cobblestone streets to the wharves to weigh and measure cargoes of coal, pacing the deck of the schooners pulled into the harbor. And he could smoke a cigar, stare at the blue sky, and make notes for his journals, watching as young women—girls really—disembarked from British ships to head north to the red brick textile mills of Lawrence, Lowell, and Haverhill. "To stand on the elevated deck or rail of a ship," Hawthorne observed with some pleasure, "and look up at the wharf, you see the whole space of it thronged with trucks and carts, removing the cargoes of vessels, or taking commodities to and from stores."

If there was no work to do, he read the *Morning Post,* a Democratic paper, or strolled over to the Boston Athenaeum and thumbed through the

Boston Custom House

magazines. In a few hours he'd stretch his long legs again, walking back to the Custom House to see if he was needed or if a letter from Sophia had arrived. Nights, he returned to Somerset Place, washed the soot from his face, and then trotted downstairs to argue politics with a cousin, also a boarder. He often ate alone at a local oyster shop, rushing home to write a message, once again, to his blessed Dove.

He said he couldn't compose fiction because, working for the government, he felt he no longer owned himself; but that wasn't the whole story. Hawthorne held on to his government job not just because he needed the money or because the country ignored its artists—though both were true—but because he liked it. He felt rejuvenated at the docks: the bustle, the sheer movement of men, or the looping of the gulls and, below, the dark ships' bellies, where the coal was stowed. All this brought him close to the young clerks and laborers who sweated at real jobs for quantifiable results. "Henceforth forever," he wrote Sophia in overblown terms, "I shall be entitled to call the sons of toil my brethren, and shall know how to sympathize with them, seeing that I, likewise, have risen at the dawn, and borne the fervor of the mid-day sun, nor turned my heavy footsteps homeward till eventide." No effete cavalier was he. Nathaniel Hawthorne, Custom House officer, was a man of substance, practical and proficient, solid and sound.

And he was in fact earning more than he had anticipated—fortunately, since he was dreaming of marriage again. Congress entitled him to collect fees for measuring salt and coal, which meant he could double his salary. "If I ever come to be worth $5000," he chuckled, "I will kick all business to the devil,—at least, till that be spent." It was a sentiment he'd repeat in later years as he swung like a pendulum between the two poles of commerce and art. He sensed as much. Writing to Sophia after a full day at the Custom House, he observed,

> It was exhilarating to see the vessels, how they bounded over the waves, while a sheet of foam broke out around them. I found a good deal of enjoyment, too, in the busy scene around me; for several vessels were disgorging themselves (what an unseemly figure is this—"disgorge," quoth as if the vessels were sick at their stomachs) on the wharf; and everybody seemed to be working with might and main. It pleased thy husband to think that he also had a part to act in the material and tangible business of this life, and that a part of all this industry could not have gone on without his presence. Nevertheless, my belovedest, pride not thyself too much on thy husband's activity and utilitarianism; his is naturally an idler, and doubtless will soon be pestering thee with his bewailments at being compelled to earn his bread by taking some little share in the toils of mortal man.

Bewailments, yes; they'd come soon enough. Meantime, Uncle Sam helped to provide an alibi for not writing. "I think, too, I am the less able to write," he confessed to O'Sullivan, "because a dozen editors of various periodicals, literary and political, are continually teazing me for articles. I have no refuge, save to declare myself no longer a literary man." Too much popularity and an increased demand for his work made Hawthorne anxious that he couldn't compete with himself or produce anything resembling what he'd already written. Or write at all.

Yet much as he implicitly liked his job at the Custom House, he detested it. Much as he wanted his credentials as a worker in the world, he hadn't achieved what he really wanted. When Bancroft praised Hawthorne as the best of the Custom House officers, "Tell it down in Herbert Street," Elizabeth told Sophia, "—Let the ears of Uncle Robert hear it." But Hawthorne colored a deep red. "What fame!" he sneered.

"Does Mr. Hawthorne ever write now?" the editor Evert Duyckinck asked Henry Longfellow. Such seemed to be the sense of Hawthorne: that he and his work vanished for long periods. In the fall of 1839, Capen had announced the forthcoming "New-England Historical Sketches" by "N. Hawthorne, Author of 'Twice Told Tales.' " Months passed, no stories. "I have a note to write Mr. Capen who torments me every now-and-then about a book which he wants me to manufacture," Hawthorne guiltily wrote to Sophia in December of that year, though he informed Longfellow he still meant to do it.

And still hoping for an appointment to the Salem post office, he deputized William Pike, the inspector of the Boston Custom House, as lobbyist. A short, thick man with bushy black hair, Pike was a sallow-looking bachelor, tender and pensive, who believed in ghosts; eventually he became a spiritualist. He also earned a reputation for the hard drinking later associated with Hawthorne. Hawthorne liked him. The best caucus speaker in the

William Pike

district, Pike was also a fixture in the Democratic Party politics of the North Shore and was considered indispensable. But Salem Democrats were a scrappy lot. Though a local leader, Benjamin Browne, supported Hawthorne, another party official, Robert Rantoul, regarded Hawthorne as unreliable, and in any case Rantoul wanted his brother-in-law for the job.

Bancroft had evidently promised Hawthorne the position but couldn't or wouldn't pull the necessary strings. "What an astounding liar our venerated chief turns out to be!" Hawthorne raged when Pike told him the news. But Hawthorne advised Pike not to protest. "As long as there is a possibility of his being of use to you, do not compel him to be your open enemy," he warned. It was the tack he often took. Recalled Pike many years later, one could never tell if Hawthorne was your friend or foe.

In March 1840, when O'Sullivan suggested Hawthorne resign from the Custom House for a clerkship in Washington, Hawthorne said he'd stay in Boston—to be nearer Sophia no doubt. He'd save his money. "I will retire on my fortune—that is to say, I will throw myself on fortune, and get my bread as I can," he told O'Sullivan. "I ought not to be an office-holder. There is a most galling weight upon me—an intolerable sense of being hampered and degraded."

Almost a decade later, after he finally got and lost a job at the Salem Custom House, he summarized the "effect—which I believe to be observable, more or less, in every individual who has occupied the position— . . . that, while he leans on the mighty arm of the Republic, his own proper strength departs from him." Government employ was a kind of charity, doled out more than earned and death to the soul.

George Hillard, an attorney, was a friend of Elizabeth and Mary Peabody. Slim, serious, witty, and vaguely afraid of women, he graduated Harvard in 1828, taught for a while, wrote for the *North American Review,* prepared the first American edition of Spenser's poetry, and never excelled in anything. In 1834 he established a law practice with Charles Sumner, who would be roused to the antislavery cause as Hillard would not, and in 1835 he married Sophia's friend Susan Howe.

In the fall of 1839, Hillard had asked Hawthorne to lodge with him and his wife on Pinckney Street, a pretty street on Beacon Hill. Hawthorne could meet Sophia there, as he happily informed her; "he thinks matters may be managed so." By now the Peabodys, or at least the Peabody sisters, knew of the engagement, but Hawthorne was still shielding his family, or himself.

Dimmed only by the death of Sophia's brother George that fall, the romance moved secretly forward, the lovers enjoying more freedom after Hawthorne moved to Pinckney Street. Sophia oversaw the decoration of his rooms, selecting a velvety rug, "the most beautiful carpet, that ever was seen short of Brussels," to warm his feet, and donating two of her oil paintings, a luminous landscape of Lake Como and another one of Lake Maggiore, to rest his eye. He surveyed the place. It was his castle, "bought," he said, "for the time being, with the profits of mine own labor." In his parlor he put his new writing bureau between the two windows and arranged his bookcase to stand on top of it. Evenings, he sat in his haircloth armchair before a coal fire that burned companionably in the grate. And he slept well in his bedroom on the mattress he preferred to a feather bed. "I do not get intolerably tired any longer; and my thoughts sometimes wander back to literature, and I have momentary impulses to write stories. But this will not be, at present." Instead he fantasized about his future home and the shelves he'd line with books like the good edition of Coleridge he'd just bought.

Two lamps with copper-colored shades threw a soft light on the page when he wrote to Sophia in the evening, long letters, alternately ardent and jolly, tender and arch, always earnest, always receptive. She, his sunny-hearted savior, had converted him from spectator to lover, from ghostly shade to palpable substance. She was the one person who convinced him that he was flesh, alive, unalienated. "Thou only has taught me that I have a heart—thou only hast thrown a light deep downward, and upward, into my soul. Thou only hast revealed me to myself; for without thy aid, my best knowledge of myself would have been merely to know my own shadow—to watch it flickering on the wall, and mistake its fantasies for my own real actions."

His confessions of love teetered between the formulaic and the heartfelt, the sportive and the passionate, depending on his mood. "Indeed, we are but shadows—we are not endowed with real life, and all that seems most real about us is but the thinnest substance of a dream—till the heart is touched." Sophia: artless, spontaneous, unconditional in her love, even "unlearned," as Hawthorne rather brutally observed. "Your wisdom is not of the earth," he wrote; "it has passed through no other mind, but gushes fresh and pure from your own, and therefore I deem myself the safer when I receive your outpourings as a revelation from Heaven. Not but what you have read, and tasted deeply, no doubt, of the thoughts of other minds," he added hastily, suddenly conscious of the insult festering in the compliment; "but the thoughts of other minds make no change in your essence, as they do in almost everybody else's essence."

Yet as the lovers drew closer, stealing kisses whenever they met, Hawthorne also warned his fiancée to "grant me freedom to be careless and wayward—for I have had such freedom all my life." He could be unapproachable, intractable, even insensitive. "Thy husband is a most unmalleable man." And moody: "Lights and shadows are continually flitting across my inward sky," he said, "and I know neither whence they come nor whither they go; nor do I inquire too closely into them."

But she melted the reserve he felt even in the company of his family. "I cannot gush out in their presence," Hawthorne explained to her, "—I cannot take my heart in my hand, and show it to them. There is a feeling within me (though I know it is a foolish one) as if it would be as indecorous to do so, as to display to them the naked breast."

She had not won them over. In Salem, Hawthorne's sisters received her coolly. Perhaps they guessed the engagement, hurt they had not been told. More than a year had passed since that fateful day at the Boston Common. It was now the spring of 1840 and Sophia herself began to resent the secrecy, but Hawthorne tersely reminded her of those "untoward circumstances."

He might also have warned her that their literary foreplay was to stretch over another two years. Two long years: it was as if Hawthorne was testing Sophia's resolve while determining the extent of his own.

CHAPTER ELEVEN

The World Found Out

*Whatever else I may repent of, therefore, let it be reckoned nei-
ther among my sins nor follies, that I once had faith and force
enough to form generous hopes of the world's destiny—yes!—and
to do what in me lay for their accomplishment; even to the extent
of quitting a warm fireside, flinging away a freshly lighted cigar,
and travelling far beyond the strike of city-clocks, through a
drifting snow-storm.*

Nathaniel Hawthorne, *The Blithedale Romance*

*Man never creates, he only recombines the lines and colors of his
own existence.*

Margaret Fuller, "The Magnolia of Lake Pontchartrain"

Curiosities of the fall season, 1840: Margaret Fuller, resident sibyl,
organizes another series of "Conversations" for Boston women. A
campaign of hard cider and log cabins pitches the Whig Ploughman of
Ohio, William Henry Harrison, into the United States presidency. Orestes
Brownson prophesies class warfare. Salem artist Charles Osgood paints
Hawthorne's portrait. And more than five hundred Friends of Universal
Reform pour into Boston's Chardon Street Chapel to dispute scriptural
authority, debate the woman question, and damn the institution of slavery.

Dr. Oliver Wendell Holmes, slim autocrat of the breakfast table, disap-
proves. "We never had a Bohemia in Boston, and we never wanted it." Most
of Boston's intelligentsia ignore the Chardon Street event, and, as ever,
Bronson Alcott marches to his own drummer. "A revolution of all Human
affairs is now in progress," he cries, and withdraws to Concord.

The previous July, Elizabeth Peabody unlocked the door to her new for-

Hawthorne at thirty-six, portrait by Charles Osgood, 1840.
"Mother says it is perfect," Louisa Hawthorne noted, "and
if she is satisfied with the likeness it must be good."

eign bookshop and lending library at 13 West Street. A stubby cobblestone passage near the Boston Common in a district not quite residential, not quite commercial, West Street would be home to the liberal Unitarian clergy, increasingly disaffected, who pondered intuition, self-culture, and perfection, the watchwords of a new faith born of German philosophic idealism and imported to America largely by Ralph Waldo Emerson, who spoke heresy in public. "God incarnates himself in man," Emerson declared at Harvard Divinity School; he wasn't asked to return for thirty years.

Backsliders like Emerson—he'd resigned the pulpit in 1832—craved a more humane form of belief, one that squarely placed divinity in the soul of the individual; goodness already dwelled there. Soon these seekers were identified as the Transcendental Club—the name came from detractors— and variously included Emerson; Bronson Alcott; Emerson's theological school acquaintance Frederick Henry Hedge; the Reverend James Freeman Clarke, founder of the periodical the *Western Messenger;* the pacific Reverend George Ripley, editor of the *Specimens of Foreign Standard Literature* series, translations of French and German philosophy, literature, and theology; the steely Orestes Brownson in his pre-Catholic socialist days; and the fervid William Henry Channing, a mellifluous apple that didn't fall too far from his illustrious uncle's tree.

These men welcomed women into the club: the poetic Sturgis sisters, particularly Ellen and the ironic Carolyn; Elizabeth Peabody of course; and the acid-tongued Margaret Fuller, a magnetic intellectual not to be slighted. Mary Peabody didn't seem interested—her heart was with Horace Mann— and despite her fizzy exuberance, Sophia stayed at the fringe although she adamantly subscribed to the un-Calvinist creed of God's munificence. Describing a glorious flock of swans to a friend, not Hawthorne, she reddened when he replied that transcendental swans often turn out to be geese. "Did you ever hear of such impertinence?" she wailed.

The club had a magazine, *The Dial.* Initially edited by Margaret Fuller, it produced its first issue that summer. By fall, though, its business and literary manager, George Ripley, was glum. He'd been reading Albert Brisbane's *Social Destiny of Man,* an American rendition of Charles Fourier's blueprint for social reform. Fourier believed that if left on their own, people would gravitate to the tasks they liked best, and so he proposed to reorganize society by placing congenial individuals into phalanxes, or small communities, where they could work at what they liked to do, benefiting themselves and society at the same time.

Though he was not yet ready to sign up Fourier—that came several years later—the idea of a reorganized society heartened Ripley, who'd been unhappy in a church that, to his mind, perpetuated poverty by turning its cheek. Unitarianism was all well and good as an antidote to Calvinism, but it hadn't gone nearly far enough when it came to improving social conditions. Ripley made all this clear when he took on the Unitarian pope, Andrews Norton, whose own Harvard Divinity School address, "A Discourse on the Latest Form of Infidelity," was intended to expose the transcendentalists, notably Emerson, as the atheists he figured they must be.

Ripley now cared less about theological war than about overhauling society, distributing its riches, like sunlight, to everyone. Religion conjoined with democracy: it would be a heaven on earth, the divine made quite real. "The true democratic principle is taking deep root in many hearts, which once loathed the name," Ripley appealed to George Bancroft; "& if the principle, in its purity, can be made popular with the party, as the party is with the people, we can hardly place bounds to our hopeful trust in the destinies of our country."

Ripley himself resigned the pulpit in March 1841 to look for a more felicitous way to change the world, or at least a small section of it. Politics and political machinations were too crude, institutional, and urban, so he devised an alternative: utopia on a pretty farm.

When Martin Van Buren, Andrew Jackson's heir, was not reelected president, that same November, Nathaniel Hawthorne resigned his post at the Boston Custom House, effective January 1, 1841. He'd not serve under Whigs nor be replaced by them.

Briefly he considered starting a magazine with Longfellow but the project never got off the ground. Longfellow didn't really want a partner—and not a party Democrat in any case—so Hawthorne occupied himself with a history book for children called *Grandfather's Chair.*

The structural idea for the book came to him the previous spring when he and David Roberts visited Susanna Ingersoll in her antique house on Salem's Turner Street. As Hawthorne's second cousin, Ingersoll knew plenty of family gossip firsthand, which she happily divulged, particularly when it included the story of the house and her claim to it. And it was a grisly tale. After the death of her parents, she had to outfox her uncle John Hathorne, who tried to seize the place, insisting it belonged to him. Word of his rapacious attempt to grab the orphan's house quickly spread over Salem. "We talk of savages," the Reverend Bentley had said in dismay. Ingersoll kept the house by never leaving it and ever afterwards remained ensconced under its dark ceilings, as if afraid her uncle might, in her absence, snatch away what she loved best.

Ingersoll mentioned to Hawthorne that the house had once had seven gables. "The expression [seven gables] was new and struck me very forcibly," Hawthorne told Horace Conolly, whom Ingersoll had adopted as her son; "I think I shall make something of it." Tickled by the phrase—particularly since he complained he didn't know what to write about—Hawthorne tucked it away for future use. But he seized on Ingersoll's suggestion to use her old oak chair as the center of his children's book.

Hawthorne liked to begin his stories with props, or found objects, as if their "homely reality," as he says in *Grandfather's Chair,* conferred legitimacy on an otherwise frivolous tale. Old newspapers, discarded manuscripts, the mansion of the royal governors, and, in the future, the infamous scarlet letter as well as the house of seven gables: they provide Hawthorne with a dense, tangible pretext for his fiction. So too *Grandfather's Chair,* where an elderly fellow recounts for his grandchildren the adventures of a chair—history reproduced as fictive furniture, the actual and the imaginary once again, each partaking of the other.

In this case, the chair, originally manufactured for an English lord, sailed to America on board the *Arbella* and subsequently served, Grandfather jests, as a seat for both theocratic and democratic rumps, sequentially of course. To Hawthorne, history is evolution, the story of oppression giving way to freedom; this is something like George Bancroft's teleological history of America, though Hawthorne handily supplied the irony that Bancroft lacks: the more sedentary, the better the ruler.

When Nahum Capen, tired of waiting for Hawthorne to finish his book, apparently withdrew his promise to publish it, Elizabeth Peabody stepped into the breach. She had a printing press in her library at West Street and so was able to publish *Grandfather's Chair* by herself in December. Excited, she pushed Hawthorne to write two sequels, which he did. *Famous Old People* and *Liberty Tree* appeared in January and March 1841, all printed by Peabody.

Like her, the Salem papers were loyal to the local author and championed his books, but in Boston, they received scant comment. Margaret Fuller wrote a limp notice in *The Dial.* The gifted author, said she, was squandering his talent.

Perhaps he was. But children's books were supposed to earn money. Not for Hawthorne. This "dullest of all books," as he dismissed it, would stoop his shoulders, so heavy were all the unsalable volumes he'd be lugging with him to George Ripley's hinterland farm.

Undiminished, the winds of change blew through Boston, prickling skin under the starched cotton. "We are all a little wild here with numberless projects of social reform," Emerson exulted to Thomas Carlyle. There would be no more pauperism, slavery, hypocrisy, no more materialism, selfishness, and no pressure to get a living rather than to live. "It is astonishing what a wide-spread desire there is for a new mode of life," Sarah Clarke exclaimed to her brother James. If abolitionist William Lloyd Garrison preferred to buckle all social questions to the overriding one of chattel slavery, George Ripley and his brainy wife, Sophia Dana Ripley, opted for community and what he said would be a "more natural union between intellectual and manual labor."

Ripley spelled out the scheme for Emerson. "Thought would preside over the operations of labor. . . . We should have industry without drudgery, and true equality without its vulgarity." The Brook Farm Institute of Agriculture and Education, as the community would formally be called, eschewed rank, status, privilege, and formal attire. It welcomed everyone, farmers, mechanics, writers, and preachers, all "whose gifts and abilities would make their services important"—and whose children, by the way, could be educated in the community school.

The real ticket of admission was camaraderie—that and a share of stock. Ripley proposed the farm be run as a joint-stock company that paid a fixed 5 percent interest to its subscribers, the subscription secured by some two hundred rolling acres, a few buildings, a brook, and a meadow scattered with trees in West Roxbury, a bucolic little village nine miles southwest of Boston. Each share in the association cost five thousand dollars. The interest on the investment, tuition from the community's prospective school, and the subscribers' labor—intellectual or manual—would cover room, board, and upkeep.

The government would be democratic. "His own mind, though that of a captain, is not of a conqueror," Margaret Fuller observed. "Mr. Ripley would never do for a patriarch," said Sarah Clarke. But the plan couldn't fail to impress. "The farming is to be conducted on the most liberal and scientific principles of English husbandry," Clarke explained to her brother, "and the earth is to yield her increase in a style hitherto unknown in New England." There would be wealth without corruption. "Luxuries are to be common to all and appropriated by none." The sick and elderly would be cared for, and there would be no hired labor or servants. "Labor is to be alleviated by machinery and good will." And the place would be ecumenical. "There are to be no religious tests or any other, and he who joins does it upon the principle of co-operation in labor and a desire for social improvement."

About a dozen people signed on. Emerson did not. "Can I not get the same advantages at home without pulling down my house?" the individualist wondered. But Hawthorne owned no property, and he no longer had an income, having surrendered the Custom House and, with it, the security of his steady wage. He might return to Salem—Ebe insisted Hawthorne always did his best writing there—but the atavistic pull of family threatened his hard-won autonomy. "Whenever I return to Salem," he anxiously wrote Sophia, "I feel how dark my life would be, without the light that should shedst upon it—how cold, without the warmth of thy love."

In Salem, under the watch of his mother and sisters, he'd have to confess his engagement.

But he did return there for a while, and sitting in his Herbert Street bedroom that fall, he adroitly composed one of his most seductive stories— again, about himself. "Here sits thy husband in his old accustomed chamber, where he used to sit in years gone by, before his soul became acquainted with thine," he wrote to Sophia. "Here I have written many tales—many that have been burned to ashes—many that doubtless deserved the same fate," he continued, imagining the biographer (himself) who might someday visit his room:

> He ought to make great mention of this chamber in my memoirs, because so much of my lonely youth was wasted here; and here my mind and character were formed; and here I have been glad and hopeful, and here I have been despondent; and here I sat a long, long time, waiting patiently for the world to know me, and sometimes wondering why it did not know me sooner, or whether it would ever know me at all—at least till I were in my grave. And sometimes (for I had no wife then to keep my heart warm) it seemed as if I were already in the grave, with only life enough to be chilled and benumbed. But oftener I was happy—at least, as happy as I then knew how to be, or was aware of the possibility of being. By and bye, the world found me out in my lonely chamber, and called me forth—not, indeed, with a loud roar of acclamation, but

rather with a still, small voice; and forth I went, but found nothing in the world that I thought preferable to my old solitude, till at length a certain Dove was revealed to me, in the shadow of a seclusion as deep as my own had been.

The letter is biblically lyrical, phrases cadenced and perfectly pitched, darks juxtaposed with lights, cold with heat, in which Hawthorne's half-life

Brook Farm, oil on wood panel by Josiah Wolcott, 1844

is redeemed through admiration and then love, while alliterative sounds—the waste and the waiting and wondering why—reinforce a tale of loneliness that lasts, or has lasted, a long, long time.

Bidding farewell to his mother and his sisters, leaving behind his old accustomed chamber—and his childhood—Hawthorne fancied himself and

Sophia in another kind of family, not their own exactly but as confederates of Mr. Ripley's utopia, where they would build their house. The Ripleys did not frown on private property. Yet Sophia was left behind. Hawthorne rode out to West Roxbury in early April without his intended bride. "Think that I am gone before," he consoled his secret fiancée, "to prepare a home for my Dove, and will return for her, all in good time."

For a while she seemed content. A communal life of toil was no place for a dove, especially one with a headache. She and Mary and her parents had joined Elizabeth on West Street, where Sophia fitted her painting room on the second floor—Elizabeth stocked art supplies as well as books in the shop—and welcomed the excitement from below. In the crowded front parlor, Dr. Peabody sold homeopathic staples like belladonna and sassafras, Fuller held her Conversations, and Washington Allston occasionally stopped by. In the bookshop, transcendentalists grabbed French or German volumes from the shelves while Elizabeth talked up the Brook Farm experiment or, in the back room, printed *The Dial.*

No transcendental fellow-traveler—although he was sighted at the meetings on West Street—and not a company man in any case, Hawthorne was one of the few charter members of Ripley's commune, a fact that surprises those onlookers who judge him from afar or in retrospect. "The whole experience stands as a thing apart and unrelated to the rest of his life," snapped Brook Farm's historian years later. Hawthorne's contemporaries were cannier. As Fuller shrewdly noted, "solitary characters tend to outwardness,—to association,—while the social and sympathetic ones emphasize the value of solitude,—of concentration,—so that we hear from each the word which, from his structure, we least expect."

Nor must Hawthorne accept the perfectibility of the individual to entertain the romance of West Roxbury. In need of a home, an income, and a place to write, Hawthorne gladly gambled on Ripley's arcadia. The union of thinker and worker was irresistible to a man whose conscience still carped about idleness and still considered writing a frivolous pastime, no matter how much he wanted to do it. Hoeing and milking and feeding and mulching are honest occupations, chores performed in the cowhide boots of a democratic manhood. Besides, he had to earn his living.

And the whole idea had the ring of O'Sullivan's vision of democracy, embracing "the essential *equality* of all humanity." Such had been Hawthorne's politics since college, a mix of Jeffersonian agrarianism and Jacksonian populism. "A true democracy tends ever in the direction of *liberty,* private as well as public," O'Sullivan wrote, and "all ranks of men would begin life on a fair field, 'the world before them where to choose, and Providence their guide.' "

To complete the circle, O'Sullivan's chummy meliorism also resembled Elizabeth Peabody's Christianity, which she used to promote Brook Farm. "The community aims to be rich," Elizabeth Peabody explained, "not in the metallic representative of wealth, but in the wealth itself, which money should represent; namely, LEISURE TO LIVE IN ALL THE FACULTIES OF THE SOUL." Religion and politics shook hands, as Ripley had hoped they would. Orestes Brownson sent his son to the Brook Farm school. So did the Bancrofts. As for Hawthorne, he could substitute Peabody's cloying definition of Brook Farm for O'Sullivan's more secular version of it, all while scribbling his tales and preparing to build a house for his bride in the habitat of the future.

Elizabeth Peabody did not join the community. Nor did Margaret Fuller. "I doubt they will get free from all they deprecate in society," Fuller wisely surmised. But Hawthorne grabbed his boots, and Louisa sewed him a blue cotton smock. One of the first pilgrims, he arrived in West Roxbury on April 12. The storm blew east, the snow fell fast and thick. "Spring and summer will come in their due season," he wrote Sophia, trying to sound optimistic, "but the unregenerated man shivers within me."

Aging Brook Farmers remembered Hawthorne as beautiful, well built, tall, and taciturn until approached. Then his face opened, friendly, even playful, particularly with the flirtatious women who tossed pillows at him when he stretched out on the sofa and tried to read. Teasing the Brook Farm children, he casually dropped coins behind his back as little boys skipped in his wake. But essentially he was a loner. "He was a sort of humanitarian monk, so to speak, at least before he married," recalled Charles Newcomb, one of Brook Farm's youthful boarders. "He was passively, rather than positively, social."

He inhabited the main farmhouse, dubbed the Hive, where George Ripley stored his vast library of rare books on open shelves. (Later Ripley was forced to sell almost the entire library to pay the community's huge debts.) Hawthorne's room was on the first floor. It had its own stove, and from Pinckney Street he brought Sophia's paintings and the deep red carpet, opulent luxury on a cold morning.

In addition to the Ripleys and Hawthorne, other early-comers included the farmers Frank Farley and William Allen, ready to till the sandy soil, and the Reverend Warren Burton. Slowly, in time, a few more pioneers unpacked their cases. Among them were Mrs. Minot Pratt, Minot Pratt, George Bradford, Lloyd Fuller (Margaret's brother), the beautiful Almira Barlow and her sons, and Charles Anderson Dana, later the disillusioned publisher of a conservative *New York Sun.* Rooting from the sidelines, Elizabeth Peabody invited a large group of potential backers to West Street and publicized the cause in the pages of *The Dial.*

She also monitored Hawthorne's activities. "Hawthorne has taken hold with the greatest spirit—& proves a fine workman," she wrote to a friend. At five o'clock in the morning he blew the horn to wake his sleepy cohorts, and before breakfast milked cows, chopped wood, and loaded manure into carts. Hungry, he devoured the buckwheat cakes, served piping hot at the large table before the hearth, before he returned to the brown fields to hoe and rake and plant till dusk, wearing the thin summer frock Louisa had sewn.

At first he enjoyed himself. He reminded Sophia that physical labor "defiles the hands, indeed, but not the soul," and to his family he signed his letters "Nath. Hawthorne, Ploughman." Amused at first, Hawthorne's family grew annoyed. "What is the use of burning your brains out in the sun, when you can do anything better with them?" queried Louisa. Ebe, too, couldn't understand why her brother worked so much longer than the mandated three hours a day. "I have never felt that I was called upon by *Mr. Ripley* to devote so much of my time to manual labor," Hawthorne justified himself to another onlooker.

Not only did Brook Farm demand the full, able-bodied commitment of all those, like himself, who wanted the experiment to succeed, but, Hawthorne declared, "there are private and personal motives which, without the influence of those shared by us all, would still make me wish to bear all the drudgery of this one summer's labor, were it much more onerous than I have found it."

The private motive was his engagement, still secret, to Sophia. But there was also his writing. Hawthorne intended to crowd his quota of labor into the summer months so that in September he could trade in his dung fork for a pen.

He had already fallen behind. "I have not written that infernal story," he wailed to George Hillard, having promised a tale for the 1842 *Token,* which Hillard was editing. Hawthorne begged off. "You cannot think how exceedingly I regret the necessity of disappointing you; but what could be done? An engagement to write a story must in its nature be conditional," Hawthorne guiltily wrote Hillard in July; "because stories grow like vegetables, and are not manufactured, like a pine table. My former stories all sprung up of their own accord, out of a quiet life. Now I have no quiet at all."

He had other plans too, and these he thought he could manage. James Munroe, the publisher of Emerson's *Nature,* would reissue *Grandfather's Chair* as the first in a series of children's books Hawthorne would edit. Elizabeth Peabody was to negotiate the deal. "We expect to make a great deal of money," he chortled to Louisa. "I wish Elizabeth [his sister] would write a book for the series."

Munroe had also consented to an enlarged version of *Twice-told Tales.* "I confess I have strong hopes of good from this arrangement with Munroe"— Hawthorne was excited, though he tried not to be—"but when I look at the scanty avails of my past literary efforts, I do not feel authorized to expect much from the future."

Sales meant everything. "How much depends on those little books!" he cried to Sophia. Increasingly dubious about Brook Farm's fiscal health and increasingly disenchanted with the whole setup, he vowed to resign utopia in November, not six months after he arrived, unless he could be sure that he'd have a house for him and Sophia by spring. "I am becoming more and more convinced, that we must not lean upon the community," he informed her. "What ever is to be done, must be done by thy husband's own individual strength."

But he waffled. By remaining at Brook Farm through fall, Hawthorne reasoned, "I shall see these people and their enterprise under a new point of view, and perhaps be able to determine whether thou and I have any call to cast in our lot among them." Telling the disappointed Ripleys of his intention to leave, he again reported to Sophia, this time awkwardly, that "the ground, upon which I must judge of the expediency of our abiding here, is not what they [the Ripleys] may say, but what actually is, or is likely to be; and of this I doubt whether either of them is capable of forming a correct opinion."

Regardless, he purchased two shares in the community, invested five hundred more dollars toward a home, and became a trustee of the estate as well as chairman of its finance committee. "My accession to these august offices does not at all decide the question of my remaining here permanently," he insisted, firm only in his decision to spend the winter in Boston. Yet as trustee of the estate, he actively helped to mismanage funds, taking two mortgages on the property for five hundred dollars more than the original price of the farm.

Upset and ambivalent, he retired to his room. September was passing, and he hadn't lifted his pen. "I have not the sense of perfect seclusion," he told Sophia, "which has always been essential to my power of producing anything. It is true, nobody intrudes into my room; but still I cannot be quiet." He walked along the Needham road or at the edge of the meadow, feet sinking into the spongy soil. He climbed a pine tree and afterwards wrote of it in his journal, as if to capture the moment when the gold of fall turned a wintry gray. "The woods have now assumed a soberer tint than they wore at my last date," he described the October landscape. "Many of the shrubs, which looked brightest a little while ago, are now wholly bare of leaves. . . . None of the trees, scarcely, will now bear a close examination; for then they look ragged, wilted, and of faded, frost-bitten hue; but at a distance, and in the mass, and enlivened by sunshine, the woods have still somewhat of the variegated splendor which distinguished them a week ago." He wrote as of the community itself: beautiful at a distance, wilted on inspection, and revived by confidence, however ill placed. "It is wonderful what a difference the sunshine makes; it is like varnish, bringing out the hidden veins in a piece of rich wood."

Day after day, he loitered, he scribbled in his journal, he rambled over the broad countryside. He traveled to West Street, to Salem, and back to Brook Farm. He rode with William Allen to Brighton to the cattle fair on a crisp morning, inspecting cows and heavy-yoked oxen, the gentlemen farmers and the field hands. He chatted amiably with Emerson and Margaret Fuller in a little glade near the woods. He surveyed from a distance the games of the participants and their picnics. "The grown people took part with mirth enough—while I, whose nature it is to be a mere spectator of sport and serious business, lay under the trees and looked on." He kept distances, drew boundaries. But he had come to like Fuller.

She was not a simple woman, not a tactful woman, not even a kind woman. Her manner was slightly deprecating, her absorption egotistical and intense. She was also brilliant, fascinating, and in her own time prized as a sizzling conversationalist whose physical presence alone defied assumptions about feminine passivity. Yet though she dressed beautifully and loved ornament, she struck friends as plain, or so they later said. And her voice had a rough nasal quality, said others, implying that her ceaseless, presumptuous talk gave offense. Edgar Allan Poe noted that when she spoke "her upper lip, as if impelled by the action of involuntary muscles, habitually uplifts itself, conveying the impression of a sneer." Fuller's naked ambition repelled the men who might have been, or were, attracted to her.

Born in 1810, Fuller read Latin at six, taught school, wrote lugubrious essays, and like her mother, a semi-invalid, suffered from migraines to escape the control of her father, a four-term congressman and amateur scholar of exacting standards. When Elizabeth Peabody left the Temple School, Fuller worked as Bronson Alcott's assistant, learning how conversation could be used as a tool of intellectual discovery that pushed auditors beyond where they thought they could go. Sarah Clarke recounted a typical exchange that took place during Fuller's Conversations for women. One of them, insisting upon her right to judge things by her feelings and ignore "the intellectual view of the matter," said "I am made so, and I cannot help it."

"Yes," says Margaret, gazing upon her, "but who are *you*? Were you an accomplished human being, were you all that a human being is capable of becoming, you might perhaps have a right to say, 'I *like* it therefore it is good'; but, if you are not all that, your judgment must be partial and unjust if it is guided by your feelings alone."

Alcott said she might as well have been born in Greece or Rome; she was no New England woman. Her self-regard was so sublime, said another acquaintance, it was virtually inoffensive. And she was as lonely as only an intellectual woman can be. "Womanhood is at present too straitly-bound to give me scope," she admitted.

Hawthorne and Fuller had first met two years earlier in Boston after Fuller published her translation of *Eckermann's Conversations with Goethe* (the fourth volume in George Ripley's series). Fuller breathed Goethe, and friends anticipated with pleasure her biography of their transcendentalist precursor but guessed her true gifts were more ephemeral: a riveting physical presence, a propensity to talk, an insatiable curiosity. She knew how to exploit these. Her Conversations were successful and lucrative. With a childlike laugh and a manner alternately clipped or beguiling, Fuller sat on a kind of tripod in a velvet gown, demanding no less of herself than the women assembled before her. What are we, as women, born to do, she wanted to know, and how did we intend to do it.

"She broke her lance upon your shield," recalled Sarah Clarke. "No woman ever had more true lovers among her own sex, and as many men she also remembered as equal friends." But a friendship with Margaret Fuller—for men and women—was fraught with the abrupt, the difficult, the intimate. Few could or would admit their attraction to her was sexual. Emerson, for all his emotional abstinence, deeply loved her; so did Sophia's mother and her two sisters. Upstaged by yet another sister surrogate, Sophia belittled Fuller, "contorted like a sybil on the tripod—tho! not so graceful as I imagined a greek sybil to be."

Himself a jealous man, Hawthorne used humor to defend against Fuller—against, that is, his fascination with her. "Would that Miss Margaret Fuller might lose her tongue!—or my Dove her ears, and so be left wholly to her husband's golden silence!" he had advised Sophia when she attended Fuller's second series of Conversations, which he waved aside as "a Babel of talkers."

But Sophia got hooked. In the spring of 1841, while Hawthorne pitched hay at Brook Farm, Sophia worshipfully copied Allston's "Lorenzo and Jessica" and Crawford's "Orpheus," which she submitted to Fuller for approval; she composed an essay for Fuller on music, and she wrote a sonnet of steamy adoration called "To a Priestess of the Temple Not Made with Hands."

Again Hawthorne intervened. This time he tried to cool Sophia's ardor by indulging his own. He seemed at first to dismiss Margaret, calling a Brook Farm cow that belonged to her a "transcendental heifer." "She is very fractious, I believe, and apt to kick over the milk pail." Yet he couldn't resist observing that he would be Fuller's "milk-maid, this evening." Sophia certainly understood the double entendre.

A latter-day Mrs. Hutchinson, Margaret Fuller was the impertinent, thoughtful kind of woman Hawthorne admired and avoided, especially since he'd broken his own lance on Mary Silsbee's shield. Yet Miss Fuller's cow, against whom the herd had predictably rebelled, "is compelled to take refuge under our protection," Hawthorne goaded his fiancée. "So much did she impede thy husband's labors, by keeping close to him, that he found it necessary to give her two or three gentle pats with a shove; but still she preferred to trust herself to my tender mercies, rather than venture among the horns of the herd. She is not an amiable cow," he concluded; "but she has a very intelligent face, and seems to be of a reflective cast of character."

Fuller laughed to find herself at Brook Farm "in the amusing position of a conservative" (the role Hawthorne assigned himself when he wrote *The Blithedale Romance,* based on his experiences in West Roxbury). Her unalloyed skepticism clearly helped Hawthorne acknowledge his own growing disillusion, and by the time Hawthorne departed Brook Farm in November 1841—again, not six months after his arrival—he and Fuller were friends, Fuller admiring Hawthorne's psychological acuity, a quality they shared. As for his writing, she didn't say too much. There was manliness and delicate tenderness, but Hawthorne's characters were airy, virginal. "This frigidity and thinness bespeaks a want of deeper experiences," Fuller discerned, "for which no talent at observation, no sympathies, however ready and delicate, can compensate."

Hawthorne left Brook Farm for the same reason he went there. He misjudged both himself and the situation. He realized the farm could never support him and Sophia. He couldn't write there. Nor could he tolerate the idea of a cold winter far from Sophia or a future of mind-numbing toil. "The real Me was never an associate of the community," he justified himself.

Sophia had been forewarned. "A man's soul may be buried and perish under a dung-heap or in a furrow in the field, just as well as under a pile of money," Hawthorne had griped. For months he had been cursing physical labor as an enslavement, the scourge of the world, "and nobody can meddle with it, without becoming proportionately brutified."

And he cursed the sense of dependency—Brook Farmers called it cooperation—which the community fostered no less than a Custom House sinecure.

For with all his goodwill toward Brook Farm, he did not share Ripley's faith in a human nature free of envy or avarice or evil. That too was a fundamental conflict in Hawthorne: as a true democrat, he believed nothing—no moneyed interest, no institution, no government—should intrude on the people's sovereignty; and yet he didn't for a moment assume people were basically good. Anyway, to him, sin was a requirement of consciousness.

If Brook Farm provided Hawthorne no financial cushion, neither did James Munroe. He did not reprint Hawthorne's children's stories. Later Hawthorne seemed to blame Elizabeth Peabody for holding out for too much money. Yet he contracted with Munroe and Company in October for a new two-volume edition of *Twice-told Tales* that paid him 10 percent of the $2.25 retail price. His reputation growing—at least among the cognoscenti—Hawthorne had expected a fair return.

The book did appear at the end of the year, thirty-nine tales in all, the sketches from the 1837 edition and sixteen more recent ones, including the four Province-House stories as well as five early pieces not published in the original volume, like "The Haunted Mind," "The Village Uncle," "The Ambitious Guest," "The Seven Vagabonds," and "The White Old Maid."

He still excluded "Roger Malvin's Burial," "My Kinsman, Major Molineux," and "Young Goodman Brown." At Sophia's suggestion, he also excluded three other stories, "The Man of Adamant," "Monsieur du Miroir," and "Mrs. Bullfrog."

The collection didn't sell. "Surely the book was puffed enough to meet with a sale," Hawthorne despaired. "What the devil is the matter?"

The reviews were laconic. As expected, O'Sullivan hailed Hawthorne's style as "a model of simplicity, ease, grace, quiet humor, and seriousness." In a backhanded way, Longfellow complimented Hawthorne's not seeing "by the help of other men's minds" and went on to note the "large proportion of feminine elements" in the stories, referring to the androgynous quality of the writing—and the man—that other reviewers discovered in Hawthorne's tales: fragility, rage, and a certain coyness, frightening to readers, seductive, inimitable.

Orestes Brownson regarded Hawthorne with suspicion. He classed Hawthorne "at the head of American Literature" and characterized the tales as "gentle, yet robust and manly; full of tenderness, but never maudlin"; yet he advised Hawthorne to "attempt a higher and bolder strain than he has thus far done." Edgar Allan Poe agreed about the need for boldness: "These effusions of Mr. Hawthorne are the product of a truly imaginative intellect, restrained, and in some measure repressed, by fastidiousness of taste, by constitutional melancholy and by indolence."

Margaret Fuller offered a similar observation, just as harsh. Hawthorne did not "paint with blood-warm colors."

Contemporaries respected Hawthorne, they admired him, reviewed him, and they recognized him as one of the most imaginative and strangest writers in America. Yet like Hawthorne himself, they held something in reserve.

Not Sophia. Her Hawthorne lived on Mount Olympus. Judicious, wise, empathetic, and aloof as no Olympian could ever be, Hawthorne was a poet "who must stand apart & observe," she told her mother; and to her sister Mary, an agnostic on the subject of Hawthorne, she said over and over that Hawthorne's purpose "is to observe & not to be observed."

But she had tired of ethereal love. "I love thee transcendantly," Hawthorne had assured her, offering little assurance in this, the third year of their underground romance. Hawthorne shuttled between Boston and Salem, between Sophia and bachelorhood, and though no longer a tenant of Brook Farm, his sojourn there suggests he was more unsure about marriage than he knew.

Once married, would he be able to write? To Sophia, he declared he wished nothing more than to leave the darkness of his room on Herbert Street "where my youth wasted itself in vain." Yet in this squalid chamber, fame had been won, on this pine table, near the old chest of drawers and the mahogany-framed mirror. For better or worse, this owl's nest of quiet solitude was where he composed his stories, safe and snug—and beyond the call of sex or entanglement. When the editors of the short-lived magazine *Arcturus* asked him for a tale, he said he doubted he should write anymore, "at least, not like my past productions; for they grew out of the quietude and seclusion of my former life; and there is little probability that I shall ever be so quiet and secluded again."

Marriage threatened everything he associated with writing. "During the last three or four years, the world has sucked me within its vortex," he noted; "and I could not get back into my solitude even if I would."

He dithered. Tell your mother and sisters of our engagement, Sophia admonished her dilatory lover in early 1842. Dodging her request, he retorted, "I do not think thou canst estimate what a difficult task thou didst propose to me." He tried to explain. "Thou wilt not think that it is caprice or stubbornness that has made me hitherto resist thy wishes. Neither, I think, is it a love of secrecy and darkness. I am glad to think that God sees through my heart, and if any angel has power to penetrate into it, he is welcome to know everything that is there."

Having changed the subject, he followed the thread of his own argument. "It is this involuntary reserve, I suppose, that has given the objectivity to my writings. And when people think that I am pouring myself out in a tale or essay, I am merely telling what is common to human nature, not what is peculiar to myself. I sympathize with them—not they with me."

Defensive, especially after the reviews of *Twice-told Tales,* Hawthorne half admitted what Sophia later surmised. "Mr. Hawthorne hid from himself even more cunningly than he hid himself from others," she would remark.

But they would marry, of that she was sure. And she succeeded at last. Hawthorne told his family of the engagement. The upstairs chamber at Herbert Street would be his no more.

Or so he thought.

CHAPTER TWELVE

_____

Beautiful Enough

He then looked the applicant in the face, and said briefly—
"Your business?"
"I want," said the latter, with tremulous earnestness, "a place!"

Nathaniel Hawthorne, "The Intelligence Office"

OURS IS A STORY never told, said Nathaniel Hawthorne to Sophia Peabody. To him—to both of them—their hearts had been created new for one another. "We are Adam and Eve," Sophia cried. Family and friends agreed, Margaret Fuller promising the couple "mutual love and heavenly trust," and their son Julian later declaring they'd found it. Occasionally, however, a skeptic sniggered. To Thomas Higginson— preacher, writer, soldier, activist, and a confidant of Emily Dickinson—the Hawthorne marriage represented nothing more than narcissism à deux: ecstatic, domestic, imprisoning. "Both Mr. and Mrs. Hawthorne came to each from a life of seclusion; he had led it by peculiarity of nurture, she through illness; and when they were united, they simply admitted each other to that seclusion, leaving the world almost as far off as before."

Wedded bliss or blanketed self-absorption; or both? We shall see.

"The execution took place yesterday," Hawthorne wrote to his sister Louisa the day after the wedding. "We made a christian end, and came straight to Paradise, where we abide at this present writing."

Louisa had accepted her brother's decision to marry; not Ebe, who stormed it was unconscionable that their mother hadn't been told of the engagement of her only son until weeks before his wedding. For three years she'd been deceived; they all had been. What could they do? Ebe informed

157

Silhouette of the newlyweds by August Edouart, 1843

Sophia that their future association would be congenial, "particularly as it need not be so frequent or so close as to require more than reciprocal good will, if we do not happen to suit each other in our new relationship." Snippy, she continued, "I write thus plainly, because my brother has desired me to say only what was true; though I do not recognize his right to speak of truth, after keeping us so long in ignorance of this affair."

Sophia was hurt. "All in good time, dearest," Hawthorne consoled.

The Hawthornes had pretended indifference to the impending marriage. "I dare say we shall and must seem very cold and even apathetic to you," Ebe admitted; "but after you have known us a little while it may be that you will discover more warmth and sympathy than is at first apparent." In this, she echoed her brother's estimate of family relations: "There seems to be a tacit law," he had said, "that our deepest heart-concernments are not to be spoken of."

Then Ebe softened and promised Sophia a reasonably warm welcome at Herbert Street, and Nathaniel assured Sophia that his mother—"our mother"—had suspected the liaison all along.

Hawthorne's stealth suggests how strenuously he resisted marriage even while protesting the reverse. If initially prompted by the imbroglio with Elizabeth Peabody, he managed to keep his engagement from his family for an abnormal amount of time, and his attitude at Brook Farm—never mind his participation in it—was just as strange; he intended to build a honeymoon cottage although he never told anyone of the plan. Yet Hawthorne did reveal his anxieties in a story, "A Virtuoso's Collection," the only tale he wrote before his wedding.

The virtuoso accumulates quaint relics of history and literature—Dr. Johnson's cat, Robinson Crusoe's parrot, Nero's fiddle, Claude's palette, and Charles Lamb's pipe—to include in his fantastical museum, itself a kind of story-land place, or emblem of fiction, where the actual and the imaginary meet. As Hawthorne's symbol of the artist, the virtuoso also resembles the solitary, unmarried Hawthorne and what he fears he'll become should he stay single, locked in his room at Herbert Street: "cut off from natural sympathies, and blasted with a doom that had been inflicted on no other human being, and by the result of which he had ceased to be human." This is the virtuoso: pitiless museum-keeper of the human heart.

Probing its depths, afraid of what he might find there, the virtuoso recurs with terrible regularity in Hawthorne's subsequent work. Great in ambition, small in humanity, frightening and compelling, the virtuoso, nothing himself, hoards what he can to assure himself of his own reality. There is ice, Hawthorne suspects, in the soul of a writer.

And Hawthorne characterizes himself as a virtuoso—or spectral bachelor—in his love letters to Sophia: "Thou art my only reality—all other people are but shadows to me." Again: "Without thee, I have but the semblance of life. All the world hereabouts seems dull and drowsy—a vision, but without any spirituality—and I, likewise, an unspiritual shadow, struggle vainly to catch hold of something real." And again: "It is thou that givest me reality, and makest all things real for me."

Hawthorne bemoaned his alienation especially when he wrote to Sophia from Salem, where the secrecy of the engagement must have bothered or titillated him the most. Anchored in his old chamber, single and secure, Hawthorne recognized the cords binding him fast, too fast. Strong and primitive feelings tied him to his mother and sisters, who were as disinclined to let him go as he was to leave them.

But Sophia beckoned. She offered adulation, connectedness, the lure of ordinary living, fatherhood, children, and a home. Shortly after she and Hawthorne made their engagement public in the spring of 1842, she conceived a plan. They would live in Concord, Massachusetts, the small town three and a half hours by stagecoach from Boston. What better place for Hawthorne, the chronicler of America's past? Near Concord's North Bridge, on April 18, 1775, embattled farmers had fired the shots heard round the world. And just half a mile east of the village green, transcendental guru Ralph Waldo Emerson held court in his home while his young friend Henry Thoreau scoured the woods for Indian relics and the apostolic Bronson Alcott composed milky Orphic Sayings for *The Dial.*

A few miles from the rickety North Bridge was the old weather-beaten parsonage occupied by Emerson's stepgrandfather, recently deceased. "I devoutly believe that it is one of GOD's lovely decrees," cried Sophia, when she learned the place was available. She and Hawthorne visited the musty house in early May, threw open the doors, and were greeted by Emerson himself. "He seems pleased with the colony he is collecting," an onlooker reported. The deal struck, Emerson dispatched Thoreau to plant a garden for the prospective tenants.

Originally scheduled for June 27, 1842, the Hawthorne wedding was initially postponed when Sophia fell ill. Hawthorne slid into a depression, short-lived, for not two weeks later, on July 9, the long-anticipated marriage ceremony took place in the Peabody parlor at West Street. Sophia's friend Cornelia Park braided the bride's auburn hair, and Sarah Clarke patted down her dress. She was thirty-two, he was thirty-eight: middle-aged. But they were so radiant, particularly Hawthorne, that James Freeman Clarke, who married them, could barely contain himself. He'd expected the author, of whom he'd heard so much, to be old and dry, not handsome or charismatic. But Hawthorne was so nervous that Sophia's Aunt Pickman hid in an adjoining room so as not to scare him away.

Apparently none of the Hawthornes or Mannings attended the ceremony, nor is there a record of any of Hawthorne's friends, although David Roberts gave Hawthorne a half dozen silver spoons and Horace Conolly an heirloom watch belonging to Susanna Ingersoll's great-grandfather. By and large, though, the wedding was a Peabody affair.

After the ceremony, the couple boarded their wedding carriage. A gust of summer shower delayed them more than an hour on the road, but they rolled into Concord at five o'clock that afternoon. They walked between the columns of black ash trees on the side of the long path that separated the Old Manse, as Hawthorne called the parsonage, from the road. The house

The Old Manse, Concord, Massachusetts

was filled with flowers, vases and baskets brimming with sweet-smelling roses and the white lilies that Elizabeth Hoar and Abigail Alcott, neighbors, had placed on stands made from the roots of trees. Sophia was delirious. "I am the happiest person on this earth," she wrote her mother the next day. Likewise, Hawthorne wrote to Louisa, "We are as happy as people can be, without making themselves ridiculous." He sent the reassurances his mother and sisters needed, or he did. "I have neither given up my own relatives," he reminded them, "nor adopted others."

Summer was their honeymoon. After breakfast Hawthorne rambled through the orchard that sloped in the back of the house and down to the drowsy Musketaquid (or Concord) River, returning to the Manse his arms full of lilies and cardinals for his bride. Or he slipped out of bed before dawn to catch the fish they'd eat fried for dinner. He planted vegetables. Green leaves slithered up the beanpoles, and soon his summer squashes appeared, the color of bleached gold. It was the first flush of fatherhood, he wrote, "as if something were being created under my own inspection, and partly by my own aid."

Afternoons, the couple raced down the avenue carrying baskets of whortleberries, and for dinner they feasted on peas and tomatoes from the

garden, purchasing their milk for four cents a quart and butter for eighteen
cents a pound. A young Irishwoman, Sarah, cooked, but when Sarah went
home to Waltham for a day, Sophia boiled her first dinner: corn and squash
and rice warmed in milk with baked apples from their trees.

Inside the Manse, Sophia lined the newly papered parlor with flowers
and hung one of her paintings on the yellow walls of Hawthorne's study,
helping him arrange the bureau and desk he'd brought from Pinckney
Street. She put the little plaster bust relief of Apollo, a wedding gift from
Caroline Sturgis, on a shelf, and from then on Hawthorne was Apollo to
Sophia, and she to him the sunny incarnation of spring. They lay under the
trees in one another's arms, and when they came back to the house, they
recited love poetry to each other, measuring their own bliss against the
words of the poets. "We did not think they knew much," said Sophia,
"though once in a while we would find a true word."

At night they sat in Hawthorne's study beneath the astral lamp and
Hawthorne read aloud from Shakespeare and Spenser and Milton, the
happy couple criticizing Milton's God but not his earth, which they embraced. Sophia danced to the tune of a music box, a wedding present from
Mary. Sexually expressive, she luxuriated in the freedom denied under her
mother's eye. "I would put on daily a velvet robe and pearls in my hair to
gratify my husband's taste," she announced, and to her mother she gloated
that her husband "fills me so completely that there can be no void." She
didn't transgress too far. "This vigilance & care are comparable only to a
mother's," Sophia tactfully wrote to Mrs. Peabody, "& exceed all other possible carefulness & watching."

"I send up a perpetual thanksgiving to Heaven that Mr. Hawthorne's
vocation keeps him beneath his own vine & figtree within instant reach of
eye & voice," Sophia wrote to Mary Foote, whose husband toiled in a newspaper office. Though the newlyweds didn't plan to do a thing—no writing,
no painting—during the summer, they charted a new routine. Mornings
would be for creative work. Downstairs in the dining room, near the
kitchen, Sophia had set up her studio, where she would paint, copying
Emerson's print of Endymion; or she would compose long chatty letters to
her mother about the joys of marriage while Hawthorne wrote in his study
just above her. They would meet at dinnertime and discuss what they'd
done, and later in the afternoon Hawthorne might climb back upstairs to
read, nap, or write in his journal.

Sitting at his desk in the study at the rear of the house, Hawthorne could
glimpse the North Bridge monument, and from another window he gazed

down through the apple orchard to the river, his passion for it not unlike Thoreau's for Walden Pond. As if prophesizing the images in Thoreau's masterpiece, *Walden,* Hawthorne in his journal compares the water's green and blue to an open eye; and bathing in the ponds was like plunging into the sky. "A good deal of mud and river-slime had accumulated on my soul," he wrote; "but those bright waters washed it all away." Sometimes the river seemed torpid, sluggish, and muddy. "This dull river," said he, "has a deep religion of its own."

As did he. His was a tender pantheism, reverential, tranquil, sexually satisfied—a "world just created," he observed, happy to see his wife, who met him at the door when he came home from the village. He responded to every change in weather, every scattered sound, in the journal he kept together with Sophia, an extended love letter written at home. Their home was Paradise.

Besides Apollo, Hawthorne was "Adam" or "my lord" to Sophia, and everything in paradise was holy, even the body. "Before our marriage I knew nothing of its capacities & the truly married alone can know what a wondrous instrument it is for the purpose of the heart," she exulted.

Hawthorne himself confessed that "my life, at this time, is more like that of a boy, externally, than it has been since I was really a boy." Surprised by physical pleasure, surprised by his sense of freedom, he brushed away more sober thoughts. "It might be a sin and shame, in such a world as ours, to spend a lifetime in this manner; but for a few summer-weeks, it is good to live as if this world were Heaven."

"The general sentiment that prevails about you is, I find, that you do not wish to see any one," Mary Peabody accused the newlyweds, "and that you have taken all decent measures to prevent such a catastrophe." Mary was wrong. Proud to have a home of his own, Hawthorne showed off his house to friends. "I felt that I was regarded as a man with a wife and a household—a man having a tangible existence in the world," he wrote in his journal.

By mid-August the Manse had opened its doors to a steady stream of guests: the Emersons, Elizabeth Hoar, the Hillards. George Bradford came from Brook Farm, and Louisa Hawthorne, traveling by coach all the way from Salem, stayed three weeks. Mrs. Peabody came, and Frank Farley and David Roberts. Elizabeth Peabody did not; Ebe did not.

Thoreau dined at the Manse. "Agreeable & gentle & meek," said

Sophia. Hawthorne considered him a singular character, wild and sophisticated in his own idiosyncratic way. "He is ugly as sin, long-nosed, queer-
mouthed, and with uncouth and somewhat rustic, although courteous
manners," Hawthorne observed. He respected Thoreau's minute devotion
to nature, "and Nature," said Hawthorne, "in return for his love, seems to
adopt him as her especial child, and shows him secrets which few others are
allowed to witness." A friend of both men, Ellery Channing, thought them
alike in "the stoical *fond* of their characters," he said. "A vein of humor had
they both; and when they laughed, like Shelley, the operation was sufficient
to split a pitcher."

Averse to small talk in the village, Hawthorne earned the reputation of
misfit, as Mary Peabody only too readily pointed out, but in Thoreau he
found an accomplice. He praised the younger man's "Natural History of
Massachusetts"—not overly transcendental—published in the July issue of

Henry David Thoreau

The Dial; he admired his scholarship; his good sense; the way he handled his skiff. In need of money, Thoreau sold Hawthorne his canoe for seven dollars, and Hawthorne asked Epes Sargent, editor of the *New Monthly Magazine,* to solicit Thoreau's contribution. He did the same with O'Sullivan and the *Democratic Review,* which published a review by Thoreau and a short essay before O'Sullivan presciently suggested he write about nature.

Hawthorne steered shy of Emerson. It was an unusual stance, since typically men and women came to Concord to pay homage to the resident sage already known for his sonorous lectures, his heretical book *Nature,* and his aphorisms. "Life is a progress, not a station," Emerson reminded his readers in his essay "Compensation." (A "man without a handle!" Henry James Sr. called him.) Standing erect, he was over six feet tall, with bright blue eyes, craggy nose, and high cheekbones. But his individualistic pith was the fruit of gnarled despair. Two of his brothers had died young; another was mentally ill. And his first wife succumbed to tuberculosis before the couple had been married two years. Fourteen months after her death, Emerson walked out to Roxbury, where she was buried, and opened her tomb. That same year, 1832, he left the pulpit.

After his remarriage in 1835, Emerson moved to Concord with his wife Lydia, whom Emerson renamed Lydian, adding the "n" to her name to make it more euphonious. There, he wrote the transcendentalist bible, *Nature,* likely starting it at the Manse. It encapsulated the credo of a divine nature, both inner and outer, ordered, infinite, knowable. "We have no questions to ask which are unanswerable," he claimed. Not entirely true, as he discovered in 1842, when a son died of scarlet fever. "I comprehend nothing of this fact," he wailed, "but its bitterness."

The Emersons lived on the dusty Lexington Road in a large white house with green-shuttered windows that burst with afternoon sun as if to remind Emerson that he'd staked his life on light, not the unbelief or grief nipping at his heels. He and Hawthorne were fated to misunderstand each other. When Elizabeth Peabody gave him "Foot-prints on the Sea-shore," Emerson complained that "there was no inside to it; he & Alcott together would make a man," and he criticized *Twice-told Tales* with grudging respect. "It is no easy matter to write a dialogue," he admitted. "Cooper, Sterling, Dickens, and Hawthorne cannot." As he came to know Hawthorne, Emerson liked him more, although he remained equivocal about the work. "N. Hawthorn's [*sic*] reputation as a writer is a very pleasing fact," Emerson wrote in his own journals, "because his writing is not good for anything, and this is a tribute to the man."

Ralph Waldo Emerson

For his part, Hawthorne described Emerson as "a great searcher for facts; but they seem to melt away and become unsubstantial in his grasp." *The Dial* put Hawthorne to sleep, and as to the recent religious controversies pitting Unitarians against transcendentalists, he couldn't have cared less. He preferred "the narrow but earnest cushionthumper of puritanical times," he half joked, to the "cold, lifeless, vaguely liberal clergyman of our own day."

To some extent Hawthorne kept Emerson at bay to needle Sophia, who rushed to Concord to sit at the wise man's knee. Hawthorne did not fancy sharing his bride's attentions, and Sophia, alert to Hawthorne's needs, began to deprecate the Concord sage. Aware of her daughter's stratagem, Mrs. Peabody warned Sophia not to yield to Hawthorne's point of view. Hackles up, Sophia retorted, "Our love is so wide & deep & equal that there could not be much difference of opinion between us upon any moral point." Soon Sophia ventured further. "Waldo Emerson knows not much of love," she saucily informed her mother. "He also as well as Mr. Hawthorne is *great*, but Mr. Emerson is not so whole sided as Mr. Hawthorne. He towers straight up from a deep pool—Mr. Hawthorne spreads abroad many branches."

In return, Sophia didn't approve of all of Hawthorne's friends. David Roberts was a bore, with his "Salem inquisitiveness & anxiety to know the price of things." But in Margaret Fuller the couple found common ground. Dear noble Margaret, as Sophia labeled her, startled the newlyweds one August afternoon when, unannounced, she walked in on them while they were locked in an embrace. Embarrassed, they unclasped and ushered the Queen, another of Sophia's names for Fuller, into an easy chair, taking her bonnet and begging her to stay for tea. She did, and entertained the Hawthornes with "Sydnean showers of soft discourse," Sophia fluttered. "She was like the moon, radiant & gentle."

Hawthorne walked Fuller back to the Emersons' and confided "he should be much more willing to die than two months ago, for he had had some real possession in life, but still he never wished to leave this earth. It was beautiful enough." Next day, Sunday, he returned to the Emersons' to drop off a book Fuller had forgotten at the Manse. On the way home, he saw Fuller, sitting on the ground in the woods, and joined her. Not at all shy in her presence, he talked about the pleasures of getting lost, the crows, the seasons, the experiences of early childhood, the mountains, and anything that seemed to come into his mind until Emerson, taking a Sunday walk, interrupted them. Hawthorne was annoyed.

Now happily married, Hawthorne was more comfortable with Margaret than he ever could have been before.

It rained in late summer. Hawthorne's spirits drooped. Sophia cheered him. "Thus, even without the support of a stated occupation, I survive these sullen days, and am happy," he wrote in relief. Warm summer days were numbered.

"I suspect he is lazy about writing—is he not?" Nathan Hale Jr., the editor of the *Boston Miscellany,* asked Evert Duyckinck. "He wrote me one article but has been shy of saying anything about another—although purse grew lean in obtaining the first."

Happy in marriage, his new home, and his sense of sheer belonging, Hawthorne realized he could not support a family simply by selling barrels of fruit from a rented orchard or by harvesting bushels of potatoes from a

Margaret Fuller

Margaret Fuller's husband, Giovanni Ossoli,
from a daguerreotype

garden planted by someone else. To have a place, one must work to keep it. Before the wedding, Hawthorne had traveled to Albany to talk with John O'Sullivan, now a state legislator, and agreed to continue writing for the *Democratic Review.* In March he had sent Hale "A Virtuoso's Collection." But of late he hadn't been doing much.

The Peabodys knew of Hawthorne's shaky finances, especially Elizabeth. When Samuel Soden, the publisher of the *Boston Miscellany,* decided to replace Hale as editor, she immediately suggested her brother-in-law. Mary sent Sophia the news, along with Elizabeth's exasperating instructions to hold out for a salary of one thousand dollars a year, paid monthly. It didn't matter. Henry Tuckerman, a mediocre essayist and travel writer, got the job, rejecting Poe's "The Tell-tale Heart" first thing.

Margaret Fuller tried to help. Perhaps her sister and Ellery Channing, soon to be married, could board with the Hawthornes. Hawthorne said no even though he'd already invited George Bradford to board at the Manse. Bradford had declined. Hawthorne told Fuller he wanted to spare Sophia unnecessary housework so she could be free to paint and sculpt; and then there was the real reason: four sensitive people under one roof "would take but a trifle to render their whole common life diseased and intolerable." Hawthorne liked Channing up to a point. "The lad seems to feel as if he were a genius," he laughed, "and, ridiculously enough, looks upon his own verses as too sacred to be sold for money."

The coffers remained empty.

Death, too, prowled on the outskirts of Arcady. On October 10 Uncle Robert died, the cause attributed to palsy. Hawthorne quickly extemporized. He could never get to Salem in time for the funeral, nor could he leave Concord with the harvest now in progress—the apples were a source of income—and he was trying to write a sketch from his old journals ("The Old Apple-Dealer") for Epes Sargent. Still beholden to Uncle Robert, Hawthorne no doubt remembered with resentment Robert's disappointment in him. He'd come to Salem pretty soon, he told Louisa, maybe toward the end of the month.

Nathaniel and Sophia did leave Paradise for Salem and Boston later that fall, family and the shade of Robert Manning calling Hawthorne back to his old accustomed chamber—and the warmth. The Manse's long central corridor created a pleasant draft in summertime, but in October the frosty place smelled of bruised apples and dead leaves. "It is a very cold house," remarked Sophia, rapidly stitching robes of wadded flannel. They purchased three airtight stoves, all they could afford. Detestable, Hawthorne thought them. Longing for an open fireplace, he made nostalgia the subject of a new *Democratic Review* sketch, "Fire-Worship." "The inventions of mankind are fast blotting the picturesque, the poetic, and the beautiful out of human life," he groaned; even the destructive was in jeopardy: "The mighty spirit, were opportunity offered him, would run riot through the peaceful house, wrap its inmates in his terrible embrace, and leave nothing of them save their whitened bones."

No more. Captive within an iron-bellied stove, fire can no longer thaw hands as cold as the virtuoso's. "A person with an ice-cold hand," Hawthorne had written in his notebooks, "—his right hand; which people ever afterwards remember, when once they have grasped it." Ice-cold, too, is the heart yearning for firesides, forever bygone. Alien, detached, isolated, this ice-man again crystallizes Hawthorne's fear of what he himself might be or, without Sophia, have become. Soon he'll populate the happy groom's fiction in great number.

Hawthorne could easily despise Concord, with its rolling meadows and deep woods, its donnish Whigs and do-gooders, "bores," he said, "of a very intense water." No sunbaked sailors roamed the street, earrings aglitter; no day laborers hauled masts and hurled epithets by the wharves; no brothels squat waterside. Instead Concord was a Hall of Fantasy, its dreamy corridors reaching all the way to Cambridge, where Longfellow had finished his small yellow packet of antislavery poems. And it swept over the hallowed streets of Beacon Hill, protesters cried out against the trumped-up arrest of mulatto George Latimer, jailed in Boston without a warrant.

Even Hawthorne's friend George Hillard, flat-footed defender of the Constitution, began to sweat, so troubled was he by the violation of Latimer's civil rights. The Latimer case sparked a violent outburst against returning fugitive slaves to their putative masters, with John Greenleaf Whittier composing abolitionist verse and the old guard nervously defending the letter of the law. Slavery had seemed an abstraction, something odious practiced somewhere else. Now white slaveholders prosecuted fugitive slaves in the capital of Boston, and slavery had come home.

Yet many New Englanders persisted in thinking slavery a southern problem, which is how Hawthorne largely regarded it. And he didn't give a fig for abolition, laughing at it in his sketch "The Hall of Fantasy," in which an abolitionist brandishes "his one idea like an iron flail." In this satire, Hawthorne also surrounds Emerson with fawning acolytes, "most of whom,"

Woodcut accompanying the broadside publication of
John Greenleaf Whittier's poem, "Our Countrymen in Chains," 1837.

Hawthorne gibes, "betrayed the power of his intellect by its modifying influence upon their own." By contrast, the narrator of the sketch, a newcomer to the Hall of Fantasy, is a Democrat who archly claims to "love and honor" such men as Alcott and Jones Very and Washington Allston; maybe he does, but only when he praises John O'Sullivan's opposition to capital punishment does he drop his supercilious tone.

Hawthorne had no close friends in Concord, and its residents, men like Emerson, good and intelligent men of serious purpose, struck Hawthorne as somewhat pretentious and spoiled, or like Ellery Channing, as amiable featherheads. Hawthorne sighed. "These originals in a small way, after one has seen a few of them, become more dull and common-place than even those who keep the ordinary pathway of life."

Displaced, Hawthorne took aim at his public-spirited neighbors, the poets, reformers, and woolly transcendentalists of sanguine persuasion, and

assailed by errant knights, vegetarians, Adventists, Grahamites, and abolitionists—residue of the evangelical movement known as the Second Great
Awakening—he salted his prose with misanthropic sarcasm. In "The Procession of Life," the narrator caustically sorts people into categories, a
strange pastime under any circumstance, though in this case the criterion
isn't rank or achievement, just disease, sorrow, crime, and dislocation. And
lambasting financiers, social distinctions, or silk-gowned professors, he
mocks American democracy. "These factory girls from Lowell," he declares,
"shall mate themselves with the pride of drawing-rooms and literary circles—the bluebells in fashion's nose-gay, the Sapphos, and Montagues, and
Nortons of the age."

His astringency reveals a deep, pervasive pessimism originating not just
in his earlier reading of Swift and Mandeville, satirists of deep dye, or his
recent perusal of Voltaire but in Hawthorne's perception of himself as an
outsider removed, in this instance, from the shallow fuzziness of reform.
Hawthorne's was a world of hard angles, first and forever.

Winter grew cold. Louisa hoped her brother might be selected for the
Salem post office, and though Hawthorne doubted he would, he assured his
family that he'd receive a political appointment in a matter of months. He
and Sophia ate their first Thanksgiving dinner alone, fortified by one
another. In the next months, while she gaily slid on the frozen river, he
skated, darting away from her in long sweeping curves. Or, wrapped in his
cloak, he was sometimes joined on the ice by Thoreau and Emerson. Sophia
watched them. But on a snowy afternoon, the sky leaden, the light in the
Old Manse slanted downward.

"All through the winter I had wished to sit in the dusk of Evening, by the
flickering firelight, with my wife, instead of beside a dismal stove. At last,
this has come to pass; but it was owing to her illness, and our having no
chamber with a stove, fit to receive her."

In February 1843 Sophia suffered a miscarriage. Fast recovering, she
chirped that "men's accidents are God's purposes." Hawthorne scribbled the
consolation into his journal, and like childish vandals, he and Sophia
scratched it onto the window of his study.

Hawthorne now sat at his desk in earnest. With no government job
forthcoming, he didn't appear in public until two in the afternoon, when he
trudged through the piled-up snow to the Athenaeum and read for an hour.
After peeking his head into the post office, he walked back home for an

early tea and to chop the wood he could not afford to buy. Mornings, often before dawn, he skated—"like a schoolboy," he told his friend Margaret Fuller—and evenings, he read to Sophia as usual. A cold house was no place for guests so the couple entertained one another. "I do suppose that nobody ever lived, in one sense, quite so selfish a life as we do," Hawthorne admitted, content.

Each day he returned to his study "with pretty commendable diligence," he noted with satisfaction, even though he disparaged what he did there. "I might have written more, if it had seemed worth while; but I was content to earn only so much gold as might suffice for our immediate wants, having prospects of official station and emolument, which would do away the necessity of writing for bread."

His pockets stayed empty. "It is rather singular that I should need an office," Hawthorne complained to Bridge; "for nobody's scribblings seem to me more acceptable to the public than mine; and yet I shall find it a tough match to gain a respectable support by my pen." Epes Sargent had offered Hawthorne five dollars per page for anything he might submit to the *New Monthly Magazine,* and Hawthorne tried to charge the same amount to James Lowell, editor of the recently founded *Pioneer,* but Lowell couldn't pay anywhere near that, and what he could pay, he paid slowly. So did Sargent and the *Democratic Review,* where Hawthorne earned only twenty dollars each for articles like "The Old Apple-Dealer" or a story like "The Antique Ring." And because he himself owed money, he couldn't send funds to his sisters or mother. His paltry finances kept him close to home, unable even to go to Boston. "It is an annoyance; not a trouble," he swaggered for Sophia's benefit in their jointly kept journal, though he did regret his meager income—and meager output—as well as the fact that no one remunerated him fairly for what he did manage to provide.

Hawthorne wanted to write two juvenile storybooks under O'Sullivan's auspices, believing New York a lucrative venue for publishing. But he didn't. Nor could he motivate himself to write anything for Poe's projected magazine, *Stylus.* He turned down the chance to compose more stories for the *Boys' and Girls' Magazine,* which had published his children's fable, "Little Daffydowndilly" (about dillydallying), and though he consented to contribute to the popular *Graham's Magazine,* hoping to pocket its generous fee, he dawdled. Pressure made him tense.

"Could I only have the freedom to be perfectly idle now—no duty to fulfil—no mental or physical labor to perform—I could be as happy as a squash, and much in the same mode," he scribbled in his journal. "But the necessity of keeping my brain at work eats into my comfort as the squash-bug do into the heart of the vines. I keep myself uneasy, and produce little, and almost nothing that is worth producing." More likely Hawthorne did not quite know what he wanted to do, and he still hoped for a political appointment, traveling to Boston and Salem when he could afford to go to jockey for it.

But nothing eased his sense of failure. Either he accused himself of not writing enough or he considered what he wrote trivial: the busy conscience was a cruel taskmaster, impossible to please. Still, through 1843, Hawthorne's sketches and tales appeared regularly, and by the end of the year, with Sophia six months pregnant, Hawthorne sat in his study all morning and in the afternoon until sunset, having stocked the pages of the *Democratic* with stories like "The New Adam and Eve," "Egotism; or, The Bosom-Serpent," "The Procession of Life," "The Celestial Rail-road," "Buds and Bird-Voices," and "Fire-Worship." Though his pace slackened slightly in 1844, he did publish "Earth's Holocaust" in *Graham's* and "Drowne's Wooden Image" in *Godey's Lady's Book*. Destitution and the imminent birth of a child had smashed through his inhibitions, or what he often termed his torpor.

But stories printed for a few dollars a page could not feed a family. Sometime after leaving the Old Manse, he quipped that he had hoped "at least to achieve a novel," if not some more serious writing while he lived there. He wrote no novel. Yet he did start what may have been conceived as a book of interrelated tales, subtitling two of them "From the Unpublished 'Allegories of the Heart.' "

He'd been speculating about the project for quite a while—the heart allegorized as a cavern, he jotted in his notebooks. "At the entrance there is sunshine, and flowers growing about it. You step within, but a short distance, and begin to find yourself surrounded with a terrible gloom, and monsters of divers kinds; it seems like Hell itself." But with a series of tales about the misalliances of men and women, Hawthorne was writing stories unlike those about bachelors, wanderers, and masqueraders, and different too from his recent satiric sketches.

Take "The Birth-mark," published in Lowell's *Pioneer* and written not six months after his marriage, during Sophia's first pregnancy. A young scientist insists on removing the crimson birthmark on his wife's left cheek that galls and obsesses him; it's the "sole token of human imperfection," says he. With sexual anxiety thinly disguised as cosmetology, he prepares a stupefying concoction, which his wife obediently drinks. The fatal red mark disappears, but the potion kills her: the ideal cannot exist in disembodied form. This is the lesson that Aylmer, the scientist, has to learn. "Our creative Mother," Hawthorne writes, "while she amuses us with apparently working in the broadest sunshine, is yet severely careful to keep her own secrets, and, in spite of her pretended openness, shows us nothing but results. She permits us indeed, to mar, but seldom to mend, and, like a jealous patentee, on no account to make."

A slap at Emerson and transcendentalism, "The Birth-mark" is also a murder story in which a man confronts marriage, and hence sexuality, with horror. Equally, he wants to prevent a birth. In this sense, Hawthorne's story is also a fantasy of abortion. The scientist kills his wife and what she produces so that he in some way can remain alone, untrammeled, asexual, and free from responsibility.

The deadly ambivalence about women and, more broadly, sexual bodies and fatherhood suffuses most of the stories that Hawthorne wrote in these years. Another example, though far less accomplished—and less sadistic—is another tale in the projected "Allegories of the Heart" series, "Egotism; or, The Bosom-Serpent." Revamping a popular sixteenth-century legend, Hawthorne coils a snake about the heart of the Poe-like Roderick Elliston, the tale's main character, who understandably shuns the general population because of his bizarre affliction. Soon, though, he wants to be noticed. "All persons, chronically diseased," writes Hawthorne, "are egotists, whether the disease be of the mind or the body."

To Hawthorne, the desire for recognition is a curse. Ambition, fame, and *la gloire* are sins of commission in Hawthorne's world. Thus, the greater Roderick's fame, the greater his torment: it's as if Hawthorne was writing the allegory of himself, an ambitious guest unhappy under his dark veil and miserable without it.

So Roderick Elliston seeks the solace of fellow sufferers. Searching for the symptoms of his own disease in everyone he meets, Roderick hopes to "establish a species of brotherhood between himself and the world," for he needs to believe that he does belong somewhere, that he's not a complete monster or deformed oddball; that he is, in effect, a man. Yet what is manhood? Elliston sees his masculinity grotesquely mirrored in ambitious statesmen, distinguished clergymen, and wealthy merchants, each of whom harbors a secret serpent. Even the envious author, who disparages the books he could never write, nurtures his own slimy snake, one that, Hawthorne jests, "was fortunately without a sting."

By seeking this fraternity, Roderick is able to sidestep the implications of his condition: Roderick is pregnant. For though Hawthorne states early in the story that the bosom-serpent symbolizes jealousy, he never bothers to make the nature of Roderick's jealousy concrete or believable—unless pro-creation is its primitive source. That is, Roderick's bosom-serpent isn't just a symbol of his manhood; the snake transforms Roderick into a woman, with a creature alive inside him that's "nourished with his food, and lived upon his life."

Written during Sophia's first pregnancy and miscarriage, Hawthorne's story conveys all the fears of coming fatherhood: that the creature about to be born is predatory, threatening; that the miracle of creation is mixed with sex and death; that a man can never do what a woman does, despite, in Hawthorne's case, an unsettling, overwhelming identification with women: his mother, his sisters, even Sophia. It's no surprise that Hawthorne's Roder-ick cannot be rid of his serpent until his wife, Rosina, appears almost willy-nilly at the story's hasty conclusion. But the ending is psychologically astute. Rosina rescues Roderick by reassuring him of his masculinity.

Bosom-serpents within the body and birthmarks on it refer again to Hawthorne's obsession with disclosure, or that which is written and borne on the body. In another story, the superbly intricate "The Artist of the Beautiful," published in the *Democratic* in 1844 but written around the time his first child was due, Hawthorne admixes sexuality and childbirth into a parable of art and artistry. The artist of the story's title is the watchmaker Owen Warland, renowned for the delicate ingenuity applied "always for purposes of grace, and never with any mockery of the useful." Loving "the Beautiful" and attempting to render a perfect depiction of it, "refined from all utilitarian coarseness," Owen might just as well have been a poet, a painter, or a sculptor, or so the story's narrator tells us. He might even have been Hawthorne, whose "demand is for perfection," said Sophia, "& noth-ing short can content him."

There is something self-centered about Owen, something infantile, insulated, and vain. With his diminutive frame, his ladylike fastidiousness, and his flapping nerves, Owen Warland is an effeminate anomaly in a world that gauges manliness, and hence productivity, by the girth of a blacksmith's big arm or the heft of his wallet.

When Annie Hovenden, whom Owen thinks he loves, marries the good-natured, thick-skinned blacksmith Robert Danforth, Owen becomes ill, gains weight, grows plump—after which episode he does eventually suc-ceed in crafting (giving birth) to a beautiful little thing, a mechanical but-terfly, perfect, lifelike, the consummation of his dreams. He brings his creation to Annie and Robert, themselves now the parents of a sturdy little child. The lovely butterfly flickers about the room, and just when it's ready to land, the child snatches it and crushes it in his little fist.

Owen is presumably defeated, his creation smashed, his butterfly vanquished not by Danforth or Annie or her scornful father but by a human child. Nature's real creation, suggests Hawthorne, threatens to overshadow, if not utterly destroy, the artist's.

After a winter of fierce cold, scant food, and little money, on March 3, 1844, Sophia Hawthorne endured ten hours of labor. She finally gave birth to a baby girl and named her Una, for Spenser's vision of purity. She had red hair.

CHAPTER THIRTEEN

Repatriation

Blessed are all simple emotions, be they dark or bright! It is the lurid intermixture of the two that produces the illuminating blaze of the infernal regions.

Nathaniel Hawthorne, "Rappaccini's Daughter"

A T ABOUT TEN O'CLOCK on the night of their third wedding anniversary, Nathaniel and Sophia Hawthorne were roused by a loud pounding at the front door. It was Ellery Channing, pale and upset. Something terrible had happened: a young woman had drowned herself in the Concord River. Her bonnet and shoes, neatly arranged, had been found on the shore. Hawthorne's boat was needed to dredge for the body.

With Channing at the oars and Hawthorne paddling, the men arrived downstream quickly. Several other townsmen had gathered, lanterns swinging, and two of them boarded Hawthorne's small boat. Hawthorne navigated, intermittently letting the boat drift while the men slowly combed the water with pronged hay rakes.

"I've got her," one man suddenly cried, and heaved his pole. In the brackish water Hawthorne saw the outline of a dress and then a body, half submerged, which the men towed to shore, banking it near a large tree. They held up their lanterns. Several men moved closer, but Hawthorne, startled, stood back. Blood oozed from the dead woman's nose and eyes. An old carpenter bent down to wipe away the thick streams, which seemed to keep flowing. One of the men fainted.

"Her arms had stiffened in the act of struggling; and were bent before her, with the hands clenched," Hawthorne later recalled. "And when the men tried to compose her figure, her arms would still return to that same position." One man had placed a large foot on her arm to force it down, but as soon as he'd moved his foot, the arm sprang back.

They wrapped her in an old quilt, and Hawthorne helped lift her onto a makeshift bier to carry her body to her father's house, a half mile down the hill. "I suppose one friend would have saved her," he fantasized; "but she died for want of sympathy—a severe penalty for having cultivated and refined herself out of the sphere of natural connections." In death as in life, he supposed, such is woman's clenched defiance—and her punishment.

Hurrying back to Sophia that unlit night, Hawthorne might easily have been warning himself against the perils of isolation. In the water he had seen a distorted image which, with stiffened arms and distended legs, spurned all Concord's pretty homilies of life and death: a poor lonely girl, homegrown expatriate, plunged beneath the river's veil.

Hawthorne knew nothing, really, of this woman, only that her name was Martha Hunt, that she was nineteen, the superintendent of a district school, and was said to be of "melancholic temperament," or so he noted, "and accustomed to solitary walks in the woods." Just like him.

After the birth of Una, Hawthorne's anxiety increased. "I find it is a very sober and serious kind of happiness that springs from the birth of a child," he confided to George Hillard. "It ought not to come too early in a man's life—not till he has fully enjoyed his youth—for methinks the spirit never can be thoroughly gay and careless again, after this great event."

It had been a difficult year. Guests to the Manse that summer admired the new baby—the daughter of a "holy and equal marriage," Fuller had purred—and tried not to notice the Hawthornes' poverty. The house was so pretty and clean, the child so affectionate, the hospitality so gracious. One could bring a gift as humble as a new potato or a baby's rattle and be treated like royalty.

Fuller colored the old gray Manse in ruddy prose, and if she saw the lines furrowing Hawthorne's brow, she didn't comment but instead reclined lazily in the *Pond-lily* and gazed moonward as he rowed. "I love him much," she wrote in her journal, "& love to be with him in this sweet tender homely scene. But I should like too, to be with him on the bold ocean shore." A single woman, depressed that summer and perennially disappointed by the men she liked, Fuller found in Hawthorne a companion "mild, deep and large." Together the two of them explored the twisted woodland paths near

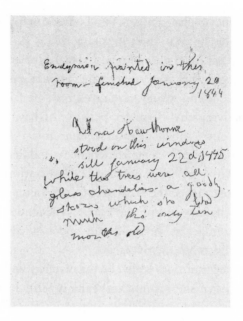

Window at the Manse,
inscribed by Sophia with a diamond

the Manse, getting lost and sharing confidences while Sophia stayed home with the baby. Trying to find words for their special relationship, Fuller uncannily settled on the fraternal image Sophia had once used: "I feel more like a sister to H. or rather more that he might be a brother to me than ever with any man before."

Hawthorne was troubled by his friendship with Fuller; he may have sensed that she thought him attractive, and he may have been attracted to her himself. He had found her intriguing at Brook Farm, though in an unquiet way. As quick as Ebe and as biting, as supportive as Elizabeth Peabody and as taxing, and as alone as Martha Hunt, Fuller embodied Hawthorne's idea of the modern woman—oppressed, confused, intelligent—who makes an appearance, nameless, in his 1844 story "The Christmas Banquet," another in the "Allegories of the Heart" series. "A woman of unemployed energy," Hawthorne describes her, "who found herself with nothing to achieve, nothing to enjoy, and nothing even to suffer. She had, therefore, driven herself to the verge of madness by dark broodings over the wrongs of her sex, and its exclusion from a proper field of action."

The characterization is Hawthorne's imaginative response to Fuller's *Dial* essay "The Great Lawsuit: Man versus Men; Woman versus Women," a first draft of the more provocative *Woman in the Nineteenth Century*. Fuller and Hawthorne agreed that "those [women] who would reform the world must show that they do not speak in heat of wild impulse," as Fuller writes; "their lives must be unstained by passionate error; they must be severe law-givers to themselves." Hawthorne sympathizes with the iconoclastic, heroic woman who poses a danger to herself or others. In fact, this modern woman stands at the center of "Rappaccini's Daughter," a story of tangled perceptions Hawthorne wrote shortly after Fuller's summertime visit.

Hawthorne observes his protagonist, Beatrice Rappaccini, from afar but knows her intimately, empathizing with her, identifying with her, and condemning her all at the same time. Her father, the renowned horticulturist Dr. Rappaccini, has raised her on a diet of poisonous plants in a poignant, stupid attempt to make her self-sufficient, and so she lives walled within his garden, strong, beautiful, but a danger to anyone not bred on the same poisons as she. Is she deadly? Hawthorne doesn't quite say. She is a threat to men, that's sure; and yet Hawthorne respects her, cursing himself, it seems, for fearing her, for desiring her: it's his version of the family romance.

Like most of Hawthorne's fiction, "Rappaccini's Daughter" is a biographical palimpsest. Dr. Rappaccini is Sophia's father and Waldo Emerson. (Concord busybodies said Lidian Emerson was poisoning herself with medicine extracted from several plants.) Rappaccini is also Fuller's father, whose stiff-backed education of Margaret was as destructive, if as well intentioned; he's Uncle Robert, another horticulturist of decided purpose; and he's Hawthorne, the father-gardener, who fusses over his wife's diet and her health. Yet Hawthorne erases most of his sources, even the discernible literary ones—his recent reading of Montaigne's essays, Eugène Sue's fiction, Frances Calderón de la Barca's *Life in Mexico,* and Shelley's *The Cenci.* "He has to contrive as hard to leave out as to put in," Sophia explained to her mother how her husband wrote his stories, "—& in every one, he circum-sails the universe for a true result."

For that "true result," Hawthorne typically settles on a single opaque image—a fire, a letter, a black veil, even a woman—around which he builds his plot. In "Rappaccini's Daughter," the image is of Beatrice in the garden; the plot concerns Giovanni Guasconti's attempt to determine her true character. Giovanni, a student, has fallen in love with Beatrice or thinks he has. Vain and shallow, Giovanni transfers his unspoken misgivings about himself onto her. "What is this being?—beautiful, shall I call her?" he stews, "—or inexpressibly terrible?" His landlady, Dame Lisabetta—Ebe?—helps feed his doubt, as does the vituperous Professor Baglioni, Dr. Rappaccini's archrival. And all of them conspire in the eventual death of Beatrice, destroyed by Giovanni's lack of faith. For like Aylmer of "The Birth-mark," Giovanni demands Beatrice drink a potion to purge her of evil. "Oh, was there not, from the first, more poison in thy nature than in mine?" Beatrice implores as she swallows the fatal draft. It's the story's central question. Destroyed like Aylmer's wife by irresolute men, Beatrice represents a woman's struggle to free herself from the Rappaccini-like garden in which she's confined.

What's a woman to do? "It somewhat startled me to overhear a number of ladies, highly respectable in appearance, proposing to fling their gowns and petticoats into the flames, and assume the garb, together with the manners, duties, offices, and responsibilities of the opposite sex," Hawthorne's narrator quips in the satire "Earth's Holocaust," about a bonfire set to purge the world of folly. The narrator is nervous, justly so: prior to overhearing these respectable ladies, he witnessed a neglected American author toss his pen and paper into the blaze. If women are wearing trousers, the narrator seems to ask, whatever will become of men, especially men of questionable manliness, like those who write for a living?

And so Hawthorne flays his weak male characters—Goodman Brown, Reuben Bourne, Roderick Elliston, Giovanni; they are repressed, insecure, cold, and self-deceived. But not necessarily Monsieur de l'Aubépine (Hawthorne), the prodigious, unknown, and fictitious French writer that Hawthorne pretends to be the "real" author of "Rappaccini's Daughter." In Hawthorne's short preface to the story, he claims to have translated de l'Aubépine's story, and with this gimmick he transforms "Rappaccini's Daughter" into one of those found objects, like Grandfather's chair, he likes to pretend he's stumbled upon. Alas, poor Monsieur de l'Aubépine, Hawthorne opines, that neglected author of *Contes Deux Fois Racontées* [*sic*] and such recent work as "L'Artiste du Beau; ou, Le Papillon Mécanique," published in *La Revue Anti-Aristocratique:* "As a writer, he seems to occupy an unfortunate position between the Transcendentalists (who, under one name or another, have their share in all the current literature of the world), and the great body of pen-and-ink men who address the intellect and sympathies of the multitude."

Neither fish nor fowl, transcendentalist nor popular pen-and-ink man, Monsieur de l'Aubépine is Hawthorne's derelict romancer, a writer of nonsense—in French, no less. (Irked by the novels of Charles Paul de Kock, which she hadn't read, Sophia put the matter squarely. "I think France is the most corrupt of all cultivated nations.")

Monsieur de l'Aubépine: foreign, a bit disreputable, and an acquired taste. What else can a scribbler without a niche hope to be?

Poverty.

It picked Hawthorne out of his study and dropped him into the kitchen, the writer as scullery maid. "My husband's time is taken up with housewifery," Sophia told her mother. "We have no woman yet, because Nathaniel feels as if he could not afford to pay one just now, & it is an ease to his mind to have as few expenses as possible." Rising before dawn, he lit the fire, took his fishing pole to the river, and then returned to prepare breakfast and wash the dishes. "He actually does everything," Sophia said.

To help, John O'Sullivan, Una's godfather, suggested Hawthorne buy the unsold copies of *Twice-told Tales* (six hundred sets) and reissue them through O'Sullivan's brother-in-law, Henry Langley, current publisher of the *Democratic Review*. O'Sullivan offered to raise the money himself. Cautiously, Hawthorne agreed. "I wish Heaven would make me rich enough to buy the copies for the purpose of burning them," he said. The plan lurched forward without much success until O'Sullivan approached James Munroe with the same offer (to raise money for the unsold volumes, undertaking the financial risk himself). But when Munroe finally reissued the books, there was no profit for Hawthorne.

He tried to work off his debts by selling apples, potatoes, and grass but earned just a few dollars after applying the rest to his rent. His only chance at a real income was another government job. Otherwise he was sure to end in the almshouse.

"My husband says that he will consent to cease to be kitchen-maid since Polk is chosen," Sophia remarked after the election. Since Louisa had heard a political appointment might be afoot, the Hawthornes decided it was a good time to show off Una in Salem while Nathaniel made himself available to local Democratic chieftains. No offers came. Instead the pastor of the First Church, Charles Wentworth Upham, circulated embarrassing stories about Hawthorne's indigence.

Demeaned and despondent, Hawthorne wanted to get back to Concord as soon as possible, "else we shall be said to have run away from our creditors," he told Sophia. "GOD gives us all that is eternal worth," she reassured him. "Sweetest husband—has He put a very heavy yoke on us?"

Though happy in marriage and fatherhood—"I am a husband!—I am a father!"—Hawthorne despaired; he couldn't provide for his little circle. "At any rate, something satisfactory *shall be done* for you," O'Sullivan kept encouraging. He asked Evert Duyckinck, now literary editor of the *New York Morning News,* to write an article on Hawthorne for the *Democratic,* and suggested Hawthorne sit for a daguerreotype. "By manufacturing you thus into a Personage, I want to raise your mark higher in Polk's administration," O'Sullivan explained.

Hawthorne, daguerreotype by John Adams Whipple [1845? 1848?]

A daguerreotype taken around this time captures the hunger in Hawthorne's gaunt face, the body taut and poised for flight. "A man in the midst of all sorts of cares and annoyances—with impossibilities to perform—and almost driven distracted by his inadequacy," Hawthorne confided to his notebook. O'Sullivan heard the cry. "Hawthorne is in a state of extreme anxiety, not to say, distress," he informed George Bancroft in the spring of 1845. But Hawthorne's name didn't sit well among Democrats, several of whom alleged the writer hadn't so much as voted during his two years in Concord.

Bancroft fiddled. Positions at the Watertown Arsenal, the Cambridge post office, the Chelsea Hospital, the naval store in Portsmouth, New Hampshire—all came and went. In April, Duyckinck's essay on Hawthorne appeared in the *Democratic.* "The poet lives and starves," Duyckinck accused, recommending that a Literary Pension Fund be established for writers. "The principle has been already recognized by our Government." Duyckinck named the government posts occupied by Washington Irving, Alexander Everett, even the mighty Bancroft himself, now Polk's Secretary of the Navy. Still nothing.

O'Sullivan was frantic. "Hawthorne is dying of starvation," he exploded in May.

That month two ministers of providence, as Sophia called them, arrived in Concord. Horatio Bridge and Franklin Pierce waltzed up the long avenue to the Manse, waving their hats in the air, come to buck up their pinched and harried friend. A job would be forthcoming, they soothed, their arms tightly wound around the rawboned writer. Bridge loaned him one hundred dollars, and Pierce begged Bancroft to send Hawthorne to the Salem post office. No reply.

O'Sullivan was livid. "It sounds badly that something fitting & worthy was asked for in vain for such a man as Hawthorne!" Bills unpaid, rent owing, Hawthorne realized he'd have to vacate the Manse.

Where to go?

Bancroft proposed an assignment in the West Indies. O'Sullivan scoffed at such "Robinson Crusoe solitude of Santa Rosa Island, away from the civilization of New England, for a pittance barely adequate, at the highest sum, to support life."

As Hawthorne's most vociferous ambassador, O'Sullivan worked tirelessly on his behalf. Countering Bancroft's absurd offer, he suggested Hawthorne be sent to the Custom House in Salem, and if the position could be managed, O'Sullivan volunteered to take care of Hawthorne himself in the interim. "There could not possibly be a better appointment in itself—one more popular with all parties—more creditable to the P[resident] & to you—more contentedly acquiesced in by rival candidates," O'Sullivan coaxed, "—and by making the promise in advance, all the difficulties are obviated of subsequent judgment between competing claims."

In August, Bancroft responded. He offered Hawthorne the clerkship at the Charlestown Navy Yard for nine hundred dollars a year. Hawthorne rejected it.

"Such is his character," O'Sullivan defended his friend, "—he would rather live on a mouldy crust than take a place below his dignity & conscious claims."

Bancroft must have been furious.

For then there was an even longer silence.

Longfellow had also approached Evert Duyckinck about a job for Hawthorne in New York. About to launch a semijingoistic project, the Library of American Books, and another venture, the Library of Choice Reading, for the publishers Wiley and Putnam, Duyckinck was flexing the literary arm of Young America. The radical wing of the Democratic Party, Young America was the antidote to Whiggish transcendentalism: libertarian, imperialistic, shortsighted, and short-lived, it backed bank reform, low tariffs, copyright reform, workingmen, and American authors. Its de facto political leader was John O'Sullivan; its literary representative, the slim New York bibliophile Evert Duyckinck, who owned one of the largest private libraries in America.

Though he had no job for Hawthorne, Duyckinck immediately recruited him to write something for the new series. Declining, Hawthorne said he had nothing to contribute himself but instead offered up Horatio Bridge's travel journal, which he'd been editing. Bridge had been serving as purser under the command of Matthew C. Perry on the USS *Saratoga,* whose mission was to patrol the African coast to suppress the illegal slave trade. Hawthorne had suggested Bridge keep a record of his experiences, which Hawthorne would help publish on Bridge's return. Bridge would pay $125 and sign over the copyrights to Hawthorne. Hawthorne would receive all profits.

The project could be a godsend. Democrats had been challenging Hawthorne's commitment to the party, and with Bancroft dragging his feet about an appointment, Bridge's memoir could bolster Hawthorne's credentials, particularly since Bridge had much to say on the slavery problem. In fact, his support of colonization as the solution to the slavery question might actually placate antislavery Democrats and pacify southern ones at the same time.

Established in 1816 by associates of Matthew Perry's family, the American Colonization Society offered emancipated slaves passage to Africa. The proposal appealed to men like Hawthorne and Bridge and even the young Abraham Lincoln, men averse both to slavery and to any action organized to end it. To them, emancipation, if it was to occur at all, must occur gradually—and somewhere else. That colonization had been blasted as segregationist and racist by antislavery's evangelist William Lloyd Garrison did not dissuade them. Rather, they figured that a nonviolent repatriation of displaced Africans promised opportunities under the law that could never exist in America. "In this point of view—as restoring to him his long-lost birthright of equality—Liberia may indeed be called the black man's paradise," Horatio Bridge wrote. Or Nathaniel Hawthorne, his editor, did.

In the acrimonious climate of 1845, colonization was a quaint idea, out of the question. Western Democrats bent on expansion and southerners wishing to extend slavery into the territories had been pushing hard to annex Texas. When Democratic presidential contender Martin Van Buren opposed annexation, he lost his party's nomination to James K. Polk, a Tennessee slaveholder. But when Polk proceeded to move toward Texas and open southern territory to slavery, John Quincy Adams, a Whig, managed to lift the congressional gag order that had blocked a slavery debate since 1834. Pandora's box was finally open.

"My husband says he has not wholly thought out the subject of the annexation of Texas," Sophia answered her mother's anxious inquiries, "but he does not think it such a calamity as many do." Sophia's remarks suggest she was trying to mollify Mrs. Peabody, a staunch Conscience (antislavery) Whig. "He says he should be glad of the separation of the South from the North, for then he should feel as if he had a country, which he can never do while that weight of slavery hangs on our skirts. He does not believe it will make any difference about perpetuating Slavery."

According to Sophia, Hawthorne didn't—couldn't—approve of slavery in America, but he didn't think annexation a "calamity," believing or hoping that slavery would wither on the vine when it inched into the far reaches of Mexico, where it wouldn't last, or where its existence didn't bother him. This was O'Sullivan's position. As the slave's labor "becomes less and less valuable," O'Sullivan charged in the *Democratic Review,* "emancipation, gradual, progressive, at last universal, will pass him over the Southern border to his more appropriate home in Mexico and the States beyond." Slavery would crawl to its inevitable end sometime, say, in 1926.

Elizabeth Peabody later insisted that Hawthorne "knew *nothing* about slavery," but he had actually been meditating on it for some time. In his 1835 sketch "Old News," Hawthorne's narrator calls slavery "a patriarchal, and almost a beautiful, peculiarity" of colonial days, observing that many emancipated slaves "would have been better advised had they staid at home, foddering the cattle, cleaning dishes—in fine, performing their moderate share of the labors of life without being harassed by its cares." Freedom is more difficult than bondage, Hawthorne's ridiculous narrator implies, romanticizing the slavery system almost as if it were a prototype of Brook Farm.

Whether the narrator speaks for Hawthorne is debatable. Certainly Hawthorne liked to hedge his bets, and his narrators are frequently the butt of his irony. But in a passage Hawthorne omitted when the story was reprinted in 1851, his narrator blandly anticipates Bridge's similar observation in *Journal of an African Cruiser:* "Slavery, as it existed in New-England, was precisely the state most favorable to the humble enjoyments of an alien race, generally incapable of self-direction, and whose claims to kindness will never be acknowledged by the whites, while they are asserted on the ground of equality."

If racial equality and emancipation are unthinkable, then colonization makes sense. "When the white man sets his foot on the shore of Africa, he finds it necessary to throw off his former prejudices," Bridge writes in *Journal of an African Cruiser*. ". . . In another city, where I might be known to few, should I follow the dictates of my head and heart, and there treat these colored men as brethren and equals, it would imply the exercise of greater moral courage than I have ever been conscious of possessing. This is sad; but it shows forcibly what the colored races have to struggle against in America, and how vast an advantage is gained by removing them to another soil."

Though Hawthorne failed to sympathize with any nonwhite population, he nonetheless despised the slave trade, which implicated both North and South. Emerson remarked that the American flag was sewn with cotton threads, and as Bridge points out in his *Journal,* "It is quite an interesting moral question, however, how far either Old or New England can be pronounced free from the guilt and odium of the slave-trade, while, with so little indirectness, they both share its profits and contribute essential aid to its prosecution." Again Bridge sounds like Hawthorne.

Journal of an African Cruiser, then, reflects sentiment of long standing: that northern states are complicit in the slave trade; that Africans, and especially African-Americans, are childlike creatures; that the white man, the flower of civilization, is a hypocritical brute. When Hawthorne read Bridge's account of how sailors from the *Saratoga* burned native villages and shot the villagers in retaliation for the death of an American trading schooner's crew, Hawthorne trembled with anger. "A civilized and educated man must feel somewhat like a fool, methinks, when he has staked his own life against that of a black savage, and lost the game," he sardonically informed Bridge. "In the sight of God, one life may be as valuable as another, but in our view, the stakes are very unequal. Besides, I really do consider the shooting of these niggers but of very questionable propriety; and am glad, upon the whole, that you bagged no game on either of those days. It is a far better deed to beget a white fellow-creature," he concluded, "than to shoot even a black one."

The incident appears in Bridge's book. Hawthorne comments in the self-mocking deadpan of his tales and sketches:

> Though the burning of villages may be a very pretty pastime, yet it leaves us in a moralizing mood, as most pleasures are apt to do; and one would fain hope that civilized man, in his controversies with the barbarian, will at length cease to descend to the barbarian level, and may adopt some other method of proving his superiority, than by his greater power to inflict suffering. For myself, personally, the "good old way" suits me tolerably enough; but I am disinterestedly anxious that posterity should find a better.

Published in June of 1845, two thousand copies in its first edition, *Journal of an African Cruiser* appeared the same month as the *Narrative of the Life of Frederick Douglass, an American Slave.* The *Narrative,* not the *Journal,* became an international sensation.

Emerson, who shrugged off Hawthorne's poverty—everyone's in debt, he said—now dispatched Caroline Sturgis to the Manse as an unofficial boarder. Hawthorne refused to take her money.

Frantic he couldn't pay for the trip, Hawthorne took Sophia and Una to Portsmouth, New Hampshire, to see Bridge, now supervisor of the Navy Yard there, who said he'd introduce Hawthorne to friends variously placed in the government and sure to help him get a government job.

Desperate for cash, Hawthorne sued George Ripley—do it "promptly and forcibly," he instructed Hillard—to recover the down payment he'd made on his Brook Farm house, a note for $530 plus interest. Hawthorne eventually won the suit, though not until the following year, and it's doubtful that he ever collected the money ($585.90) granted by the court.

And the Hawthornes had been evicted. This was polite Concord, so they were told their landlord, the Reverend Samuel Ripley, wanted his house back. "We are actually turned out of roof & home," Sophia sobbed.

The truth was that they had not paid the rent in a very long time.

Sophia wrapped up their frayed clothes, the coffeepot, the mattress, the crockery, a looking glass, and all her sadness about leaving the Manse. "I have got weaned from it, however, gradually, by the perplexities that have vexed my husband's soul for the last year, & have really made the spot painful to him."

Uncertain as wandering Arabs, said Hawthorne, he and his family left the gray parsonage, unsure where their tent might next be pitched. Fortunately, O'Sullivan delivered one hundred dollars of the money he owed Hawthorne for his contributions to the *Democratic,* and with Bridge loaning another sum ($150 now, $100 the previous May), Hawthorne was at least able to ride out of Concord "with flying colors," as he put it, on the second of October.

They headed to Herbert Street. They had nowhere else to go. The spare rooms at the Peabody home had been rented. So Nathaniel took his old chamber, and Sophia and Una rented a front room on the lower floor, sixteen by sixteen and nine feet high, right below the Hawthorne parlor. They paid Uncle William Manning, who owned the house, ten dollars each quarter. Sophia was grateful. "I besieged Heaven with prayers that we might not find it our duty to separate, whatever privations we must awkwardly suffer in consequence of remaining together."

Restored to his bedroom, the forty-one-year-old Hawthorne must have seen his homecoming as the defeat it was. Once more he'd come back to Salem, a deflated storyteller seeking shelter under his mother's roof.

"Here I am again established in the old chamber where I wasted so many years of my life," he confided to Bridge, reverting to the old refrain. But as of old, there were compensations. "I find it rather favorable to my literary duties," he added.

Placing a quire of paper on his desk, Hawthorne began to write, borne back into the past. This time, though, his subject was the gray parsonage, drenched in memory's afterglow. It wouldn't be easy.

———

CHAPTER FOURTEEN

Salem Recidivus

"We public men," replies the showman, meekly, "must lay our account, sometimes, to meet an uncandid severity of criticism."

Nathaniel Hawthorne, "Main-street"

I AM TURNED OUT of office!" Hawthorne was horrified. It had taken almost two years to get his government post, and now he'd lost it.

Hawthorne's appointment as surveyor of the Salem Custom House finally came in March 1846, five months after the Hawthornes had returned to Salem. Prominent Democrats had been besieging Polk. The chairman of the Essex County Democratic Committee had written the president; so had Senator John Fairfield of Maine and Franklin Pierce and the publishers of the *Salem Advertiser,* who praised Hawthorne as a pure and primitive Democrat, a phrase likely intended as a compliment. Friends like William Pike, Hawthorne's crony in the Boston Custom House, and Horace Conolly, now chairman of the second congressional district committee, argued that Hawthorne's appointment would heal party rifts in Salem. Even Benjamin Browne, whose job at the Salem post office Hawthorne had tried to steal, threw his support to the writer. In gratitude, Hawthorne edited Browne's "Papers of an Old Dartmoor Prisoner" for the *Democratic Review.* "I have grown considerable of a politician by the experience of the last few months," Hawthorne sheepishly declared in early March.

Nor did Whigs oppose Hawthorne's candidacy. George Hillard backed Hawthorne, and Charles Sumner pleaded with Elizabeth Bancroft: "Poor Hawthorne (that sweet, gentle, true nature) has not wherewithal to live."

It was true. With Sophia pregnant again, the baby due in the spring of

1846, Hawthorne was almost frantic. "What a devil of a pickle I shall be in," he told Bridge, "if the baby should come, and the office should not!" His suit against Ripley had not been tried, so he couldn't anticipate any cash from that direction, and though the publishers sent him a small royalty from the second edition of *Journal of an African Cruiser,* he still owed Bridge money.

And he couldn't write. On Herbert Street, he struggled over a preface for a new collection of short stories that Evert Duyckinck, inspired by O'Sullivan, had solicited on behalf of Wiley and Putnam's Library of American Books. Nothing materialized. Frustrated, Duyckinck goaded the dilatory author. "MSS! MSS! Mr. Wiley's American series is athirst for a volume of Tales."

The past year had chipped away at his confidence. He answered Duyckinck, apologetic. "I have reached that point in an author's life, when he ceases to effervesce; and whatever I do hereafter must be done with leaden reluctance, and therefore had better be left undone."

Overlooking the self-pity, Duyckinck suggested Hawthorne expand the collection to two volumes. Hawthorne appreciated the offer, particularly since he didn't think he'd be writing any more stories: self-pity again, but understandable. "It is rather a sad idea," he said, "—not that I am to write no more in this kind, but that I cannot better justify myself for having written at all."

Then, in March, Hawthorne learned he'd been appointed surveyor at the Salem Custom House. His salary—twelve hundred dollars per year plus incidental fees—was modest but allowed for some luxuries, and besides, the job itself entailed no great expenditure of time. His mood considerably brightened, and on April 9, 1846, Hawthorne swore the oath of office fully expecting to be able to write and free himself at last from debt. Six days later he sent the preface "The Old Manse" to Duyckinck, overdue by almost a year.

"The Old Manse" is an elegiac evocation of time past and passing, for the Manse itself had come to represent a last summer in the haze, lovely, enchanted, doomed to slide into the meaner seasons of obligation and middle age.

"Ah," writes Hawthorne, "but there is a half-acknowledged melancholy, like to this, when we stand in the perfected vigor of our life, and feel that

Time has now given us all his flowers, and that the next work of his never idle fingers must be—to steal them, one by one, away!"

The Manse is another of Hawthorne's old houses, fragrant with the spirit of former tenants and, perched on the banks of the past, fit emblem of his imagination. In the Manse, one is not compelled, Hawthorne explains, to "subserve some useful purpose." Rather, the writer fishes in the nearby river, picks apples from his orchard, and on a rainy day pokes around a garret stocked with Latin folios and old books bound in black leather. From the upstairs window of his study he dreams of bygone soldiers near the North Bridge, battle smoke barely dispersed in the wind. And he mulls over a tale he heard about a young woodchopper who, happening upon a wounded British soldier, splits his head with an ax for no apparent reason. Out of such stuff are stories made.

Days at the Manse float on a cloud of leisure, fantasy, and lazy liberty. But the inhabitant of the Manse has matured into a man of regret. He never wrote a novel or produced any great work while living there. "The treasure of intellectual gold, which I hoped to find in our secluded dwelling," Hawthorne admits, "had never come to light. No profound treatise of ethics—no philosophic history—no novel, even, that could stand, unsupported on its edges. All that I had to show, as a man of letters, were these few tales and essays, which had blossomed out like flowers in the calm summer of my heart and mind. Save editing (an easy task) the journal of my friend of many years, the African Cruiser, I had done nothing else."

For his sin, the writer is expelled from the Manse and cast into a world of smiling public men in another edifice, the Custom House. "As a storyteller, I have often contrived strange vicissitudes for my imaginary personages," he grins, "but none like this."

Hawthorne doesn't say—he can't say—that he'd maneuvered ceaselessly for this new berth or that the honeymoon years at the Manse may have been conceived from the start as a vacation forced on him by a hostile administration. Nor would he admit that he could never tolerate Eden for too long anyway, or that the Salem Custom House was a retreat no less than the Manse, and not just from economic privation but from the agonies of literature.

On June 5 Hawthorne's new collection, *Mosses from an Old Manse,* was published in two volumes, sold individually or as a set, the title stamped in gold on the spine. In addition to the preface, the collection contained most of the stories written at the parsonage along with "Young Goodman Brown" and "Roger Malvin's Burial," reprinted at last. "I am jogging onward in life, with a moderate share of prosperity," he wrote to Bridge, "and am contented and happy." Life was good again.

Hoping to earn more money and broaden his readership, Hawthorne sent advance copies to Margaret Fuller in New York, where she wrote for Horace Greeley's *New-York Daily Tribune,* as well as to Edgar Allan Poe, Henry Tuckerman, and Rufus Griswold, the tubercular editor of *Graham's.* The response was mostly favorable. Notices in *Graham's Magazine* and the *Harbinger* complimented the book, with William Henry Channing emphasizing Hawthorne's tragic vision: "No masks deceive him. And plainly, the mockeries of life have cost him sleepless nights and lonely days." Lest Hawthorne's reputation as a Democrat nettle readers, Charles Wilkins Webber, writing in the *American Whig Review,* recommended *Mosses* as "the specific remedy for all those congestions of patriotism which relieve themselves in uttering speeches."

In her large review, posted on the front page of the *Tribune,* Margaret Fuller refused to give a full-throttled endorsement to Hawthorne's work; this, after her hesitant review of *Twice-told Tales,* may account for the chill soon to settle over her friendship with the Hawthornes. Commending stories like "The Birth-mark," "Rappaccini's Daughter," and "Young Goodman Brown," she nonetheless found Hawthorne's style "placid" and his command of language "indolent." The coup de grâce: "Hawthorne intimates and suggests, but he does not lay bare the mysteries of our being."

Eight years after Fuller's premature death, Hawthorne retaliated with vitriolic pleasure. Writing in his notebooks in 1858, he characterized his former friend as lacking "the charm of womanhood" and a humbug, talented, yes, but arrogantly determined to "make herself the greatest, wisest, best woman of the age; and to that end, she set to work on her strong, heavy, unpliable and, in many respects, defective and evil nature, and adorned it with a mosaic of admirable qualities, such as she chose to possess." Continuing for pages, he savored his own portrait of the woman he once cared for: "But she was not working on an inanimate substance, like marble or clay; there was something within her that she could not possibly come at, to re-create and refine it; and by and by this rude old potency bestirred itself, and undid all her labor in the twinkling of an eye. On the whole, I do not know but I like her the better for it;—the better, because she proved herself a very woman, after all, and fell as the weakest of her sisters might."

Hawthorne rewrote Margaret Fuller's life, the ambitious guest as fallen woman.

Fuller wasn't alone in criticizing Hawthorne's work. Edgar Allan Poe liked Hawthorne's precision and fluency but not the hermetic, rarified quality of the stories. Scorning the New England drawing rooms and the dainty prose applauded there, Poe tendered his advice: "Get a bottle of visible ink, come out from the Old Manse, cut Mr. Alcott, hang (if possible) the editor of *The Dial,* and throw out of the window to the pigs all his odd numbers of *The North American Review.*"

With Texas admitted into the Union in December 1845, James K. Polk ordered American troops, led by Zachary Taylor, to cross the border into Mexico. To John Quincy Adams, the invasion was morally reprehensible, but to John O'Sullivan, America was simply spreading freedom and democracy, like spilled ink, over the continent. O'Sullivan wanted no bloodshed, but Polk didn't seem to mind and in the spring of 1846 declared all-out war.

That same spring, Hawthorne was climbing the wide granite staircase

Hawthorne's office, Salem Custom House

Salem Custom House, erected 1819, Derby Street

of the Salem Custom House, a massive brick building that overlooked the ocean, its small windowed cupola bright on a sunny morning and with a huge gilt eagle, arrows and thunderbolts in each claw, poised to take flight from its roof. Each morning, Hawthorne entered the arched doorway at about ten o'clock, looked at the morning papers, and swapped stories with the custom officers, chairs tipped back, until the ships arrived.

He liked his new life and joked to George Curtis, former Brook Farmer and Concord resident, that he'd use the Custom House barge as a private yacht. Ellery Channing came to visit, watching in awe as Hawthorne tread the docks, proof glass in hand, and tested the strength of the rum to be exported to the African coast. Natives shall have "as good liquor as anybody gets from New England," the new surveyor insisted. Just as often, though, the docks were empty and there was nothing to do. The officers hung around, talking, smoking, reading the papers. Hawthorne might write a couple of letters until one o'clock, when he descended the Custom House steps and walked home to Herbert Street.

For the last months of her pregnancy, Sophia had taken Una and gone to

Boston to the home of Sophia's sister Mary and her husband, Horace Mann. (Mary had married Mann in 1844.) The Manns were in Wrentham for the summer, where Horace's sister lived. Hawthorne too stayed at the Mann's place at 77 Carver Street, commuting to work on the railroad, disembarking in Salem and then going over to Herbert Street, where he bathed and break-fasted before his duties began. It was inconvenient but good for Sophia: near Back Bay, Carver Street was also near Mrs. Peabody and Sophia's solicitous homeopath, Dr. William Wesselhoeft, as well as far from the Hawthorne women. Sophia tolerated Louisa but felt nervous around Ebe, who lavished too much attention on Una from Sophia's point of view, sneaking the girl candy and allowing her, against Sophia's distinct instructions, to pad into Mrs. Hawthorne's chilly, uncarpeted room. And the Hawthornes had even brought their airtight stoves with them; it was time to move.

On June 22, 1846, just after sunrise, Sophia gave birth to a baby boy. Called the Black Prince by his father for his dark curls and apple-red cheeks, Julian was not named for almost six months, by which time he'd been car-ried back to Salem and its best neighborhood. But the house and yard at 18 Chestnut Street were cramped, and as soon as the air blew cold, the Hawthornes huddled indoors, banging into one another. Hawthorne, who had no study, complained he couldn't write. He couldn't afford to move either, his expenses in Boston having been greater than he'd anticipated, his Custom House fees less. Salem shipping was in its final death throe.

Hawthorne had to borrow money to pay off the rent he still owed for the Manse. Sophia owned few dresses and no warm coat, and when the Hawthornes did finally move into a bigger place in the fall of 1847, they refrained from decorating the downstairs parlor and the guest room because they had no money for furniture. Nonetheless, Sophia was pleased. "This small income that comes from external business is far better than our for-mer income which was coined out of fine imaginings & profound searching thoughts," she declared. "That gold always seemed to me too precious to spend for earthly goods & the pressure upon the brain was too great."

The sunny three-story house at 14 Mall Street was large enough to accommodate Hawthorne's mother and sisters, who may have moved there to help Hawthorne economize, if he was now paying their rent, or to free them from Uncle William. Sophia now claimed not to mind. The Hawthornes were too polite to get underfoot. And she was genuinely grate-ful her husband could finally establish himself in a study on the third floor, "as quiet up there as if among the stars," Sophia observed, "& still, yet within my reach." It had been nearly a year since he'd touched his desk, she said. "He—the poet, the waiter upon the Muse—the heaven gifted seer—to spend his life in the Custom-house & Nursery!"

As a matter of fact, Hawthorne had been writing, albeit sporadically, publishing occasional reviews in the *Salem Advertiser*, mainly of books in Duyckinck's series. Work for the *Democratic Review* had all but dried up since O'Sullivan had married and sold it, so Hawthorne asked Longfellow to alert him to opportunities "to add something to my income." And when he repaid a loan from Francis Shaw, the philanthropist who helped finance Brook Farm, he similarly asked Shaw to keep him apprised of opportunities for work, probably editorial.

Yet Hawthorne strolled Salem streets with a swelling sense of accomplishment, and no doubt he appreciated the irony of his position: by scribbling tales in his lonely bedroom, he'd won a political appointment and, indirectly, a wife and children. He was also secretary of the Salem Lyceum, and he invited to Salem speakers from Daniel Webster to Henry Thoreau. He himself declined invitations, however, especially from Salem's gentry. Conscious of his rising social cachet, he was confident enough to defy it. "His taste was more democratic than aristocratic," a Salem writer commented; "he preferred gin to champagne." Aristocratic Salem felt the snub.

Local Democrats capitalized on Hawthorne's association with the party. They submitted Hawthorne's name as a member of the Democratic Town Committee and advertised him as a delegate to the state party convention. That he did not attend these functions was of no real concern; his name reflected glory. And though he contributed what few reviews he wrote mainly to the *Salem Advertiser*, the Democratic paper, Hawthorne billed himself as "high & dry out of the slough of political warfare," or so Sophia alleged to Mary Mann. ". . . He took his office because it was presented to him, but not a word or look would he be persuaded to give for it as a pledge of action."

Mary's husband had also entered government service. After the death of John Quincy Adams, Horace Mann had been elected to complete Adams's term in Congress, and the following fall, 1848, Mann ran for the seat himself, backed by a coalition of Cotton (proslavery) and Conscience Whigs. The Manns and the Hawthornes disagreed on political matters, especially slavery; like the Hawthornes, the Manns weren't abolitionist but they did want to stop the extension of slavery and to meliorate the condition of the slave as rapidly, and legally, as possible.

Waiting for her husband to return from Washington, Mary Mann provided room and board to Chloe Lee, an African-American student refused lodging everywhere else. Sophia appreciated Mary's "Christian motive" but protested loudly when Mary invited Miss Lee to dinner. Unthinkable. "I think your white guests have rights as well as your black one," Sophia seethed. "I could scarcely eat my supper, so intolerable was the odor wafting from her to me." Black skin, as she pointed out to her benighted sister, "is the one natural barrier between the races."

Of her husband's response to this or similar episodes, Sophia said nothing. Nor does Hawthorne himself offer his own account of the dinner. But Rose Hawthorne, having heard of the Chloe Lee incident, would recall that "once, at the table of Horace Mann, he [her father] was expected to sit down to dinner with a Negro slave. He did; but that table lost its attractiveness for him, thenceforth."

In his third-floor study at Mall Street, away from the racket and the merciless baby linen, Hawthorne wrote every afternoon.

"When shall you want another article?" Hawthorne asked Charles Wilkins Webber at the end of 1848. Webber was starting a new magazine, the *American Review.* "Now that the spell is broken, I hope to get into a regular train of scribbling."

It's likely he sent Webber "The Unpardonable Sin," later known as "Ethan Brand," the story of a man who searches everywhere to discover the worst mankind can do. Elizabeth Peabody had rejected the tale as too morose for her own journal, *Aesthetic Papers;* Henry Thoreau's lecture "Resistance to Civil Government" (subsequently titled "Civil Disobedience") was more to her taste. So Hawthorne substituted "Main-street," a historical overview of Salem told by a showman-artist who exhibits scenes from the past with a turn of a mechanical crank: one rotation and William Hathorne orders the whipping of the Quaker Ann Coleman, ten stripes in Salem, ten in Boston, and ten in Dedham; two turns and the Salem witches march up Main Street to Gallows Hill. Hawthorne's Salem forebears were on the loose again.

Hawthorne was composing quite a bit. When he came downstairs after a stint of writing, he brought his journal with him to record the movements of his children. Una was of special interest. Mercurial and alternately imperious and gentle, affectionate and tempestuous, she scampered helpfully about the house until reprimanded, and then she threw herself against the walls, uncontrollable. If her parents locked her in a room, she emerged sassy and willful. "In short, I now and then catch an aspect of her," Hawthorne writes, "in which I cannot believe her to be my own human child, but a spirit strangely mingled with good and evil, haunting the house where I dwell." By contrast, Julian was steady, good-natured, forgettable: "The little boy is always the same child, and never varies in his relation to me." But Una reflected back her father's turmoil, his ambition, his frustration, even his ennui. "I'm tired of little Una Hawsorne," the child cried.

Wondering if this child was beautiful or terrible—the same question Giovanni had posed in "Rappaccini's Daughter"—Hawthorne would change Una into Pearl, the illegitimate daughter of Hester Prynne, a spritelike, demonic girl, source both of salvation and of bleak terror.

If Una stirred Hawthorne's imagination, so did Elizabeth Peabody's newest protégé, Dr. Charles Kraitsir, a Hungarian linguist whose theory was that language, functioning as an image of the human mind, reveals the essential unity of all peoples. "If it [language] is Babel," Kraitsir wrote, "it is because men have abandoned themselves to chance, and lost sight of the principle by which language was constructed." In 1846 Peabody had published his knotty pamphlet, *Significance of the Alphabet,* and in *Aesthetic Papers* tried hopelessly to explain his theory.

The alphabet and language—the letter "A," in fact—would be a theme of *The Scarlet Letter,* though Hawthorne is less interested in the origin of language than in its manifold interpretations. People may be alike, but when they express themselves, the results are often perplexing and ambiguous, as he suggests, sending Pearl's skulking father into the night where he sees the letter "A" emblazoned across the sky, his guilt writ large. "But what shall we say," Hawthorne reasons, "when an individual discovers a revelation, addressed to himself alone, on the same vast sheet of record! In such a case, it would only be the symptom of a highly disordered mental state, when a man, rendered morbidly self-contemplative by long, intense, and secret pain, had extended his egotism over the whole expanse of nature, until the firmament itself should appear no more than a fitting page for his soul's history and fate."

As Hawthorne mulled over ideas soon to become *The Scarlet Letter,* Kraitsir's theories were ultimately of less interest to him than the salacious details of the man's domestic life: a loveless marriage, an abandoned wife, and the hapless daughter that Elizabeth Peabody, in her headlong way, decided to rescue.

To Peabody, Kraitsir leaped directly from the pages of *Jane Eyre;* he was Mr. Rochester dogged by an uncaged Bertha, for Kraitsir's wife was the incurable madwoman who, according to Peabody, "has broken all the commandments," meaning she seduced several students while Kraitsir was teaching at the University of Virginia. "I wonder he do not divorce himself from a woman who has dishonored him," Sophia marveled with reason. He did not. Instead Kraitsir quit his job, deposited his wife and daughter in Philadelphia, and settled himself in Boston, where he thrived under Elizabeth Peabody's protection, quaking, claimed Peabody, lest the crazy Mrs. Kraitsir rush into his new classroom one day, shiny knife in hand.

Peabody figured she could free Kraitsir of his troubles by assuming guardianship of the child, and with this delirious scheme in mind, she boarded a train for Philadelphia, a flurry of skirts, to inform Mrs. Kraitsir of her plan. The meeting was a disaster. Incensed, Mrs. Kraitsir followed Peabody back to Boston, where Peabody and Kraitsir tried to have her committed to the McLean Asylum. Mrs. Kraitsir rallied friends; the friends rallied the press.

Cited as the third party in a failing marriage, Peabody found herself at the center of a sensational storm. "Every body seems to think Dr. Kraitsir very dilatory, weak, even craven not to justify himself & Elizabeth by the

Elizabeth Palmer Peabody [1850s]

revelation of the whole," Sophia tartly told her mother. Former supporters of Peabody averted their eyes while the penny press made a pretty penny, Peabody said, at her expense. "Though everybody respectable take our part," she claimed, "they do not come out in the newspapers, because this is vulgar they think."

Her name pilloried, her honor questioned, Peabody did not bow her head. She refused to exonerate herself in a public statement. "Wondrous strength and generosity of a woman's heart," Hawthorne would soon write in *The Scarlet Letter,* as if referring to Peabody's tenacious defense of a very weak man.

Margaret Fuller, Una Hawthorne, the Kraitsir affair; Puritans, pariahs, and in Salem, a household of women: the scene is set for *The Scarlet Letter.*

Biographical legend insists that *The Scarlet Letter* was composed in a white heat after Hawthorne lost his job at the Custom House. Sophia, however, stated otherwise. "The Photographic study of the children in 1848 was at the very time he was writing *The Scarlet Letter*!" she recalled shortly after Hawthorne's death, "when he used to come from his labor of pain to rest by observing the sports and characteristics of the babies and record them."

Actually, it does appear that Hawthorne began *The Scarlet Letter* and possibly *The House of the Seven Gables* before the Custom House debacle. Horace Conolly distinctly remembered Hawthorne composing "at odd times, when he felt in the vein, as he called it. This [*The House of the Seven Gables*] and the 'Scarlet Letter' were written both, in Mall St.," recollected Conolly, "during the years 1846–7 and 8." Again Sophia corroborates Conolly's version of events. Having finished "The Unpardonable Sin," Hawthorne started another story, she said, or "rather went on with another, & finally it grew so very long that he said it would make a little book—So he had to put that aside & begin another." Presumably this was the first draft of one or both of his early novels. But everything was shelved when the clamor of 1848 reached up to his third-floor study.

Free trade, free labor, free soil, free men and women: 1848 was a year of revolutions abroad and at home. "Kings, princes and potentates flying dismayed to the right and left, and nation after nation rising up demanding freedom," actress Fanny Kemble reported from Europe. That July, in America, more than three hundred women and men assembled in Seneca Falls, New York, in the boiling heat to demand suffrage, equal pay, and a woman's right to divorce and own property. In Buffalo the next month, Free-Soilers, as they were called, split the Democratic Party. Riding high on the Wilmot Proviso, which forbade slavery in the territory acquired from Mexico, these antislavery Democrats from New York lined up with Conscience Whigs to choose Martin Van Buren as their presidential candidate, so fed up were they with Lewis Cass, the Democratic Party nominee, and politics as usual.

Van Buren didn't carry a single state. Instead Zachary Taylor, a Whig, won the presidency in November. Hawthorne read the handwriting on the wall. Aware that he'd alienated a number of Democrats and that Salem Whigs wanted him out, he began to plot his defense. He was a writer, not a politician. How dare he be removed from office on political grounds? He asked Hillard to mobilize prominent Whigs in his behalf, and he began to do the same.

It was no use.

On June 8, 1849, Hawthorne received the telegram. He had been fired.

In Boston with the children, Sophia had not yet heard. "She will bear it like a woman," Hawthorne informed Hillard, "—that is to say, better than a man."

Foul, cried the press, when it learned Hawthorne had been sacked. "An act of wanton and unmitigated oppression by the Whigs," charged William Cullen Bryant's *New York Evening Post,* a Democratic paper. "There stands, at the guillotine, beside the headless trunk of a pure minded, faithful, and well deserving officer, sacrificed to the worst of party proscription," reproved the *Boston Post,* and the *Albany Atlas* yelped that "the man who would knowingly commit such an act would broil a humming bird, and break a harp to make the fire."

Dissenters laughed, contemptuous both of the issues and of Hawthorne's profession. "Not one of Mr. Hawthorne's 'twice told tales' has been more repeated than the sickly sentimentality evinced when a 'literary man' is turned out of office. He has no more right to be pensioned than an honest, hard working day laborer."

But testimonials flooded the Secretary of the Treasury's office in Washington. "The office has given us a compliment to letters & genius, & I earnestly hope it may be continued on the same generous & graceful policy," claimed Rufus Choate, a Whig conservative. The scholar George Ticknor, also a conservative, said he detested all forms of patronage but regretted Hawthorne's poverty, and as for politics, "I am satisfied that while he is a Democrat, he is a retired, quiet, and inoffensive one." Another supporter called Hawthorne an elegant gentleman devoted only to literature, and Democratic firebrand John O'Sullivan testified, "I should as soon have dreamed of applying to a nightingale to scream like a vulture, as of asking Hawthorne to write politics."

Hawthorne spoiled for a fight. "If they will pay no reverence to the imaginative power when it causes herbs of grace and sweet-scented flowers to spring up along their pathway," he warned, "then they should be taught what it can do in the way of producing nettles, skunk-cabbage, deadly night-shade, wolf's bane, dog-wood." Charged with malfeasance, he shot back that he had never written political articles, nor had he undertaken any overtly political action except voting. (He couldn't deny his appointment had been political, though.) He did not pay Democrats in the Custom House more than Whigs, he said. As for the allegation that he had actively sought office, he denied that too, requesting Hillard to publish his full rebuttal in the *Boston Advertiser* under the rubric of a letter to a friend. "He seems to be all in a rouse," said Elizabeth Peabody.

By the end of June, there seemed to be a stay of execution: "He is either to be reinstated if he will consent—or to be presented with a better office," Sophia thought. Angry, Hawthorne considered compromise unacceptable; he kept the job or nothing.

With Hawthorne intransigent, the Whigs redoubled their effort under the direction of the smooth-talking Reverend Charles Wentworth Upham ("that oily man of God," Charles Sumner reportedly called him). The Whig Ward Committee reconvened, unanimously declaring Hawthorne a two-bit politician and party hack who screamed nonpartisanship when his job was threatened.

Haranguing continued on both sides. Hawthorne wanted the surveyorship back. It was a matter of pride. Upham wanted him gone. He had his own pride to consider. And that Hawthorne had also intervened for Zachariah Burchmore, secretary of Salem's Democratic Party, when Burchmore almost lost his job, raised the stakes even higher. Local Whigs argued that Hawthorne's apolitical posture was a charade "supported by all the talent which Mr. Hawthorne may have possessed."

To block the reinstatement, Upham drafted a huge document, a "Memorial of the Whigs of Salem in regard to Mr. Hawthorne." The case against Hawthorne was scrupulously mounted. Not only had Hawthorne as surveyor superintended discrepancies in pay, which Upham itemized, he had demanded his own officials kick back their extra salary to pay party dues and support the *Salem Advertiser*—sheer and incontrovertible improprieties. Boston Whigs began to huff and puff and then to backpedal. "I was yesterday informed upon authority which I cannot distrust, that Mr. Hawthorne has been, while in office, the agent of party measures of the most objectionable character, acting perhaps rather as the instrument of other than for his own impulses, but in such a manner as to destroy all claim to the plea of neutrality." Edward Everett retracted his letter of support.

All the Sturm und Drang, bitter and intense, makes one wonder what really motivated the attack on Hawthorne, a man Salem knew well, or too well. There is no simple or completely satisfying answer. Enmity in Salem was, as ever, historical; Sophia speculated that George Devereux conspired against Hawthorne "on account of an ancient family feud between Hawthornes & Devereux!" But the animus against Hawthorne seems personal, not just historical and decidedly not abstract. Charles Upham, who had promised Hawthorne immunity should administrations change, was motivated by injuries near at hand, and Horace Conolly went so far as to cross party lines to jockey for Hawthorne's removal. Even Hawthorne's friend Caleb Foote voted to dump him.

Evidently Hawthorne's position as a writer-politician infuriated these men, who preferred artists to know their place and keep to it. If Hawthorne wanted to be a writer, fine; but he couldn't be a writer and a backroom politician at the same time. So with the political means at their disposal, Hawthorne's foes sent the man of letters packing, straight back to the dreamy region he had vainly claimed as his defense.

CHAPTER FIFTEEN

Scarlet Letters

I am a citizen of somewhere else.

Nathaniel Hawthorne, *The Scarlet Letter*

Hawthorne had returned to Salem like a bad penny, he said, only to find himself ignominiously cast out of the job he'd sorely wanted. Then, following close on the heels of that failure, came the death of his mother. Sorrow, loss, bitterness, and shame: they helped complete *The Scarlet Letter*, the book toward which all Hawthorne's earlier work had been tending, a book as sleek as a Greek tragedy and as passionate as anything Hawthorne wrote, before or after.

Hawthorne also wished to muster all his literary skill to avenge himself on his enemies, "to make such a defence to the Senate as will ensure the rejection of my successor," as he told Horace Mann, "and thus satisfy the public that I was removed on false or insufficient grounds. Then, if Mr. Upham should give me occasion—or perhaps if he should not—I shall do my best to kill and scalp him in the public prints."

He'd have to wait. In July, when the temperature shot to one hundred degrees, his mother had lain in her bed, half-conscious and unable to breathe. Sophia sat at her bedside, fanning off flies. Hawthorne kept at a distance while his desolate sisters whisked past him, though occasionally he tiptoed into his mother's darkened room. Late in the day, on July 29, he crept over the threshold and stood stock-still. His mother had shrunken in just the last forty-eight hours. Louisa motioned to a nearby chair, but Hawthorne kneeled at his mother's bedside. Stretching out her frail hand, which he clasped, she murmured something that sounded like a request to take care of his sisters. Tears scalded his eyes. "I tried to keep them down;" he wrote in his journal, "but it would not be—I kept filling up, till, for a few moments, I shook with sobs." He stayed in the darkened room a long time. "Surely it is the darkest hour I ever lived," he moaned.

"I love my mother," he had also confided to his journal; "but there has been, ever since boyhood, a sort of coldness of intercourse between us, such as is apt to come between persons of strong feelings, if they are not managed rightly." In some ways, mother and son remained afraid of one another after all these years, or at least of the intensity of their feelings. But there they were. Sophia recognized them. "There was the deepest sentiment of love & reverence on both sides," she said.

Through an opening in the curtains, Hawthorne spied his young daughter playing outdoors, curls coppery in the warm sunlight. "And then I looked at my poor dying mother; and seemed to see the whole of human existence at once, standing in the dusty midst of it."

Shaken, he left the room. He wasn't able to recover himself. Sophia diagnosed brain fever. His soul seemed crushed, his heart pierced. Elizabeth Manning Hawthorne died two days later.

He had no job and no income. Horatio Bridge asked John Jay, American attorney for *Blackwood's Magazine,* if Hawthorne might become an occasional contributor. O'Sullivan sent another hundred dollars of the money he still owed the author, and Sophia had saved some of the Custom House salary, at least enough for bread and rice. She didn't quail. She didn't mind accepting donations from friends like Ann Hooper or Francis and Anna Shaw, whether in cash or clothes. Nor did she shrink from peddling her artwork. With Elizabeth acting as unofficial agent, Sophia began to hand-decorate lampshades, painting mythological scenes copied from John Flaxman's illustrations to sell to acquaintances in Boston. "I hope to get money—from people of refined taste & full purses," she happily announced.

Lampshades sold at five and ten dollars apiece couldn't feed a family for very long. George Hillard passed the hat among friends, from whom he collected a substantial sum. He did not mean to insult Hawthorne, he wrote when he mailed Hawthorne the draft. "It is only paying, a very imperfect measure, the debt we owe you for what you have done for American Literature." Hawthorne read Hillard's letter while walking home from the post office. Again tears burned his eyes as his face reddened in gratitude and the cold January wind.

As Hillard suspected, Hawthorne took the gift hard. "It is something else besides pride that teaches me that ill-success in life is really and justly a matter of shame," Hawthorne thanked his friend. "I am ashamed of it, and I ought to be. The fault of a failure is attributable—in a great degree, at least—to the man who fails." He was the man who failed.

James T. Fields was the man who succeeded. Son of a ship's captain who, like Hawthorne, lost his father at an early age, in 1849 Fields was just thirty-two and already a publishing meteor. From his native Portsmouth, New Hampshire, he'd come to Boston in 1832 as an ambitious, energetic boy, smart and well read but too poor for college. He apprenticed himself to the booksellers Carter and Hendee, whose Boston location was already famous as the Old Corner Bookshop at the juncture of Washington and School Streets. When Carter and Hendee sold out to William Davis Ticknor, Fields was included in the bargain, and by 1843 the indispensable Fields was junior partner, having brought De Quincey and Tennyson to America with lucrative results; soon the firm was considered the most prestigious imprint in the country.

This self-made litterateur was soon granted admittance to Boston's blue-hearted elite. Few could resist his sterling taste or commercial shrewdness. He was genial, loyal, and tactful. He was also a mediocre poet. Invited to speak at the Salem Lyceum while Hawthorne was its secretary, in the spring of 1849, he soon requested a story from Hawthorne for *The Boston Book,* a compilation of work by local authors. Hawthorne supplied "Drowne's Wooden Image." Evidently this is how they met.

Contact between the two men must have been amiable, for when Fields learned of Hawthorne's dismissal from the Custom House, he instantly called on several politicians he knew—Fields made a habit of knowing influential people—to rally their support. Rebuffed, as he later recounted, he clambered aboard the Salem train to flush more stories out of Hawthorne. Hawthorne sat despondently at Mall Street, warming himself near the stove, spirits sunk. Fields inquired about his work. Hawthorne muttered there was none. Fields asked again, promising to print two thousand copies of anything Hawthorne gave him.

Hawthorne adamantly insisted he had written nothing, a strange response for a man chained to his desk that fall. "He writes immensely," Sophia had reported to her mother. "I am almost frightened about it." Nine hours a day every day, Hawthorne exorcised the scourge of the past months. But according to Fields's memoirs, Hawthorne brushed the young editor aside.

James T. Fields

Defeated, Fields tramped down the wooden stairs. In his version of events, Hawthorne scrambled after him, and before Fields reached the bottom, the author pressed a roll of manuscript in Fields's hand, *The Scarlet Letter* nearly finished. On the train back to Boston, Fields read the story and returned to Salem like a bullet, having realized he possessed something more spellbinding, and salable, than just another tale about the Puritans.

Slated for a collection of a half dozen stories to be called "Old-Time Legends, Together with Sketches Experimental and Ideal" (Hawthorne's original title for the book), *The Scarlet Letter* would secure both Hawthorne's and Fields's respective reputations as eminent writer and purveyor of eminent writers.

Sophia later disputed Fields's account of events partly out of pique. "I have heard that he has made the absurd boast that *he* was the sole cause of the Scarlet Letter being published!!!!" she guffawed in 1871. "Or that *he* encouraged Mr. Hawthorne that it was a good book!! This is entirely a mistake. It was Mr. Whipple, the clever critic, and really literary man of careful culture, who came to Salem with Mr. Fields and told him what a splendid work it was—and then Mr. Fields begged to be the publisher of it."

Whether on his own or encouraged by his friend and literary consultant Edwin Whipple, Fields launched a collaboration between himself and Hawthorne that lasted the rest of Hawthorne's life. For Hawthorne, the timing was right. He had lost his most recent literary ally, John O'Sullivan, to reckless political and economic ventures, like the asinine attempt to invade Cuba that temporarily landed him in jail. And Hawthorne needed literary allies, whether Goodrich or Bridge or Elizabeth Peabody, to clap him on the back and promote him or his work however they could. The wonder is not that Hawthorne needed them but that they were there. Just when O'Sullivan and Bridge retreated, Fields appeared as if on cue.

Hawthorne sent him an introductory essay to include with the book. "In the process of writing," he informed Fields, "all political and official turmoil has subsided within me, so that I have not felt inclined to execute justice on any of my enemies." Justice was served: in his introduction, Hawthorne skewers with Daumier-like wit the desiccated Whig officers at the Custom House, thick-witted political appointees grown even more dull on the job. As he promised Horace Mann he would, Hawthorne dispatches his enemies without compunction and yet claims, with false modesty, that he always kept "the inmost Me behind its veil."

"The Custom-House," as the captious essay was called, reveals a good deal about Hawthorne and his professional uncertainties. Convinced that a government sinecure dried up his ability to write—or ready to say it had—Hawthorne claims he considered resigning. "My imagination was a tarnished mirror. It would not reflect, or only with miserable dimness, the figures with which I did my best to people it." Leaning on the strong arm of the Republic, he'd sold his independence—and compromised his writing—for "a little pile of glittering coin out of his Uncle's pocket." The sacrifice cost him self-respect. "I endeavoured to calculate how much longer I could stay in the Custom-House," Hawthorne rationalized after the fact, "and yet go forth a man." The irony is that he's then fired, his situation resembling "that of a person who should entertain an idea of committing suicide, and, altogether beyond his hopes, meet with the good hap to be murdered."

The "decapitation," as he provocatively called his firing, revived him.

He could now compose—in the full tide of anger. Ambivalent scribbler no longer, Hawthorne is avenger, scalper, judge, and adjudicator, working "as if the devil were in me," said he, "if it were only to put my enemies to the blush."

Hawthorne said he purchased steel pens and ink, determined to become "a citizen of somewhere else," by which he meant a literary man. But his imagination is no salutary place, cozy and forgiving, and as we have seen, Hawthorne wasn't particularly comfortable there with the ancestors—all male—who peer scornfully over his shoulder just as he settles at his desk. "What is he?" he hears them snort. "A writer of story-books! What kind of a business in life,—what mode of glorifying God, or being serviceable to mankind in his day and generation,—may that be? Why, the degenerate fellow might as well have been a fiddler!"

In "The Custom-House" and in *The Scarlet Letter*—indeed, in all his work—Hawthorne soothed his nagging conscience by staking out that middle ground, as we have seen, he called a "neutral territory, somewhere between the real world and fairy-land, where the Actual and the Imaginary may meet, and each imbue itself with the nature of the other." In this neutral territory, moonlight falls on familiar objects, remaking them "so they lose their actual substance, and become things of intellect." Here, Hawthorne is neither petty bureaucrat nor low-down fiddler; nor is he the soulless purveyor of objects and emotions. Rather, the dim coal fire brings warmth to "the cold spirituality of the moonbeams, and communicates, as it were, a heart and sensibilities of human tenderness." Snow-images and ice figures have become real people at last.

He continues the saga. Rifling through the attic of the Custom House, he uncovers a treasure more valuable than anything in the garret of the Old Manse. He finds a muse in the eighteenth-century person of Jonathan Pue, a far more tolerant ancestor than any of the grim Hathornes. He was also a Custom House surveyor and, like Hawthorne, an amateur antiquarian. In a whimsical conceit, Hawthorne pretends to have found Pue's papers one rainy day among the dusty records stored and forgotten in the Custom House attic. With them is a mysterious relic, a bit of tattered cloth shaped like the letter "A." Puzzled, Hawthorne clutches it to his own breast, as if to array himself in its meaning or infuse it with his own, but the red letter scorches him and he drops it to the floor.

He peruses the scroll of faded manuscript in which the scarlet token had been rolled. These curled pages contain the letter's eerie history, diligently collected by Pue from aged persons who recalled the letter's bearer. Do right by this woman's tale, admonishes Surveyor Pue, sounding like Hamlet's ghost. And thus the irrepressible Hester Prynne is born.

Conceived as a story, *The Scarlet Letter* was written "all in one tone," said Hawthorne. "I had to get my pitch, and then could go on interminably." Finished after the death of his mother, *The Scarlet Letter* is Hawthorne's tribute to her, written with grief, guilt, and unabashed freedom.

Though its prose is slightly formal, its phrasings aphoristic and rhythmically exact, the story's smoldering emotions are so volatile that Hawthorne regulates them in the book's shapely design. The tale of Hester Prynne unfolds in twenty-four short chapters, with the first, twelfth, and the last symmetrically organized around the scaffold on which Hester appears to suffer for the crime of adultery. Similarly, the plot of the story shuttles between interior and exterior locations—one chapter, for example, is called "The Interior of a Heart"—suggesting how the private and public worlds are so often at tragic variance.

Condemned by the vigilant magistrates of colonial Boston to wear the scarlet badge of shame, Hester climbs onto the scaffold in the book's opening scene, more proud than penitent, a bright red letter "A" on her breast, a young baby in her arms. Self-reliant and brave, Hester conceals the identity of her lover, the pious and passive Reverend Arthur Dimmesdale, but though she protects him from civic disgrace, she can't save him from the scourge of his own guilty self. Gifted with eloquence and steeped in weakness, Dimmesdale is pale, obsessive, and craven; he refuses to take responsibility for his crime, rationalizing that men such as he retain such "zeal for God's glory and man's welfare, they shrink from displaying themselves black and filthy in the view of men; because, thenceforward, no good can be achieved by them."

The rationalizations are wasted upon the man to whom he confides them, none other than Hester's long-lost husband, now called Roger Chillingworth. Chillingworth arrives in Boston just as his wife, holding another man's child, stands dishonored before the town. Hester immediately recognizes him as he raises his finger to his lips, signaling her to keep quiet. She says nothing, thereby colluding with the man who will wreak vengeance on her lover.

Characters bound together by love and hate keep one another's secrets. Chillingworth tells Hester, the young wife he emotionally abandoned, that "we have wronged each other," and if he does not forgive her betrayal—Chillingworth is not a man of mercy—he at least recognizes that "between thee and me, the scale hangs fairly balanced." But as Hester knows, Chillingworth intends to expose her lover and uncover his secret sin, even if that means he must possess Dimmesdale's soul, steal into his dreams, violate his most private self. Exquisite connoisseur of revenge, Chillingworth becomes Dimmesdale's constant companion, his physician and adviser, his friend and housemate.

Figuratively, Chillingworth, no less than Hester, is Dimmesdale's lover and Hawthorne's double. "Mr. Dimmesdale, whose sensibility of nerve often produced the effect of spiritual intuition, would become vaguely aware that something inimical to his peace had thrust itself into relation with him," writes Hawthorne. "But old Roger Chillingworth, too, had perceptions that were almost intuitive; and when the minister threw his startled eyes towards him, there the physician sat; his kind, watchful, sympathizing, but never intrusive friend."

The literary sources of *The Scarlet Letter,* from Walter Scott to Goethe to William Cowper to Andrew Marvell, Cotton Mather, Thomas Hutchinson, and Joseph Felt (chronicler of Salem), Hawthorne had completely digested, making them, like his characters, resolutely his. And certain elements of the story had been in place for a while. In his 1837 tale "Endicott and the Red Cross," Hawthorne wrote of a woman condemned to wear the telltale "A" who, like Hester Prynne, embroiders the shameful symbol with insolent golden thread, and a germ of Hester Prynne existed in his "Mrs. Hutchinson," published seven years before "Endicott." "Edward Fane's Rosebud" (published anonymously in 1837) tells of a young woman married to an older man, like Hester and Chillingworth; later, a distinguished clergyman keeps his hand over his breast in "Egotism; or, the Bosom-Serpent," and the fiendlike Ethan Brand serves as the prototype of Chillingworth, who takes after Hawthorne's virtuoso collector and Dr. Rappaccini. The list goes on.

But now Hawthorne's characters take on a life and a passion of their own. Dimmesdale lashes himself with voluptuous passion until his brain reels with spectral visions; his guilt so inflames his sermons that young women swoon with a pale fervor they mistake as religious. The stormy, implacable intransigeance of the birdlike Pearl, Hester's unruly child, reflects the illicit desire with which she was conceived. And Hester too, despite her punishment, simmers. She would fling off the past, casting aside the scarlet stigma in a moment, should Dimmesdale consent to leave

Boston with her and her daughter. Reunited with her lover after seven long years, Hester entreats Arthur in one of the novel's most heartbreaking moments, "What we did had a consecration of its own. We felt it so! Hast thou forgotten it?"

Magisterial and fierce, Hester Prynne is both sinning and sinned against, a woman able to love, to yearn, and to endure the consequences of her offense. Poised, she glides through seventeenth-century Boston bearing her punishment in humble silence while advertising her sin like an open secret, as indeed she must. Even more important, she suffers the weakness of those around her. "None so ready as she to give of her little substance to every demand of poverty; even though the bitter-hearted pauper threw back a gibe in requital of the food brought regularly to his door."

She persists; she endures. "In all seasons of calamity, indeed, whether general or of individuals, the outcast of society at once found her place. She came, not as a guest, but as a rightful inmate, into the household that was darkened by trouble; as if its gloomy twilight were a medium in which she was entitled to hold intercourse with her fellow-creatures." Like Hawthorne's mother, whom she resembles in stature, Hester Prynne lives on the fringes of society, which is where, as we have seen, Hawthorne as artist places himself: an outcast radical who holds dear the rules he has broken: "It is remarkable," observes Hawthorne, "that persons who speculate the most boldly often conform with the most perfect quietude to the external regulations of society."

Like Hawthorne, Hester is also a quiet rebel whose isolation grants her a certain freedom of thought, particularly concerning the plight of women, with whom she, and he, identify: "Was existence worth accepting, even to the happiest among them," Hester asks as if she were a doughty Margaret Fuller, deciding that society should be completely overhauled, torn down and rebuilt. In the thirteenth chapter of the book, "Another View of Hester," she becomes a radical visionary, wishing to free both men and women from the injustice of mean convention: "The world's law was no law for her mind," Hawthorne declares.

> It was an age in which the human intellect, newly emancipated, had taken a more active and a wider range than for many centuries before. Men of the sword had overthrown nobles and kings. Men bolder than these had overthrown and rearranged—not actually, but within the sphere of theory, which was their most real abode—the whole system of ancient

prejudice, wherewith was linked much of ancient principle. Hester Prynne imbibed this spirit. She assumed a freedom of speculation, then common enough on the other side of the Atlantic, but which our forefathers, had they known of it, would have held to be a deadlier crime than that stigmatized by the scarlet letter.

Hester's revolutionary program is just the kind of misty-eyed vision that Hawthorne resentfully censures. To him, the apostate Hester Prynne is a fallen creature punishable not just by parochial Puritans but by him. When she begins to think too much and question too deeply, Hawthorne converts into marmoreal coldness all the tenderness he calls "essential to keep her a woman." Male or female or both, Hawthorne restrains all such seekers as heartless, friendless, exiled from the human community. And it is with them that he deeply identifies.

Yet Hester is not a vengeful Chillingworth, an unfeeling Ethan Brand, or even a virtuoso museum keeper who merchandizes history and art. She is ardent, loyal, and so seductive that Hawthorne must bind her once luxuriant hair into her cap much as he binds his passionate prose into a style coolly elegant and austerely composed. For he is not only Hester but Dimmesdale too, repressing the desires of a prodigal nature.

Then Hawthorne reneged. It was a typical gesture, complicating his work, rendering even his conservatism ambiguous. The sturdiest of Hawthorne's heroines and the most ably imagined, Hester endures alienation, exclusion, and the forfeiture of her sexuality but relinquishes neither passion nor richness of soul even when, at the story's conclusion, she sews the scarlet letter back on her breast. To be sure, Hawthorne loved and hated her, admired and punished her, branded and redeemed her and then left her quite as bereft as he likely imagined his mother must have been—as he himself had been. Softly, she stole into his novel, a ghost "beloved, but gone hence," he writes in "The Custom-House," "now sitting quietly in a streak of this magic moonshine, with an aspect that would make us doubt whether it had returned from afar, or had never once stirred from our fireside."

Now he was bereft again.

Like Hawthorne's mother, his sister, and Hawthorne himself, Hester Prynne knows herself to be different. "There was wild and ghastly scenery all around her, and a home and comfort nowhere." If she cannot conceal her difference—just the identity of her lover—she can conform when she again takes up the scarlet letter, "of her own free will." With the letter voluntarily clamped to her breast as if her very identity depended on it, Hester condoles with the downcast, soothes the afflicted, and tells women in particular of a fairer day when they will live together with men in "mutual happiness." To some readers, her new employment suggests she represents the fundamental nature of America: working within the social order to change it, she consigns herself to the public trust. More important, she allows Hawthorne to reassert control over his book. But propitious as her last act may appear to be, Hester ultimately triumphs only by taking up the mark—and mask—identifying her as woman.

Hawthorne too had taken up the mantle of respectability in the rough-and-tumble world of the Custom House, converting his sense of vocational homelessness into camaraderie—only to find the Custom House a symbol of failed purpose. Then, like Hester, he converts a token of shame into an emblem of art, kaleidoscopic and complex, that reveals the shallowness of cultural labels: ambition, atonement, autonomy, and of course American author.

"A book one reads shudderingly," Mary Mann described *The Scarlet Letter.* "Among other things, it reveals Hawthorne."

The evening Hawthorne read the last chapter of *The Scarlet Letter* to Sophia, she went to bed with a terrible headache—a good sign of the book's success, he said, though he worried about its shadowy darkness. "To tell you the truth," he confided to Bridge, "—it is positively a h–ll fired story, into which I found it almost impossible to throw any cheering light."

In February, Hawthorne sent the last three chapters of the manuscript to Fields. "Mr. Fields!" Sophia blurted. "I expect to hear, after he has read this, that he was exploded & gone off like a sky-rocket—so great was his enthusiasm about the rest of the romance." Exhilarated, Fields had advised Hawthorne to forget about the other old-time legends and let the story stand on its own. Though skeptical, Hawthorne complied, and suggested that the book's title be printed in red ink.

The Scarlet Letter was published on March 16, 1850, to wide and continuous acclaim. Two weeks later, Fields reported to Hawthorne that the first edition of twenty-five hundred copies had sold out and that another two thousand copies of *The Scarlet Letter* were being printed. Fifteen hundred copies of the second edition sold in three days. Sophia trumpeted

Hawthorne's success. "Nathaniel's fame is perfectly prodigious," she crowed.

"Glorious," Fields had described the book to Evert Duyckinck, prompting Duyckinck to publish part of "The Custom-House" in his new magazine, the *Literary World,* in order "to force a little breath among the coals," said Fields, "& raise a conflagration." In local quarters, there was one. "The Custom-House" was unmanly and mean-spirited, accused the *Salem Register,* and Hawthorne a self-important boor to air his grievance publicly. "If I escape from town without being tarred-and-feathered," Hawthorne laughed, "I shall consider it good luck." In the second edition of the book, he prepared a preface and recanted nothing. "The only remarkable features of the sketch are its frank and genuine good-humor," he deliberately shrugged.

About the novel, critics were kinder. The *Salem Gazette* called the book thrilling, and Fields's well-placed friends, like Evert Duyckinck, also praised the book with genuine admiration. Edwin Whipple wrote the review that Hawthorne admired most, comparing the introductory essay to the work of Joseph Addison and Charles Lamb and then hailing *The Scarlet Letter* as piercing "directly through all the externals to the core of things." Another appreciative acquaintance, George Bailey Loring, devoted six pages to *The Scarlet Letter* in the *Massachusetts Quarterly Review,* excoriating Dimmesdale's cowardice and commending Hester's ability to love. Orestes Brownson, however, complained that Hawthorne misunderstood the meaning of Christian pardon, Christian remorse, and Christian confession, not a surprising lapse in a popular Protestant writer, said Brownson, himself a Catholic convert. The *Church Review and Ecclesiastical Register* was more direct about Hawthorne: "He perpetrates bad morals."

Overall, though, reviewers adopted Hawthorne's point of view: when judged by *The Scarlet Letter,* Hawthorne's dismissal from the Custom House must be reckoned a boon to American literature. There was another lesson here: the real world and fairyland don't mix, except in literature.

CHAPTER SIXTEEN

The Uneven Balance

This possibility of mad destruction only made his domestic kindness the more beautiful and touching.

Nathaniel Hawthorne, "Fire-Worship"

"THOU DIDST much amiss, to marry a husband who cannot keep thee like a lady," Hawthorne lamented to his wife. Nomads once again, they would pack their worldly goods and head westward—western Massachusetts, that is—hoping to recover from the agony of the last months.

All of them were tired, especially Sophia; she hadn't even known where they'd be living come spring. And with the children squealing in her ears, her husband lashed to his desk, requests for lampshades multiplying—Elizabeth had even gone so far as to suggest she paint hand-screens—she collapsed with pleurisy shortly after the publication of *The Scarlet Letter.*

Life seemed forever changed. The Mall Street household was breaking up. Louisa sorted what to take to Aunt Dike's, and Ebe went to Manchester, north of Salem, where she could walk along the shore unmolested by busybodies. Hawthorne also wanted to get out of "abominable" Salem. "I detest this town so much that I hate to go into the streets, or to have people see me," he told Bridge.

They had investigated Portsmouth, New Hampshire, near Bridge and his wife, but not finding anything affordable, Sophia began to consider a place in the Berkshire mountains. Her friend the wealthy Caroline Sturgis had married the wealthy New York broker William Aspinall Tappan in 1847, and they were staying at Highwood, the estate of Anna and Samuel Ward, in the small village of Lenox, population circa fifteen hundred. Having bought property nearby, the Tappans were building their own cottage—as mansions were called locally—on the acreage known as Tanglewood. Caroline Tappan began to recruit Sophia to the Berkshire community: the writer Catharine Maria Sedgwick lived in Stockbridge among a clan of Sedgwicks that included Theodore, the senator, who paced the village green when not in Washington, and Catharine's sister-in-law Elizabeth, who superintended a well-known school for young ladies in Lenox. Actress Fanny Kemble had purchased a cottage, the Perch, in the woods; Oliver Wendell Holmes's grandfather kept a farm in Pittsfield; Fanny Longfellow's family owned property in Stockbridge. The Hawthornes would not be alone.

"To give up the ocean caused rather a stifling sensation," Sophia admitted; "but I have become used to the idea of mountains now." Hawthorne wavered. Depressed, dreading further debt, and by no means sanguine about earning his keep, he uneasily imagined himself eating food from his own garden and paying the rent with proceeds from the sale of Sophia's lampshades. But in the Berkshires there would be no real garden, with snow falling early and fast during the bottomless winter.

Nonetheless, when the Tappans offered the Hawthornes the handyman's small red house on the edge of their property at no cost, Hawthorne accepted with dignity, stipulating he'd pay fifty dollars for the rent. "I infinitely prefer a small right to a great favor," he later explained as he folded away his dream of a house by the sea. "Had this wish of his been fulfilled," Julian would plaintively write years later, "it might have made great differences."

At the end of May, the Hawthornes chugged into the airy hills, decamping from the train, their clothes soaked in soot, and descended on the Tappans, who brushed the dust from their garments and put the entire east wing of Highwood at their disposal while the red house was being repaired. Julian rode a hobbyhorse covered with real horsehair, and Una walked through jade-green woods, birds bursting into "ecstatic song" (Sophia's phrase). Hawthorne, worn and weary, lapsed into a nervous fever, his eyes glazed, his face pale as cement. "Belladonna finally conquered the enemy," Sophia exhaled in relief, "and though he is not so vigorous yet as in former days before the last day began (it is a year now since he was expelled from the Custom House) yet he is reviving very fast."

About ten days later, an old oxcart lugged the Hawthornes' furniture through the rickety black gate of their new home, a little red box that sat like a district schoolhouse on the northern end of the Stockbridge Bowl (the familiar name for Lake Mahkeenac). The house was one of the poorest, oldest shanties in Lenox, Ellery Channing later remembered, "with uneven floors, and so ill-built that the wind could not be kept out." Sophia was delighted.

She hung her reproductions above the mantel and in the bedrooms and halls; she draped crimson curtains over the windows and covered the center table with ruby-red cloth; she placed a purple-and-gold-colored carpet given by Caroline in the small front room and in the low-studded drawing room set out the bowl and pitcher Hawthorne's father had brought from India. In Hawthorne's study she arranged the red acanthus-leaf carpet, a secretary, an ottoman, and a cane-bottomed rocker. The rooms were tiny; the house was tiny, but its views were fresh and breezy, and the dining room window, like the one in the upstairs bedroom, looked out on the buttery lake, its color changing by the hour. In the background loomed Monument Mountain, a headless sphinx draped in a rich Persian shawl.

"My house is an old red farm house, (as red as the Scarlet Letter)," Hawthorne wrote to Zachariah Burchmore, a friend from Custom House days. He might as well have been living on the moon as in Lenox. The air was pure, too pure. "I find it very agreeable to get rid of politics and the rest of the damnable turmoil that has disturbed me for three or four years past," he said; "but I must plead guilty to some few hankerings after brandy and water, rum and molasses, an occasional cigar, and other civilized indulgences of the like nature."

Come to visit, Horatio Bridge cleared out the barn and hen coop, and he hammered bookshelves and mended tables, but he didn't think rural solitude healthy for Hawthorne. "He has gone to Lenox, where I fear he will settle down for three or four years," Bridge confided to Frank Pierce. "Perhaps he may remain there unless, at the end of this administration, he should have a good office tendered him," he hinted. Released on bail after the Cuban fiasco, O'Sullivan surprised the Hawthornes when he knocked at the red shanty's door. Hawthorne stayed grumpy. "Mr. Hawthorne thinks it is *Salem* which he is dragging at his ankles still," Sophia remarked.

Moody under the best of circumstances, Hawthorne had left friends and family in the wake of embarrassment, penury, and spleen, having endured what Sophia considered the most trying year of his life. It wasn't quite over. In July came news of Margaret Fuller's death. She had gone to Europe in 1846 as the *New-York Tribune*'s foreign correspondent, and once in Italy, set about writing an eyewitness history of the Roman revolution, "the daily bulletin of men and things," she said. To proper Bostonians, though, Fuller's name continued to raise eyebrows no matter what she did, even marrying, particularly since she concealed her marriage from friends, who tried to squash vicious gossip. That she gave birth to a son whet the appetite of scandalmongers even more: Fuller's child must be illegitimate, his father an uneducated bumpkin without talent of any kind. "Think of the dry, forlorn old maid changed into a Marguerita Marchesa d'Ossoli!" snickered Fanny Longfellow. Fuller drew herself up. "I pity those who are inclined to think ill," she retorted from a distance, "when they might as well have inclined the other way, however let them go."

With her son ill, the revolution in shambles, and the pope restored, Fuller decided to come home. She sailed with her family from Leghorn on the ill-fated *Elizabeth*. En route, its captain died of smallpox; and that wasn't the worst of it. Approaching Fire Island, New York, in the wee hours of July 18, the *Elizabeth*, hitting a southwestern gale, was dashed into a sandbar. A cargo of Carrara marble split the ship's hold, and the boat began to crumple into a mass of planks and swollen splints. Women and men jumped overboard, and the crew desperately clung to wooden planks, but Fuller, it was said, refused to leave the deck. Some think that Ossoli had already drowned and she was suicidal. Sophia pictured her sitting with her hands upon her knees, waves breaking over her water-soaked nightdress.

Neither her body nor Ossoli's was found, and the sailor who tried to swim ashore with their little boy was washed onto the beach that morning with the dead child.

"Oh was ever any thing so tragical, so dreary, so unspeakably agonizing as the image of Margaret upon that wreck, alone," cried Sophia. Emerson sent Thoreau and Ellery Channing to New York to hunt for Fuller's body and her manuscript. Channing dried the papers washed up on the shore but found nothing that amounted to a book.

Sophia calmed herself. "I am really glad she died," she concluded without feeling, "—there was no other peace or rest to be found for her—especially if her husband was a person so wanting in force & availability."

Evert Duyckinck, soon to visit the red shanty, remarked that Sophia Hawthorne looked like Margaret Fuller though she definitely seemed cut from much sturdier cloth.

The day Margaret Fuller's ship was tossed to bits, Herman Melville's aunt handed him a copy of Hawthorne's *Mosses from an Old Manse*.

It was an auspicious gift, for the two men were soon to meet at a picnic arranged by their Stockbridge neighbor, David Dudley Field. On a Friday in early August, Field was returning to the Berkshires from New York when he happened to see Evert Duyckinck and the essayist Cornelius Mathews on the train. They were going to spend a few days with Melville and his family on the Pittsfield farm owned by Melville's cousin.

James T. Fields and his wife were scheduled to stop by the Hawthornes' that same week, and Oliver Wendell Holmes was vacationing at his summer home. Why not arrange a climb up Monument Mountain with the literati and their guests, Dudley Field wondered. He'd do it.

The date was set for Monday, August 5, a day soon to be promoted as an American *Déjeuner sur l'Herbe* (without the scandal): Hawthorne, fully clothed, pursues the Great Carbuncle while Herman Melville, Mr. Neptune, rapturously pursues Mr. Noble Melancholy. It's a good story: friendship forged in the blue mountains between two of the most singular of all American writers, attended by a retinue of lesser-knowns. Cornelius Mathews wrote the first account of it for Duyckinck's *Literary World;* revelers convene in the summer sun before a thunderclap and a sheet of rain send them scampering. Gaily, they all yell out puns and rhymes as they run for cover. Dr. Oliver Wendell Holmes (Mr. Town Wit) is the most droll; James T. Fields, the most inept (his patent leather shoes slip on the slick stones); and Herman Melville is the daredevil who sprints from rock to jutting rock.

The party descended the cliffs to reassemble at Dudley Field's home, where Field supplied dry clothes, a three-hour dinner, and a good deal of wine. According to Duyckinck, Dr. Holmes baited the group with witticisms about Englishmen being superior to Americans. Melville stoutly defended the Americans while Hawthorne looked amiably on. Later James Fields remembered that Hawthorne took the part of the American.

Afterwards the group headed over to Ice-Glen, a mountain cranny, for another lark led this time by Joel Tyler Headley, a popular historian, who depicted the "remarkable literary column," as did Fields twenty-five years after the fact. "Hawthorne was among the most enterprising of the merrymakers," Fields claimed; "and being in the dark much of the time, he ventured to call out lustily and pretend that certain destruction was inevitable to all of us." The cleft was so deep that nothing melted within, Hawthorne observed, and looked "as if the Devil had torn his way through a rock & left it all jagged behind him." Grumbling about his bulky size, Fields again slid on the stones. Dr. Holmes shouted, If you'd give your authors another 10 percent, you wouldn't have so much fat.

Of the group, Melville captured Sophia's fancy. "Mr. Typee is interesting in his aspect quite," she told Elizabeth, referring to Melville's first book.

"I see Fayaway in his face." Besides *Typee,* the young author had published four other books: a novel, *Omoo,* had appeared in 1847, a year after *Typee,* and like it was based on his experiences as a sailor in the South Seas, this time in Tahiti and Eimeo; his novel *Mardi* came out in 1849, the same year as his autobiographical *Redburn* (Defoe on the ocean, Duyckinck said). Just recently *White-Jacket* had appeared, and now he was trying to write a strange sort of a book about whaling, having grown tired of his reputation as the writer who'd lived among cannibals.

He also had pedigree. "He is married to a daughter of Judge Shaw— Judge Lemuel Shaw," Sophia bragged to her mother, "& has a child of a year & half—Malcolm. He is of Scotch descent—of noble lineage—of the Lords of Melville & Leven, & Malcolm is a family name." In America the family had distinguished itself during the Revolution, with one grandfather dump- ing tea in Boston Harbor and the other raising his musket in defense of Fort Stanwix. But those days were long gone. Melville's father, a wholesaler of high-class imports, had died bankrupt when Herman was twelve, forcing him to leave school and work as a bank clerk, a sales clerk, and a school- teacher. He studied civil engineering and surveying but found no employ- ment on the Erie Canal project, as he'd hoped, so in 1839 set sail on a merchant ship bound for Liverpool, as recounted in *Redburn.* Back at home, he again taught for a while, traveled to Illinois, and then signed on to the *Acushnet,* a whaler headed for the South Seas. In 1842 he jumped ship in the Marquesas, and eventually returned, after a series of remarkable adven- tures, to Boston as a sailor in the United States Navy.

Hawthorne liked the bushy-bearded young man—utterly himself— and asked him to spend a few days at the red house. Generally suspicious of literary men (Longfellow was an exception), Hawthorne much preferred the retired sea dogs of Salem to any highfalutin tribe in Concord or the Berk- shires. Plus, like Melville, he loved the sea, which represented raw adventure and a test of manhood perfectly balanced by death, certain and uncertain.

And here Melville was, bearded and bronzed, a man who led the kind of life Hawthorne could only dream about: afloat on some craft or other, bat- tling typhoons and enduring doldrums, dropping anchor in exotic, distant lands. Mixing with salts, young and old, on board ship, men and women on land, Melville was the coxswain, not a dry-docked Custom House inspec- tor, come back to tell all, striding off the gangplank into a garret where he could dip his pen into the inkpot and be, of all things, a writer. He was also a willing acolyte, fourteen years Hawthorne's junior, fatherless, and so hungry for literary companionship that he eagerly projected onto the older author the preoccupations assailing him while he wrote his book about whales.

"We landsmen have no variety in our lives," Hawthorne once said of himself. Ready to drink a bottle of brandy and "talk ontological heroics" in the barn, Melville struck Hawthorne as unashamed, sexual, tender, and individual, a spendthrift stylist and prolific author liberally "tolerant of codes of morals that may be little in accordance with our own," Hawthorne had written in his review of *Typee*. Melville was no landsman.

When Duyckinck returned to New York City, he carried the first installment of Melville's review of *Mosses from an Old Manse*.

Though it's not clear when Melville began the review, whether before or after meeting Hawthorne, it's obvious that Melville was smitten with Hawthorne and his work. "Already I feel that this Hawthorne has dropped germinous seeds into my soul," Melville lustily writes. Pretending to be a Virginian on vacation in New England, he says he's just read Hawthorne's book while lying on the new-mown clover near the barn. And he's ecstatic. "He expands and deepens down, the more I contemplate him," Melville writes of Hawthorne, "and further and further, shoots his strong New-England roots into the hot soil of my Southern soul."

The eroticism is unmistakable; so too Melville's canny perception of Hawthorne's work, "the rich and rare distilment of a spicy and slowly-oozing heart," he called it. Without compunction, Melville dares liken Hawthorne to Shakespeare—"Some may start to read of Shakspeare and Hawthorne on the same page"—since most readers don't really understand either writer anyway, their insights being too grave, ornery, and hard to swallow whole. "For in this world of lies," Melville utters in crescendo, "Truth is forced to fly like a sacred white doe in the woodlands; and only by cunning glimpses will she reveal herself, as in Shakespeare and other great masters of the great Art of Telling the Truth—even though it be covertly and by snatches."

Melville will set the record straight. "For spite of all the Indian-summer sunlight on the hither side of Hawthorne's soul, the other side—like the dark half of the physical sphere—is shrouded in blackness, ten times black." Melville understands despondency and vile doubt; they stalk him too, and he knows that what most reviewers term morbidness is the clear-eyed admission that all the tanks have been drained. It's a perception that "derives its force from its appeals to that Calvinistic sense of Innate Depravity and Original Sin," he continues, "from whose visitations, in some shape or other, no deeply thinking mind is always and wholly free. For, in certain moods, no man can weigh this world without throwing in something, somehow like Original Sin, to strike the uneven balance."

Melville's Man of Mosses (as he referred to Hawthorne in his review) is a man of brooding unbelief.

Was he writing of Hawthorne or himself? With insatiable hunger, Melville devoured the world, and when he wrote of Hawthorne, he wrote of both of them. For in his magniloquent prose, Melville pictured Hawthorne as a mate bobbing like him on the troubled seas of publishing, recognition, and posterity. "What I feel most moved to write, that is banned,—it will not pay," he would confide to his new friend. "Yet, altogether, write the *other* way I cannot."

Recognizing a fellow traveler when he met one, Melville boldly predicted that Hawthorne augured greatness for American literature. Washington Irving was a grasshopper compared to him. "Let him write like a man, for then he will be sure to write like an American," Melville boomed, sounding like John O'Sullivan and Emerson, who sounded like one another. "Let us away with this leaven of literary flunkeyism toward England." As for Hawthorne, he is the flesh and blood of the land. The scent of beech and hemlock and tar is in his soul, where Niagara roars and the prairies stretch far and wide.

Hawthorne may have hoodwinked the multitude with his tidy tales, but he didn't outfox everyone; certainly not Herman Melville. "For genius, all over the world, stands hand in hand," Melville declared, "and one shock of recognition runs the whole circle round."

Melville's magnetism held the entire Hawthorne family in its grip long after Hawthorne and Melville ceased to see one another. Said Julian Hawthorne in retrospect, "There were few honester or more lovable men than Herman Melville."

"A man with a true warm heart & a soul & an intellect—with life to his finger-tips—earnest, sincere & reverent, very tender & modest," Sophia described him. "—And I am not sure that he is not a very great man—but I have not quite decided upon my own opinion."

Houseguest at the red shanty, Melville was the essence of good manners, "careful not to interrupt Mr. Hawthorne's morning when he was here,"

Herman Melville

Sophia reported to her mother. "He told me he was naturally so silent a man that he was complained of a great deal on this account; but that he found himself talking to Mr. Hawthorne to a great extent—He said Mr. Hawthorne's great but hospitable silence drew him out—that it was astonishing how *sociable* his silence was."

When Sophia learned that Melville wrote the review of *Mosses* in the *Literary World,* he could do no wrong. "He is an invaluable person, full of daring & questions, & with all momentous considerations afloat in the crucible of his mind," she again described him. "He tosses them in, & heats his furnace sevenfold & burns & stirs, & waits for the crystalization with a royal indifference as to what may [toss up], only eager for truth, without previous prejudice. This ocean-experience has given sea-room to his intellect, & he is in the mere boyhood of his possibilities."

When he spoke, she said, people and places and even objects sprang to life. Melville told the Hawthornes a story about a man and a large oak cudgel, and shortly after Melville left the house, she found herself looking in the bedroom for the stick. "When conversing, he is full of gesture & force, & loses himself in his subject—There is no grace nor polish—once in a while his animation gives place to a singularly quiet expression out of these eyes, to which I have objected—an indrawn, dim look, but which at the same time makes you feel that he is at that instant taking deepest note of what is before him—It is a strange, lazy glance, but with a power in it quite unique."

Sophia seemed to praise Melville more than her husband did, although he appreciated Melville's work. "No writer ever put the reality before his reader more unflinchingly than he does in 'Redburn,' and 'White Jacket,' " Hawthorne wrote to Duyckinck. " 'Mardi' is a rich book, with depths here and there that compel a man to swim for his life." Melville was no ordinary writer, but Hawthorne did wish the younger man wouldn't seem in such a blasted hurry: "One scarcely pardons the writer for not having brooded long . . . so as to make it a good deal better." For many years this was the standard criticism of Melville's work.

During the next fifteen months the two men enjoyed a friendship that echoes in the halls of American literature, where it's been probed, sexualized, and moralized, Hawthorne cast as a repressed and withholding fatherfigure, ungenerous to a fault, and Melville, needy son, rebuffed by the elder writer. Whenever Melville effused, Hawthorne shrank, or so it seems.

Melville loved Hawthorne, of this there can be no doubt. And Hawthorne loved his male friends; he didn't need to categorize or condemn his feelings, or to fear them. He also cared for Melville. But Hawthorne did not love Melville, not the way—whatever way that was—that Melville needed love.

Yet Melville left his mark on Hawthorne. Characterizing Holgrave in *The House of the Seven Gables,* Hawthorne drew upon his neighbor: scantily educated, left early to his own guidance, a former country schoolmaster and a man who "had never lost his identity, homeless as he had been—continually changing his whereabouts." Of course, Melville figures much more importantly in Hawthorne's *Blithedale Romance,* where Hawthorne incorporates him into the character of brawny Hollingsworth: "There was something of the woman moulded into the great, stalwart frame of Hollingsworth," Hawthorne writes; "nor was he ashamed of it, as men often are of what is best in them."

In that novel, Coverdale's rejection of Hollingsworth's bid for friendship gives rise to the flat-footed speculations about Hawthorne's rejection of Melville. There's no real evidence for this. Hawthorne's letters to Melville do not survive, a fact that leads nowhere, especially not to the assumption that Melville destroyed them in a pique of unrequited love. He likely burned them at Hawthorne's behest, as Hawthorne's other friends—Peabody, Pierce, Bridge—all would.

But Melville was—is—an engulfing spirit whose whirlpool of feelings sucked in everything and everyone near him. He plummeted from doubt to depression or leaped from desire to enthusiasms as broad as his compassion, as grievous as his solitudes, as polymorphous as his experiences on board ship or in the South Sea Islands. Whatever Melville told Hawthorne of all this, whatever Hawthorne surmised, or whatever he feared about Melville, Hawthorne was a fastidious man who depended on regulation—regular living, regular loving, rituals of predictable routine—as if to contain or curb his own sense of the underside of things, that stuff of terror and despair and dissolution (or so he thought). He constantly flirted with it in his work, but he also wanted a life of pattern, order, comfort, much like many of his beleaguered characters. In fact, the allure of his best prose derives from the tension between regulation and psychological—even ontological—pandemonium. Over and over, Hawthorne reassured himself that he preferred the road taken: "Persons who have wandered, or been expelled, out of the common track of things, even were it for a better system, desire nothing so much as to be led back," he writes in *The House of the Seven Gables.* "They shiver in their loneliness, be it on a mountain-top, or in a dungeon."

And Hawthorne's male friends—Horatio Bridge, John O'Sullivan, and Frank Pierce—were men who negotiated the world by defending themselves in ways Melville could and would not. They were men comfortable with their ability to compete with others and men whose ambitions facilitated Hawthorne's rather than got in his way.

Melville read *Twice-told Tales,* telling Duyckinck that "their deeper meanings are worthy of a Brahmin. Still," he added, "there is something lacking—a good deal lacking to the plump sphericity of the man. What is that?—He does'nt patronise the butcher—he needs roast-beef, done rare." Hawthorne's work—a little light and delicate—needed meat on the bone.

It didn't matter. In one of those rare acts of literary generosity and friendship, Melville would dedicate *Moby-Dick,* his novel of metaphysics and whaling, to Hawthorne "in token for my admiration of his genius."

Two men, differently timed, together for a brief interlude; and they'd write far different books when each returned to his study. Hawthorne called *Moby-Dick* a book with a gigantic conception; it was the kind of book he'd never write.

The publication of *The Scarlet Letter* had salvaged Hawthorne's pride and helped to fill his purse, but he had a new book to finish, barely begun, that worried him. And Fields was at his elbow. "You are aware how much depends upon getting ready in season," he nudged. "I intend this fall to sell a good many thousand for you of whatever you choose to give the public." Hawthorne resisted. "I must not pull up my cabbage by the roots, by way of hastening its growth," he replied with a touch of asperity.

Yet Hawthorne trusted Fields, who continued to insinuate himself into Hawthorne's career—or, rather, he determined that the former short story writer should have one. Fields kept the lid open on his cashbox so far as Hawthorne was concerned, should he need to borrow on credit. He acted as impresario, talking up Hawthorne's talents, his future, even his physique. "His form is only second to Daniel Webster's in robustness," Fields would tell a friend, hastening to add that "he blushes like a girl when he is praised." He rallied Hawthorne's spirits. "We intend to push your books a-la-Steam Engine," he said, "and do better for you than any other house." Fields was reissuing the entire *Grandfather's Child* series originally published by Elizabeth Peabody as *True Stories from History and Biography* and *Biographical Studies.* After the publication of Hawthorne's new novel, which he wanted to advertise as soon as possible, Fields planned to reprint *Twice-told Tales* with a new author's preface. And he persuaded Hawthorne to round up more stories for yet another collection to appear after writing his book of children's stories, *A Wonder Book.*

When the houseguests departed and the weather cooled, Hawthorne began to write in earnest, even going so far as to puzzle over his new book's title, which likely he remembered from his visit to Susanna Ingersoll years before: "The House of the Seven Gables." Fields approved, and so it remained. But it wouldn't be ready before January, for he wanted to polish many of the passages and make sure each detail was finished "with the minuteness of a Dutch picture," he said. He also wished to make the book a little lighter than *The Scarlet Letter* in order to win, he hoped, an even larger audience. To do this, he had to stop writing for a while. "There are points when a writer gets bewildered," he sighed, "and cannot form any judgement of what he has done, nor tell what to do next."

Meantime, he rejected an offer from *Graham's* to write a new story, he rejected a proposal from Emerson to write for a new magazine, he rejected an offer from Greeley's *Tribune*. No longer would he disperse his talents, such as they were, on unprofitable enterprises, thanks to Fields's business acumen and unconditional support.

He did compose a new preface for *Twice-told Tales* in his recognizable style: muted irony, authorial detachment, sardonic nonchalance, and modesty mixed with a dollop of hauteur. Affecting to spurn anything as base as self-disclosure, popularity, or ostentation, he drew attention to himself and his career, reminding the reader with just a trace of bitterness that he'd been "for a good many years, the obscurest man of letters in America," who'd tried his utmost "to open an intercourse with the world." The author is Oberon, disappointed and unloved but able to console himself with those few but fit readers who, caring for his stories, care for him.

The autobiographical preface is also lightly powdered with self-pity. But Hawthorne wrote sincerely, up to a point. Sensitive to criticism, imagined or real, Hawthorne strikes preemptively, disputing the criticism he pretends to accept. With typical disingenuousness, he wonders how his stories managed to have any vogue at all, and he denigrates his early tales—"pale tint of flowers that blossomed in too retired a shade"—much in the manner of Poe and Fuller. "Instead of passion, there is sentiment," he echoes them; "and, even in what purport to be pictures of actual life, we have allegory." Defiantly, he goes on: "The book, if you would see anything in it, requires to be read in the clear, brown, twilight atmosphere in which it was written; if opened in the sunshine, it is apt to look exceedingly like a volume of blank pages."

Disparagement of this sort is hardly an inducement to turn the page. But Hawthorne knows that *Twice-told Tales* is being reissued by the most ambitious publisher in Boston. So much for the influence of Fuller or Poe, both of whom were dead. And was his work so pallid? "Every sentence, so far as it embodies thought or sensibility," Hawthorne smoothly continues, "may be understood and felt by anybody, who will give himself the trouble to read it, and will take up the book in a proper mood." As Melville had.

In this mild-mannered way, Hawthorne threads his preface with indelible cords of revenge, much like Hester Prynne when she sews her "A" with golden thread. "The spirit of my Puritan ancestors was mighty in me," he reiterates again and again.

Man of compassion, man of ice; man of forgiveness, man of spite: "Nobody would think that the same man could live two such different lives simultaneously," Hawthorne once told Sophia, referring to the disparity between his inner and external life. Alienation, duplicity, and the sense of living double, not being what one seems or what others take one to be: these were the hallmark of Hawthorne's prose, and through it, a persona that "on the internal evidence of his sketches," he wrote, "came to be regarded as a mild, shy, gentle, melancholic exceedingly sensitive, and not very forcible man, hiding his blushes under an assumed name, the quaintness of which was supposed, somehow or other, to symbolize his personal and literary traits."

Hawthorne knew what he was doing, he knew these half-truths became him. As did empathy, passion, fiery aggression, and the embittered loneliness of an outsider turned exile, the fugitive alone, a shadow, whether in the company of his beloved family, a responsive readership, or the keen-witted Herman Melville.

CHAPTER SEVENTEEN

The Hidden Life of Property

What we call real estate—the solid ground to build a house on—is the broad foundation on which nearly all the guilt of this world rests.

. . .

But, for this short life of ours, one would like a house and a moderate garden-spot of one's own.

Nathaniel Hawthorne, *The House of the Seven Gables*

T HE BOOK IS an affliction," Catharine Sedgwick sniffed at *The House of the Seven Gables.* "It affects one like a passage through the wards of an insane asylum."

Hawthorne had returned home, at least in imagination, for the setting of his new novel, and though he insisted in the book's preface that it had "a great deal more to do with the clouds overhead than with any portion of the actual soil of the County of Essex," he fooled no one. The setting of the book is vintage Salem, so much so that amateur literary sleuths steeped in New England lore quickly identified Hawthorne's seven-gabled house as the Ingersoll place on Turner Street.

In *The Scarlet Letter,* he had focused on his mother and more broadly the complex predicament women faced as wives, mothers, daughters, and sexual beings. In *The House of the Seven Gables,* he again shook the family tree, this time to confront his paternal legacy: class, heredity, and the all but incestuous business of living in one spot for generations, tyrannies and injustice handed down generation after generation like a congenital disease.

Hawthorne combined Susanna Ingersoll's story about her Turner Street house with tales about his great-grandfather, the hanging judge, and the malediction supposedly uttered by Sarah Good when the Reverend

Nicholas Noyes had called her a witch. "I'm no more a witch than you're a wizard!" she reportedly cried. "And if you take my life God will give you blood to drink!" Translating this into the prophecy that Matthew Maule, the accused wizard, hurls at his nemesis, Colonel Pyncheon in *The House of the Seven Gables,* Hawthorne also dug up the Hathorne legend that a curse—much like Sarah Good's, much like Matthew Maule's—had robbed the family of a putative patrimony, nine thousand acres of land in eastern Maine. "The impalpable claim, therefore, resulted in nothing more solid than to cherish, from generation to generation, an absurd delusion of family importance," Hawthorne explains, as if writing of the family pretensions for which he castigated them and himself.

The book's main character is a seven-gabled house, its timbers oozy "as with the moisture of a heart" that rises phoenixlike from Hawthorne's Province-House, another pretentious mansion, and from his "Tales of the Province-House" Hawthorne also took the doddering royalist Esther Dudley, whom he rewrites as Hepzibah Pyncheon, both of them anachronisms. But the mansion is no place of grace. It was built on property stolen twice over, first from the Indians and then from the carpenter Matthew Maule, whose greedy persecutor, Colonel Pyncheon, not only expropriated Maule's land but brought down Maule's curse on his family: "The wrong-doing of one generation lives into the successive ones, and, divesting itself of every temporary advantage, becomes a pure and uncontrollable mischief," Hawthorne announces in the book's preface: Sophoclean tragedy on a New England stage.

The novel opens on the terrible morning when Hepzibah "is to be transformed into the plebeian woman." Humiliated and terrified, she barely swallows her pride to open a cent-shop, the only recourse, Hawthorne notes, for a woman in circumstances as diminished as hers. Readying herself and her store for its first customer, poor Hepzibah clumsily drops her gingerbread elephants and scatters a tumbler of marbles over the floor, every awkward attempt to retrieve them an index of her state of mind. The narrator recounts the bumbling operation, barely suppressing his laughter, but if he humiliates the gawky, scowling Hepzibah, Hawthorne deeply pities this woman, so much like relatives of his own, displaced in a rapacious nation "where everything is free to the hand that can grasp it."

"In this republican country," Hawthorne writes, "amid the fluctuating waves of our social life, somebody is always at the drowning point." The waves were, of course, cresting on the issues of property and ownership at the bottom of American politics. The Compromise of 1850 had been passed in September of that year to put a lid on the slavery issue by admitting California into the Union as a free state and leaving the question of slavery in New Mexico and Utah to referendum. The Compromise also settled Texas boundary disputes, outlawed the slave trade (not slavery) in the District of Columbia, and mollified the proslavery South with the stringent Fugitive Slave Law (an enactment of Hell, abolitionists called it), which Hawthorne himself was dead against.

In his novel, he concerns himself with the Compromise obliquely and at a distance, as in the case of Jaffrey Pyncheon's political ambitions or the gingerbread Hepzibah sells, made in the shape of Jim Crow. Instead he focuses on his own demons: hapless aristocrats at loggerheads with their avaricious relatives. For Hepzibah is awaiting the appearance of her defrauded brother Clifford, wrongly incarcerated almost a lifetime by the rich and deceitful cousin Jaffrey.

Clifford Pyncheon is prey partly because of the "feminine delicacy of appreciation" that renders him poetic, soft, even voluptuous, and reminds the reader of Hawthorne's Owen Warfield in "The Artist of the Beautiful." Clifford, like Owen, is not a manly man; he is an aesthete confused by the crudities of getting and spending. His opposite is the unctuous, aggressive Jaffrey Pyncheon, the man of consummate materialism who never mistakes shadow for substance. In public, Jaffrey beams his waxy smile; in private, he breaks his wife's spirit on their honeymoon. (Ebe saw the Reverend Charles Upham, Hawthorne's Custom House nemesis, in Jaffrey's grin.) Clifford in his damask dressing gown, Judge Jaffrey with his gold-headed cane: the Pyncheon men—victim and victimizer, idealist and materialist—incarnate the poles of conventional manhood for Hawthorne.

Enter Holgrave, the reconciler. A lodger in the house of seven gables, he has what the Pyncheons lack. He is ardent, youthful, and radical, a man at home in the modern world who nevertheless lives in the creaky old house, temporarily of course. "I dwell in it for awhile," he says, "that I may know the better how to hate it." Despising the house and what it represents, he wails, "Shall we never, never get rid of this Past?" The plaint comes straight from Hawthorne's notebooks. "We read in dead men's books! We are sick of dead jokes, and cry at dead men's pathos! We are sick of the same men's diseases, physical and moral, and die of the same remedies with which dead doctors killed their patients!" Build therefore your own house, Holgrave counsels, mouthing the kind of Emersonian self-reliance Hawthorne finds seductive and vapid. But Holgrave's raison d'être is the very past he hates: he's Matthew Maule's descendant, come to nurse ancestral wounds.

Holgrave resembles Hester Prynne, Hawthorne's ultimate outsider and another character who eventually makes her peace with society, more or less, as Holgrave will. For though he insists that "once in every half century, at longest, a family should be merged into the great, obscure, mass of humanity, and forget all about its ancestors," he falls in love with the fresh-faced Phoebe, a Pyncheon country cousin recently domiciled in the house.

Tamed by Phoebe (Hawthorne's pet name for Sophia), Holgrave renounces his wanton ways, declaring himself a conservative eager to set out trees and make fences, even, he says, to build a house for another generation. So the novel closes with Holgrave looking forward. Hawthorne, however, is not so sanguine about Holgrave's prospects. Adopting Phoebe's morally neat desire for "a house and a moderate garden-spot of one's own," Holgrave does not pick up Hawthorne's reference to Voltaire or his irony. Cultivating a garden rank with plebeian vegetables and aristocratic flowers may be the best one can do: mitigated pleasures destined for our world.

If one can have even those. Hawthorne has rigged a set of circumstances—a convenient death, a will, an inherited fortune—to remunerate his characters for their troubles, allowing Hepzibah and Clifford and Phoebe and Holgrave to light out for the territory of a romancer's conjuring, a pastoral world of happily ever after from the contingencies of time or age and the vicissitudes of fortune.

That province of make-believe is the utopian dream that Hawthorne abandoned years before, except in fiction. And one cannot be sure he hasn't given it up there too. At the conclusion of the novel, he cynically conveys Holgrave and company in a dark-green barouche to Jaffrey Pyncheon's elegant country-seat, not a garden-spot of their own but another house, redolent both of the past and of what's to come.

Produced less than a year after *The Scarlet Letter, The House of the Seven Gables* is a book of middle age, for time is the novel's cardinal theme, time and its relentless passage in a world hell-bent on progress. Eyes filmy and dim, Clifford cannot flee himself or his past, and all the newfangled appurtenances—the railroad and the electric telegraph—cannot undo what's been done. "No great mistake, whether acted or endured, in our moral sphere," Hawthorne writes, "is ever really set right."

Doubtless begun as one of the tales to be included with *The Scarlet Letter, The House of the Seven Gables* is the first novel Hawthorne produced as such, which helps account for its curious repetitions (the story of Matthew

Maule's martyrdom told more than once) and its almost static temper. Ellery Channing joked to Emerson that Hawthorne took one hundred forty pages to describe an event; "a cough took up ten pages, and sitting down in a chair six more." But with such set-pieces as a wizened Hepzibah Pyncheon opening her shop or a smug Judge Pyncheon sitting dead in his chair, this singular novel goes where books have not yet tread, stopping time entirely.

Chapter 18 is a case in point: planting a corpse in his book, Hawthorne halts his story as the narrator speaks of life and death and the sure oblivion that opens beneath our feet. Meantime, our pocket-watches, like Jaffrey Pyncheon's, tick indifferently on:

> There is still a faint appearance at the window; neither a glow, nor a gleam, nor a glimmer—any phrase of light would express something far brighter than this doubtful perception, or sense, rather, that there is a window there. Has it yet vanished? No!—yes!—not quite! And there is still the swarthy whiteness—we shall venture to marry these ill-agreeing words—the swarthy whiteness of Judge Pyncheon's face. The features are all gone; there is only the paleness of them left. And how looks it now? There is no window! There is no face! An infinite, inscrutable blackness has annihilated sight! Where is our universe? All crumbled away from us; and we, adrift in chaos, may hearken to the gusts of homeless wind, that go sighing and murmuring about, in quest of what was once a world!
>
> Is there no other sound? One other, and a fearful one. It is the ticking of the Judge's watch.

"There is a certain tragic phase of humanity, which, in our opinion, was never more powerfully embodied than by Hawthorne," Melville remarked. "We mean the tragicalness of human thought in its own unbiased, native, and profounder workings."

Hawthorne is like the daguerreotypist Holgrave, who wants to reveal people's characters, not just their looks. Holgrave is a contemporary sorcerer, or romancer, manipulating time, the better to discover its secrets, like Hawthorne does. Calling the novel a romance, as he had in *The Scarlet Letter,* Hawthorne says he does not dramatize events unsheathed in the spick-and-span light of common day, like Dickens or Balzac do. Rather, as romancer—an American Walter Scott crossed with Goethe and E. T. A. Hoffmann (though he would never have said so)—he claims in the preface to *The House of the Seven Gables,* that he, unlike a novelist, manages "his atmospherical medium as to bring out or mellow the lights and deepen and enrich the shadows of the picture," salting his dish (he changed his metaphor) with "the Marvellous rather as a slight, delicate and evanescent flavor."

To the extent that Holgrave is a reconciler, he represents the artist who (again like Hawthorne) squares the actual and the imaginary, time and eternity, being and nothingness. To Hawthorne, then the work was balanced, its writing a kind of exorcism, and he consequently considered *The House of the Seven Gables* "a more natural and healthy product of my mind" than *The Scarlet Letter.*

Hawthorne finished the book at the end of January, mailed it to Fields, and then suffered the "blue devils" in its wake. "How slowly I have made my way in life!" he wrote to Horatio Bridge. "How much is still to be done!"

"There is a grand truth about Nathaniel Hawthorne. He says NO! in thunder; but the Devil himself cannot make him say *yes,*" Melville bellowed after reading *The House of the Seven Gables.* "For all men who say *yes,* lie; and all men who say *no,*—why, they are in the happy condition of judicious, unencumbered travellers in Europe; they cross the frontiers into Eternity with nothing but a carpet-bag."

In the fall, after Melville had purchased 160 acres and a farm he dubbed Arrowhead in Pittsfield, Massachusetts, he and Hawthorne exchanged letters and visits across the country roads, Melville rumbling over to Lenox in his pine-board wagon, drinking champagne foam (a concoction of champagne, beaten eggs, and loaf sugar) at the Hawthorne house and promising "mulled wine with wisdom, & buttered toast with story-telling" in return. In a March snowstorm, Hawthorne drove off with Una and brought to Melville Archibald Duncan's *The Mariner's Chronicle,* a book owned by his uncle Richard: it was a gift of affection and regard.

The friendship had not waned. "I mean to continue visiting you until you tell me that my visits are both supererogatory and superfluous," Melville wrote Hawthorne, happy to tote from Pittsfield a bedstead and a clock to the red shanty. And Sophia watched with approval as this "fresh, sincere, glowing mind" spoke to Hawthorne about God and the Devil and life "so he can get at the truth," she said, "for he is a boy in opinion—

having settled nothing yet." Yet there was no "mush of concession" in him, she said.

During a trip to New York that spring, Melville overheard much praise of Hawthorne's *House of the Seven Gables.* "So upon the whole, this N.H. is in the ascendant," Melville reported with a touch of envy. "My dear Sir, they begin to patronize. All Fame is patronage." Hawthorne was doing well. Not he. He was completing *Moby-Dick* in a spasm of energy and jitters. "Though I wrote the Gospels in this century," he predicted, "I should die in the gutter." But he approved of *The House of the Seven Gables* ("genialities peep out more"), and Sophia loved it.

Publication was delayed. Fields figured he needed three or four thousand bound copies ready for purchase at the Old Corner Bookstore, it being bad policy to run out of a new book. He expected it to be popular. Having reissued *Twice-told Tales,* which sold almost two thousand copies, he was creating a market for Hawthorne, as he'd said he would, stolid and powerful as a locomotive, by hawking the novel in the South when he traveled there and making sure every newspaper pirating a copy of the preface to *Twice-told Tales* ran a wood engraving of Hawthorne's face.

Hawthorne disliked these although he'd been pleased with Cephas Thompson's portrait from which they were taken. Painted in Boston in 1850, the portrait depicts Hawthorne as seated, composed, in command of himself and his surroundings. He wears a standing white collar, black coat and waistcoat, and a silk bow-tie. His greenish gray eyes, the color of the sea on an overcast day, meet the spectator in the way a shy man defies his shyness. The forehead is high, the hair thinning. The face itself is long, a smile—or a grimace—playing about his mouth.

Fields commissioned Thomas Phillibrown to make a steel engraving from this portrait, which magnified the sadness in Hawthorne's eye, or so Sophia thought, but Hawthorne approved enough to have it sent with the presentation copies of *The House of the Seven Gables* going to friends. Sophia gave Melville a copy.

Fields finally released the novel during the second week of April. "A weird, wild book, like all he writes," Longfellow remarked, and James Russell Lowell predicted Salem would soon build Hawthorne a monument "for having shown that she did not hang her witches for nothing." Evert Duyckinck told readers of the *Literary World* that Hawthorne carries "his lantern, like Belzoni among the mummies, into the most secret recesses of the heart."

Of the reviewers, most perceptive was Edwin Whipple, if one excuses him for not being able to see what Melville had. To Whipple, the first hun-

Hawthorne at forty-six, portrait by Cephas Thompson, 1850,
"drawing sad sweetness," said Sophia Hawthorne, "which
makes me catch my breath as I gaze at it. No one has ever
drawn or painted anything of Mr. Hawthorne comparable to
this, & Mr. Thompson must have a wondrous perception &
have seen all he has there expressed."

dred pages of *The House of the Seven Gables* were brilliant in conception and execution, combining the humor of "The Custom-House" with the pathos of *The Scarlet Letter.* But the rest of the book was shaky, the characters weak. Holgrave was a stick and Clifford Pyncheon a nattering bore. From England, however, Fanny Kemble wrote to the Hawthornes that *The House of the Seven Gables* caused as much of a ruckus as *Jane Eyre,* and the *Athenaeum* ranked Hawthorne one of the most original novelists of modern times. Ebe Hawthorne delivered the starchest, best compliment of all: "It is evident that you stand in no awe of the public," she praised her brother, "but rather bid it defiance, which is well for all authors, and all other men to do."

On May 20, 1851, just about a month after the publication of *The House of the Seven Gables,* Sophia produced what Hawthorne called "a little work"— a new baby. Squalling and kicking, Rose Hawthorne entered the world, "the daughter of my age," her forty-six-year-old father remarked wryly, "if age and decrepitude are really to be my lot."

Sophia had definitely wanted another child; her sister Mary had three. It's not clear what Hawthorne wanted. According to Elizabeth Peabody, Sophia claimed that her husband was so anxious over her health he thought she should bear only three children, each after a prescribed interval. The story, even if true, smacks of apology. Nonetheless, something prompted Elizabeth Peabody to conclude that "Mr. Hawthorne's passions were under his feet," as if he had none.

Whatever transpired in the bedroom, Hawthorne's insistent worries about how to feed a growing family contributed in no small measure to his blues. "I have never yet seen the year, since I was married, when I could have spared even a hundred dollars from the necessary expense of living," he told Peabody when she tried to make him buy life insurance. *The House of the Seven Gables* sold for a dollar, with Hawthorne receiving a 15 percent royalty, but despite the advance brouhaha, sales lagged, and Fields couldn't peddle the English rights. Hawthorne, who earned just a little over one thousand dollars the first year of publication, had to draw on his account with the publisher to settle old debts.

Sophia was tired, the baby cried, and always a tight fit, the little red shanty began to shrink even further. The walls were too thin, the ceilings too low. And Hawthorne was lonely for his friends. All winter, the snow was deep, the paths impassable. In spring, the muddy lanes were hard to navigate. "I feel remote, and quite beyond companionship," he complained to Longfellow. The fans who opened his gate were a nuisance. He generally refused invitations, and he seldom went to the village except to visit the post office. Joseph Smith, a Stockbridge resident, remembered Hawthorne's rare appearance in town. "Mr. Hawthorne, even for a man of letters, leads a remarkably secluded life," Smith observed. "I'm afraid the de'il will carry him off if he walks so much in solitary places," Caroline Tappan joshed.

Sophia welcomed callers from Boston come to see the Tappans, but if too many people, especially literary ones, were to flock to the Berkshires, she complained to her mother, "I dare say we shall take flight." It was an uncommon outburst. Sophia didn't want to leave Lenox although Hawthorne longed to inhale ocean breezes, pace the moist docks, plunge his feet into the sand. And talk with his buddies. "He seems older, & I think he has suffered much living in this place," Ellery Channing reported to his wife after seeing Hawthorne in Lenox. ". . . I think he has felt his lack of society."

He returned to work. He still considered the children's market a lucrative one, and since Fields's republication of his juvenile tales (renamed *True Stories*) enjoyed a press run of forty-five hundred, he expected even more of a profit for a new children's book. It took Hawthorne only six weeks to write his irresistible retelling of classical myths, *A Wonder Book for Girls and Boys*.

Later in the summer, Sophia headed for West Newton with Una and the baby, leaving Hawthorne alone with the frisky Julian, now five, and their black cook, Mrs. Peters. The two males—one sturdy and small, the other almost six feet tall—walked daily to the lake, where they amused themselves flinging stones into the water and picking wildflowers. Julian was especially thrilled when Melville, galloping down the road, stopped, bent down, and scooped him up into the saddle. Melville stayed through tea, and after supper he and Hawthorne smoked cigars in the sacred precincts of the sitting room, talking deep into the night about "time and eternity, things of this world and of the next, and books, and publishers, and all possible and impossible matters."

In Melville's presence, Hawthorne yearned even more for the magically curative powers of the sea. Should his writing turn profitable, he fantasized, he might buy a house by the coast. He asked friends to look for something priced between fifteen hundred and two thousand dollars, if not on the ocean then with easy access to it. "I find that I do not feel at home among these hills, and should not like to consider myself permanently settled here," he explained to William Pike. To Sophia, he dropped the veil. "I hate Berkshire with my whole soul, and would joyfully see its mountains laid flat."

There was little argument from Sophia. She and Caroline Tappan had been quarreling without words for several months. Sophia thought Caroline (like Ebe) induced Una to deceive and disobey, and while Sophia was in West Newton, Caroline had been dropping by the red farmhouse, arms heavy with newspapers and books to loan Hawthorne for his next novel. Perhaps she stayed too long, ruffling Sophia's feathers more. Caroline responded by asserting droit du seigneur. She had seen the Hawthornes' servant, Mary Beekman, carrying a basket of fruit and peremptorily asked if the fruit was to be given away or sold, the latter a breach of etiquette, to be sure, and an abuse of her largesse. She sent a note to Sophia; wouldn't Sophia prefer to receive kindness than assume rights? she asked.

"The right of purchase is the only safe one," Hawthorne sharply replied, referring not to the fruit but to his demeaned position as tenant farmer. He wanted a roof of his own, his own garden-spot, and Tappan provided just the excuse he needed. "I am sick to death of Berkshire," he sputtered to Fields. ". . . I have felt languid and dispirited, during almost my whole residence."

Within two weeks Hawthorne took off for Boston and put in motion plans to remove his family from the hated hills.

"Did Mr. Hawthorne tell you *all* the reasons why we are disenchanted of Lenox?" Sophia was soon asking Mary Mann.

Since Mary and her family were bound for Washington, Horace having been reelected to Congress on the Free-Soil ticket, Mary had offered to rent their place in West Newton to the Hawthornes. They had declined. The price was too high, and thinking they might stay in the Berkshires another two years—the length of the presidential term—they figured they'd take Fanny Kemble's house, offered for the same rent they paid the Tappans. But they didn't. They bolted.

Reasons other than Tappan apples hustled the Hawthornes from Lenox. "When a man is making his settled dispositions for life, he had better be on the mainland, and as near a rail-road station as possible," Hawthorne confessed to Bridge, meaning more than he let on. With the presidential election upcoming in 1852, Hawthorne wanted to be a stone's throw from Boston, partly to keep his political hat close to the ring. Like him, many Democrats had been biding their time in local caucuses, hoping their time would come again soon; if they could reunite the party, they might recapture the presidency, and after the sudden death of New Hampshire favorite Levi Woodbury in September—just when Hawthorne decided to return to the Boston area—they thought Frank Pierce might be their man. Hawthorne may have heard from Pierce himself that he would consider a bid, and in any case, William Pike and Zachariah Burchmore, still active in the cause, each kept an eye on the prize.

So too Hawthorne. Neither Free-Soiler nor abolitionist, he commended Burchmore for not defecting to the antislavery movement—as he had not, steering much the same course as when he edited *Journal of an African Cruiser.* "I have not, as you suggest, the slightest sympathy for the slaves," he reassured Burchmore; "or, at least, not half so much as for the laboring whites, who, I believe, as a general thing, are ten times worse off than the Southern negros."

With his opposition to the antislavery movement, Hawthorne embarrassed many of his acquaintances and later his fans. "How glad I am that

Sumner is at last elected!" he wrote Longfellow about the protracted fight to send that Free-Soiler to the United States Senate. "Not that I ever did, nor ever shall, feel any pre-eminent ardor for the cause which he advocates," he crisply added, "nor could ever have been moved, as you were, to dedicate poetry—or prose either—to its advancement." Nonetheless, he signed a Free-Soil petition protesting the Fugitive Slave Law. A firm believer in states' rights, he regarded any law absurd that ceded control to the federal government, particularly one that allowed slave owners or their representatives to enter free states, arrest runaways—kidnap them, according to the abolitionists—and haul them back South like so much bundled hay. "This Fugitive Law is the only thing that could have blown me into any respectable warmth on this great subject of the day." He paused—"If it really be the great subject."

Elizabeth Peabody smiled to learn of Hawthorne's signature, but as far as he was concerned, in so doing he had "bade farewell to all ideas of foreign consulships, or other official stations." He said he didn't care a "d— for office," suggesting the opposite.

The Mann offer began to sound good. Visiting West Newton, Hawthorne temporized. From there, he and Sophia could more reasonably look at last for their own place. "Ticknor & Co. promise the most liberal advances of money, should we need it, towards buying the house," he reassured his wife and himself.

Sensing his urgency, she quickly acquiesced. "I begin to unlove the lake now I think it has done harm to Mr. Hawthorne & my chief desire is to get as far from it as possible, when a little while ago it caused a real pang to think of leaving it."

In the fall, they sold much of their furniture at auction, including Hawthorne's mahogany writing desk, and gathered the remaining household goods, leaving behind their five cats and a sorrowful Melville. There was nothing to be done about Melville, of course; he had a family of his own. Early in November, Hawthorne met Melville for dinner at the Lenox hotel, and that night Melville presumably gave Hawthorne his inscribed copy of *Moby-Dick*, cooked, Melville hinted, partly at Hawthorne's fire. "I have written a wicked book," Melville was to tell him, "and feel spotless as a lamb." The letter (lost) that Hawthorne wrote in praise of *Moby-Dick* drove the younger author to rapture: "Your heart beat in my ribs and mine in yours, and both in God's," Melville surged with hopeful intimacy, demanding in the next breath, "Whence come you, Hawthorne? By what right do you drink from my flagon of life?"

Melville was doomed to disappointment. It came first in Duyckinck's patronizing notice of *Moby-Dick* in the *Literary World*. "What a book Melville has written!" Hawthorne wrote Duyckinck in protest. "It hardly seemed to me that the review of it, in the Literary World, did justice to its best points." If Hawthorne volunteered to review it, Melville waved him aside. "Don't write a word about the book," he admonished. Hawthorne took Melville at face value. Melville lovers never forgave him.

Leaving the Berkshires, Hawthorne began slowly to pull away from the parched Berkshire sailor who ceaselessly sought answers to questions his contemporaries did not pose. "It is strange how he persists—and has persisted ever since I knew him, and probably long before—in wandering to and fro over these deserts, as dismal, as dismal and monotonous as the sand hills amid which we were sitting," Hawthorne commented five years later in a searching analysis of Melville—and of himself. "He can neither believe, nor be comfortable in his unbelief; and he is too honest and courageous not to try to do one or the other."

A man who himself knew of desert places, Hawthorne must have wondered whether he faced them with Melville's soul-rending honesty. "But truth is ever incoherent," Melville had told him, "and when the big hearts strike together, the concussion is a bit stunning." Hawthorne warded off Melville's tribute with a characteristic blend of hard-shell irony and finical decorum. Melville, said he, is "a person of very gentlemanly instincts in every respect, save that he is a little heterodox in the matter of clean linen."

On a sunless November morning, the Hawthorne wagon lumbered out of the red shanty. Julian, twisting around in his seat, looked back and saw their five household cats sitting on the ridge of the hill, abandoned to the gray snowflakes.

"I suppose it is Sophia's plan," the waspish Ebe Hawthorne wrongly surmised; "it is so much like the Peabodys never to be settled." She was half right in her second guess: "If Nathaniel buys a place she will have some excuse for leaving it in a year or two."

CHAPTER EIGHTEEN

Citizen of Somewhere Else

*It was impossible, situated as we were, not to imbibe the idea
that everything in nature and human existence was fluid, or fast
becoming so; that the crust of the Earth, in many places, was
broken, and its whole surface portentously upheaving; that it
was a day of crisis, and that we ourselves were in the critical
vortex.*

Nathaniel Hawthorne, *The Blithedale Romance*

A S PROMISED, Fields kept the pot boiling. He published an illustrated
Wonder Book in November, paying a 15 percent royalty, and he dug
Hawthorne's early pieces out of old *Tokens* for a new volume, *The Snow-
Image and Other Twice-told Tales,* that appeared in December. A trim col-
lection of fifteen stories and sketches, the latter contained "Main-street"
and "Ethan Brand" and the two weaker stories, "The Great Stone Face" and
"The Snow-Image," all written after Hawthorne left the Manse; though
it also included "The Devil in Manuscript" and "My Kinsman, Major
Molineux," it was the flimsiest demonstration of Hawthorne's talent to date
and the least popular commercially.

But he felt he was finally on the map and could now be generous. In the
dedicatory letter prefacing *The Snow-Image,* Hawthorne named Horatio
Bridge as the knight-errant who, by subsidizing Hawthorne's first collection, had single-handedly rescued him from oblivion. "If anybody is responsible for my being at this day an author, it is yourself," he thanked Bridge.
Yet neither the notoriety of *The Scarlet Letter* nor the critical success of *The
House of the Seven Gables* could sweeten Hawthorne's bitterness over years of
neglect and anonymity that he believed he'd suffered. "I sat down by the
wayside of life," Hawthorne wrote, "like a man under enchantment, and a

shrubbery sprung up around me, and the bushes grew to be saplings, and the saplings become trees, until no exit appeared possible, through the entangling depths of my obscurity."

Its whistle shrieking, the iron-black railroad delivered the Hawthornes into the small village of West Newton after a twenty-minute ride from Boston, and in a five-minute walk from the depot along the edge of the cow pasture, they arrived at the Mann house. Mary had planted rosebushes in the yard, now crunchy with snow, and had fitted the house with a furnace that toasted the entire downstairs. There was a separate bathing chamber with a pump, and next to that, a water closet. Sophia complained about the steamy air, but Una and Julian preferred modern conveniences to the buckets of cold water in Lenox their parents had called a bath.

With his family of five to support and Fields irrepressible, Hawthorne shut himself up in his new study, door locked, from breakfast until four every day. Having found an audience, he didn't wanted to lose it. He meant "to put an extra touch of the devil" into the new book, he confided to Bridge, "for I doubt whether the public will stand two quiet books in succession, without my losing ground. As long as people will buy, I shall keep at work; and I find that my facility of labor increases with the demand for it." His subject would be Brook Farm.

Having divested himself of mothers in *The Scarlet Letter* and fathers in *The House of the Seven Gables,* Hawthorne was free to reconstruct "the most romantic episode" of his life, or so he wrote in the introduction to *The Blithedale Romance,* as the new book would be named. Brook Farm rose up in imagination as "essentially a day-dream, and yet a fact," he continued, reverting to the way he intermingled fiction and reality in what he defined as romance, that psychological place of grace where idle dreamers and men of the world commingle. After the Berkshire retreat and his tenancy in the house of seven gables, Hawthorne was ransacking the present, or near present. And living in West Newton, in the vicinity of Brook Farm, among aficionados of reform like the Manns and the Peabodys, Hawthorne may have wanted to distance himself from them; he didn't tell Sophia what he was writing, or if he did, she pretended not to know so as not to tell her family.

He'd begun his book the previous summer, and with it in mind, and Duyckinck and Melville in tow, he visited the Shaker village in Hancock, Massachusetts. Ushered through the main house by a somber village elder, the men padded over well-oiled wooden floors. Hawthorne was repelled when he peeked into the same-sex dormitories and glimpsed the narrow beds in which two men or two women slept with one another. "The Shakers are and must needs be a filthy set," he wrote, working himself into a harangue. "And then their utter and systematic lack of privacy; the close conjunction of man with man, and supervision of one man over another—it is hateful and disgusting to think of; and the sooner the sect is extinct the better."

Years earlier, of course, he had teasingly threatened to join the Shakers and in stories like "The Canterbury Pilgrims" wrote sympathetically of them, depicting the community more as a refuge from sex than a sexual hellhole; so, too, in "The Shaker Bridal." There, the Shakers are lost sheep, not reprobates. Now the bloom was off the rose. But Hawthorne was still interested in corporate living—alternative forms of sodality and experimental sexual groups—although he frequently shrank from what engaged him most, reducing his world to spectacle. "Insincerity in a man's own heart makes all his enjoyments, all that concerns him, unreal; so that his whole life must seem like merely a dramatic representation. And this would be the case, even though he were surrounded by true-hearted relatives and friends," Hawthorne had written as a young man. Except around Sophia, he hadn't changed. To give himself was to lose himself, and he couldn't afford to lose what he wasn't sure he had in the first place.

A psychological roman à clef, *The Blithedale Romance* is a book about male friendship and mesmerism, utopian idealism and erotic women, women authors and passive men, none of them able to confront precisely what they want. Such is the dilemma of Miles Coverdale, Hawthorne's first-person narrator, who believes he can best hold himself together by holding himself apart and conceives the world as theater, the book's dominant image. Melancholy and distrustful, this caviling poet is perpetual loner, a prurient bachelor who spurns the desires he affects to embrace. He's a citizen of somewhere else, as Hawthorne wrote of himself in "The Custom-House," scuttling between rented rooms in Boston—themselves a metaphor for dislocation—and Blithedale, Hawthorne's ironic name for Brook Farm, where Coverdale is resident spy.

Coverdale, like Hawthorne, recounts his experiences in retrospect, as if Blithedale/Brook Farm were the vestige of a different, more hopeful, more innocent time. By 1852 the community had long since disbanded. After Hawthorne left, it turned to Fourier for guidance, sputtering along for a while in makeshift phalanxes until bankruptcy and fire razed the place. Utopia folded its tent in 1847, its youthful members having put away child-ish things, its older members altering their sights. George W. Curtis, a stu-dent at Brook Farm in 1842, would sail the Nile and come back with a successful travel book, *Nile Notes of a Howadji;* Charles A. Dana was en route, via the Whiggish *New-York Tribune,* to the *Sun;* and the Ripleys were in New York too, where George himself wrote for Greeley's paper. Brook Farm hadn't been such a bad place; certainly it did no harm, its adherents developing how they would, but Hawthorne saw the experiment as doomed to failure from the start. "Persons of marked individuality—crooked sticks, as some of us might be called—are not exactly the easiest to bind up into a faggot."

The fictional Brook Farm is assembled from such crooked sticks. The pallid seamstress Priscilla, a washed-out version of Sophia, also resembles Hawthorne's sister Louisa, meekly devoted to personalities more powerful. Priscilla moonlights as a medium, the Veiled Lady, her occupation deriving from the spiritualism vogue that had sprouted in upstate New York a few years before when the infamous Fox sisters claimed that the "rappings" ema-nating from underneath the table (they were cracking their knuckles) came directly from the dead. Elizabeth Peabody, a reed in every zeitgeist, had decided Una would make a fine medium. Hawthorne growled that he'd defy all of Hell to disprove the rappers' testimony, if it came to that.

For many years Sophia denied that Hawthorne based Priscilla's half sis-ter Zenobia, another inmate of Blithedale, on Margaret Fuller although eventually she acknowledged that Hawthorne "felt Margaret Fuller's pres-ence" when writing his book. Zenobia, beautiful and brainy, plaits a white flower in her indignant hair and asks, "Did you ever see a happy woman in your life?" Proud Zenobia is Hawthorne's hothouse advocate of women's rights, more seditious and at the outset more successful, it seems, than Hes-ter Prynne. But by drawing on the life of Zenobia's namesake, the queen of Palmyra, Hawthorne creates a sexy, independent heroine only to cast her in a mawkish melodrama, and he precipitously banishes her and her ideas, sending her to an early and surprising death when Hollingsworth, the radi-cal reformer, rejects her love, and she drowns herself like Ophelia or Martha Hunt.

The reason is obvious. To Hawthorne, social renegades and apostles of change—even Zenobia—are fanatical monsters of sentiment and vanity. "They have no heart, no sympathy, no reason, no conscience. They will keep no friend, unless he make himself the mirror of their purpose; they will smite and slay you, and trample your dead corpse under foot, all the more readily, if you take the first step with them, and cannot take the second, and their third, and every other step of their terribly straight path." Hollingsworth, single-minded philanthropist committed to the reform of criminals, is true to type. Compounded of William Henry Channing, a dabbler in Brook Farm who preached there in the woods and became, for a while, a prison reformer attractive to a number of women, Sophia included, and the abolitionist Samuel Gridley Howe, who achieved a certain renown by exhibiting his pupil, the blind and deaf child Laura Bridgman (for a time Sophia and Elizabeth Peabody had hoped Hawthorne would write about her), Hollingsworth also bears the gentle imprint of Howe's best friend and Hawthorne's brother-in-law, Horace Mann, in whose house Hawthorne finished the book.

Black-browed Hollingsworth is Hawthorne's doppelgänger too. The name of Hollingsworth is that of a Hawthorne distant relative; Hollingsworth's profession, that of blacksmith, is the same as that of Hawthorne's Manning grandfather and uncle Richard. And like all of Hawthorne's characters, he is an updated rendition of Hawthorne's other obsessives—Chillingworth, Ethan Brand, the virtuoso—each a man of concentrated purpose twisted by a monomaniacal devotion to some pursuit, be it vengeance, history, sin, or art, but always a "cold, spectral monster which he had himself conjured up, and on which he was wasting all the warmth of his heart, and of which, at last—as these men of a mighty purpose so invariably do—he had grown to be the bond-slave."

Mostly, though, Hawthorne drew on himself for Coverdale, whose observations come straight from Hawthorne's journals. One never really knows why he, like Hawthorne, signs on to the Blithedale community, except perhaps in a spasm of visionary enthusiasm, for like Hawthorne, Coverdale prefers to stay insulated in his rooms, comforted with a good bottle of claret behind a thick curtain of cigar smoke. His métier is concealment; he watches others, himself unseen. (*The Blithedale Romance* is a book about seeing: women and men hide behind veils, flaunting their invisibility.) Coverdale spies on Hollingsworth and Zenobia from his treetop hermitage, hungrily glimpsing Zenobia's white shoulder while he denies his naked attraction to her.

Coverdale does admit to loving his masculine rival, Hollingsworth, but when Hollingsworth asks him to "strike hands" and join him in his great reformer's project so as to "never again feel the languor and vague wretched-ness, of an indolent or half-occupied man," Coverdale casts him off, too terrified to share in life or love. Yet he finds the proposal dangerously seduc-tive and leaves Blithedale so as not to confront it, forever the frosty solipsist clinging to the wayside, treasuring his sterile fantasies above all else. But whatever else he may be, Coverdale is the first modern antihero, an antebel-lum Prufrock, self-regarding, anxiety-ridden, paralyzed, and mistaken.

Decidedly one of Hawthorne's most peculiar books and certainly one of the most unique novels yet written in America, *Blithedale* is as personal as anything Hawthorne ever produced, a fantasy of what-might-have-been from the conflicted position of what is. The family man with three children, a well-known and admired writer, regards himself as displaced and out of time, a spectator never quite able to get what he wants. Had he not married, he seems to suggest, he might have become the world-weary Coverdale—Holgrave without Phoebe—a writer of lukewarm stuff who permits his "colorless life," as he says of Coverdale, "to take its hue from other lives." And with no native inclination toward industry, as he once confided to Sophia, Hawthorne perceives himself as constantly having to battle the dreamy nature he continues to condemn.

Brook Farm had promised a way out, bringing together dreamers and laborers in a joint-stock company far from the go-getting herd. It didn't work. To Hawthorne, Brook Farm spawned the same society, peopled by the same problems, he'd hoped to leave behind, his own included. Worse: with its assertive women and womanish men, and men who love men, and women, like Priscilla, who love women like Zenobia, Blithedale is society's grotesque obverse. "While inclining us to the soft affections of the Golden Age," Coverdale notes, "it seemed to authorize any individual, of either sex, to fall in love with any other, regardless of what would elsewhere be judged suitable and prudent." He can't stand it. "No sagacious man will long retain his sagacity," he justifies his peremptory leave-taking, "if he live exclusively among reformers and progressive people, without periodically returning into the settled system of things, to correct himself by a new observation from that old stand-point."

Hawthorne is the one who loses perspective. *Blithedale* fails precisely because Hawthorne stands too close to his material to shape it. He neither manages to salvage a believable plot from Coverdale's passive narration nor does he develop the characters enough to rescue them from its improbabili-ties. Plots within plots, rich men brought low, love triangles, and suicide: the mechanics of intrigue tumble atop one another, as if Hawthorne were

Professor Westervelt, the novel's evil genie, a spiritualist hack who gulls his audience and fleeces them: in other words, a fraud.

Hawthorne knew his strengths as a writer did not lie in consistently sustained narrative, and for that reason refused to write serially in magazines. "In all my stories, I think, there is one idea running through them like an iron rod, and to which all other ideas are referred and subordinate," he explained. There is no iron rod in *Blithedale*. Not even Coverdale could help. He tries to think about the future but fails and, emotionally dead, withdraws from his own subject matter. He rakes through the cold ashes of America's grand utopian moment with itchy intolerance, so much so that, after the first few chapters of his memoir, Blithedale is no longer integral to his story.

However, many of Hawthorne's contemporaries saw in Hawthorne's new production a social issue stormier than anything as benign as the socialist experiment at Brook Farm. Identifying with Coverdale, the Reverend Theodore Parker, who kept a brace of pistols in his desk to assist fugitive slaves, thought the book written just for him. Friends agreed. Though Parker detested slavery, he did not truckle to abolitionists like William Lloyd Garrison, and Garrison could be none other than Hollingsworth. "He thinks Garrison will flinch at Hawthorne's picture of the philanthropist," Mary Mann reported to her husband with pleasure.

To Mann and friends, Hawthorne's quarry in *Blithedale* was not the counterfeit arcadia of the 1840s nor the troublesome relations between women and men. It was a fractious America, a present-day America, where abolitionists were called philanthropists and fanatics. Blithedale was the abolition movement that Hawthorne adamantly refused to join.

No sooner had the Hawthornes settled in West Newton than Hawthorne was ready to leave. The winter was especially severe. Sophia stopped her home instruction of Una and Julian to drive through pathless snow each day and tend to her now bedridden mother, who grew feebler by the hour. When the snow began to melt, stale water spewed into the house from defective drains. Sophia fretted about the disease that might invade her own little circle, Mr. Peabody came to spread lime on the ground, and Hawthorne worried about paying the rent. "He is very anxious to get into a home of his own, where his mind will be free to follow the calling on which his bread depends," Mrs. Peabody commented, ready to let them go.

In February they wrapped themselves in flannel and wool and rode by

sleigh to Concord to inspect the old Alcott place, "Hillside," so named for
the steep incline at the rear of the house, at the top of which stretched a dark
wood of locust trees, acacia, and tall dark pine. In years to come, Hawthorne would love that hill, climbing it and pacing the ridge for hours, or
lying down under an umbrella of tree to dream about unwritten books.

A. Bronson Alcott

A wizard gardener, Alcott had cut terraces into the hill, planting flowers
and vegetables in manicured profusion. Ice now covered the brown tufts of
branch and the withered vines hung over the house, the raggediest he'd ever
seen, Hawthorne said, and he promptly offered to buy it for fifteen hundred
dollars. Hawthorne rechristened it "The Wayside." "I never feel as if I were
more permanently located than the traveller who sits down to rest by the
road," he mused. The words were prophetic.

Built before the Revolutionary War, the old clapboard farmhouse shook
with the clatter of wagon wheels, so close was it to the Lexington road.
Inside, the ceilings hung low and damp. Sunshine crawled into corners only
at rare intervals, and though Alcott had built extra rooms, new stairs, a

shower-bath, and a veranda, the house felt boxy, and small, even smaller than the red shanty. It was a mess, too. Not fit for a menagerie of cattle, Sophia moaned, wrinkling her nose at the residue of the Alcotts and whatever creatures had been inhabiting the place since they'd left.

There was no time to lose. The Manns were returning to Massachusetts, and the house had to be made spick-and-span for the new inhabitants. Sophia went to Concord with the three children on the first Sunday in June, took a large room at the Middlesex Hotel, and hired a hack to drive over to the Lexington road, where she had employed a woman to clean and a man to do the heavy lifting. She and her workers dragged out the mattresses stored in the barn, swept and washed the floors, and varnished the oak walls to a happy gloss. The next day she found two more women to help her wash windows. The water was pure, the pump quiet, and Sophia bragged that within weeks her skin looked like whipped marble.

A pretty grapevine curled over the front porch and the honeysuckle twisted around the piazza. Locust trees in white blossom covered the hillside. For her husband's study, Sophia bought a lapis and gold rug that she laid carefully on the floor just before Hawthorne opened the gate—his gate—to the first house he'd ever owned.

Sophia had proudly hung her portrait of Endymion in his workroom and set up a pedestal for the bust of Apollo. There wasn't much furniture since his desk and secretary had been sold in Lenox. No matter. On the first of May, he'd finished the last part of the manuscript and scrawled its tentative title, "Hollingsworth: A Romance," on the first page, sending it to Whipple for a preliminary glance. (Fields had gone to Europe to recover from the death of his wife.) Whipple later recalled that he offered a few suggestions, mainly about Hollingsworth—that, for instance, he ought to be punished more severely for his brutal rejection of Zenobia. "I hate the man ten times worse than you do," Hawthorne presumably replied, "but I don't now see how such a nature can feel the remorse he ought to feel." According to Whipple, though, Hawthorne modified the book's conclusion enough to satisfy him—and the public.

The book's title had to be changed too. Fields nixed "Hollingsworth." Hawthorne weighed other options: "Zenobia" was an impossibility, since a novel by that name had just been published. " 'Miles Coverdale's Three Friends';—this title comprehends the book, but rather clumsily," Hawthorne said. " 'The Veiled Lady'—too melodramatic; and, besides, I do not wish to give prominence to that feature of the romance. 'Priscilla'—she is such a shrinking damsel that it seems hardly fair to thrust her into the vanguard and make her the standard-bearer. 'The Blithedale Romance'—that would do, in lack of a better."

Fields responded with typical ebullience, buoying Hawthorne's spirits with his uncorked faith in his talent and reporting from London that he'd successfully managed a deal with Chapman and Hall, Dickens's publishers, for two hundred pounds—money to help Hawthorne pay for the new house, Sophia happily noted. The publication date was set in advance of the American one to prevent pirating.

Just weeks after Hawthorne's forty-eighth birthday in July, *The Blithedale Romance* sold out its first five thousand copies. Emerson thought the book unworthy of Hawthorne's talent, but when Melville returned to Pittsfield from Nantucket and found his copy waiting, he wrote to Hawthorne right away. "Especially at this day," Melville said, "the volume is welcome, as an antidote to the mooniness of some dreamers—who are merely dreamers—Yet who the devel aint a dreamer?"

Friends praised *Blithedale*. William Pike compared it favorably to *The Scarlet Letter* for its penetration into the "the moody silences of the heart." George Hillard considered Zenobia a splendid creature, and like many of the book's critics, wished Hawthorne hadn't gotten rid of her so ruthlessly. Admiring *Blithedale*'s originality, Washington Irving, to whom Hawthorne had mailed a copy, sent Hawthorne a useful warning: "You have a formidable rival to contend with in yourself, those [earlier] works having attained a height of excellence which it will be difficult if not impossible to surpass, and the public always requiring an author in a new work to surpass himself."

By and large, however, reviewers agreed. Hawthorne had not surpassed himself, far from it. Clumsy, sneering, gloomy: they heaped up epithets and in America focused on the novel's unhealthiness. "Morbid" was a favorite accusation. Even Duyckinck's *Literary World* didn't like the book's tone, and in England the *Westminster Review* flogged Hawthorne for denuding politics and morality with superciliousness. "Would he paint an ideal slave-plantation merely for the beauty of the thing, without pretending to 'elicit a conclusion favourable or otherwise' to slavery?" the writer—George Eliot?—quotes with contempt from Hawthorne's preface, comparing *Blithedale* unfavorably with Harriet Beecher Stowe's wildly popular *Uncle Tom's Cabin*.

Sophia groaned. And she disagreed about Stowe. "I have felt all along that Mrs. Stowe's book was overrated—that it was not profound but exciting—too much addressed to the movable passions—not to the deeper soul," she grumbled. "Also that it would do no good to the slave. Time will show."

Fields grumbled too. "Let us hope there are no more Blithedales," he confided to a friend. "The writer of *Uncle Tom's Cabin* is getting to be a millionaire."

CHAPTER NINETEEN

─────────

The Main Chance

Look ever to the main chance. English proverb.

signed, Nathaniel Hawthorne
Concord, December 31, 1852

H IS FACE the shape of a baked potato, Franklin Pierce earned a reputation for sociability—too much sociability, if rumors about his
drinking were true. And they were. Sophia Hawthorne didn't care. "My
own experience, in my young girlhood, with the morphine that was given
to me to stop my headaches," she archly announced, "has given me infinite
sympathy and charity for persons liable to such a habit."

Critics of Pierce included Sophia's mother. "It is mysterious to me how
General Pierce with a face beaming with benevolence & sweetness can
enjoy the horrors of battle, the groans of his murdered fellows—the triumphs of blood—," she had shuddered during the Mexican War. "Smooth
it over as you will, it is only legal murder." Other Boston Whigs were more
serene, at least initially. Pierce, they laughed, was nothing but the hero of
"many a hard-fought bottle." Emerson would call him paltry.

As brigadier general in the Mexican War, the handsome Pierce earned a
dubious renown in the battle of Contreras when he was thrown by his
horse, which then stumbled and fell on him. His knee and pelvis injured,
Pierce fainted from the pain, missed the call to battle, and was called a coward by a subordinate. The label stuck, even though Pierce, hobbling, found
a stray horse, rejoined his troops, and fought on until the next day, when, as
bad luck would have it, he twisted his injured knee and passed out again.

Hawthorne's friend George Hillard considered Pierce "just an average
man—such as are found in every considerable town in the U.S.—of popular
manners & convivial habits, but as a statesman, an orator, or even a lawyer,

of no account at all." A mediocrity. Yet Pierce's early life had been crowned with success. At the age of twenty-seven he had been appointed to the bench of the New Hampshire Supreme Court; in 1833, at the age of twenty-nine, he was elected New Hampshire's representative to Congress, and in 1837 the blue-eyed politician became the youngest member of the United States Sen-

Franklin Pierce, president-elect, at the age of forty-eight, 1852

ate. Five years later, though, he tendered his resignation, withdrawing more or less from public office. He declined an appointment in Polk's administration as attorney general, and he refused to be nominated governor of New Hampshire because, he said, he loved his wife, who mistrusted both politics and her husband's predilection for hard liquor. It was a lethal combination, obligatory from Pierce's point of view.

The daughter of Jesse Appleton, Bowdoin College's second president, Jane Appleton Pierce was a chronically depressed woman, all fire and brimstone turned against herself. Hawthorne didn't much like her but respected Frank's devotion, bound as it was with personal tragedy. The Pierces had lost their first child, a son, three days after his birth; their second son died of typhus in 1843 at the age of four; and ten weeks before Pierce's inaugural as the fourteenth president of the United States, their third son and only remaining child was killed in a train wreck right before their eyes. Jane Pierce had reason to be depressed.

The heartbreak inevitably affected Pierce's performance as president, but it never changed his outlook. A Democrat of the Jacksonian school, Pierce stood four-square by states' rights, limited federal control, and unfettered territorial expansion. He read the Constitution as a strict constructionist, helped purge the Democratic Party in New Hampshire of Free-Soilers, and fully backed all parts of the Compromise of 1850. As Hawthorne bluntly put it, Pierce "dared to love that great and sacred reality—his whole, united, native country—better than the mistiness of a philanthropic theory."

Southern Democrats were grateful for his support, and northern Democrats, pleased by his imperturbability, suggested Pierce for the vice presidency in 1852. Pierce insisted that he was still unavailable. It was a good strategy. Politicians, especially New Englanders, weren't supposed to be too obvious or hungry. "He has a subtle faculty of making affairs roll onward according to his will," Hawthorne observed, "and of influencing their course without showing any trace of his action." At the Democratic convention in Baltimore that June, the dark horse candidate was suddenly praised as the party's unifier, and Pierce won the nomination with 282 votes on the forty-ninth ballot. He received the news by telegram. His wife fainted.

A farmer from the Granite State was said to predict the future with Yankee foresight. Frank does well enough for New Hampshire, he nodded, "but he'll be monstrous thin, spread out over the United States."

News of Pierce's nomination quickly reached Hawthorne, who immediately wrote his old friend that "it has occurred to me that you might have some thoughts of getting me to write the necessary biography." Not wishing to sound too eager (the same strategy Pierce had used), Hawthorne downplayed his qualifications. "I should write a better life of you after your term of office and life itself were over, than on the eve of an election," he joked. Pierce wasn't fooled.

Though another biographer stood in the wings—a Connecticut writer, David Bartlett—Pierce promptly accepted Hawthorne's offer. Likely he anticipated it. Stopping at the Tremont Hotel in Boston, not far from the Corner Bookstore, Pierce was surrounded by well-wishers, party hacks, politicians, office-seekers, and friends in the plush mahogany public rooms, all of whom he refused to meet, but he did receive Hawthorne, whom he hadn't seen in over two years. The dark-browed writer entered the room— or so the story goes—clasped Pierce's hand, and then flopped on one of the lounges. "Frank," he said, "I pity you." Pierce smiled his affable smile. "I pity myself," he replied.

After a couple of seconds Hawthorne replied, "But, after all, this world was not meant to be happy in—only to succeed in!"

Gentlemen of genius and renown (so Sophia said) traipsed in and out of the Wayside volunteering Pierce anecdotes for the biography. And they urged Hawthorne, the candidate's unofficial prime minister, to exert his influence. Pierce mustn't be so apathetic; Van Buren and Lewis Cass had been sure they'd be elected, and look what happened to them. "I want you to scare Pierce a little," pleaded one operative, requesting that Hawthorne arrange meetings between Pierce and Democratic representatives in New York, Ohio, and Pennsylvania. Hawthorne reportedly held a reception at the Wayside, introducing Pierce to local backers.

The matter of Hawthorne writing a campaign biography, however, was to be kept quiet—probably until *The Blithedale Romance* was published, so as not to prejudice reviewers.

Hawthorne's publishers had contracted to bring out the campaign biography, paying Hawthorne a flat fee of three hundred dollars. With Fields abroad, Hawthorne had been consulting with the firm's senior partner, William Davis Ticknor. Six years younger than Hawthorne, he looked older, almost paternal, his forehead sloping down from a shiny pate and a fringe of white whiskers coating his chin like a bib. Ticknor's daughter thought him handsome, as daughters do, but his look, like his manner, was understated and subdued. A milder man than Fields though no less charming, Ticknor was cordial, sharp-witted, adept with balance sheets, accounts, patrons, and writers. Hawthorne trusted him.

And Ticknor fully backed Pierce. Fields's politics, insofar as he was political at all, may have inclined elsewhere. (Fields's biographer insists unconvincingly that Fields inclined to nothing but literature.) Hawthorne cautiously explained that he simply must write the campaign biography of a friend with whom he'd been "intimate through life." Besides, he added gratuitously, tipping his hand, "I seek nothing from him."

Indeed he should not, snorted Louisa Hawthorne. At the Salem depot, she bumped into Horace Conolly and David Roberts on the platform, the two of them bursting with talk of the exotic diplomatic posts Hawthorne should receive at the hand of a President Pierce. She dismissed the conjectures in a huff. Its mention soiled her skirts. Roberts thought her ridiculous. She didn't care. "I told him I hoped he would have nothing to do with an office," she proudly reported to Ebe.

If Louisa's disdain represented the family's view—politics paved the way to hell, not glory—small wonder that Hawthorne kept his worldly aspirations to himself.

After much hesitation, Louisa decided to come to the Wayside, choosing the most indirect route possible. She would stop in Concord when coming home from Saratoga Springs, New York, where she and her uncle John Dike would take the waters. Then they'd steam down the Hudson River from Saratoga to New York aboard the *Henry Clay,* and Louisa would head up north to Concord by herself.

On the afternoon of July 28, a calm and sunny day, the *Henry Clay* raced a rival ship, the *Armenia,* on the river, steam belching, crew scurrying, passengers cowering. Out of control, the *Clay* soon slammed into the *Armenia.* People screamed. Metal ripped, wood crackled, but the *Clay* continued the race. A wall of flame leaped from the boiler room. Men and women ran for the lifeboats. There were none. Fire licked the wheelhouses. The steamer couldn't slow down. It plowed forward, heading straight for the riverbank. A group of passengers huddled together and waited for the crash. Others leaped into the water, hoping to swim for their lives. Many jumped to their deaths, Louisa Hawthorne among them.

As soon as he could, John Dike telegraphed Salem. He reclaimed a small brooch, a mourning pin, stained and blackened by the salt water.

William Pike did not carry it when he caught the early train for Concord. He traveled alone and light. The railroad coach dropped him near the Wayside gate shortly before seven in the morning. Sophia had not yet come down for breakfast, but seeing Pike through the window, she called out his name and waved him onto the piazza. There he stood, flushed and nervous, when she and Hawthorne opened the door. Louisa is dead, drowned, he blurted out the story. Hawthorne listened, face leeched of color. Write Pierce, Hawthorne told Pike; he'd have to delay the biography. Then he shut himself in his study.

That afternoon one could glimpse him plodding on the hilltop at the rear of the house, hands clasped behind his back, head sunk.

Hawthorne went to Salem, but with Pike confused about the time of the service, he arrived too late for the funeral. "I was glad," Sophia placated herself, "it would have been so painful for him to go through any ceremony & to hear all the Calvinistic talk." Mrs. Peabody warned Sophia to keep her rationalizations to herself. Ebe seemed dazed. Hawthorne escorted her back to Beverly, where she now lived, in a chaise.

If Hawthorne dreamed that the Wayside might soothe his restless soul, Louisa's death sent him in search of distant pastures yet again. No longer did he equivocate about the matter of a consular post. As he told William Ticknor, "We are politicians now; and you must not expect to conduct yourself like a gentlemanly publisher." The gloves were off.

Ticknor began to advertise Hawthorne's *Life of Pierce* in August knowing that the rival campaign biography would preempt Hawthorne's. But Hawthorne's slim book, 144 pages in all, bore the most prestigious imprimatur in America, that of Ticknor, Reed and Fields, and, of course, that of Hawthorne himself, whose other work Ticknor cagily advertised on the frontispiece.

"Being so little of a politician that he scarcely feels entitled to call himself a member of any party," Hawthorne introduces himself in the biography. He is a cordial nonpartisan concerned only for the welfare of his country and does not voluntarily undertake the writing of the book. Politics are "too remote" from the romancer's "customary occupations."

Whigs chuckled. Such a suave introduction: it was Hawthorne's newest romance.

He continued. His task, as he saw it, was to explain why Pierce, despite all his civil and military appointments, remained so little known. (Who is

Franklin Pierce, cried the newspapers, and how had a man of Pierce's passable talents risen so high?) Hawthorne, however, interpreted Pierce's failings as proof of good character. The man may not be a brilliant strategist, a brilliant orator, or a natural leader; but he is of great heart and conviction, earnest, steadfast, generous, a man who waits "for the occasion to bring him inevitably forward," Hawthorne claimed; bumptious, yes, but steady, manly, whole, and far preferable to Dimmesdale or Hollingsworth.

Not to the Manns. To them, Pierce was a knave, "a thorough, unmitigated, irredeemable pro-slavery man," Horace Mann stormed. How could Hawthorne back him? Mary Mann said Hawthorne was writing the biography only out of friendship. Mann wanted to know whether his brother-in-law would ignore the need—the anguish—of enslaved millions for mere personal considerations. "Is Hawthorne such a man?"

Hawthorne was. "If he makes out Pierce to be either a great or a brave man, then it will be the greatest work of fiction he ever wrote," Mann declared. Certainly Hawthorne didn't share Pierce's views. But he did. To one who never felt quite at home, the symbolic loss of one—the dissolution of the Union—was intolerable. Conceived in liberty and hope, the Union was the only rationale possible for a bloody, fratricidal American revolution that pitted not just governments but family members against one another. And despite satires depicting American vulgarity, avarice, and idiocy, Hawthorne could just as easily summon a rhetoric of manifest destiny, the country as hallowed experiment, the Constitution its covenant.

To Hawthorne, the Constitution must never be sundered or sullied by the stupidity of common mortals who set themselves up as gods, like the witch judges or the tuneless mobs that tarred and feathered Tories or the opponents of slavery, like Whig senator William Seward, waving the banner of what he in his arrogance calls a "higher law." For the Constitution preserves the Union precisely by keeping its various elements in check, ensuring the rule of law and order essential to the social good and preventing mass hysteria, demagoguery, and the petty tyranny of petty men.

Like Daniel Webster, Hawthorne considered the Compromise of 1850 the best means of protecting the Constitution from abolitionist agitators in the North and the slaveholding intransigents of the South. No surprise, then, that in the campaign biography he portrayed Pierce as the "unshaken advocate of Union, and of the mutual steps of compromise which that great object unquestionably demanded." As for the Fugitive Slave Law he once berated, Hawthorne fell prudently silent. So did Pierce.

Yet Hawthorne didn't for a minute condone slavery. Rather, he consid

ered himself a hardheaded realist who understood, as the impractical philanthropists did not, that once passed, the Compromise laws—all of them—
needed to be upheld. "The fiercest, the least scrupulous, and the most
consistent of those, who battle against slavery," Hawthorne insisted, "recognize the same fact that he [Pierce] does. They see that merely human wisdom and human efforts cannot subvert it, except by tearing to pieces the
Constitution, breaking the pledges which it sanctions, and severing into
distracted fragments that common country, which Providence brought into
one nation through a continued miracle of almost two hundred years, from
the first settlement of the American wilderness until the Revolution."

Human wisdom and effort can't abolish slavery? What then? Hawthorne still favored a gradual approach, as he indicated in *Journal of an
African Cruiser.* The institution of slavery, though execrable, if let alone, will
disappear like a dream, he now said, "by some means impossible to be anticipated, but of the simplest and easiest operation, when all its uses shall have
been fulfilled."

This is an incredible statement for a man cynical about humanity and
its enlightenment. Hawthorne saw no other way. "There is no instance," he
insists, "in all history, of the human will and intellect having perfected any
great moral reform by methods which it adapted to that end." That is slavery is preferable to whatever nefarious system might rise—or be used—to
replace it. "The evil would be certain," Hawthorne continues in his most
exhortatory vein, "while the good was, at best, a contingency." In *Blithedale,*
he wrote almost the same thing: "Little as we know of our life to come, we
may be very sure, for one thing, that the good we aim at will not be attained.
People never do get just the good they seek. If it come at all, it is something
else, which they never dreamed of, and did not particularly want."

Hawthorne defends passivity and inaction, the one a psychological
state, the other a political one, and both of them consistent with the
proslavery argument. Emancipation would inevitably lead to crime,
poverty, and bloody violence; and once freed, the emancipated slave would
not be able to find a livelihood or a home. Thus, any action taken on behalf
of abolition only serves to aggravate the situation of those "whose condition
it aimed to ameliorate, and terminating, in its possible triumph—if such
possibility there were—with the ruin of two races which now dwelt together
in greater peace and affection, it is not too much to say, than had ever elsewhere existed between the taskmaster and the serf."

Recall that Hawthorne had written almost the same thing seventeen
years earlier in his sketch "Old News," where he deemed slavery a "patriar-

chal, and almost a beautiful, peculiarity" of early American life, not admirable, to be sure, but not without its benefit for the slave; an inferior people is better off enslaved. Latter-day Hawthorne fans may want to read him as tongue-in-cheek; in his own days, his sisters-in-law did not. Appalled, Mary Mann and Elizabeth Peabody, realizing they could no longer speak their minds to Sophia, decided that Pierce had led the befuddled romancer down a primrose path of moral obliquity.

Hawthorne as master ironist, or a naïve romancer out of his element: the evidence suggests he was neither. He meant what he said and knew what he meant.

Doubtless Hawthorne considered blacks an inferior race, as did most of his New England compeers, whether Oliver Wendell Holmes, at one smug extreme, or Theodore Parker at the antislavery other. Strange and disappointing, though, is Hawthorne's complete lack of empathy for the slave. His conscious sympathies lay with the laboring white man who would certainly lose his job to an emancipated black man. And doubtless Hawthorne identified with the southern white slaveholder to the extent that he romanticized an agrarian planter class as more cultured and genteel than its busy Yankee counterpart, those no-nonsense industrialists, slick and utilitarian, or their Brahmin brothers, their privileged eyes foggy with reform. Yet like most people, Hawthorne regarded himself as well-intentioned and fair-minded, a neo-Jeffersonian patriot devoted to "preserving our sacred Union, as the immovable basis from which the destinies, not of America alone, but of mankind at large, may be carried upward and consummated."

"The biography has cost me hundreds of friends, here at the north, who had a purer regard for me than Frank Pierce ever gained, and who drop off from me like autumn leaves, in consequence of what I say on the slavery question." Hawthorne wrote to Bridge. "But they were my real sentiments, and I do not now regret that they are on record."

In the process of writing Pierce's biography, Hawthorne decided that Pierce possessed the character of a great ruler. "There are scores of men in the country that seem brighter than he is; but Frank has the directing mind, and will move them about like pawns on a chess-board, and turn all their abilities to better purpose than they themselves could."

Hawthorne was wrong on several counts.

Reviews of Hawthorne's book split along party lines. The *Springfield Republican* dubbed it fiction; the *Democratic Review* liked it, and *Harper's New*

Monthly Magazine deftly sidestepped politics to speak of literary form. The *New York Herald* called Hawthorne a hack, and the *New York Times,* a Whig paper, dismissed Hawthorne as a partisan still harboring a grudge against the village custom house. As for the biography, the *Times* continued, it exposed the real Frank Pierce: average student, lackluster attorney, unsuccessful soldier, boring speaker, doughface (as southern sympathizers were called) politician: "This is the marrow of Mr. Hawthorne's panegyric."

While the press debated the biography's demerits, Hawthorne went up to Maine to join Pierce at Bowdoin's commencement and semicentennial celebration. "All my cotemporaries [*sic*] have grown the funniest old men in the world," Hawthorne wrote home to Sophia. "Am I a funny old man?" Exhausted from writing, grieving Louisa's death, tired of Peabody politics, and cranky about domestic life, he had looked forward to the tall academic pines, scented as they were with another era. And he liked spending time with Pierce.

It seems an unlikely pairing—poky politician, stylish writer; one outgoing, the other introspective—but only at first glance. Hawthorne was more relaxed and jovial, Pierce more considerate and caring, than most people knew. "He is deep, deep, deep," said Hawthorne of Pierce. Mostly, though, these two men—out of step with their milieu though in step with their times—sought and found in each other the comfort of a thirty-year friendship and the full acceptance neither had quite discovered elsewhere, despite all their success. "I love him," Hawthorne said. It was a simple statement of easy truth.

Pierce commissioned George Healy, portraitist of the famous, to paint Hawthorne and paid one thousand dollars, a goodly sum. Pierce, who cherished the picture, kept it on exhibit in Washington during his entire term of office, and for more than a century it remained in the Pierce family, Hawthorne glancing outward, somber, not sad, his eyebrows black as crows, his eyes impenetrable. During the sitting, a visibly nervous Hawthorne grew more comfortable. At his request, Mrs. Healy read one of Edward Bulwer-Lytton's works, or Hawthorne chatted amiably with the painter, comparing notes about their early, unsuccessful days when Hawthorne said he couldn't afford more than plain wooden furniture that Sophia painted in her artistic way.

Healy thought Hawthorne looked like a poetical Daniel Webster, if shyer and more feminine, as befitted a writer; perhaps Healy confused the two men and their politics, although several others, like Fields and Ellery Channing, had noticed the similarity. It was flint.

*Hawthorne at forty-eight, portrait by George P. A. Healy, 1852, commissioned
by President-elect Franklin Pierce and shown in the White House.*

After Brunswick, Hawthorne rode down the coast to the rocky Isles of
Shoals, nine miles off the coast of Rye Beach, New Hampshire, and accessi-
ble by ferry from Portsmouth. Pierce introduced Hawthorne at the small
hotel, Leighton's, perfect for escape. He stayed there twelve days, waking
each morning to the caw of gulls and the soft sound of water lapping at the
shore. White sun and stinging salt burned out his malaise, and back at

the Wayside, he said he was ready to start a new romance. It was to be "in the *Scarlet Letter* vein," Fields purred with delight.

"I am beginning to take root here, and feel myself, for the first time in my life, really at home," Hawthorne confided to Longfellow while he set his sights on foreign shores.

Tuesday, November 2, 1852, was a day of dull rain and clammy fog in Boston, except for Democrats. Franklin Pierce defeated both his Whig opponent, Winfield Scott, and Free-Soil Democrat John P. Hale, whom he detested. Hawthorne began making plans. Sophia and the children would go to the Manns for Thanksgiving; he invited Pike to join him in Concord for a bachelor's holiday. They talked politics. The scramble for appointments had begun.

From distant Concord, Hawthorne pulled Salem's political levers. He dickered with George Bailey Loring, Democratic Party leader, who wanted Ephraim Miller's position in the Custom House, and he worked to keep Miller in the Custom House, hoping to appease Loring with the postmaster's job. He backed Nathaniel James Lord, president of the Essex County Democrats, for district attorney and advised Zach Burchmore to go to the Boston Custom House, hoping Loring would then support him. ("Do not let my name be mixed up with the above business," he admonished Burchmore.) The maneuvering took skill, patience, and circumspection. "A subtile boldness with a veil of modesty over it, is what is needed," Hawthorne confided to one aspirant. It was the method he used.

And it worked. Everyone was happy with what they received, including Hawthorne's ne'er-do-well uncle William Manning, who landed a job as superintendent of repairs—janitor—in the Custom House.

Literary friends also looked to Hawthorne for their ration of spoils. Richard Stoddard, a young poet Hawthorne had met the previous summer, wanted an office of some sort; Charles Wilkins Webber asked for help with an appointment in South America; Ellery Channing hoped to go to Rome or Naples; and with *Pierre,* his new novel, a disaster, Melville half hoped for a foreign post. In November he visited Concord, and soon afterwards Hawthorne took Melville's name to Washington. Nothing came of Hawthorne's efforts on Melville's behalf, and it's impossible to know how strongly he pushed, though for years he felt guilty about not succeeding. "However, I failed only from real lack of power to serve him," he later told himself on seeing Melville again, "so there was no reason to be ashamed."

As for himself, Hawthorne was reasonably certain he'd be given the consulship in Liverpool. He spoke longingly of England, noted Henry Bright, a young Englishman visiting Concord, and Hawthorne explained to Bridge that he'd received "several invitations from English celebrities to come over there; and this office would make all straight"—meaning it was a position he could afford, given the salary and fees. Fields sulked. "We shall have no more romances from his pen at present."

Sophia pretended not to know of Hawthorne's plans, or if she did, kept mum so as not to distress her mother. But Mrs. Peabody died in early January. Two months later, in March, news of Hawthorne's assignment hit the newspapers. Ecstatic at the prospect of Europe—at long last—Sophia shunted aside criticism, real and perceived, about Hawthorne's appointment. He had not jockeyed for it, she snapped; it belonged to him by right. Not that the plum of a post had anything to do with Pierce's friendship or the biography, she asserted with sticky innocence. "Bargain & sale are not terms or ideas to influence such a man as he or my husband & since I know it & them, I do not care a fig what low minded people may say or think up on the subject."

On March 26, 1853, the United States Senate approved Pierce's nomination of Nathaniel Hawthorne as United States consul in Liverpool. Hawthorne accepted the position. He torched old letters and papers, as well as hundreds of letters Sophia had written him before they married. It was a key gesture: covering his traces so as to reinvent the past.

CHAPTER TWENTY

This Farther Flight

And England, the land of my ancestors! Once I had fancied that my sleep would not be quiet in the grave until I should return, as it were to my home of past ages. . . .

Nathaniel Hawthorne,
"Fragments from the Journal of a Solitary Man"

THREE YEARS at the Manse, back to Salem and briefly to Boston, where Julian was born; to Salem yet again; to Lenox, West Newton, and Concord. "Then this farther flight to England, where we expect to spend four years, and afterwards another year in Italy—during all which time we shall have no real home," Hawthorne mused, sitting quietly in a suburb of Liverpool on a showery evening. He half sighed. "I felt that I should never be quite at home here."

After banishing himself from Salem in 1850, Hawthorne found no peace anywhere, said Julian: "Partly necessity or convenience, but partly, also, his own will, drove him from place to place; always wishing to settle down finally, but never lighting upon the fitting spot."

Before departure there was much to do: farewell dinners, a three-week stay in Washington to confer with Pierce, the packing, the waiting, the settling of accounts, and of course the correcting of proofs for *Tanglewood Tales,* a sequel to *A Wonder Book.* But one must ask why, just at the point when his career was flourishing—he'd written four books and two volumes of children's stories within the last three years—why Hawthorne was trading the writer's life for the drudgery of civil service. Hawthorne wouldn't publish again for seven more years.

In Concord, Moncure Conway, a starstruck Harvard student, recognized Hawthorne—"Who else could have those soft-flashing unsearchable eyes, that *beauté du diable* at middle age?"—though Hawthorne's dapper dress surprised him until he recollected that "Prospero had left his isle, temporarily buried his book, and was passing from his masque to his masquerade as consul at Liverpool and man of the world." Only to romantics like Conway was the consulship in Liverpool a masquerade, an excuse, a temporary and slightly embarrassing deviation on the path of continued literary acclaim. What Conway and others failed to realize was that Hawthorne needed the consulship as much as he needed to write.

For one thing, there was the money. Writing still seemed to Hawthorne the self-absorbed pastime of a monkish patrician who did not have to bother about how to feed, clothe, and educate three children and to provide for a wife in the manner she deserved. For another thing, Hawthorne was not by nature prolific. "A life of much smoulder, but scanty fire," he would characterize his career with a modicum of truth. The world of publishing, as Fields demonstrated, was a whistle-stop world; and to keep up, Hawthorne had to be a kind of aristocratic huckster, like Hepzibah in *The House of the Seven Gables*. He preferred the narcotic of government officialdom: reputable, responsible, lucrative, and far easier than writing.

With its solid floors, cigar smoke, and ribald tales, it was also a world, like the Custom House, into which men could escape, pretending they were youthful and unencumbered and successful in whatever ways success mattered or didn't. Sure, Hawthorne had said Uncle Sam robbed him of his manhood and the ability to stand on his own, but the Custom House had once represented manhood too: a steady income, a definable niche, and the community of seamen, like Hawthorne's father, formerly at the center of Salem life. Of course, government appointments are ephemeral, and Hawthorne reckoned that an eventual rotation of office would oblige him to return to his writing desk, as if he had no choice but to revert to the vocation he profoundly loved but respected only in fitful doses.

The consulship thus promised to resolve the conflict between the artist and the laborer much as Brook Farm had—but at a better wage and with the premium of prestige due a man of middle age. Hawthorne calculated he might save as much as thirty thousand dollars after four years in office. Since merchandise sailing from the port of Liverpool to America required the consul's signature, and since each signature paid the consul a two-dollar fee, Hawthorne could "bag" (his term) enough gold to return to America to write unimpeded by financial worry.

And anyway, what to write? After *The House of the Seven Gables,* history—his own or the nation's—no longer inspired him, and he'd long ago stopped scribbling small masterpieces like "My Kinsman, Major Molineux" or "The Minister's Black Veil." He'd ceased writing stories of twisted love like "The Birth-mark" and "Rappaccini's Daughter," and Coverdale was yet another crafty nincompoop on yet another pilgrimage: no more. When Fields prepared to republish *Mosses from an Old Manse* under the Ticknor and Fields imprint, Hawthorne reread his tales with dismay. "I am a good deal changed since those times; and to tell you the truth, my past self is not very much to my taste, as I see myself in this book." But his present self had produced the disappointing *Blithedale,* and though the campaign biography served him well, it was a one-time occupation.

"The American stamp is pretty strong on you," Ellery Channing observed of Hawthorne, referring to his work. "Could you feel at ease in European circumstances?" he asked. The question was academic. Hawthorne booked staterooms for himself, his family, and two servants on the Cunard paddle-wheel steamer *Niagara,* bound for Liverpool, and they sailed from Boston on July 6, 1853, two days after Hawthorne's forty-ninth birthday. The next day, as the vessel chugged out of Halifax, four cannons fired a salute to the new consul. The die was cast.

"I do not like England," Una Hawthorne moped. Her father didn't much like it either. "To tell you the truth," he wrote William Ticknor, "I believe we are all very homesick."

Liverpool loomed on the shore, warehouses standing like upended coffins in an overcast dawn. It rained constantly, a brown, half-hearted, chilly rain that shook the bones. With William Ticknor as temporary factotum, the Hawthornes disembarked onto the sopping dock, tired and nervous and excited after their ten-day journey. They collected their trunks and carpetbags and piled into a cab, but their rooms weren't yet ready at Mrs. Blodget's genteel boardinghouse, a Fields recommendation, so for the next ten days they huddled indoors at the Waterloo Hotel, shrinking from the city's soiled air. Sophia and the children caught cold.

Liverpool was poor, crowded, soggy, and drab, a city on the edge of Empire. They couldn't possibly live there. They crossed the Mersey—"the color of a mud-puddle," Hawthorne griped—for the suburb of Rock Ferry and registered at the Royal Rock Hotel, a fine hostelry, more what they had had in mind, with its broad walks and mannerly flowers and the nearby park where furry donkeys waited politely in a row. "There we shall remain," Sophia declared, "till we find a house & home."

Sophia recovered her breathlessness, wooed by English pomp and rural opulence. The coaches of a well-to-do Liverpool merchant whisked the Hawthornes outside the grimy port to a country manor, Poulton Hall, about three miles distant, where a merchant lived among twenty-five bedrooms and two sisters sensible enough to praise *The Scarlet Letter* as the most moral book they'd ever read. At another manor, they dipped their fingers in bowls of blue Bohemian glass and dined on fish, turkey, and chicken served by elegant footmen in full-court dress who held the shining domes of silver dishes. Hawthorne had already given three speeches at affairs of note, Sophia happily buzzed, including a dinner with His Worship the city mayor at the Town Hall. "People who have not heard of Thackeray here, know Mr. Hawthorne," Sophia wrote to her father. England had its satisfactions.

Hawthorne stepped into his new life with noticeably less verve. Each morning, he left the Rock Ferry station at half past nine and crossed the Mersey on a little steamer, arriving at his post about a half hour later. Located in the Washington Buildings on Brunswick Street—"the most detestable part of the city"—the consular office consisted of two rooms on the first floor, one for him and an outer chamber for his treasured clerk, Henry J. Wilding, and the indispensable vice-consul, Samuel Pearce, two Englishmen of experience. Hawthorne's own office, about twelve feet by fifteen, reminded him of an old-fashioned barbershop. On the walls were nondescript pictures and maps as well as two lithographs, one of Zachary Taylor and one of the Tennessee State House. An American eagle skulked over the mantelpiece, and a barometer pointed hopefully to "Fair." It continued to rain.

Hawthorne's consular duties included various maritime and mercantile tasks, all related to Liverpool's strategic position in Anglo-American trade. (It was the port of entry for cotton and sugarcane and American politics.) Mostly, though, the consul interpreted protocol, clarified the finer points of maritime law, paid postage on unclaimed letters from Americans, and provided passage home to stranded seamen. He investigated the numerous complaints about the conditions aboard American ships and took the deposition of a battered sailor in Liverpool's North Hospital. He placed a young American who'd been wandering about the streets in a hospital for the insane, and he arranged the forlorn funeral of an American sea captain who died in a Liverpool boardinghouse. "The duties of the office," he noted, "carried me to prisons, police-courts, hospitals, lunatic asylums, coroner's inquests, death-beds, funerals, and brought me in contact with insane people, criminals, ruined speculators, wild adventurers, diplomatists, brother-consuls, and all manner of simpletons and unfortunates, in greater number and variety than I had ever dreamed of as pertaining to America."

If anyone came calling for Hawthorne the author (as opposed to the consul), the clerk was to say he was out.

What Hawthorne liked best was tallying fees. "The autograph of a living author has seldom been so much in request at so respectable a price," he chortled, constantly aware how little authors were valued at home. It was with pride that he repaid George Hillard the money Hillard had raised after Hawthorne lost his job at the Salem Custom House, and he loaned Horatio Bridge three thousand dollars.

In September the Hawthornes moved to Rock Park, the affluent housing project near the waterfront, a kind of suburban fortress protected by police guards to keep out the riffraff. Their place was a large stone semidetached structure, three stories high and surrounded by dense hedges, originally renting for two hundred pounds. The landlady lowered the price when she discovered the United States consul had his eye on it, "instead of Mr. Nobody," said Sophia, "so much influence has rank & title in dear old England."

The Hawthornes counted pennies. Tea alone cost a dollar a pound (four-shilling tea was tasteless) and potatoes sold at thirty cents a peck. Though he and Sophia had always hired someone to help with chores or cooking—except during their poorest Manse days—Sophia said their new rank demanded a staff of at least housemaid, nursemaid, cook, and a gardener to tend the rare roses. "We do not live in 'great style,' " Sophia hastily explained to her father, "—neither do we intend to have much company. We really could not afford it." When Elizabeth put Hawthorne's income at forty thousand dollars, Sophia quickly trimmed her sister's sails. "So very far from this is the truth that it really is *funny* & melancholy at the same time," she scolded. "And Mr. Hawthorne must lay aside a good part of this income, or we should return ruined." To Mary she explained that "we live as economically as we possibly can—no carriage—no 24 dinners (dinner of 24) no liveried footmen." Living in the backwoods of Ohio with her children and Horace, now president of Antioch College, Mary must have raised an eyebrow.

Hawthorne relied on Ticknor to invest Hawthorne's earnings as he saw fit. In fact, if not for the money, Hawthorne professed he'd "kick the office to the devil, and come home again. I am sick of it," he wrote in December,

Hawthorne lodgings in Rock Park, Rock Ferry

"and long for my hillside, and—what I thought I never should long for—my pen!"

True, he had little time to write stories, but he had no real intention of trying. Instead he recorded long accounts of English life. Hawthorne shivered in revulsion, fear, and stupefaction as he walked the Liverpool streets. Winter came on, cold. He saw the raw feet of scantily clad children, a beggar without arms or legs pleading for a sixpence, a woman in a hand wagon (good subject for a romance), and a half-starved, half-frozen boy trying to sell dirty newspapers. Smudged young girls furtively grabbed the coal that fell from carts and hid the precious cargo in their aprons. A man stood barelegged playing a fife hoping for a halfpenny. Hawthorne looked in the apple stalls, fruit not fit for a pig. Appalled and fascinated, he returned home to his warm sitting room fire and wrote, certain he'd "got hold of something real, which I do not find in the better streets of the city."

He supposed he might one day transform his casual impressions into fiction since his notebooks had always been a source of stray facts capable of sparking a tale. It was no different now, except that Hawthorne was trying to match his fantasy of England against what he saw. The déjà vu of rural churches came from his reading about them, he told himself. "Or perhaps the image of them, impressed into the minds of my long-ago forefathers, was so deep that I have inherited it; and it answers to the reality."

His forefathers were constantly present, sometimes closer than the streetpeople of Liverpool. "My ancestor left England in 1630," Hawthorne ruminated, "I return in 1853. I sometimes feel as if I myself had been absent these two hundred and eighteen years—leaving England just emerging from the feudal system, and finding it on the verge of Republicanism. It brings the two far separated points of time very closely together, to view the matter thus." England was the root, he the branch.

Yet the country was resolutely itself, its gay pageantry repulsive to him, a democrat. And it was strangely soothing too. "How comfortable English-men know how to make themselves," Hawthorne observed, "locating their dwellings far within private grounds, with secure gateways and porter's lodges, and the smoothest roads, and trimmest paths, and shaven lawns, and clumps of tress, and every bit of the ground, every hill and dell, made the most of for convenience and beauty, and so well kept that even winter cannot disarray it—." But the puritan in him could never condone smug luxury. ". . . I doubt whether anybody is entitled to a home in so full a sense, in this world." To Ticknor, he wailed, "I HATE England."

Still, the poets entombed among dim stones in Westminster Abbey had been old friends, and Hawthorne stopped for a night in Lichfield to visit the birthplace of Dr. Johnson. "I set my foot on the worn steps, and laid my hand on the wall of the house, because Johnson's hand and foot might have been in those same places." This England, his England, is the place where he came alive so many years ago; this England, his England, is the magic green Forest of Arden, best home of all.

The English had heard stories. They had read Frederika Bremer's impressions of the good-looking American author, his nose fine, his eyes clear as the Stockbridge Bowl, and the bitter smile on his lips spoiling the lower part of his face. Others had heard tales of his shyness. William Story told Elizabeth Barrett Browning that Hawthorne spoke only through his pen, and James Fields told his friend Mary Russell Mitford that Hawthorne was so thin-skinned Fields dared not criticize his writing lest he toss it in the flames. And how well Fields remembered those awful days—only four years ago—when the Hawthornes were starving, until, that is, Fields discovered *The Scarlet Letter.* "Was Hawthorne aware of his Columbus," Story asked James Lowell. "Browning seemed somewhat to have suspected a rat."

At an official function, Hawthorne is said to be standing slightly to the left,
behind the central figure, below, who is celebrating the laying of the
foundation stone of the Liverpool Free Public Library, 1857.

In Liverpool, Hawthorne gained a reputation for refusing invitations although he did develop a close friendship with Henry Arthur Bright, the precocious twenty-two-year-old who'd met the author in Concord in the fall of 1852. Then, Hawthorne had hardly talked to him, but once in Liverpool he was grateful for his company and all his kindnesses, great and small. "Bright was the illumination of my dusky little apartment, as often as he made his appearance there!" Hawthorne would write. Bright took Hawthorne to the theater, accompanied him on his rambles, brought him magazines, oddments, and gossip, and conveyed to Sophia invitations to country houses. She responded gratefully, sprinkling him with adjectives:

"interesting, sincere, earnest, independent, warm and generous hearted; not at all dogmatic, and with ready answers."

He liked pre-Raphaelite poetry, Balzac, and flowers, and though he wrote an occasional piece for the *Westminster Review*—later for the *Examiner* and *Athenaeum*—Bright had no pretensions of a literary career. Instead he was the cream of the Liverpool merchant class, educated at Trinity, a Liberal, a Unitarian, and in 1857 a partner in the family shipping business, Gibbs, Bright, & Company. He was also a humanitarian. He published a pamphlet, *Cruelties on High Seas,* to try to protect sailors from physical and emotional abuse on board ship, and he shared Hawthorne's interest in politics, particularly as they were unfolding in America. Another of his pamphlets, *Free Blacks and Slaves: Would American Abolition be a Blessing?,* answered its own question with a definite no.

Buffering the consul from Liverpool society, Bright looked to Hawthorne as to a father, and Hawthorne responded, tenderly cuffing him when he wrote a milk-warm review of De Quincey, that "poor old man of genius," Hawthorne cried in sympathy, "to whom the world is in arrears for half-a-century's revenue of fame!" Bright hadn't served the old man at all. "You examine his title-deeds, find them authentic, and send him away with the benefaction of half-a-crown!"

The callow youth made Hawthorne feel spry himself. He and Sophia had begun to shave a couple of years from their ages, and when Elizabeth Peabody sent congratulations on Sophia's birthday, Sophia erupted. Never refer to her age, nor to Hawthorne's. "He wants to know nothing about the birth days you are so fond of."

Hawthorne put the matter somewhat differently. "I have had enough of progress," he wrote Longfellow; "—now I want to stand stock still; or rather, to go back twenty years."

By and large, Hawthorne was a diligent consul, attending to affairs of office with dispatch and decorum. During his first two years in office he hardly left his post, so scrupulous was he about any imputation of impropriety; he did not travel or sightsee beyond the boundaries of Liverpool, and each day spent almost eight hours at his dingy desk. In the summer of 1854, when Sophia and the children went to the Isle of Man for two weeks to recover from whooping cough, Hawthorne joined them only on weekends. His desires were simple: perform well, avoid attention, count his money.

Nothing is perfect, particularly in government service, and even the most conscientious consul is not above reproach. About two hundred soldiers, shipwrecked from the United States vessel *San Francisco,* landed in Liverpool in need of passage home, but since they were soldiers, not sailors, they did not fall under the jurisdiction of the consul, who didn't quite know what to do with them. According to Hawthorne, when the ship's officers requisitioned two thousand dollars to furnish provisions, he supplied the items himself, dispatching his clerk to make the purchases, and he found temporary lodging for the soldiers, which, according to Sophia, he paid out of pocket.

The soldiers' transportation to America was more ticklish. Hawthorne telegraphed James Buchanan, American minister to Great Britain, to ask if Buchanan would take over the matter. Replying that the troops fell outside his purview, Buchanan passed the buck back to Hawthorne, suggesting he open an account at Baring Brothers for the soldiers' relief. Furious, the captain of the *San Francisco* went to see Buchanan, and someone leaked to the American press that Hawthorne had avoided all responsibility for the soldiers, having referred everything to his clerk, an Englishman, no less. Moreover, if the *San Francisco*'s captain hadn't traveled to London to importune Buchanan, no action on behalf of the shipwrecked soldiers would have been taken at all.

Hawthorne himself was furious. But he knew that to exonerate himself he would have to shift responsibility back onto Buchanan—not a good political move—so he sent exculpatory letters to Bridge and Ticknor, instructing them to publish them if, and only if, necessary. Ticknor and Bridge knew what to do. They leaked Hawthorne's letters to the press in just the right proportions, and the affair soon passed over, leaving Hawthorne's reputation and his cordial relations with Buchanan intact.

The affair left Hawthorne slightly shaken. He did not want to repeat the Salem Custom House debacle. This was a "devilish good office," he told Ticknor again and again. He'd netted ten thousand dollars in almost a year, a tidy sum, and could salt away even more—if "those Jackasses at Washington (of course I do not include the President under this polite phrase) will but let it alone."

They would not. A new agreement between Britain and America allowing merchandise to travel to Canada without the consul's signature reduced Hawthorne's fees by one-quarter. And John O'Sullivan, the American chargé d'affaires in Portugal, brought Hawthorne word of change slated for the diplomatic corps. If passed by Congress, new consular laws would direct the American consul in Liverpool to hand over all fees to the government and then to subsist on a fixed salary of seventy-five hundred dollars, not nearly enough, declared Sophia, for a family of five—and a consul's family at that. "For God's sake, bestir yourself," Hawthorne wrote to Ticknor, "and get everybody to bestir themselves, to restore matters to the former footing. I am not half ready to begin scribbling romances again, yet."

Hoping Pierce might forestall passage of the bill so that he could come home flush, he really didn't want to alter his situation: the money was good; the work, though boring, wasn't difficult; he didn't miss writing. Bridge and Ticknor lobbied on Hawthorne's behalf, but the bill slouched toward passage regardless.

As far as Bridge was concerned, Hawthorne's talents were buried in Liverpool. He asked Ticknor to mobilize Hawthorne's literary friends, like Longfellow, to encourage him to get back to work, real work. "H. ought to go to Italy, and write."

An American claimant searches for patrimony and permanence, much like the many claimants Hawthorne met in the consul's office. They were mostly deluded individuals, convinced of their kinship to British nobility on the basis of an old mug or an illegible document. But if their absurd claims seemed pathetic, Hawthorne recognized in them the tag end of a comparable wish.

"The American shall be a person of high rank, who has reached eminence early: a Governor; a congressman; a gentleman; give him the characteristics and imperfections of an American gentleman," Hawthorne mused. The threat of the consular bill sent Hawthorne back to fiction, his subject the American abroad, a comparison of New World and Old. "He shall, I think, be unmarried," Hawthorne continued his ruminations. "He searches for relatives, burrows in books of records, consults heralds; for there is a misty idea, as in so many cases, that a great estate and perhaps title is due to him."

Hawthorne would endow the American with a secret powerful enough to destroy the English branch of the family, but he didn't know what the secret was or how it could be used: family misdeeds, centuries old, to demonstrate the bankruptcy of aristocratic institutions? But were these institutions so bad? Sometimes he trembled at the thought of a place "where no change comes for centuries, and where a peasant does but step into his father's shoes, and lead just his father's life, going in and out over the old threshold, and finally being buried close by his father's grave, time without end." And then he added, "Yet it is rather pleasant to know that such things are."

"Royalty," he observed on another occasion, "has its glorious side."

His attitude toward England was ambivalent, hotly so. Perhaps therein lies the claimant's secret, an insatiable yearning for another place that left him perpetually homeless. But since Hawthorne could not consciously reconcile his conflicted sense of England—his sense of belonging, his sense of displacement—the secret remained unnamed.

In April of 1855, he was playing with yet another idea for a story, having heard the legend of a bloody footstep in the entrance of Smithells Hall. "The tradition is that a certain martyr, in Bloody Mary's time, being examined before the then occupant of the Hall, and committed to prison, stamped his foot in earnest protest against the injustice with which he was treated," Hawthorne jotted the tale in his notebooks. "Blood issued from his foot, which slid along the stone pavement of the hall, leaving a long footmark printed in blood; and there it has remained ever since, in spite of the scrubbings of all after generations."

The image was tailor-made for Hawthorne, who'd considered the idea of a footstep soaked in blood in the early 1840s as a possible starting point for a story. Now its appeal was amplified by the image of a man stamping his foot in anger and frustration, like Rumpelstiltskin. For Hawthorne was frustrated. He'd been happy of late, he noted querulously—"more content to enjoy what I had; less anxious for anything beyond it, in this life"—but he couldn't shake loose a recurrent dream. He was at school, realizing he'd been there far too long and had "quite failed to make such progress in life as my contemporaries have; and I seem to meet some of them with a feeling of shame and depression that broods over me, when I think of it, even at this moment."

Hawthorne had begun to weary of town life, as he'd said of Robin Molineux, wondering if he'd sold his soul for immunity, or easy cash. Then he learned the provisions of the new consular bill wouldn't take effect for a while because Pierce considered parts of it unconstitutional.

Hawthorne set down his pen. He decided not to quit his post just yet.

To economize, he gave up the Rock Park house and dismissed all the servants save Fanny Wrigley, Rose's nursemaid. From now on his family could live more cheaply in boardinghouses and rented rooms. Trunkloads of household goods were shipped back to America. Sophia was crestfallen. "Now we are fixtures in Liverpool till next spring *at least*," Sophia moaned.

Italy drifted away into an amorphous future. Having endured the death of her father at a distance, she endured Liverpool beyond all sufferance, despising the Mersey, the fog, the smut, the noxious fumes that rose from the putrid streets. She refused to go outdoors. Night air filled her lungs with peril. She immersed herself in cold water, drank cod-liver oil, and complained that the racking cough that killed her mother had crept into her lungs.

In June the Hawthornes went to the Royal Leamington Spa in Warwickshire, where they rented a house at 13 Lansdowne Crescent, hoping Sophia might recuperate. (Hawthorne estimated the lodgings would cost only seven guineas a week.) Surrounded by lissome trees, she was calmer, and soon she and Hawthorne began to act like tourists, visiting Warwick, Stratford, Coventry, and the Lake District in July. "I have a right to some recreation," he defended himself nervously. "I shall be within reach of telegraphic notices, and can always make my appearance at the consulate within a few hours."

But Sophia's cough deepened in Leamington, and when the family returned to Rock Ferry in August, neither she nor Hawthorne was happy. Sarah Clarke visited and took Hawthorne aside to tell him his wife was sicker than he knew; he should not subject her to another winter of clammy damp. It was decided. Sophia should accept O'Sullivan's offer and go to sunny Lisbon. Hawthorne asked Pierce for a leave of absence.

As Pierce's unofficial envoy, Bridge replied to Hawthorne's request. Pierce would consider giving O'Sullivan's post to Hawthorne. O'Sullivan had tired of it. Hawthorne rejected the offer. He knew nothing about diplomatic protocol, didn't speak Portuguese; and he couldn't afford it in any case.

Sophia sailed to Portugal without him. "The doctors said I *must* leave England this winter, if I would escape destruction," she guiltily told her sister Mary. "So I had no choice, you see—& I tried to behave well—as my life is very important to some persons." Una and Rose accompanied her, and Julian stayed in England with his father.

The five of them hugged one another in early October, standing on the wooden deck as the ship's whistle blew. Hawthorne and Julian walked off the gangplank to the shore, Julian's little hand in his father's. "This is the first great parting that Sophia and I have ever had," Hawthorne acknowledged to himself in bewilderment. Father and son boarded the Southampton train, Hawthorne glimpsing through the window a fragment of rainbow. Then it dropped to darkness.

CHAPTER TWENTY-ONE

Truth Stranger Than Fiction

*Thus far, no woman in the world has ever once spoken out her
whole heart and her whole mind. The mistrust and disapproval
of the vast bulk of society throttles us, as with two gigantic hands
at our throats!*

Nathaniel Hawthorne, *The Blithedale Romance*

ALL WOMEN, as authors, are feeble and tiresome," Hawthorne bitterly
exploded. "I wish they were forbidden to write, on having their faces
deeply scarified with an oyster-shell."

With more and more authors peddling their work, each claiming a
readership that threatened his, Hawthorne directed his nasty outburst at the
ink-stained Amazons who'd always upset him, now more than ever. There
were three hundred thousand copies of Harriet Beecher Stowe's antislavery
novel, *Uncle Tom's Cabin*, circulating the first year of its publication, 1852; by
comparison, *The Scarlet Letter* had sold barely seven thousand; the same was
true of *The Blithedale Romance*.

The admission of women into men's professions, particularly writing,
was another instance of philanthropy run amok. "A false liberality which
mistakes the strong division lines of Nature for arbitrary distinctions," he'd
written in "Mrs. Hutchinson," "and a courtesy, which might polish criticism but should never soften it, have done their best to add a girlish feeble-
ness to the tottering infancy of our literature."

Maria Susanna Cummins's *The Lamplighter*, selling forty thousand
copies in two months, triggered another blast. "America is now wholly given
over to a d—d mob of scribbling women," Hawthorne cried in 1855, "and I
should have no chance of success while the public taste is occupied with their
trash—and should be ashamed of myself if I did succeed." Better to stay in

Liverpool, despite the reduction in revenue, than compete with women who wrote sentimental claptrap about current affairs. They'd trounce him, no question, which was no doubt another reason Hawthorne did not yet resign the consulship, as he often said he would.

Hawthorne's anxiety about women writers—and writing generally—tangled him in a paradox. If his fiction did not sell, he was not an adequate provider; if it did, he was writing trash like Stowe and company, which not only violated his definition of romance, it linked him, once again, to the scribbling women he despised. Effete and unread; or popular and a female scribbler, which is to say hack: either way, he was the loser.

But Hawthorne's prejudices were at least two-sided. Though he didn't approve of women authors, he didn't condescend to them either, and he made the same demands on them as he made on himself: "truth of detail," combined with "a broader and higher truth." Of course, a higher truth was exactly what Mrs. Stowe was after, only in her case she defined it as the higher truth of emancipation. Hawthorne's aims were different. He said he wanted to keep politics out of art, even in *Blithedale,* a questionable position in this novel, as reviewers of it had been quick to point out—and a Whiggish one, in which the artist is a gentleman, not a politician. But the figure of the artist as uninvolved spectator still suited him.

Disappointed when he saw a group of pre-Raphaelite paintings, he complained that "with the most lifelike exhibition, there is no illusion." Mimicry is not art, romance is: the imagination applied to the actual, transporting raw experience beyond itself. Thus defined, romance is a hedge against realism, abject, political, indecent realism, and just what he couldn't stomach in Julia Ward Howe's poems, *Passion Flowers:* "a whole history of domestic unhappiness," Hawthorne cringed. "What a strange propensity it is in these scribbling women to make a show of their hearts, as well as their heads, upon your counter, for anybody to pry into that chooses!"

Or, to switch metaphors, the writer is something of a wolf in sheep's clothing, his outer garment elegantly sewn, with sentences stitched into paragraphs, affected, quaint, a bit outdated and entirely masterful. But passion is a bodice ripper. *The Scarlet Letter,* as we have seen, is its best example, desire throbbing under the well-articulated surface, much like the anarchical heart that beats beneath Hester's "A," each indispensable to the other.

Hawthorne believed in privacy—no doubt about it—and self-control and discretion, but writing, really good writing, depends on the inmost me stealing forth like a bosom-serpent that crawls out of its hole. Hawthorne knew that. "Be true! Be true! Be true!" he admonishes at the end of *The*

Scarlet Letter. All writers need be true, even women, who do write well when they "throw off the restraints of decency, and come before the public stark naked, as it were"—like Julia Howe. Hawthorne also appreciated Fanny Fern and her snappy satire of the publishing industry, *Ruth Hall.* "The woman writes as if the devil was in her," Hawthorne praised Fern; "and that is the only condition under which a woman ever writes anything worth reading."

But a proper lady keeps her clothes on, which is why she shouldn't write. "It does seem to me to deprive women of all delicacy," he repeated himself to Sophia; "it has pretty much such an effect on them as it would to walk abroad through the streets, physically stark naked." Admiring Sophia's travel journals, he stringently opposed their publication. "Neither she nor I would like to see her name on your list of female authors," Hawthorne would tell Ticknor. Sophia went on record to agree. "I think it is designed by GOD that woman should always spiritually wear a veil, & not a coat & hat," she tartly informed Elizabeth Peabody. When Una began to scribble stories—she said she *must* be a romance writer—Sophia specifically ignored them. "I have such an unmitigated horror of precocious female story tellers & poets," she said, "—that in every way I pass over with indifference what she does in this way."

Shielding her children from the steam pressure of modern life, Sophia plied them with dance and fencing lessons, and she offered French, geography, and music in small doses, rejecting the strenuous regime that had been forced on her. She pushed aside Mary's objections. "My principle is not to wear out young twigs with hanging millstones on them."

Nor did she want Una, in particular, to learn of slavery. "The repose of art is better for her now than the excitement of human wrongs and rights," Sophia reprimanded Elizabeth, who sent letters stuffed with stories of abuse and degradation. Una obeyed her parents but despaired of her ignorance, and soon she was complaining of a pain in her head. Overprotected, melancholy, and approaching puberty, she thought she might be losing her mind.

"Life has never been light and joyous to her," her father commented with regret and doubtless some recognition.

John O'Sullivan resided with his wife, mother, and sister-in-law in a grand house in one of Lisbon's most desirable neighborhoods. He employed a staff of ten, rode in a carriage lined with cerulean damask, and frequently entertained royalty in the starched blue uniform he buttoned high, his white collar barely visible. His only ornament was the uniform's gold buttons with the United States seal. He appeared at court with his family and their house-guest, Mrs. Hawthorne, whom he introduced to the king. She wore a violet brocade trimmed with lace and purple ribbons, and around her neck she tied a black velvet ribbon hung with a diamond pendant that twinkled in the light. Hawthorne had told her to spare no expense.

"Oh, my wife, I do want thee so intolerably," he pined for Sophia. "Nothing else is real, except the bond between thee and me. The people around me are but shadows. I am myself but a shadow, till thou takest me in thy arms, and convertest me into substance." Hawthorne as ghost: it was the familiar cry. And after Sophia sailed to Portugal, he tossed in his dreary bed at night, plagued by forebodings of desertion and death. "I have learned what the bitterness of exile is, in these days," he confided to his journal as fall crept into winter, "and I never should have known it but for the absence of my wife." When Sophia praised O'Sullivan as being as radiant as the sun, Hawthorne sullenly reminded his wife that he had a heart that burned hot for her.

"Heretofore," he added glumly, "thou has had great reason to doubt it."

Liverpool had taxed the marriage. Sophia had been miserable. Haw-thorne did not write, travel, or come home for eight long hours a day, a sep-aration Sophia detested, having married a man who, she'd thought, would stay close by her side. The rancid city had offered little in the way of amuse-ment and even less in the fulfillment of expectations; at most, the Haw-thornes had attended a couple of dinners and visited a couple of manorial homes. A talisman, the English porcelain they'd purchased had arrived in Massachusetts broken to bits. Sophia had been inconsolable. "What a mill-stone I was in England," Sophia confessed from Portugal, "but with what divine patience you bore up beneath my weight."

Lonely, guilt-ridden, and depressed, Hawthorne treated himself to a twenty-day vacation in London at the end of March. His cicerone was Fields's friend Francis Bennoch, a merchant prince, generous and deferen-tial without being obsequious, somewhat like Henry Bright though closer in age to Hawthorne. Born in Scotland in 1811, Bennoch cultivated literary or artistic people and, in the case of the painter Robert Haydon, helped sup-port them financially. He also wrote a little poetry himself. Commuting each day from his suburban home to his wholesale silk and ribbon firm in London, he scribbled verses in the railroad carriage, oblivious to the clack and bounce. In 1841 he published a book of poems, *The Storm and Other Poems*. Wordsworth recommended against a literary career, but Bennoch hadn't harbored any illusions about his talent. He remained a trader, a speculator, and a local politician, maintaining, as Hawthorne did not, an easy intercourse between art and economy—until his firm's bankruptcy in 1857 indicated his talent did not lie in business either.

Julian Hawthorne remembered Bennoch as one of the best-looking men in England, his forehead steep, his brow bushy, and his "sparkling black eyes full of hearty sunshine and kindness." (The description makes him sound like Hawthorne.) Rose Hawthorne recalled a short, fat man who sounded like a pack of chickens when he chuckled at his own jokes, which he often did. He was sitting in his London office in the early spring of 1856 when Hawthorne walked through the door, much changed since the two men had been introduced two years earlier. Bennoch hardly recognized him. He was heavier, his hairline had veered farther north, and the strands of hair around his ears shimmered with demonstrable silver. But the face retained its smoothness, the eyes their inward look.

"I never saw a man more miserable," Bennoch recalled many years later; "he was hipped, depressed, and found fault with everything; London was detestable; it had but one merit—it was not so bad as Liverpool." To prove Hawthorne wrong, Bennoch showed him the curiosities, like Barber Surgeon's Hall and St. Giles Church in Cripplegate, and he stage-managed Hawthorne's entrance into literary society, inviting him to a dinner at the Milton Club, where Hawthorne met the editor of the *London Illustrated News,* the songwriter Charles Mackay, and S. C. Hall, the editor of the *Art Union Monthly Journal.* After Hawthorne delivered a speech—he disliked public speaking but was rather good, provided he drank enough—he went to a supper party at the home of Eneas Dallas, editorial writer for the *Times.* "They have found me out," Hawthorne reported to Sophia, "and I believe I should have engagements for every day, and two or three a day, if I staid here through the season."

At Mackay's invitation, Hawthorne met the writer Douglas Jerrold at the Reform Club, and at a dinner at the lord mayor's arranged by Bennoch, Hawthorne sat mesmerized by the lord mayor's beautiful sister-in-law until he was again called upon to speak. Afterwards he decided he'd made fool of himself: talking "in one's cups" was a ridiculous custom. Bennoch also contrived a series of expeditions that included a military camp in Hampshire, a meal with the author Martin Tupper in Surrey, and in Hastings a meeting with Theodore Martin and his wife, the actress Helena Faucit. A botheration and a satisfaction, Hawthorne called the engagements, pleased with himself and hoping Sophia would be pleased—or envious.

Unperturbed by London's literary establishment, as long as it excluded Tennyson, Thackeray, Eliot, and Dickens, Hawthorne relied completely on Bennoch for his entry into it. "If this man has not a heart, then no man ever had," Hawthorne said. His feelings about Bennoch never changed, and Bennoch entered Hawthorne's spangled pantheon—Bridge, Pierce, O'Sullivan, Fields—as a "friend whom I love as much as if I had know him for a life-time."

Dissension, the pop of gunfire, and confused alarms that rose and fell: slavery's fire bell clanged not just in the night but during the day, every day. Hawthorne was glad to be in England. "If anything could bring me back to America, this winter, it would undoubtedly be my zeal for the Anti-slavery cause," he quipped dryly in December of 1855; "but my official engagements render it quite impossible to assist personally."

Pierce's presidency had been a sorry disaster, fiasco following abysmal fiasco. Particularly abominable was the Kansas-Nebraska bill. Introduced by Illinois senator Stephen A. Douglas (partly because the senator hoped to maneuver a transcontinental railroad through his state), the bill allowed the inhabitants of the Nebraska territory, which included Kansas, their own referendum for or against slavery. In so doing, the bill effectively repealed the Missouri Compromise of 1820 and allowed slavery to extend its reach into territories previously considered untouchable. Charles Sumner condemned the bill as a slaveholders' plot; Douglas retorted that Senator Sumner represented "the pure unadulterated representatives of Abolitionism, Free Soilism, and Niggerism." William H. Seward, the savvy antislavery senator from New York, tried to outmaneuver Douglas by urging southern Whigs to demand total repeal of the compromise.

"I must say that the tone and standard of public morals at Washington are very, very low," George Hillard, a Whig, glowered. "The antislavery Seward and the proslavery Douglas are alike calculating, ambitious, and time-serving." The poet William Cullen Bryant, editor of the Democratic *New York Evening Post,* denounced the bill as despicable, and George Bancroft called "this cruel attempt to conquer Kansas into slavery . . . the worst thing ever projected in our history." It passed in May of 1854 with Pierce's blessing.

Sophia Hawthorne was among the minority who embraced, or said they did, an impartial view. "How insane all America seems to us about the Nebraska bill," she disdainfully informed Mary Mann. Pierce had supported the bill to preserve the Union and maintain the sovereignty of states' rights. To Mary Mann, the old saw was objectionable. But Sophia informed her sister with a certain contemptuousness that she knew certain "persons"—Hawthorne?—"angelic in goodness & humanity & of the purest motives, who agree with the advocates of this bill. Not because it promotes the extension of slavery—of course not," she quickly added, "—but because they think it constitutional & right—& that it would be a ruinous precedent to legislate against it." Mary assumed that Pierce had bamboozled Hawthorne once again.

While Sophia pretended equanimity, Hawthorne did not. "I find it impossible to read American newspapers (of whatever political party) without being ashamed of my country," he groaned, protesting more than once that if it weren't for his children, he'd never go back. In Boston federal marshals had nabbed the fugitive slave Anthony Burns, and when Theodore Parker condemned the arrest to a roaring crowd at Faneuil Hall, the crowd swooped down on the courthouse where Burns was being held. The Reverend Thomas Wentworth Higginson butted its thick oak door with a wooden beam. He was clubbed. A shot rang out. A marshal's deputy was stabbed to death. "Oh how much harm to the wretched slave, these crazy men do!" Sophia wailed. "Mr. Parker was far more the murderer of that officer than the man who shot him."

The situation was even worse in Kansas. Proslavery men fought against the abolitionist recruits sent into the territory by New England emigrant aid societies, Bible in one hand and a rifle in the other, according to Stephen Douglas. With Pierce and Douglas backing the proslavery regime, the antislavery Free-Soilers set up their own legislature, claiming that border Missourians—ruffians—were terrorizing voters and rigging the local elections. In the spring of 1856, a posse of proslavery men mobbed the Free-Soil town of Lawrence, Kansas, burned the hotel, sacked the governor's house, and demolished two antislavery newspaper offices. Pierce's friend Jefferson Davis, the secretary of war, dispatched federal troops to the territory. Kansas teetered on the brink of civil war.

In Washington, Sumner inveighed for two days against the crimes in Kansas, drubbing colleagues like South Carolina's Andrew Butler, a man with chalk-white hair and genteel manners. Two days later, on May 22, Butler's less dignified protégé, Congressman Preston Brooks, avenged the honor of his slandered kinsman and their state when he entered the Senate chamber, walked over to the wooden desk where Sumner sat, and whacked him senseless with a gutta-percha cane.

"To say the truth," Hawthorne groaned again, "there is no inducement to return to our own country, where you seem to be on the point of beating one another's brains out."

Sophia came back to England on June 9, 1856, still coughing. Resuming life in Liverpool was out of the question, so the Hawthornes tumbled here and there—Blackheath, Southport, Old Trafford, Bath—in search of health, recreation, and some ineffable quality associated with home. It was impossible to find.

His family installed, for the moment, in a boardinghouse run by the parsimonious Mrs. Hume in Shirley, near Southampton, Hawthorne commuted to Liverpool. In July the Hawthornes took over the Bennochs' place in Blackheath while the Bennochs vacationed in Germany. Blackheath was a pretty suburban enclave within easy reach of London, perfect for Sophia, so glad to be in range of "stupendous, grand London, the epitome of the world, the centre of all things," that she ventured out at night in a low-cut blue silk carrying a portable respirator. She wanted to meet Jenny Lind.

The Bennoch place was too small for the family, but Hawthorne placed Una, Rose, and Rose's nursemaid in rooms nearby and stayed in Blackheath as often as consular business allowed. Like Sophia, he took advantage of London, strolling its narrow streets, relaxed and happy, stopping for ice cream, breakfasting or eating lunch here and there with a small group of literati like Bennoch's friend Monckton Milnes, Keats's first biographer and an expert in autographs and pornography.

Shortly after moving to Blackheath, Hawthorne went to London to call on a countrywoman, Delia Bacon, at her lodging house on Spring Street, Hyde Park. As he stood in Miss Bacon's third-floor parlor, he thumbed through books on a table, waiting for an elderly woman to appear. Later he remembered being agreeably disappointed. Miss Bacon was dark-haired, intelligent, demure, graceful. With that wild glint in her eye, she might even have been a Hester or a Zenobia. "Unquestionably, she was a monomaniac," Hawthorne would write. He stayed an hour and rather liked her.

Delia Bacon was in England intending to prove that William Shakespeare—the ignorant groom—had not authored the plays attributed to him, which were in fact composed by a consortium of revolutionaries including Francis Bacon (no relation) who larded the texts with their secret, seditious codes.

"I want some literary counsel," she had written Hawthorne the preced-

*Outing at Oxford, photograph by Philip Delamotte, summer 1856. Hawthorne
at the far right, slightly apart from the group. "I was really a little startled at
recognizing myself so apart from myself," he noted after seeing the picture.
Sophia Hawthorne is standing at the far left, her face half visible.*

ing May, "and such as no Englishman of letters is able to give me." Thomas
Carlyle was sympathetic but ineffectual, so she turned to the American consul in Liverpool—what else should a literary man be doing in official office
if not assist a fellow author—and asked him to evaluate a portion of her
manuscript.

He said he would, warning her that he didn't share her point of view.
"But I feel that you have done a thing that ought to be reverenced," he
replied graciously, "in devoting yourself so entirely to this object, whatever
it be, and whether right or wrong, and by so doing, you have acquired some
of the privileges of an inspired person and a prophetess." Though Delia
Bacon was just the sort of scribbling woman Hawthorne could esteem—all
the more since she wrote nonfiction—it's not clear how much about her he

already knew: born on the American frontier in 1811; placed in a foster home in Connecticut; a student of Catharine Beecher's estimable Female Seminary, where she professed her faith; a teacher and a onetime playwright. In 1831 she had submitted a story, "Love's Martyr," for the Philadelphia *Saturday Courier*'s literary prize that beat out a tale by Edgar Allan Poe. That was the year she published her own version of American history in *Tales of the Puritans,* influenced, as Hawthorne had been, by John Neal. Then malaria left her with the scourge of all intellectual women, delicate health.

In 1845 she met with more bad luck. Courted by Alexander MacWhorter, a Yale theology student ten years her junior, Bacon accepted his proposal of marriage. MacWhorter, "too weak to bear the ridicule," scoffed Harriet Beecher Stowe, "of marrying a woman older than himself," quickly withdrew the offer. That was a disappointment Bacon could bear. His distributing her love letters among his friends was a humiliation her brother simply had to avenge. Ignoring his sister's embarrassment, Leonard Bacon, the pastor of the First Congregational Church, pit himself against the divines at Yale College by publicly accusing MacWhorter of personal misconduct. The subsequent ecclesiastical trial acquitted him by a vote of 24 to 23, a victory for Yale College more than for MacWhorter, whom the tribunal reprimanded. It also tacitly acknowledged his guilt, warning him not to try the same stunt again.

That wasn't all. Another defender of Bacon, Catharine Beecher, took up the pen for her in a book entitled *Truth Stranger Than Fiction,* its title yet another humiliation.

Bacon wasn't licked. She moved to Boston, where she lectured on history to men as different as George Hillard and William Henry Channing. They loved her. A respected woman in the mold of Margaret Fuller—minus Fuller's off-putting conceit and her feminism—she devoted herself to genius not her own, namely, whoever it was that wrote Shakespeare's plays. Convinced more than ever of the hoax, Bacon enlisted the queen of causes, Elizabeth Peabody, and Peabody conveyed her to Emerson. Emerson consented to act as Bacon's agent and passed her on to Hawthorne, then packing for Liverpool. Hawthorne wasn't interested.

No matter; Bacon showed up in London herself, financed by a wealthy lawyer enthralled with her theory. Iconoclasm was contagious, especially among Americans who didn't mind toppling a British giant, or letting a crackpot woman try. "Delia Bacon, with genius but mad," was, according to Emerson, one of the two greatest originals "America has yielded in ten years." The other was Walt Whitman.

In stodgy London, Bacon attracted supporters like Carlyle, but book publishers were not as amused as he. She canvassed the magazines and with Emerson's help placed a feisty article, "William Shakespeare and His Plays: An Inquiry Concerning Them," in the January 1856 issue of *Putnam's Monthly*, but despite strong sales, the magazine declined to print her next article. It wanted hard evidence. Bacon was discouraged. And when Emerson lost three of the articles she sent him, she began to doubt his loyalty to the cause. That's when she wrote to the American consul.

"If you really think that I can promote your object, tell me definitely how, and try me," Hawthorne responded; "and if I can say a true word to yourself about the work, it shall certainly be said; or if I can aid, personally, or through any connections in London, in bringing the book before the public, it shall be done." He sent ten pounds.

He did find her book remarkable, if only for its nutty logic. "It is a very singular phenomenon," he later concluded; "a system of philosophy growing up in this woman's mind without her volition—contrary, in fact, to the determined resistance of her volition—and substituting itself in the place of everything that originally grew there." Motivated by his long-standing rivalry with Emerson as well as Bacon herself, he approached several London publishers.

Eager to get on with it, Bacon moved to Stratford, convinced that she should clinch her case by opening Shakespeare's tomb, where she figured she might find the documents Francis Bacon had buried there. She stole into the Holy Trinity Church one evening, a candle and a lamp in her hand, and sat by Shakespeare's grave but did nothing until the oil in her lamp burned low and she fumbled out of the church. Sophia Hawthorne was crestfallen. Bacon's quixotic enterprise ended with a whimper.

Disappointed with herself, Bacon railed at Hawthorne. He had betrayed her, she believed, just like all the rest, when he said she should accept money from her brother Leonard; how dare he think she'd take anything from a nonbeliever? Insulted by Hawthorne's suggestion, she had to accept another five pounds—filthy lucre—from him. Bewildered and a bit offended himself, Hawthorne pledged to continue to help her publish her book. "The more absurdly she behaves," he confided to Bennoch, whom he had enlisted as intermediary, "the more need of somebody to help her."

Hawthorne would neither cast Bacon off nor take credit when he secured a publishing contract from Parker and Son. Nor would he balk at assuming financial responsibility for her book, which Parker required as a condition. (To cover his investment, Hawthorne demanded that Ticknor bring out half the agreed-on copies—five hundred in all—doubtless hoping to offset inevitable losses.) He also consented to write a preface for the book, another crucial item for the negotiations with Parker. "How funny, that I should come in front of the stage-curtain, escorting this Bedlamite!" he said to Bennoch.

But his attention, like his affection, was divided. With the Bennochs re-occupying their house in the fall, the Hawthornes had to pitch their tent elsewhere. "It is a strange, vagabond, gypsey sort of life, this that we are leading; and I know not whether we shall finally be spoilt for any other," Hawthorne reflected wistfully. The wind howled bleakly as he and his family resettled in the coastal resort of Southport, twenty miles north of Liverpool, where Sophia could inhale ripe, salty air and Hawthorne travel home by rail each night from the office.

Their rooms at 15 Brunswick Terrace faced the great promenade and the sea, and Sophia was comfortable for a while in their two shabby floors. Small donkey carts pulled her over the beach, and the saltwater baths subdued her dry cough. It then started to rain. Melville came and went in the drizzle en route to the Holy Land in search of succor. His literary ebullience soured by failure, Melville dimly hoped Hawthorne might help place his new book, *The Confidence-Man.* "He certainly is much overshadowed since I saw him last," Hawthorne observed somewhat regretfully, inviting him to Southport, where he stayed for three days. Temporarily warmed by reminiscence, cigars, and a tumbler of ale, the two men sat and talked, not quite comfortable in a hollow among the hills. "If he were a religious man," Hawthorne astutely observed in his journal, "he would be one of the most truly religious and reverential; he has a very high and noble nature, and better worth immortality than most of us."

A few days later, he took Melville to Chester and they walked along the wall, ate veal pies in a confectioner's shop, toured the cathedral. They puffed on cigars and drank stout at the Yacht Inn, where they were shown the window on which Jonathan Swift had etched a screed against the clergy with the diamond of his ring. Melville had a good time.

But the flowers of friendship had faded. Melville was no longer young and hopeful, an acolyte in love.

Melville stowed his trunk at the consulate and sailed a few days later with only a carpet bag. "I do not know a more independent personage," commented Hawthorne with elegiac affection. The two men saw each other once more, when Melville claimed his trunk. Hawthorne did not record the final meeting.

In a matter of weeks the Hawthornes were restless. Southport was seedier than they thought, the surrounding countryside marshy and flat, and Sophia was bored. Elizabeth had offered to come to England to help out, but Sophia said she'd hate such "an utterly stupid, uninteresting, lonely place, where there is no society, no life, no storied memories, & no scenery." Hawthorne would nod. "Our life here has been a blank," he groused, astray and adrift.

In the winter of 1857, thieves broke into their house, taking nothing more than a few silver cups, a spoon, a shoulder of mutton, and Hawthorne's topcoat and boots. A few days later two men were arrested while pawning Hawthorne's clothes. "I rather wished them to escape," he remarked.

Escape was on his mind. On February 13, 1857, he resigned as consul, effective six months later on the last day of August. He'd have spent four years in office, which is what he'd intended, his purse not bursting but full enough so that he could head with clear conscience for Italy, where the exchange rate happened to be quite good.

Franklin Pierce sought and lost the Democratic Party nomination for president to James Buchanan, who ran against a splintered Whig Party. A remnant of the Whigs rallied around Millard Fillmore on the anti-Catholic, nativist American Party ticket; the rest went over to John C. Frémont and the newly organized Republicans, an amalgam of Conscience Whigs and disgruntled Democrats all galvanized by Pierce's failed Kansas policy. "Free Speech, Free Press, Free Soil, Free Men, Frémont, and Victory," their slogan ran.

Whether or not Frémont won, observed Evert Duyckinck, "the moral victory at any rate will be for Free Soil."

But since Pierce's political life was over, so was Hawthorne's.

Hawthorne was lying when he said the whole thing mattered little to him. He detested both the Free-Soilers who abandoned the Democratic Party and the proslavery forces of its southern wing. "For the sake of novelty, and to put down the Southerners," he rasped to Ticknor, "I should like well enough to try Frémont; but it would be a dangerous experiment for the country." And Sophia believed the white supremacist propaganda about the slave rebellions Frémont's election would indubitably incite "because the negroes received an idea or instruction that he would aid them with an army."

Buchanan won. "The country will stand, & . . . Mr. Buchanan will be wise & strong," Sophia consoled Mary Mann.

With Pierce leaving office and his own departure imminent, Hawthorne felt far less compunction about dodging consular business, which meant he could gratify pleasures long deferred. He and Sophia and Julian traipsed through Yorkshire at Easter time, to Lincolnshire and Newstead Abbey in May, to Glasgow and Dumbarton Castle and Loch Lomand and Edinburgh in the summer. (Cranky with so much sightseeing, Una was left behind with Rose and a servant.) At the end of July, the entire family quit Southport, renting rooms near Victoria Station in Old Trafford, outside of Manchester, so Hawthorne could finish out his term while the rest of the family explored Prince Albert's exhibition of British art in the immense hymn to iron and glass erected for the occasion.

Hawthorne also quit himself of Bacon, having finished the preface to her book. "No man or woman has ever thought or written more sincerely than the author of this book," he wrote, damning Bacon's undertaking with half praise. She wanted him to rewrite his lukewarm endorsement; Hawthorne refused, and Bacon's publisher reneged. Bennoch saved the day, coaxing Groombridge and Sons, publisher of the *Westminster Review,* to bring out Bacon's tome, *The Philosophy of the Plays of Shakspere Unfolded,* in the spring of 1857. Hawthorne paid twenty-five pounds toward advertising.

The press savaged the book as wild and silly and dull, and Hawthorne's preface was taken to be ironical. "I do not repent what I have done," he had written Ticknor. Without Shakespeare, Bacon's paranoia lost its object. She stopped eating, dressing, and changing the linens on her bed. The mayor of Stratford contacted Hawthorne, as American consul, and Hawthorne wrote to Leonard Bacon, paid her bills, and arranged a September passage back to America. By then Bacon, completely mad, had to be committed to a private sanatorium.

Hawthorne would salute Delia Bacon. "I fell under Miss Bacon's most severe and passionate displeasure, and was cast off by her in the twinkling of an eye," he later recalled, carefully choosing his words. "It was a misfortune to which her friends were always particularly liable; but I think that none of them ever loved, or even respected, her most ingenuous and noble, but likewise most sensitive and tumultuous character, the less for it."

So much for female authorship: it seemed a cruel object lesson, even for a sensitive writer who cast off his own tumultuous women, like Zenobia, in the twinkling of an eye.

CHAPTER TWENTY-TWO

Questions of Travel

Continent, city, country, society:
the choice is never wide and never free.
And here, or there . . . No. Should we have stayed at home,
wherever that may be?

Elizabeth Bishop, "Questions of Travel"

MR. H CAME this evening, and I was quite surprised to see so *handsome* a man as he is. He has the most beautiful brow and eyes, and his voice is extremely musical," exclaimed Ada Shepard, a student of languages fresh out of Antioch College come to Europe to tutor the Hawthorne children. The Hawthornes were the most charming couple, Sophia as wise as Elizabeth Peabody, although, thank goodness, more conventional. Lovable Una, her hair the color of cherry wood, read everything with a comprehension far beyond her thirteen years; at eleven Julian was a Hercules in miniature; and if not so remarkable, Rose was at least sweet.

But the road to Rome was paved with delays.

After the Manchester exhibition, the Hawthornes went back to Leamington Spa again, where they'd stayed in the spring and summer of 1855. They expected to leave for France in a week or two, or Sophia and the children would go to Paris while Nathaniel waited in Liverpool for his successor, Nathaniel Beverly Tucker. Events conspired against them. Tucker didn't come until October, and Hawthorne's trusted clerk, Henry Wilding, took ill with a nervous fever. With Wilding unavailable, administrative particulars fell to Hawthorne, who wanted to make sure he pocketed everything the government owed him before he left England. So he would stay as long as necessary.

At last, on November 11, 1857, the Hawthornes put Leamington behind them—but not England. They spent the entire month in London, Sophia and the children having gotten the flu. "It seems as though the fates have decided that we shall never reach the continent," despaired Ada Shepard, "for cause after cause of delay springs up, and still we stay, stay, stay." December passed. Not until before sunrise on January 5, their dozen trunks and half dozen carpetbags summarily labeled, did the Hawthorne tribe climb into two hansom cabs and roll through gaslit streets to the railway station. On to France at last.

Paris was fabulous, for a while. "The splendor of Paris, so far as I have seen, takes me altogether by surprise," Hawthorne penned in his journal three days later. The grand buildings, gold and Doric, and the motley street life were so different from the austerities of a top-hatted London. For a week, quartered in the excellent Hôtel du Louvre, Hawthorne explored the magnificent, interminable Louvre, just steps away, he traversed stately avenues and busy bookstalls, and he poked his nose into Notre-Dame. But the biting cold made him nostalgic for English drizzle. A generous and kind man, according to Ada Shepard, he was also critical and hard to please. Soon bored with Paris, he railed against the narrow little fireplaces at the hotel, and suddenly the plane trees of the Champs-Elysées looked straggly.

Longing for home, he and his family packed up again, their piles of luggage bundled into yet another railroad car for yet another journey, vagabonds all over again.

The Eternal City huddled in January's icy glare. Hawthorne shivered as he sat in front of one of the big hearths in his ten-room apartment in the Palazzo Laranzani at 37, Via Porta Pincia. "How I dislike the place," he snarled, "and how wretched I have been in it." The cold of Paris and the cold of Rome were the meteorological barometer of his distress.

The Hawthorne entourage had crawled into Rome just two weeks earlier, on January 20, their carriage bowed by a spectacular quantity of luggage, their limbs half frozen, and poor Maria Mitchell, an American astronomer in their party, dumbfounded by Hawthorne's impracticality, his indecision, his silences. "Had Mr. Hawthorne been as agreeable in conversation as he is in writing," she remarked in irritation, "it could have made the day pleasant."

Arrive they finally did, their *vetturino* rattling and Julian so hungry he wished the dome of St. Peter's a mutton chop. Wearily, they settled into Stillman's Hotel near the buzzing Piazza di Spagna, but within hours, it seemed, Sophia sprang into health, cough gone, headache vanished, and virtually skipped into the city of her dreams. Rome: it was rife with Domenichino, Guido Reni, Raphael, and Michelangelo. John Flaxman had studied there and Washington Allston; Madame de Staël's Corinne lingered at the fountains with Oswald, as did Margaret Fuller. And now, after years of wishing and hoping, Sophia had her turn at last.

Indefatigable sightseer, she bounded forth, released from the dolor of England with its fog of consular routine. For Rome opened its arms to women. Women models and sculptors and tourists strolled the crooked streets, an omnipresent Madonna grinning down on all of them. "How could wise and great Mr. Emerson say such a preposterous thing as that it was just as well not to travel as to travel!" Sophia asked in annoyance, "and that each man has Europe in him, or something to that effect?" She tossed her head. "Mere transcendental nonsense—such a remark."

Hawthorne lagged behind. Exhausted, crabby, and chilled by a low-grade fever, he wound himself in his overcoat and morosely sat before the fire with an open volume of Thackeray on his lap, which Maria Mitchell suspected he used to ward off noisome intruders.

He adjusted to new environs slowly. The locals seemed alien, the language impenetrable, the bread sour, the cigars bad, the monuments chipped and unclean. The city's small square paving stones tormented his aching feet, fleas pinched him, and every single alley terminated in a piazza where a grotesque fountain squirted jets of water from a ridiculous hunk of sculpture. "Of course there are better and truer things to be said," he admitted; "but old Rome does seem to lie here like a dead and mostly decayed corpse, retaining here and there a trace of the noble shape it was, but with a sort of fungous growth upon it, and no life but of the worms that creep in and out."

Rome as corpse: it was an image to which he would return.

Looking back to England, he slipped into provincial comparisons. English ruins were better than Roman ruins; Norman churches superior to Italian ones; English damp more tolerable than Roman chill. And like any traveler face to face with sites anticipated for years, Hawthorne reluctantly relinquished his own fancies for the real thing, which never measured up. The golden bubble of St. Peter's dome loomed larger in daydream, and as for the half-ruined face of the Coliseum, "Byron's celebrated description is better than the reality."

Actually, Rome baffled him. Tin hearts hung at the shrines of saints, Romans urinated near marble monuments, cheap wooden confessionals stood in St. Peter's: sublime and absurd, devout and heathen, ancient and modern heaped together in a riot. Green peas, onions, cauliflower, apples, almonds, and fish were sold in the nasty Piazza Navona, but in the Borghese gardens, where the tall stone pines looked like islands of green in the air, he could smell the ilex and sweet cypress. "Take away the malaria," Hawthorne gibed, "and it might be a very happy place."

He and Sophia traipsed through the endless galleries to see countless pictures, Sophia wanting to embrace everything, the paintings at the Capitol, the Borghese Gallery, and the Rospigliosi, Sciarra, and Doria Pamphili palaces. Hawthorne bleakly stood in attendance. "There is something forced, if not feigned, in our tastes for pictures of the old Italian school," he muttered, never criticizing his wife's aesthetic taste though not exactly sharing her raptures over the innumerable Magdalens, Holy Infants, Crucifixions, and Flights into Egypt. That was bad enough. The "general apotheosis of nakedness" piqued him beyond endurance.

Hawthorne was a prude. He blanched before the tinted Venus in the English sculptor John Gibson's studio: "This lascivious warmth of hue quite demoralizes the chastity of the marble," he cringed, feeling "ashamed to look at the naked limbs in the company of women." He was also a boor. Unvarnished and unframed pictures depressed him, and he liked the work of Cephas Thompson, who had painted his portrait in 1850, much better than anything else he saw, except maybe very old masters. He hated Giotto. But his parochialism and his harangues weren't wholly laughable. Unlike many of his contemporaries, he preferred the warmth of Donatello over the slippery, frigid beauty of most classical statues, for when he trudged through the Vatican Sculpture Gallery, "the statues kept, for the most part, a veil around them, which they sometimes withdrew, and let their beauty glow upon my sight." The illumination swiftly disappeared, leaving nothing in its wake but grubby marble.

An exception was Praxiteles' copy of a Faun, or Resting Satyr, in the Capitol and another copy in the Borghese, where Hawthorne mulled over the "strange, sweet, playful rustic creatures, almost entirely human, yet linked so prettily, without monstrosity, to the lower tribes by the long, furry ears, or by a modest tail." Fit subject for a romance, he reflected, rich and poetical and freakish and "a natural and delightful link betwixt human and brute life, and with something of a divine character intermingled." Three weeks later, he walked back over to the Capitoline Museum to look at the Faun again, its androgynous form leaning on a tree trunk, pointed ears lightly sexual, his mouth voluptuous, his entire comportment seductive and amiably sly. Hawthorne thought he might write a short, fantastic tale about it.

Resting Satyr [Standing Faun], Praxiteles

Grief, desire, cruelty, and the heart-twisting beauty of time past in every stone, every square, every broken brick: slowly Rome began to wear down Hawthorne's xenophobia, luring him into crevices "which will make me reluctant to take a final leave of it," he confided to Ticknor as if surprised at himself. Clutching *Murray's Handbook*—guidebook of choice for all self-respecting American tourists—he frequently strayed from its proscriptions, moseying along the Pincian or lolling along the banks of the yellow Tiber, stopping to watch a man fish. He drew from his pocket the bronze match-box Una had given him and lit his cigar as he surveyed the city from the hillside and then descended the Spanish Steps to stop at his bank, Pakenham and Hooker, and read the American newspapers. He reentered the Pantheon to stand beneath the dome that stood open to the sky, silently worshipping nature and art, blue air and icy marble, and at night, with Sophia, he rambled through the city, moonlight sprinkling magic over the Fountain of Trevi (Bernini was an acquired taste) and the grand Arch of Constantine.

Even Rome's expressive Catholicism, visible everywhere, began to thaw Hawthorne's Protestant frost. Peasant and soldier, each entered a church and kneeled before a shrine to ask the mediation of some saint, too humble to plead to God directly. "In the church of San Paulo yesterday I saw a young man standing before a shrine, writhing and wringing his hands in an agony of grief and contrition," Hawthorne observed. "If he had been a protestant, I think he would have shut all that up within his heart, and let it burn there till it seared him." American expatriates muttered in gossipy consternation that the Hawthornes genuflected before false gods.

Hawthorne made no special friends like Bright or Bennoch in Rome, although he liked Thompson and he respected another Massachusetts man, William Wetmore Story, whose character he studied in his notebooks, for he was as interested in the makers of art as in their work. American artists, in particular, were flocking to the Eternal City, where there was an abundance of marbles, models, and skilled labor, all for a pittance. But they came too because Rome was far, far away from home, where, as Story put it, "the sky itself is hard and distant."

Friend to both Margaret Fuller and James Lowell, who were not friends of one another, Story was at the center of the American art colony in Rome, where he successfully navigated—or helped spawn—its internecine rivalry. ("Their public is so much more limited than that of the literary men," reasoned Hawthorne, "that they have better excuse for these petty jealousies.") A Salem native and the son of the late Supreme Court justice Joseph Story, William Story and his wife, Emelyn, had lived in Rome on and off since 1847, becoming permanent expatriates in 1856 when Story threw over his career in the law for poetry and sculpture.

The Storys occupied ten stately rooms on an upper floor in the sumptuous Barberini Palace, sheltered from Roman weather by exuberant palms. "With sparkling talents, so many that if he choose to neglect or fling away one, or two, or three, he would still have enough to shine with;—who should be happy, if not he?" mused Hawthorne, wondering if Story had actually been blessed with too much. "The great difficulty with him, I think, is a too facile power," he observed cannily; "he would do better things, if it were more difficult for him to do merely good ones."

Bald, bearded, slightly gray, and slender, Story had just begun his massive statue of Cleopatra when he first ushered the Hawthornes into his studio, separate from his home, on the Via Sistina. "He is certainly sensible of something deeper in his art than merely to make beautiful nudities and baptize them by classic names," pronounced Hawthorne. "I cannot say now what I think of the Cleopatra, but I am proud of it as an American work," Sophia remarked patriotically, "—and I think it will render immortal William Story."

Like all of the other expatriate sculptors, Story drenched himself in the neoclassicism beloved by expatriates and partly inspired by the archaeological findings of the last thirty or so years, including the discovery of the Venus de Milo in 1820. Plus, neoclassicism suited an American Protestant middle class: elegant, uncluttered, edifying, and silent, if one was for it, or the frozen tedium of sublime dummies, if one wasn't. Devoid of ostentation, the high-minded work of the American neoclassicists praised heroic deeds, heroic suffering, and American history. Hawthorne looked at Joseph Mozier's famed Pocahontas and his Wish-ton-Wish, modeled after a character in James Fenimore Cooper, but preferred Mozier's somewhat less pretentious schoolboy mending a pen. The sculptor's "cleverness and ingenuity appear in homely subjects," observed Hawthorne, "but are quite lost in attempts at a higher ideality."

Not true of another Salem native, Louise Lander, who asked Hawthorne to sit for her. She modeled his head for a bust altogether too idealizing, commented Maria Mitchell. Lander insisted on puffing out Hawthorne's cheeks where several missing teeth had sucked them hollow. Years later, Julian Hawthorne alleged that an American art critic, deciding that the lower part of the face had been incorrectly molded, instructed the marble cutters to change it, Lander and Hawthorne being out of town at the time. "The likeness was destroyed," recalled Julian; "and the bust, in its present state looks like a combination of Daniel Webster and George Washington."

In early 1858 Lander basked in the Hawthornes' hospitality, rambling with Sophia through various artists' studios or joining the family for dinner and an evening of Beethoven. Like many of her countrywomen, Lander walked around Rome with astounding ease. "A young woman, living in almost perfect independence, thousands of miles from her New England home, going fearless about these mysterious streets, by night as well as by day, with no household ties, no rule or law but that within her," Hawthorne marveled, "yet acting with quietness and simplicity, and keeping, after all, within a homely line of right." Lander was not alone. She was part of what Henry James, writing of William Story, condescendingly named "that white Marmorean flock" of women artists daring to be themselves—and daring to compete with men.

One of these women, the twenty-eight-year-old Harriet Hosmer—Hatty to friends—had been in Rome since 1852, one of the "jolly bachelors" who lived in Charlotte Cushman's large house on the Corso. A former student of John Gibson, she shared his studio on the Via Fontanella, near the Spanish Steps, where she entertained the gawking public in men's clothing, a man's shirt, collar, tie, and a close-fitting brown jacket "like a boy," observed

Maria Mitchell, "buttoned by boy buttons and furnished with boy pockets." On top of short vivacious hair she planted a little black velvet cap. "She was indeed very queer," commented Hawthorne, "but she seemed to be her actual self, and nothing affected nor made-up; so that, for my part, I give her full leave to wear what may suit her best, and to behave as her inner woman prompts." Una sniffed, "I think Miss Hosmer altogether too masculine, and did not take a fancy to her at all."

Una bristled at the idea of emancipated women. So did William Story. "Hatty takes a high hand here with Rome," Story wrote, distilling his annoyance, "and would have the Romans know that a Yankee girl can do anything she pleases, walk alone, ride her horse alone, and laugh at their rules." Such liberty galled him almost as much as Hosmer's vulgar, enviable commercial sense. Her star sculpture, a roguish Puck sitting on a toadstool, was replicated by the hundreds and sold prodigiously, especially to British aristocrats.

Hosmer petrified expatriate competitors still shaken by the specter of Margaret Fuller, who invited salacious prattle eight years after her death. Joseph Mozier bubbled with slander about Fuller and her handsome moron of a husband, "entirely ignorant even of his own language," sneered Mozier, "scarcely able to read at all, destitute of manners; in short, half an idiot." No manuscript of Fuller's had been lost in the sinking of the *Elizabeth;* it was her literary powers that bottomed way before the boat had sailed. Hawthorne recorded the vitriol in his journal with certain pleasure, and when published years later by Julian, these comments set off a nasty scandal of their own. But Hawthorne had softened his tone. "The amelioration of society depends greatly on the part that women shall hereafter take," he wrote a few weeks later in a new romance. He rather liked the idea; then again, he didn't.

Engulfed by art and artists and the heavy weight of the past, Hawthorne tried reaching for his pen. A recurring cold kept him in bed in the morning, sick and tired. The overcast or showery weather continued, and despite the incessant sightseeing and journalizing, he jotted in his pocket diary that he "did nothing of importance, as usual."

"I doubt greatly whether I shall be able to settle down to serious literary labor as long as I remain abroad," he warned Ticknor; "at all events, not in Italy." Yet at about the same time as his tête-à-tête with Mozier, he was sketching out the idea of a romance. "Mr. Hawthorne commenced a new book yesterday," Ada Shepard marked the calendar on April 13, even though Hawthorne had already started two weeks earlier. "None of us yet know what its subject is to be."

This new book comes down to us as "The Ancestral Footstep," a title bequeathed by Rose Hawthorne and her husband when they published the extant manuscript in 1882, eighty-eight pages from a copybook, with some missing leaves, and interesting for its raw incompletion. The disarray throws light onto Hawthorne's messy worktable.

As is typical, Hawthorne begins with the donnée, or an image—in this case, the bloody footstep—around which he composes various episodes, each one entered into his notebook on a different day and dated, as if each passage were an entry in a diary. Had he finished the story, he would in all likelihood have destroyed his copybook, erasing his trials, errors, and quandaries once he transcribed his results into clean copy. But he did not. He proceeded by fits and starts after April 1, not writing continuously except for two weeks in May, and even then was unsatisfied. The story was of the American claimant again, which Hawthorne now intended to introduce to his reader as an anecdote he'd supposedly heard at the consulate presented with "touches that shall puzzle the reader to decide whether it is not an actual portrait." His reader would also have to puzzle over the story, whose hero, Hawthorne noted, should make "singular discoveries, all of which bring the book to an ending unexpected by everybody, and not satisfactory to the natural yearnings of novel-readers."

This hero, Middleton, is a politician so disenchanted with civic life that he's come abroad to refresh himself, much as Franklin Pierce was doing, by returning to the country of his ancestors. (In an early sketch, Hawthorne planned to make his hero a veteran of the Mexican War.) Middleton, moreover, is aware of an old family legend about two brothers in love with the same woman (an inversion of Hawthorne's relations with the Peabody sisters). In a jealous rage, one brother reputedly killed his sibling on the threshold of the family manor, where, before dying, the slain brother leaves his bloody print. But the slain brother is, in fact, alive, having fled with the woman to America, where he changed his name, "so remorseful, so outraged, that he wished to disconnect with all the past, and begin life quite anew, in a new world."

Bemused by it all, Middleton decides to investigate the English branch of the family, descended from a third brother, and in so doing, Middleton realizes his connection to the past: "He rather felt as if he were the original emigrant, who long resident on a foreign shore, had now returned, with a heart brimful of tenderness, to revisit the scenes of his youth, and renew his tender relations with those who shared his own blood." Also to Middleton's surprise, he finds he is rightful heir to a titled estate. But here's the rub. The discovery requires a good deal of turmoil and bloodshed; and the really serious question, from the novelist's point of view, is "what shall be the nature of this tragic trouble, and how can it be brought about."

Hawthorne was stumped. One thing was certain, though. Middleton is Hawthorne's Hamlet, wondering whether to act or retreat, whether to stir up the past or leave it alone and "withdraw himself into the secrecy from which he had emerged; and leave the family to keep on, to the end of time perhaps, in its rusty innocence; rather than to interfere." Perhaps Middleton affects a middle way between the desire to dig up the past, taking active responsibility for what he finds there, and the desire to stay aloof, an unmolested spectator distant to alarms.

Sophia herself had compared Hawthorne to the brooding Dane. "He [Hamlet] lived so completely in his own inner world, that he found it impossible to break forth into a deed of violence, though he was morally convinced he should punish the criminal," she wrote to Elizabeth. ". . . To you alone in this world I would say that this made me think of another person of the contemplative, meditative, introspective order—tender also— who would probably do very much as Hamlet did in those circumstances." Elizabeth knew of whom Sophia spoke.

In "The Ancestral Footstep," however, Hawthorne tips the scales, and not toward action. Little good comes from trying to alter the course of events, given our imperfect knowledge of what we do, Hawthorne claimed in his biography of Pierce. "The progress of the world, at every step, leaves some evil or wrong on the path behind it, which the wisest of mankind, of their own set purpose, could never have found the way to rectify."

As yet another attempt to justify inaction, or a life lived wholly in the present, "The Ancestral Footstep" hints that Hawthorne was himself unhappy, as always, with his decision. The past intrudes in present life every day, at every juncture, demanding something: the impossible settling of old accounts by means as reprehensible as the initial crime. Again and again, Hawthorne picked at the same psychological issues. But in social terms, these issues weren't peculiar to Hawthorne. The question of a regrettable past and uncertain future confronted all Americans in 1858: what to do about ancestral crimes like slavery?

"The moral, if any moral were to be gathered from these paltry and wretched circumstances," Hawthorne decides in his unfinished "Ancestral

Footstep," "was 'Let the past alone; do not seek to renew it; press on to higher and better things—at all events to other things; and be assured that the right way can never be that which leads you back to the identical shapes that you long ago left behind. Onward, onward, onward!"

Hawthorne didn't sit still long enough to write much. In May he was negotiating for a place to rent in Florence for the summer and the means to get there, by way of Spoleto and Perugia. He and Sophia thought they might be able to nose about the countryside without the children (the children could always revisit Italy as adults, they rationalized). In the winter they'd all return to Rome, and the following spring, 1859, they'd go home. Home: "blessed words," Una skeptically remarked, aware that in her family, plans fluttered as quickly as her adolescent pulse.

Expectations of Florence ran high, and the trip didn't disappoint: blood-red poppies and the silvery glisten of olive trees, deep valleys and ravines and white buildings the color of New England snow. "What a land!" said Sophia, always amazed, "where rainbows are broken up, and tossed among the mountains and valleys, just for beauty." At the suggestion of the sculptor Benjamin Paul Akers, Hawthorne enlisted the assistance of Hiram Powers, another sculptor, who obligingly leaped into action. The Hawthornes, somewhat like strayed sheep, had found their shepherd.

Across the street from Powers on the Via Fornace, the Casa del Bello was vacant and furnished, the lower floor dotted with as many as fifteen easy chairs in an abundantly frescoed, high-ceilinged set of rooms arranged around a courtyard. One of the three parlors doubled as Hawthorne's study, delighting him with its view of the green garden that fireflies lit after dark—all for fifty dollars a month. Florence was not only lovely, its air like sherbet, opined Sophia, but cheap, the very "Paradise of cheapness," observed Nathaniel, "which we vainly sought in Rome." Their servant charged only six dollars a month, and for one dollar and twenty cents a day, the Hawthornes ordered dinner from a nearby cookshop. Tolerable red wine cost mere pennies, cigars or fresh dark cherries equally reasonable. "What can man desire more!" Hawthorne murmured happily, content for the first time in months.

Sophia too was happy. Their illustrious neighbors the Brownings, though soon off to France, had welcomed them at Casa Guidi, Elizabeth Barrett petite and expressive, a spiritualist with fairy fingers (Sophia commented) serving the strawberries and cake. Herself a rival invalid, Sophia coughed once in a while, taking umbrage, as of old, when anyone remarked on how well she looked. Still, she admired herself in white muslin, perfect for the steamy weather. The whole family was picture perfect: Una's own white dress billowed on the sofa while she read Tennyson, Julian busily scribbled his history of shells, and little Rose, now seven, jumped rope in the Boboli Gardens or picked tea roses for her mother.

"Mr. Hawthorne has become himself again," Sophia exulted to Mary. "He did not *live* in Rome, he only existed—besides that he had a perpetual cold. Here I find him again as in the first summer in Concord at the old Manse." He was writing.

"Every day I shall write a little, perhaps," Hawthorne outlined his plans, "—and probably take a brief nap, somewhere between breakfast and tea."

Mornings, he sauntered over Florentine streets, stopping here and there, or wandered at leisure through the Uffizi Gallery, returning to the Venus de' Medici as to a mistress, aghast to learn that Powers, an opinionated man impressed with himself, compared her unfavorably to his own handiwork. Powers tickled Hawthorne. He spouted off about flying machines, Swedenborg, Andrew Jackson, the laying of the Atlantic cable, which Powers could've done better—shrewd Yankee talk, said Hawthorne, "full of bone and muscle," transcribing in his journal the sculptor's tirades. Yet Powers was conspicuous among American sculptors, having zoomed to fame and a comfortable life after his *Greek Slave* toured America in 1847 to handsome receipts and a storm of publicity guaranteeing a hit in London. How not? Stripped naked, hands chained, a cross dangling in her rumpled clothing, the five-foot-tall Greek woman is a triumph of prurient eroticism, with everybody allowed to look. And best of all, in her chaste, white-marbleish way, she alludes ever so obliquely to the real-life slavery on everyone's mind.

Hawthorne struggled to keep up with all the art talk, so sophisticated and knowing. But "after admiring and being moved by a picture, one day," he admitted, "it is within my experience to look at it, the next, as little moved as if it were a tavern-sign." Yet in the Uffizi galleries, he could relax with the Dutch masters, for Dutch realism was neither abject nor a misty ideality perceived, if perceived at all, only by the cognoscenti. "Until we learn to appreciate the cherubs and angels that Raphael scatters through the blessed air, in a picture of the Nativity, it is not amiss to look at a Dutch fly settling on a peach, or a humble-bee burying himself in a flower," he observed. "For my part," Hawthorne soon concluded, "I wish Raphael had painted the Transfiguration in this style."

Nor did he not see why the two styles couldn't—shouldn't—be com-

THE VIRGINIAN SLAVE.

INTENDED AS A COMPANION TO POWER'S "GREEK SLAVE."

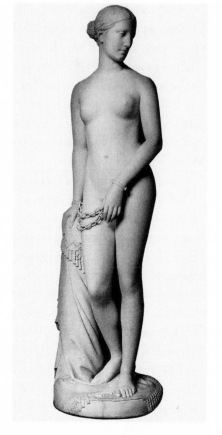

"The Virginian Slave," parody, Punch,
London

The Greek Slave, *Hiram Powers*

bined. "Had it not been possible for Raphael to paint General Jackson!" he observed with dry wit. This would be the actual and the imaginary combined, just what he wanted for his new romance; he did not "wish it to be a picture of life; but a Romance, grim, grotesque, quaint," he said. ". . . It might have so much of the hues of life that the reader should sometimes think it was intended for a picture; yet the atmosphere should be such as to excuse all wildness."

The romance came haltingly when it came at all. "I feel an impulse to be at work," he recorded two weeks after arriving in Florence, "but am kept idle by the sense of being unsettled, with removals to be gone through, over and over again, before I can shut myself into a quiet room of my own, and turn the key."

Hawthorne caught cold, complained of the heat, grew tired of city life, its art and conversation charming him no longer. More disruption, another illness, and another move. Isabella Blagden, a friend of the Brownings, knew of a villa near hers in Bellosguardo that might be just the thing. Her neighbor Count Montauto, a man long on title and short of cash, had decided to rent his home, "big enough to quarter a regiment," Hawthorne wrote James Fields, with a wonderful "moss-grown-tower, haunted by owls and by the ghost of a monk," from which he could look out to the brown Arno Valley.

The Hawthornes loaded their carpet bags with their clothes and on August 1 climbed the Bellosguardo hill, a mile outside the Roman gate to the north of Florence. Sophia had arranged to rent the Villa Montauto for two months at twenty-eight dollars a month. Marching through dusty streets with Una and Julian, Hawthorne arrived at the villa, found the iron gate locked, located a *contadino* who scrambled up a ladder and into a window and out again with the keys. The gate swung wide, and Hawthorne ascended the rickety staircase to the wide square tower, from whose battlements he and Julian were soon flinging pieces of lime, watching them fall. The view was fine, peaceful, beautiful, quiet: a spectator's jewel.

Each member of the Hawthorne house took a suite of rooms, Hawthorne claiming three on the ground floor, one for a writing closet. He stayed there for several weeks, sketching out a new book until September, when he announced to Fields that he had planned two romances, one or both of which might be ready for the press in a few months—if, that is, he wasn't in Italy. "I find this Italian atmosphere not favorable to the close toil of composition," he explained, "although it is a very good air to dream in."

In the misty mornings, Hawthorne felt as if the valley itself were dreaming, and at the end of September, as the full moon gleamed softly over the Tuscan hill, it was time to move on. Hawthorne socialized a bit and listened politely as visitants from the spirit world blew through the Florentine valley, overturning tables and conveying messages from the dead. Notified that she possessed the power to interpret their messages, Ada Shepard sent tidings from Sophia's two dead brothers, her father (recently deceased), and from the garrulous Mrs. Peabody, who reported that she hadn't seen Byron yet.

The party over and the spirits departed, Hawthorne shook Hiram Powers's smooth hand, picked his way through streets scented with green lemon and walked through the Pitti Palace and the Uffizi "with a sad reluctance to bid them farewell forever." Then he changed his mind. "I am not loth to go away," he said, "—impatient rather; for taking no root, I soon weary of any soil that I may be temporarily deposited in. The same impatience I sometimes feel, or conceive of, as regards this earthly life."

On Friday, October 1, 1858, Hawthorne left the ancient tower in the early morning haze, his sights set again on Rome, Eternal City of memory, art, and contagion.

CHAPTER TWENTY-THREE

Things to See and Suffer

Hawthorne entices, appalls.

Emily Dickinson

APPROACHING the city, St. Peter's radiant in the sky-blue distance, the Hawthornes asked their driver—they called him the Emperor—to stop the horses. One by one they stepped out of the carriage. Sophia went first. "ROME ROME ROME." Only capital letters would do. "I can now understand the irresistible attraction it has to those who return a second time," she cried. "Now that I have known it once, Rome certainly does draw into itself my heart," Nathaniel admitted.

Incorrigible realist, he added, "Besides, we are to stay here six months."

Quite a long time, noted the imperturbable Sophia, "to such Arabs as we have been lately."

The Hawthornes climbed back into the carriage, the Emperor cracked his leather whip, and six horses, heads bent forward, galloped toward the Porta del Popolo.

He now liked the crowded Corso, a noble street, he said. He scaled the marble steps of the Capitoline Museum without a murmur and marched valiantly through the picture galleries. Even the roasted chestnuts, sold on the street, tasted good to him.

The lodgings were satisfactory. That helped. Cephas Thompson had found the Hawthornes a seven-room apartment at 68 Piazza Poli. Equipped with a facsimile of a Franklin stove and plenty of carpets—there had been none in the Palazzo Laranzani—it promised warmth, especially in Hawthorne's study, and comfort. Late at night, when the city fell quiet,

Hawthorne could hear the splash of the Trevi Fountain, just a block away, as he drifted to sleep.

The American colony welcomed them, the Storys, Hatty Hosmer, Joseph Mozier, and of course Thompson, the latter bursting with the Louisa Lander scandal. Lander, it seems, had been living with a man on "uncommonly good terms" and posing as a model in risqué clothes, it was said, to show off her good figure. Punctilious, the American expatriate community appointed William Story to interview anyone who could vouch for Miss Lander's drowning reputation, and Hawthorne rather hoped Lander would acquit herself. She wouldn't stoop to such folly and refused to be interviewed.

So the Hawthornes turned their backs. "Miss Lander's life (as she truly observes) lies between her Maker and herself," Hawthorne conceded in a formal letter, perhaps never sent. Until she cleared her name, he continued, his prose as rigid as toy soldiers, his pronouns third-person stiff, the Hawthornes simply could not admit her to their home. "Any attempt at social intercourse with her former friends (especially where young people and

The Hawthorne family [late 1850s, early 1860s]

children are included in the number) should have been preceded by a full explanation and refutation of those reports," Hawthorne declared.

Lander left Rome.

Hawthorne's good mood fell apart. Lander's disgrace, the pitiless drizzle, another bout of grippe: Rome flattened the soul. "I have suffered more in Rome from low spirits than almost anywhere else," he told Franklin Pierce. Yet the persistent influenza and distemper—sporadic, provoking—paled next to the long death struggle of Una.

It began on the Thursday after their arrival. Sophia was descanting about Praxiteles' Faun in her journal. Suddenly she dropped her pen mid-sentence and snapped the book shut. Five days later, on October 26, slimy rain clung to the windows, and Una burned with fever.

They moved her into Hawthorne's study. She first was diagnosed incorrectly and then—correctly—with malaria, or Roman fever, a disease that smolders, subsides, and then darts back to rack the body with chill, the mind with delirium. Una rallied and relapsed. She chanted "like a tragic heroine," her father despaired, "—as if the fever lifted her feet off the earth." Every two hours she was given quinine. "The ill effects of the large doses . . . were probably quite as lasting and injurious as those of the fever itself," Julian concluded, with good reason, years later.

In three weeks, she seemed well enough to take a drive with Mrs. Story, but at the end of November her face flushed purple and her temperature shot back up.

Malaria probably toppled Ada Shepard in January. With Sophia exhausted from nursing both girls, Hawthorne still managed somehow to closet himself in his study, writing an hour or two each day on a romance begun the day of Una's illness. "I have been trying to tear [it] out of my mind," he told Fields; writing kept him from going mad. In February he finished a rough draft. "As for my success, I can't say much," he wrote to Fields; "indeed, I don't know what to say at all. I only know that I have produced what seems to be a larger amount of Scribble than either of my former Romances, and that portions of it interested me a good deal while I was writing them; but I have had too many interruptions, from things to see and things to suffer, that the story has developed itself in a very imperfect way, and will have to be revised hereafter."

Soon Hawthorne himself was in bed. "I never knew that I had either bowels or lungs, till I came to Rome," he grimly wrote to Ticknor, "but I have found it out now, to my cost." Sophia suspected that he too had malaria, although he seemed to be stronger, sipping beef broth, quite unlike the stricken Una, so slow to recover. Weakness shook her hand as she walked with her father down the Corso at Carnival time, two invalids in the pestilential city.

Carnival revelry: not for him. Hawthorne wanted to leave Rome as quickly as possible. Mid-April sounded good. They could hire a carriage to take them to Geneva and Paris, then cross the Channel to England, stop over in London, and swing the Wayside gate open in July. By August he'd be revising his new book and outlining another to pay for the renovations he was imagining now that they'd lived in the Villa Montauto.

It was a good plan, foiled in March. Una had crashed. Dr. Franco diagnosed galloping consumption. "God help us!" Hawthorne scribbled in his pocket diary. He gestured toward Sophia. "I don't know what will become of her when she loses hope," he winced. But Sophia, resolute, kept vigil at Una's side, day and night, for two weeks. "I am going to die now," the girl murmured to her mother. "There is no use in living," she repeated. "Goodbye, dear." Sophia said nothing. Una said "Goodbye, dear" again and faced the wall, waiting for death.

Not healthy herself, Ada replaced Sophia at Una's bedside while fending off the advances of Dr. Franco, their lecherous homeopath. It must have been a confused, unhappy household. Sophia watched over Una and sidestepped Nathaniel, whose eye she avoided lest they both break down; Ada dodged Dr. Franco, who kept lunging after her for a kiss; Julian raged against fate in the privacy of his room; and Rose, bewildered, lonely Rose, said or did nothing of note. Long afterwards, Julian remembered his father trying hard to keep up appearances, shuffling cards for whist every night until, hammered by grief, he put them down. "We won't play any more," he announced.

Early in April, Dr. Franco told Sophia that Una might not survive the night. "It is not natural that the young should die," she sobbed. "I always knew I was not worthy of her." It was Sophia's finest hour. She resolved to tell Hawthorne what Franco had said—"drop the thunderbolts gently at his feet"—and when she did, Hawthorne passed a quivering hand through his hair. "I do not remember what I said then," she recalled, "but I left him & went back to my post."

For the sake of Nathaniel and the children, Sophia contrived to stay silent, organized, and stalwart, propped up by the expatriate community that rallied to her side in all the ways meaningful to her, a line of well-wishing carriages constantly at the Piazza Poli door, itself crowded with cards and flowers and fussing friends. Even Mrs. Browning, who rarely emerged from her villa, rushed to the Hawthorne house.

And there was Franklin Pierce, come to relieve her of Hawthorne. The former president and his wife, vacationing in Rome, refused to leave the city until Una improved. At least once a day, sometimes as many as three times, Pierce called at 68 Piazza Poli to draw Hawthorne outdoors. Hawthorne grabbed his hat and meandered with Pierce over the winding streets, two friends of thirty-five years, Pierce attentive lest Hawthorne pout too long. Sophia said she owed her husband's sanity to him. "No one else could have supplied his place."

Hawthorne discussed Pierce's presidential prospects, which seemed nil to Hawthorne, and though Pierce protested he'd never run again—his usual strategy—Hawthorne knew Pierce would likely jump at the chance. Hawthorne didn't necessarily think it a bad idea. Pierce had fully risen to what the office demanded, he reasoned. True, Pierce had not risen beyond what the office demanded, nor was he a political visionary, but Pierce knew, according to Hawthorne, "with a miraculous intuition of what ought to be done, just at the time for action. His judgment of things about him is wonderful." Other Americans, most of them, disagreed violently. Said one of the old party faithful who'd since lost faith, "The Kansas outrages are all imputable to him, and if he is not called to answer for them here, 'In Hell they'll roast him like a herring.' "

Hawthorne didn't care a fig for such calumny. "I did not know what comfort there might be in the manly sympathy of a friend," he wrote in his journal; "but Pierce has undergone so great a sorrow of his own, and has so large and kindly a heart, and is so tender and so strong, that he really did us good, and I shall always love him the better for the recollection of these dark days."

Never again would Pierce receive better or more genuine praise.

May arrived, sweet-smelling and nonchalant. Una's fever had broken. Thin and wan, she had raised her weary head, cherry-wood hair all gone, lopped off at doctor's orders. Hands trembling, she had asked for her knitting needles. Dr. Franco was outraged. He forbade her to sew or read or talk, and the Hawthornes must remain in Rome, he insisted, for the recuperation.

But Hawthorne needed a change of air and circumstance almost as much as Una. "He says he should die if he should come to Rome another winter," Sophia reported to Elizabeth Peabody. He wasn't well. "The malaria certainly disturbs him, though it is undeveloped." He walked the Pincian Hill and stood, cigar in hand, looking down at the ancient, complex city. How he hated Rome; how he loved it. "But (life being too short for such questionable and troublesome enjoyments)," said he, "I desire never to set eyes on it again."

Maybe so, but he was to occupy himself with it—or it with him—for the next six months.

On June 23, 1859, the Hawthornes touched British soil, and once they'd arrived in London, the trusty Bennoch directed the lot of them to a boardinghouse on Golden Square, near Piccadilly. Hawthorne arranged passage to America for mid-August and busied himself with Fields, in London with his second wife, and Pierce, now in London too. Pierce presented Hawthorne with a slim whalebone cane topped in silver for their walks together, past and future. Sophia stayed indoors, having enveloped herself in a nervous headache. "My fatigue is something infinite," she explained. "All I can do is to sit in parks, and muse over pictures, and preserve silence."

She had been the only one sorry to leave Rome.

She excused herself from most invitations, and in her absence Hawthorne brought Julian with him to breakfast at the Fieldses', where they met Mrs. Annie Adams Fields for the first time. She was a bright young woman, and at twenty-five, seventeen years younger than her husband. Slender where Fields was portly, calm where he was talkative, Brahmin where he was plebeian, she had married the publisher in 1854. "I have known her since childhood," Fields had crowed at the time, "and have held her on my knee many and many a time." Just a girl then, in five years she had matured into an observant woman independent in thought and action, should she choose to exercise them. She did not. The quintessence of Boston's Back Bay, Annie Fields was gracious, reserved, literary, secure, and tactful, the perfect idolatrous complement for the city's liveliest publisher.

She liked Hawthorne. Bashful and mild, she thought him, and thoroughly unpretentious. Speaking in a low voice, he talked about his new novel, face twitching with evident apprehension. Or perhaps infirmity. In any case, he'd prepared friends for his altered appearance. He'd grown a mustache—Sophia said it made him look like a bandit—and his hair was frizzled with gray. The Italian adventure, he told Bennoch, left him wrinkled, shabby, travel-worn, and bald. "He is entirely unchanged in heart & genius," Pierce loyally reported to Horatio Bridge. "Can anything better be said of any man?"

Fields sold Hawthorne's new book to the British firm of Smith & Elder, which offered six hundred pounds for the rights. "It was a proposition gratifying to his pride & agreeable enough to his purse and was of course accepted," Pierce informed Bridge of the deal. But it meant Hawthorne wouldn't return to America right away, having agreed to stay in England to revise the book and hand it over for typesetting. In turn, Smith & Elder would send advance sheets to Ticknor & Fields. (Again, the issue was copyright. To protect it, the British and American editions of a book had to appear simultaneously.) Since the book wouldn't be finished at least until the fall, much too late for an Atlantic crossing, Hawthorne would have to stay until spring.

Foiled again. "I think of Mamma," Una rationalized, "& that comforts me, for I really believe it is the saving of her life to stay."

Hawthorne, London, photograph by
J. J. E. Mayall, London, 1860

For the summer the Hawthornes settled in Redcar, Yorkshire, a fishing village turned seaside resort. "It is as bleak and dreary a strip of sand as we could have stumbled upon, had we sought the whole world over," Hawthorne cheerily informed Bennoch; "and the gray German ocean tumbles in upon us, within twenty yards of our door." Far from the fuss of London, he could write as if a young man again striding over Salem Point.

They rented a two-story house—"a nutshell," Sophia called it—on High Street near the waterfront. Ada Shepard had returned to America but fortunately Fanny Wrigley, Rose's former nursemaid, had come to help out, for Sophia slept most of the day unless dragged along the beach in her bath chair. Hawthorne disappeared after breakfast for six hours at a stretch, and after dinner he hiked along the shore or took Julian swimming. In the evening he walked out again to the water. "The sea entirely restored Mr. Hawthorne," Sophia was glad to report to Elizabeth.

In the middle of October, with spirits up and summer over, the Hawthornes went back to Leamington for the winter, and Hawthorne dispatched most of the manuscript (429 pages) to Smith & Elder. "As usual he thinks the book good for nothing, and based upon a very foolish idea which nobody will like or accept," Sophia reported to Elizabeth after reading a large chunk of it. Aversion aside, he set about finishing it, and accepted Sophia's minor suggestions, like changing the color of Italian houses, which she said he'd got wrong, and altering the name of a main character from Graydon to Kenyon. On November 9, 1859, he sent the remaining 79 pages to the publisher.

The book had no title. Hawthorne toyed with several, including "Monte Beni; or, The Faun: A Romance." ("Monte Beni is our beloved Montauto," Sophia explained to Elizabeth.) He also played with "The Romance of a Faun," "Marble and Life; a Romance," "Marble and Man; a Romance," and his favorite, "St. Hilda's Shrine," which Ticknor used when he advertised the book in America. Fields suggested "The Romance of Monte Beni," but Smith & Elder preferred "Transformation," which they claimed Hawthorne himself had recommended. He denied it. If anything, he'd offered "*The* Transformation." But he went along, begging Ticknor at least to call the American version of the book "The Marble Faun."

Published as *Transformation* (a good title) in England on February 28, 1860, the new novel appeared in America, bound in maroon and gold, a week later—still within the copyright limit—as *The Marble Faun*. The subtitle to both editions had been Fields's idea: "The Romance of Monte Beni."

Whatever its title, the novel was so modern it baffled many of its first readers and many contemporary ones too, for age and time and the unbearable illness of Una, or mortality, are its main constituents, all wrenched from Hawthorne's Italian experiences and his overpowering sense of despair. "A wonderful book," sighed Longfellow; "but with the old, dull pain in it that runs through all Hawthorne's writings."

It's an exquisite sentence (if a periodic sentence this long can be called exquisite) and lyrical, biblical, confident, heartfelt.

"When we have once known Rome," Hawthorne writes about two thirds through *The Marble Faun,*

> and left her where she lies, like a long decaying corpse, retaining a trace of the noble shape it was, but with accumulated dust and a fungous growth overspreading all its more admirable features;—left her in utter weariness, no doubt, of her narrow, crooked, intricate streets, so uncomfortably paved with little squares of lava that to tread over them is a penitential pilgrimage, so indescribably ugly, moreover, so cold, so alley-like, into which the sun never falls, and where a chill wind forces its deadly breath into our lungs;—left her, tired of the sight of those immense, seven-storied, yellow-washed hovels, or call them palaces, where all that is dreary in domestic life seems magnified and multiplied, and weary of climbing those staircases, which ascend from a ground-floor of cook-shops, coblers' stalls, stables, and regiments of cavalry, to a middle region of artists, just beneath the unattainable sky;—left her, worn out with shivering at the cheerless and smoky fireside, by day, and feasting with our own substance the ravenous little populace of a Roman bed, at night;—left her, sick at heart of Italian trickery, which has uprooted whatever faith in man's integrity had endured till now, and sick at stomach of sour bread, sour wine, rancid butter, and bad cookery, needlessly bestowed on evil meats;—left her, disgusted with the pretence of Holiness and the reality of Nastiness, each equally omnipresent;—left her, half-lifeless from the languid atmosphere, the vital principle of which has been used up, long ago, or corrupted by myriads of slaughters;—left her, crushed

down in spirit with the desolation of her ruin, and the hope-lessness of her future;—left her, in short, hating her with all our might, and adding our individual curse to the Infinite Anathema which her old crimes have unmistakably brought down;—when we have left Rome in such mood as this, we are astonished by the discovery, by-and-by, that our heart-strings have mysteriously attached themselves to the Eternal City, and are drawing us thitherward again, as if it were more familiar, more intimately our own home, than even the spot where we were born!

The tension of leaving—of having left—resolved by the pleasure of coming back: here and in the entire novel, Hawthorne expresses his deep ambiva-lence about Rome, for Rome to Hawthorne had become something beyond itself and its daily annoyances, something beyond the noise and confusion and the long sweep of history; it had become dear in the ways that home is dear and home is hateful, both for the very same reasons.

Rome, Salem, Hawthorne: the past is never dead. In Rome the physical evidence of the past is written into every paving stone, making it for Hawthorne a fitting emblem of romance. And Italy itself exists as much in the imagination as in the real world, as Hawthorne writes in the preface to *The Marble Faun;* it's "a sort of poetic or fairy precinct, where actualities would not be so terribly insisted upon, as they are, and must needs be, in America." As was his wont, Hawthorne repeated, almost verbatim, the def-inition of romance in "The Custom-House" as something that takes place "between the real world and fairy-land," and Rome is that place.

It's also a rotting corpse, which suggests, by implication, the death of romance.

Hawthorne had used the image of the corpse before, not just in his notebook entries but in *The House of the Seven Gables,* where Holgrave wails that the past sits on the present like a giant's dead body. In that book, how-ever, the past inhabits the present in a predictable, almost orderly fashion: the misdeeds of one generation creating havoc in the next and, obversely, Holgrave reincarnating the best of Matthew Maule. Rome is different; it's a "casual sepulchre," streets piled with "continually recurring misfortunes" stacked on top of one another willy-nilly and depressing even to the most adroit storyteller—like Hawthorne—who encounters a "heap of broken rubbish"—his term, not Eliot's—wherever he looks. Meaninglessness lurks in every fallen column, chipped statue, dim fresco, all "far gone towards nothingness." Art is nothing but a "crust of paint over an emptiness," and a "pit of blackness . . . lies beneath us, everywhere": thoughts of a brain in a dry season.

No matter how one reads *The Marble Faun*—and there are myriad ways to analyze it—its author seems distraught and depressed. Conscious that he hasn't "appeared before the Public," as he puts it, in seven or eight years, Hawthorne is aware that much has changed. He has changed; it has changed. And he knows he must match or exceed his previous novels, as Washington Irving had bluntly said; it's the curse of a popular author. But he felt old and tired. He constantly complained of languor or ennui. "It is strange that, when he never was ill before in his life, he should suffer so much from colds, &c., in Italy," Ada Shepard remarked. He lied about his age. Applying for his Italian passport in 1857, he gave it as fifty-one—he was then fifty-three—and Sophia's as forty-two; she was forty-eight.

Earlier in life, Hawthorne had taken solace in nature. No more; the sky is unattainable, and though the Alban Mountains stand far from "all this decay and change," as he writes in *The Marble Faun*'s opening chapter, they don't compensate for the depredations of time. "We all of us, as we grow older, lose somewhat of our proximity to Nature," rationalizes Kenyon. "It is the price we pay for experience." Another character, disillusioned, disagrees. Experience teaches nothing. Nature teaches nothing. " 'The sky itself is an old roof, now,' answered the Count; 'and, no doubt the sins of mankind have made it gloomier than it used to be.' "

Miriam, Hilda, Kenyon, and the Count of Monte Beni, a.k.a. Donatello: Hawthorne uses the four characters to structure this long, discursive book. The first and last chapters bear their four names, as if to say that events in between have changed all of them. Regardless, there is something abstract about the novel, something inert: too much change amounts to stasis, it seems; and so it is with character, like that androgynous faun carved in marble.

Modeled loosely on William Story, the man of marble, cold and stiff, is Kenyon, the American sculptor who anchors the novel's plot but, except for his occasional moralizing, isn't much of a force within it. Although he wishes to "climb heights and stand on the verge of them," Kenyon is an artist without style, locked into a moral code and afraid to take a risk. Rather, Donatello, the young Count of Monte Beni, takes the plunge—or, more literally, initiates his own inevitable fall into experience, having left a Tuscan home "guiltless of Rome" and come to the Eternal City, where he falls in love with the mysterious, guilt-ridden Miriam.

Said to look remarkably like the Faun of Praxiteles, Donatello is at the outset of the novel a prelapsarian creature of sensuality, mirth, amiability, and warmth, and seems to share with the mythical faun a heritage "neither man nor animal, and yet not monster, but a being in whom both races meet, on friendly ground!" In fact, according to local legend, Donatello's first Monte Beni ancestor was a sylvan creature, the sensual child of nature like Donatello. No one is quite sure whether Donatello has inherited, among other attributes, the pointy, metonymic ears of his bestial forefather.

It's clear, however, that Donatello, the living embodiment of Praxiteles' Faun, represents for Hawthorne a prior, ornery self (his own, perhaps), mixture of pagan and primitive, human and animal; and he represents the Catholicism that Hawthorne associated with Italy and, more specifically, with Italians: simple, passive, affectionate and, at bottom, savage. When Donatello melodramatically heaves Miriam's antagonist over the Tarpeian Rock, a precipice from which the ancient empire's traitors were supposedly flung, he is the Italian male that Hawthorne dreads, unpredictable, tempestuous, violent. He is also inversely linked to the man that he kills, a nameless figure from Miriam's past who initially appears in the novel wearing goatskin breeches. Later this nameless figure wears the penitent brown cowl of a Capuchin monk, and by the book's end Donatello is similarly dressed.

Sharing Donatello's crime is the beautiful artist Miriam Schaefer, herself a woman of mixed heritage. No one knows who she is, where she's from, whether she's a German princess or an octoroon whose "burning drop of African blood in her veins so affected her with a sense of ignominy, that she relinquished all and fled her country"—an odd and significant choice of parentage linking her directly to contemporary America's slavery debate. She is associated more specifically with Emma Salomons, a sister-in-law of the lord mayor of London, whom Hawthorne met while dining at the Salomonses' residence in the spring of 1856. Bennoch later recalled that "he could not keep his eyes off, the beautiful young woman, whispering to him 'How lovely!' "

Here is Hawthorne's own description of—and reaction to—Emma Salomons:

> She was, I suppose, dark, and yet not dark, but rather seemed
> to be of pure white marble, yet not white; but the purest and
> finest complexion (without a shade of color in it, yet anything
> but sallow or sickly) that I ever beheld. Her hair was a won-
> derful deep, raven black, black as night, black as death; *not*

raven black, for that has a shiny gloss, and her's had not; but it was hair never to be painted, nor described—wonderful hair, Jewish hair. . . . [L]ooking at her, I saw what were the wives of the old patriarchs, in their maiden or early married days— what Rachel was, when Jacob wooed her seven years, and seven more—what Judith was; for, womanly as she looked, I doubt not she could have slain a man, in a good cause—what Bathsheba was; only she seemed to have no sin in her—per- haps what Eve was, though one could hardly think her weak enough to eat the apple. I never should have thought of touch- ing her, nor desired to touch her; for, whether owing to dis- tinctness of race, my sense that she was a Jewess or whatever else, I felt a sort of repugnance, simultaneously with my per- ception that she was an admirable creature.

Immediately repulsed by the woman who attracts him, Hawthorne again recoils from his own desire, and once again desire, repugnance, fear, and, in this case, a dash of anti-Semitism infuse his portrait of dark-haired beauties like Hester and Zenobia who seduce and terrify their creator; women who look provocatively like his mother and his sister Ebe; women who speak with the force of a Margaret Fuller; and beautiful women, he writes in *The Marble Faun,* "such as one sees only two or three, if even so many, in all a lifetime; so beautiful, that she seemed to get into your consciousness and memory, and could never afterwards be shut out, but haunted your dreams, for pleasure or for pain."

Miriam, her latest incarnation, is exotic, different. Across her face falls "a Jewish aspect; a complexion in which there was no roseate bloom, yet neither was it pale." As Hawthorne copied the remainder of Miriam's description from his notebooks, he rendered her into his femme fatale: Miriam sketches Jael driving the nail through Sisera and Judith holding the head of Holofernes. "Over and over again," notes the narrator of *The Mar- ble Faun,* "there was the idea of woman, acting the part of a revengeful mis- chief toward man." But naturally, like Hester and Zenobia before her, Miriam is also Hawthorne himself: artist, criminal, outsider.

Pursued by a grim demon—a father figure of some kind, her con- science, or the residue of a sorrowful past—Miriam, in Hawthorne's moral economy, bears as much responsibility for the murder as the passionate Donatello. "I did what your eyes bade me to do," Donatello accuses her after he murders her stalker. Miriam cannot deny that she wished her

Beatrice Cenci, *portrait attributed to Guido Reni*

demon dead. In this, she is associated with Beatrice Cenci, the tragic six-teenth-century murderess of her incestuous father, a woman "fallen and yet sinless," as Hawthorne had described her when looking at the portrait of her, attributed to Guido Reni, in the Barberini Palace.

Slender and brown-haired, girlish-looking and sometimes strikingly beautiful, Hilda is Miriam's obverse, an American in Rome who dwells in a medieval tower on the Via Portoghese, where, quite like a virgin high priest-ess, she tends the local shrine that sits atop the battlement. There, a lamp illumines the Madonna's image and, according to Hawthorne, must at all costs stay lit or the tower will become the property of the Catholic Church. But if Hilda sleeps in a dovecote high above the jumbled ruin of Rome, she moves through the city with Hatty Hosmer's insouciance—though one friend of Hosmer's friends tartly remarked he could not fancy her "with doves and a pet Madonna."

An optimistic idealist like Sophia, Hilda is too humble and loyal, we are told, to consider herself on a par with great artists or, presumably, even minor ones. As a consequence, she is a copyist content, like Sophia, to reproduce sections of the works of the Old Masters and subsist on reflected glory. But she is talented. Every artist and souvenir-monger in Rome wants to copy the portrait of Beatrice Cenci; only Hilda reproduces its solitary despair. Hilda, however, will condemn Beatrice—how could a murderess, even if an incest victim, be guiltless?—and in so doing slashes Miriam with a morality-wielding innocence that, says Miriam, cuts "like a sharp steel sword." Innocence without experience is an impossible taskmaster; Hilda is a prig.

In this, Hilda resembles Una, whose brittle high-mindedness often troubled her parents. A reserved young woman with "a great horror of very demonstrative people," Una by her own admission set her standards high, so high that her mother had expressed concern for the "ideal which it will take the angels to satisfy." Unafraid and unmolested—that is, until she witnesses the crime at the heart of the novel—Hilda, again like Una, confronts not a crime per se but the scourge of illness which robs her of her youth—or her father the illusion of her infinite girlhood. And so like Una, Hilda suffers her own painful confrontation with experience, grief, and death, finding temporary succor in the Catholic confessional—this time like Hawthorne, who once noted in its presence that "if I had had a murder on my conscience or any other great sin, I think I should have been inclined to kneel down there."

He decides against it.

On the edge of her own moral precipice, Hilda smugly declaims, "I am a daughter of the Puritans," and safely binds herself to the Anglo-Saxon Kenyon, content to "live and die in—the pure, white light of Heaven!" For Kenyon has long loved Hilda, and Hilda can set him straight. At novel's end, Kenyon wonders if sin is merely an element of human education, a fortunate fall. With transcendental speed and sureness, Hilda answers that such an idea mocks all religious and moral law, destroying "whatever precepts of Heaven are written deepest within us." Kenyon backs off. He's just a lost and lonely man, he replies, far from home, who needs Hilda to guide him hither.

Though she's shrugged it off for most of the novel, Hilda evidently accepts his suit. The couple decides to return to America while Miriam, a female penitent behind a veil, stands at a distance from these happy Anglo-Saxons. Donatello has disappeared, either into the pit of Roman justice or to a monastery. Of his future or Miriam's, who knows?

And so the novel ends. "Hilda had a hopeful soul, and saw sunlight on the mountain-tops," the narrator concludes.

One can almost hear him snicker.

Hawthorne's completed novel swims against its most pious nostrums. Of course, the surface of *The Marble Faun* aims to please. Perhaps to fill up George Smith's stipulation that he produce three volumes, Hawthorne included long passages of description that the novel's critics found distracting, undigested, or downright boring. The *Westminster Review* said it had the flavor of a newsletter sent to the American public. Nonetheless, not even a month after its English publication, the book entered a third printing, and in Leipzig the publisher Bernhard Tauchnitz reprinted a popular illustrated edition of *Transformation* for the German market. Pretty soon sightseers to Rome were packing it into their carpetbags.

James Russell Lowell roundly praised the book as Christian parable. The *Boston Daily Courier* called Hawthorne a Yankee Aeschylus, the *New York Times* (which didn't like the book) called him Paracelsus, and Edwin Whipple, in a retrospective of Hawthorne's career, claimed that if Hawthorne had written nothing else, *The Marble Faun* alone would rank him among the masters of English composition. The *New-York Tribune* thought Hilda "the loveliest type of American womanhood," though when Henry Fothergill Chorley in the *Athenaeum* wrote she was Phoebe's cousin, Sophia curtly rapped his knuckles.

Regardless, Hawthorne irritated readers by leaving the conclusion of his novel deliberately vague. The ending was cloudy, inconclusive, uncertain, and even Henry Bright accused it of "a want of finish." Who was the man hunting Miriam, and for what ancient crime? Why does Hilda disappear after delivering a packet to the Palazzo Cenci? Why does she resurface during the Carnival? What happens to Miriam and Donatello? Do they marry, and how many children did they have, Sophia mimicked the stupid critics.

"How easy it is to explain mysteries," Hawthorne replied, "when the author does not more wisely choose to keep a veil over them." He did, however, add a postscript in the second English edition of the book, although he insisted that his own ending "was one of its essential excellencies that it left matters so enveloped in a fog." He wasn't joking. As he had indicated in his notes to "The Ancestral Footstep," he wanted a conclusion "not satisfactory to the natural yearnings of novel-readers," and, what's more, in the final chapter of *The Marble Faun* he had pointed out that "the actual experience of even the most ordinary life is full of events that never explain themselves; either as regards their origin or their tendency."

Like Rome, then, *The Marble Faun* is a series of fragments, intentionally so: "The charm lay partly in their very imperfection; for this is sugges-tive," writes Hawthorne, "and sets the imagination at work; whereas, the finished picture, if a good one, leaves the spectator nothing to do, and, if bad, confuses, stupefies, disenchants, and disheartens him." Plotline and character and rumination and guidebook are shored against one another—not just like an unfinished picture but also like the body parts strewn throughout the novel, statues without noses, skulls, a model of Hilda's hand, and the headless Venus discovered in the Campagna. For Hawthorne writes of flotsam and waste as well as imagination, the latter a sign of hope, like nature. But the rubbish of Rome, history stacked high and ringed by Roman fever, is an emblem of grinding, incessant decay.

So too writing: "The very dust of Rome is historic, and inevitably settles on our page, and mingles with our ink," Hawthorne observes. In a chapter cagily called "Fragmentary Sentences," the narrator says he, as writer, pieces together as best he can those ephemeral, unknown, uncertain things—feelings, conversations, human desire—all slated for extinction.

> In weaving these mystic utterances into a continuous scene, we undertake a task resembling, in its perplexity, that of gath-ering up and piecing together the fragments of a letter, which has been torn and scattered to the winds. Many words of deep significance—many entire sentences, and those possibly the most important ones—have flown too far, on the winged breeze, to be recovered.

"I really put what strength I have into many parts of this book," Hawthorne told James Fields. Acknowledging its grim modernity as no reviewer could, he sighed, "The devil himself always seems to get into my inkstand, and I can only exorcise him by pensfull at a time."

Writing as restoration, memorialization, and a defense against ruin: these are doomed to failure. And that, finally, is the lesson of Rome.

The Marble Faun is Hawthorne's last completed novel.

Between Two Countries

*The years, after all, have a kind of emptiness, when we spend too
many of them on a foreign shore. We defer the reality of life, in
such cases, until a future moment, when we shall again breathe
our native air; but, by-and-by, there are no future moments; or,
if we do return, we find that the native air has lost its invigorating quality, and that life has shifted its reality to the spot where
we have deemed ourselves only temporary residents. Thus,
between two countries, we have none at all.*

Nathaniel Hawthorne, *The Marble Faun*

As soon as he settled in Concord in the summer of 1860, Hawthorne
was pining for England, cold, drizzly, fog-laden England, the place
he'd once called, in a fit of distemper, beer-soaked and sodden.

Hawthorne recognized what a gift his tenancy had been. "The sweetest
thing connected with a foreign residence is," he told Ticknor, "that you have
no rights and no duties, and can live your own life without interference of
any kind." Yet before leaving John Bull, he ached for America so bitterly,
said Sophia, that he couldn't work for thinking of it.

America: that was the place he described in the preface to *The Marble
Faun* as a country "where there is no shadow, no antiquity, no mystery, no
picturesque and gloomy wrong, nor anything but a common-place prosperity, in broad and simple daylight."

No gloomy wrong? No shadow? Mary Mann took exception. "How
could he say in his beautiful preface that his country had no wrong to
mourn over?" What about slavery? And why doesn't he write about it? "I
hope the time will come when he will use his wizard's pen in our holy
cause," Mary prodded Sophia, "for I think no country ever presented such a

subject for literature, and with his power of representing the action of conscience, he might be almost the besom of destruction to Slavery."

Hawthorne preferred not to, although the days of sweet immunity were decidedly numbered.

Mary Mann and Elizabeth Peabody (especially the latter) had been plying their sister with long letters about the odium of slavery. "I wholly and utterly abominate slavery," Sophia hotly defended herself against the implicit criticism. "I disagree, however, with those who would abolish it with a civil war or any evil deed whatever—and I believe GOD will not smile on any violence, for its good intention."

In 1857 a Missouri slave, Dred Scott, sued for his freedom, arguing all the way to the Supreme Court that his residence in free states or territories had made him free. In a stunning 7–2 decision, the Court ruled that blacks were nothing more than property and as such had no rights of citizenship, meaning they could not petition the courts; and it declared unconstitutional all congressional acts excluding slavery from the territories, meaning that slavery might exist anywhere it wanted. A staggering blow to Free-Soil and antislavery activists, the decision deepened the rift in the Democratic Party and strengthened the palm of the Republicans, who looked forward with some hope to the next round of elections.

Mary Mann received a letter from Sophia seeming to praise Chief Justice Roger Taney's decision. Horrified, Mann attacked. Sophia parried. "Because I suggested that he *might* have decided according to his conscience, you think, I advocate him and his decision," she replied; her only concession: "I may have said or perhaps have thought in my letters that it may have been intended by Providence that the inferior race were designed to serve the superior—*But not as slaves!*"

Though unremitting, Sophia's racism was not exceptional. By and large, northern Democrats and many Republicans wishing to abolish slavery were not comfortable with the consequences. Debating Stephen Douglas for a seat in the Senate, Abraham Lincoln himself had reminded audiences that he had "no purpose to introduce political and social equality between the white and black races." Emancipation would produce an irreparable sectional split or, worse yet, amalgamation. "You surely must know that there are advocates of amalgamation, & also that there are abolitionists who uphold that the black race is virtually equal to the white," Sophia reminded Elizabeth. "I did not suppose *you* did either, and I was wondering how *anyone* could."

Sophia, more than her husband, feared a multiracial society; likely Hawthorne feared it, and so did Mary Mann and Elizabeth Peabody, who, to their credit, considered slavery atrocious enough to risk it. And they

Mary Peabody Mann

hoped to recruit the Hawthornes to the holy cause, still convinced that Pierce, the knave, had warped Hawthorne's judgment—"You always speak as if he were an ignorant baby and very weak," Sophia reproved Mary—and that Hawthorne had overmastered hers. "My husband meddles with my ideas no more than the stars," Sophia insisted.

But meddling was what they did. Each of them. Sophia and Nathaniel forbade their children to read newspapers, and of Hawthorne's novels, Una was not permitted *The Scarlet Letter* or *Blithedale*. As for Elizabeth's wanting to tell Una about the young girls, chained and naked, sold on the block, Sophia emphatically refused. "I have read of those auctions often," she assured the intemperate Elizabeth, "and even the worst facts were never so bad as absolute nudity."

Hawthorne meddled too. Reading Sophia's mail, he returned to Elizabeth one of her sermons on abolition without "bothering" his wife about it. "No doubt it seems the truest of truth to you," he charged; "but I do assure you that, like every other Abolitionist, you look at matters with an awful squint, which distorts everything within your line of vision." As far as he was concerned, the abolitionists were a mob of rabble-rousers of no good to anyone, least of all the slave. His mind had not changed; if anything, his position had grown more entrenched. "We go all wrong, by too strenuous a resolution to go all right," he writes in *The Marble Faun*, reiterating phrases from his Franklin Pierce biography and from "The Ancestral Footstep." He paraded the same phrases past Elizabeth Peabody. "Vengeance and beneficence are things that God claims for himself," he scolded her. "His instruments have no consciousness of His purpose; if they imagine they have, it is a pretty sure token that they are not His instruments."

No friend of the South, he nonetheless counseled inaction, converting into a moral weapon the passivity he had criticized, year in, year out, in himself. Action, he seemed to be saying, carried with it an inevitable penalty, the same penalty—or myth of penalties—in so many of his stories; even his tales for children are fables of punishment disbursed to the proud and the rich, the vain and the arrogant. Better to do nothing—ignore the prick of conscience—than to unleash the catastrophic unknown, easy to associate with dark-skinned slaves, a strange and alien race; better to hope that Providence would take the problem out of human hands.

Something else lay beneath Hawthorne's suave if illogical (and plainly racist) invocation of Providence. He was a fatalist, apprehensive of action— associated with aggression—skeptical of result. And stories like "The Birthmark" reveal a Hawthorne suspicious of the unfettered self strewing its narcissism where it may and eradicating the so-called blemishes of nature. Hawthorne knew, of course, that, unlike Georgiana's mole, slavery was no natural state of affairs. Little matter. Abolition was slavery's real foe, its moral urgency another instance of noxious pride. "The good of others, like our own happiness, is not to be attained by direct effort, but incidentally," he chided Elizabeth Peabody in terms familiar to both of them. ". . . I am really too humble to think of doing good; if I have been impertinent enough to aim at it, I am ashamed."

Since the first days of marriage, Hawthorne had been weaning his bride from her family (and from Emerson), deflating their transcendentalism with prickly humor. "We human beings cannot venture to assert what is 'highest laws,' " Sophia stood up to Elizabeth. ". . . I know all you would say and do say about Absolute Law—and that men's laws are not LAW—Yes I know all that—I also have thought about such things, and can also float in a 'fluid consciousness.' " Sophia delivered the final blow. What are higher laws anyway, she charged, but another form of "transcendental slang."

Times had changed. Transcendentalism had sprouted in the shale of New Hampshire and on the plains of Kansas, with John Brown its standard-bearer, saluted by Thoreau as "a transcendentalist above all, a man of ideas and principles." A longtime abolitionist, Brown was a humorless man (unlike Thoreau), decisive and without mercy. In 1855 the tall, gaunt Brown, gunpowder in his eye, joined five of his sons (he had sired twenty children) in the bleeding territory of Kansas, arriving in Osawatomie with a wag-onload of rifles and artillery sabers. After proslavery forces sacked the city of Lawrence, Brown, then fifty-six, rounded up four sons and two other men to ride out to Pottawatomie County, where they dragged five settlers from their cabins and hacked them to death with cavalry broadswords.

Boston seemed not to know about the midnight massacre or at least didn't have all the cold-blooded facts. Or it chose not to know. When Brown went east to raise money, a bowie knife stuck in his boot, the free-dom fighter was invited into Boston drawing rooms by velvet-chair aboli-tionists although a secret group of prominent citizens, including Thomas Higginson and the schoolteacher Franklin Sanborn, were privy to Brown's plans. In May of 1859, Old Brown, speaking at the Concord Town Hall, inspired so much confidence, observed Bronson Alcott, that the good peo-ple of Concord donated to his cause without asking for particulars. "I think him equal to anything he dares," Alcott himself admitted, "the man to do the deed if it must be done, and with the martyr's temper and purpose."

The deed was done. On October 16, 1859, in Harpers Ferry, Virginia, Brown and nineteen others, including several of his sons, seized ten slaves and their owner, hoping to spark a slave insurrection. They stormed the squarish federal armory, but rather than strike and flee, Brown and his men stayed near the arsenal for thirty-six hours, an amazing strategic blunder. The local militia quickly cut off any escape route, forcing Brown and his gang to withdraw into a small fire engine house in the armory yard. Brevet Colonel Robert E. Lee and a squadron of twelve marines offered Brown a chance to surrender; the next day they battered down the door. Seventeen people died, including two of Brown's sons, two slaves, the slave owner, a marine, and three residents of Harpers Ferry. Brown, who'd been stabbed with a decorative dress sword, was taken prisoner.

The country convulsed. The United States Senate issued warrants, including one for Frank Sanborn, who hid for a night at the Wayside, then occupied by Mary Mann. Exonerated, Sanborn gloated, but not over the fate of Brown, who'd been summarily tried, found guilty, and sentenced to death. Bells tolled—though not in Concord—on the day of Brown's execution, a day, Emerson supposedly said, that "will make the gallows as glorious as the cross."

This sort of mawkishness, ill informed and dangerous, revolted Hawthorne. "Nobody was ever more justly hanged," said he. Anyone with a modicum of common sense, he continued, "must have felt a certain intellectual satisfaction in seeing him hanged, if it were only in requital of his preposterous miscalculation of possibilities."

Hawthorne delivered this bolt of dry sarcasm after he returned to the Wayside, where he would build himself a third-story tower, twenty feet square, a sky-parlor he called it, modeled roughly on the tower at the Villa Montauto. There, he'd write high above the fray, entering his sanctum through a trapdoor, he told Longfellow, on which he'd plant his chair.

He was facetious about the trapdoor, to a degree. During much of his adult life, he had tried to simulate the conditions of the prolific early years, melodramatically characterized as spent in the lonely seclusion of his room. He needed seclusion, in other words, in order to write, seclusion and peace of mind. Little by little, he was to have neither.

"I should like to sail on and on forever, and never touch the shore again," Hawthorne had presumably told James Fields when they crossed a dark green ocean, heading back to New England, at long last. It had been seven years.

He'd been apprehensive about his homecoming. "I fear I have lost the capacity of living contentedly in any one place," he confided to Ticknor. Maybe he should purchase a house near Boston. "I am really at a loss to imagine how we are to squeeze ourselves into that little old cottage of mine," he fretted, wondering if, on the other hand, he should stay in Concord and build another house—not that he could afford it.

Nor could he shake off a disabling pessimism. His journal was blank. "I feared his depression of spirits concerning himself would cause a fixed illness," Sophia would tell Annie Fields. Dark foggy mornings, bone-piercing chill, and everywhere muck: "Surely, the bright severity of a New-England winter can never be so bad as this," he had hoped when still in England. But on board the ship *Europa,* he spent most of the trip in his cabin either sick or, more likely, intentionally unavailable to fellow passengers like Harriet Beecher Stowe. After he docked, he saw Longfellow, who thought him bewildered and sad, though tan and fit. "It is the school-boy's blue Monday," the poet smiled; "vacation over and work beginning."

In Concord he was hustled to Emerson's for a strawberries-and-cream party with Thoreau and Sanborn, and Emerson soon whisked him to Boston to attend the dinners of the Saturday Club, to which he'd been elected. Officially formed in 1855, it was a coterie of men, like Longfellow and James Russell Lowell and Edwin Whipple, come together to exchange witticisms over food and drink the last Saturday of each month. There were no women and no Bohemia at the table, said George William Curtis, just camaraderie and the sense of having-arrived. Hawthorne enjoyed himself. "It is an excellent institution," he explained to Henry Bright, "with the privilege of first-rate society, and no duties but to eat one's dinner."

Of Hawthorne, it was remembered that he was reserved and attractive—"even if a Democrat." Henry James Sr. recalled Hawthorne at one of the dinners, eyes pinned to his plate, eating furiously to avoid conversation. "He has the look all the while—, or would have to the unknowing," James keenly remarked, "—of a rogue who suddenly finds himself in a company of detectives."

Hawthorne stood out as an anomaly to a roomful of anomalies.

Of the Saturday Club's members and their guests, Hawthorne had little control except the right of refusal: refusal to talk, refusal to come. When Nathaniel Prentiss Banks, outgoing Republican governor of Massachusetts and something of a nativist, was invited to a dinner, Hawthorne declined. "Beyond a general dislike to official people," Hawthorne gingerly chose his words, "I have no objection to the Governor, and I care very little about his politics; although just now, in the ruin and dismemberment of the party to which I have been attached, it might behove me to show a somewhat stronger political feeling than heretofore;—at least, a strong one enough to preclude me from joining in what I presume to be an acquiescent compliment to the Governor's public course, as well as to his private character."

More pleasing was the welcome-home banquet for Hawthorne arranged by Ticknor and Fields, who invited both Pierce and the Saturday Clubbers, who deplored him. Pierce was a lout. "He is used to public speaking, and so he public-speaks in tête-à-tête, doing the appropriate gestures," James Russell Lowell lampooned the former president. The sleek and jaunty Lowell was editor of the *Atlantic Monthly,* a new literary periodical with a decided antislavery, anti-Pierce bias, though its publishers, the firm of Phillips and Sampson, capitalized more on the literary than the political scene. Dr. Holmes, Emerson, the historian John Lothrop Motley, Whipple, and Stowe had all been canvassed as early contributors, as had Hawthorne; and in England so had Rossetti, Ruskin, and Mrs. Gaskell.

Hawthorne had declined this invitation too. When Lowell pestered him again in the summer of 1859, he received the same polite refusal. But Ticknor had purchased the floundering magazine (for ten thousand dollars), and Fields exercised his charm. Hadn't Hawthorne said he'd like to do something with his English journals? Hawthorne responded with a chuckle, throwing back Fields's earlier admonishments against magazine work, but promised to write a piece soon.

On the lookout for female writers, Fields also tried Sophia. "I am very anxious that not only the author of sundry great books which you and I and the public like so much should write for 'The Atlantic' but that his wife should also send some papers for its pages," he gallantly declared. Startled, Sophia dashed off an unambiguous reply. "You forget that Mr. Hawthorne is the Belleslettres portion of my being, and besides that I have a repugnance to female authoresses in general, I have far more distaste for myself as a female authoress in particular." Only the threat of starvation, she coyly added, would bring her before the public.

"Perhaps I may yet starve her into compliance," Hawthorne told Fields. "I have never read anything so good as some of her narrative and descriptive epistles to her friends." But to Bennoch, he more fully bared his feelings. "I don't know," he said, "whether I can tolerate a literary rival at bed and board."

Mr. Wetherbee and Mr. Watts set to work on the small, dank Wayside, extending it upward by three stories and to the west by two. Bronson Alcott raced over from his place next door, called Orchard House and nicknamed Apple Slump by the Hawthornes, and cut paths and planted gardens in the rear of the house, lopping off branches of trees as he chatted about grapes and the consanguinity of people and plants. For ten dollars Henry Thoreau surveyed the property, Julian in tow, where the dozens of fir trees and larches shipped from England had taken root.

*The Wayside, complete with author's tower. Sophia and Nathaniel Hawthorne
appear in the left-hand corner of the photograph [1861].*

Indoors, a hodgepodge of boxes and lumber and trunks littered the
rooms. Hawthorne was wretched, said Mary Mann, but Sophia kept serene
and calm, "doing exactly as she pleases." "Mrs. H is as sentimental and muff-
ing as of old," Louisa Alcott observed, "wears crimson silk jackets, a rosary
from Jerusalem, fire-flies in her hair and the dirty white skirts with sacred
mud of London still extant thereon." When the cook proved unsatisfactory,
Hawthorne refused to eat if Sophia entered the kitchen. Una took charge.

The Alcotts, except Bronson, were generally churlish on the subject of
their neighbors. "Una is a stout English looking sixteen year old with the
most ardent hair and eyebrows, Monte Bene airs and graces and no accomplishments but riding," said Louisa. She was wrong. Una's accomplishment
was anger, aggrieved and ferocious. Sophia had agreed to let Julian attend
Frank Sanborn's Concord school even though she objected to coeducation
as "bad for her darling son," Sanborn recalled, "whose character she did not
quite appreciate." Una was another affair. Emerson asked why Una did not
go to Sanborn's school and laughed aloud at the reason: there was to be no
coeducation for girls.

"Her Byronic papa forbid her to distinguish herself in any manner again," observed Louisa Alcott pointedly, "and she is in a high state of wrath and woe." Sophia conferred with a physician. Raging, Una consulted with the doctor privately, reporting in jubilation to a Salem cousin that he "is going to talk to Papa and tell him his mind, and then I shall be free as air!" (Papa was then visiting Pierce in New Hampshire.) And she'd be in Salem soon, she added; any longer in "this killing place," and she'd explode in "brain fever."

As a temporary compromise—they didn't want Una in Salem just yet— her parents offered to send her to Mary Mann, now living on Sudbury Road, about a mile away. Later Hawthorne himself would bring Una to Ebe's in Montserrat, and in September the two of them could visit Horatio Bridge and his wife. But in Portsmouth, Una thrashed and screamed. She had to be restrained. And no one knew why. Had a stifling letter from her mother set her off? Or her father's repressive solicitude? Had some delicate mechanism, damaged in Rome and strained by adolescence, finally broken?

At the Wayside, Louisa Alcott and her mother tended Una's bedside, for Sophia was traveling in New Hampshire with Mary Mann. A Concord homeopath prescribed cold-water baths. Poor Una, screaming again, this time when dunked in a tub of frigid water. Hawthorne sent for Dr. Osgood, a noted Boston physician, who wisely suggested a change of scene, and Una went back to Mary Mann's. Concord folk whispered madness. Hawthorne was unnerved. "His spirits are so shocked that he thinks he cannot recover from it," Sophia said.

In desperation herself, Mary Mann hired Mrs. C. M. Rollins, a "phreno-pathist" who juggled phrenology, magnetism, and the galvanic battery, a primitive form of shock therapy. Mrs. Rollins attributed Una's malady to a liver complaint and "slight affection of the heart," exacerbated by Roman fever. Una was subdued, her family mollified. In fact, Hawthorne was so impressed, he tried the battery himself.

"I lose England without gaining America," the melancholy Hawthorne wrote to Francis Bennoch.

When the carpenters left, he clambered up the steep wooden staircase to his tower-garret and for months closeted himself there while the family below adjusted to Concord life. Defeated, Una attended Bronson Alcott's series of "Conversations" at Mr. Sanborn's (one dollar for six), and at home, said Ellery Channing, she sewed coarse towels like a penitent. Julian hiked to Sanborn's school, and on Sundays, Sophia read the Bible to the children, huddled in the "Chapel," a small alcove where the front door had been before the renovation. Weekdays, she mended hoops, wrote letters, visited her sisters on Sudbury Road, and over time painted her designs on all the woodwork, chairs, tables, pedestals, whatever would take her brush. She encouraged the children to do the same.

Callers, including Ticknor and Pierce, opened the front gate and wiped their boots on the piazza. Or Hawthorne saw them in Boston, his top hat over his thinning hair when he headed to the Old Corner Bookstore, where he smoked with Ticknor behind the green curtain separating the shop and the offices. Or he strolled up Beacon Hill and stopped by the Fieldses' cozy

James T. Fields, Hawthorne, and William D. Ticknor,
photograph by James Wallace Black [1861–62]

Charles Street home. Sophia recorded these small events in her diary as well as flushed sunsets and blizzardy evenings when Nathaniel read Walter Scott aloud, Ticknor having sent a set of the "Waverley" novels for the new bookshelves.

Mostly, though, he stayed aloft. Hawthorne never goes out, said Bronson Alcott, who saw him only by chance when at the Wayside or on the sled paths, where Hawthorne scurried "as if he feared his neighbor's eyes would catch him as he walked." The Sage of Apple Slump was a chronic talker, and Hawthorne was likely dodging an hour's harangue. "He seems not at home here in his temperament and tendencies," Alcott continued, wiser than he knew, when he heard Hawthorne was writing about England. "See how he behaves, as if he were the foreigner still, though installed in his stolen castle and its keeper, his moats wide and deep, his drawbridges all up on all sides, and he secure from invasion."

As promised, Hawthorne reworked an essay from his English journals, published in the October 1860 *Atlantic* as "The Haunts of Burns," about visiting the homestead of the Scottish poet, and he'd been scavenging English journals for a new romance, reworking "The Ancestral Footstep" into a story about the "unconquerable interest, which an American feels in England, its people, and institutions."

This time the protagonist is an orphan, Ned Etherege, plucked from an almshouse by a strange doctor who lives with his niece in a cobwebby place that abuts a graveyard, like the Peabody house and the Charter Street cemetery. No surprise, then, that Ned grows up fantasizing about "hereditary connections and the imposing, imaginative associations of the past, beautifying and making venerable the mean life of the present," even as he, an American democrat, tells himself "not to be ashamed of springing from the lowest, but to consider it as giving additional value and merit to every honorable effort and success that he had thus far made, in the struggle of life."

As an adult, Ned's longings center on England. "Oh home, my home, my forefather's home! I have come back to thee!" he shouts, approaching the threshold of an old English manor, Braithwaite Hall. He supposes himself its long-lost heir but eventually will learn that the title belongs to someone else. You can't go home again.

"Is there going to be a general smash?" Hawthorne asked Ticknor in December. Abraham Lincoln, the rail-splitting Republican, had been elected president by less than 40 percent of the popular vote and without a single southern state. One by one, the southern states began to secede.

"Secession of the North from Freedom would be tenfold worse than secession of the South from the Union," the temperate Longfellow was ablaze. John O'Sullivan begged Frank Pierce to get back into politics and work toward "*Reunion*" to rid the country of "this wicked & crazy Republicanism." Pierce proposed meeting with the other living ex-presidents— Buchanan, Fillmore, Tyler, and Van Buren—to try to settle the "quarrel." The *New York Herald* groaned, "It was the imbecility and political chicanery of some of these very men that brought about the present evils."

Alarmed, Hawthorne feigned disinterest, writing Henry Bright in England "how little I care about the matter. New England will still have her rocks and ice." Besides, he added, "the Union is unnatural, a scheme of man, not an ordinance of God; and as long as it continues, no American of either section will ever feel a genuine thrill of patriotism, such as you Englishmen feel at every breath you draw." After England, America no longer seemed a political marvel, divinely sanctioned, as he'd argued in the Franklin Pierce biography. "How can you feel a heart's love for a mere political arrangement," he mused.

Hawthorne loved his country, he hated it, and he wanted to flee. But flee to what? To a place where shifting political tides don't uproot everything one holds dear every four years? And where is that? England, where he has no birthright and for whose hierarchies he has no conscious respect? Or perhaps the place is to be found up the steep steps in a sky-parlor, with the hillside jutting to the north and the meadow, softly dappled, to the south.

For a while, Hawthorne was able to escape in the sky-parlor, speculating with gallows humor that his new book might be finished by the time New England was a separate nation. But it progressed slowly. "There is still a want of something, which I can by no means describe what it is," he wrote after completing a couple of opening scenes. Starting and stopping and starting over again, he squirms. "The story must not be founded at all on remorse or guilt," he reminds himself, "—all that I've worn out." He couldn't sufficiently motivate his characters. Who, for instance, is the lord of the old manor, Braithwaite Hall? He must be a miserable cad—he's part Italian—or else a thug, or else wicked in some way; or maybe he is poisoned by a Bologna sausage, Hawthorne jokes harshly.

He cobbled together a stronger version of Ned's story, placing it just after the American Revolution, a metaphor for fratricidal conflict, Tory against rebel instead of North against South. In this draft, Hawthorne concentrates on the old doctor, Ned's stepfather. He's a self-involved Englishman called Dr. Ormskirk or Grimshawe or Grimsworth, who cultivates in his ward a longing for the past—easy to do, because Ned seeks psychic compensation for what he does not and can never have, namely, a sense of connectedness with the world.

Just as significant, however, is the way that the doctor and Ned are the same person, at least symbolically: the doctor looks back into the past with anger and grief; Ned wants from that same past a homeland, a parentage, an escape from ontological solitude. And both of them are Hawthorne, old and young: the fifty-six-year-old writer in the present and the writer years before, daydreaming in Salem over ancient boneyards.

Ned is a shy, imaginative child not like other boys. "I want you to be a man; and I'll have you a man or nothing," the old doctor shouts at him. But the brandy-swilling doctor is no paragon of unsplotched masculinity; he's angry, tyrannical, and, like many a Hawthorne character, an outcast persecuted by the community partly because he cannot tolerate its small-minded conformities. When a street brat flings a mud ball at him, he catches the boy and pounds him with a stick. Cruelty meets with cruelty, aggression with counteraggression; the only recourse against a violent and unhappy manhood seems passivity: doing nothing.

By comparison, the Old World looks good, with its tokens of "learned ease," the euphemism for aristocracy. England is the imagination of refuge, safe and snug, like Hawthorne's high tower. Ned, grown man and republican, nervously defends his preference. He's earned the right, hasn't he, to subside in a "quiet recess of unchangeable old time, around which the turbulent tide of war eddied, and rushed, but could not disturb it. Here, to be sure, hope, love, ambition, came not; but here was—what just now, the early wearied American could appreciate better than aught else—here was rest."

Having labored for four long years in Liverpool and, before that, in two different Custom Houses; having lost his job in one of them along with the comforts, however stultifying, of his hometown; having jockeyed for appointments that never came and blistering his hands at Brook Farm to purchase a fair share of disillusion there and elsewhere, Hawthorne sought rest. He didn't not want to be pelted by anyone or anything. He wanted— he told himself he'd always wanted—to write, far above the noisome crowd.

But secession and the sundered Democrats were the agonizing, unfathomable reality.

On Saturday, April 13, 1861, a day of showers and shine, Sophia shouted that Fort Sumter and the South had fired on each other.

Hawthorne put away his manuscript.

CHAPTER TWENTY-FIVE

—————

The Smell of Gunpowder

*If a group of chosen friends, chosen out of all the world and all
time for their adaptedness, could go on in endless life together,
keeping themselves mutually warm in their high, desolate way,
then none of them need ever sigh to be comforted in the pitiable
snugness of the grave.*

Nathaniel Hawthorne, "Septimius Felton"

HAWTHORNE CREDITED James T. Fields with helping him find an
audience. "My literary success, whatever it has been or may be, is the
result of my connection with you," Hawthorne thanked his friend in 1861.
"Somehow or other, you smote the rock of public sympathy on my behalf."
Before Fields, Hawthorne had been known mainly to a small band of writers and intellectuals; Edgar Allan Poe had called him "the example, par
excellence, in this country, of the privately-admired and publicly under-
appreciated man of genius." That was in 1847; Hawthorne was forty-three.
When he was forty-six, Fields published *The Scarlet Letter,* and Hawthorne
entered the most prolific period of his life.

Like Sophia, Fields supplied the appreciation and encouragement—and
publishing wherewithal—Hawthorne needed in order to write and to face
the consequences of writing: what it meant, how he felt about it, the uneasy
anticipation of reviews or sales. Fields knew Hawthorne was a perfectionist
unwilling to release any of his work to the public before he had polished it
to a high gloss, as if its unsullied surface protected him from rejection. He
weighed each word, balanced each sentence, scrutinized each character for
motive and depth and meaning. Extant manuscripts reveal his vigilance,
how he organized each scene, wringing from it nuance, embedding it with
significance until at last it satisfied him. "I am sensible that you mollify me

343

with a good deal of soft soap," Hawthorne grinned, "but it is skillfully applied and effects all that you intend it should." The two men understood one another.

But sitting beneath the spirelike ceiling of his tower, he found it difficult to work. He felt restless, anxious, confined. His tower was too hot in summer, too cold in winter. "He always, I believe, finds fault," Ellery Channing had once observed; the man who wrote compellingly of a sense of place could find none for himself.

"The war continues to interrupt my literary industry," Hawthorne ruefully informed Ticknor, saying he wished he could perform some "useful labor"—an old theme going back to his youth—and he proclaimed that if he were younger, he'd volunteer. His own blood was up. In milder moments, he confessed that he didn't quite understand "what we are fighting for, or what definite result can be expected." The elimination of slavery? "It may be a wise object," Hawthorne nominally agreed with Horatio Bridge. Writing to Francis Bennoch, he was less sure. "We seem to have little, or, at least, a very misty idea of what we are fighting for," he repeated. "It depends upon the speaker, and that, again, depends upon the section of the country in which his sympathies are enlisted." Southerners fight for states' rights; westerners, for the Union; northeasterners, to end slavery. "One thing is indisputable; the spirit of our young men is thoroughly aroused."

If Hawthorne fancied himself shouldering a musket, the vision didn't last. "I wish they would push on the war a little more briskly," he joked without humor. "The excitement had an invigorating effect on me for a time, but it begins to lose its influence." Throughout the spring and summer of 1861, news from Washington was contradictory and disheartening, and though he complained to Horatio Bridge that "all we ought to fight for is, the liberty of selecting the point where our diseased members shall be lopt off," he bristled with patriotism, almost against his will, in the face of Henry Bright's English insolence. "Every man of you wishes to see us both maimed and disgraced," he snapped, "and looks upon this whole trouble as a god-send—if only there were cotton enough at Liverpool and Manchester." As for Bright's qualms about rising death tolls, Hawthorne sourly replied, "People must die, whether a bullet kills them or no."

Hawthorne's friends in England gasped. "If this is the literary tone of the United States," said Richard Monckton Milnes, "what must be the rowdy?" Hawthorne didn't care; he'd quit idealizing the sceptered isle, its green hedge primly clipped, and put away his unfinished tales about American claimants and English patrimony. To continue with the Grimshawe manuscript was folly while drums of war beat at the Concord Common and Julian marched off each morning to drill at the town armory. Far easier was rooting around in his English journals for essays, especially since Fields now sat in the editor's chair at the *Atlantic*. Hawthorne sent him "Near Oxford" and "Pilgrimage to Old Boston," and in the next two years produced nine essays in all, seven of which were published in the *Atlantic*—"capital papers," Fields would approve, for a "delectable *Book*."

In December he consented to being photographed. "He allowed the photographer to poke about his sacred face and figure," Sophia reported to

Hawthorne at fifty-seven, 1861

Fields, "arranging even the hairs of his head and almost his eyelashes, and turning his brow as if on a pivot. He was as docile as the dearest baby," she marveled, "though he hates to be touched any more than anyone I ever knew." A wide-brimmed felt hat in his hand, Hawthorne stares as if afraid to move from his seat lest an epithet fall from his expressionless mouth. His hair lies in thick, graying abundance on the side of his head; brows darkening his eyes but not the circles underneath them. Hawthorne admired the photographer's handiwork enough to mail a copy of the finished product to Bridge.

Sophia Hawthorne, 1861

Una, Julian, and Rose Hawthorne, 1861

The photographer poked at Sophia too. Bent slightly forward in a chair, collar finely scalloped, brooch in center place, and her skirts spread voluminously about her, she looks as plain as she believed she was. "I have no features," she lamented. True: nothing of her ebullience, her stubbornness, or her unconditional enthusiasm peeps from mouth or eye. Instead she seems either ready to assist the fussy photographer—or to run away.

The Hawthorne children look fretful. Una, handsome at seventeen, sneers; ten-year-old Rose frowns; and Julian, an attractive boy of fifteen, looks as though he might burst into tears: children at wartime, nervous and sad.

Paymaster general of the United States Navy in charge of provisions and clothing, Horatio Bridge invited Hawthorne to visit him and his wife, stationed in Washington, D.C., to glimpse the war firsthand. Hawthorne pleaded lassitude of mind or body, hard to say which, and a new romance, he hinted, in the works. Mostly, though, he paced lugubriously on the hillside. Worried, Sophia took the invitation as a godsend and asked Ticknor if he'd accompany her husband to Washington.

The two men set out on the railroad the first Thursday in March, chugging through a frostbitten Massachusetts to New York and then on to a balmy Philadelphia. At each stop, the number of soldiers increased, young men with smooth cheeks and scratchy uniforms as eager for news as the two travelers. Ticknor managed everything. He bought gloves for the two of them; he arranged their transportation; he paid their bills. "He says this is the only way he can travel with comfort," Ticknor wrote to his wife, "and it is no trouble to me."

Though Hawthorne wanted somehow to participate in the war, he also wanted to shut it out. So he watched. From the sooty window of the railway car, he saw jerry-built fortifications, cannons of iron, and smoky canvas tents, all flying by, and when he stepped off the train in the Washington station, it was still swarming with soldiers and muskets even though he and Ticknor had missed the sixty thousand men who'd waded into muddy Virginia just hours before. Hawthorne had refused to travel at night, and they had been delayed. Ticknor was disappointed.

Thanks to Horatio Bridge and other connections, Ticknor and Hawthorne lost no more time. They joined Representative Charles Russell Train and the Massachusetts delegation for the presentation of an ivory-handled leather whip, made in Pittsfield, Massachusetts, to Abraham Lin-

coln, the homeliest man Hawthorne had ever seen. "If put to guess his calling and livelihood," Hawthorne would subsequently write, "I should have
taken him for a country schoolmaster." Lank, loose-limbed, and awkward,
Lincoln appeared before the delegation, his hair rumpled, his frock coat
rusty and unbrushed. His feet sloshed in shabby slippers. As for his vaunted
perspicacity, Uncle Abe, as Hawthorne called him, would "take an antagonist in flank, rather than to make a bull-run at him right in front,"
Hawthorne loved his puns. "On the whole, I like this sallow, queer, sagacious visage, with the homely human sympathies that warmed it; and, for
my small share in the matter, would as lief have Uncle Abe for a ruler as any
man whom it would have been practicable to put in his place."

Next day, Hawthorne was taken to Virginia, where he and Ticknor heard
the commander address his troops, and the day after that, they splattered
through the bleating rain to the military base at Harpers Ferry. A document
signed by Secretary of War Stanton authorized their passage by steamer to
Fortress Monroe, the naval base near Newport News; on another excursion,
they pressed south again, this time to Manassas, as a guest of the Baltimore
& Ohio Railroad, along with the writer Nathaniel Parker Willis and the
reporter Benjamin Perley Poore, several members of Congress, several officials of the railroad, several newspaper editors, an English correspondent,
and the Bridges. It was a group of do-gooders, spectators, and enthusiasts
straight out of the pages of "The Celestial Rail-road."

Hawthorne felt good. He lingered in Washington, willing to sit for the
painter Emanuel Leutze, who was applying the final dabs to his manifest-
destiny mural in the House of Representatives. Leutze supplied Hawthorne
with several glasses of champagne and several cigars to achieve a ruddier,
more affable image—though not much of a likeness—than anything
achieved at Mathew Brady's Gallery of Photographic Art. Those pho-
tographs, taken by Alexander Gardner, show Hawthorne grimmer and
grayer, his skin as wrinkled as crumpled paper around the large, weary eyes
that reveal nothing. He stands erect in a Napoleonic pose, white collar
caressing his face, coat lapels a snazzy velvet. Yet of the several pictures of
Hawthorne taken that day, all stern, there is a special one. Hawthorne's
hand rests on a table as his lower body slowly washes into whiteness; here, he
seems approachable, palpable, evanescent, and mortal, all at the same time.

Revived, Hawthorne opened the back door to the Wayside on April 10, and
in less than a month produced for the *Atlantic* a tour de force called

"Chiefly About War Matters by a Peaceable Man." He'd lost none of his satirical power. The essay is Swiftian, corrosive and funny, and directed at the foibles both of humankind and, more precisely, the *Atlantic* readership.

Generals are bullet-headed, the *Monitor* a rattrap, war a savage feat of recidivism. "Set men face to face, with weapons in their hands, and they are as ready to slaughter one another now," Hawthorne writes, "after playing at peace and good will for so many years, as in the rudest ages, that never heard of peace-societies, and thought no wine so delicious as what they quaffed from an enemy's skull." When the Army of the Potomac finally crossed the river after months of delay, it encounters no one: "It was as if General McClellan had thrust his sword into a gigantic enemy, and beholding him suddenly collapse, had discovered to himself and the world that he had merely punctured an enormously swollen bladder." And Hawthorne's proposals for the conduct of war are venomously comic: send old men to war instead of the young: "As a general rule, these venerable combatants should have the preference for all dangerous and honorable service in the order of their seniority," he writes, "with a distinction in favor of those whose infirmities might render their lives less the worth keeping."

Fed up with political poltroonery, Hawthorne rails at one side and excoriates the other. War spills blood, despoils the landscape, sends bumpkins into battle unaware of any noble cause, if noble it is, given the country's prodigality in "sacrificing good institutions to passionate impulses and impracticable theories." Once again Hawthorne offers his chilling proscription: "Man's accidents are God's purposes. We miss the good we sought, and do the good we little cared for."

As for the freeing of slaves, Hawthorne refuses to beat the drum. "I wonder whether I shall excite anybody's wrath by saying this?" Hawthorne inquires in his deadpan tone, likening a group of contrabands (fugitive slaves) to rustic fauns with nice manners: Donatello in blackface. Donatello and the contrabands are primitive creatures, almost androgynous, without consciousness or complexity—domesticated savages apt to revert to type, capable of murder and mayhem. No doubt about it: to Hawthorne, blacks and Italians and Jews are inferior to Anglo-Saxons, whom he doesn't much like either.

Yet any of them are liable to change—or conversion—and emancipation will provide a rite of passage for former slaves. But transformation into what, he asks, and at whose behest? A skeptic about the war, about emancipation—in fact, about everything—Hawthorne readily admits he lives in a society as racist as himself. "Whosoever may be benefited by the result of this war," he writes, "it will not be the present generation of negroes, the childhood of whose race is now gone forever, and who must henceforth fight a hard battle with the world, on very unequal terms."

These unequal terms are his point. And what he means by unequal terms lies at the heart of a national hypocrisy that, in one incarnation or another, has always been Hawthorne's subject, whether he writes about Puritans, Tories, rebels, or transcendentalists. America is conceived in liberty and oppression, and with this insight Hawthorne moves beyond a consideration of local politics, beyond even his own racism, to the extent that it's possible, to a fine-tuned perception of America's heritage. The slaves are "our brethren," he writes, "as being lineal descendants from the May Flower, the fated womb of which, in her first voyage, sent forth a brood of Pilgrims upon Plymouth Rock, and, in a subsequent one, spawned Slaves upon the southern soil:—a monstrous birth, but with which we have an instinctive sense of kindred."

En route to New York in May when Hawthorne sent "Chiefly About War Matters" to the *Atlantic,* Fields approved it on faith. "This is somewhat to be regretted," Hawthorne told Ticknor, "because I wanted to benefit of somebody's opinion besides my own, as to the expediency of publishing two or three passages in the article." He explained he'd already omitted several "which I doubted the public would bear. The remainder is tame enough in all conscience, and I don't think it will bear any more castration." Nor would he decline responsibility for what he wrote and felt. "I think the political complexion of the Magazine has been getting too deep a black Republican tinge," he went on, "and that there is a time pretty near at hand when you will be sorry for it. The politics of the Magazine suit Massachusetts tolerably well (and only tolerably) but it does not fairly represent the feeling of the country at large."

Returning home, a wide-eyed Fields read Hawthorne's description of President Lincoln as homely, coarse, and unkempt. That, of all things, was unacceptable. Fields assured Hawthorne that he liked the article—no question there—but said he and Ticknor both thought "it will be politic to alter yr. phrases with reference to the President, to leave out the description of his awkwardness & general uncouth aspect."

"What a terrible thing it is to try to let off a little bit of truth into this miserable humbug of a world!" Hawthorne grumbled, submitting to the editorial knife. He cut the description of Uncle Abe and for Fields's sake modified a few more passages, as when he describes a nameless officer as sitting on his horse like a meal-bag, and "the stupidest looking man he ever saw." But he warned Fields that should he collect the sketch into a book, "I shall insert it in all its original beauty."

Hawthorne also inserted a series of editorial footnotes, written by himself in the voice of a dull-witted editor who, as a Massachusetts patriot, misunderstands the author's satire or condemns it. In place of the Lincoln passage, then, Hawthorne-as-editor notes that "we are compelled to omit two or three pages, in which the author describes the interview, and gives his idea of the personal appearance and deportment of the President. . . . It lacks reverence, and it pains us to see a gentleman of ripe ages, and who has spent years under the corrective influence of foreign institutions, falling into the characteristic and most ominous fault of Young America."

To a man without faith or the conviction of a just cause—or what passes for either—war degenerates into butchery, massacre without meaning or end. And so the Peaceable Man and his editor together lampoon the slaveholding South and the censorious North; and together they lampoon Fields as editor and Hawthorne as writer and an entire country, bloodlusting and blind. "Can it be a son of old Massachusetts who utters this abominable sentiment?" Hawthorne, as editor, writes of the Peaceable Man. "For shame!"

"What an extraordinary paper by Hawthorne in the Atlantic!" Charles Eliot Norton (son of Andrews Norton) wrote to George William Curtis, editor of *Harper's Weekly* magazine. "It is pure intellect, without emotion, without sympathy, without principle."

" 'A fig for your kindly feelings,' might the escaping fugitives say to him," William Lloyd Garrison's *Liberator* scorned Hawthorne. "He says he would not have turned them back, and yet 'should have felt almost as reluctant, on their own account, to hasten them forward to the stranger's land' "! A nice balancing of considerations, truly! But the fugitives, it seems, had no difficulty whatever in determining 'on their own account,' whether to remain in the house of bondage."

Hawthorne dashed off another piece, much briefer, for a short-lived local weekly, the *Monitor,* in which he celebrated the North—or, rather, the northern soldier, having met on his trip from Manassas "the sons of Northern yeomen," a whole division of them, about fifteen thousand, who displayed gallantry toward the women in Hawthorne's party. He contrasted these regiments with the chivalrous southern soldiers who swept the battlefields for human bones to send home to their sweethearts or mothers for souvenirs. But he hadn't changed his position; this piece was no sop to the North; barbarity on either side revolted him.

"Chiefly About War Matters" offended most *Atlantic* readers not because it frequently seems prosouthern but because it is so virulently and unequivocally antiwar—and this during a war fought for such a palpable moral good. "If ever a man was out of his right element, it was Hawthorne in America," observed Edward Dicey, the thirty-year-old correspondent Hawthorne had met during his trip to Virginia. Dicey remembered that Hawthorne seemed to feel more at ease with him, an Englishman, than with his fellow Americans. "It was impossible for a man like Hawthorne to be an enthusiastic partisan," Dicey justified Hawthorne, who in these days needed the support. "Nobody disliked slavery more cordially than he did," Dicey insisted; "and yet the difficulty of what was to be done with the slaves weighed constantly upon his mind."

Dicey visited Concord in June. Hawthorne had returned to his tower, descending once in a while to plant sunflowers or entertain *Atlantic* contributors come to call. One of them, Rebecca Harding, who'd published "Life in the Iron Mills" in the magazine, had written Hawthorne just before his trip to Washington. He'd graciously answered, and that spring she took the train to Concord to knock at the door of the Wayside, where Emerson and Bronson Alcott had gathered in the little parlor, the latter standing before the fireplace, white hair cascading over his shoulders. He rambled on and on about the war as Hawthorne calmly sat astride a chair, chin resting on folded arms, shrewd laughter tucked in his eye. He was a stranger, Harding later recalled, even in his own home, like Banquo's ghost among the thanes.

He pulled himself to his feet, she remembered. " 'We cannot see that thing at so long a range. Let us go to dinner,' and Mr. Alcott suddenly checked the droning flow of his prophecy and quickly led the way to the dining-room."

Whenever Hawthorne went to Boston, he stopped by the Fields home at 37 Charles Street, a "fostering roof" (the phrase belongs to Henry James Jr.) that overlooked the river. From the front windows, boats sailing the river tilted by as the Fieldses sat with friends, *Atlantic* contributors, and other writers come to feel important, entertained, comforted, indispensable. Fields sent Hawthorne a typical note of thanks after Hawthorne met Anthony Trollope at a Fields soiree: Trollope had fallen in love with Hawthorne, "the handsomest Yankee that ever walked the planet."

Merry and smart though he was—and powerful—Fields did not accomplish his magic alone. Annie Fields bore the real brunt of making a salon: fresh cloths on the mahogany, clean linens on the bed, plump cushions, ready wit, and of course making sure the larder brimmed with enough food and wine for guests who might, at the last minute of course, spend the weekend. She covered her table in flowers from the wide garden at the back

Annie Adams Fields, 1861

of the house and showed to her guests Leigh Hunt's old brown Boccaccio. Always welcome, Una and Julian often stayed on Charles Street in pampered style, or Sophia lay on their couch in the parlor to watch the moon rise over the river. For Hawthorne, Annie reserved the extra bedroom with a view of the water and fed him hot chowder.

With her graces and background, her easy learning, her beauty, and her adulation of Hawthorne, Annie Fields was the sort of woman Sophia could appreciate. She coaxed rather than criticized, inspiring confidences impossible for Sophia to share with her sisters. For Annie Fields would not cross her, especially about Nathaniel or the children. Quite the reverse: both Annie Fields and Sophia Hawthorne needed heroes.

Sophia also needed affection, the kind Hawthorne was less and less capable of giving. Cloistered within his tower or in the downstairs library, curtains drawn, and on occasion able to eat only a little potato at dinnertime, Hawthorne seemed to shrink inside himself, unavailable and unavailing. With her sisters nearby and the war and Sanitary fairs and the children growing up, Concord largely fulfilled her need for sociability. But none of it replaced the profound intimacy with her husband that had lit the early days of their marriage. And like Hawthorne, she craved something more, something different: in her case, the female sympathy that Annie Fields provided. "I love you with a mighty love," Sophia opened her heart to Annie. "You embellish my life."

When Hawthorne was in his tower, Sophia sat at her own desk, gushing to Annie, "I *will* say just what I choose and you must hear it as you can. For how absurd for me to have these facts on the tip of my pen, and from a foolish conventional reticence, repair from letting them crystalline on the paper when I wish to do so." Annie objected. Sophia should restrain herself. Sophia could not.

The intensity of their friendship, as binding for a time as that of Hawthorne and Pierce, could not survive Hawthorne's death. For Sophia and Annie, intimacy required four people, not two. Sophia eventually quarreled with James Fields and severed all ties with the Fieldses. No one was more hurt than Annie. In 1871, after Sophia's death, she put her own sorrow into wobbly verse, remembering "that grief,/Which thou with mortal insight dealt to me,/Leaving a gaping wound without relief,/While yet we drifted on life's misty sea."

Probably not even Pierce's wife loved him as Hawthorne did. Princlie Frank was Hawthorne's anagram for Pierce; it was the small things that Pierce did that made him such. On the iron-cold day of Jane Pierce's funeral, Pierce, in mourning, leaned over to Hawthorne and to protect him from the biting wind drew up the collar of his coat.

Except for "Chiefly About War Matters," Hawthorne spent the rest of 1862 and the first half of 1863 mining his English notebooks for *Atlantic* essays instead of writing his new romance. Fields had promised to pay one hundred dollars for articles of ten pages, and for anything more than that, another ten dollars per page. (Hawthorne's reminiscence of Delia Bacon, "Recollections of a Gifted Woman," netted $150, no small sum. In 1863, three hundred dollars bought exemption from the draft, and a nice house could be had for three thousand, which Hawthorne just about spent to renovate the Wayside.)

"Have you not almost enough for a book prepared?" Fields angled. "And when will you like to publish a volume?" Though Hawthorne was dubious about the literary value of the sketches, he churned them out. He handed Fields "A London Suburb" in January, "Up the Thames" in February, and "Outside Glimpses of English Poverty" by mid-April. For the projected book, he proposed to rewrite an essay on his visit to Uttoxeter, published in *The Keepsake* in London in 1857, and he set about another sketch, "Civic Banquets," which he completed in June. And he composed an autobiographical piece, "Consular Experiences," to be saved for the collection, which already had a title: "*Our Old Home:* a series of English Sketches," combining, or so he said, intellectual ice with the wine of memory.

Come what may, he also proposed to dedicate them in a prefatory letter to Franklin Pierce, who made this book possible, in deference "to my own life-long affection for him."

That summer Hawthorne went to see Pierce in Concord, New Hampshire, and on July 4, Hawthorne's fifty-ninth birthday, Pierce mounted a wooden dais festooned with flags at Capitol Square to deliver an Independence Day speech. Declaring himself weary of carnage and war, the ex-president flayed the present administration as despotic, Lincoln as a demagogue, and, in a burst of alliteration, depicted the war as "fearful, fruitless, fatal." In the words of Pierce's biographer, the speech was a consummate literary feat in a lifetime of platitudes. But while Pierce disgorged his jeremiad, rumors of the Union's hard-fought victory at Gettysburg gripped the crowds. Pierce the Copperhead—as Republicans called rabid Peace Democrats—had managed to destroy what little reputation he had.

Doubtless, however, the fracas merely hardened Hawthorne against Pierce's detractors. "He will not relent," Annie Fields noted, partly in anger, partly in admiration. Fields predicted disaster; one book dealer, a large one, said he wouldn't order any book with a dedication to Franklin Pierce. Hawthorne did not yield. "Such adherence is indeed noble," Annie Fields stiffly noted. "Hawthorne requires all that popularity can give in a pecuniary way for the support of his family."

Later that month, rioters protesting the draft stormed New York City.

Before federal troops could restore some semblance of order, about two thousand people lay dead, including one hundred blacks lynched or otherwise killed. "The negroes suffer in NY," Sanborn told Moncure Conway, "but they are enlisting in the South at the rate of a regiment a week at least." Smaller riots broke out in Boston while edgy soldiers roved the cobblestones. On July 18, at Fort Wagner, South Carolina, Colonel Robert Gould Shaw, the son of Francis and Anna Shaw (who'd donated money to the Hawthornes several times in the 1840s), was shot through the heart. Killed with most of his regiment, the proud black troop known as Massachusetts Fifty-fourth, he was thrown into an unmarked grave. "Higginson is only slightly wounded," Sanborn reported of another of the Fifty-fourth's white officers, gratuitously adding, "Hawthorne has behaved badly and is a copperhead of the worst kind."

"He is in despair about the war and the country," said Henry Yates Thompson, an Englishman visiting Concord, "and he is a copperhead of copperheads. Mr. Hawthorne has all the prejudices about the negroes—'the smell, their intellects are inferior', etc., etc.'" Hawthorne was an anathema.

Fields presumably asked Ellery Channing to make Hawthorne retract the dedication. A coward, Channing begged Elizabeth Peabody to do it. Devoted to him after all these years, unafraid of his moods or his repugnant politics, she pleaded with him that it would hurt the cause. Amused and touched, he waved away her objections in a letter that reveals his respect for her. Of all people, he wrote, she should recognize Pierce's sterling qualities, which, he implied, were like hers: "There is a certain steadfastness and integrity with regard to a man's own nature (when it is such a peculiar nature as that of Pierce) which seems to me more sacred and valuable than the faculty of adapting one's self to new ideas, however true they may turn out to be."

Hawthorne was intransigent.

He added that he was not proslavery. Nor did he consider himself a Peace Democrat seeking reconciliation with the South; far from it. The recent northern victories, he feared, would drive the South into the arms of the Peace Democrats and bring about a coalition that would prolong slavery for at least another hundred years, "with new bulwarks" no less. Meantime, the North would think they'd won a victory "and never know they had shed their blood in vain, and so would become peace Democrats to a man. In that case, woe to the Abolitionists!"

To him, disunion now seemed the only viable alternative.

But he wasn't sure. So he requested that Peabody keep his views to herself. He'd always depended on her discretion. As for anything else, well, she could read what he had to say in his dedication to Pierce.

As loyal as Hawthorne was to Pierce, Fields was to Hawthorne. If Hawthorne insisted on the dedication, so be it—although the editor did suggest his author emend the last paragraph. "It would be a piece of poltroonery in me to withdraw either the dedication or the dedicatory letter," Hawthorne answered. If Pierce's name was enough to scuttle the book, the more reason to stand by him. "I can only say that I would gladly sacrifice a thousand or two of dollars rather than retain the good will of such a herd of dolts and mean-spirited scoundrels."

Yet he was no martyr. He'd strike the last paragraph of his dedicatory letter, which Fields thought contentious:

> Can it be that no man shall hereafter reach that elevated seat!—that its platform, which we deemed to be so firmly laid, has crumbled beneath it!—that a chasm has gaped wide asunder, into which the unbalanced Chair of State is about to fall! In my seclusion, accustomed only to private thoughts, I can judge little of these matters and know not what to hope, although I can see much to fear. I might even deem it allowable in the last resort, to be contented with half the soil that was once broad inheritance. But you, as all men may know by the whole record of your life, will hope stedfastly while there shall be any shadow or possibility of a country left, continuing faithful forever to that grand idea which, as you once told me, was the earliest that your brave father taught you; and whether the Union is to be henceforth a living giant, or a mangled and dismembered corpse, it will be said of you that this mighty Polity, or this miserable ruin, had no more loyal, constant, or single minded son than Franklin Pierce.

To Fields's amazement, the dedication didn't hurt advance sales of *Our Old Home*. Before its publication date, September 19, he put a second edition to press, and in October he reported that the confounded book continued to sell "bravely." But Pierce's name curdled in the mouths of every northerner. Just days before the publication of *Our Old Home*, a group of soldiers had discovered a letter that Pierce had written to Jefferson Davis in

1860 fomenting secession. If the South seceded from the Union, Pierce had told Davis, fighting would break out in the North, and the Democrats would side with him. "I have never believed that actual disruption of the Union can occur without blood," Pierce wrote; "and if through the madness of northern abolitionists that dire calamity must come, the fighting will not be along Mason & Dixon's line merely. It will be within our own borders, in our own streets."

According to Elizabeth Peabody, she and Mary Mann subscribed to the *Evening Post,* which published the treasonous letter on September 19 and then again on October 7. The sisters promptly showed the item to Sophia, who declared the letter a forgery and left their house in a snit. Once home, she sent for the paper, saying Hawthorne wanted to see it. From then on, Peabody insisted, Hawthorne never uttered Pierce's name to his sisters-in-law. He didn't denounce him; he just wanted to avoid an argument.

Early in October, *Harper's Weekly* requested that Hawthorne absolve himself of "Pierce's infamy" by saying he hadn't known of it when writing his dedication. Hawthorne would do no such thing. "I was very sorry to see what Hawthorne said," lamented George Curtis on reading the dedication. "He has a kind of moral blindness like color blindness, and except when he insults us all, as in this letter, we can do nothing but spit and pass on." In the review of *Our Old Home* that Curtis may have written, he praised Hawthorne's sinewy style and condemned his point of view: "That one of the most gifted and fascinating of American writers should fail to see, or to care for, the very point of our contest is monstrous."

Franklin Sanborn or Moncure Conway expressed bafflement in the pages of *Commonwealth,* which they coedited. How could Hawthorne call Pierce a patriot, they gaped in disbelief. Like everyone commenting on Hawthorne's new book, they duly trotted out the references to Addison, Gibbon, and Lamb when characterizing Hawthorne's graceful style. But grace has its limits: "His perception is quick but partial; he relates better than he observes, and observes better than he generalizes," said *Commonwealth.*

Reviewers relished the book's personal tone, especially the autobiographical sketch "Consular Experiences," and the *North American Review,* among others, praised "images reflected from the mirror and mottled with the intense idiosyncrasies of the writer." Readers agreed that Hawthorne finds nooks and crannies overlooked by most travel writers; his England exists not on the map but in the evanescent envelope of consciousness. "What was he to Liverpool, or Liverpool to him?" asked Henry Bright.

But Hawthorne's decision to pay tribute to Pierce ruffled most every feather. Charles Eliot Norton said the dedicatory letter "reads like the bitterest of satires; and in that I have my satisfaction. The public will laugh. 'Praise undeserved' (say the copybooks) 'is satire in disguise'—& what a blow his friend has dealt to the weakest of our Presidents." Harriet Beecher Stowe was indignant. "Do tell me if our friend Hawthorne praises that arch traitor Pierce in his preface & your loyal firm publishes it," she admonished Fields. "I never read the preface and have not yet seen the book, but they say so here & I can scarcely believe it of you—if I can of him." Calling the book pellucid but not deep, Emerson sliced out its dedication.

Bright too was offended, though not about Pierce. Hawthorne talked like a cannibal, he said. Bright couldn't brook Hawthorne's cynical, contemptuous (Bright's words) treatment of the "bulbous, long-bodied, short-legged, heavy-witted" Englishman (Hawthorne's words), to say nothing of Englishwomen, whom Hawthorne had compared to overblown cabbage-

Nathaniel Hawthorne, two years before his death.
"Things and men look better at a distance than close at hand."

roses "massive with solid beef and streaky tallow" and "made up of steaks and sirloins." Bright wasn't alone. Hawthorne's acrid humor, his jeers at the British class system, at the aristocracy, and at Englishwomen were not meant to please, and they didn't. "Whether it be that Nathaniel loved our British beer, not wisely, but too well," retorted *Blackwood's,* "and has found that it permanently disagrees with him; or whether the British beef has destroyed his digestion, and left his liver hopelessly deranged, we know not; but the same dyspeptic way of viewing things English accompanies him into all scenes." *Punch* also poked fun at Hawthorne—a Liverpool Lovelace— whose indictment of British women must have been a momentary weakness. "Can any created woman be terrible to you?" the magazine reveled in deadpan. "Away, eater of hearts." Never mind, Mr. Punch soothed. "You are strong enough in your own works to bear being supposed a descendant from a gorilla, were heraldry unkind."

Daily, Hawthorne was vilified either in letters or in reviews from across the sea. It must seem rather queer to him whose books had always been adored, Una remarked. Sophia wondered how much the "carping" (her term) bothered him. She didn't know. Fields did. Hawthorne told him not to send any more reviews.

Having miscalculated the extent of his own hostility, he was startled by the hostility he reaped. "But they do me great injustice in supposing that I hate them," he told Fields. "I would as soon hate my own people."

Except that, in a way, he did.

"It is impossible to possess one's mind in the midst of a civil war to such a degree as to make thoughts assume life. I hear the cannon and smell the gunpowder through everything."

Though he'd easily plundered his journals for publishable sketches, Hawthorne struggled with his fiction not just because the war rang loudly in his ears or because on some days he felt unaccountably ill. He also knew the days of romance, diction elegant and sentences poised, were numbered. He'd implied as much in *The Marble Faun.* "I feel as if this great convulsion were going to make an epoch in our literature as in everything else (if it does not annihilate all)," he wrote to Francis Bennoch, "and that when we emerge from the war-cloud, there will be another and better (at least, a more national and seasonable) class of writers than the one I belong to. So be it."

This class of writers included Rebecca Harding and William Dean Howells. But the youthful Howells hadn't written much, and Hawthorne soon tired of Harding's work, or so Sophia confided to Annie Fields. "Mr. Hawthorne cannot read her [Miss Harding's] productions now, they are so distasteful to him from her bad style and slimy gloom."

Had he lived, Hawthorne himself might have been a charter member in a new class of American journalist, modern, cold, dispassionate, satiric. "Chiefly About War Matters" signaled a new style and direction. But something else was on his mind—immortality, the tacit, impossible aim of him and everyone else in the throes of catastrophe.

CHAPTER TWENTY-SIX

———————

A Handful of Moments

Thou hast nor youth nor age;
But, as it were, an after-dinner's sleep,
Dreaming on both.

Measure for Measure, Act 3, Scene 1

I doubt, if it had been left to my choice, whether I should have
taken existence on these terms; so much trouble of preparation to
live, and then no life at all; a ponderous beginning, and nothing
more.

Nathaniel Hawthorne, "Septimius" manuscripts

INSOFAR AS ANYONE can know, Hawthorne knew he was going to die. Soon.

He hated the war and continued to fear it, disgusted by its slaughter, distrustful of its aim. He sat in his study alone for hours. "There seemed to be a stream rushing past him, which, even if he plunged into the midst of it, he could not be wet," he wrote not long after cannons blasted in Charleston Harbor. "He himself felt strangely ajar with the human race, and would have given much, either to be in full accord with it, or to be separated from it forever."

He was to have his wish.

Six years after Hawthorne's death, in 1870, Sophia Hawthorne published her husband's private notebooks, justifying her decision with a peculiar metaphor: she was an intruder in the writer's study, rifling through his drawers, hoping to find souvenirs of character in his old journals since they provide an "open sesame" to his work. Knowing the end of Hawthorne's life is near, biographers too have pored over frazzled papers, sure in retrospect to have discovered a man who exhausted his talent. But unlike the crude claimant manuscripts, the unfinished "Septimius" manuscript is supple, sharp, and, though incomplete, still complex: a series of fragments, as Hawthorne foretold in *The Marble Faun,* whose "charm lay partly in their very imperfection." He stopped revising "Septimius" about two-thirds through a second draft and likely intended one more revision to iron out inconsistencies, but as it stands, it's a work of gritty mourning, national identity, and agnosticism, and it contains the ripest, most coruscating of his satires, including—significant from a biographical point of view—his most seeing self-portrait to date.

"Septimius" opens in 1775 on the afternoon of the battle of Lexington and Concord, one war a substitute for another, all interchangeable, as Hawthorne contrasts the birth of the Union with what he assumed would be its end. The hero of the story is Septimius Felton, a divinity student of waning faith consumed by his fixation on death, "believing nothing, although a thin veil of reverence had kept him from questioning some things," like unanswerable riddles, the visitations, Melville had said, speaking of Hawthorne, from which no deeply thinking mind is ever free.

This is Hawthorne's cri de coeur, uttered while he and, as he supposed, his world faced certain extinction.

Septimius shoots a young British officer on that fateful April day and, rushing to the soldier's side, cradles him in his arms and takes from him, at the officer's request, a bloodstained, crumpled page. Though he can't make it out, the page appears to be a recipe for immortal life, and Septimius, from that moment on, begins a frantic effort to decipher the ingredients. Such mad pursuit is not new to Hawthorne, whose stories tell of quixotic potions and deadly cures; even the ambitious guest, hungry for fame, mortgages the blankness of death with it.

The ambitious guest was punished for his wish to be remembered; but it's not remembrance that Septimius—or Hawthorne—craves, or not entirely; he wants to wrest some meaning from life, itself too short to offer much. But once he's concocted the brew, he doesn't drink it. That fate falls to Sybil Dacy, a woman come to Concord to avenge the death of her lover, the same young British officer Septimius has killed. Unbeknownst to him, she splashes the elixir with poison, but having fallen in love with him, she drains the cup herself, leaving Septimius, mortal, to live out his spate of days all alone.

The external impulse for Hawthorne's story came from Thoreau, who once remarked that the Wayside had been inhabited by a man who thought he'd never die, and, earlier, from James Lowell, who told Hawthorne of the youthful patriot who axed a wounded British soldier for no apparent reason. He'd written of the latter legend in his preface to *Mosses from an Old Manse,* and in a sense he was rewriting it now, for "Septimius" incorporates elements of almost all of Hawthorne's previous work: alchemical or scientific crusades waged in solipsistic splendor; mighty women who drink poison to please, or punish, hapless men; hapless women themselves destroyed for their beauty or their strength.

In fact, in "Septimius" Hawthorne throws open the door to his cabinet of obsessions. A doctor of dubious background eggs Septimius forward; a muscular young soldier contrasts with a meditative, and murderous, student; a crusty old woman, descending from the slave Tituba, cooks up her own rotten liquor; and a legend, that of the bloody footstep, leads once again to an English estate, this time through the slain officer, who happens to be Septimius's kin. It's a mixed-up plot, to be sure, but the tale is fundamentally "an internal one," says Hawthorne, "dealing as little as possible with outward events."

Melancholia and stark existential dread are the nub of the Septimius story, less about the search for an elixir than about the impossibility of maintaining belief in anything—especially his own work. "We are the playthings and fools of Nature," Hawthorne recasts *King Lear,* "which she amuses herself with, during our little lifetime, and then breaks for mere sport." The "Septimius" manuscripts tell a simple, plangent tale of writing—Hawthorne's writing, or what he called "the mud of his own making" in a recent letter to Fields.

Hawthorne wrote; he could not write; and he wrote about his failure. "A man no sooner sets his heart on any object, great or small, be it the lengthening out of his life interminably, or merely writing a romance about it," Hawthorne explains, "than his fellow beings, and fate and circumstance to back them, seem to conspire to hinder, to prevent, to throw in each his obstacle, great or small according to his power." But like his story, the hindrances were internal. ". . . Mocking voices call us back, or encouraging voices cease to be heard, when our sinking hearts need them most; so unaccountably, at last, when we feel as if we might grasp our life-long object by merely stretching out our hand, does it all at once put on an aspect of not being worth our grasp; by such apparently feeble impediments are our hands subtly bound; so hard is it to stir to-day, while it looks as if it would be easy to stir to purpose tomorrow."

Then, unbidden, an awful thought bangs at the door: "You are deluding yourself. You are toiling for no end."

Revising the first draft of his story, Hawthorne tinkered with names (Septimius Felton becomes Septimius Norton), pruned the biographical, and twisted the plot as he honed his skepticism to a mean edge. But the second draft proceeded with difficulty, and it's painful to read. Passage after passage spills with hopelessness. "We are all linked together in a chain of Death, and feel no remorse for those we cause, nor enmity for that we suffer," Hawthorne comments. "And the Purpose? what is Purpose? Who can tell when he has actually formed one."

Writing meant everything to Hawthorne and yet cost everything. It was his heart of darkness, an isolation no one could fathom or relieve; it was a source of shame as much as pleasure and a necessity he could neither forgo nor entirely approve. He wondered if Julian was embarrassed by his father's profession, as Walter Scott's son reportedly was, and when Rose began to compose stories of her own, Hawthorne stood over her, "dark as a prophetic flight of birds," she remembered years later. "Never let me hear of your writing stories!" he roared.

And what is fiction anyway? Over and over, Hawthorne grapples with the question in stories like "Fancy's Show Box," in his prefaces, his notebooks, in *The Marble Faun*. "He did not write stories in the usual style, marrying people all off at the end," Mary Mann remarked. "He hunted out the hidden processes of actions." Hence come the unsettling conclusions of *The Scarlet Letter* and *The Marble Faun* or the satiric endings of *Fanshawe* and *The House of the Seven Gables*; hence, too, comes Hawthorne's insistence that he writes romance, not sentimental gibberish, not popular books, and decidedly not the beef-and-ale novels of Anthony Trollope, "just as real," he remarked, "as if some giant had hewn a great lump out of the earth and put it under a glass case, with all its inhabitants going about their daily business."

He took pleasure in Trollope's work. But it wasn't for him. Like Septimius, Hawthorne mistrusts the sturdy fibers of the actual world—the stuff of realism, to say nothing of the facile stuff of human progress, human order, and human knowledge. "In short, it was a moment, such as I suppose all men feel (at least, I can answer for one)," admits Hawthorne in his "Septimius" story, "when the real scene and picture of life swims, jars, shakes, seems about to be broken up and dispersed, like the picture in a smooth pond, when we disturb its smooth mirror by throwing in a stone; and though the scene soon settles itself, and looks as real as before, a haunting doubt keeps close at hand, as long as we live, asking—'Is it stable? Am I sure of it? Am I certainly not dreaming? See; it trembles again, ready to dissolve.' "

Nor are romance writers themselves exempt from doubt—and self-doubt:

> They make themselves at home among their characters and scenery, and know them better than they know anything actual, and feel a blessed warmth that the air of this world does not supply, and discern a fitness of events that the course of human life has not elsewhere; so that all seems a truer world than that they were born in; but sometimes, if they step beyond the limits of the spell, ah! the sad destruction, disturbance, incongruity, that meets the eye; distortion, impossibility, everything that seemed so true and beautiful in its proper atmosphere, and nicely adjusted relations, now a hideous absurdity.

The yellow of the sunset ferments, manifest destiny implodes, and ambitious dreams of grandeur fade to black, obliterated by an avalanche of time, indifference, or triviality. Emerson found Hawthorne pacing on top of the hill. The two men followed his tracks back to the Wayside, Hawthorne remarking "*This path is the only remembrance of me that will remain.*"

Hawthorne is the chronicler of imagination, an imagination of unbelief and dislocation. Wakefield had come home to find he had none.

Though Sophia represented the person who once upon a time drew him into the daily life he wanted, its warm hearth—and real passion—melting the chill in his heart, Hawthorne hadn't shown her the proofs of *Our Old Home*. An anagram he contrived out of her name is not entirely auspicious: "a hope while in a storm—aha!!"

Loneliness had not abated. It returned, full throttle.

Fortunately for Hawthorne, Sophia never lost her faith. Nor did Fields. When Hawthorne confided the germ of his "Septimius" idea, Fields pushed forward with characteristic brio, hoping to publish installments of the book in the *Atlantic*. Hawthorne held back. "I don't mean to let you have the first chapters," he replied, "till I have written the final sentence of the story." Regardless, Fields brightly announced in the *Atlantic* prospectus of 1862 that a new romance by Hawthorne would soon appear, and Edward Dicey later remembered Hawthorne speaking of his new book that same spring, but by the end of 1862 Hawthorne had ceased to mention it and instead siphoned gloom into humor. Bringing Rebecca Harding to Sleepy Hollow, Concord's new-sprung graveyard, he squatted on the emerald grass and, as she recalled, chuckled. "Yes," he said, "we New Englanders begin to enjoy ourselves—when we are dead."

His physical powers were dwindling. Like Sisyphus in reverse, Hawthorne reputedly dragged logs of wood down from the top of his hillside to its bottom in an effort to recover his strength. He agonized about money. "It is a pain to him to be so hard driven in his present unenergetic condition," Sophia informed her sister Elizabeth, "and he doubts if we can at any rate easily make the ends meet." He told Ticknor, "I expect to outlive my means and die in the alms-house," and when Annie Fields one day offered to brush the dust from Hawthorne's coat, he flinched. "No, no," he said, "I never brush my coat, it wears it out." He refused to buy wine for himself, hire someone to help clear the meadow, vacation in the mountains, pay for Una's music lessons. "I do not know what I shall do with him," Sophia confessed to Annie.

Age clasped his throat. "It is a new and strange thing to myself to be old," he wrote in his second "Septimius" manuscript, "& I have not yet convinced myself of it." If he was young yesterday, why not to-day? Death was everywhere. The soil was drenched in blood, and daily newspapers barked long lists of names. James Lowell had lost two nephews, one of Henry James's sons—Julian's friend Wilky—had been wounded, and so had the son of Oliver Wendell Holmes. More than five thousand men died at Antietam, with eighteen thousand wounded or missing. At Gettysburg the casualties had totaled more than forty thousand. "Life, which seems such a priceless blessing, is made a jest, emptiness, delusion, a flout, a farce, by this inopportune Death."

By the summer of 1863, Hawthorne had abandoned the "Septimius" manuscript. He rationalized the decision in the opening pages of *Our Old Home:* "The Present, the Immediate, the Actual has proved too potent for me," he writes. "It takes away not only my scanty faculty, but even my desire for imaginative composition, and leaves me sadly content to scatter a thousand peaceful fantasies upon the hurricane that is sweeping us all along with it."

Hurricane without, tumult within: the green world up in smoke.

Less than a month after the publication of *Our Old Home* in the fall of 1863, Sophia reported that Hawthorne was very "negative." "I am afraid that Concord is not the best place for him," she confided to Annie Fields, "and that he requires a city-life, with a secure retreat in its midst as well." But he left home reluctantly and socialized with difficulty. "Una thinks it is the greatest misfortune to him to live so secluded," Mary Mann reported to her eldest son, "that he ought to be where he cannot help seeing people, and she has the right of it."

Moncure Conway remembered meeting Hawthorne at the Fieldses'. Hawthorne preferred reading Defoe's ghost stories in the guest room to joining the company in the parlor. This in itself was not unusual; Hawthorne had long ago earned a reputation as a loner. These days, however, much had changed. His Democratic acquaintances scorned his defense of the war while others detested his sympathy with the South. Yet his political party had been debased by obsequiousness, racism, and sectional strife. Friends, too. John O'Sullivan made no secret of his southern allegiances, and Pierce continued to cleave to his stale interpretation of the Union. "He thus had no party," Conway concluded of Hawthorne, "—then nearly equivalent to having no country."

Demoralized, he mounted the steps to his tower to begin another story, also about immortality, and in the fall of 1863 he outlined it for Fields: he'd begin by describing the Wayside and Thoreau, recently felled by tuberculosis—"How Thoreau would scorn me for thinking that I could perpetuate *him!*"—and then proceed to the tale. Fields leaped. A chapter for the December *Atlantic,* he queried, going so far as to suggest a title: "The New Tithonus, The Deathless Man." He knew Hawthorne was worried about taxes and bills—Julian had just entered Harvard—so he promised two hundred dollars for a chapter of it. But as Fields pressed forward, Hawthorne pulled away. Let's just call the story "Fragments of a Romance," he countered, and proposed February for the *Atlantic* installment.

In November, Fields dispatched a check. By then Hawthorne had fallen alarmingly ill. Sophia guessed typhus. Hawthorne suspected some kind of "bedevilment." He feared he was losing his mind. Thanksgiving passed blankly. "I am amazed that such a fortress as his stomach should give way."

Sophia was confused. Sometimes despondent, at other times she considered Hawthorne merely cranky or slightly indisposed. "He cannot bear anything," she admitted to Una, "and he must be handled like the airiest venetian glass."

Understandably, she wanted to minimize his symptoms, and because she fluttered her ailments more dramatically, it was easy to do. But he drained her patience. Homemade remedies failed to nourish his body or hike his spirits. Hawthorne groused about his pens, his writing paper, the weather, the war, and the broken fence on the roadside. Sophia soundlessly placed a book by his plate at teatime, grateful to Fields, who kept Hawthorne well stocked. "He is not a very manageable baby," she soon complained to Horatio Bridge, "because he has so long been a self-reliant man."

In December, Hawthorne delivered a listless new tale, "The Dolliver Romance," to Fields by hand. An elderly apothecary, Dr. Dolliver, dabbles with elixirs, striving "amid the sloth of age and the breaking-up of intellect, to earn the competency which he had failed to accumulate even in his most vigorous days." Looking backward with half-shut eye, "The Dolliver Romance" perfunctorily draws on Hawthorne's past, its ghosts unappeased. Dolliver's name is that of the blind organist at Salem's First Church who played in Hawthorne's youth; he lives in the Peabody house, next to the Charter Street graveyard; his shop stands on Main Street; his mentor is Salem's seventeenth-century physician John Swinnerton. Dolliver's deceased aunts correspond to Hawthorne's aunts, one of whom died in her "virgin bloom, another in autumnal maidenhood, yellow and shriveled with vinegar in her blood." Even Hawthorne's mother rises again, the "forlorn widow, whose grief outlasted even its vitality, and grew to be a merely torpid habit."

Hawthorne said he'd never finish "Dolliver" either because he didn't like it, as he told Annie Fields, or because he knew he couldn't. Fields rallied him, but once back at home, Hawthorne lay on the couch until noon. Sophia feared the new story would be sad. It struck Annie Fields that way. Hawthorne guessed as much too, but more to the point, he had no idea where he was going with it. So old Dolliver hovers between youth and age, sipping without comprehension the strange elixir that, for a while, shores him against his ruin.

When Hawthorne could, he ascended to his hillside to trudge back and forth for an hour or so. Some days he insisted only a trip to Europe would cure him; the Wayside was the death of him. "I wish, with all my heart, that our dear little Wayside domain could be sold advantageously for his sake," Sophia repined, "and that he could wander on sea beaches all the rest of his days." Other days, he believed he'd never write again. "I am tired of my own thoughts and fancies, and my own mode of expressing them," he moaned. And what avails a literary reputation anyway, he muttered to Henry Longfellow. Even the best achievements grow cold.

The new year, 1864, dawned gray and icy. Frost crinkled the windowpanes of the Wayside. Longfellow was slowly emerging from the horrible death of his wife at Craigie House, in Cambridge, where they had been happily living until one hot day in July when, while sitting in the library, Fanny Longfellow had dropped a lit match or drop of burning wax onto her light summer dress. It whooshed into flame. She ran to Longfellow's study, where he woke from his nap and threw a rug over her, holding it close with his own body, to try to put out the fire. She died the next day.

Doubled over in sorrow for three long years, Longfellow, sensing the mood of a fellow sufferer, proposed to Fields that he and Ticknor arrange a small dinner with Hawthorne, just the four of them, "two jovial Publishers, and two melancholy authors."

Fields drove out to frozen Concord the first week of January. Hawthorne sat gazing into the fireplace, his gray dressing gown twisted about a shrinking torso. Pierce journeyed from New Hampshire. "I cannot help thinking that mental causes are at the bottom of his illness." Mary Mann decided Hawthorne's Copperhead views would kill him. "I suppose he would rather die than recant, whatever may be his convictions." Ebe recommended he wear heavier clothes and consume animal food, and Ticknor wanted to take the broken-down author to Havana. In the interim, he bought him an easy chair.

No one knew what to do, no one knew what was wrong, and at this remove, his devastating array of symptoms is hard to diagnose. Some biographers have reasonably suspected cancer, others a brain tumor; Hawthorne was soon unable to walk or write without shaking. But with a boring pain in his stomach and a rumble in his intestines, Hawthorne may have had ulcerative colitis or an infection acquired in Italy, where his complaints first surfaced and which he later treated by fasting, causing malnutrition. Several descendants speculate about dysentery or the developing stages of syphilis. Odd, though, is the resemblance between Hawthorne's symptoms and those of his uncle Richard Manning and, it seems, his uncle Robert. "This mode of death has been an idiosyncrasy with his family," Hawthorne wrote in *The House of the Seven Gables,* one of his eeriest foreshadowings.

In February he announced to Fields that he was clear-eyed and ready for the future, small though it may be. There was to be no new romance. "Say to the Public what you think best, and as little as possible," Hawthorne instructed Fields, his humor briefly rekindled at his own expense: ". . . 'Mr. Hawthorne's brain is addled at last, and, much to our satisfaction, he tells us that he cannot possibly go on with the Romance announced on the cover of the Jany Magazine." Doubtless Field did not laugh.

In March, Emerson came to visit, full of talk about inner strength. Hawthorne was too weak to pull on his boots; his illness, whatever the cause, had entered its terminal stage.

Assisted by Sophia, he traveled to Boston again aboard the smoky local train and informed David Roberts that he would've liked to have seen his children fully grown, though he would not. Annie Fields recorded him commenting in low tones that "I think we could bear it if we knew our fate. At least I think it would not make much difference to me now what became of me." He was wraithlike, shriveled, spectral. His eyesight was blurred, his hearing dull, his hand trembly. At night Annie Fields heard the floorboards creak. Hawthorne was pacing.

It seemed impossible that the stalwart William Ticknor, only fifty-three, a publishing giant and good man come to take an enfeebled Hawthorne on a journey for his health, it seemed impossible that William Ticknor would die in Hawthorne's stead, as if the gods determined to toy with Hawthorne one last time.

During his mission of mercy, Ticknor's seemingly robust health sputtered under the weight of a cold caught sometime before he left Boston. The cold deepened to pneumonia in the bitter rains pummeling New York. Hawthorne, however, felt better, or said he did, writing to his daughter Rose that he'd been swallowing oysters whole, a feat of appetite intended to reassure his family; who knows if it was true.

When churning seas capsized their Cuban plan, Hawthorne and Ticknor headed south. In Philadelphia they drove out to Fairmount Park in the vacant April sun, Ticknor wrapping his coat about Hawthorne. That night, back at the Hotel Continental, Ticknor's breath snagged. Hawthorne called a physician and sat down beside his friend's bed, never letting go of his hand. On the morning of April 9, when an acquaintance, the publisher George William Childs, called at the hotel, he found Hawthorne wandering the corridors dazed, crying that it was all a terrible mistake. Someone had shuffled the cards badly, dealt them blindly. Childs wondered if Hawthorne was mad.

After Childs learned that Ticknor had died that morning, he stayed with Hawthorne, afraid to leave him for a moment. Later he conveyed the author to another friend, who accompanied the grief-soaked Hawthorne back to Boston.

Blanched and haggard, he trekked from the little train station in Concord to the Wayside, face streaming with sweat and guilt. The last ribbon of hope had disappeared. The gleam had gone from his eye, Sophia said. Only weariness, infinite weariness, hung on.

Hawthorne could no longer walk across the room without tottering. He could not digest food. The pain in his stomach kept him from lying down at night. Yet he managed to ask George Hillard to organize his finances, and before journeying with Ticknor had stipulated that Ebe should receive $180 per annum from his estate. Years later, Rose remembered that her father began to burn old letters and to make small farewell speeches to Una and Sophia, though they did not understand the import at the time.

Fewer than two weeks after Ticknor's death, Hawthorne insisted on another trip, as if to simulate a motif from his stories—or duplicate his trip with Ticknor and this time get it right. The widowed Franklin Pierce, whose own health had been precarious, was available. This pleased Sophia, although Bronson Alcott, who'd recently seen Hawthorne at his gate, thought him far too ill for travel. But Sophia naïvely—or desperately—put stock in the curative power of a private carriage rolling by boyhood haunts, the two chums then revived at the Isles of Shoals, where Hawthorne could sniff the salty sea. In confidence, she begged Pierce to convince her husband that he wouldn't spend his last days in the almshouse, as he feared. Not just money but the necessity of gainful employment hounded him, the Furies never placated by former success. "He has become very nervous and intolerable to himself," said Mary Mann, "which makes him distressing to others."

Sophia asked Fields, also confidentially, if he could arrange for Dr. Holmes to examine Hawthorne on the sly.

From the perspective of his faltering health, Hawthorne's "Septimius" and "Dolliver" manuscripts may be read as an argument for and against suicide, the search for elixirs not of life but of death. "If sometimes it impels the dark man to self-violence," Hawthorne writes of life in "Septimius," "it is because he cannot any longer bear the anticipation of losing it, and rushes to the reality."

In "Dolliver," he writes of death: "He had the choice to die, and chose it."

Gossips supposed that Hawthorne and Pierce consumed too much alcohol the night Hawthorne died, drink as fatal as any imagined potion. And they didn't even know that two months earlier he'd commented regretfully—or prophetically—that men no longer came together to get drunk. "Think of the delight of drinking in pleasant company," he had said to Annie Fields, "and lying down to sleep a deep strong sleep."

"Men die, finally, because they choose not the toil and torment of struggling longer with Time, for mere handsfull of moments," Hawthorne wrote. He may have sipped a final elixir with Pierce or, worn out, may have folded a secret remedy into his portmanteau to season his last drink quite decisively. "His death was a mystery," Ellery Channing maintained. Elizabeth Peabody weighed in, as was her wont, recollecting that just before his death Hawthorne had said, "A man's days are in a man's hands."

The morning of Hawthorne's funeral, she remarked that he very much wanted to die before he turned sixty. He was fifty-nine.

Like the end of one of his best tales, any account of Hawthorne's death is inconclusive. Even so, everywhere he left clues as if he were the weird epicenter of his most ambiguous work, his life—as indeed he was.

About two weeks earlier, on Tuesday, May 10, a carriage stopped at the Wayside gate. Hawthorne looked shrunken and battered, but he stepped out of the house in military posture, upright and unaided. In Rose Hawthorne's memory her father stood one last time "like a snow image of an unbending but an old, old man." Sophia covered her face with her hands and wept. "My father did not like to die," Rose recalled, "though now he wished to do so."

Sophia accompanied Hawthorne into Boston to rendezvous with Pierce. They stopped by Charles Street for an affectionate farewell, and as planned, Oliver Wendell Holmes called at the Bromfield House, Hawthorne's hotel.

The two men chatted for half an hour, Hawthorne complaining of indigestion with seeming unconcern. His mental powers were keen, his talk no more or less hesitant than usual, his bashfulness still much like a girl's, Holmes reported publicly. In private, he said he sensed a shadow had passed over Hawthorne's mind. He then ushered Hawthorne to a nearby apothecary where, Holmes claimed, he treated him to some innocuous medicine as one treats a child to ice cream. But the shark's tooth was on him, Holmes later told Annie Fields. There was nothing more to be done.

Pierce joined Hawthorne in Boston, and the two friends sped to Andover, Massachusetts, to see Pierce's sister-in-law and then to Concord, New Hampshire, where they waited for the weather to clear. When the clouds scattered, they headed to Franklin, Laconia, and Center Harbor. At sunset on Wednesday, May 18, their coach rumbled into Plymouth.

Hawthorne had grown so frail he had to be lifted out of the carriage— Sophia was never told this—and into the huge, white-shingled Pemigewassett Inn. Remnants of daylight streamed through the windows. Shadows lengthened. Pierce signed the brown leather guest register for both of them.

"Happy the man that has such a friend beside him, when he comes to die!" Hawthorne forecast his own end in *The Blithedale Romance*. Hawthorne chose his old friend for his deathbed companion. Pierce undoubtedly knew it.

It would be a boon, Hawthorne had said to him, to pass away without a struggle. Later, however, Pierce told Sophia that Hawthorne's only intimation of mortality occurred when he, Pierce, had noted that the wind, blowing from the east, promised a change. "Not in my day," Hawthorne had replied.

After Hawthorne's death, Pierce provided, as if by rote, the history of Hawthorne's last night. Hawthorne had hardly eaten after arriving at the inn; he took a cup of tea with toast and went to bed. At ten Pierce himself climbed upstairs, his room separated from Hawthorne's by a door, which he left open. The lamp was lit. A few hours passed. Pierce rose and paused at the threshold of the chamber. Hawthorne seemed peacefully asleep, right palm tucked beneath his cheek. At three or four in the morning, Pierce got up again, and this time stole into his friend's room. Hawthorne lay in the same position, so Pierce placed his hand on his forehead. It was cold.

Pierce sent for a doctor and alerted two guests in the hotel whom he knew. They confirmed what he had felt beneath his fingers. He wired James Fields, not bearing to deliver the news to Sophia with the staccato cruelty of a short telegram.

Later that day, May 19, the birthday of Hawthorne's father, Pierce was packing Hawthorne's clothes and noticed an old pocketbook at the bottom of Hawthorne's valise. In it lay Pierce's picture.

"I need not tell you how lonely I am," Pierce would write to Bridge, "and how full of sorrow."

The Painted Veil

*Lift not the painted veil which those who live
Call Life; though unreal shapes be pictured there
And it but mimic all we would believe
With colours idly spread,—behind, lurk Fear
And Hope, twin Destinies; who ever weave
Their shadows o'er the chasm, sightless and drear.
I knew one who had lifted it . . . he sought,
For his lost heart was tender, things to love
But found them not, alas; nor was there aught
The world contains, the which he could approve.
Through the unheeding many he did move,
A splendour among shadows, a bright blot
Upon this gloomy scene, a Spirit that strove
For truth, and like the Preacher, found it not.*

Percy Bysshe Shelley, Sonnet

E LIZABETH PEABODY, who'd introduced Sophia to Nathaniel, was obliged to take him away. To her fell the task of announcing his death.

She traveled to Concord from Boston on the local train, collected Mary at Sudbury Road, and together they walked to the Wayside. They intended to tell Una as softly as they could and let her deliver the blow to Sophia when and however she thought best. It happened differently.

Sophia was downstairs eating her dinner. Hearing footsteps clatter on the piazza, Una jumped from the table. "What's happened?" she cried, seeing Aunt Mary's expression. "Papa is gone," Mary answered. Una didn't understand. "He is dead, dear," Mary repeated. From the dining room Sophia heard a commotion and raised her voice to ask what was the matter. Una's face was the color of paper. Sophia called out again. "She says Papa is dead!" Una wailed.

"No, it's not true," Sophia struck out at her sisters, those sisters who, like two Fates, never let her alone. And now they were trying to snip her very life cord. "Go away—it can't be true—how do you know?" Sophia denied and wept and pleaded. The two sisters disappeared into another room while Rose, tears running down her pink cheeks, hugged her mother. Una sat in white terror, figuring that any minute Sophia would drop dead.

Half an hour later, Sophia had calmed. The mystery had been solved. She saw the hand of God in it. With Hawthorne dying away from home, she'd been spared the ugliness of death—this she didn't say—and as for Mr. Hawthorne, who'd once skated in the frigid dawn and chopped wood all afternoon, her now shattered husband had been spared a helpless old age. "He peacefully closed his eyes for a quiet earthly slumber," Sophia decided, "and opened them in the better world, without a motion or jar, without a farewell or a regret." The book was shut.

Pierce's letter came. It contained information about Hawthorne's last day that would become a mantra. Hawthorne had died in his sleep without desiring anything or anyone, hungry only for the rest he'd sought for so long.

Thenceforward Sophia referred to her husband's death as a euthanasia, or easy passing. The present meaning of the word had not yet come into use.

When Julian learned there was trouble at home, he assumed his mother had been stricken. It never occurred to him his father could die. "He had been frail of late, to be sure, but there seemed to be nothing specific the matter with him," Julian later remembered, as if uncertain still. Fathers were invincible.

But Julian's world had cracked open. "Trifling details stood out, meaningless, stones in the desert," he would recall. James Fields took the dazed boy to Concord in the unhappy rain.

Saturday, May 20, was Rose Hawthorne's thirteenth birthday. It rained. Franklin Pierce brought Hawthorne's body back to Boston. Sophia was not to know it had been embalmed.

She insisted that it not be transferred to Concord until Monday noon, when it could be conveyed directly to the church, not the Wayside, for the funeral. "Sophia does not wish to think of the body or any of the circumstances," Mary Mann explained to one of her sons. "Julian & Una do not even consult her but do every thing themselves, and she likes to leave it to them." Una scribbled a note to the Reverend James Freeman Clarke requesting that he conduct the service. Elizabeth Peabody added a hasty postscript. Sophia, she wrote, "cannot bear to think of any body but you. You must come, dear James."

From Charles Street, Fields had been contacting Hawthorne's friends and the members of the Saturday Club. He and Judge Hoar orchestrated the funeral. Sophia asked Annie Fields for help with the widow's weeds. Annie got her a soft-crowned hat, veil, gloves, and a cloak.

It was raining on Sunday too, but Monday sparkled, the air fresh and sweet, the sky a robin's-egg blue. The village was thronged with spectators, who strolled arm in arm to the Old Manse, already a tourist site. Some of the onlookers rowed on the lazy river nearby, its bank spread with purple flowers. But at three o'clock, mourners deserted the sunshine and filed into the Church of the First Parish, where Louisa Alcott had arranged the flowers in blazing shades of white: lilies of the valley, Hawthorne's favorite, and luxurious apple blossoms picked from orchards at the Manse. Huge vases of them stood in each of the church windows. "It looked like a happy meeting," Oliver Holmes murmured to Emerson.

Bronson Alcott listed some of the mourners in his diary: Henry Longfellow, Louis Agassiz, Charles Eliot Norton, George Hillard, Edwin Whipple, James Russell Lowell. Judge Rockwell Hoar was there of course, and the other Concord neighbors, Emerson, Ellery Channing, Frank Sanborn. "We shall be alone soon," Charles Sumner wrote Longfellow in despair. David Roberts had come from Boston, and William Pike from Salem with Hawthorne's remaining uncle, William Manning. Recently injured, Horatio Bridge was absent. Franklin Pierce sat with the family.

Ebe Hawthorne was also absent. Cut deep by the news of her brother's death, she grieved by herself in Beverly, the hamadryad alone, too heartbroken to manage Concord.

Hawthorne lay before the pulpit, girdled in lilies and white tea roses braided with orange blossoms. On top of the casket Fields had placed the manuscript of "The Dolliver Romance." Mary Mann sang, and James Freeman Clarke spoke of Hawthorne's special gift. He was the friend of sinners not because he excused sin but because he loved the sinner, and he loved perfection too, though he himself never found it. Julian, his hand cold, held on to his mother's warmer one.

Afterwards Sophia said the service was a festival of life, she and Hawthorne reborn as the new Adam and Eve.

Sixteen pallbearers, eight on a side, carried the casket out of the church. Hawthorne was buried in Sleepy Hollow cemetery under an awning of white pine.

Hawthorne's personal estate amounted to twenty-six thousand three hundred twenty-two dollars and sixty-one cents. It included eight hundred dollars' worth of furniture, a two-hundred-dollar library, several shares in local banks, two United States coupon bonds, several promissory notes, and stock in the Boston & Maine Railroad and in the Jamaica Plain Gas Company. The Wayside and its seventeen acres added twenty-five hundred dollars. His copyrights, taken together, were estimated at another twenty-five hundred.

He died with one hundred twenty dollars cash on hand. It wasn't a tremendous amount but would have kept the almshouse away.

They had watched the flesh melt from his bones, but Hawthorne's friends were strangely surprised when they heard of his death, which they considered sudden. Perhaps like Julian they regarded him as a fixture, remote to be sure but likely to make himself real or human at some later date. Emerson articulated it best. "I thought I could well wait his time & mine for what was so well worth waiting," he told Sophia. But even when talking to her, he couldn't cough up fulsome praise. "As he always appeared to me superior to his own performances," Emerson continued, "I counted this yet untold force as insurance of a long life."

In the privacy of his journal, he reminisced about the "tragic element" of Hawthorne "that might be fully rendered, in the painful solitude of the man—which, I suppose, could no longer be endured, & he died of it."

By and large, literary acquaintances who outlived Hawthorne devoted a good portion of their reminiscences to complimenting his work. "I don't think people have any kind of true notion yet what a Master he was, God rest his soul!" said James Russell Lowell. "Shakespeare, I am sure, was glad to see him on the other side." As for his person, they hedged. He was enigmatic, they said, sparing themselves the further admission that Hawthorne was not their friend or, worse yet, that they hadn't understood him in the least. "It was pleasant to meet Hawthorne on the street in Concord, but I recall no conversation of importance with him, nor did I seek any," recollected Moncure Conway, "having long felt that his genius was to be got at only in his pages."

With their inveterate affection for *dulce et decorum,* many of Hawthorne's contemporaries had to struggle with Hawthorne's quirks, and though they genuinely respected his work, they despised much of what he stood for: doubt, darkness, and the Democratic Party. Think of it: his era produced Frederick Douglass, Abraham Lincoln, Henry Thoreau, Margaret Fuller, Sojourner Truth, Garrison, Greeley, Stowe, Walt Whitman, and of course Emerson. So in Hawthorne's presence—or in their memory of it—friends discreetly sidestepped his political vagaries. William Dean Howells, Lincoln's campaign biographer, met Hawthorne only once, when he climbed Hawthorne's hill and talked while Hawthorne companionably smoked his cigar. Howells remembered Hawthorne as shy, affable, impossible to describe. It was like talking to an apparition. "We are always finding new Hawthornes," Howells later wrote, referring to Hawthorne's work as well as his person; "but the illusion soon wears away, and then we perceive that they were not Hawthornes at all."

Said Sophia Hawthorne, "I never dared to gaze at him, even I, unless his lids were down. It seemed an invasion into a holy place. To the last he was in a measure to me a divine Mystery, for he was so to himself."

But not everyone was as infatuated with Hawthorne as Sophia. Charles King Newcomb, from Brook Farm days, regarded Hawthorne as a "self-centered, self-reproductive, & soliloquial person," and the women's rights advocate Caroline Healey Dall called him an egotist. To Charles Norton, Hawthorne was a strange mixture of callousness and sensitivity, and to Louisa Alcott he seemed a "beautiful soul in prison trying to reach his fellow beings through the bars." He was a puzzlement. "There can be companionship without speech," insisted Hillard, longtime Whig and faithful friend. Mary Mann made her peace. "He was a man of natural tenderness & imaginative nature," she declared, "rather than a man of lofty principles."

He had a penchant for tugging on loose threads yet rued the undone string; he anatomized what most of us try to conceal and pretended disinterest; similarly, he affected to veil his face, which he did not; yet neither did he unburden himself. How could he? His combativeness took myriad forms, guilt transforming his irascibility into satire or subtlety or, at times, sweetness. He mixed together pain and pleasure in one full cup; it was a secret of his art.

He was watchful and wary, decent and courteous and as provincial as

Hepzibah Pyncheon, whom he loved and hated as himself. Silence never scared him. He sought fellowship while spurning it, and if taciturn with people he didn't like, he talked volubly to the friends he loved without embarrassment or regret. Plus, disclaimers notwithstanding, he enjoyed politics and public office, the latter a strange sanctum for a man of poetry, or so said acquaintances who didn't fret about money or manhood or acknowledge that America intervened in both. "Nobody would think that the same man could live two such different lives simultaneously," Hawthorne had written his fiancée in 1840.

Once read, his stories never vanish: the minister dons his veil, Wakefield perambulates around London, and the birthmark, like Hawthorne, entices and appalls. Of all writers, female or male, in nineteenth-century America, Hawthorne created a woman, Hester Prynne, who still stands, statuesque, the heroine par excellence impaled by courage, conservatism, consensus: take your pick. Yet there she is. And her creator's legacy, like hers, is one of success even though Hawthorne apprehended banal failure wherever he looked, particularly in his own desultory career.

James T. Fields swiftly smoothed out the wrinkles in Hawthorne's reputation. Less than a month after Hawthorne's death, he prepared to publish "The Dolliver Romance" in the July *Atlantic* along with a tribute from Oliver Wendell Holmes, and in the August number he featured Longfellow's poem about Hawthorne's funeral. In subsequent years, he stoked the Hawthorne fire whenever and however he could, encouraging Sophia to transcribe her husband's journals for publication and scratching out a small essay of his own. He truly admired Hawthorne's writing and truly cared for Hawthorne; if he protected his investment by keeping Hawthorne's name honored and alive, so be it.

Shortly after Hawthorne's death, his old friend George William Curtis sent Fields an essay commemorating Hawthorne's life and work. Curtis was by then the brother-in-law of Robert Gould Shaw, having married a daughter of Hawthorne's early benefactors, Frances and Sarah Shaw. He'd also campaigned for Frémont and Lincoln, and as political editor of *Harper's Weekly* he tackled a subject Fields preferred to leave alone. What kind of person could stand by as the country buckled under the weight of cruelty, battle, slavery, and blood, Curtis wondered. "Is he human? Is he a man?"

Hawthorne died in 1864; the war had not ended, and Hawthorne's peers did not yet know how or when it would. But they knew of Hawthorne's reluctance to rally to their great cause and join in what Curtis believed was civilization's lurching struggle toward freedom. "What other man of equal power," Curtis demanded, "who was not intellectually constituted precisely as Hawthorne was, could have stood merely perplexed and bewildered, harassed by the inability of positive sympathy, in the vast conflict which tosses us all in its terrible vortex?" Curtis had no answer except to regard his beloved Hawthorne as a faunlike Donatello, locked in his tower. Dry and indifferent but without pride or arrogance, Hawthorne loved humankind in the abstract, not the particular. "His genius obeyed its law," Curtis concluded weakly.

Fields refused to print the piece. "I said probably too precisely what I thought for a moment so near his death," Curtis exclaimed, and mailed it to Charles Norton, now editor of the *North American Review*. Norton tried his hand at the paradox of Hawthorne. "His genius continually, as it seems to me, overmastered himself," Norton observed, "and the depth & fulness of his feelings were forced into channels of expression in which they were confined & against which they struggled in vain."

Had Hawthorne squeezed refractory emotions into channels much too narrow? No: those channels helped to create emotion by harnessing what they unleashed. And yes, in a way, insofar as Hawthorne outlived his idiom; the idea of romance seemed fusty now, even naïve. The world had altered a good deal since Independence Day, 1804. Hawthorne knew it. But he hankered after dark ancestral houses plunked down in forests, like Arden, where nothing changes, not even rot. This was his stay against nastiness and evil, meaninglessness and damned folly. But no matter its elegance, the fantasy of home—community, consolation, belonging, place—wore thin. Or out. And yet, comfortless, Hawthorne painted a dark corner of the contemporary world: terrifying, terrible, and grand.

Notes

Books and articles about Hawthorne are voluminous—and have been appearing at an astonishing rate ever since Hawthorne's death in 1864. As a consequence, I try to confine my citations to the primary sources consulted or quoted. Otherwise the notes (already lengthy) would be longer than this book. However, I do cite secondary sources when I think they might amplify some particular issue or guide further reading, for I'm obviously indebted to decades and decades of superb critical writing about Hawthorne's work.

Anyone interested in my evaluation of recent Hawthorne scholarship may consult the annual *American Literary Scholarship,* 1997–2001, edited by David J. Nordloh and Gary Scharnhorst (Duke University Press). I learned a great deal from writing this chapter during the last five years; and I'm grateful to the editors, two fine scholars quick with humor and help.

I used the Hawthorne family letters in the possession of Evelyn Hamby, with permission, before the archive was sold to Stanford University, where it now resides. With permission, I've quoted from these materials, crediting both Mrs. Hamby and Stanford.

In quoting any primary materials, I've retained the writer's original spelling so that the reader may better hear the author's voice, and as a consequnce I keep the use of [*sic*] to a minimum.

COMMONLY USED ABBREVIATIONS

The following abbreviations are used for frequently cited names:

ECH:	Elizabeth Clarke Manning Hawthorne (mother)
EH:	Elizabeth Hawthorne (sister Ebe)
MLH:	Maria Louisa Hawthorne
JH:	Julian Hawthorne
NH:	Nathaniel Hawthorne

SH:	Sophia Peabody Hawthorne
RH:	Rose Hawthorne Lathrop (Mother Mary Alphonsa)
UH:	Una Hawthorne

HB:	Horatio Bridge
ED:	Evert Duyckinck
RWE:	Ralph Waldo Emerson
AF:	Annie Adams Fields
JTF:	James T. Fields
MF:	Margaret Fuller
GH:	George Hillard
HWL:	Henry Wadsworth Longfellow
HM:	Herman Melville
EPP:	Elizabeth Palmer Peabody
Mrs. EPP:	Elizabeth Peabody, mother-in-law
FP:	Franklin Pierce
MM:	Mary Mann
WDT:	William D. Ticknor

For frequently cited libraries or manuscript depositories,
the following abbreviations are used:

AAS: American Antiquarian Society, Worcester, Massachusetts

Amherst: Amherst College Archives and Special Collections, Amherst College, Amherst, Massachusetts

Antioch: Antiochiana, Antioch College Library, Antioch College, Yellow Springs, Ohio

Bancroft: Bancroft Library, University of California at Berkeley

BY: Yale Collection of American Literature, Beinecke Rare Book and Manuscripts Library, Yale University, New Haven, Connecticut

BPL: Rare Books Department, Boston Public Library, Boston

Berg: Berg Collection of English and American Literature, New York Public Library, New York

Bowdoin: George J. Mitchell Department of Special Collections and Archives, Bowdoin College Library, Bowdoin College, Brunswick, Maine

Butler: Rare Book and Manuscripts Library, Butler Library, Columbia University, New York

Houghton: Houghton Library, Harvard University, Cambridge, Massachusetts

Huntington: Huntington Library, San Marino, California

LC: Library of Congress, Washington, D.C.

MHS: Massachusetts Historical Society, Boston

Morgan: Pierpont Morgan Library, New York

NHHS: New Hampshire Historical Society, Concord, New Hampshire

NYPL: Manuscripts and Archives Division, The New York Public Library, Astor, Lenox and Tilden Foundations, New York

OSU: Rare Books and Manuscripts Library of The Ohio State University Libraries, Columbus

PE: Phillips Library (formerly Essex Institute), Peabody Essex Museum, Salem, Massachusetts

Rosary Hill: Rosary Hill Home, Hawthorne, New York

Smith: Peabody Family Papers, Sophia Smith Collection, Smith College, Northampton, Massachusetts

Stanford: Department of Special Collections, Stanford University Libraries, Stanford, California

UVA: Alderman Library, University of Virginia, Charlottesville

The following abbreviations are used for frequently cited books:

Unless otherwise indicated, quotations from Hawthorne's letters published in *The Letters of Nathaniel Hawthorne,* ed. William Charvat et al., in the *Centenary Edition of the Works of Nathaniel Hawthorne,* vols. XV–XVIII (Columbus: Ohio State Univ. Press), will be cited as C followed by the volume number. I have also provided recipient and date.

American Claimant Manuscripts: The Ancestral Footstep, Etherege, Grimshawe in the *Centenary Edition of the Works of Nathaniel Hawthorne,* ed. Edward H. Davidson and Claude M. Simpson, vol. XII (Columbus: Ohio State Univ. Press, 1977), cited as *American Claimant Manuscripts.*

American Notebooks, ed. Claude Simpson, in the *Centenary Edition of the Works of Nathaniel Hawthorne,* vol. VIII (Columbus: Ohio State Univ. Press, 1972), cited as *AN.*

The Elixir of Life Manuscripts in the *Centenary Edition of the Works of Nathaniel Hawthorne,* ed. Edward Davidson, Claude Simpson, and L. Neal Smith, vol. XIII (Columbus: Ohio State Univ. Press, 1977), cited as *Elixir of Life.*

English Notebooks, ed. Thomas Woodson and Bill Ellis, in the *Centenary Edition of the Works of Nathaniel Hawthorne,* vols. XXI and XXII (Columbus: Ohio State Univ. Press, 1997), cited as *EN* (followed by vol. 1 or 2, to specify volume number).

The French and Italian Notebooks, ed. Thomas Woodson, in the *Centenary Edition of the Works of Nathaniel Hawthorne,* vol. XIV (Columbus: Ohio State Univ. Press, 1980), cited as *FIN.*

Our Old Home, ed. Claude Simpson and Fredson Bowers, in the *Centenary Edition of the Works of Nathaniel Hawthorne,* vol. V (Columbus: Ohio State Univ. Press, 1970), cited as *OOH.*

True Stories from History and Biography, ed. Roy Harvey Pearce and Fredson Bowers, in the *Centenary Edition of the Works of Nathaniel Hawthorne,* vol. VI (Columbus: Ohio State Univ. Press, 1970), cited as *True Stories.*

Hawthorne's novels, cited by title, all appear in *Nathaniel Hawthorne: Collected Novels,* ed. Millicent Bell (New York: Library of America, 1983).

Hawthorne's tales and sketches, cited by title, all appear in *Nathaniel Hawthorne: Tales and Sketches,* ed. Roy Harvey Pearce (New York: Library of America, 1996), also cited as *Tales.*

Horatio Bridge, *Personal Recollections* (New York: Harper & Bros., 1893), cited as *Personal Recollections.*

James T. Fields, *Yesterdays with Authors* (Boston: Houghton Mifflin, 1882), cited as *Yesterdays*.

Julian Hawthorne, *Hawthorne and His Circle* (New York: Harper & Bros., 1903), cited as *HHC*.

Julian Hawthorne, *Nathaniel Hawthorne and His Wife*, 2 vols. (Boston: Houghton Mifflin, 1884), cited as *NHHW.*

Rose Hawthorne Lathrop, *Memories of Hawthorne* (Boston: Houghton Mifflin, 1897), cited as *Memories.*

CHAPTER ONE: THE PRISON DOOR—INTRODUCTORY

3. The second-born child: Exhibits A and B, Southern District Court Criminal Dockets C 4–5, National Archives, New York City.

4. "always handicap"; "To be the son": James Russell Lowell to JH, Nov. 28, 1885, in C. E. Frazer Clark Jr., ed., *Hawthorne at Auction, 1884–1971* (Detroit: Gale Research, 1972), p. 136; Henry James, "Julian Hawthorne," in *Henry James: Literary Criticism*, vol. 1, *Essays on Literature, American Writers, English Writers,* ed. Leon Edel (New York: Library of America, 1984), p. 295.

4. "This idea is": *The House of the Seven Gables,* p. 511.

4. Like him: See MM to Horace Mann Jr., Jan. 8, 1865, Antioch; see also UH to Horace Mann Jr., Oct. 4, 1859, BY.

4. "The more I feel": UH to EPP, Oct. 4, 1859, BY.

4. Una had worshipped: See SH to Mrs. EPP, June 9, 1850, Berg.

4. "It was impossible": Thomas Wentworth Higginson, *Part of a Man's Life* (Boston: Houghton Mifflin, 1905), p. 268.

5. "Theirs is the greater": "Wise Flays Hawthorne," *New York Times,* Mar. 13, 1913, p. 3.

5. His conviction disgraced: "Hawthorne Seeks Apology," *New York Times,* Oct. 17, 1913, p. 20.

5. "In such extremities": JH, *The Subterranean Brotherhood* (New York: McBridge, Nast, 1914), p. 16.

5. "I was sure": "Convict Three Men in Hawthorne Case," *New York Times,* Mar. 15, 1913, p. 2.

5. "It is a very common": "Etherege," *American Claimant Manuscripts,* p. 328.

5. "his tendencies": Feb. 1, 1849, *AN,* p. 420.

6. In 1908 . . . he managed: Hawthorne's letters to prospective dupes usually included this sentence: "I have dropped literature, and taken up the development—and the exploitation—of a mine." See, for instance, JH to Paul Hodgeland, Sept. 24, 1908, Minnesota Historical Society.

6. "Why not go on": JH, *Confessions and Criticisms* (Boston: Ticknor & Fields, 1886), p. 9.

6. "I think we take"; "a bread-and-butter calling": JH, *Confessions and Criticisms,* p. 16; "Julian Hawthorne Dead on Coast, 88," *New York Times,* July 15, 1934, p. 22.

6. "better than I do": JH, diary, July 3, 1879, Bancroft.

6. "I cannot sufficiently": JH, *Confessions and Criticisms,* p. 16.

6. Friends thought she: SH to FP, Mar. 31, 1865, NHHS; see Charlotte Cushman to EPP, July 25, 1869, MHS.

6. "But he is he": RH to Clifford Smythe, Apr. 6, 1913, courtesy Evelyn Hamby; Stanford.

6. "I know that he really": Vernon Loggins, *The Hawthornes* (New York: Columbia Univ. Press, 1951), p. 331.

6. "I am consoled": RH to JH, Mar. 15, 1913, Bancroft.

7. "What had I to do": JH, *The Subterranean Brotherhood*, p. 11.

7. "She is to be": NH to William B. Pike, July 24, 1851, *C* XVI, p. 464.

7. "I think you inherited": SH to RH, May 20, 1868, Morgan.

7. Rose wanted to write: *Memories,* pp. 422–23.

7. "I have not the smallest": SH to EPP, Feb. 16, 1851, Berg.

8. "The men of our family": EH to Rebecca Manning, Mar. 2, 1874, PE.

8. "Love is different": RH, "For a Lord," *Harper's Bazaar* 25:31 (July 30, 1892), p. 615.

8. George . . . got a job: Factual details about Rose Hawthorne Lathrop and George Lathrop's life during this period, where not otherwise indicated, are taken from Theodore Maynard, *A Fire Was Lighted: The Life of Rose Hawthorne Lathrop* (Milwaukee: Bruce Publishing, 1948), chap. 3, or Maynard's research notes and primary documents in the Theodore Maynard Collection, Georgetown University Library.

8. "abrupt and strange"; "usefulness": JH, "A Daughter of Hawthorne," *Atlantic Monthly* 142 (Sept. 1928), p. 372; RH to Charlotte Holloway, Apr. 22, 1895, Berg.

8. "He was as earnest": RH, memoir, Morgan.

8. "I gave up": RH to Katherine Lee Bates, Apr. 11, 1902, Amherst Archives.

8. "From close observation": RH, "Resolution," manuscript, courtesy Evelyn Hamby; Stanford.

9. "The ice in the blood": Flannery O'Connor, *Mystery and Manners* (New York: Farrar, Straus & Giroux, 1969), p. 219. It should be noted that on February 4, 2003, Mother Alphonsa was proposed a candidate for sainthood.

9. Una Hawthorne installed: UH to EPP, n.d., Berg; *NHHW,* vol. 2, p. 371.

9. "I do indeed love": UH to Rebecca Manning, Apr. 18, 1871, PE.

9. "Sometimes I wish": *Memories,* p. 354.

9. "Her natural bent": Jan. 28, 1849, *AN,* p. 411.

9. "If there were not": Feb. 6 [1849], *AN,* p. 422.

9. She was educated . . . A few years later: SH to Mrs. EPP, July 15, 1851, Berg; SH to EPP, Oct. 26, 1853, Berg.

10. To vanquish the vanquishers: In his perceptive reinterpretation of the Hawthorne marriage, Walter Herbert reads Una's "misery" as "a parable of the psychic entrapment of women." See T. Walter Herbert, *Dearest Beloved: The Hawthornes and the Making of the Middle-Class Family* (Berkeley: Univ. of California Press, 1993), p. 176.

10. Calm again: EH to Rebecca Manning, Dec. 31 [1861], PE.

10. "insanity"; "nearly took": Nathaniel Cranch Peabody (SH's brother) to Dora Inwood, Oct. 11, 1871, PE.

11. "She will fulfil": SH to EPP, Oct. 31, 1854, Berg.

10. When the effort: See Valerie Bonham, *A Joyous Service: The Clewer Sisters & Their Work* (Windsor, England: Valerie Bonham and the Community of St. John the Baptist, 1989), p. 43. Sister Mary Ashpitel, who presided over St. Andrew's Cottage, where Una died, was an especial friend.

10. "Has Una had": JH, diary, Feb. 3, 1877, Bancroft.

10. "The idea that you": UH to Mrs. Horton, Aug. 6 [1877], PE.

10. "almost at the time": RH to EH, n.d. [1877], Rosary Hill.

12. From afar: RH to EH, n.d. [1877], Rosary Hill. It may have been similar, especially if father and daughter suffered from a similar infection or from ulcerative colitis. See Chapter 26.

CHAPTER TWO: HOME .

13. Called Naumkeag: For information and statistics on early Salem, see C. H. Webber and W. S. Nevins, *Old Naumkeag* (Salem, Mass.: A. A. Smith, 1877); Samuel Eliot Morison, *The Maritime History of Massachusetts* (Boston: Houghton Mifflin, 1921); and *Salem: Maritime Salem in the Age of Sail* (National Park Service, Peabody Museum, and Essex Institute: National Park Handbook 126, 1987).

14. Bandanna handkerchiefs: In addition to Samuel Morison, see Luther S. Luedtke, *Nathaniel Hawthorne and the Romance of the Orient* (Bloomington: Indiana Univ. Press, 1989), chap. 1, for a good composite history of the Salem trade.

14. Generals, jurists: Charles E. Trow, *The Old Shipmasters of Salem* (New York: G. P. Putnam's Sons, 1905), p. 49. See also James Duncan Phillips, *Salem and the Indies: The Story of the Great Commercial Era of the City* (Boston: Houghton Mifflin, 1947), who irately defends Salem against its imagined detractors: "It is not the flamboyant morons of Hollywood or Broadway, however smart, who make for the eventual good of a community," Phillips observes, "but people of taste, culture, and mental activity, living decent, restrained lives" (p. 191).

14. One Salem daughter: Eleanor Putnam, *Chronicles of Old Salem,* ed. Arlo Bates (Boston: Houghton Mifflin, 1899), p. 27.

14. Nathaniel Hathorne, as the name: See William Bentley, *The Diary of William Bentley, D.D., 1784–1819* (reprint, Gloucester, Mass.: Peter Smith, 1962), vol. 3, p. 5.

14. "No family": Bentley, *Diary,* vol. 3, p. 167.

14. "Azure, a lion's head": "The White Old Maid," in *Tales,* p. 320.

14. William Hathorne was a man: For an account of the early years and political and civic accomplishments of Major William Hathorne (1606/7–1681), see Loggins, *The Hawthornes,* pp. 29–95, and Margaret B. Moore, *The Salem World of Nathaniel Hawthorne* (Columbia: Univ. of Missouri Press, 1998), pp. 28–37, as well as the related excerpts in Sidney Perley, *A History of Salem, Massachusetts,* 3 vols. (Salem, Mass.: Sidney Perley, 1928); for his son John Hathorne (1641–1717), see Loggins, *The Hawthornes,* pp. 96–141, and Moore, *The Salem World of Nathaniel Hawthorne,* pp. 37–46, as well as Joseph B. Felt, *Annals of Salem* (Salem, Mass.: W. & S. B. Ives, 1827); NH to WDT, Mar. 16,

1855, *C* XVII, p. 319. James T. Fields recalls having seen a copy of Sidney's *Arcadia* in Nathaniel Hawthorne's library. See *Yesterdays,* p. 62, and "Grandfather's Chair," in *True Stories,* p. 32.

14. 200-acre land grant: Copies of the land grant stipulation can be found in *Essex Institute Historical Collections* 4 (1862), p. 113.

15. He voted to banish: Felt, *Annals of Salem,* p. 179.

15. He ordered Ann Coleman: Perley, *A History of Salem,* vol. 2, p. 254; Felt, *Annals,* pp. 183, 195.

15. For his own pains: Perley, *A History of Salem,* vol. 2, p. 250. See also Land Grant to William Hauthorne [*sic*], UVA.

15. "Let us thank God": "Main Street," *Tales,* p. 1039.

15. "I cannot remember": Fragments [from the letters of EH] in the hand of JH, Bancroft.

15. "dim and dusky grandeur": *The Scarlet Letter,* p. 126.

16. According to his family: Putnam, *Chronicles of Old Salem,* p. 27. See, among other sources, Loggins, *The Hawthornes,* p. 133. NH uses these legends, as well as stories about Hathorne's claim to land, in *The House of the Seven Gables.* See also Chapter 17.

16. Federalists and Republicans: M. C. D. Silsbee, *A Half-Century in Salem* (Boston: Houghton Mifflin, 1887), p. 2. See also Morison, *The Maritime History of Massachusetts,* p. 174.

16. "The jealousy & envy": Bentley, *Diary,* vol. 1, p. 248.

16. In 1804 the Federalists . . . The congregation: Bentley, *Diary,* vol. 3, pp. 96–97; *Salem: Maritime Salem in the Age of Sail,* p. 58.

17. The bride, Betsy Manning: Elizabeth was born on March 7, 1802. Betsy Hathorne's pregnancy and its possible impact on her is mentioned in James Mellow, *Nathaniel Hawthorne in His Times* (Boston: Houghton Mifflin, 1980), p. 12, as possibly accounting for her later, so-called reclusive tendencies; it is discussed more specifically in Nina Baym, "Hawthorne and His Mother: A Biographical Speculation," *American Literature* 54 (1982), pp. 1–27. However, since the Mannings and the Hathornes were neighbors and friends, it is unlikely that the Hathornes would have judged the pregnant ECH as harshly as she suggests. See also Gloria Erlich, *Family Themes and Hawthorne's Fiction* (New Brunswick, N.J.: Rutgers Univ. Press, 1984) p. 188; unfortunately, Erlich also takes for granted an estrangement between the families. Yet Baym does try to quell the speculation concerning the supposed rift between the Hathornes and Elizabeth Hathorne after the death of the captain by saying ECH was not "overly fond of his family" (p. 63). On similarly scant evidence, Arlin Turner, *Nathaniel Hawthorne* (New York: Oxford Univ. Press, 1980), p. 11, mentions the "distance and coolness" between ECH and her Hathorne relatives after the captain's death. Since EPP is evidently the sole source of the presumed estrangement, it should be handled with care. See also Moore, *The Salem World of Nathaniel Hawthorne,* p. 71, who provides a balanced view of the pregnancy and discounts rumors about any disaffection. But none of these critics mentions the close relations between ECH and her sisters-in-law.

18. Old even by Salem standards: Daniel Hathorne (1731–1796) and Rachel Phelps

(1734–1813) married in 1756. In 1772 Hathorne purchased the house on Union Street from his father-in-law, Jonathan Phelps. Daniel and Rachel Phelps Hathorne had eight children: Rachel (1757–1823), Daniel (1759–1763), Sarah (1763–1829), Eunice (1765–1827), Daniel (1766–1804), Judith (1770–1827), Ruth (1778–1847), and Nathaniel (1775–1808). See *Vital Records of Salem,* vol. I, pp. 45–48; Loggins, *The Hawthornes,* pp. 168–89; Moore, *The Salem World of Nathaniel Hawthorne,* pp. 50–55. Rachel married the wealthy merchant Simon Forrester, befriended by her father even before Forrester first came to America.

18. The Hathorne place sat: Elizabeth Manning, "The Boyhood of Hawthorne," *Wide Awake* 33:6 (Nov. 1891), p. 500.

18. Not surprisingly: Bentley, *Diary,* vol. 2, p. 323; shipping records, PE.

18. Robert Manning put: Nathaniel Hathorne (father), Manning invoice, shipping papers, PE.

18. He was also hitching: For an overview of the Manning family and a genealogy, see William H. Manning, *The Manning Families of New England* (Salem, Mass.: Salem Press, 1902), pp. 714–32.

18. She was a bashful: *Personal Recollections,* p. 33; *Yesterdays,* p. 43.

18. "strange reserve": NH to SH, Feb. 27, 1842, *C* XV, p. 611. ECH's own correspondence does not suggest that she was undemonstrative or cold.

19. "capacity for placid": EH to JTF, Dec. 13 and 16 [1870], BPL. Hildegarde Hawthorne, *Romantic Rebel* (New York: Appleton-Century-Crofts, 1932), p. 11.

19. "looked as if"; "full of sensibility": EPP to Thomas Wentworth Higginson, n.d., Berg; EPP to Francis Henry Lee, 1882, PE.

19. Hathorne's father: Loggins, *The Hawthornes,* p. 176; *Salem Gazette,* Apr. 26, 1796.

19. By then his son: "Domestic Affairs," *Salem Gazette,* May 3, 1796.

20. "In Storms when": Nathaniel Hathorne, logbook, 1795–96, PE. Hathorne was at the time chief mate on the *Perseverance,* which was owned by brother-in-law Simon Forrester and which traveled to Batavia, Manila, and Canton.

20. "I hear your darter": EPP to JH, transcript by JH, notebooks, Morgan.

20. "inclined to melancholy": *Yesterdays,* p. 43.

20. Granite, he said: *NHHW,* vol. I, p. 96.

20. Hathorne had brought home: As first mate on the *Herald* under Captain Nathaniel Silsbee, Hathorne had been authorized by President John Adams in 1800 to subdue or seize any French ships within jurisdictional limits of the United States. JH, flyleaf of logbook, Nathaniel Hathorne, Bancroft. JH writes of his own father: "In particular he was interested in the fight with the French privateer, recorded on Nov. 3rd or 4th 1800, when Hathorne's ship, *The Herald,* beat her off when she was attacking the ship *Cornwallis* of the British East India Co."

20. From these books: Nathaniel Hathorne, logbooks, Bancroft and PE.

20. Having shipped . . . third child: Maria Louisa Hathorne was baptized on March 18, 1808, First Church Records.

20. In 1804, after the birth: Walter Muir Whitehill, *The East India Marine Society*

and the Peabody Museum of Salem: A Sesquicentennial History (Salem, Mass.: Peabody Museum, 1949), p. 162.

20. In 1808 no ships: For the tribulations faced by Salem in this period, see Morison, *The Maritime History of Massachusetts,* chap. 13. For a partisan view, see Phillips, *Salem and the Indies,* chap. 17.

21. On April 10: Bentley, *Diary,* vol. 3, p. 353.

21. "I remember very well": EH to UH, Nov. 12, 1865, transcript by JH, notebooks, Bancroft.

21. "died in India": SH to EPP, n.d., Morgan.

21. Captain Hathorne had died: Nathaniel Hathorne, shipping papers, PE.

21. "He left very little": EH to UH, Nov. 12, 1865, transcript by JH, notebooks, Bancroft.

21. In later years: Elizabeth Manning, "The Boyhood of Hawthorne," p. 504; ECH to Richard Manning III, Jan. [26], 1820, PE.

21. "The billowy Ocean"; "those for whom we weep": "Poetry," *Spectator,* Sept. 25, 1820, PE, quoted in *Miscellaneous Prose and Verse, C* XXIII, p. 44; "The Ocean," n.d., in *Miscellaneous Prose and Verse, C* XXIII, p. 6.

21. "Of what mysteries," "Of sunken ships": "Foot-prints on the Sea-shore," in *Tales,* p. 568.

22. "The rovers of the Sea": See EH to UH, Feb. 26, 1865, transcribed by JH, Bancroft. JH omits part of this passage in *NHHW,* vol. 1, pp. 123–24, which he loosely transcribes, and George Parsons Lathrop has changed "rovers" to "pirates" in his summary of NH's early work. See George Parsons Lathrop, *A Study of Nathaniel Hawthorne* (1876; reprint, New York: AMS Press, 1969), p. 134.

22. "The weather not looking": Nathaniel Hathorne, logbook, inscribed by NH in 1825, Huntington.

22. A friend recalled: JTF, *Yesterdays,* p. 92; F. B. Sanborn, *Recollections of Seventy Years* (Boston: Richard G. Badger, 1909), p. 523.

22. "came fresh": NH to SH, Apr. 3, 1940, *C* XV, p. 434.

22. He wanted to do "everything": Richard Manning Jr. (father) to Richard Manning III (son), Feb. 4 [1804], PE. Richard Manning III is henceforward referred to as Richard Manning.

23. "There were four Uncles": EH to JTF, Dec. 12 [1870], BPL. The aunts and uncles were Mary, born June 1, 1778; William, Nov. 27, 1780; Elizabeth Clarke Manning (Hawthorne's mother), Sept. 6, 1780; Richard, July 31, 1782; Robert, July 19, 1784; Maria, June 18, 1786; John, Feb. 10, 1788; Priscilla, Jan. 10, 1790; and Samuel, Dec. 17, 1791.

23. According to relatives: Rebecca Manning, "Some Facts about Hawthorne," PE.

23. It was a singular case: After Maria Manning's death in May 1814, the Reverend Dr. Bentley also noted that "the d. [daughters] have united elsewhere [First Church] & the youngest became one of the fanatics." See Bentley, *Diary,* vol. 4, p. 257.

23. "All have something": Mary Manning to Richard Manning, Dec. 14, 1814, PE.

23. Reputedly he removed: RH, "Memoir," Morgan.

23. At one time he owned: EH to UH, Dec. 20, 1865, transcribed by JH, Bancroft.

23. He played . . . theological questions: Manning Hawthorne, "A Glimpse of Hawthorne's Boyhood," *Essex Institute Historical Collections* 83 (1947), p. 160. See also undated newspaper clipping, John M. Conklin, "Hawthorne," address at the Franklin Literary Society, pp. 7–8, PE.

24. He was especially good-looking: EH to JTF, Dec. 12 [1870], BPL.

24. Forrester angrily informed: EH to JTF, Dec. 12 [1870], BPL.

24. In later life: NH to SH, Apr. 14, 1844, *C* XVI, p. 30.

24. "Study the hard lessons": Robert Manning to NH, Aug. 14, 1813, Berg.

24. On Saturday, April 17 . . . The funeral: Bentley, *Diary,* vol. 4, p. 163; *Salem Gazette,* Apr. 20, 1813.

24. No more would: EH to JTF, Dec. 13, 1870, BPL; See Bentley, *Diary,* vol. 4, p. 163.

24. "The heart never breaks": "Grimshawe," in *American Claimant Manuscripts,* p. 439.

24. The Maine holdings: Manning legal papers, estate of Richard Manning, PE. Taken together, the property was assessed at more than thirty thousand dollars, a figure that did not include Manning's personal worth of about twenty thousand dollars, judging from promissory notes, mahogany furniture, his jewelry and his pewter, three tea sets from China, and his horse and carriage.

25. "Uncle Richard he can grow": Robert Manning to NH, Aug. 14, 1813, Berg.

25. "I do not forget": Richard Manning to ECH, Jan. 29, 1815, PE.

25. "I should rather live": Richard Manning to Robert Manning, Dec. 18, 1820, PE.

25. So he put off moving: Robert Manning was also encumbered by the family stage business, run for a time by Samuel and William Manning until "illicit trade" (likely gunrunning) threatened to bankrupt it, and Robert was forced to take it over in early 1815. See Bentley, *Diary,* vol. 4, p. 307, and (Salem) *Essex Register,* Jan. 4, 1815, p. 2.

25. It seems a strange choice—except: His twenty-seven-year-old aunt, the beloved and intelligent Maria Manning, died May 20, 1814.

26. In one of his early: See "Sights from a Steeple," in *Tales,* pp. 42–48.

26. Less than six weeks: EH to JTF, [Salem, Dec. 12, 1870], BPL.

26. "work at his Trade": Joseph Lakeman to Nathaniel Wells, Feb. 25, 1814, BY. Wrote NH: "I had an Uncle John, who went a voyage to sea, about the beginning of the war of 1812, and has never returned to this hour" (*EN,* vol. 1, June 30, 1854, pp. 98–99).

26. With Grandfather Manning dead: EH to JTF, Dec. 13 and 16 [1870], BPL.

26. "Like a lame man": "The Gentle Boy," in *Tales,* p. 119; the story's troubled depiction of Ilbrahim's mother has been exhaustively examined elsewhere: see, for instance, Frederick C. Crews, *The Sins of the Fathers: Hawthorne's Psychological Themes* (New York: Oxford Univ. Press, 1966), and Edwin Haviland Miller, *Salem Is My Dwelling Place* (Iowa City: Univ. of Iowa Press, 1991).

26. "Nathaniel was particularly": EH to JTF, Dec. 12 [1870], BPL.

26. "Everybody thought": EH to UH, Nov. 23, 1865, transcribed by JH, Bancroft.

27. Legend says: Elizabeth Manning, "The Boyhood of Hawthorne," p. 503.

27. There was talk: See, for instance, Putnam, *Chronicles of Old Salem,* p. 54.

27. Robert and Priscilla Manning . . . sent all three: In 1808 both NH and EH were sent to Elizabeth Carlton, on Union Street, for instruction. During 1810–11, NH attended the school of Francis Moore, on Herbert Street. EH was instructed by Nathaniel's future mother-in-law, Elizabeth Peabody, and then by her sister, the more orthodox Amelia P. Curtis, 1812–15. Receipts and, in the case of EH, certificates of merit may be found in PE and the Berg. Because no receipts are available for MLH, much less is known about her education, but eventually she too was taught by Mrs. Curtis.

27. "One of the peculiarities": Quoted in *NHHW,* vol. 1, p. 95.

27. During school recess: *Personal Recollections,* pp. 34–35.

27. Taking refuge: JH, notes, PE.

28. "If he had been educated": EH to UH, Nov. 12, 1865, transcribed by JH, Bancroft.

28. "He used to invent": EH to JTF, Dec. 13 and 16 [1870], BPL.

28. By the winter of 1815: See Mary Manning to Richard Manning, Dec. 14, 1814, PE; ECH to Richard Manning, Jan. 20, 1815, Bowdoin.

28. Thrilled by the news: Richard Manning to Robert Manning, Nov. 16, 1814.

CHAPTER THREE: THE FOREST OF ARDEN

29. Of the three Hathorne: NH to SH, Apr. 14, 1844, *C* XVI, p. 31.

29. "I have a better opinion": EH to UH, Mar. 1, 1865, transcribed by JH, Bancroft.

29. "You are learning": Robert Manning to EH, Aug. 14, 1813, Berg.

29. "Elizabeth in particular"; an early teacher: Richard Manning to Robert Manning, Nov. 10, 1816, PE; Certificate of Merit, Oct. 1814, signed by A. P. Curtis, preceptoress, Berg. Amelia Curtis was Sophia Peabody's aunt.

29. "Useful knowledge"; "if you ever": EH to UH, June 19, 1868, transcribed by JH, Bancroft; EH to Rebecca Manning, n.d., PE.

30. "Elizabeth is not available": SH to Mrs. EPP Sept. 27, 1849, Berg. Manning Hawthorne, "Aunt Ebe: Some Letters of Elizabeth M. Hawthorne," *New England Quarterly* 1:20 (1947), p. 215.

30. She rose late: EH to UH, Dec. 20, 1865, transcribed by JH, Bancroft; EH to UH, Mar. 10 [1872], transcribed by JH, Bancroft.

30. "People can talk": EH to Mary Manning, Aug. 1816, Bowdoin.

30. "The only argument": EH to UH, Mar. 1, 1865, transcribed by JH, Bancroft.

30. "The very best way": EH to UH, June 7, 1872, Huntington.

30. "I am something": EH to Rebecca Manning, Aug. 7, 1875, PE.

30. "I should not like to feel": EH to SH, June 15, 1842, Berg.

30. "it was a love disappointment": JH, notebook, Morgan; see Norman Holmes Pearson, "Elizabeth Peabody on Hawthorne," *Essex Institute Historical Collections* 94 (1958), p. 263.

30. "The beautiful Miss": "Domestic Intelligence," Jan. 1822, *Spectator,* in *Miscellaneous Prose and Verse, C* XXIII, p. 53.

30. Nathaniel may have: Briggs married Hepsebeth Collins, whose name antici-

pates Hepzibah Pyncheon's in *The House of the Seven Gables*. Alluding to Elizabeth Hawthorne, the unwed "Hepzibah" devotes herself not to a Captain Briggs but to her brother. For information on Briggs, see "Catalogue of Portraits in the Museum of Salem," *Essex Institute Historical Collections* 73 (1937), pp. 187–88.

30. As her nephew: JH, "My Aunt Elizabeth Hawthorne," typescript, Bancroft.
30. "She is the most sensible": NH to WDT, May 17, 1852, *C* XVIII, p. 456.
31. "The only thing I fear": *NHHW,* vol. 1, p. 5.
31. "You must never expect": NH to SH, Apr. 17, 1839, *C* XV, p. 298.
31. As children: Copybook, circa 1815, UVA. An untitled poem of Nathaniel's reads: "The charms of sweet Music no pencil can paint/They calm the rude Savage, enliven the Saint,/Make sweeter our pleasures, more joyous our joy/ With raptures we feel, yet those raptures ne'er cloy." See *Miscellaneous Prose and Verse, C* XXIII, p. 3.
32. "made it the habit": EPP to Francis Henry Lee, n.y. [1885], PE.
32. If the Hathornes took: Rebecca Manning, "Some Facts about Hawthorne," PE; Hawthorne-Manning, receipts, PE. They included boarding expenses dated from July 1, 1808, to July 1, 1815. Interestingly, NH's board, at $1.50 per week, was the most expensive; EH cost her mother 28 pence per week, and Maria Louisa, 18 pence.
32. "improving property": Mary Manning to Richard Manning, Dec. 14, 1814, PE.
32. "You say he is": Richard Manning to Robert Manning, May 3, 1815, PE. Many of Richard Manning's letters link him to NH, as the family no doubt did as well.
32. Linked once again: See EH to Richard Manning, May 29, 1815, Bowdoin.
32. Having married Susan Dingley . . . "Manning's Folly": Richard Manning to Robert Manning, Aug. 16, 1815, PE; Ernest Knight, *The Origin and History of Raymondtown* (Norway, Maine: Oxford Hills Press, 1974), p. 81. Robert Manning shipped the glass from Salem; its origin is unknown.
33. "Stay here one summer": EH to Mary Manning, Aug. 1816, Bowdoin.
33. "It is true we": ECH to Priscilla Manning, Sept. 14, 1816, Bowdoin. A week earlier, in Richard Manning to Robert Manning, Sept. 9, 1816, PE, her brother had said that ECH has "almost concluded to send for her Furniture & remove with Samuel on the [Bridgton] Farm," even though he would have preferred to see her settled in a more profitable place closer by.
33. To that end, she asked: EH to Miriam Manning, Oct. 28, 1816, Bowdoin.
33. The Hathornes packed: See Richard Manning to Robert Manning, Nov. 10, 1816, PE. It's not clear where NH went to school at this time; Worcester had given up his classes, and even Ebe did not yet know when she wrote her grandmother in October asking for details. For some interesting speculations, see Moore, *The Salem World of Nathaniel Hawthorne,* pp. 85–86.
34. Plain, symmetrical: Richard Manning to Robert Manning, Feb. 25, 1818, PE; Jeremiah Briggs to Robert Manning, Mar. 21, 1818, PE.
34. "I do not feel": EH to Priscilla Manning Dike, Dec. 15, 1818, Bowdoin. Priscilla Manning had married John Dike the year before.

34. He tracked bears . . . Aunt Mary warned: Mary Manning to ECH, Nov. 17, 1818, PE.

34. One could live best: EH to UH, Feb. 14, 1862, Bancroft.

34. "I ran quite wild": *NHHW,* vol. 1, pp. 95–96.

35. "It did him": EH to JTF, Dec. 12 [1870], BPL.

35. "upon any and all": Samuel T. Pickard, *Hawthorne's First Diary, With an Account of its Discovery and Loss* (Boston: Houghton Mifflin, 1897), p. 37. The date of the inscription is given as June 1, 1816, which accords with the Hathornes' first visit to Raymond.

35. "clumsy," "singularly destitute": *NHHW,* vol. 1, p. 94.

35. She remembered . . . Uncle Robert Manning's son: See Richard C. Manning to HB, Feb. 16, 1871, Bowdoin.

35. "a literary curiosity": Samuel T. Pickard, "Is 'Hawthorne's First Diary' a Forgery?," *Dial* 33 (Apr. 16, 1902), p. 155; Samuel T. Pickard to Joseph McDonough, July 24, 1906, Univ. of Rochester Library.

36. Indeed it is: Pickard admitted, "I am puzzled, and have lost hope of ever solving the mystery." Not only did Manning's literate inscription seem suspect, but he had learned that one of the incidents recounted had not occurred until 1828. Pickard tentatively concluded, then, that only parts of the diary may have been genuine. See Pickard, "Is 'Hawthorne's First Diary' a Forgery?," p. 155. The matter remains a mystery despite Gloria Erlich's meticulous case against Pickard, suggesting he was the author of the entire hoax. See "Who Wrote Hawthorne's First Diary?" *Nathaniel Hawthorne Journal,* 1977, ed. C. E. Frazer Clark Jr., pp. 37–70.

36. "I have made": *Hawthorne's First Diary,* p. 97.

36. "This morning I saw": *Hawthorne's First Diary,* p. 68.

36. "Since the loss": *Hawthorne's First Diary,* p. 49.

36. "I was almost sorry": *Hawthorne's First Diary,* p. 88.

36. We glimpse Robert Manning: William H. Manning, *The Manning Families of New England* (Salem, Mass.: Salem Press, 1902), p. 729.

37. "An orchard has": Preface to *Mosses from an Old Manse,* in *Tales,* p. 1130.

37. In it, Manning praises: Robert Manning, *The Book of Fruits* (Salem, Mass.: Ives & Jewett, 1838), p. 10.

38. "Though he had": "Passages from a Relinquished Work," in *Tales,* pp. 175–76.

38. He corrected the grammar: Mary Manning to Robert Manning, Dec. 1, 1818, PE.

38. "The older 'dear uncle' ": Robert Manning to NH, Aug. 14, 1813, Berg.

38. Richard went to Portland; "dolefull complaints": Richard Manning to Robert Manning, Jan. [19], 1819, PE; Robert Manning to Miriam Manning, Mar. 9, 1819, PE.

38. "I have no chance": Richard Manning to Robert Manning, Apr. 28, 1819, PE.

38. The Mannings ignored him: Richard Manning to Robert Manning, Dec. 18, 1820, PE.

38. "I am sorry": NH to Robert Manning, May 16, 1819, *C* XV, p. 111.

39. "He sighs for": Mary Manning to ECH, July 6 [1819], Bowdoin.

39. "I have no employment": Robert Manning to MLH, Feb. 8, 1820, Bowdoin.
39. "Aunt Mary is continually" . . . "If I ever": NH to ECH, Mar. 7, 1820, *C*XV, p. 117.
39. "It seems very lonesome": NH to Robert Manning, July 26, 1819, *C*XV, p. 112.
39. "How often do I": NH to MLH, Mar. 21, 1820, *C*XV, p. 119.
39. "Oh how I wish": NH to ECH, Mar. 7, 1820, *C*XV, p. 117.
39. "I shall never be": NH to MLH, Sept. 28, 1819, *C*XV, p. 114.
39. "I dreamed the other": NH to ECH, Mar. 13, 1821, *C*XV, p. 138.
39. "pressed to explain": Mellow, *Nathaniel Hawthorne in His Times,* p. 611.
40. "having spent so much": *NHHW,* vol. 1, p. 97.
40. "Tell Ebe she's not": NH to MLH, Sept. 28, 1819, *C*XV, p. 114.
40. A "Departed Genius": See, for instance, NH to MLH, Sept. 28, 1819, *C*XV, p. 114.
40. "that lone cottage": "Poetry," Aug. 21, 1820, *Spectator,* in *Miscellaneous Prose and Verse, C*XXIII, p. 24.
41. "and when Robin": "My Kinsman, Major Molineux," in *Tales,* p. 80.
41. "Those may be my rhymes": NH to MLH, Sept. 28, 1819, *C*XV, p. 114.
41. "One thing only": ECH to Richard Manning Jan. 20, 1815, Bowdoin.
41. Salem offered: See NH to ECH, Mar. 6, 1821, *C*XV, p. 137.
42. "How far preferable": Sept. 4, 1820, *Spectator,* in *Miscellaneous Prose and Verse, C*XXIII, p. 26.
42. "raises man above": [Jan. 31, 1822], *Spectator,* in *Miscellaneous Prose and Verse, C*XXIII, pp. 51, 52.
42. "What do you think": NH to ECH, Mar. 13, 1821, *C*XV, p. 138–39.

CHAPTER FOUR: THE ERA OF GOOD FEELINGS

43. "I have almost": NH to EH, Oct. 31, 1820, *C*XV, p. 132.
43. "We must not have": Mary Manning to ECH, Feb. 29, 1820, Bowdoin.
43. "So you are in": NH to ECH, Mar. 7, 1820, *C*XV, p. 117.
44. "Much time & money": Robert Manning to ECH, Oct. 24, 1820, PE.
44. "with all my might": NH to EH, Oct. 31, 1820, *C*XV, p. 132.
44. "Do you not regret": NH to ECH, Mar. 6, 1821, *C*XV, p. 137.
44. "Shall you want me": NH to ECH, Mar. 7, 1821, *C*XV, p. 117.
44. "How proud you would": NH to ECH, Mar. 13, 1821, *C*XV, pp. 138–39.
44. "An angel would fail": EH to ECH, May 14, 1822, Bowdoin.
44. At Harvard: See Manning Hawthorne, "Nathaniel Hawthorne at Bowdoin," *New England Quarterly* 13:1 (1940), p. 247; *Bowdoin College Catalogue,* 1825, Bowdoin.
45. "I am quite reconciled"; "shut out": NH to ECH, Mar. 13, 1821, *C*XV, p. 138; NH to ECH, June 19, 1821, *C*XV, p. 150.
45. "I encouraged him": Robert Manning to Miriam Lord Manning, Oct. 5, 1821, PE.
46. "a short, thick little": NH to EH, Oct. 28, 1821, *C*XV, p. 159.
46. Uncle Robert hunted . . . paid the bill: Robert Manning to Miriam Lord Manning, Oct. 5, 1821, PE. In guaranteeing the payment of all NH's expenses, Robert Manning was joined by his brother-in-law John Dike and his brother

Samuel Manning, at least in 1823. See the expense contract sent to Bowdoin from these men, Sept. 28, 1823, PE.

46. "has money enough": NH to William Manning, Oct. 9, 1821, *C*XV, p. 155.

46. "I am very well": NH to EH, Oct. 28, 1821, *C*XV, p. 159.

47. "to induce your Son": William Allen to ECH, May 5, 1822, PE.

47. He resented regulations: *Laws of Bowdoin College*, 1822, Bowdoin.

47. In 1826: Wilmot Brookings Mitchell, *A Remarkable Bowdoin Decade* (Brunswick, Maine: Bowdoin College, 1952), p. 25.

47. "Meeting for this day": NH to EH, Oct. 28, 1821, *C*XV, p. 160.

48. Longfellow's more dissolute: See Louis C. Hatch, *The History of Bowdoin College* (Portland, Maine: Loring, Short & Harmon, 1927), p. 310.

48. Nathaniel Hathorne, an Athenaean: *Personal Recollections*, p. 32.

48. One of them, Franklin Pierce: See Ralph Waldo Emerson, *The Journals and Miscellaneous Notebooks of Ralph Waldo Emerson, 1860–1866*, ed. Linda Allandt, David Hill, et al. (Cambridge, Mass.: Belknap Press of Harvard Univ. Press, 1982), vol. 15, p. 361.

48. "noisy, foul-mouthed": Quoted in Thomas Woodson, "Introduction," *C*XV, p. 35.

49. "I got it from Stowe's": Nehemiah Cleaveland, *History of Bowdoin College*, ed. Alpheus Spring Packard (Boston: J. R. Osgood, 1882), p. 92.

49. "seemed always," "power of sympathy": "Jonathan Cilley," in *Miscellaneous Prose and Verse, C* XXIII p. 111. Commissioned by their friend John Louis O'Sullivan for the *Democratic Review*, this memorial to Cilley originally appeared in that publication in September 1838.

49. "elder brother," "simplicity of one": "Jonathan Cilley," in *Miscellaneous Prose and Verse, C*XXIII, p. 116.

49. "If Nathaniel Hathorne": *Personal Recollections*, p. 47.

50. "stretched in his own blood": "Jonathan Cilley," in *Miscellaneous Prose and Verse, C*XXIII, p. 118.

50. "shrinking almost": Samuel P. Benson to JTF, Dec. 18, 1870, copy, Bowdoin.

50. "I know not whence": Preface to *The Snow-Image*, in *Tales*, p. 1155.

50. "stands and looks": HWL, journals, Mar. 17 [1836 or 1838, Bridge on way to Washington], MS Am 1340(194), Houghton.

50. "Polished, yet natural": July 5, 1837, *AN*, p. 33.

50. Bridge long remembered: *Personal Recollections*, p. 46.

51. "so much of danger": *Personal Recollections*, p. 5.

51. "two idle lads": Preface to *The Snow-Image*, in *Tales*, p. 1155.

51. "the best friend": NH to HB, Feb. 8, 1838.

51. Then, after they ate: For admission, according to the *Bowdoin College Catalogue*, Mar. 1822, students were already expected "to write Latin grammatically, and to be well versed in Geography, in Walsh's *Arithmetic*, Cicero's *Select Orations*, the *Bucolics*, the *Georgics*, and the *Aeneid* of Virgil, Sallust, the *Greek Testament* and the *Collectanea Graeca Minora* [of the late Professor Andrew Dalzel]. They must produce certificates of their good moral character." See also Jesse Appleton, "Miscellaneous and Literary Intelligence," *North American Review* 2 (1816), p. 433.

51. By their senior year . . . They studied: See *Bowdoin College Catalogue* and Mitchell, *A Remarkable Bowdoin Decade*, pp. 17–18.

51. "timidity prevented": Samuel P. Benson to JTF, Dec. 18, 1870, copy, Bowdoin.

52. "He stood hardly": *Personal Recollections*, p. 33.

52. "In Latin and Greek": Samuel P. Benson to JTF, Dec. 18, 1870, copy, Bowdoin.

52. Otherwise he shirked: See Richard Harwell, *Hawthorne and Longfellow: A Guide to an Exhibit* (Brunswick, Maine: Bowdoin College, 1966), p. 12.

52. "enchanting topicks": Thomas C. Upham, *American Sketches* (New York: David Longworth, 1819), p. 11.

52. "reluctant step": George Thomas Packard, "Bowdoin College," *Scribner's Monthly* 12 (1876), p. 52.

52. "I love Hawthorne": Cleaveland, *History of Bowdoin College*, p. 303.

53. "I *know* that": EH to ECH, May 14, 1822, Bowdoin.

53. "As steady as": NH to EH, Aug. 5, 1822, *C* XV, p. 174.

53. His braggadocio . . . "De Patris": Minutes, Executive Government, Bowdoin College, July 26, 1824. The speech is in the Bowdoin College Library.

54. He often stopped: George J. Little to unknown, n.d., PE.

54. "I verily beleive": NH to EH, Oct. 1, 1824, *C* XV, p. 184.

54. "rarely sought": *Personal Recollections*, p. 47.

54. "My term bills": NH to EH, Oct. 1, 1824, *C* XV, p. 185.

54. "Uncle Richard seemed": NH to EH, July 14, 1825, *C* XV, p. 194.

54. "I am perfectly satisfied": EH to NH, July 14, 1825, *C* XV, p. 195.

54. "The family had before": NH to EH, July 14, 1825, *C* XV, p. 194. NH alludes to his embarrassment at unmerited praise in "Roger Malvin's Burial," calling it a "miserable and humiliating torture." See "Roger Malvin's Burial," in *Tales*, p. 97.

55. "say this for the purpose," "I did hope": NH to EH, July 14, 1825, *C* XV, p. 194.

55. Bridge declined . . . Nathaniel was Commander: *Personal Recollections*, p. 41.

55. The graduation took place: Courtesy Carolyn Moseley, Bowdoin College Archives.

57. "Already has a voice": Lawrance Thompson, *Young Longfellow* (New York: Macmillan, 1938), p. 71.

CHAPTER FIVE: THAT DREAM OF UNDYING FAME

58. "without mercy": Preface to *Twice-told Tales*," in *Tales*, p. 1150; see also NH to Cornelius Mathews and ED, Dec. 22, 1841, *C* XV, p. 600.

58. "I am as tractable": NH to Charles W. Webber, Dec. 14, 1848, *C* XVI, p. 251.

58. "He always puts": MM to Horace Mann Jr., Apr. 24, 1864, Antioch.

59. "formed several plans": *Personal Recollections*, p. 67.

59. "Uncle Manning's counting-house": *Personal Recollections*, p. 67.

59. But even before graduating: "The Ocean" and "Moonlight," in *Miscellaneous Prose and Verse*, *C* XXIII, pp. 6–7. Both were published before his graduation, the former appearing in the *Salem Gazette*, Aug. 26, 1825, and the latter in the *Gazette*, Sept. 2, 1825.

59. Then he'd walk . . . Or he'd hike: George Holyoke to G. M. Williamson, Nov.

10, 1901, BY; Rebecca Manning, "Some Facts about Hawthorne," PE; EH to UH, Feb. 26, 1865, transcribed by JH, Bancroft; EH to JTF, Dec. 26 [1870], BPL.

59. Ebe recalled: See Chapter 2; EH also remembered that two stories, "Alice Doane" and "Susan Grey," were tales of witchcraft, EH to UH, Feb. 26, 1865, transcribed by JH, Bancroft. "Alice Doane" is likely an earlier version of the story "Alice Doane's Appeal," published in *The Token* in 1835. For the best account and possible dating of NH's early tales, see Nelson F. Adkins, "The Early Projected Works of Nathaniel Hawthorne," *Papers of the Bibliographical Society of America* 39 (1945), pp. 119–55, and Nelson F. Adkins "Notes on the Hawthorne Canon," *Papers of the Bibliographical Society of America* 60 (1966), pp. 364–67. Although most scholars agree with Adkins and the *Centenary* editors in doubting that NH wrote "The Interrupted Nuptials," published on Oct. 12, 1827, in the *Salem Gazette,* the crudely melodramatic story could represent NH's earliest style; and with its tale of a sister and brother about to wed one another, it thematically fits the sketchy outline of "We Are Seven." See C. E. Frazer Clark Jr., " 'The Interrupted Nuptials': A Question of Attribution," *Nathaniel Hawthorne Journal,* 1971, ed. C. E. Frazer Clark Jr., pp. 49–66.

59. "That wild fellow": "P's Correspondence," in *Tales,* p. 1020.

59. "It is American": John Neal, *American Writers: A Series of Papers Contributed to Blackwood's Magazine,* ed. Fred Lewis Pattee (Durham, N.C.: Duke Univ. Press, 1937), pp. 10, 200. See also David Reynolds, *Beneath the American Renaissance* (Cambridge, Mass.: Harvard Univ. Press, 1989), pp. 198–214.

59. However, in his earliest: John Neal's own Quaker upbringing and the mistreatment he endured in boyhood bear comparison to Hawthorne's tale of the woebegone Quaker child of "The Gentle Boy." See Benjamin Lease, *That Wild Fellow John Neal and the American Literary Revolution* (Chicago: Univ. of Chicago Press, 1972).

60. Two of the stories: "The Hollow of the Three Hills" was published without attribution in the *Salem Gazette* (Nov. 12, 1830), and "An Old Woman's Tale" appeared without attribution in the *Gazette* (Dec. 21, 1830). The setting of "The Hollow of the Three Hills" suggests a very early composition date, for its visionary landscape loosely refers to Portland, Maine, a city set in a hollow among two hills—as well as Boston, the standard interpretation.

60. "Then came a measured": "The Hollow of the Three Hills," in *Tales,* p. 33. See Dan McCall, *Citizens of Somewhere Else* (Ithaca, N.Y.: Cornell Univ. Press, 1999), chap. 2, whose fine analysis of this story also links it to several Dickinson poems and to John Gibson Lockhart's *Adam Blair,* an understated connection.

60. "Oho!": "An Old Woman's Tale," in *Tales,* p. 33.

60. Identifying with: See Horace Conolly to William D. Northend to Henry Johnson, n.d., Bowdoin.

61. "All really educated men": "New York University," in *Hawthorne as Editor,* ed. Arlin Turner (University: Louisiana State Univ. Press, 1941), p. 195. Likely the comment is NH's, or at least was approved by him, if written by EH.

61. His reading . . . He relished: EH to JTF, Jan. 28, 1871, BPL.

61. They used Aunt Mary Manning's: The most complete list of the borrowings from the Salem Athenaeum remains Marion L. Kesselring, "Hawthorne's Reading, 1828–1850," *Bulletin of the New York Public Library* 53:2 (Feb. 1949), pp. 55–71, 121–38, 173–94. But Kesselring, like later biographers, tends to forget that these books served the entire Hawthorne family, who were avid readers. For example, the course in French literature that Kesselring says Hawthorne planned for himself was doubtless planned by EH for herself, and many of the novels were doubtless intended for LH or ECH and perhaps other family members. When she visited relatives, LH, herself a proud reader, told her mother in mock horror that "I heard a young lady the other day talking about Goldsmith the author of Rasselas!" Then she asked plaintively, "Have you read anything new since I came away? There is nothing to read here. I should really like a good book" (LH to ECH, Aug. 12, 1827, Berg).

61. "I am sure nobody": EH to UH, Feb. 26, 1865, transcribed by JH, Bancroft.

61. "fantastic dreams": "The Hollow of the Three Hills," in *Tales*, p. 7.

62. "The knowledge, communicated," "Fancy must": "Sir William Phips," in *Tales*, p. 12.

62. "a mood half savage": *Personal Recollections*, p. 68.

62. In another version of events: EH to UH, Feb. 26, 1865, transcribed by JH, Bancroft. See also Lathrop, *A Study of Nathaniel Hawthorne*, p. 135.

62. "inexorable": *Personal Recollections*, p. 68.

62. "He did not wish": JH, "Hawthorne's Philosophy," holograph manuscript, Huntington. See also J. Donald Crowley, "Historical Commentary," in *Twice-told Tales, C* IX, p. 486.

62. Presumably he put: AF to JH, Feb. 27, 1904, bMS Am 1745(4), Houghton.

62. Similarly, he burned: See, for example, *Personal Recollections*, p. 69. See also SH to JTF, Oct. 14, 1865, BPL: "If he journalized before 1835, he destroyed the books."

62. "Knowing the impossibility": "Passages from a Relinquished Work," in *Tales*, p. 183. See Chapter 6: three tales sent to Samuel Goodrich in 1830, "Alice Doane," "The Gentle Boy," and "My Uncle Molineux," were doubtless modified versions, if not the actual stories, originally intended for *Seven Tales*.

63. On March 30, 1826: Elizabeth Manning, "The Boyhood of Hawthorne," p. 501.

63. In 1825: Nathaniel Hathorne, logbook, inscribed by NH in 1825, Huntington.

63. "Nath. Hawthorne": See the logbook of NH's father, inscribed by NH in 1825 as "Nathaniel Hathorne, Salem 1825; Nathaniel Hawthorne," Huntington. He also inscribed his name "Nath. Hawthorne" on the 1825 *Memoir of the Life of Josiah Quincy* (Boston: Hilliard, 1825). Hawthorne likely changed the spelling of his name when he reached his majority, although I have found no corroborating legal documents.

63. "We were in those days": EH to UH, Feb. 26, 1865, transcribed by JH, Bancroft.

63. When Samuel introduced . . . a great-uncle: Colonel John Hathorne (1749–1834), the nephew of NH's grandfather Daniel, was a moderately wealthy mer-

chant involved in the shipping, dry goods, and goldsmith businesses (the possible model for Peter Hovenden in "The Artist of the Beautiful") and a gentleman farmer who retired to his estate near Salem Neck. He remained a close friend of the Reverend William Bentley and a Republican. His children died young, with the exception of Ebenezer (1789–1858), a Custom House clerk and Democrat whom NH knew. But doubtless NH's animosity toward the Hathornes came in part from the stories told him by his second cousin Susanna Ingersoll. See Chapter 11.

63. "Perhaps that is": Horace Conolly to William D. Northend to Henry Johnson, n.d., Bowdoin. In old documents, the name was variously spelled Hathorn, Hathorne, Harthorne, and Hawthorne.

63. Whatever the reason: George William Curtis, who met Hawthorne at Brook Farm, wrote soon after Hawthorne's death that he'd changed the spelling of his name after discovering the original spelling. See George William Curtis, "Nathaniel Hawthorne," *Essays from the North American Review,* ed. Allen Thorndike Rice (New York: D. Appleton, 1879), p. 336; the essay originally appeared as "Hawthorne," *North American Review* 99 (Oct. 1864), pp. 539–57.

64. The other youth: Another model for the character is his classmate Gorham Deane, who died before graduation, and to a lesser extent Cotton Mather's brother Nathanael, buried at Charter Street. Cotton Mather said that "study kill'd him." See Kenneth Silverman, *Cotton Mather and His Times* (New York: Harper & Row, 1984), pp. 76–77. The inscription is still visible, its irony intact and not lost on Hawthorne: "An Aged person that had seen but Nineteen Winters in the World." See also "Lost Notebook," n.d., in *Miscellaneous Prose and Verse, C* XXIII, p. 205.

64. Made for and by: Walcott also bears comparison with Bridge, who began to call himself Edward in his letters to Hawthorne. Also, taking the epigraph of the first chapter from *Love's Labour's Lost,* Hawthorne compares the all-male Harley College to the commonwealth of learning ridiculed by Shakespeare. Thus Hawthorne implies that Fanshawe ultimately chooses not just celibacy but a celibacy sanctioned by (and performed in) the company of men.

64. "dreams of undying fame": *Fanshawe,* p. 18.

64. "The road, at all times": *Fanshawe,* p. 89.

64. "She knew not": *Fanshawe,* p. 97.

65. "tie that shall": *Fanshawe,* pp. 99, 111.

65. "drew her husband": *Fanshawe,* p. 114.

65. "Theirs was a long": *Fanshawe,* p. 114.

65. Grandmother Manning died: In addition, at her death Maria Manning had bequeathed half of the property due her from their father's estate.

65. "It was my fortune": Quoted in *NHHW,* vol. 1, p. 96, and corroborated almost verbatim in Richard Stoddard, "Nathaniel Hawthorne," *National Magazine* 2:1 (1853), p. 18.

66. Reportedly given: Master's degree, Huntington. One suspects that some sort of proof of advanced scholarship was required, although the degree was conferred routinely, according to the *Laws of Bowdoin College,* 1825 printing, courtesy Carolyn Moseley: "Law 61. Every Bachelor, who, in the third year after the

first degree given to his class, having preserved a good moral character, shall attend at commencement and perform the appointed public exercises, unless excused, may receive the degree of Master of Arts. The part to be performed by a Bachelor shall be presented to the President for his examination as early as the Monday before commencement. The candidates for a Medical degree shall also, unless excused, attend at commencement, and must possess a good moral character. Law 62. Each candidate for the second degree shall pay the sum of five dollars for the public dinner. Candidates for either degree shall pay five dollars each to the Treasurer for the President. Candidates for either degree, if they seasonably request it, may be furnished with a diploma, signed by the President and Secretary of the Trustees, for which three dollars shall be paid to the Treasurer, one of which is for the President."

When Hawthorne was awarded his degree, so were John S. C. Abbot, Samuel P. Benson, Cyrus H. Coolidge, David Hayes, William Hale, John D. Kinsman, Josiah S. Little, Stephen Longfellow, Henry W. Longfellow, Thomas Macdougall, George W. Pierce, and Edward J. Vose.

Hawthorne's master's degree was recorded in the Sept. 3, 1828, Votes of the Trustees.

66. "I wish to God": Horace Conolly to William D. Northend to Henry Johnson, n.d., Bowdoin.

66. "not going to work"; "as so much": EH to JTF, Dec. 13 and 16 [1870], BPL; Rebecca Manning, "Some Thoughts about Hawthorne," PE.

66. "not to be forgotten" . . . "He could have borne": "The Ambitious Guest," in *Tales,* p. 301.

66. "it is our nature": "The Ambitious Guest," in *Tales,* p. 303.

66. "The story had been told": "The Ambitious Guest," in *Tales,* p. 306.

66. "Who has not heard": "The Ambitious Guest," *Tales,* p. 306.

67. "Fame—some very": "Lost Notebook," in *Miscellaneous Prose and Verse,* *C* XXIII, p. 169.

67. They were all killed: NH visited the scene of the disaster in 1832 but may have begun the story, or an early version of it, much earlier. "The Ambitious Guest" first appeared in the *New-England Magazine* 8 (June 1835), but the date of the composition of this and other early stories is far from certain. I would date it quite early, perhaps shortly after the Willey disaster and/or around when *Fanshawe* was written. Parts of "The Ambitious Guest" also resemble *Fanshawe* (which EH said was begun early, in college). The villain dies below a precipice in an unmarked grave, "but the legend, though my version of it may be forgotten, will long be traditional in that lonely spot, and give to the rock, and the precipice, and the fountain, an interest thrilling to the bosom of the romantic wanderer" (p. 108).

Although many scholars assume Hawthorne destroyed most of the manuscripts for "We Are Seven," I tend to think that he probably saved ample portions of them to rework later, as in the case of "Alice Doane." There is also reason to believe that some of Hawthorne's unattributed work has yet to be discovered. In any case, given the obscure chronology of composition, I tend to group several stories thematically and on occasion, as in the case of

"The Ambitious Guest" and "Roger Malvin's Burial," I willingly entertain the notion that some stories were conceived or composed earlier than traditionally assumed and then recycled for the later volume, *Provincial Tales*. Certainly Hawthorne did just this when gathering materials for *Twice-told Tales* and *Mosses from an Old Manse*.

68. The surrogate father's: "Roger Malvin's Burial," first published in 1831 in *The Token* (dated 1832). See also Nina Baym, *The Shape of Hawthorne's Career* (Ithaca, N.Y.: Cornell Univ. Press, 1976), pp. 15–53.

68. "I have loved you": "Roger Malvin's Burial," in *Tales*, p. 90.

68. "mental horrors": "Roger Malvin's Burial," in *Tales*, p. 98.

69. "one secret thought": "Roger Malvin's Burial," in *Tales*, p. 98.

69. "not unlike a gigantic gravestone": "Roger Malvin's Burial," in *Tales*, p. 88.

69. "The vow that": "Roger Malvin's Burial," in *Tales*, p. 107.

69. Fusing psychological obsession: Frederick Crews, *The Sins of the Fathers*, pp. 80–95, remains the best psychological reading of the story; similarly, Michael Colacurcio's historicist reading, in *The Province of Piety* (Durham, N.C.: Duke Univ. Press, 1995), pp. 107–30, has not been surpassed, but see Diane Naples, " 'Roger Malvin's Burial': A Parable for Historians?," *American Transcendental Quarterly* 13 (1972), pp. 45–48. Gloria Erlich usefully follows Crews but insists on interpreting Roger Malvin solely as Robert Manning, when the initials "RM" refer to Grandfather Manning as well as his two sons; see Erlich, *Family Themes and Hawthorne's Fiction*, pp. 113–17.

69. "Your tears" . . . "sin was": "Roger Malvin's Burial," in *Tales*, p. 107.

69. "Your father": EH to UH, Feb. 26, 1865, transcribed by JH, Bancroft.

70. A stalwart Democrat: EH to UH, Feb. 26, 1865, transcribed by JH, Bancroft; EH to JTF, Dec. 26 [1870], BPL.

70. "At that time": According to EH, NH met "Susan" circa 1833. See EH to UH, transcribed by JH, Feb. 14, 1862, Bancroft.

70. "I should have feared": EH to JTF, Dec. 26 [1870], BPL.

70. Children of the night: See "The Interrupted Nuptials," published Oct. 12, 1827, *Salem Gazette*.

70. "they know not what": "Alice Doane's Appeal," in *Tales*, p. 206.

71. "Thoughts meant": "Alice Doane's Appeal," in *Tales*, p. 207.

71. "my very," "with indisputable": "Alice Doane's Appeal," in *Tales*, p. 209.

71. "as if a fiend": "Alice Doane's Appeal," in *Tales*, p. 211.

71. The women don't: "Alice Doane's Appeal," in *Tales*, p. 216.

71. "We are a people": "Alice Doane's Appeal," in *Tales*, p. 206.

71. The narrator: A fine discussion of the artist in Hawthorne's work remains Millicent Bell, *Hawthorne's View of the Artist* (Albany: State Univ. of New York, 1962).

CHAPTER SIX: STORYTELLER

73. "By some fatality": EH to UH, Feb. 26, 1865, transcribed by JH, Bancroft.

73. They moved: The family sold Mary Manning the Herbert Street property for two thousand dollars on June 2, 1829; she converted the house for tenants.

73. "When sorrow": MM to Sarah Forbes, May 29, 1864, MHS.

73. "I, being heir": "Passages from a Relinquished Work," in *Tales*, p. 175.

74. By that spring: Conolly insisted that Hawthorne's visit to the graves of the Connecticut "regicides," Edward Whalley, William Goff, and John Dixwell, inspired his story "The Gray Champion." See Horace Conolly to William D. Northend, transcribed by Miss Pendleton, Nov. 1901, Bowdoin. See also Manning Hawthorne, "Hawthorne and 'The Man of God,'" *Colophon* 2:2 (winter 1937), p. 263.

74. "a fair prospect": Quoted in Benjamin Lease, *That Wild Fellow John Neal* (Chicago: Univ. of Chicago Press, 1972), p. 133.

74. "the superstitions": NH to Samuel Goodrich, Dec. 20, 1829, *C* XV, p. 199.

74. He mailed a few: The fullest account of Goodrich's business practices and its relation to Hawthorne appears in Wayne Allen Jones, "The Hawthorne-Goodrich Relationship," *Nathaniel Hawthorne Journal*, 1975, ed. C. E. Frazer Clark Jr., pp. 91–140.

74. "which seemed to me": Samuel G. Goodrich, *Recollections of a Lifetime* (New York: Miller, Orton & Mulligan, 1856), vol. 2, p. 270.

74. More likely: See Cleaveland, *History of Bowdoin College*, p. 304. Of course, by the time these men looked backward, there was no dearth of self-congratulatory friends eager to credit themselves with engendering Hawthorne's career. Regardless, Cheever and Hawthorne knew each other at Bowdoin and in Salem, although, as Hawthorne's sister pointed out, they were "not in the . . . same set [at Bowdoin]." Cheever supported capital punishment and abolition, and in 1835 published a temperance article about a fictional deacon who owned a distillery. John Stone, the Unitarian deacon who in fact did own a distillery, sued for libel. Cheever was flogged and jailed for thirty days, during which time Hawthorne, who did not share his views about temperance or abolition, visited him, according to EH. See EH to JTF, Dec. 26 [1870], BPL.

74. "unsettled": Goodrich, *Recollections of a Lifetime*, vol. 2, p. 271.

74. "You do not anticipate": NH to Samuel Goodrich, Dec. 20, 1829, *C* XV, p. 199.

75. Other stories: See also Richard P. Adams, "Hawthorne's *Provincial Tales*," *New England Quarterly* 30 (1957), pp. 39–57, and Baym, *The Shape of Hawthorne's Career*, pp. 30–40, whose inclination, as she puts it, is "to stick with the known group [which includes "The Wives of the Dead"] and reject the others." I am not convinced about putting "The Wives of the Dead" in this group. "The Wives of the Dead" appeared in an early *Token* but the rest were published separately in 1835, after Hawthorne abandoned any hope of a collection. The *Centenary* editors assume that the publication date precludes their inclusion in *Provincial Tales;* I disagree. However, "The Wedding-Knell" may also have been one of the stories, or a version of one, originally written for *Provincial Tales*.

75. "It was near": "My Kinsman, Major Molineux," in *Tales*, p. 68.

75. "Deep as Dante": "Hawthorne and His Mosses, by a Virginian spending July in Vermont," *Literary World*, Aug. 17, 24, 1850, pp. 125–27, 145–57, in *Nathaniel Hawthorne: The Contemporary Reviews*, eds. Buford Jones and John Idol (New York: Cambridge Univ. Press, 1994), p. 113.

75. "without the help": "My Kinsman, Major Molineux," in *Tales,* p. 87. Exegesis of this story is a cottage industry. My discussion profits from Colacurcio, *The Province of Piety,* pp. 135–53; Roy Harvey Pearce, "Robin Molineux on the Analyst's Couch: A Note on the Limits of Psychoanalytic Criticism," *Criticism* 1 (1959), pp. 83–90, and T. Walter Herbert Jr., "Doing Cultural Work: 'My Kinsman, Major Molineux' and the Construction of the Self-made Man," *Studies in the Novel* 23:1 (spring 1991), pp. 20–27. Readers interested in a historical interpretation of the novel should consult Colacurcio and Peter Shaw, *American Patriots and the Rituals of Revolution* (Cambridge, Mass.: Harvard Univ. Press, 1981), pp. 18–21, 126–29, 210–31.

76. "the loudest there": "My Kinsman, Major Molineux," in *Tales,* p. 87.

76. He rejected "Alice Doane": Samuel Goodrich to NH, Jan. 19, 1830, quoted in *NHHW,* vol. 1, p. 132.

76. "born to do": NH to EPP, Aug. 13, 1857, *C* XVIII, p. 89.

76. For his part, Goodrich: Goodrich, *Recollections of a Lifetime,* vol. 2, pp. 269–70.

76. Goodrich paid him: The stories are: for the *Token* dated 1831, "Sights from a Steeple," "Dr. Bullivant," and "The Haunted Quack"; for the *Token* dated 1832, "The Wives of the Dead," "Roger Malvin's Burial," "Major Molineaux," and "The Gentle Boy"; and "The Canterbury Pilgrims," "The Seven Vagabonds," and the sketch "Sir William Pepperell" for the 1833 *Token.* See also Jones, "The Hawthorne-Goodrich Relationship," p. 102.

77. "particularly" he rationalized: Samuel G. Goodrich to NH, May 31, 1831, quoted in *NHHW,* vol. 1, p. 132.

77. Historical sketches: I tend to agree with Donald C. Gallup ("On Hawthorne's Authorship of 'The Battle-Omen,'" *New England Quarterly* 9:4 [Dec. 1936], pp. 690–99), who places "The Battle Omen" among NH's early sketches. It appeared in the *Gazette* on Nov. 2, 1830; "The Hollow of the Three Hills" on Nov. 12, 1830; "Sir William Phips" on Nov. 23, 1830; "Mrs. Hutchinson" on Dec. 7, 1830; "An Old Woman's Tale," Dec. 21, 1830; and "Dr. Bullivant," Jan. 11, 1831. The *Gazette's* Federalist/Whig politics may have influenced Hawthorne's attitudes toward these figures, or at least deepened his own satire. By this time the *Gazette* was edited by NH's friend Caleb Foote. NH to Carey & Lea, Jan. 27, 1832, *C* XV, p. 222.

77. "He never liked": EH to JTF, Dec. 26 [1870], BPL.

77. "was resolved not": JH, "Hawthorne's Philosophy," holograph, Huntington.

77. He'd planned: EH to UH, Feb. 26, 1865, transcribed by JH, Bancroft.

77. "I nourished": EH to JTF, Dec. 12 [1870], BPL; "The Journal of a Solitary Man," in *Tales,* pp. 490–91.

78. So he got hold: EH to JTF, Jan. 28, 1871, BPL; *Personal Recollections,* p. 68.

78. His argument . . . "medium" . . . "naked mind": "Mrs. Hutchinson," in *Tales,* pp. 18–19. Note that Hawthorne uses almost identical language in the "Custom-House" introduction to *The Scarlet Letter.* Overall the sketch also bears comparison with Harriet Vaughn Cheney's "A Peep at the Pilgrims," to which he may be responding; see Reynolds, *Beneath the American Renaissance,* p. 344. And the matter of Hawthorne's identification with women is provocatively explored by Robert K. Martin, "Hester Prynne, C'est Moi," in *Engender-*

ing Men, eds. Joseph Boone and Michael Cudder (New York: Routledge, 1990), pp. 122–39.

79. "It is one of my": "Passages from a Relinquished Work," in *Tales,* p. 183.

79. "a flash": "Mrs. Hutchinson," in *Tales,* p. 23.

79. "relinquishing the immunities": "Passages from a Relinquished Work," in *Tales,* p. 183.

79. But "Mrs. Hutchinson": The monomaniacal mother of the gentle boy is somewhat more complex. For an extended, if reductive, discussion of her role, see Miller, *Salem Is My Dwelling Place.*

79. Funeral bells: I refer to "The Wedding-Knell," "The May-Pole of Merry Mount," "The White Old Maid," "The Prophetic Pictures," and "The Minister's Black Veil."

79. "I very often say": Richard Manning to Mary Manning, Feb. 18, 1831, PE.

80. "The loss of Brother": Robert Manning to Mary Manning, Aug. 22, 1830, PE.

80. "Brother William": Mary Manning to Priscilla Dike, Mar. 17, 1831, PE.

80. "on account of a book": From this leg of the journey came the story "The Canterbury Pilgrims," in which a young couple fleeing the Shakers meet with a group of pilgrims, who gloomily foretell what the couple can expect from the clutches of the world. Merchant, yeoman, yeoman's wife, and poet: all lament their fortunes, most notably the poet, who cries "shame upon the unworthy age." See "The Canterbury Pilgrims," in *Tales,* p. 159. NH to FP, June 28, 1832, *C* XV, p. 224.

80. With two hundred . . . To judge from: NH to ECH, Sept. 16, 1832, *C* XV, p. 226. Sketches like "The Notch of the White Mountains," "Old Ticonderoga," "My Visit to Niagara," and "The Canal-Boat," published in 1835–36, provide a rough itinerary; some of these sketches were later republished as "Sketches from Memory" in *MOM.* The best reproduction, though speculative, of NH's itinerary is the excellent article by Nelson F. Adkins, "The Early Projected Work of Nathaniel Hawthorne," pp. 119–55. My discussion is indebted to this essay. For an overview of the framework of *The Story Teller* and an itemization of what section of the collection may have been published where, see also Turner, *Nathaniel Hawthorne,* chap. 7.

80. "extemporaneous fictions": "The Seven Vagabonds," in *Tales,* p. 152.

80. "dull race": "Sketches from Memory," in *Tales,* p. 347.

81. "I had not of": "The Seven Vagabonds," in *Tales,* p. 141.

81. "I manufactured": "Passages from a Relinquished Work," in *Tales,* p. 183.

81. He flirts: "Passages from a Relinquished Work," in *Tales,* p. 185.

81. "We kept together": "Passages from a Relinquished Work," in *Tales,* p. 182.

81. According to his sister-in-law: Moncure Conway, *Life of Nathaniel Hawthorne* (London: Walter Scott [1890]), p. 32.

81. These sketches: "The Canterbury Pilgrims" and "The Seven Vagabonds," along with the biographical sketch "Sir William Pepperell," all appeared in the 1833 *Token,* which had merged with the *Atlantic Souvenir,* bought by Goodrich the previous year. "Sketches from Memory by a Pedestrian, No. 1" appeared in the *New-England Magazine,* November 1834, with the second installment appearing the following month as "Sketches from Memory by a Pedestrian,

No. 2." "Mr. Higginbotham's Catastrophe" was published alone in *Twice-told Tales* in 1837, and the remainder of the "Sketches from Memory" were published in *Mosses from an Old Manse*, second edition, as "Passages from a Relinquished Work." See also the argument that Park Benjamin, not Joseph Buckingham, was responsible for Hawthorne's early publication in the magazine: Lillian B. Gilkes, "Hawthorne, Park Benjamin, and S. G. Goodrich: A Three-Cornered Imbroglio," *Nathaniel Hawthorne Journal*, 1971, pp. 83–112. Having looked at the Benjamin archive at Columbia University, I tend to agree with her.

81. "So they tore up": Conway, *Life of Nathaniel Hawthorne*, p. 32.

81. "It had been long": "Fragments from the Journal of a Solitary Man," in *Tales*, p. 497. Published originally in the *American Monthly Magazine*, July 1837, this section, "My Return Home," appears to have been written earlier. The rest of the story provides a frame, evidently added later, to correspond in part with "The Devil in Manuscript." See note below.

82. "It was only after": EH to JTF, Dec. 26 [1870], BPL.

82. It features a cadaverous: *Personal Recollections*, p. 49. Elizabeth Peabody assumed Hawthorne was given the name by classmates who recognized his talent and beauty, but HB insisted Hawthorne took the name himself. The section of the *Story Teller* series in which Oberon appears, "Fragments from the Journal of a Solitary Man," was not published until July 1837 in the *American Monthly Magazine*. (Interestingly, Hawthorne never republished it in his collected stories.)

82. Hawthorne's Oberon: A motive for Oberon's return and his outlook also lies in Walter Scott's "The Lay of the 14th Minstrel," canto 6: "Breathes there the man with soul so dead"; Hawthorne quotes it in his story. Says Oberon, "I am to die 'Unwept, unhonored, and unsung' " ("The Journal of a Solitary Man," in *Tales*, p. 490).

82. "Adopt some great": "Fragments of the Journal of a Solitary Man," in *Tales*, p. 499.

82. "I have become": "The Devil in Manuscript," in *Tales*, p. 331. The story was published in the November 1835 issue of the *New-England Magazine* along with "Sketches from Memory I," evidently another piece of *The Story Teller*. The following month the magazine printed "Sketches from Memory II"; both detailed his journey through Vermont and western New York.

82. "the beaten path," "a strange": "The Devil in Manuscript," in *Tales*, p. 331.

83. "like a father," "Would you": The Devil in Manuscript," in *Tales*, pp. 333, 334.

83. "the obscurest": Preface to *Twice-told Tales*, in *Tales*, p. 1150.

83. "public opinion," "and felt": "Passages from a Relinquished Work," in *Tales*, p. 176.

84. "In the depths": "The Haunted Mind," in *Tales*, p. 202; in "The Devil in Manuscript" this tale is obliquely mentioned as one of those to be burned.

84. And with a psychological: See [William Henry Channing], "Mosses from an Old Manse," *Harbinger* 3:3 (June 27, 1846), pp. 43–44, quoted in *Nathaniel Hawthorne: The Contemporary Reviews*, p. 75. The phrase was much liked and often quoted by Sophia Hawthorne.

84. Nowhere is this more: Published in the 1836 *Token* and appearing the preceding fall. In "One Hundred Fifty Years of 'The Minister's Black Veil,'" *Nathaniel Hawthorne Review* 13:2 (fall 1987), pp. 5–12, Lea Bertani Vozar Newman suggests the story could've been written in 1829, but other scholars suggest that the tale may have been part of the *Story Teller* series. See also Adkins, "The Early Projected Works of Nathaniel Hawthorne," pp. 119–55.

84. "two folds," "probably did not": "The Minister's Black Veil," in *Tales*, p. 372. Two excellent and very different interpretations of the story may be found in Colacurcio, *The Province of Piety*, pp. 314–85, and J. Hillis Miller, *Hawthorne and History* (Cambridge, Mass.: Basil Blackwell, 1991), esp. pp. 56–128.

84. "He has changed": "The Minister's Black Veil," in *Tales*, p. 373.

85. "I can't really feel": "The Minister's Black Veil," in *Tales*, p. 372.

85. "that a simple": "The Minister's Black Veil," in *Tales*, p. 374.

85. "Have I dreaded": "The Canterbury Pilgrims," in *Tales*, p. 159.

85. "So far as I am": Preface to *Mosses from an Old Manse*, in *Tales*, p. 1147.

CHAPTER SEVEN: MR. WAKEFIELD

86. "Crafty nincompoop": "Wakefield," in *Tales*, p. 294.

86. Wakefield is a drab; "his place": "Wakefield," in *Tales*, p. 297; "Sights from a Steeple," in *Tales*, p. 43.

87. "Amid the seeming": "Wakefield," in *Tales*, p. 298.

87. And Boston women: FP to George Pierce, July 30, 1830, Bowdoin. Among other sources I've gleaned much information about Boston from William and Jane Pease, *Web of Progress: Private Values and Public Styles in Boston and Charleston, 1828–1843* (New York: Oxford Univ. Press, 1985).

87. "It is no small point": HB to NH, Feb. 20, 1836, quoted in *NHHW*, vol. 1, p. 133.

87. "a truly Yankee idea": "Fashionable Wigs," *American Magazine of Useful and Entertaining Knowledge* 2 (Boston: Bewick, 1836), p. 284.

88. "I approve": NH to EH, Mar. 22 [23], 1836, *C* XV, p. 243.

88. "There was little": "The Duston Family," *American Magazine of Useful and Entertaining Knowledge* 2 (Boston: Bewick, 1836), p. 397.

88. "You should not make": NH to EH, Mar. 22 [23], 1836, *C* XV, p. 243.

88. "You may extract": NH to EH, Feb. 10, 1836, *C* XV, p. 234.

88. "The Bewick Co.": NH to EH, Feb. 10, 1836, *C* XV, p. 234.

88. "Ebe should have": NH to LH, Mar. 3 [1836], *C* XV, p. 239.

88. "I am ashamed": NH to LH, Feb. 5, 1836, *C* XV, p. 232.

89. "For the Devil's sake": NH to LH, Feb. 15, 1836, *C* XV, p. 236.

89. "a good-natured sort": NH to LH, Feb. 15, 1836, *C* XV, p. 236.

89. "If you are willing": NH to EH, May 5, 1836, *C* XV, p. 245.

89. "It is a poor": NH to EH, May 12, 1836, *C* XV, p. 247.

89. For eight contributions: "The Great Carbuncle" may have been one of the *Story Teller* series.

89. "The brevity": For pertinent correspondence, see *NHHW*, vol. 1, p. 137. "Editorial Notice," in Turner, *Hawthorne as Editor*, p. 224.

89. This is how: "Lost Notebook," Aug. 31, 1836, in *Miscellaneous Prose and Verse,* *C* XXIII, p. 148.

90. "Brighter days": *Personal Recollections,* p. 70.

90. "My worshipful self": NH to EH, Jan. 25, 1836, *C* XV, p. 230. The *Register* reprinted "The Gentle Boy" in May 1835 and on June 4, 1835, "The Ambitious Guest." (It's not clear whether Hawthorne was paid.)

90. "What is the plan": HB to NH, quoted in *NHHW,* vol. 1, pp. 138–39.

90. "It is a singular": *Personal Recollections,* p. 70.

90. "How few have": [Park Benjamin], "Critical Notices," *American Monthly Magazine* 8 [n.s. 2] (Oct. 1836), pp. 405–7. Benjamin knew that Hawthorne intended to publish just such a volume—perhaps he'd even encouraged him to do so—and, knowing this, took the opportunity to compare Hawthorne and Nathaniel Willis, to Hawthorne's advantage to goad Samuel Goodrich, for Willis was Goodrich's friend.

90. "I fear you are": HB to NH, Oct. 22, 1836, quoted in *NHHW,* vol. 1, p. 142.

90. "You have the blues": HB to NH, Oct. 16, 1836, quoted in *NHHW,* vol. 1, p. 140.

91. "desperate coolness": HB to NH, Oct. 22, 1836, quoted in *NHHW,* vol. 1, p. 142.

91. "It will cost": Samuel G. Goodrich to HB, Oct. 20, 1836, Bowdoin.

92. "You will have more": *Personal Recollections,* p. 73.

92. "I expect, next summer": *Personal Recollections,* p. 73.

92. "an editorship": HB to NH, Feb. 1, 1837, quoted in *NHHW,* vol. 1, p. 149.

92. "I rejoice": HB to NH, Dec. 25, 1836, quoted in *NHHW,* vol. 1, p. 147.

93. "best worth offering": NH to HWL, Mar. 7, 1837, *C* XV, p. 249.

93. By June: NH to HWL, June 4, 1837, *C* XV, p. 253.

93. "spoken of in the highest": J. B. Russell to NH, Mar. 17, 1837, *NHHW,* p. 151.

93. "The *Boston Daily Advertiser*": See *Nathaniel Hawthorne: The Contemporary Reviews,* pp. 20–23.

93. "It had the credit": HB to NH, Mar. 19, 1837, quoted in *NHHW,* vol. 1, p. 151.

93. "There is little": [Horatio] B[ridge], "Twice-told Tales," *Age* 6:17 (Apr. 5, 1837), p. 3.

93. "aerial," "this fault": [Horatio] B[ridge], "Twice-told Tales," *Age* 6:17 (Apr. 5, 1837), p. 3.

93. "the soul," "rose": [Park Benjamin], "Twice-told Tales," *American Monthly Magazine* 5 (Mar. 1838), p. 281; see also SH to EPP, Apr. 23, 1838, Berg.

93. "the veterans": "The Gray Champion," in *Tales,* p. 237.

93. "Quakers, esteeming": "The Gentle Boy," in *Tales,* p. 109.

94. And though reviewers: See Kesselring, "Hawthorne's Reading, 1828–1850," pp. 55–71, 121–38, 173–94. My own investigations of Hawthorne's borrowings coincide. Samuel Johnson's style also influenced Hawthorne's.

94. "We were not": NH to HWL, Mar. 7, 1837, *C* XV, p. 249. Hawthorne refers to Longfellow's travel book.

95. "Though something": HWL to NH, Mar. 9, 1838, PE.

95. Although the review: HWL, *North American Review* 45 (July 1837), pp. 59–73.

95. "the whole Maine delegation": HB to NH, Mar. 26, 1837, quoted in *NHHW,* vol. I, p. 153.

95. "not subject": HB to J. Reynolds, Mar. 28, 1837, quoted in *NHHW,* vol. I, pp. 154, 156. See also FP to HB, Apr. 20 and May 2, 1837, Bowdoin.

95. "set your heart," "you will be": HB to NH, Apr. 7, 1837, quoted in *NHHW,* vol. I, p. 157.

96. "What! suffer": Jonathan Cilley to NH, Nov. 17, 1836, quoted in *NHHW,* vol. I, p. 144.

96. "Why should you": HB to NH, Dec. 25, 1836, quoted in *NHHW,* vol. I, p. 147.

96. "For the last ten" . . . "I have made a captive": NH to HWL, June 4, 1837, *C* XV, p. 251–52.

97. "I have now": NH to HWL, June 4, 1837, *C* XV, p. 251.

97. "I confess that": HB to NH, Apr. 14, 1837, quoted in *NHHW,* vol. I, p. 158.

97. "intellectual style": HWL, diary, June 15, 1839, MS Am 1340(194), Houghton.

97. "a grave & beautiful": SH, journal, Nov. 9, 1832.

97. "much that is": "The Letters of Ann Gillam Storrow to Jared Sparks," *Smith College Studies in History* 6:3 (Apr. 1921), pp. 230–31.

98. "She was a handsome": JH, notebook, Morgan.

98. It was Mary Silsbee: EPP recalls that NH met Silsbee through O'Sullivan, which would place their meeting after April 19, 1837 (see *NHHW,* vol. I, p. 159)—and after NH announced to Bridge his intention of marrying. However, the extant correspondence among all parties leads me to believe that NH met Silsbee earlier.

98. "With her father": M. C. S. [Mary Crowninshield Silsbee] Sparks, *Hymns, Home, Harvard* (Boston: A. Williams, 1883), p. 294. I have not discovered the tale.

99. What's more: "Lost Notebook," in *Miscellaneous Prose and Verse, C* XXIII, p. 166.

99. Hawthorne did plan: July 5, 1837, *AN,* p. 34.

99. "My circumstances": July 5, 1837, *AN,* p. 34. JH, notebook, Morgan.

99. "Then here is," "so independent": July 5, 1837, *AN,* p. 34.

99. "Of female society," "has never yet," "We live": July 13 [1837], *AN,* pp. 44, 46.

99. "A man tries": "Lost Notebook," in *Miscellaneous Prose and Verse, C* XXIII, pp. 176, 175.

CHAPTER EIGHT: THE WEDDING KNELL

101. Her charity: Henry James, *The Bostonians* (New York: Library of America, 1985), pp. 824–27; 1165–70.

101. One could see: See Lilian Whiting, *Boston Days* (Boston: Little, Brown, 1902), pp. 181–82, and M. A. De Wolfe Howe, *Later Years of the Saturday Club, 1870–1920* (Boston: Houghton Mifflin, 1927), pp. 156–57.

101. "the joy of the Ideal": EPP to MM, Aug. 19 [1877], typescript, Antioch.

101. Sarah Clarke: Sarah Clarke to Ednah Dow Cheney, Jan. 22, 1894, Smith.

102. "Miss Peabody": EH to her cousins, [1875], PE.

102. Peabody told her own: JH, notebooks, Morgan. See Norman Holmes Pearson,

"Elizabeth Peabody on Hawthorne," *Essex Institute Historical Collections* 94 (July 1958), p. 264.

102. "and with no regard": EPP to SH, July 31, 1838, Berg.

102. "I think she": EH to her cousins, April [1875], PE.

102. "Presently Louisa": EPP to Thomas Wentworth Higginson, Berg. See also Pearson, "Elizabeth Peabody on Hawthorne," p. 256.

102. By then she'd heard: EPP to Francis Lee [1885], in *The Letters of Elizabeth Palmer Peabody*, ed. Bruce Ronda (Middletown, Conn.: Wesleyan Univ. Press), pp. 420–21. EPP later recalled that the pretext for bringing Hawthorne to Charter Street was to ask about the terms of the *Democratic Review*. Either Silsbee or Hawthorne may have introduced Peabody to O'Sullivan. Her unsigned review of Emerson's *Nature* and "The American Scholar" appeared in the *Democratic Review* in February 1838.

103. On Saturday evening: The content of this story dates it as a first meeting, especially since Peabody notes that Hawthorne invited her to call on his sisters, promising to take her home. Also, the conversation takes place after a meeting at Judge White's, which accords with Sarah Clarke's memory of the first meeting. Doubtless, then, a reasonable reconstruction of events suggests Peabody had called on the Hawthornes but, as she said, never called again despite the invitation to do so. Then she met Hawthorne himself at Judge White's, in the presence of Sarah Clarke. He walked Peabody home, telling him something about himself, and sometime after this conversation—how long is not known—he called at the Peabody house. See JH, notebook, Morgan, quoted in Pearson, "Elizabeth Peabody on Hawthorne," pp. 262–67.

103. "He has a temple" . . . "He has promised": MM to George Mann, Nov. 16, 1837, Berg.

103. False in particulars: JH, notebook, Morgan, quoted in Pearson, "Elizabeth Peabody on Hawthorne," p. 261.

103. Your brother has no: EPP to Thomas Wentworth Higginson, n.d., Berg. See also Pearson, "Elizabeth Peabody on Hawthorne," p. 256.

103. "An extreme shyness": EPP to Horace Mann, Mar. 3 [1838], MHS.

103. "His early & his college": EPP to William Wordsworth, Feb. 1838, quoted in Margaret Neussendorfer, "Elizabeth Palmer Peabody to William Wordsworth: Eight Letters, 1825–1845," *Studies in the American Renaissance* (1984), pp. 197–98.

104. "He is a man": EPP to Horace Mann, Mar. 3 [1838], MHS.

104. "I see that you": EPP to EH, n.d., quoted in *JHHW*, vol. 1, p. 166.

104. Fidelity of purpose: EPP, "Mental Photograph in 20 Questions," Aug. 1871, UVA.

104. "Not that you can": NH to HB, Feb. 8, 1838, *CXV*, p. 262.

104. Hawthorne's intended trip . . . quarrel: JH, notebook, Morgan. The episode is recounted in Norman Holmes Pearson, "Hawthorne's Duel," *Essex Institute Historical Collections* 94 (1958), p. 232.

104. "And you, Master Edward": *Fanshawe*, p. 59. Hawthorne or his sister also condemned dueling in the *American Magazine of Useful and Entertaining Knowledge* 2 (Boston: Bewick, 1836), p. 504.

105. At age eighty: She may also have the story of Frank White's death by dueling, which Hawthorne confided to his notebooks of the time. See "Lost Note-book," in *Miscellaneous Prose and Verse,* C XXIII, p. 193.

105. "real heart felt": Jonathan Cilley to Deborah Cilley, Oct. 1, 1837, Thomaston Historical Society.

105. "My labors": Jonathan Cilley to Deborah Cilley, Feb. 22, 1838, Thomaston Historical Society.

105. The ostensible reason: Much of this account is taken from "The Martyrdom of Cilley," *Democratic Review* 1:4 (Mar. 1838), pp. 493–508, and the various papers in the Thomaston Historical Society.

106. "to put the brilliant": *Personal Recollections,* pp. 19–21.

106. The uproar didn't: "Jonathan Cilley," in *Miscellaneous Prose and Verse,* C XXIII, p. 119.

106. John O'Sullivan remembered: John Louis O'Sullivan to Henry A. Wise, Nov. 24, 1843, Maine Historical Society.

106. Hawthorne supplied: The twenty stories were "Foot-prints on the Sea-shore," "Snow-flakes," "Chippings with a Chisel," "Howe's Masquerade," "Edward Randolph's Portrait," "Lady Eleanore's Mantle," "Old Esther Dudley," "John Inglefield's Thanksgiving" (published under the pseudonym "Rev. A. A. Royce"), "The New Adam and Eve," "Egotism; or, The Bosom-Serpent," "The Procession of Life," "The Celestial Railroad," "Buds and Bird-Voices," "Fire-Worship," "The Christmas Banquet," "The Artist of the Beautiful," "A Select Party," "A Book of Autographs," "Rappaccini's Daughter," and "P.'s Correspondence."

106. "one of the truest": NH to William C. Bennett, Sept. 12, 1854, C XVII, p. 256.

106. "The Devil has": NH to SH, Feb. 7, 1856, C XVII, p. 438.

107. "The Best Government": In addition to the back issues of the *Democratic Review,* the best sources of information on O'Sullivan include Robert Dean Sampson's dissertation, "Under the Banner of the Democratic Principle: John Louis O'Sullivan, the Democracy, and the *Democratic Review*" (Urbana: Univ. of Illinois, 1995), and Edward L. Widmer, *Young America: The Flowering of Democracy in New York City* (New York: Oxford Univ. Press, 1999).

107. "The eye of man," "Democracy is the cause": "The Best Government Is That Which Governs Least," *United States Magazine and Democratic Review* 1:1 (Oct. 1837), pp. 9, 11.

107. "I cannot believe": HWL, journal, Oct. 25, 1838, MS Am 1340(194), Houghton.

107. "as gentle as a girl": John O'Sullivan to William Meredith, June 22, 1849, U.S. Treasury—Personnel: Notable Persons, Nathaniel Hawthorne, National Archives.

107. According to O'Sullivan: John Louis O'Sullivan to Henry A. Wise, Nov. 24, 1843, Maine Historical Society.

108. "We would not yoke": [EPP], "Twice-told Tales," *New-Yorker* 5:1/105 (Mar. 24, 1838), p. 2. She also uses this phrase in the interesting fragment, subsequently quoted, of the letter in *NHHW,* vol. 1, p. 165, and the phrase "better for a man

to be harnessed to a draycart" dates the letter as having been written around the time of the review. Moreover, internal evidence further suggests that the letter was written shortly after Cilley's death, but unfortunately I haven't found the original letter.

108. "such a view," "he has been": EPP to EH, n.d., quoted in *JHHW*, vol. 1, pp. 165–66.

108. At the time of Cilley's death: In *NHHW*, vol. 1, p. 165, JH quotes from this letter of Elizabeth Peabody and from which he excises substantial portions. See also NH to EPP, July 20, 1863, *C* XVIII, p. 591.

108 "he felt as if": *NHHW*, vol. 1, p. 174. Julian Hawthorne obviously printed the story without investigating it deeply, as his fanciful narration of Cilley's duel reveals. (Remarkably, a number of historians swallow the story.) But Julian writes that Cilley's challenger was Henry Wise, not Graves; he misstates the cause of the argument, and alleges that Cilley hesitated before accepting the challenge, which he did not. Further, the analogy between Hawthorne and Cilley is skewed. Hawthorne did not receive the challenge, he sent it; it was O'Sullivan who refused to fight—as Cilley could have done, had he conferred with O'Sullivan. In fact, into this period of hesitation Julian inserts an incredibly fanciful, apolitical interpretation of his father and his father's friends: "At length, however," JH writes, "some one said, 'If Hawthorne was so ready to fight a duel without stopping to ask questions, you certainly need not hesitate'; for Hawthorne was uniformly quoted by his friends as the trustworthy model of all that becomes a man in matters of honorable and manly behavior."

108. "knew something": NH to John L. O'Sullivan, Nov. 5, 1838, *C* XV, p. 278.

108. "provided I have time": NH to HWL, Mar. 21, 1838, *C* XV, pp. 266–67.

109. "He is much": HWL, journal, Mar. 24–25, 1838, MS Am 1340(194), Houghton.

109. Meantime, though: See Bruce A. Ronda, *Elizabeth Palmer Peabody: A Reformer on Her Own Terms* (Cambridge: Harvard Univ. Press, 1999), chap. 4.

109. "one great moral" . . . "He says": EPP to Horace Mann, Mar. 3 [1838], MHS.

110. "We want something": Horace Mann to EPP, Mar. 10, 1838, MHS.

110. The gossips of Salem: NH to J. L. O'Sullivan, Apr. 19, 1838, *C* XV, p. 272.

110. A family silhouette: Anna Q. T. Parsons, "Reminiscences of Miss Peabody," *Kindergarten Review* 14 (1904), p. 539.

110. Of course, no silhouetted: *HHC*, pp. 17–18.

110. "on acct of his engagement"; "Sophia never knew": Laura Johnson to AF, July 7, 1864, Laura Winthrop Johnson Papers, NYPL; Carolyn H. Dall to Mr. Niles, Jan. 24, 1894, quoted in Carroll A. Wilson, *Thirteen Author Collections of the Nineteenth Century and Five Centuries of Familiar Quotations* (New York: Charles Scribner's Sons, 1950), p. 131.

110. "An engagement": Norman Holmes Pearson, "Hawthorne's Two Engagements" (Northampton, Mass.: Smith College, 1963), p. 12.

110. "Everybody thought": Carolyn H. Dall, "Reminiscences of Rebecca Hull Clark," p. 59, MHS.

112. "Circumstances are such": MM to Sally Gardiner, Apr. 10, 1838, MHS.

112. "And afterwards": JH, notebook, Morgan; see Pearson, "Elizabeth Peabody on Hawthorne," p. 265.

112. "Rather, I should say": SH to EPP, May 2, 1838, Berg.

CHAPTER NINE: THE SISTER YEARS

113. But the general: See SH to EPP, Sept. 23, 1825, courtesy Kent Bicknell. For my subsequent description of the Peabody family, I have drawn on the typescript of Nathaniel Cranch Peabody's reminiscences in the Mann archive, Antioch, as well as its collection of Peabody family correspondence; the incomplete Mary Mann reminiscence, Antioch; the Peabody papers at the Berg; Julian Hawthorne's transcriptions of Elizabeth Peabody's reminiscences, Morgan; Louise Hall Tharp's fine *The Peabody Sisters of Salem* (Boston: Little, Brown, 1950); Claire M. Badarocco's 1978 Ph.D. thesis, " 'The Cuba Journal' of Sophia Peabody Hawthorne, Volume I" (Rutgers Univ.); and Ronda, *Elizabeth Palmer Peabody: Reformer on Her Own Terms*.

113. Better yet, the "Peabodie Race": SH to EPP, Sept. 23, 1825, courtesy Kent Bicknell.

114. Dr. Peabody turned: SH to Maria Chase, Apr. 15, 1825, Peabody Family Papers, Smith.

114. "It is dreadful": SH, journal, 1832, Berg.

114. That left Nathaniel Peabody: See Ronda, *Elizabeth Palmer Peabody: A Reformer on Her Own Terms*, p. 14. Despite the seeming cruelty of the comment, Ronda pays fair tribute to Nathaniel Peabody.

115. "I wish you now": EPP to SH, June 23, 1822, Berg.

115. The throbbing increased: MM, typescript reminiscences, Antioch.

115. "They would think": SH to EPP, [1823], Berg.

115. "I thank you": SH to EPP, [1822–29], Berg.

116. "I have often told": SH to EPP, July 1833, Berg.

116. "Your loveliness": SH to MM, Feb. 2, 1851, Berg.

116. Trim and tasteful: Lilian Whiting, *Boston Days* (Boston: Little, Brown, 1902), p. 22.

116. The cannons boomed: Nathaniel Cranch Peabody, reminiscences, typescript, Antioch.

116. The physician, Walter Channing: JH, notebook, Morgan.

116. "I only fear": Mrs. EPP to MM, [1827], Antioch.

117. "Home is best": Mrs. EPP to EPP and MM, Jan. 26, 1827, Antioch.

117. She struck visitors: MM to Maria Chase, n.d., Peabody Family Papers, Smith.

117. "I still keep": SH to Maria Chase, [Oct. 16, 1829], Peabody Family Papers, Smith.

117. "Superior to what": SH to Mrs. EPP, May 12, 1832, Berg.

117. "I am rather": SH to EPP, June 1822, Berg.

117. Painting and pain: MM to Maria Chase, Jan. 17, 1830, Peabody Family Papers, Smith.

117. "Her nature was": NCP, reminiscences, typescript, Antioch.

118. "One is, it would": MM to Horace Mann, July 29 [1834], MHS; SH to Mrs. EPP, Mar. 21 [1834], Berg.

118. "It gives queer ideas": "Lost Notebook," in *Miscellaneous Prose and Verse,* C XXIII, p. 205.

119. "a decent respectability": "Grimshawe," in *American Claimant Manuscripts,* p. 347.

119. Only Sophia: Sarah Clarke to James Freeman Clarke, Dec. 31, 1837, and Jan. 1, 1838, MHS.

119. "Mr. Hawthorne endeavored": SH to Thomas Bailey Aldrich, Oct. 28, 1866, bMS Am 1429(2008–2009), Houghton.

119. The Peabodys offered: [Elizabeth Peabody], *Holiness; or, The Legend of St. George: A Tale from Spenser's Faerie Queene,* by a mother (Boston: E. R. Broaders, 1836).

119. "Mary told Louisa Hawthorne": SH to EPP, Apr. 20, 1838, Berg.

120. "I opened my door," "He has a celestial": SH to EPP, Apr. 23, 1838, Berg.

120. "He had taken": SH to EPP, Apr. 23, 1838, Berg.

120. "To be the means": SH to EPP, Apr. 23, 1838, Berg.

120. "I had a delightful": SH to EPP, Apr. 26, 1838, courtesy Evelyn Hamby; Stanford.

120. "I like to hear": EPP to SH, [May 1838], courtesy Evelyn Hamby; Stanford.

120. "I am diverted": SH to EPP, May 10, 1838, Berg.

120. "He thought it 'providential' ": SH to EPP, May 10, 1838, Berg.

120. "It makes me faint": SH to EPP, May 3, 1838, Berg.

121. "too bad," "insufferable," "not fair": SH to EPP, [spring 1838], courtesy Evelyn Hamby; Stanford; SH to EPP, May 14–16, 1838, Berg.

121. Just as often: SH to EPP, May 14–16, 1838, Berg.

121. She gave him: SH to EPP, July 23, 1838, Berg.

121. "a flower": JH, notebook, Morgan.

121. "He has him in his mind": EPP to SH, [May 1838], courtesy Evelyn Hamby; Stanford.

121. "a rose bathed": [Park Benjamin], "Twice-told Tales," *American Monthly Magazine* 5 (Mar. 1838), pp. 281–83.

121. What did Benjamin: [EPP], "Twice-told Tales," p. 1.

121. "I was astonished": SH to EPP, [spring 1838], courtesy Evelyn Hamby; Stanford.

121. "coquetting": EPP to EH, fragment, [fall 1838], Berg.

121. But that spring: "Lost Notebook," June 15 [1838], in *Miscellaneous Prose and Verse,* C XXIII, p. 202.

122. "On visiting": "Lost Notebook" [spring 1838], in *Miscellaneous Prose and Verse,* C XXIII, p. 208.

122. "A story to show": "Lost Notebook" [entry written circa 1838], in *Miscellaneous Prose and Verse,* C XXIII, p. 192.

122. "break off all intercourse": NH to John Louis O'Sullivan, Nov. 5, 1838, C XV, p. 278.

122. "sense that all": NH to John Louis O'Sullivan, Nov. 5, 1838, C XV, pp. 278–79.

122. Much like Hawthorne's: SH to NH, Dec. [6, 1838], UVA.

122. "See if I don't!": "Lost Notebook," in *Miscellaneous Prose and Verse,* C XXIII, p. 214.

122. The *"fervor scribendi"*: SH to EPP, [June 1838], courtesy Evelyn Hamby; Stanford.

123. Inspired by Sophia's account: SH to EPP, May 14 and 28, 1838, Berg. For superb analyses of history and art in "Tales of the Province-House," see Evan Carton, "Hawthorne and the Province of Romance," *ELH* 4 (1980), pp. 331–54, and on Hawthorne and history, see Colacurcio, *The Province of Piety,* part 3.

123. "Never, surely": "Lady Eleanore's Mantle," in *Tales,* p. 656.

123. Yet Helwyse: According to family legend, the Hawthorne ancestor Ebenezer Hathorne delivered smallpox into Salem in 1717.

124. "pale, ethereal creature," "enthusiasm": "Edward Randolph's Portrait," in *Tales,* p. 642. Her name also suggests the tolerant colonial governor Sir Henry Vane.

124. "We are no longer": "Old Esther Dudley," in *Tales,* p. 677.

125. The terrible conflict: See also Colacurcio, *The Province of Piety,* part 3. In his otherwise intelligent study of Hawthorne and history, Michael Colacurcio condescends toward John O'Sullivan and the *Democratic Review,* partly to render Hawthorne, as an author, more canny than O'Sullivan, which he was—as an author. But not as a politician. O'Sullivan was a complex, shrewd man who should not be dismissed by facile retrospective or wishful readings. It is not true that Hawthorne wrote for O'Sullivan under duress or without any very real commitment to Democratic politics. Hawthorne's allegiance to the Democrats and to O'Sullivan (not Bancroft), as well as his ironic sense of history and grim view of human nature, present the compelling paradox that is his character. Colacurcio's analysis, moreover, derives from several biographical falsehoods, such as the undocumented assertion that Elizabeth Peabody delivered O'Sullivan's invitation to Hawthorne to write for the *Democratic Review.* Even Elizabeth Peabody, who told several different but related versions of her meeting Hawthorne, does not suggest as much. See, for instance, EPP to Francis Lee [1885], in *The Letters of Elizabeth Palmer Peabody,* pp. 420–21. Moreover, the evidence suggests, as Peabody does, that Hawthorne introduced Peabody to O'Sullivan, who corresponded with her through Hawthorne. Assuming the opposite, Colacurcio then deduces that Bancroft, via Peabody, had already been jockeying on Hawthorne's behalf for a political appointment; this happened somewhat later, though not by much. In any event, the proleptic interpretation of Hawthorne's politics and Colacurcio's mistaking O'Sullivan for Bancroft, plus his misunderstanding Hawthorne's relation to both of them, seriously mar his argument, although much of his interpretation of the Province-House tales and of Hawthorne's irony is sensitive—and the best to date.

125. "Your life has been": "Old Esther Dudley," in *Tales,* p. 676. Published after I wrote this chapter, David T. Haberly's "Hawthorne in the Province of Women," *New England Quarterly* 74 (Dec. 2001), pp. 580–621, presents an argument about "Old Esther Dudley" somewhat similar to mine, although his biographical speculations are dubious.

125. "not to show": "Old Esther Dudley," in *Tales,* p. 677.

CHAPTER TEN: ROMANCE OF THE REVENUE SERVICE

126. "I rejoice": SH to EPP, Nov. 25 [1838], courtesy Evelyn Hamby; Stanford.

126. "thousand brothers in one": SH to EPP, Nov. 25 [1838], courtesy Evelyn Hamby; Stanford.

126. "I wish you could": MM to Sally Gardiner, Dec. 10, 1838, MHS.

126. Hawthorne's sacred "Word": SH to EPP, Nov. 25 [1838], courtesy Evelyn Hamby; Stanford.

126. And back on Charter Street: SH to EPP, Nov. 25 [1838], courtesy Evelyn Hamby; Stanford.

126. "No two could be": MM to Sally Gardiner, Dec. 10 [1838], Antioch.

127. "If, after so high": NH, *The Gentle Boy* (New York: G. P. Putnam, 1838).

128. "Now does that not": SH to NH, Dec. 6–7, 1838, UVA.

128. "I am afraid" . . . "Besides": EPP to EH, [Oct. 19, 1838], PE; see Norman Holmes Pearson, "A Good Thing for Hawthorne," *Essex Institute Historical Collections* 100 (Oct. 1964), p. 304.

128. "sort of man": EPP to EH, [Oct. 19, 1838], PE.

129. "the quiet of nature" . . . "as a matter": EPP to Elizabeth Bliss Bancroft, Nov. 6, 1838, LC.

129. Sitting in the square parlor: MM to SH, Jan. 5, 1839, Berg.

129. "He wants to come": SH to EPP, Feb. [1839], courtesy Evelyn Hamby; Stanford.

129. "January Fourth 1839": "Lost Notebook," in *Miscellaneous Prose and Verse*, *C* XXIII, p. 218.

129. "I had a parting": NH to SH, Mar. 6, 1839, *C* XV, p. 290.

130. "My surest hope": NH to SH, Apr. 30, 1839, *C* XV, p. 305.

130. "How did I live": NH to SH, Apr. 30, 1839, *C* XV, p. 303.

130. "It is I who": NH to SH, May 26, 1839, *C* XV, p. 317.

130. "I felt it": NH to SH, July 3, 1839, *C* XV, p. 320; July 24, 1839, *C* XV, p. 329.

130. "naughty" . . . "with pent-up love": NH to SH, Aug. 8, 1839, *C* XV, pp. 333, 335.

130. In fact, they wouldn't: Edwin Haviland Miller, in *Salem Is My Dwelling Place*, p. 165, oddly asserts that the lovers kept their engagement a secret to protect their two mothers. However, Hawthorne seems not to have concealed his intentions regarding Mary Silsbee, and Sophia Peabody had openly courted and rejected earlier suitors. As always, James Mellow is more temperate and reasoned in his speculations, suggesting Hawthorne could hardly afford to support a wife and, besides, still suffered embarrassment over his recent affair with Mary Silsbee (although he did not seem fazed when he announced to O'Sullivan that he'd fallen in love with Sophia). See Mellow, *Nathaniel Hawthorne in His Times*, pp. 159–60. Arlin Turner offers no explanation for the secrecy.

130. "brother measurers": NH to SH, July 3, 1839, p. 323.

130. Such elaborate chicanery: Word of the engagement remained part of Boston scuttlebutt for many years. See, for example, Johnson to AF, July 7, 1864, Laura Winthrop Johnson Papers, NYPL, and chap. 8.

130. "I have great comfort": NH to SH, Apr. 30, 1839, *C*XV, p. 305.

131. "What a trustful": [June 1853], *AN, C*VIII, p. 552.

131. "having fallen in love": NH to John Louis O'Sullivan, May 19, 1839, *C*XV, p. 312.

131. "She is a good old soul": NH to John Louis O'Sullivan, May 19, 1839, *C*XV, p. 312.

131. "a thing I had set": EPP to SH, June 23, 1839, courtesy Evelyn Hamby; Stanford.

131. "I am very sorry": SH to EPP, June 29, 1839, courtesy Evelyn Hamby; Stanford.

131. "to enjoy such elements": EPP to SH, June 23, 1839, courtesy Evelyn Hamby; Stanford.

131. "I have often doubted": SH to EPP, July [1839], courtesy Evelyn Hamby; Stanford.

131. "We will wait": NH to SH, July 24, 1839, *C*XV, p. 329.

131. "The world might": NH to SH, July 24, 1839, *C*XV, p. 330.

132. "It is true": EPP to Amelia Boelte, May 2, 1886, quoted in *The Letters of Elizabeth Palmer Peabody,* pp. 431–32.

132. "with as much confidence," Tongue in cheek: NH to HWL, Jan. 12, 1838, *C*XV, p. 287.

132. But he was still: See NH to George P. Morris, [Jan. 11, 1839], *C*XV, p. 285; NH to HWL, Jan. 1839, *C*XV, p. 288.

132. "Uncle Sam is rather": NH to HWL, May 16, 1839, *C*XV, p. 310.

132. "To stand on": Feb. 19 [1839], *AN,* p. 193.

133. "Henceforth forever": NH to SH, July 3, 1839, *C*XV, p. 320.

134. "If I ever come": NH to John Louis O'Sullivan, May 19, 1839, *C*XV, p. 312.

134. "It was exhilarating": NH to SH, Apr. 3, 1840, *C*XV, pp. 434–35.

134. "I think, too": NH to John Louis O'Sullivan, May 19, 1839, *C*XV, p. 314.

135. "Tell it down": EPP to SH, June 23, 1839, courtesy Evelyn Hamby; Stanford.

135. "What fame!": SH to EPP, July 5 [1839], courtesy Evelyn Hamby; Stanford.

135. "Does Mr. Hawthorne ever": ED to HWL, Nov. 14, 1840, bMS Am 1340. 2 (1734), Houghton.

135. In the fall of 1839: *Christian Examiner* 27 (Sept. 1839), pp. 132–35.

135. "I have a note"; he informed Longfellow: NH to SH, Dec. 18, 1839, *C*XV, p. 388; HWL, journal, Jan. 4, 1840, MS Am 1340(195), Houghton.

135. He also earned: See Franklin B. Sanborn to Samuel T. Pickard, June 18, 1901, Autograph File, Houghton.

135. Hawthorne liked: Feb. 19 [1839], *AN,* p. 191.

136. "As long as there": NH to William Pike, Feb. 10, 1840, *C*XV, p. 410.

136. Recalled Pike: "The Dinner," Norman Holmes Pearson manuscripts file, n.d., BY.

136. "I will retire": NH to John Louis O'Sullivan, Mar. 15, 1840, *C*XV, p. 418–19.

136. "effect—which": "The Custom House," in *The Scarlet Letter,* p. 153.

136. "he thinks matters": NH to SH, Oct. 23, 1839, *C*XV, p. 358.

137. "the most beautiful": SH to George Peabody, Nov. 3–5, 1839, Berg.

137. "bought" he said: NH to SH, Dec. 11, 1839, *C*XV, pp. 385–86.

137. "I do not get": NH to SH, Nov. 17, 1839, *C*XV, p. 364.

137. "Thou only has": NH to SH, Oct. 4, 1840, *C*XV, p. 495.

137. "Indeed, we are but": NH to SH, Oct. 4, 1840, *C*XV, p. 495.

137. "Your wisdom is not": NH to SH, 1839, *C*XV, p. 343.

138. "grant me freedom": NH to SH, July 30 [1839], *C*XV, p. 332.

138. "Thy husband is": NH to SH, Mar. 30, 1840, *C*XV, p. 431.

138. "Lights and shadows": NH to SH, May 19, 1840, *C*XV, p. 462.

138. "I cannot gush": NH to SH, Feb. 27, 1842, *C*XV, pp. 611–12.

138. "untoward circumstances": NH to SH, June 2, 1840, *C*XV, p. 469.

CHAPTER ELEVEN: THE WORLD FOUND OUT

139. Salem artist Charles Osgood: "The portrait came home a fortnight ago," Louisa Hawthorne writes Hawthorne, "and gives great delight": see LH to NH, May 10, 1841, Berg. Most scholars speculate that Robert Manning commissioned the portrait, although Hawthorne's mother may have. For a good discussion, see Rita Gollin, *Portraits of Nathaniel Hawthorne: An Iconography* (De Kalb: Northern Illinois Univ. Press, 1983), p. 20.

139. "We never had": Quoted in Margaret Armstrong, *Fanny Kemble: A Passionate Pilgrim* (New York: Macmillan, 1938), p. 326. Although Holmes had not yet published his famous poems, in 1831 and 1832 he used the phrase in two essays published in the *New-England Magazine.*

139. "A revolution of all Human": See EPP to John S. Dwight, Sept. 20, 1840, BPL; Bronson Alcott to Samuel J. May, Aug. 10, 1840, in *The Letters of Bronson Alcott,* ed. Richard L. Hernnstadt (Ames: Univ. of Iowa Press, 1969), p. 53.

141. "God incarnates": Ralph Waldo Emerson, "The Divinity School Address," in *Selected Writings,* ed. Brooks Atkinson (New York: Modern Library, 2000), p. 67.

141. Soon these seekers: The best introduction to the transcendental movement is Barbara L. Packer, "The Transcendentalists," in *The Cambridge History of American Literature,* ed. Sacvan Bercovitch (New York: Cambridge Univ. Press, 1995), pp. 329–603.

141. "Did you ever hear": SH to Mrs. EPP, July 4, 1841, Berg.

142. "The true democratic": George Ripley to George Bancroft, Sept. 20, 1837, MHS.

142. Politics and political: For the subsequent discussion of Brook Farm, I have drawn on the invaluable material contained in Zoltán Haraszti, *The Idyll of Brook Farm as Revealed by Unpublished Letters* (Boston: Boston Public Library, 1937); Henry Sams, *Autobiography of Brook Farm* (Englewood Cliffs, N.J.: Prentice-Hall, 1958); John Van der Zee Sears, *My Friends at Brook Farm* (New York: Desmond FitzGerald, 1912); Lindsay Swift, *Brook Farm* (1900; reprint, New York: Corinth Books, 1961); Anne C. Rose, *Transcendentalism as a Social Movement, 1830–1850* (New Haven, Conn.: Yale Univ. Press, 1981); and Carl J. Guarneri, *The Utopian Alternative: Fourierism in Nineteenth-Century America* (Ithaca, N.Y.: Cornell Univ. Press, 1991), as well as Joel Myerson, "James Burrill Curtis and Brook Farm," *New England Quarterly* 51:3 (Sept. 1978), pp. 396–423; Joel Myerson, "An Ungathered Sanborn Lecture on Brook Farm," *American Transcendental Quarterly,* suppl. (spring 1975), pp. 1–10; Joel Myerson, "Two

Unpublished Reminiscences of Brook Farm," *New England Quarterly* 48:2 (June 1975): pp. 253–60; Amelia Russell, "Home Life of the Brook Farm Association," *Atlantic Monthly* 42 (Oct.–Nov. 1878), pp. 458–66, 556–63; Ora Gannett Sedgwick, "A Girl of Sixteen at Brook Farm," *Essex Institute Historical Collections* 85 (1949), pp. 394–404. Interested readers should also consult *The Brook Farm Book: A Collection of First-Hand Accounts of the Community,* ed. Joel Myerson (New York: Garland, 1987).

142. "We talk of savages": Bentley, *Diary,* vol. 4, p. 71.

143. "The expression [seven gables]": NH to Horace Conolly, May 1840, *C* XV, p. 456.

143. But he seized: As early as 1838, he had proposed a similar idea to Longfellow for their collaboration on a book of fairy tales. "Ought there not to be a slender thread of story running through the book, as a connecting medium for the other stories?" NH to HWL, Mar. 21, 1838, *C* XV, p. 266.

143. The gifted author: [MF], "Grandfather's Chair: A History for Youth," *Dial* 3 (Jan. 1841), p. 405.

143. "dullest of all books": NH to SH, Nov. 27 [1840], *C* XV, p. 504.

144. "We are all": *The Correspondence of Emerson and Carlyle,* ed. Joseph Slater (New York: Columbia Univ. Press, 1964), pp. 283–84.

144. "It is astonishing": Sarah Clarke to James Freeman Clarke, Dec. 6, 1840, bMS Am 1569.3(12), Houghton.

144. "more natural union": George Ripley to RWE, Nov. 9, 1840, quoted in Sams, *Autobiography of Brook Farm,* p. 6.

144. "Thought would preside": Sams, *Autobiography of Brook Farm,* pp. 3, 8.

144. "His own mind": MF to William Henry Channing, Oct. 25–28, 1840, quoted in *The Letters of Margaret Fuller,* ed. Robert N. Hudspeth (Ithaca, N.Y.: Cornell Univ. Press, 1983–94), vol. 2, p. 174.

144. "The farming" . . . "There are to be": Sarah Clarke to James Freeman Clarke, Dec. 6, 1840, bMS Am 1569.3(12), Houghton.

145. "Can I not get": RWE to William Emerson, *The Letters of Ralph Waldo Emerson,* vol. 2, 1836–1841, ed. Ralph Rusk (New York: Columbia Univ. Press, 1939), p. 365. Sarah Clarke informed her brother that because the Brook Farm venture brought Emerson "to a crisis"—of conscience—he wished to adopt the Alcott family into his own, improve his own property for their support, and unite everyone, including servants, in common and equal labor. See Sarah Clarke to James Freeman Clarke, Dec. 23, 1840, bMS Am 1569.3(12), Houghton.

145. "Whenever I return": NH to SH, Jan. 27, 1841, *C* XV, p. 517.

145. "Here sits thy husband" . . . "He ought to make": NH to SH, Oct. 4, 1840, *C* XV, p. 494.

147. "Think that I": NH to SH, Apr. 13, 1841, *C* XV, p. 527.

147. "The whole experience": Swift, *Brook Farm,* p. 174.

147. "solitary characters": *Memoirs of Margaret Fuller Ossoli,* ed. RWE, William H. Channing, and James Freeman Clarke (London: Richard Bentley, 1852), vol. 2, p. 269 (henceforward given as *Memoirs*).

147. "the essential *equality*": [John O'Sullivan], "Dr. Channing's Recent Writings," *Democratic Review* 9:40 (Oct. 1841), p. 319.

147. "A true democracy": [O'Sullivan], "Dr. Channing's Recent Writings," p. 320; [John O'Sullivan], "The Course of Civilization," *Democratic Review* 6:21 (Sept. 1839), p. 215.

148. "The community aims": EPP, "Plan of the West Roxbury Community," *Dial* 2 (Jan. 1842), p. 364.

148. "I doubt they will": MF to William H. Channing, Mar. 29, 1841, *The Letters of Margaret Fuller,* p. 194.

148. "Spring and summer": NH to SH, Apr. 13, 1841, *C*XV, p. 526.

148. Teasing the Brook Farm: Sears, *My Friends at Brook Farm,* p. 117; Ora Gannett Sedgwick, "A Girl of Sixteen at Brook Farm," *Atlantic Monthly* 85:400 (Mar. 1900), pp. 395–97.

148. "He was a sort": *The Journals of Charles King Newcomb,* ed. Judith Kennedy Johnson (Providence, R.I.: Brown Univ. Press, 1946), pp. 149, 151.

149. "Hawthorne has taken hold": EPP to John S. Dwight, Apr. 26, 1841, BPL, quoted in *The Letters of Elizabeth Palmer Peabody,* p. 250.

149. "defiles the hands": NH to SH, May 4, 1841, *C*XV, p. 542.

149. "What is the use": LH to NH, June 11, 1841, Berg.

149. "I have never felt": NH to David Mack, July 18, 1841, *C*XV, p. 552.

149. "there are private": NH to David Mack, July 18, 1841, *C*XV, p. 552.

149. "I have not written": NH to GH, July 16, 1841, *C*XV, p. 550.

150. "We expect": NH to LH, Aug. 3, 1841, *C*XV, p. 555.

150. "I confess": NH to SH, Aug. 22, 1841, *C*XV, p. 563.

150. "How much depends" . . . "I am becoming": NH to SH, Aug. 22, 1841, *C*XV, p. 563.

150. "I shall see": NH to SH, Sept. 22, 1841, *C*XV, p. 575.

150. "the ground, upon which": NH to SH, Sept. 25, 1841, *C*XV, p. 578.

150. "My accession to these": NH to SH, Sept. 29, 1841, *C*XV, p. 582.

151. "I have not the sense": NH to SH, Sept. 22, 1841, *C*XV, p. 575.

151. "The woods have" . . . "It is wonderful": Oct. 18 [1841], *AN,* pp. 217–18.

151. "The grown people": Sept. 28 [1841], *AN,* p. 202.

151. "her upper lip": Quoted in Bell Gale Chevigny, *The Woman and the Myth: Margaret Fuller's Life and Writings* (Boston: Northeastern Univ. Press, 1994), p. 162.

152. "Yes," says Margaret: Sarah Clarke to James Freeman Clarke, Dec. 14, 1839, bMS Am 1569.3(12), Houghton.

152. Her self-regard: Carolyn Healey Dall, diary, Feb. 3, 1851, MHS; JTF to Mary Russell Mitford, Aug. 12 [n.y.], Huntington.

152. "Womanhood is": *Memoirs,* vol. 1, p. 297.

152. "She broke her lance": Sarah Clarke, reminiscences, University of Wisconsin at Madison, Special Collections.

153. "contorted like a sybil": SH to George Peabody, Oct. 27, 1839, Berg.

153. "Would that Miss Margaret": NH to SH, Jan. 13, 1841, *C*XV, p. 511.

153. In the spring of 1841: Carolyn Healey Dall, journals, Apr. 15, 22, 29, 1841, MHS.

153. "transcendental heifer," "she is very fractious": NH to SH, Apr. 13, 1841, *C*XV, p. 527.

153. "is compelled to take": NH to SH, Apr. 16 [1841], *C*XV, p. 531. See also the interpretation of the Fuller-Hawthorne relationship in Thomas Mitchell, *Hawthorne's Fuller Mystery* (Amherst: Univ. of Massachusetts Press, 1998).

153. "in the amusing position": *Memoirs,* vol. 2, p. 77.

153. "This frigidity": [Margaret Fuller], "Record of the Month," *Dial* 3 (July 1842), pp. 130–31.

154. "The real Me": NH to SH, Sept. 3, 1841, *C*XV, p. 565.

154. "A man's soul": NH to SH, June 1, 1841, *C*XV, p. 545.

154. "and nobody can meddle": NH to SH, Aug. 12, 1841, *C*XV, p. 556.

154. The book did appear: It also included "The Sister Years," "Snow-flakes," "Peter Goldthwaite's Treasure," "Chippings with a Chisel," "The Shaker Bridal," "Night Sketches," "Endicott and the Red Cross," "The Lily's Quest," "Footprints on the Sea-shore," "Edward Fane's Rosebud," and "The Threefold Destiny."

155. "Surely the book": NH to GH, Nov. 26, 1843, *C*XVI, p. 11.

155. The reviews were laconic: [John O'Sullivan], "Twice-told Tales," *Democratic Review* 10:44 (Feb. 1842), p. 198; [HWL], "Twice-told Tales," *North American Review* 54:115 (Apr. 1842), pp. 496–99; Orestes Brownson, "Literary Notices and Criticisms," *Boston Quarterly Review* 5:2 (Apr. 1842), p. 252.

155. "These effusions": [Edgar Allan Poe], "Twice-told Tales," *Graham's Magazine* 20:5 (May 1842), p. 299.

155. "paint with blood-warm colors": [Fuller], "Record of the Month," p. 132.

155. "who must stand": SH to Mrs. EPP, Oct. 9, 1842, Berg. "Is to observe" is quoted in the same letter.

155. "I love thee": NH to SH, Sept. 14, 1841, *C*XV, p. 569.

156. "where my youth": NH to SH, Sept. 3, 1841, *C*XV, p. 565; NH to SH, Jan. 27, 1841, *C*XV, p. 517.

156. "at least, not like": NH to Cornelius Mathews and ED, Dec. 22, 1841, *C*XV, p. 600.

156. "During the last three": NH to Cornelius Mathews and ED, Dec. 22, 1841, *C*XV, p. 600.

156. "I do not think": NH to SH, Feb. 27, 1842, *C*XV, pp. 612–13.

156. "It is this": NH to SH, Feb. 27, 1842, *C*XV, pp. 612–13.

156. "Mr. Hawthorne hid": SH to unknown recipient, [June 1864], Berg.

CHAPTER TWELVE: BEAUTIFUL ENOUGH

157. To him—to both: See, for instance, NH to SH, Apr. 6, 1842, *C*XV, p. 620.

157. "We are Adam": SH to Mrs. EPP, July 10, 1842, Berg.

157. "mutual love": See MF to SH, June 4 [1842], *The Letters of Margaret Fuller,* vol. 3, p. 66.

157. "Both Mr. and Mrs. Hawthorne": Thomas Wentworth Higginson, "Wedded Isolation," *Woman's Journal,* Dec. 20, 1884, p. 407. See also Henry James, "Nathaniel Hawthorne," in *Literary Criticism,* vol. 1, p. 388.

157. "The execution": NH to LH, July 10, 1842, *C*XV, p. 639.

158. "particularly as it": EH to SH, May 23, 1842, Berg.

158. "All in good time": NH to SH, May 27, 1842, *C*XV, p. 626.

158. "I dare say we": EH to SH, June 15, 1842, Berg.

158. "There seems to be": NH to SH, Feb. 27, 1842, *C*XV, p. 611.

159. "our mother": NH to SH, June 9, 1842, *C*XV, p. 628.

159. "cut off from": "A Virtuoso's Collection," in *Tales*, p. 713, published originally in the May issue of the *Boston Miscellany.*

159. There is ice: See "Lost Notebook," in *Miscellaneous Prose and Verse*, *C*XXIII, p. 221; see also "There is a splinter of ice in the heart of a writer" (Graham Greene, *A Sort of Life* [New York: Simon & Schuster, 1971], p. 188).

159. "Thou art"; "Without thee"; "It is thou": NH to SH, Oct. 4, 184[1], *C*XV, p. 584; Jan. 13, 1841, *C*XV, p. 511; Sept. 3, 1841, *C*XV, p. 565.

160. "I devoutly believe": SH to MF, May 11, 1842, MS Am 1086 v. XVI, Houghton.

160. "He seems pleased": Sarah Clarke to MF, May 25, 1842, MS Am 1086 v. XVII, Houghton.

160. But Hawthorne was so nervous: MM to SH, July [11–12], 1842, Berg.

160. Apparently none of the Hawthornes: George Holden file, PE. The watch may have belonged to Joseph Hathorne.

161. "I am the happiest"; "We are as happy": SH to Mrs. EPP, July 10, 1842, Berg; NH to LH, July 10, 1842, *C*XV, p. 639.

161. "as if something": Aug. 10 [1842], *AN*, p. 329.

162. "We did not think": SH to Mary Foote, Dec. 18, 1842, courtesy Evelyn Hamby; Stanford.

162. "I would put on"; "fills me": SH, diary, Dec. 1, 1843, Berg; SH to Mrs. EPP, Aug. [6], 1842, Berg.

162. "This vigilance": SH to Mrs. EPP, Aug. [6], 1842, Berg.

162. "I send up": SH to Mary Foote, Apr. 6, 1843, courtesy Evelyn Hamby; Stanford.

163. "A good deal of mud": Aug. 15 [1842], *AN*, p. 337. See also Sept. 24 [1843], *AN*, p. 395.

163. "This dull river": Aug. 7 [1842], *AN*, p. 321.

163. "world just created": Aug. 7 [1842], *AN*, p. 322.

163. "Before our marriage": SH, notebooks, [1842–43], Morgan. See Patricia Valenti, "Sophia Hawthorne's *American Notebooks*," *Studies in the American Renaissance*, 1996, ed. Joel Myerson (Charlottesville: Univ. Press of Virginia), p. 133.

163. "It might be a sin": Aug. 13 [1842], *AN*, pp. 333–34.

163. "The general sentiment": MM to SH, July 17, 1842, Berg.

163. "I felt that I": Aug. 15 [1842], *AN*, p. 334.

163. Mrs. Peabody came: See MM to SH, [Apr. 1845], Berg.

163. "Agreeable & gentle": SH to Mrs. EPP, Aug. 30–Sept. 4, 1842, Berg.

164. "He is ugly as sin": Sept. 1 [1842], *AN*, pp. 353–54.

164. "A vein of humor": William Ellery Channing, *Thoreau: The Poet-Naturalist* (Boston: Charles Goodspeed, 1902), p. 273.

165. "Life is"; "man without": "Compensation," in *Emerson: Essays & Poems*, ed. Joel Porte (New York: Library of America, 1996), p. 300; James quoted in Louis

Menand, *The Metaphysical Club: A Story of Ideas in America* (New York: Farrar, Straus & Giroux, 2001), p. 83.

165. "We have no questions": *Nature,* in *Emerson: Essays & Poems,* p. 7.

165. "I comprehend nothing": *Emerson in His Journals,* ed. Joel Porte (Cambridge, Mass.: Harvard Univ. Press, 1982), p. 280.

165. "It is no easy matter": Sept. 18–32, 1839, quoted in *Emerson in His Journals,* p. 288.

165. "N. Hawthorn's reputation": Sept. 1842, quoted in *Emerson in His Journals,* p. 288.

166. "a great searcher": Aug. 15 [1842], *AN,* p. 336.

166. "the narrow but earnest": Aug. 16 [1842], *AN,* p. 339.

166. "Our love is so wide": SH to Mrs. EPP, Aug. 30–Sept. 4, 1842, Berg.

167. "Waldo Emerson knows": SH to Mrs. EPP, Sept. 3 [1843], Berg. For a discussion of Hawthorne and Emerson, see Larry Reynolds, "Hawthorne and Emerson in 'The Old Manse,' " *Studies in the Novel* 23 (Spring 1991), pp. 403–24.

167. "Salem inquisitiveness": See SH to Mrs. EPP, Oct. 2, 1842; see also SH to Mrs. EPP, Aug. 13 and 20–21, 1843, Berg.

167. Dear noble Margaret: SH to MF, May 11, 1842, MS Am 1086 v. XVI, Houghton.

167. "Sydnean showers": SH to Mrs. EPP, Aug. 22, 1842, Berg.

167. "he should be much more": "Margaret Fuller's 1842 Journal: At Concord with the Emersons," ed. Joel Myerson, *Harvard Library Bulletin* 21 (July 1973), p. 325.

167. "Thus, even without": Aug. 28 [1842], *AN,* p. 349.

167. "I suspect": Nathan Hale Jr. to ED, Aug. 29, 1842, Duyckinck Family Papers, NYPL.

169. "would take but a trifle": NH to MF, Aug. 25, 1842, *C* XV, p. 648.

169. "The lad seems": Sept. 2 [1842], *AN,* p. 357.

169. he was trying to write a sketch: "The Old Apple-Dealer," based on earlier notebook jottings, appeared in Sargent's *New Monthly Magazine* in January 1843.

169. He'd come to Salem: NH to LH, Oct. 12, 1842, *C* XV, p. 653.

169. "It is a very cold": SH to Mary Wilder Foote, Dec. 30, 1842, courtesy Evelyn Hamby; Stanford.

170. "The mighty spirit": "Fire-Worship," in *Tales,* pp. 841, 843, published originally in the *Democratic Review,* Dec. 1843.

170. "A person with an ice-cold": n.d., *AN,* p. 235.

170. "bores," he said: "The Old Manse," preface to *Mosses from an Old Manse,* in *Tales,* p. 1147.

170. "his one idea": "The Hall of Fantasy," in *Tales,* p. 741, originally published in *The Pioneer* 1:2 (Feb. 1843). When revising the story for inclusion in *Mosses from an Old Manse,* Hawthorne shortened it, omitting the copious references to contemporaries like Catharine Sedgwick, John Neal, Mrs. Abigail Folsom, and John O'Sullivan.

170. "most of whom," Hawthorne gibes: See "The Hall of Fantasy," pp. 55–56.

Emerson, at this time, didn't entirely disagree with Hawthorne: "The abolitionists with their holy cause; the Friends of the Poor; the ministers at large;
the Prison Discipline Agents; the Soup Societies; the whole class of professed
Philanthropists—it is strange & horrible to say—are an altogether odious set
of people, whom one would be sure to shun as the worst of bores & canters."

171. By contrast, the narrator: See "The Hall of Fantasy," p. 52. Recently O'Sullivan
had been sparring publicly with the Reverend George B. Cheever, Hawthorne's classmate, over the issue of capital punishment, which O'Sullivan
fiercely opposed.

171. "These originals": Sept. 2 [1842], *AN,* p. 357.

172. "These factory girls": "The Procession of Life," in *Tales,* p. 798, published originally in the *Democratic Review,* Apr. 1843.

172. "All through the winter": n.d., *AN,* p. 238.

172. "men's accidents": n.d., *AN,* p. 236.

173. "like a schoolboy": NH to MF, Feb. 1, 1843, *C*XV, p. 670.

173. "with pretty commendable": Mar. 31, 1843, *AN,* p. 367.

173. "It is rather singular": NH to HB, May 3, 1843, *C*XV, p. 688.

173. "It is an annoyance": Mar. 31, 1843, *AN,* p. 367.

173. "Could I only have": June 23 [1843], *AN,* pp. 387–88.

174. "at least to achieve": "The Old Manse," in *Tales,* p. 1123.

174. "At the entrance": n.d., *AN,* p. 237.

174. "sole token of human": "The Birth-mark," in *Tales,* p. 780, published originally in *The Pioneer,* Mar. 1843.

175. "Our creative Mother": "The Birth-mark," in *Tales,* p. 769.

175. "All persons, chronically": "Egotism; or, The Bosom-Serpent," in *Tales,* p. 785,
published originally in the *Democratic Review,* Mar. 1843.

175. "establish a species," "was fortunately," "nourished with": "Egotism; or, The
Bosom-Serpent," in *Tales,* pp. 786, 788, 790.

176. Rosina rescues Roderick: As his double, she also suggests that Roderick is part
woman. Hawthorne evidently had Poe's "The Fall of the House of Usher" in
mind.

176. "always for purposes": "The Artist of the Beautiful," in *Tales,* p. 909, published
originally in the *Democratic Review,* June 1844.

176. Loving "the Beautiful": "The Artist of the Beautiful," in *Tales,* p. 909.

176. "demand is for perfection": Dec. 7, 1843, "A Sophia Hawthorne Journal,
1843–1844," ed. John McDonald, *Nathaniel Hawthorne Review,* 1974, p. 8.

176. When Annie Hovenden: Robert Danforth, a "man of earth and iron," may
resemble Hawthorne's grandfather Manning, who had been a blacksmith, or
Uncle Richard before his injury; both men must have seemed huge figures of
strength to a frail or lame boy. The name "Robert" refers to uncles; the
"Danforth," an old New England name, evokes Hathorne/Hawthorne. See
also "The Artist of the Beautiful," in *Tales,* p. 921.

177. She finally gave birth: In 1836 Mrs. Elizabeth Palmer Peabody had published a
child's version of *The Faerie Queene,* called *Holiness; or, The Legend of St.
George: A Tale from Spenser's Faerie Queene.* Before her marriage Sophia had
taken Una and St. George as the subjects of her paintings.

CHAPTER THIRTEEN: REPATRIATION

178. "And when the men": The entire passage is taken from N.d., *AN*, pp. 261–67.

179. "I suppose one friend": *AN*, p. 266.

179. "melancholic temperament": *AN*, p. 261.

179. "I find it is": NH to GH, Mar. 24, 1844, *C* XVI, pp. 22–23.

179. "holy and equal" . . . One could bring: " 'The Impulses of Human Nature':
Margaret Fuller's Journal from June through October 1844," ed. Martha L.
Berg and Alice De V. Perry, *Proceedings of the Massachusetts Historical Society*
102 (1990), p. 89.

179. Fuller . . . reclined lazily: Or so we gather from her bowdlerized journal.

179. "I love him much": " 'The Impulses of Human Nature': Margaret Fuller's
Journal from June through October 1844," p. 89.

179. "mild, deep and large": " 'The Impulses of Human Nature': Margaret Fuller's
Journal from June through October 1844," p. 85.

180. "I feel more like": " 'The Impulses of Human Nature': Margaret Fuller's
Journal from June through October 1844," p. 108.

180. "A woman of unemployed energy": "The Christmas Banquet," in *Tales*, p. 865,
originally published in the *Democratic Review*, Jan. 1844. Pitting his proto-
feminist next to a "half-starved, consumptive seamstress," Hawthorne anticipates the juxtaposition of Zenobia and Priscilla in *The Blithedale Romance*.

181. "those [women] who would": See "The Great Lawsuit," in *The Essential
Margaret Fuller*, ed. Jeffrey Steele (New Brunswick, N.J.: Rutgers Univ. Press,
1992), p. 30.

181. Rappaccini is also: See " 'The Impulses of Human Nature': Margaret Fuller's
Journal from June through October 1844," p. 109. See also SH, notebook,
[May 1843], Morgan.

181. Yet Hawthorne erases: For a good overview of the sources in "Rappaccini's
Daughter," see Carole Marie Bensick, *La Nouvelle Beatrice: Renaissance and
Romance in "Rappaccini's Daughter"* (New Brunswick, N.J.: Rutgers Univ.
Press, 1985); for a reading of the story that focuses on Hawthorne's relationship
with Fuller, see Mitchell, *Hawthorne's Fuller Mystery*, pp. 93–124.

181. "He has to contrive": SH to Mrs. EPP, [Mar. 1844], Berg.

181. "What is this being?": "Rappaccini's Daughter," in *Tales*, p. 993, originally published in the *Democratic Review*, Nov. 1844.

182. "Oh, was there not": "Rappaccini's Daughter," in *Tales*, p. 1005.

182. "It somewhat startled": "Earth's Holocaust," in *Tales*, p. 893, originally published in *Graham's Lady's and Gentleman's Magazine*, May 1844. Misty-eyed
reformers set the blaze, thinking it will eradicate the world's misery and injustice. As an image, the bonfire recalls the vengeful blaze of "The Devil in
Manuscript," a fire sparked by despair, neglect, and revenge. There's another
interesting motif in "Earth's Holocaust," too. Hawthorne couples women's
independence with his own professional anxiety: just before a group of ladies
discard their petticoats, a neglected American author pitches pen and paper
into the flames "and betook himself to some less discouraging occupation."

182. Alas, poor Monsieur de l'Aubépine: "Rappaccini's Daughter," in *Tales*, p. 975.

182. "I think France": SH to Mrs. EPP, Apr. 6, 1845, Berg.

183. "My husband's time": SH to Mrs. EPP, Aug. 19, 1844, Berg.

183. "We have no woman": SH to LH, Oct. 27, 1844, Berg.

183. "He actually does": SH to Mrs. EPP, Aug. 19 [1844], Berg.

183. "I wish Heaven": NH to GH, May 29, 1844, *C* XVI, p. 41.

183. The plan lurched: See John Louis O'Sullivan to James Munroe, June 12, 1844, BPL.

183. He tried to work: See NH to Samuel Ripley, Oct. 3, 1845, *C* XXIII, p. 457.

183. "My husband says": SH to Mrs. EPP, Nov. 20, 1844, Berg.

183. "else we shall": NH to SH, Dec. 20, 1844, *C* XVI, p. 73.

183. "GOD gives us": n.d. [June 1843?], SH, joint notebooks, Morgan.

183. "I am a husband!": NH to SH, May 19, 1844, *C* XVI, p. 44.

183. "At any rate": John Louis O'Sullivan to NH, Mar. 21, 1845, quoted in *NHHW,* vol. 1, p. 285.

184. He asked Evert Duyckinck: Hawthorne's tale "A Select Party," published in the July 1844 issue of the *Democratic Review,* also appeared in the first issue of the *New York Morning News.* Duyckinck solicited stories from Hawthorne for his magazine *Arcturus* 3 (Apr. 1842), p. 394.

184. "By manufacturing you": John Louis O'Sullivan to NH, Mar. 21, 1845, quoted in *NHHW,* vol. 1, p. 285.

185. "A man in the midst": n.d., *AN,* p. 253.

185. "Hawthorne is in a state": John Louis O'Sullivan to George Bancroft, Apr. 19, 1845, MHS.

185. "The poet lives": ED, "Nathaniel Hawthorne," *Democratic Review* 16 (Apr. 1845), pp. 376–77.

185. "Hawthorne is dying": John Louis O'Sullivan to George Bancroft, May 10, 1845, MHS.

185. "It sounds badly": John Louis O'Sullivan to George Bancroft, May 31, 1845, MHS.

185. "Robinson Crusoe solitude": John Louis O'Sullivan to George Bancroft, July 11, 1845, MHS.

185. "There could not possibly": John Louis O'Sullivan to George Bancroft, July 11, 1845, MHS.

186. "Such is his character": John Louis O'Sullivan to George Bancroft, Aug. 24, 1845, MHS.

186. Bridge would pay . . . Hawthorne would receive: See *Personal Recollections,* pp. 87–89.

187. "In this point": Horatio Bridge, *Journal of an African Cruiser,* ed. Nathaniel Hawthorne (New York: Wiley & Putnam, 1845), p. 164. The governor of Liberia was John Brown Russwurm, 1826 graduate of Bowdoin, fellow Athenaean, and acquaintance of Hawthorne and Bridge. See Patrick Brancaccio, " 'The Black Man's Paradise': Hawthorne's Editing of the *Journal of an African Cruiser,*" *New England Quarterly* 53 (1980), pp. 23–41.

187. "My husband says": SH to Mrs. EPP, Mar. 6, 1845, Berg.

187. "becomes less and less": See [John O'Sullivan], "The Re-Annexation of Texas: In Its Influence on the Duration of Slavery," *Democratic Review* 15 (July 1844),

pp. 11–16. It's important to note that O'Sullivan was a staunch supporter of Van Buren for the 1844 presidential nomination, which Van Buren, having opposed the annexation of Texas, lost. The pacifistic O'Sullivan also dreaded war with Mexico.

188. "knew *nothing* about slavery": EPP to HB, June 4, 1887, quoted in *The Letters of Elizabeth Palmer Peabody,* p. 445.

188. "a patriarchal" . . . "would have been better": "Old News," in *Tales,* p. 257, originally published in installments in the February, March, and May 1835 issues of the *New-England Magazine.*

188. "Slavery, as it existed": See "Old News," in *New-England Magazine* 8 (Feb. 1835), pp. 81–88; (Mar. 1835), pp. 170–78; (May 1835), pp. 365–70. See also "Effect of Colour on Odours," *American Magazine of Useful and Entertaining Knowledge* 2 (July 1836), p. 468, where the author writes—with irony?—that "negroes should suffer more, in proportion to their numbers, than whites, by all sorts of pestilence, and unwholesome smell." Even if ironic, the passage is cruel and unfunny.

188. "When the white man": *Journal of an African Cruiser,* p. 164.

188. "It is quite an interesting": See *Emerson in His Journals,* p. 356; *Journal of an African Cruiser,* p. 112.

189. "A civilized and educated": NH to HB, Apr. 1, 1845, *C* XVI, p. 26.

189. "Though the burning": *Journal of an African Cruiser,* p. 85.

189. Emerson, who shrugged off: SH to NH, Sept. 7, 1845, Berg. See also RWE to Carolyn Sturgis, Aug. 2, 1845, in *The Letters of Ralph Waldo Emerson,* vol. 8, 1845–59, ed. Eleanor M. Tilton (New York: Columbia Univ. Press, 1991), p. 44.

190. "promptly and forcibly": NH to GH, Sept. 6, 1845, *C* XVI, p. 119.

190. Hawthorne eventually won: A fire destroyed much of the property at Brook Farm in March, just days before the suit was heard in Concord. Hawthorne claimed $800 in damages, and the court granted him $560.62 plus costs of $25.28. The judgment seems not to have been paid, then or later. See *Hawthorne vs. Ripley and Dana,* Mar. 9, 1846, University of Rochester Library. For a full discussion of Hawthorne's suit, see Robert F. Metzdorf, "Hawthorne's Suit Against Ripley and Dana," *American Literature* 12 (1940), pp. 235–41.

190. "We are actually": SH to LH, Sept. 1, 1845, Berg.

190. "I have got weaned": SH to Mrs. EPP, Sept. 7, 1845, Berg.

190. Uncertain as wandering Arabs: "The Old Manse," in *Tales,* p. 1148.

190. "with flying colors": NH to HB, Oct. 7, 1845, *C* XVI, p. 122.

190. "I besieged Heaven": SH to Mrs. EPP, Sept. 7, 1845, Berg. Sophia would pay room and board to William Manning, Mary Manning's beneficiary. After her, the rooms at Herbert Street unoccupied by the Hawthornes were owned and rented out by him.

190. "Here I am again": NH to HB, Oct. 7, 1845, *C* XVII, p. 122.

CHAPTER FOURTEEN: SALEM RECIDIVUS

191. "I am turned out": NH to GH, June 8, 1849, *C* XVI, p. 273.

191. publishers of the *Salem Advertiser:* Varney Parsons & Co. to James K. Polk, Oct. 29, 1845, Personnel File of Nathaniel Hawthorne, record group 56, U.S.

Treasury Department Records, National Archives and Records Service (hereafter cited as National Archives).

191. Even Benjamin Browne: H. L. Conolly to Thomas Bowles, Oct. 25, 1845, National Archives.

191. In gratitude, Hawthorne: Published in installments from January to September 1846. Hawthorne hoped to interest Duyckinck in their publication in book form, to no avail.

191. "I have grown considerable": NH to HB, Mar. 1, 1846, *C* XVI, p. 148.

191. "Poor Hawthorne": Charles Sumner to Elizabeth Bancroft, Jan. 9, 1846, [copy], MHS.

192. "What a devil": NH to HB, Feb. 21, 1846, *C* XVI, p. 142.

192. "short stories that Evert Duyckinck . . . had solicited: ED to NH, Mar. 21, 1845, Duyckinck Family Papers, NYPL.

192. "MSS! MSS!" ED to NH, Oct. 2, 1845, Bowdoin.

192. "I have reached that point": NH to ED, Dec. 24, 1845, *C* XVI, p. 136.

192. "It is rather": NH to ED, Jan. 24, 1846, *C* XVI, p. 140.

192. Then, in March: The political maneuvering had continued unabated. According to one Democratic Party member, G. W. Mullet, Hawthorne hadn't been considered for the Custom House until arrangements had been concluded with others, which had to be undone. Mullet himself helped out by voluntarily withdrawing his application for the naval officer in favor of Hawthorne, and when the offer was rejected he managed to convince his friend Richard Lindsay to withdraw his name for surveyor, promising he'd do the same. They both then promoted Hawthorne's candidacy for surveyor and that of Howard for naval officer. See G. W. Mullet to George Holden, Oct. 1, 1883, PE. See also Carl E. Prince and Mollie Keller, *The U.S. Customs Service: A Bicentennial History* (Washington, D.C.: Department of the Treasury, 1989), p. 109: "James Polk recognized a political ornament when he saw one."

192. "Ah," writes Hawthorne: "The Old Manse," in *Tales*, p. 1142.

193. "subserve some useful": "The Old Manse," in *Tales*, p. 1126.

193. "The treasure of intellectual gold": The Old Manse," in *Tales*, p. 1148.

193. "As a storyteller": "The Old Manse," in *Tales*, p. 1148.

194. In addition to the preface: Hawthorne continued to exclude "My Kinsman, Major Molineux" but not "Mrs. Bullfrog" or "Monsieur du Miroir," both originally published in the 1837 *Token*, and "The Virtuoso's Collection." He did not, however, include more recent stories like "The Antique Ring," "A Good Man's Miracle," or "A Book of Autographs." The book sold in cloth as two-volumes-in-one for $1.25 and also appeared in printed paper wrappers, with the volumes sold separately or together.

194. "I am jogging": NH to HB, Oct. 26, 1846, *C* XVI, p. 188.

194. "No masks deceive him": See NH to ED, July 1, 1845, *C* XVI, p. 106. See also H. T. Tuckerman, "Nathaniel Hawthorne," *Lippincott's Magazine* 5 (May 1870), p. 502, and [William Henry Channing], "Mosses from an Old Manse," *Harbinger* 3 (June 27, 1846), pp. 43–44, quoted in *Nathaniel Hawthorne: The Contemporary Reviews*, p. 76.

194. "the specific remedy": See [Charles Wilkins Webber], "Hawthorne," *American*

Whig Review 4 (Sept. 1846), pp. 296–316, quoted in *Nathaniel Hawthorne: The Contemporary Reviews,* pp. 79–93. In his long encomium, Webber elevated Hawthorne above all party lines, doubtless aware, all protestation to the contrary, of Hawthorne's affiliation and friends. "We do not know, nor do we care, to what Party Nathaniel Hawthorne ostensibly belongs," Webber postured, "—we should judge, not to any. If he has identified himself with any, it should be the Whig Party—for he is a Whig and can't help himself. If it be the fact that he is ranked among the Loco-Focos [radical Democrats], it is the result of sheer accident or that indifference which is so characteristic of those Literary men of all countries who feel how much about the petty ends of Faction their sacred mission is, and accept from *their Government*—of whatever Party— whatever it has to offer, as a right."

194. In her large review: SH had already cooled to Fuller, resenting the latter's call for female independence and equality in *Woman in the Nineteenth Century,* the book-length version of her essay in *The Dial.* "Altogether ignoble," Sophia sneered. "I suspect a wife only can know how to speak with sufficient respect of man," she told her mother, "—I think Margaret speaks of many things that should not be spoken of." See SH to Mrs. EPP, Mar. 6, 1845, Berg.

194. "Hawthorne intimates": [MF], "Mosses from an Old Manse," *New York Daily Tribune,* June 22, 1846, p. 1.

194. "the charm of womanhood" . . . "But she was not": Apr. 3, 1858, *FIN,* pp. 156–57.

195. "Get a bottle": Edgar Allan Poe, "Tale-Writing: Nathaniel Hawthorne," *Godey's Magazine and Lady's Book* 35 (Nov. 1847), p. 256.

195. To John Quincy Adams: See John L. O'Sullivan, "Annexation," *Democratic Review* 17 (July–Aug. 1845), pp. 2–10.

196. He liked his new life: NH to George William Curtis, June 12, 1846, courtesy Kent Bicknell.

196. "as good liquor": Frank Sanborn, reminiscence, Aug. 28, 1901, Sanborn Collection, Concord Free Public Library.

197. Called the Black Prince: SH to Mrs. EPP, [Oct. 6, 1846], Huntington; Sophia's letter contains the scribbling of names by NH: "Hawthorne Hawthorne Francis Hawthorne, Henry Hawthorne, Walter Hawthorne, Wilfred Hawthorne, George Hawthorne, Herbert Hawthorne, Arthur Hawthorne, Edward Hawthorne, Horace Hawthorne, Robert Hawthorne, Lionel Hawthorne, Bundleblock Hawthorne." For the house on Chestnut Street, see Nevins S. Winfield, "The Homes and Haunts of Hawthorne," *New-England Magazine* 9 (1893), p. 292.

197. Salem shipping was: See Luther S. Luedtke, *Nathaniel Hawthorne and the Romance of the Orient,* p. 19.

197. "This small income": SH to Mrs. EPP, Dec. 19, 1847, Berg.

197. "as quiet up there": SH to Mrs. EPP, Sept. [9–]10, 1847, Berg.

198. As a matter of fact: Hawthorne's reviews and short pieces have been collected in *Miscellaneous Prose and Verse, C* XXIII, pp. 235–57: "Melville's *Typee*," Mar. 25, 1846; "Calvert's *Scenes and Thoughts in Europe* and Dickens's *Travelling Letters,*" Apr. 29, 1846; "Simms's *Views and Reviews; Hood's Poems,*" May 2,

1846; "Whittier's *Supernaturalism of New England,*" Apr. 17, 1847; "A Ball at Ballardvale," Oct. 6, 1847; "Evangeline," Nov. 13, 1847; "A Salem Theatrical," May 3, 1848; "A Salem Theatrical," May 10, 1848; and later "Webber's *The Hunter-Naturalist,*" Dec. 10, 1851.

198. Hawthorne asked Longfellow: NH to HWL, Nov. 11, 1847, *C* VI, p. 215; see Francis Shaw to NH, Jan. 26, 1848, Berg.

198. Yet Hawthorne strolled: NH to HWL, Nov. 11, 1847, *C* VI, p. 215.

198. "His taste was": George Batchelor, "The Salem of Hawthorne's Time," *Salem Gazette,* Mar. 11 and 18, 1887.

198. "high & dry": SH to MM, Oct. 15, 1848, Berg.

199. "I think your white guests": SH to MM, Jan. [16], 1848, Berg. Though she was well intentioned, Mary Mann's attitudes are not above reproach, for she contradictorily defended her action by noting that "the more I know of Miss Lee's beautiful soul, which is snowy white before God . . . the more I mourn for her that it is clothed in such an integument, and the more glad I am, that I have had an opportunity of seating her at my table with the magnates of the land, and showing the respect I bear to merit irrespective of colour," MM to SH, [Jan. 1848], Antioch.

199. He did; but that table: RH, memoir, Morgan.

199. "When shall you want": NH to Charles Wilkins Webber, Dec. 14, 1848, *C* XVI, p. 251. The *Centenary* editors reasonably suggest that the story was "The Unpardonable Sin." See J. Donald Crowley, "Historical Commentary" on *The Snow-Image, C* XI, pp. 382–83.

200. "In short, I now" . . . "I'm tired": June 20, 1847, *AN,* p. 398.

200. "If it [language] is Babel": Charles Kraitsir, *Significance of the Alphabet* (Boston: E. P. Peabody, 1846), p. 3.

200. The alphabet and language: Despite its cursory and often erroneous assumptions, Patricia Crain's *The Story of "A"* (Palo Alto, Calif.: Stanford Univ. Press, 2000.), chap. 5, attempts to deal with these issues.

200. "But what shall we say": *The Scarlet Letter,* p. 252.

201. "has broken all": See EPP to Ann Sargent Gage, [Mar. 1849]; EPP to Ann Sargent Gage, Feb. 15, 1849, Gage Family, Additional Papers, AAS.

201. "I wonder he do": SH to Mrs. EPP, Mar. 8–9, 1849, Berg.

201. "Every body seems": SH to Mrs. EPP, Mar. 8–9, 1849, Berg.

202. "Though everybody respectable": EPP to Ann Sargent Gage, Feb. 15, 1849, Gage Family, Additional Papers, AAS. Scandal clung to EPP, so much so that Henry James Jr., hearing of it, incorporated the Kraitsir affair into his fictionalized EPP in *The Bostonians.* See James, *The Bostonians,* p. 826: "There was a legend that an Hungarian had once possessed himself of her affections, and had disappeared after robbing her of everything she possessed. This, however, was very apocryphal, for she had never possessed anything, and it was open to grave doubt that she could have entertained a sentiment so personal."

202. "Wondrous strength": *The Scarlet Letter,* p. 176.

202. "The Photographic study": SH to JTF, Aug. 19, 1866, BPL. Similarly, Norman Holmes Pearson believed Hawthorne "had started writing *The Scarlet Letter before* his dismissal (although not before the possibility of it became clear) and

then put it aside as more suitable for a novel than a short tale." See Norman Holmes Pearson to Dean A. Fales, Aug. 4, 1865, BY.

202. "at odd times": William D. Northend to Henry Johnson, Horace Conolly recollections, copy, Bowdoin. The ample parallels between both novels and the tales written during this period suggest Conolly is right. Compare, for instance, the attempt in "Main-Street" to "give a reflex of the very life that is flitting past us!" and the point of view, says Hawthorne in *The House of the Seven Gables,* "in which this Tale comes under the Romantic definition, lies in the attempt to connect a by-gone time with the very Present that is flitting away from us" (*The House of the Seven Gables,* p. 351).

202. "rather went on with": SH to Mrs. EPP, Mar. 8–9, 1849, Berg.

202. "Kings, princes and potentates": Armstrong, *Fanny Kemble: A Passionate Victorian,* p. 311. Her notorious divorce from Pierce Butler, who sued on the grounds of desertion, was argued by Hawthorne's Whig ally in the Custom House fight, Rufus Choate, and it included allegations of Butler's adultery as well as their fight over custody of the children; it may be yet another source for *The Scarlet Letter.*

203. "She will bear it": NH to GH, June 8, 1849, *C* VI, p. 273.

203. Foul, cried the press: The standard compilation of relevant data can be found in Stephen Nissenbaum, "The Firing of Nathaniel Hawthorne," *Essex Institute Historical Collections* 114:2 (Apr. 1978), pp. 57–86.

203. "Not one of Mr. Hawthorne's": Quoted in "The Removal of Mr. Hawthorne," *Salem Register,* June 20, 1849, p. 2.

203. "The office"; "I am satisfied"; Another supporter; "I should as soon": Rufus Choate to William Meredith, June 9, 1849, National Archives; George Ticknor to William Meredith, June 19, 1849, National Archives; Amory Holbrook, June 12, 1849, National Archives; John O'Sullivan, June 22, 1849, National Archives.

204. "If they will pay": NH to HWL, June 5, 1849, *C* VI, p. 270.

204. "He seems to be": EPP to Mrs. EPP, June 15, 1849, Antioch.

204. "He is either to be": SH to Mrs. EPP, June 21, 1849, Berg.

204. With Hawthorne intransigent: SH to Dr. Nathaniel Peabody (father), July 4, 1848, Berg.

204. The Whig War Committee: Charles W. Upham to William Meredith, July 9, 1849, National Archives.

204. "supported by all": Charles Upham et al., to William Meredith, June 25, 1849, National Archives.

205. "I was yesterday": Edward Everett to William Meredith, June 27, 1849, MHS.

205. "on account of an ancient": SH to Dr. Nathaniel Peabody, July 4, 1849, Berg.

CHAPTER FIFTEEN: SCARLET LETTERS

206. "to make such a defence": NH to Horace Mann, Aug. 8, 1849, *C* XVI, p. 293.

206. "I tried to keep," "I love my mother": July 29, 1849, *AN,* p. 429.

207. "There was the deepest": SH to MM, Aug. 12, 1849, Berg.

207. "And then I looked": July 29, 1849, *AN,* p. 429.

207. "I hope to get": SH to MM, Nov. 4, 1849, Berg.

207. "It is only paying": GH to NH, Jan. 17, 1850, quoted in *NHHW,* vol. 1, pp. 354–55.
207. "It is something else": NH to GH, Jan. 20, 1850, *C* XVI, p. 310.
208. "He writes immensely": SH to Mrs. EPP, Sept. 27, 1849, Berg.
209. Slated for a collection: NH to JTF, Jan. 15, 1850, C XVI, p. 306; see *Yesterdays,* pp. 48–51.
209. "I have heard": SH to Richard Manning, Feb. 12, 1871, PE. Some years after Hawthorne's death, Sophia accused Fields of cheating her of Hawthorne's royalties.
210. "In the process of writing": NH to JTF, Jan. 15, 1850, *C* XVI, p. 305.
210. "the inmost Me": *The Scarlet Letter,* p. 121.
210. "My imagination," "a little pile," "I endeavored," "that of a person": *The Scarlet Letter,* pp. 148, 152, 153, 155.
211. "as if the devil": NH to Horace Conolly, June 17, 1850, *C* XVI, p. 345.
211. "a citizen of somewhere else": *The Scarlet Letter,* p. 157.
211. "What is he?" *The Scarlet Letter,* p. 127.
211. "neutral territory," "so they lose," "the cold": *The Scarlet Letter,* pp. 149, 150.
212. "all in one tone": NH to JTF, Nov. 3, 1850, *C* XVI, p. 371.
212. "zeal for God's glory": *The Scarlet Letter,* p. 232.
213. "we have wronged": *The Scarlet Letter,* p. 182.
213. "Mr. Dimmesdale, whose": *The Scarlet Letter,* p. 229.
213. The literary sources of *The Scarlet Letter:* See also Larry J. Reynolds, "*The Scarlet Letter* and Revolutions Abroad," *American Literature* 57 (1985), pp. 44–67, for a cogent account of Hawthorne's use of the revolutions of 1848.
213. In his 1837 tale: Early journal entries tell of the woman who, "by the old colony law, was condemned always to wear the letter A, sewn on her garment, in token of her having committed adultery." See n.d., *AN,* p. 254. Hawthorne doubtless read of the practice in Joseph Felt's *Annals of Salem.*
214. "What we did had": *The Scarlet Letter,* p. 286.
214. "None so ready," "In all season": *The Scarlet Letter,* p. 256.
214. "It is remarkable," "Was existence worth": *The Scarlet Letter,* pp. 259–60.
214. "The world's law," "essential to keep her": *The Scarlet Letter,* p. 259.
215. "beloved, but gone hence": *The Scarlet Letter,* p. 149.
215. "There was wild and ghastly": *The Scarlet Letter,* p. 261.
215. "of her own free," "mutual happiness": *The Scarlet Letter,* p. 344.
216. To some readers: See, for instance, the enormously influential Sacvan Bercovitch, *The Office of "The Scarlet Letter"* (Baltimore: Johns Hopkins Univ. Press, 1991); see also Gary Scharnhorst, ed., *The Critical Response to Nathaniel Hawthorne's "The Scarlet Letter"* (Westport, Conn.: Greenwood, 1992).
216. "A book one reads": MM to Horace Mann, Mar. 20, 1850, MHS.
216. "To tell you the truth": NH to HB, Feb. 4, 1850, *C* XVI, p. 311.
216. "Mr. Fields!": SH to EPP, [Feb. 3, 1850], Berg.
216. Exhilarated, Fields: See SH to EPP, [Feb. 3, 1850], Berg.
217. "Nathaniel's fame": SH to LH, Apr. 28, 1850, Berg.
217. "Glorious" . . . "& raise": JTF to ED, Mar. 5, 1850, Duyckinck Family Papers, NYPL.

217. "If I escape": NH to HB, Apr. 13, 1850, *C* XVI, p. 329.

217. "The only remarkable": *The Scarlet Letter,* p. 119.

217. "directly through": [Edwin Percy Whipple], "Review of New Books," *Graham's Magazine* 36:5 (May 1850), pp. 345–46, quoted in *Nathaniel Hawthorne: The Contemporary Reviews,* p. 124.

217. "He perpetuates bad morals": [Arthur Cleveland Coxe], "The Writings of Hawthorne," *Church Review and Ecclesiastical Register* 3:4 (Jan. 1851), in *Nathaniel Hawthorne: The Contemporary Reviews,* p. 146.

CHAPTER SIXTEEN: THE UNEVEN BALANCE

218. "Thou didst much amiss": NH to SH, Apr. 26, 1850, *C* XVI, p. 333.

218. And with the children: Letters from MM to Horace Mann, Mar. [15]–23, 1850, MHS, do not suggest that Sophia Hawthorne had suffered another miscarriage, as sometimes alleged. See Miller, *Salem Is My Dwelling Place,* p. 551.

218. "I detest this town": NH to Horace Mann, Aug. 8, 1849, *C* XVI, p. 293; NH to HB, Feb. 4, 1850, *C* XVI, p. 312.

219. "To give up the ocean": Quoted in *NHHW,* vol. 1, p. 353, Sept. 2, 1849.

219. "I infinitely prefer": NH to Caroline Sturgis Tappan, Sept. 5, 1851, *C* XVI, p. 481.

219. "Had this wish": *HHC,* p. 20.

219. "Belladonna finally conquered": SH to Mrs. EPP, June 9, 1850, Berg.

219. "with uneven floors": Quoted in Franklin B. Sanborn, *Recollections of Seventy Years* (Boston: Richard G. Badger, 1909), vol. 2, p. 523.

220. She hung her reproductions . . . In the background: SH described it thus, SH to EPP, Aug. 8, 1850, Berg. See also Oct. 13 [1850], *AN,* p. 298.

220. "I find it very agreeable": NH to Zachariah Burchmore, June 9, 1850, *C* XVI, p. 340.

220. "Perhaps he may remain": HB to FP, Nov. 4, 1850, LC.

220. "Mr. Hawthorne thinks": SH to Mrs. EPP, Aug. 1, 1850, Berg.

220. "the daily bulletin": Quoted in *The Letters of Margaret Fuller,* vol. 5, p. 194.

221. "Think of the dry": Fanny Longfellow, *Mrs. Longfellow: Selected Letters and Journals of Fanny Appleton Longfellow,* ed. Edward Wagenecht (New York: Longmans, Green, 1956), p. 159.

221. "I pity those": Quoted in *The Letters of Margaret Fuller,* vol. 6, p. 77.

221. Approaching Fire Island: Details of the shipwreck in various books often contradict one another, so I have reconstructed events from various newspaper accounts in the New York press.

221. "Oh was ever any thing": SH to Mrs. EPP, Aug. 1, 1850, Berg.

221. "I am really glad": SH to Mrs. EPP, Sept. 10, 1850, Berg.

221. Evert Duyckinck, soon to visit: ED to Margaret Duyckinck, Aug. 9, 1850, Duyckinck Family Papers, NYPL.

222. The date was set: See Cornelius Mathews, "Several Days in Berkshire," *Literary World* 7 (Aug. 24 and 31 and Sept. 7, 1850), pp. 145–47, 166, 185–86.

222. Dr. Oliver Wendell Holmes: Mathews, "Several Days in Berkshire," p. 145.

222. Later James Fields: *Yesterdays,* pp. 52–53; in addition to Mathews and Fields, I

have used J. T. Headley, "Berkshire Scenery," *New-York Observer,* Sept. 14, 1850, and the letters of ED to Margaret Duyckinck, NYPL, and SH to EPP, [summer 1850], Berg, to reconstruct events.

222. "remarkable literary column"; "Hawthorne was among": See Headley, "Berkshire Scenery"; *Yesterdays,* p. 53.

222. "as if the Devil": SH to EPP, Aug. 8, 1850, Berg.

222. "Mr. Typee is interesting": SH to EPP, Aug. 8, 1850, Berg.

223. Defoe on the ocean: ED to George Duyckinck, Sept. 5, 1849, Duyckinck Family Papers, NYPL.

223. "He is married": SH to EPP, [Sept. 1850], Berg.

224. "We landsmen": NH to HB, [Dec. 1846], *C*XVI, p. 195.

224. "tolerant of codes": HM, *Correspondence,* ed. Lynn Horth (Chicago: Northwestern Univ. Press and Newberry Library, 1993), p. 186; "Melville's *Typee,*" in *Miscellaneous Prose and Verse, C*XXIII, p. 235.

224. Melville was no landsman: NH to HB, [Dec. 1846], *C*XVI, p. 195.

224. "Already I feel," "He expands": "Hawthorne and His Mosses, by a Virginian spending July in Vermont," in *Nathaniel Hawthorne: The Contemporary Reviews,* p. 112.

224. "the rich and rare": "Hawthorne and His Mosses," in *Nathaniel Hawthorne: The Contemporary Reviews,* p. 106.

224. "Some may start," "For in this world": "Hawthorne and His Mosses," in *Nathaniel Hawthorne: The Contemporary Reviews,* p. 108.

224. "For spite of all": "Hawthorne and His Mosses," in *Nathaniel Hawthorne: The Contemporary Reviews,* p. 108. For a cogent discussion of the racial implications of this metaphor, see Bruce Neal Simon, "The Race for Hawthorne" (Ph.D. diss., Princeton Univ., 1998).

224. "derives its force": "Hawthorne and His Mosses," in *Nathaniel Hawthorne: The Contemporary Reviews,* pp. 107–8.

225. "What I feel most moved": HM to NH, [June 1], 1851, in Melville, *Correspondence,* p. 192.

225. Recognizing a fellow traveler: "Hawthorne and His Mosses," in *Nathaniel Hawthorne: The Contemporary Reviews,* p. 110.

225. "Let him write": "Hawthorne and His Mosses," in *Nathaniel Hawthorne: The Contemporary Reviews,* p. 111.

225. "For genius, all over": "Hawthorne and His Mosses," in *Nathaniel Hawthorne: The Contemporary Reviews,* p. 111.

225. "There were few": *HHC,* p. 33.

225. "A man with a true": SH to Mrs. EPP, Sept. 4, 1850, Berg.

225. "careful not to interrupt": SH to EPP, [Sept. 1850], Berg.

227. "He is an invaluable": SH to Mrs. EPP, Oct. 24, 1852, courtesy Evelyn Hamby; Stanford.

227. "When conversing, he is full": Jay Leyda, *The Melville Log: A Documentary Life of Herman Melville* (1951; reprint, New York: Harcourt, Brace, 1969), vol. 1, pp. 393–94.

227. "No writer ever put": NH to ED, Aug. 29, 1850, *C*XVI, p. 362.

227. During the next fifteen months: See also Brenda Wineapple, "Hawthorne and Melville; or, The Ambiguities," *ESQ* 46:1, 2 (2000), pp. 75–98. Although this issue is devoted in its entirety to the Hawthorne-Melville friendship, it focuses primarily on Melville's end of the equation, repeating much of the tired speculation of Miller. More useful is Hershel Parker, *Herman Melville*, vol. 2, 1851–1891 (Baltimore: Johns Hopkins Univ. Press, 2001), pp. 130–32, 136–61.

228. "had never lost": *The House of the Seven Gables*, p. 504.

228. "There was something of the woman": *The Blithedale Romance*, p. 667.

228. He likely burned them: See HM to NH, July 22, 1851, in Melville, *Correspondence*, p. 199, where Melville suggests Hawthorne's letters to him were unguarded, lengthy, and well received.

228. "They shiver": *The House of the Seven Gables*, p. 472.

228. "their deeper meanings": HM to ED, Feb. 12, 1851, quoted in Melville, *Correspondence*, p. 181.

229. Hawthorne called *Moby-Dick: A Wonder Book for Girls and Boys*, *C* VII, p. 169: "On the hither side of Pittsfield sits Herman Melville, shaping out the gigantic conception of his 'White Whale,' while the gigantic shape of Graylock looms upon him from his study-window."

229. "You are aware": JTF to NH, Aug. 20, 1850, Berg.

229. "I must not pull": NH to JTF, Aug. 23, 1850, *C* XVI, p. 359.

229. "His form is only": JTF to Mary Russell Mitford, Sept. 30, 1851, quoted in James C. Austin, *Fields of the Atlantic Monthly* (San Marino, Calif.: Huntington Library, 1953), p. 209.

229. "We intend to push": JTF to NH, Jan. 14, 1851, Berg.

230. "with the minuteness" . . . He also wished: NH to JTF, Nov. 3, 1850, *C* XVI, p. 371.

230. "There are points": NH to JTF, Dec. 9, 1850, *C* XVI, p. 378.

230. He did compose . . . "for a good many years": Preface to *Twice-told Tales*, in *Tales*, p. 1150.

230. "Instead of passion": Preface to *Twice-told Tales*, in *Tales*, pp. 1151, 1152.

230. "The book, if you would": Preface to *Twice-told Tales*, in *Tales*, pp. 1151–52.

230. "Every sentence, so far": Preface to *Twice-told Tales*, in *Tales*, p. 1152.

231. "The spirit of my": See, for instance, *EN*, vol. 1, p. 193.

231. "Nobody would think": NH to SH, Jan. 1, 1840, *C* XVI, p. 395.

231. "on the internal evidence": Preface to *Twice-told Tales*, in *Tales*, p. 1153.

CHAPTER SEVENTEEN: THE HIDDEN LIFE OF PROPERTY

232. "The book is an affliction": quoted in Joel Pfister, *The Production of Personal Life* (Stanford, Calif.: Stanford Univ. Press, 1991), p. 157.

232. "a great deal more": *The House of the Seven Gables*, p. 353.

233. "I'm no more a witch": Loggins, *The Hawthornes*, p. 133.

233. "The impalpable claim": *The House of the Seven Gables*, p. 366. More recently the Hathorne clan included an eccentric sister and a brother, both unmarried, and a quarrel over a will that mysteriously disappeared.

233. "The wrong-doing of one generation": *The House of the Seven Gables*, p. 352.

233. "is to be transformed": *The House of the Seven Gables,* p. 383.

233. "where everything is free": *The House of the Seven Gables,* p. 508.

233. "In this republican country": *The House of the Seven Gables,* p. 384.

234. Ebe saw the Reverend Charles Upham: EH to NH, May 3, 1851, Berg. So did others. See George Holden, Aug. 18, 1883, notes, PE: according to Elizabeth Peabody (an unreliable source), Upham was annoyed that Hawthorne didn't attend his church, although the Hawthorne family had a pew. Another story, also from Peabody, has Upham advising Hawthorne before his marriage that "a wife should be kept in subjection and brought up to wait upon the husband, [but] that this would be found especially desirable in the case of Sophia, as she had been in delicate health, and therefore petted and indulged at home." Hearing this, Hawthorne was indignant—again, according to Peabody.

234. "I dwell in it": *The House of the Seven Gables,* p. 510.

234. "Shall we never": *The House of the Seven Gables,* p. 509. See also N.d., *AN,* p. 252: "To represent the influence which Dead Men have among living affairs;— for instance, a Dead Man controls the disposition of wealth; a Dead Man sits on the judgment-seat, and the living judges do but repeat his decisions; Dead Men's opinions in all things control the living truth; we believe in Dead Men's religion; we laugh at Dead Men's jokes; we cry at Dead Men's pathos; every-where and in all matters, Dead Men tyrannize inexorably over us."

235. "once in every half century": *The House of the Seven Gables,* p. 511.

235. "a house and a moderate": *The House of the Seven Gables,* p. 486.

235. "No great mistake": *The House of the Seven Gables,* p. 621.

235. Doubtless begun as one: See NH to JTF, Jan. 15, 1850, *C* XVI, p. 306. He counted circa two hundred manuscript pages to be included with "The Scarlet Letter" for a volume of tales. See Chapter 15.

236. "a cough took up": Quoted in Edward W. Emerson, *The Early Years of the Saturday Club* (Boston: Houghton Mifflin, 1918), p. 211.

236. "There is still a faint": *The House of the Seven Gables,* p. 589. The passage seems to me to anticipate the "Time Passes" section of Virginia Woolf's *To the Light-house;* Woolf clearly knew of Hawthorne's work, and her father, Leslie Stephen, wrote eloquently of him in "Hawthorne and the Lessons of Romance," *Cornhill Magazine* 26 (Dec. 1872), pp. 717–34.

236. "There is a certain": HM to NH, [Apr. 16], 1851, in Melville, *Correspondence,* p. 186.

237. "his atmospherical medium": *The House of the Seven Gables,* p. 351.

237. "a more natural and healthy": NH to ED, Apr. 27, 1851, *C* XVI, p. 421. See Holgrave's observation, when he reads from a story he'd written: "As one method of throwing it [his emotion] off, I have put an incident of the Pyncheon family-history, with which I happen to be acquainted, into the form of a legend, and mean to publish it in a magazine" (*The House of the Seven Gables,* p. 512).

237. "How slowly I have": NH to HB, Mar. 15, 1851, *C* XVI, p. 407.

237. "There is a grand truth": HM to NH, [Apr. 16], 1851, in Melville, *Correspondence,* p. 186.

237. "mulled wine": HM to NH, [Jan. 1851], in Melville, *Correspondence*, p. 176.

237. "I mean to continue": HM to NH, [June 1851], in Melville, *Correspondence*, p. 190.

237. "fresh, sincere" . . . "much of concession": SH, Apr. 11, 1851, diary, Berg; SH to EPP, May 10, 1851, Berg.

238. "So upon the whole": HM to NH, [June 1], 1851, in Melville, *Correspondence*, p. 193.

238. "Though I wrote": HM to NH, [June 1], 1851, in Melville, *Correspondence*, p. 192.

238. But he approved: HM to NH, [Apr. 16], 1851, in Melville, *Correspondence*, p. 185.

238. "A weird, wild book"; "for having shown": HWL, journal, Apr. 16, 1851, MS Am 1340(204), Houghton; *NHHW*, vol. 1, p. 391.

238. "his lantern": [ED], "House of the Seven Gables," *Literary World* 8 (Apr. 26, 1851), p. 334.

239. From England: "The House of the Seven Gables," *Athenaeum* 24 (May 1851), in *Nathaniel Hawthorne: The Contemporary Reviews*, p. 164.

239. "It is evident": EH to NH, May 3, 1851, courtesy Evelyn Hamby; Stanford.

240. "the daughter of my age": NH to HB, July 22, 1851, *C*XVI, p. 462; NH to EPP, May 25, 1851, *C*XVI, p. 441.

240. "Mr. Hawthorne's passions": JH, notebook, Morgan.

240. "I have never yet seen": NH to EPP, May 25, 1851, *C*XVI, p. 440.

240. Hawthorne, who earned: See *The Cost Books of Ticknor and Fields, 1832–1858*, ed. W. S. Tryon and William Charvat (New York: Bibliographical Society of America, 1949), pp. 188–203.

240. "I feel remote": NH to HWL, May 8, 1851, *C*XVI, p. 431.

240. "Mr. Hawthorne, even for a man": Godfrey Greylock [Joseph E. A. Smith], *Taghconic; or, Letters and Legends about our Summer Home* (Boston: Redding, 1852), p. 101; *The Letters of Ralph Waldo Emerson*, vol. 8, p. 265.

240. "I dare say": SH to Mrs. EPP, Sept. 7, 1851, Berg.

241. "He seems older": Ellery Channing to Ellen Channing, Oct. 30, 1851, MHS.

241. "time and eternity": Aug. 1, 1851, *AN*, p. 448.

241. Should his writing: SH to EPP, Oct. 2, 1851, Berg; NH to HB, July 22, 1851, *C*XVI, p. 462.

241. "I find that": July 29 [1851], *AN*, p. 439.

241. Sophia thought Caroline: See SH to EPP, fragment, [Aug. or Sept. 1858], Berg.

241. She sent a note: See NH to Caroline Sturgis Tappan, Sept. 5, 1851, *C*XVI, p. 480–82.

242. "The right of purchase": NH to Caroline Sturgis Tappan, Sept. 5, 1851, *C*XVI, p. 483.

242. "I am sick to death": NH to JTF, Sept. 13, 1851, *C*XVI, p. 486.

242. "Did Mr. Hawthorne": SH to MM, Sept. 23, 1851, Berg.

242. Since Mary and her family: Horace Mann had run on the Free-Soil ticket, having alienated Webster and other Whigs by his opposition to the Compromise of 1850.

242. "When a man is making": NH to HB, Oct. 11, 1851, *C*XVI, p. 495.

242. "I have not, as you": NH to Zachariah Burchmore, July 15, 1851, *C*XVI, p. 456.

242. "How glad I am": NH to HWL, May 8, 1851, *C*XVI, p. 431.

243. "This Fugitive Law": NH to HWL, May 8, 1851, *C*XVI, p. 431.

243. "bade farewell to all": NH to Zachariah Burchmore, July 15, 1851, *C* XVI, p. 456.

243. "d— for office": NH to Zachariah Burchmore, July 15, 1851, *C*XVI, p. 456.

243. "Ticknor & Co. promise": NH to SH, Sept. 23, 1851, *C*XVI, p. 492.

243. "I begin to unlove": SH to EPP, Oct. 2, 1851, Berg.

243. Early in November: See Hershel Parker, *Herman Melville*, vol. 1, 1819–1851 (Baltimore: Johns Hopkins Univ. Press, 1996), pp. 879–83.

243. "I have written a wicked": HM to NH, [Nov. 17, 1851], in Melville, *Correspondence*, p. 212.

243. "Your heart beat": HM to NH, [Nov. 17, 1851], in Melville, *Correspondence*, p. 212.

244. "What a book Melville": NH to ED, Dec. 1, 1851, *C*XVI, p. 508.

244. "Don't write a word": HM to NH, [Nov. 17, 1851], in Melville, *Correspondence*, p. 213.

244. "It is strange": Nov. 20, 1856, *EN*, vol. 2, p. 163.

244. "But truth is ever": HM to NH, [Nov. 17, 1851], in Melville, *Correspondence*, p. 213.

244. "a person of very gentlemanly": Nov. 20, 1856, *EN*, vol. 2, p. 163.

244. On a sunless November morning: *NHHW*, vol. 1, p. 430. The story seems apocryphal, for when Caroline Tappan suggested she leave an annoying pet rabbit in the woods, Hawthorne dryly observed that "she would not for the world have killed Bunny, although she would have exposed him to the certainty of lingering starvation, without scruple or remorse." He and Julian rescued the rabbit the next day. See Aug. 2 [1851], *AN*, p. 451.

244. "I suppose it is": EH to LH, [fall 1852], PE.

CHAPTER EIGHTEEN: CITIZEN OF SOMEWHERE ELSE

245. As promised, Fields: See, for instance, JTF to NH, Mar. 12, 1851, Berg: "To 'keep the pot boiling' has always been the endeavor of all true Yankees from the days of the Colonies down to the present era. Will it now be a good plan for you to get ready a volume of tales for the fall, to include those uncollected stories, The Snow Image, the piece in the mag. got up by Audubon's son & friend, etc. etc. and add to it any others not yet printed?"

245. A trim collection: *The Snow-Image and Other Twice-told Tales* cost seventy-five cents and gave Hawthorne 10 percent on royalty. See *The Cost Books of Ticknor and Fields*, pp. 210, 234, 409.

245. "If anybody is responsible," "I sat down": Preface to *The Snow-Image*, in *Tales*, p. 1155.

246. With his family of five: SH to LH, Dec. 1, 1851, *C*XVI, p. 511.

246. "to put an extra touch": NH to HB, July 25, 1851, *C*XVI, p. 462.

246. "the most romantic," "essentially a day-dream": *The Blithedale Romance*, p. 634.

247. "The Shakers are": Aug. 8 [1851], *AN,* p. 465.

247. "Insincerity in a man's": "Lost Notebook," n.d., in *Miscellaneous Prose and Verse, C* XXIII, p. 173.

248. "Persons of marked individuality": *The Blithedale Romance,* p. 686.

248. Hawthorne growled: See Mrs. EPP to EPP, Jan. 12, 1851, Antioch; SH to EPP, Feb. 3, 1851, Berg.

248. "felt Margaret Fuller's presence": Maria Mitchell, Jan. 30, 1858, journal, BY. In a sense, Hawthorne created his own memorial to Fuller in *Blithedale,* just as, shortly after Fuller's death, her friends James Freeman Clarke, William Henry Channing, and Ralph Waldo Emerson set to work on a multi-volume collection, *Memoirs,* celebrating Fuller's life through a highly selective tissue of her letters and journal entries. Hawthorne did not contribute; one supposes, however, that he was asked.

248. "Did you ever see": *The Blithedale Romance,* p. 683.

248. But by drawing on: Zenobia's drowning death comes as much from Ophelia's as from Hawthorne's own journal entries made after the drowning of Martha Hunt.

248. "They have no heart": *The Blithedale Romance,* p. 693.

249. "cold, spectral monster": *The Blithedale Romance,* p. 679.

249. Coverdale spies: *The Blithedale Romance,* p. 672.

249. "strike hands," "never again": *The Blithedale Romance,* p. 749.

250. "colorless life": *The Blithedale Romance,* p. 846.

250. And with no native: NH to SH, July 10, 1840, *C* XV, p. 481.

250. "While inclining": *The Blithedale Romance,* p. 694.

250. "No sagacious man": *The Blithedale Romance,* p. 755.

251. "In all my stories": NH to Charles Putnam, Sept. 16, 1851, *C* XVI, p. 488.

251. "He thinks Garrison": MM to Horace Mann, Aug. 15, 1852, MHS.

251. "He is very anxious": Mrs. EPP to MM, Feb. 25, 1852, Antioch.

252. Ice now . . . the raggediest: NH to ED, June 15, 1852, *C* XV, p. 548. Hawthorne bought the house from the trustees for Mrs. Abigail Alcott and her cousin Samuel Sewall, who owned the title, with the approval of Ralph Waldo Emerson. Hawthorne also purchased from Emerson eight acres of farmland across the road for five hundred dollars.

252. "I never feel": Study for "Septimius," n.d., Berg, quoted in *Elixir of Life,* p. 499. No one has definitively dated the notes to the "Septimius" manuscripts or the manuscripts themselves. I wouldn't be at all surprised if the romance begun in October 1852 wasn't a very early version of these manuscripts, inspired by Thoreau's comment on the Wayside. This romance, or notes for it, may or may not still exist.

253. The water was pure: SH to Mrs. EPP, [spring 1852], courtesy Evelyn Hamby; Stanford.

253. "I hate the man": See [E. P. Whipple], review of *Yesterdays, Boston Globe* (Mar. 7, 1872), pp. 4–5.

253. " 'Miles Coverdale's Three Friends' ": NH to E. P. Whipple, May 2, 1852, *C* XVI, p. 536.

254. Fields responded: SH to LH, July 17, 1852, Berg.

254. "Especially at this day": HM to NH, July 15, 1852, in Melville, *Correspondence*, p. 231.

254. "the moody silences": William Pike to NH, July 18, 1852, courtesy Evelyn Hamby; Stanford.

254. "You have a formidable": Washington Irving to NH, Aug. 9, 1852, Houghton, quoted in *C* XVI, p. 571.

254. "Would he paint": [George Eliot or Rufus Griswold], "Contemporary Literature of America," in *Nathaniel Hawthorne: The Contemporary Reviews*, p. 207.

255. "I have felt": SH to Mrs. EPP, Oct. 31, 1852, Berg.

255. "Let us hope": JTF to Mary Mitford, Oct. 24, 1852, Huntington.

CHAPTER NINETEEN: THE MAIN CHANCE

256. "My own experience": SH to Mrs. EPP, n.d., BY, quoted in *NHHW,* vol. 1, p. 483.

256. "It is mysterious": Mrs. EPP to SH, Mar. 20 [1848], Berg.

256. Emerson would call: *The Journals and Miscellaneous Notebooks of Ralph Waldo Emerson,* vol. 15, p. 60.

256. As brigadier general in the Mexican War: I am indebted to Roy Franklin Nichols, *Franklin Pierce* (1931; reprint, Philadelphia: Univ. of Pennsylvania Press, 1958), and Larry Gara, *The Presidency of Franklin Pierce* (Lawrence: Univ. Press of Kansas, 1991), for background on Pierce and the general anecdotes in this chapter.

256. "just an average man": GH to Frances Lieber, June 9, 1852, Huntington.

258. "dared to love": "The Life of Franklin Pierce," in *Miscellaneous Prose and Verse, C* XXIII, p. 292.

258. "He has a subtle faculty": NH to HB, Oct. 13, 1852, *C* XVI, p. 605.

258. "but he'll be monstrous": Quoted in Conway, *Life of Hawthorne,* p. 146.

259. "it has occurred to me": NH to FP, June 9, 1852, *C* XVI, p. 545.

259. The dark-browed writer: My account is based on the seemingly reliable account in Maunsell B. Field, *Memories of Men and of Some Women* (New York: Harper & Bros., 1874), p. 159; a far less reliable account appears in Henry T. Tuckerman, "Nathaniel Hawthorne," *Lippincott's Magazine* 5 (May 1870), p. 505. The latter part of the story was told to James Russell Lowell by Pierce himself in 1860; see James Russell Lowell to Grace Norton, misdated June 12, 1860, in *The Letters of James Russell Lowell,* ed. Charles Eliot Norton (New York: Harper & Bros., 1894), vol. 1, p. 303.

259. Hawthorne reportedly held: On the gathering at the Wayside, see Sanborn, *Recollections of Seventy Years,* vol. 2, p. 514. Sanborn not only reports long after the fact, he was not even an eyewitness; nonetheless, Concord locals were likely invited to the Wayside to meet Pierce, and certainly party operatives were always welcome. Thoreau remembers Pierce visiting the Wayside that July. See *The Correspondence of Henry David Thoreau,* ed. Walter Harding and Carl Bode (New York: New York Univ. Press, 1958), p. 283. [Zachariah Burchmore] to NH, July 9, 1852, NHHS; FP to Charles O'Connor, June 23, 1852, courtesy Kent Bicknell.

260. Fields's biographer insists: Given the tenor of the *Atlantic Monthly*, I disagree.

260. "intimate through life": NH to JTF, June 17, 1852, *C* XVI, p. 551.

260. "I told him I hoped": LH to EH, July 16, 1852, Berg.

260. If Louisa's disdain: Early biographers of Hawthorne also tended toward this view, so uncomfortable were they with the political side of Hawthorne's career and personality. See, for instance, Moncure Conway, *The Life of Hawthorne*, p. 145, who not only assumes Pierce forced Hawthorne to write the biography— "Hawthorne has an angry consciousness that he has been persuaded to descend from the sanctum of his genius"—but adds, more honestly, that "to the present writer it appears that Hawthorne descended from his height to write the book, and remained on that lower level while writing it."

260. On the afternoon of July 28: The summary of events is based on several matching reports of the accident in the New York press.

260. As soon as he could . . . Then he shut himself: For these events, see SH to Mrs. EPP, July 30, 1852, Berg.

261. "I was glad": SH to Mrs. EPP, Aug. 5, 1852, Berg.

261. "We are politicians now": NH to WDT, Aug. 25, 1852, *C* XVI, p. 588.

261. Ticknor began to advertise: Pierce had initially welcomed and encouraged David W. Bartlett before turning against him. Regardless, Bartlett's *Life of Gen. Franklin Pierce, of New-Hampshire, the Democratic President of the United States* (Buffalo, N.Y.: G. H. Derby, 1852) did appear before Hawthorne's, although Ticknor made sure that Hawthorne's gleaned the lion's share of reviews and sales. For an account of Bartlett, see Scott Caspar, "The Two Lives of Franklin Pierce," *American Literary History* 5:2 (summer 1993), pp. 203–30.

261. "Being so little" . . . "customary occupations": "The Life of Franklin Pierce," in *Miscellaneous Prose and Verse, C* XXIII, p. 273.

262. Hawthorne, however, interpreted . . . bumptious: "The Life of Franklin Pierce," in *Miscellaneous Prose and Verse, C* XXIII, p. 289.

262. "a thorough, unmitigated" . . . "Is Hawthorne": Horace Mann to MM, July 26, 1852, MHS.

262. "If he makes out": Horace Mann to MM, Aug. 20, 1852, MHS.

262. "higher law": See Allan Nevins, *Ordeal of the Union* (New York: Charles Scribner's Sons, 1947), vol. 1, pp. 298–302.

262. "unshaken advocate": "The Life of Franklin Pierce," in *Miscellaneous Prose and Verse, C* XXIII, p. 350.

262. So did Pierce: In the winter of 1852, when pressed, Pierce admitted he considered the law inhumane. Once nominated, however, he dodged the issue and pretended he couldn't remember what he had said.

263. "The fiercest, the least scrupulous": "The Life of Franklin Pierce," in *Miscellaneous Prose and Verse, C* XXIII, pp. 350–51.

263. "by some means impossible": "The Life of Franklin Pierce," in *Miscellaneous Prose and Verse, C* XXIII, p. 352.

263. "There is no instance," "The evil would be certain": "The Life of Franklin Pierce," in *Miscellaneous Prose and Verse, C* XXIII, p. 351.

263. "Little as we know": *The Blithedale Romance*, p. 698.

263. "whose condition it aimed": "The Life of Franklin Pierce," in *Miscellaneous Prose and Verse, C* XXIII, p. 351. Compare Sophia Hawthorne's views: "As regards the Compromise and the Fugitive Slave Law, it is his [Pierce's] opinion that these things must be now allowed—for the sake of the slave! One of his most strenuous supporters said that, 'viewed in itself, the Fugitive Slave Law was the most abominable of wrongs'; but that it was the inevitable fruit of the passionate action of the Abolitionists, and, like slavery itself, must be for the present tolerated. And so with the Compromise,—that it is the least of the evils presented. It has been said, as if there were no gainsaying it, that no man but Webster could ever be such a fool as really to believe the Union was in danger. But General Pierce has lately, with solemn emphasis, expressed the same dread; and it certainly seems that the severance of the Union would be the worst thing for the slave" (*NHHW,* vol. 1, p. 483). One wonders if Pierce's "strenuous supporter" was Hawthorne himself.

263. "patriarchal, and almost a beautiful": "Old News," in *Tales,* p. 257. See Chapter 13.

264. His conscious sympathies: Hawthorne expresses a strange sort of (supremacist) sympathy, even if one reads him ironically, in the 1837 sketch "Sunday at Home." Describing church congregations dispersing after a Sabbath service, he writes: "No; here, with faces as glossy as black satin, come two sable ladies and a sable gentleman, and close in their rear, the minister, who softens his severe visage, and bestows a kind word on each. Poor souls! To them, the most captivating picture of bliss in Heaven, is— 'There we shall be white!' " (in *Tales,* p. 419).

264. "preserving our sacred Union": "The Life of Franklin Pierce," in *Miscellaneous Prose and Verse, C* XXIII, p. 370.

264. "The biography has cost": NH to HB, Oct. 13, 1852, *C* XVI, p. 605. As for Sophia, she stood fast. "He does the thing he finds right, & lets the consequences fly." SH to Mrs. EPP, Sept. 10, 1852, Berg.

264. "There are scores": NH to HB, Oct. 13, 1852, *C* XVI, pp. 605–6.

264. Reviews of Hawthorne's book: "New Publications," *Springfield Republican,* Sept. 20, 1852, p. 2; *United States Magazine and Democratic Review,* Sept. 31, 1852, pp. 276–88; "Literary Notices," *Harper's New Monthly Magazine,* Nov. 1852, p. 857; "Degradation of Literary Talent," *New York Herald,* Sept. 23, 1852, p. 1; "Hawthorne's Memoir of Mr. Pierce," *New York Times,* Sept. 25, 1852, p. 1.

265. "All my cotemporaries": NH to SH, Sept. 3, 1852, *C* XVI, p. 593.

265. "He is deep": NH to HB, Oct. 13, 1852, *C* XVI, p. 606.

265. "I love him": NH to HB, Oct. 13, 1852, *C* XVI, p. 607.

265. At his request, Mrs. Healy: George Healy to George Holden, Sept. 1885, PE.

267. "in the *Scarlet Letter* vein": JTF to Mary Russell Mitford, Oct. 24, 1852, Huntington. Scholars surmise that Hawthorne may have seriously entertained Melville's suggestion that he write the story of Agatha Hatch Robertson, which Melville had first encountered during a trip to Nantucket the summer before. A patient Griselda, Robertson nursed a shipwrecked sailor back to health, married him, and then waited for him to return to her—although he'd married

another woman. There's room for speculation regarding Hawthorne's plans but no clear indication as to what he may have had in mind, although Fields's letter is suggestive.

267. "I am beginning to take": NH to HWL, Oct. 5, 1852, *C*XVI, p. 602.

267. "Do not let my name": NH to Zachariah Burchmore, Dec. 9, 1852, *C* XVI, p. 620.

267. "A subtile boldness": NH to R. H. Stoddard, Mar. 16, 1853, *C*XVI, p. 649.

267. Nothing came of Hawthorne's efforts: Leyda, *The Melville Log*, p. 464. During this visit Melville continued to press Hawthorne to write the story of Agatha Hatch Robertson, but Hawthorne evidently turned it down, possibly because of his own consular plans. Hershel Parker assumes that Melville himself used the story in the now lost manuscript *Isle of the Cross*. See Hershel Parker, *Herman Melville: A Biography*, vol. 2, 1851–1891 (Baltimore: Johns Hopkins Univ. Press, 2002), pp. 136–61. Doubtless the subject of a possible appointment for Melville from Pierce was broached at this time, although the larger Melville family did not begin lobbying until the spring; see also Laurie Robertson-Lorant, *Melville* (New York: Clarkson Potter, 1996), p. 327.

267. "However, I failed only": Nov. 20, 1856, *EN*, vol. 2, p. 162.

268. "several invitations": NH to HB, Oct. 13, 1852, *C*XVI, p. 605; *Happy Country This America: The Travel Diary of Henry Arthur Bright*, ed. Anne Henry Ehrenpreis (Columbus: Ohio State Univ. Press, 1978), p. 398.

268. "We shall have no more": JTF to Mary Russell Mitford, Dec. 11, 1852, Huntington.

268. "Bargain & sale": SH to Dr. Nathaniel Peabody, Mar. 20, 1853, Berg.

268. He torched old letters: JTF to ED, Apr. 16, 1853, Duyckinck Family Papers, NYPL; June 1852, *AN*, p. 552.

CHAPTER TWENTY: THIS FARTHER FLIGHT

269. "Then this farther flight": Sept. 2, 1853, *EN*, vol. 1, pp. 33–34.

269. "Partly necessity": *NHHW*, vol. 1, p. 429.

269. proofs for *Tanglewood Tales:* First published in England by Chapman and Hall, in America the book was published by Ticknor, Reed and Fields and contained six stories: "The Minotaur," "The Pygmies," "The Dragon's Teeth, "Circe's Palace," "The Pomegranate Seeds," and "The Golden Fleece."

270. "Who else could have": Moncure D. Conway, *Autobiography, Memories, and Experiences* (Boston: Houghton Mifflin, 1904), p. 135.

270. "A life of much smoulder": NH to JTF, Feb. 25, 1864, *C*XVIII, p. 641.

271. "I am a good deal": NH to JTF, Apr. 13, 1854, *C*XVII, p. 201.

271. "The American stamp": *NHHW*, vol. 1, p. 434.

271. "I do not like England": UH to Rebecca Manning, n.d., PE.

271. "To tell you the truth": NH to WDT, July 22, 1853, *C*XVII, p. 101.

272. "There we shall remain": SH to Dr. Nathaniel Peabody, Aug. 6, 1853, Berg.

272. Hawthorne had already given: SH to Dr. Nathaniel Peabody, Aug. 9 and 17, 1853, Berg. See Aug. 15, 1853, *EN*, vol. 1, p. 17: "After the removal of the cloth, the Mayor gave various toasts, prefacing each with some remarks—the first of course, the Sovereign, after which 'God Save the Queen' was sung; and there

was something rather ludicrous in seeing the company stand up and join the chorus, their ample faces glowing with wine, enthusiasm, perspiration, and loyalty."

272. "People who have not heard": SH to Dr. Nathaniel Peabody, Oct. 21, 1853, Berg.

272. Each morning, he left: Aug. 9, 1853, *EN,* vol. 1, p. 13.

272. Located in the Washington Buildings: NH to William Pike, Sept. 13, 1853, *C* XVII, p. 119; NH to Henry Bright, Jan. 4, 1858, *C* XVIII, p. 133.

272. An American eagle: Aug. 4, 1853, *EN,* vol. 1, p. 4.

272. "The duties of the office": "Consular Experiences," in *OOH,* p. 31.

273. "The autograph of a living author": Aug. 10, 1853, *EN,* vol. 1, p. 16.

273. "instead of Mr. Nobody": SH to Dr. Nathaniel Peabody, Aug. 26, 1853, Berg.

273. Tea alone cost: SH to Dr. Nathaniel Peabody, Oct. 4, 1853, Berg.

273. "We do not live": SH to Dr. Nathaniel Peabody, Oct. 4, 1853, Berg.

273. "So very far from this": SH to Dr. Nathaniel Peabody, Oct. 4, 1853, Berg.

273. "we live as economically": SH to MM, Mar. 17–24, 1855, Berg.

273. "kick the office": NH to WDT, Dec. 8, 1853, *C* XVII, p. 152.

274. "got hold of something": Aug. 20, 1853, *EN,* vol. 1, p. 19.

275. "Or perhaps the image": June 22, 1855, *EN,* vol. 1, p. 188.

275. "My ancestor left England": Oct. 9, 1854, *EN,* vol. 1, p. 138.

275. "How comfortable Englishmen": Feb. 19, 1855, *EN,* vol. 1, p. 156. A fine study of Hawthorne's changing attitudes toward the English is Frederick Newberry, *Hawthorne's Divided Loyalties* (Rutherford, N.J.: Fairleigh Dickinson Univ. Press, 1987); accounts of his daily activities can be found in Raymona E. Hull, *Nathaniel Hawthorne: The English Experience, 1853–1964* (Pittsburgh: Univ. of Pittsburgh Press, 1980), still the best book of its kind despite the more recent but compendious Bryan Homer, *An American Liaison: Leamington Spa and the Hawthornes, 1855–1864* (Rutherford, N.J.: Fairleigh Dickinson Univ. Press, 1997).

275. "I HATE England": NH to WDT, Nov. 9, 1855, *C* XVII, p. 401.

275. "I set my foot on": July 4, 1855, *EN,* vol. 1, p. 222.

275. They had read Frederika Bremer's: Frederika Bremer, *The Homes of the New World; Impressions of America,* trans. Mary Howitt (1853; reprint, New York: Negro Universities Press, 1968), vol. 2, p. 597.

275. William Story told: *The Letters of Elizabeth Barrett Browning to Mary Russell Mitford, 1836–1854,* ed. Meredith B. Taymond and Mary Rose Sullivan (Winfield, Kan.: Wedgestone Press, 1983), vol. 3, p. 391; JTF to Mary Russell Mitford, Sept. 30, 1851, Huntington; *The Correspondence of Mary Russell Mitford with Charles Boner and John Ruskin,* ed. Elizabeth Lee (London: T. Fisher Unwin, 1914), p. 194.

275. James Fields told; "Was Hawthorne aware": JTF to Mary Russell Mitford, Sept. 30, 1851, Huntington; *The Correspondence of Mary Russell Mitford with Charles Boner and John Ruskin,* p. 216; William Story to James Russell Lowell, Aug. 10, 1853, quoted in *Browning to His American Friends,* ed. Gertrude Reese Hudson (New York: Barnes & Noble, 1965), p. 277.

276. "Bright was the illumination": *OOH,* p. 39.

276. Bright took Hawthorne; "interesting, sincere": Aug. 4, 1853, *EN,* vol. 1, p. 4; *Memories,* p. 229.

277. "poor old man" . . . "You examine": NH to Henry Bright, Apr. 4, 1854, *C*XVII, p. 198

277. "He wants to know": SH to EPP, [Sept. 1854], Berg.

277. "I have had enough": NH to HWL, Aug. 30, 1854, *C*XVII, p. 250.

278. According to Hawthorne; according to Sophia: See NH to HB, Mar. 30, 1854, *C*XVII, pp. 187–89; *Memories,* pp. 281–83.

278. "those Jackasses at Washington": NH to WDT, Apr. 30, 1854, *C*XVII, p. 210.

278. If passed by Congress . . . not nearly: SH to EPP, Mar. 24, 1855, Historical Society of Pennsylvania.

279. "For God's sake, bestir": NH to WDT, Mar. 30, 1854, *C*XVII, p. 190.

279. Hoping Pierce might forestall: Pierce objected to the bill on constitutional grounds, arguing that it abrogated executive prerogative, ceding it to the legislative branch of government. See Graham Stuart, *The Department of State* (New York: Macmillan, 1949), pp. 120–21, and Warren Ilchman, *Professional Diplomacy in the United States* (Chicago: Univ. of Chicago Press, 1961), p. 33.

279. "H. ought to": HB to WDT, Feb. 26, 1855, Berg.

279. "He shall, I think": "Study 1," in *American Claimant Manuscripts,* p. 473. I agree with the *Centenary* editors, who speculate that this sketch must have been written circa April 1855, given its similarity to an entry in his *English Notebooks* dated April 12, 1855, vol. 1, p. 163. I also believe the two other studies for the story, numbered by the *Centenary* editors "2" and "3," may have been written sometime during Hawthorne's consular service, for I imagine he began outlining ideas for the American claimant just when he feared he would be leaving his consular office prematurely.

279. "where no change": June 24, 1855, *EN,* vol. 1, pp. 191–92.

280. "Royalty": Mar. 24, 1856, *EN,* vol. 1, p. 429.

280. "Blood issued": Apr. 7, 1855, *EN,* vol. 1, p. 160.

280. The image was tailor-made: See *AN,* p. 239: "The print in blood of a naked foot to be traced through the street of a town."

280. He'd been happy . . . "quite failed": Dec. 28, 1854, *EN,* vol. 1, p. 148.

280. "Now we are fixtures": SH to MM, May 9–10, 1855, Berg. See also SH to EPP, Mar. 24, 1855, Historical Society of Pennsylvania.

281. "I have a right": NH to WDT, May 27, 1855, *C*XVII, p. 347; NH to WDT, June 9, 1855, *C*XVII, p. 353.

281. Sarah Clarke visited: MM to Horace Mann, Aug. 7, 1856, MHS.

281. "The doctors said I *must*": SH to MM, Nov. 13, 1855, Berg.

281. "This is the first": Oct. 11, 1855, *EN,* vol. 1, pp. 388, 390.

CHAPTER TWENTY-ONE: TRUTH STRANGER THAN FICTION

282. "All women, as authors": NH to JTF, Dec. 11, 1852, *C*XVI, p. 624. The ostensible catalyst for the remark was Camilla Crosland's latest books, *Lydia: A Woman's Book* and *English Tales and Sketches,* published by Ticknor, Reed and Fields and sent to Hawthorne.

282. "A false liberality": "Mrs. Hutchinson," in *Tales,* p. 18.

282. "America is now wholly": NH to WDT, Jan. 19, 1855, *C* XVII, p. 303. For a recent cogent analysis of Hawthorne's famed outburst, see Nina Baym, "Again and Again, The Scribbling Women," in *Hawthorne and Women*, ed. John L. Idol Jr. and Melinda M. Ponder (Amherst: Univ. of Massachusetts Press, 1999), pp. 20–35, and in particular the observation about Grace Greenwood and a "female discourse," in opposition to Hawthorne's, "in which the woman writer moves from the home fires to the public sphere without apology, registering absolutely no sense of impropriety."

283. "truth of detail," "a broader": July 26, 1857, *EN*, vol. 2, p. 345.

283. Of course, a higher truth: In 1854, when Congress was debating the Kansas-Nebraska bill, Stowe published in *The Independent* "An Appeal to Women of the Free States of America, on the Present Crisis on Our Country" and also circulated petitions to defeat the bill. See Joan D. Hedrick, *Harriet Beecher Stowe: A Life* (New York: Oxford Univ. Press, 1994), pp. 256–57.

283. "with the most lifelike": July 26, 1857, *EN*, vol. 2, p. 345.

283. "a whole history": NH to WDT, Feb. 17, 1854, *C* XVII, p. 177.

283. "Be true!": *The Scarlet Letter*, p. 341.

284. "throw off the restraints": NH to WDT, Feb. 2, 1855, *C* XVII, p. 308.

284. "The woman writes as if": NH to WDT, Feb. 2, 1855, *C* XVII, p. 308.

284. "It does seem to me": NH to SH, Mar. 18, 1856, *C* XVII, p. 457.

284. "Neither she nor I": NH to WDT, June 5, 1857, *C* XVIII, p. 64.

284. "I think it is designed": SH to EPP, Dec. 29, 1850, Berg.

284. "I have such an unmitigated": SH to EPP, Oct. 31, 1854, Berg.

284. "My principle is not": SH to MM, Aug. 28 [1857], Antioch.

284. "The repose of art": SH to EPP, Aug. 7–12, 1857, Berg.

284. "Life has never been": NH to SH, Dec. 13, 1855, *C* XVII, p. 418. On Una's headaches, see UH to NH, Dec. 18 [1856], Berg. The letter is misdated 1858.

285. She wore a violet brocade: See UH to MM, Oct. 31, 1855, Berg, and *NHHW*, vol. 2, p. 88.

285. Hawthorne had told her: NH to SH, Nov. 3, 1855, *C* XVII, p. 398.

285. "Oh, my wife": NH to SH, Apr. 7, 1856, *C* XVII, p. 465.

285. "I have learned": Jan. 16, 1856, *EN*, vol. 1, p. 406.

285. Hawthorne sullenly reminded; "Heretofore": NH to SH, Apr. 7, 1856, *C* XVII, p. 465.

285. "What a mill-stone": SH to NH, [1856], fragment, courtesy Evelyn Hamby; Stanford.

285. His cicerone was: Mitford, *The Correspondence of Mary Russell Mitford with Charles Boner and John Ruskin*, p. 226.

285. He also wrote a little poetry: See Bennoch's preface, *Poems, Lyrics, Songs and Sonnets* (London: Hardwicke and Bogue, 1877).

286. "sparkling black eyes": *HHC*, p. 92.

286. Rose Hawthorne recalled: *Memories*, p. 308.

286. "I never saw a man": Francis Bennoch, "A Week's Vagabondage with Nathaniel Hawthorne," *Nathaniel Hawthorne Journal*, 1971, ed. C. E. Frazer Clark Jr., p. 33.

286. "They have found me out": NH to SH, Apr. 7, 1856, *C* XVII, p. 463.

286. Afterwards, he decided: Apr. 13, 1856, *EN,* vol. 1, p. 485.

287. "If this man has": May 24, 1856, *EN,* vol. 2, p. 37.

287. "friend whom I love": Nov. 10, 1857, *EN,* vol. 2, p. 404.

287. "If anything could bring": NH to WDT, Dec. 7, 1855, *C* XVII, p. 414.

287. "the pure unadulterated": Quoted in Nevins, *Ordeal of the Union,* vol. 2, p. 114. Among the books I've consulted in this and subsequent chapters, particularly useful are George Frederickson, *The Inner Civil War* (New York: Harper & Row, 1965); Eric Foner, *Free Soil, Free Labor, Free Men* (New York: Oxford Univ. Press, 1995); Roy Franklin Nichols, *The Disruption of American Democracy* (New York: Macmillan, 1948); David M. Potter, *The Impending Crisis, 1848–1861,* ed. Don E. Fehrenbacher (New York: HarperPerennial, 1976); Leonard L. Richards, *Gentlemen of Property and Standing* (New York: Oxford Univ. Press, 1970).

287. "I must say": GH to Francis Lieber, Mar. 2, 1854, Huntington.

287. "this cruel attempt": Quoted in Nevins, *Ordeal of the Union,* vol. 2, p. 490.

287. "How insane all": SH to MM, July 3, 1854, Berg.

288. "persons angelic in goodness": SH to MM, July 3, 1854, Berg. The remaining sections of this letter strongly suggest that her arguments were derived from Hawthorne: "I have no doubt that this measure of President Pierce will be considered a wise, courageous & disinterested one, as far as he is concerned, & that it will be seen that he dared to do what he believed his duty against the fiercest hue & cry—There was very much such a condemnation of President Jackson about the Bank—& the result proved his wisdom & foresight though he was accused of every mean & base motive all the time."

288. "I find it impossible": NH to HB, Dec. 14, 1854, *C* XVII, p. 292; see NH to WDT, July 7, 1854, *C* XVII, p. 237.

288. "Oh how much harm": SH to Dr. Nathaniel Peabody, July 4–5 [1854], Berg.

289. "To say the truth": NH to William Pike, July 17, 1856, *C* XVII, p. 521.

289. "stupendous, grand" . . . She wanted to meet: SH to MM, Aug. 12, 1856, Berg.

289. Monckton Milnes: See James Pope-Hennessy, *Monckton Milnes: The Years of Promise* (New York: Farrar, Straus & Cudahy, 1955), p. 4.

289. "Unquestionably, she was": "Recollections of a Gifted Woman," in *OOH,* p. 106.

289. "I want some literary": Delia Bacon to NH, May 8, 1856, Folger, quoted in Vivian Hopkins, *Prodigal Puritan: A Life of Delia Bacon* (Cambridge: Harvard Univ. Press, 1959), p. 200. For information on Delia Bacon, I am grateful to the Folger Shakespeare Library, and indebted to Vivian Hopkins's biography and Theodore Bacon's *Delia Bacon* (Boston: Houghton Mifflin, 1888).

290. "But I feel": NH to Delia Bacon, May 12, 1856, *C* XVII, pp. 488–89.

291. "too weak to bear": Harriet Beecher Stowe to NH, Dec. 18, 1862, bMS Am 2010 129, Houghton.

291. "Delia Bacon, with genius": RWE to Caroline Sturgis Tappan, Oct. 13, 1857, quoted in *The Selected Letters of Ralph Waldo Emerson,* ed. Joel Myerson (New York: Columbia Univ. Press, 1997), p. 395.

292. "If you really think": NH to Delia Bacon, May 2, 1856, *C* XVII, p. 488.

292. "It is a very singular": "Recollections of a Gifted Woman," in *OOH,* p. 106.

292. "The more absurdly": NH to Francis Bennoch, Oct. 27, 1856, *C*XVII, p. 569.

293. "How funny": NH to Francis Bennoch, Oct. 27, 1856, *C*XVII, p. 570. See also NH to WDT, Nov. 6, 1856, *C*XVII, p. 574.

293. "It is a strange": Sept. 9, 1856, *EN*, vol. 2, p. 149.

293. His literary ebullience: See Parker, *Herman Melville*, vol. 2, pp. 297–98.

293. "He certainly is": Nov. 20, 1856, *EN*, vol. 2, p. 170.

293. "If he were a religious": Nov. 20, 1856, *EN*, vol. 2, p. 163.

293. "I do not know": Nov. 20, 1856, *EN*, vol. 2, p. 170.

294. "an utterly stupid": SH to EPP, Nov. 19, 1856, Berg.

294. "Our life here": May 10, 1857, *EN*, vol. 2, p. 209.

294. "I rather wished them": Mar. 1, 1857, *EN*, vol. 2, p. 182.

294. "the moral victory": ED to George Duyckinck, Oct. 20, 1856, NYPL. He was right: Frémont won a whopping 114 electoral votes.

294. "For the sake of novelty": NH to WDT, Aug. 15, 1856, *C*XVII, p. 531.

294. "because the negroes": SH to MM, Dec. 30 [1856]–Jan. 2 [1857], Berg.

295. "The country will stand": SH to MM, Dec. 30 [1856]–Jan. 2 [1857], Berg.

295. "No man or woman": Preface to Delia Bacon's *The Philosophy of the Plays of Shakspere Unfolded,* in *Miscellaneous Prose and Verse, C*XXIII, p. 395.

295. She wanted him: See SH to EPP, Apr. 27, 1857, Berg.

295. "I do not repent": NH to WDT, Apr. 9, 1857, *C*XVIII, p. 49.

295. By then Bacon: NH to WDT, June 19, 1857, *C*XVIII, p. 74. Bacon did not return to America until a young nephew, who arrived in England, could accompany her, and then shortly after her return, on April 2, 1858, she died, faithful to the end to the truth as she saw it.

295. "I fell under Miss Bacon's": "Recollections of a Gifted Woman," in *OOH,* p. 114.

CHAPTER TWENTY-TWO: QUESTIONS OF TRAVEL

296. "Mr. H. came": Ada Shepard to Henry Clay Badger, Oct. 14, 1857, BY.

296. Lovable Una: See Ada Shepard to Henry Clay Badger, Oct. 4 and 7, 1857, BY.

297. "It seems as though": Ada Shepard to Kate [Shepard], Dec. 6, 1857, BY.

297. "The splendor" . . . But the biting: Jan. 8, 1858, *FIN*, p. 13.

297. A generous and kind man: Ada Shepard to Henry Clay Badger, June 3, 1858, BY.

297. Longing for home: Jan. 12, 1858, *FIN*, p. 34.

297. "How I dislike": Feb. 3, 1858, *FIN*, p. 54.

297. The Hawthorne entourage . . . "Had Mr. Hawthorne": Maria Mitchell, journal, Jan. 15, 18, and 19, 1858, BY.

297. Arrive they finally did: Maria Mitchell, journal, Jan. 19, 1858, BY.

298. "How could wise and great": SH to EPP, May 27, 1858, Berg.

298. Hawthorne lagged . . . Exhausted: *Maria Mitchell: Life, Letters, and Journals,* ed. Phebe Mitchell Kendall (Boston: Lee & Shepard, 1896), p. 90; Maria Mitchell's lectures to her students, BY.

298. "Of course there are better": Feb. 3, 1858, *FIN*, p. 54.

298. "Byron's celebrated description": See *The Marble Faun*, p. 980.

299. "Take away the malaria": Nov. 3, 1858, *FIN*, p. 496.

299. "There is something forced" . . . "general apotheosis": Feb. 25, 1858, *FIN*, pp. 115, 111.

299. "This lascivious warmth": Apr. 3, 1858, *FIN*, p. 157.

299. He was also . . . "the statues kept": Apr. 12, 1858, *FIN*, pp. 165–66.

299. "strange, sweet" . . . "a natural": Apr. 1, 1858, *FIN*, pp. 173–74.

299. Three weeks later: JH to W. T. H. Howe, July 22, 1931, Bancroft; Apr. 22, 1858, *FIN*, pp. 178–79.

300. "which will make me": NH to WDT, Apr. 14, 1858, *C*XVIII, p. 140.

300. Clutching *Murray's Handbook: Murray's Handbook of Rome and Its Environs* (London: John Murray, 1858); Hawthorne often quotes Murray's descriptions and views in his journals.

300. "In the church of San Paulo": Feb. 7, 1858, *FIN*, p. 60.

301. American expatriates: Ada Shepard to Lucy Shepard, Aug. 6, 1858, BY.

301. "the sky itself": William Wetmore Story to James Russell Lowell, Dec. 30, 1855, quoted in Henry James, *William Wetmore Story and His Friends* (Boston: Houghton Mifflin, 1903), vol. 1, p. 298.

301. "Their public": May 21, 1858, *FIN*, p. 220.

301. "With sparkling talents": Oct. 4, 1858, *FIN*, p. 448.

301. "He is certainly sensible": Feb. 14, 1858, *FIN*, p. 73.

301. "I cannot say": SH, Roman journal, Feb. 18, 1858, Berg.

301. Like all of the other expatriate: For this chapter I've consulted Paul R. Baker, *The Fortunate Pilgrims: Americans in Italy, 1800–1864* (Cambridge, Mass.: Harvard Univ. Press, 1964); Van Wyck Brooks, *The Dream of Arcadia: American Writers and Artists in Italy* (New York: E. P. Dutton, 1958); Hugh Honour, *Neo-Classicism* (New York: Viking Penguin, 1987); Joy S. Kasson, *Marble Queens and Captives: Women in Nineteenth-Century American sculpture* (New Haven, Conn.: Yale Univ. Press, 1990); Theodore E. Stebbins Jr., ed., *The Lure of Italy: American Artists and the Italian Experience, 1760–1914* (Boston: Museum of Fine Arts, 1992); William Vance, *America's Rome* (New Haven, Conn.: Yale Univ. Press, 1989); Nathalia Wright, *American Novelists in Italy: The Discoverers: Allston to James* (Philadelphia: Univ. of Pennsylvania Press, 1965).

302. "cleverness and ingenuity": Apr. 3, 1858, *FIN*, p. 153.

302. Lander insisted on puffing: Maria Mitchell, journal, Mar. 9, 1858, BY.

302. "The likeness was destroyed": *NHHW*, vol. 2, p. 183. For a refutation of JH's story, see John Idol Jr. and Sterling Eisminger, "Hawthorne Sits for a Bust by Maria Louisa Lander," *Essex Institute Historical Collections* 114 (1978), pp. 207–12.

302. "like a boy": Maria Mitchell, journal, Feb. 4, 1858, BY.

303. "She was indeed": Apr. 3, 1858, *FIN*, p. 158.

303. "I think Miss Hosmer": UH to EPP, Feb. 24, 1858 [misdated 1859], BY.

303. "Hatty takes a high hand": William Wetmore Story to James Russell Lowell, Feb. 11, 1853, quoted in James, *William Wetmore Story*, vol. 1, p. 254.

303. "entirely ignorant": Apr. 3, 1858, *FIN*, p. 156.

303. "The amelioration of society": "The Ancestral Footstep," in *American Claimant Manuscripts*, p. 70.

303. "did nothing of importance": Pocket diary, Apr. 30, 1858, *FIN*, p. 594.

303. "I doubt greatly": NH to WDT, Apr. 14, 1858, *C* XVIII, p. 140.

303. Yet at about the same time . . . "Mr. Hawthorne commenced": Mozier visited the Hawthornes on April 2; Hawthorne wrote of Fuller in his journal the next day. While Ada Shepard noted April 13 (Ada Shepard to Henry Clay Badger, Apr. 14, 1858, BY), the extant "Ancestral Manuscript" bears a date of April 1, with an earlier leaf having been cut out. Hawthorne's remarks about women and social change were written on May 14, 1858.

304. This new book comes: Rose Hawthorne Lathrop and her husband George Lathrop published the manuscript partly to fend off Julian's latest gambit, passing off some of the fragments discovered among his father's papers as a newly discovered work. (These fragments, cobbled together, became known as *Doctor Grimshawe's Secret*). For textual information and details about the publishing history of these drafts, see *C* XII, pp. 491–515, 523–34. For more information on the squabble between the Lathrops and Julian Hawthorne, see Brenda Wineapple, "The Biographical Imperative; or, Hawthorne Family Values," *Biography and Source Studies* 6, ed. Frederick Karl (New York: AMS Press, 1998), pp. 1–13.

304. "touches that shall puzzle": "The Ancestral Footstep," in *American Claimant Manuscripts,* p. 87.

304. "singular discoveries": "The Ancestral Footstep," in *American Claimant Manuscripts,* p. 11.

304. "so remorseful": "The Ancestral Footstep," in *American Claimant Manuscripts,* p. 50.

304. "He rather felt": "The Ancestral Footstep," in *American Claimant Manuscripts,* p. 60.

305. "what shall be the nature": "The Ancestral Footstep," in *American Claimant Manuscripts,* p. 53.

305. "withdraw himself": "The Ancestral Footstep," in *American Claimant Manuscripts,* p. 18.

305. "He [Hamlet] lived so": SH to EPP, Apr. 22, 1857, Berg.

305. "The progress of the world": "The Life of Franklin Pierce," in *Miscellaneous Prose and Verse, C* XXIII, p. 352.

305. "The moral, if any": "The Ancestral Footstep," in *American Claimant Manuscripts,* p. 56.

306. "blessed words": UH to Richard Manning Jr., May 3, 1858, PE.

306. "What a land!": SH, *Notes in England and Italy* (New York: G. P. Putnam & Son, 1869), p. 487.

306. The Hawthornes . . . like strayed: UH to MM, July 19, 1858, BY.

306. "Paradise of cheapness": June 3, 1858, *FIN,* p. 283.

306. "What can man": June 4, 1858, *FIN,* p. 283.

306. Their illustrious neighbors: SH, *Notes in England and Italy,* p. 344.

307. "Mr. Hawthorne has become": SH to MM, June 7–10, 1858, Berg.

307. "Every day I shall": June 4, 1858, *FIN,* p. 283.

307. Powers tickled Hawthorne . . . "full of bone": June 13, 1858, *FIN,* p. 314; June 7, 1858, p. 290.

307. "after admiring": June 10, 1858, *FIN,* p. 307.

307. "Until we learn": June 15, 1858, *FIN,* p. 317.

307. "For my part": June 15, 1858, *FIN,* pp. 317–18.

308. "Had it not been": July 8, 1858, *FIN,* p. 367.

308. "wish it to be": "The Ancestral Footstep," in *American Claimant Manuscripts,* p. 58.

308. "I feel an impulse": June 13, 1858, *FIN,* p. 316.

309. Hawthorne caught cold: See SH to MM, June 7–10, 1858, Berg; and SH to EPP, Aug. 14, 1858, Berg.

309. "big enough to quarter": NH to JTF, Sept. 3, 1858, *C*XVIII, p. 150.

309. Marching through . . . The view: Aug. 4, 1858, p. 390; Aug. 2, 1858, p. 383, in *FIN.*

309. "I find this Italian": NH to JTF, Sept. 3, 1858, *C*XVIII, p. 151.

309. Ada Shepard sent tidings: Manuscripts enclosed in RH to Clifford Smythe, July 3, 1925, courtesy Evelyn Hamby; Stanford.

309. "with a sad reluctance": Sept. 28, 1858, *FIN,* p. 429.

309. "I am not loth": Sept. 29, 1858, *FIN,* p. 436.

CHAPTER TWENTY-THREE: THINGS TO SEE AND SUFFER

311. "ROME ROME ROME": SH, notebooks, Oct. 18, 1858, Berg.

311. "Now that I," "Besides": Oct. 17, 1858, *FIN,* p. 488.

311. "to such Arabs": SH, notebooks, Oct. 18, 1858, Berg, quoted in *Passages from the English Notebooks,* ed. Sophia Hawthorne (Boston: Fields, Osgood, 1870), p. 541.

312. "uncommonly good terms": John Rogers Jr. to Henry Rogers, Feb. 13, 1859, New-York Historical Society.

312. Punctilious, the American expatriate: See a note regarding the work of the so-called committee of investigation, Dec. 27, 1858, among the William Wetmore Story papers, Harry Ransom Humanities Research Center, University of Texas at Austin: Lander evidently committed an unpardonable sin against society, or the committee, when she refused to let Benjamin Appleton, an American physician, testify in the form of an affidavit sworn before the United States ambassador. Appleton declined to testify in any other way. It's not clear why Appleton insisted on an affidavit nor why Lander insisted he speak only before the committee, but the stalemate effectively disabled the committee, allowing, it seems, Lander neither defense nor recourse.

312. "Miss Lander's life": NH to Louisa Lander and Elizabeth Lander, Nov. 13, 1858, *C*XVIII, p. 158. For a highly speculative reading of Hawthorne's relation to Lander, unsupported by evidence but entertaining, see T. Walter Herbert's otherwise excellent *Dearest Beloved: The Hawthornes and the Making of the Middle-Class Family,* pp. 231–34.

313. "I have suffered more": NH to FP, Oct. 27, 1858, *C*XXVIII, p. 156.

313. She first was diagnosed: At the time, it was assumed that breathing bad air (*mala aria*) caused malaria; hence it was assumed that Una took ill after sitting to sketch in the Colosseum, somewhat like her descendant Daisy Miller. Oddly, contemporary critics repeat the account, although it is known that

malaria is caused by a parasitic virus transmitted to humans through infected mosquitoes, which Una may have contracted before returning to Rome.

313. "like a tragic heroine": Nov. 2, 1858, *FIN*, p. 495.

313. "The ill effects": *NHHW*, vol. 2, p. 210. Acting as an antiseptic, quinine retards the progress of the disease, but when taken in large doses over long periods, it can produce gastric disorders and disorders of the nervous system, including vertigo, apprehension, confusion, delirium, excitability, and vision and hearing problems. Because quinine can depress the nervous system and the heart, it's possible the effects of the drug were a material cause in Una Hawthorne's final illness and death. See Gordon MacPherson, ed., *Black's Medical Dictionary* (London: A. & C. Black, 1992), p. 493. I am also indebted to Carolyn Kelly Patten's fine unpublished paper "Una Hawthorne: Seeking a Purpose," written for my Hawthorne graduate seminar at NYU in 1997.

313. "I have been trying": NH to JTF, Feb. 3, 1859, *C*XVIII, p. 160.

313. "As for my success": NH to JTF, Feb. 3, 1859, *C*XVIII, pp. 160–61.

313. "I never knew": NH to WDT, Mar. 4, 1859, *C*XVIII, p. 163.

314. "God help us!": Apr. 8, 1859, *FIN*, p. 657.

314. "I don't know": Ada Shepard to Henry Clay Shepard, Apr. 9, 1859, BY; SH to EPP, July 3–4, 1859, Berg.

314. But Sophia . . . Una said: SH to EPP, July 3–4, 1859, Berg.

314. "We won't play any more": *NHHW*, vol. 2, p. 208.

314. "It is not natural": SH to MM, Apr. 9, 1859, Berg.

314. "I do not remember": SH to EPP, July 3–4, 1859, Berg.

315. Even Mrs. Browning: The foregoing is paraphrased from SH to EPP, July 3–4, 1859, Berg.

315. "No one else could": SH to EPP, July 3–4, 1859, Berg.

315. "with a miraculous": Mar. 23, 1859, *FIN*, p. 512.

315. "The Kansas outrages": Quoted in Nevins, *Ordeal of the Union*, vol. 2, p. 455.

315. "I did not know what": Apr. 19, 1859, *FIN*, p. 518.

316. "He says he should die": SH to EPP, [Apr. 24, 1859], Berg.

316. "But (life being": May 29, 1859, *FIN*, p. 524.

316. "My fatigue": SH to JTF, June 26, 1859, BPL.

316. "I have known her": Thomas Tryon, *Parnassus Corner: A Life of James T. Fields* (Boston: Houghton Mifflin, 1963), p. 211.

316. She liked Hawthorne: AF, diary, June 27, 1859, MHS.

316. He'd grown . . . The Italian adventure: Ada Shepard to Henry Clay Badger, June 23, 1858, BY; NH to Francis Bennoch, June 17, 1859, *C*XVIII, p. 178.

317. "He is entirely": FP to HB, Sept. 11, 1859, Bowdoin.

317. "It was a proposition": FP to HB, Sept. 11, 1859, Bowdoin.

317. Again, the issue: Clark, *Hawthorne at Auction, 1894–1971*, p. 127.

317. "I think of Mamma": UH to EPP, Aug. 13, 1859, BY.

318. "It is as bleak": NH to Francis Bennoch, July 23, 1859, *C*XVIII, p. 182.

318. Hawthorne disappeared . . . In the evening: See UH to Ada Shepard, July 29, 1859, Antioch.

318. "The sea entirely": SH to EPP, July 31, 1859, Berg.

318. "As usual he thinks": SH to EPP, [Oct. 1859], Berg.

318. Aversion aside . . . minor suggestions: See, for instance, "Textual Introduction" to *The Marble Faun*, *C* IV, pp. xxv, lxviii.

318. "Monte Beni is our": SH to EPP, Feb. 27, 1860, Berg.

318. He also played: NH to JTF, Oct. 10, 1859, p. 196; NH to WDT, Dec. 1, 1859, *C* XVIII, p. 206. The Hawthornes had visited St. Hilda's Abbey while in Whitby, just before moving to Redcar, in July 1859, from which the name of Hilda was likely taken, especially because Una at the time was reading Scott's *Marmion*. See UH to Ada Shepard, July 29, 1859, Antioch. Also, local legend explains that the lamp atop the medieval tower, built circa 1000, at the Palazzo Scapucci commemorates the Madonna's rescue of a child once imprisoned in the tower by, of all things, a monkey. In Hawthorne's day, the monkey tower's inhabitant stoked the lamp; today a neighborhood organization uses electricity. It also claims that the monkey was named Hilda. See NH to WDT, Dec. 1 and 22, 1859, *C* XVIII, pp. 206, 211; see also *Bookseller's Medium and Publisher's Advertiser* 2 (Feb. 1, 1860), p. 223.

318. But he went along: NH to WDT, Feb. 3, 1860, *C* XVIII, p. 222; see SH to MM, Apr. 27, 1860, Berg, which implies that Hawthorne did suggest "The Transformation"—not as good a title, it seems, as "Transformation."

319. "A wonderful book": Quoted in Edward W. Emerson, *The Early Years of the Saturday Club*, p. 213.

319. "When we have known": *The Marble Faun*, pp. 1123–24.

320. "a sort of poetic"; "between the real"; It's also: *The Marble Faun*, p. 855; *The Scarlet Letter*, p. 149; *The Marble Faun*, p. 855.

320. "casual sepulchre" . . . "heap of broken": *The Marble Faun*, p. 945.

320. "far gone," "crust," "pit": *The Marble Faun*, pp. 1104, 1135, 987.

321. No matter how: I have found Joseph Riddel's discussion of *The Marble Faun* instructive; see Joseph Riddel, *Purloined Letters: Originality and Repetition in American Literature*, ed. Mark Bauerlein (Baton Rouge: Louisiana State Univ. Press, 1995). Millicent Bell's eloquent "*The Marble Faun* and the Waste of History," *Southern Review* 35:2 (spring 1999), pp. 354–70, dovetails with much of my thinking about the novel; "new historicist" interpretations of the novel include Robert S. Levine, "Antebellum Rome in *The Marble Faun*," *American Literary History* 2:1 (spring 1990), pp. 19–38, and Nancy Bentley, *The Ethnography of Manners: Hawthorne, James, Wharton* (New York: Cambridge Univ. Press, 1995), chap. 2. More recently issues of race and gender are discussed in the essays collected in Robert K. Martin and Leland S. Person, ed., *Roman Holidays: American Writers and Artists in Nineteenth-Century Italy* (Iowa City: Univ. of Iowa Press, 2002). For intelligent speculation about Hawthorne and Una, see Herbert, *Dearest Beloved: The Hawthornes and the Making of the Middle-Class Family*, chaps. 13–17; I don't think Herbert's speculations wrongheaded, though I think he overstates his case—so much so that I cannot include it in my narrative of the making of *The Marble Faun* without more palpable or textual evidence. I do think, however, that if one were to pursue this line of inquiry, it would be equally useful to contemplate the sprightly

Julian as a model for the sprightly, beautiful Donatello and to wonder if the fantasy of incest includes sons as well as daughters.

321. "appeared before the Public": *The Marble Faun*, p. 853.

321. And he knows he must: Washington Irving to NH, Aug. 9, 1852, Houghton, quoted in *C* XVI, p. 571; see Chapter 18. Richard Brodhead, *The School of Hawthorne* (New York: Oxford Univ. Press, 1986), chap. 4, expertly discusses Hawthorne's need to surpass himself in terms of the larger culture issue of canon-making and Hawthorne's collaboration with his own institutionalization. In this regard, see also Jane Tompkins's justly renowned "Masterpiece Theater: The Politics of Hawthorne's Literary Reputation," in *Sensational Designs* (New York: Oxford Univ. Press, 1985), chap. 1.

321. "It is strange": Ada Shepard to Henry Clay Badger, June 23, 1858, BY.

321. Applying for his Italian passport: See NH to Benjamin Moran, Sept. 15, 1857, *C* XVIII, p. 97.

321. "We all of us": *The Marble Faun*, p. 1059.

321. " 'The sky itself' ": *The Marble Faun*, pp. 1067, 1104.

321. Modeled loosely on William Story: Hawthorne places in Kenyon's studio, for instance, Story's sculpture *Cleopatra*. He also attributes Benjamin Paul Akers's *The Dead Pearl Diver* to Kenyon as well as Harriet Hosmer's *The Clasped Hands*.

321. "climb heights and stand": *The Marble Faun*, p. 1068.

321. "guiltless of Rome": *The Marble Faun*, p. 1044.

322. "neither man nor animal": *The Marble Faun*, p. 861.

322. Later this nameless figure: Toward the end of the novel, Donatello again sybolically resembles the Model when he wears the white robes of the penitent and a "featureless mask over the face" (*The Marble Faun*, p. 1179).

322. "burning drop of African blood": *The Marble Faun*, p. 870.

322. "he could not keep": Francis Bennoch to George Holden, Dec. 3, 1885, UVA.

322. "She was, I suppose": *EN*, vol. 1, pp. 481–82. Another source for Miriam may have been Henriette Deluzy-Desportes, the governess involved in the scandalous Praslin murder in Paris in the summer of 1847. The evidence is circumstantial but interesting; see Nathalia Wright, "Hawthorne and the Praslin Murder," *New England Quarterly* 15:1 (1942), pp. 5–14. After the Duc de Praslin murdered his wife, who had fired the governess, and then killed himself before being tried for his crime, Mlle. Deluzy was arrested. Though proven innocent of any wrongdoing, she remained under so much suspicion that she eventually left France for America, where she married the son of one of Hawthorne's Berkshire neighbors, David Dudley Field. Though Sophia Hawthorne did suggest that Hawthorne had a well-known case in mind when conceiving of Miriam, its exact identity remains unknown.

323. "such as one sees": *The Marble Faun*, p. 891.

323. "a Jewish aspect": *The Marble Faun*, p. 891.

323. "Over and over again": *The Marble Faun*, p. 890.

323. "I did what your eyes": *The Marble Faun*, p. 997.

324. "fallen and yet sinless": Feb. 20, 1858, *FIN*, pp. 92–93; see also *The Marble*

Faun, p. 906. Hawthorne looted his own journals for fresh descriptions of everything from the worshippers at St. Peter's to the blue-coated French soldiers quartered on the ground floor of the Barberini Palace to his and Sophia's stumbling onto the bier of a dead monk in the darkly cool Capuchin church, reproduced in the chapter "The Dead Capuchin." And of course he used his and Una's experiences at the Carnival for the novel's chapter "A Scene in the Corso" which, given Kenyon's state of mind, appear to him as the "emptiest of mockeries" when contrasted with the esprit of the previous year: this too was Hawthorne's experience, for the Carnival in the second instance took place during Una's siege.

324. "with doves": Sir Henry Layard to Miss Hosmer, London, June 27, 1860, in Harriet Hosmer, *Letters and Memories,* ed. Cornelia Carr (New York: Moffat, Yard, 1912), pp. 159–60.

324. As a consequence: Sophia took offense at her sister Elizabeth's suggestion that Sophia was Hilda: "Mr. Hawthorne had no idea of portraying me in Hilda," she claimed, adding the inadvertently amusing comment that "whatever resemblance any one sees is accidental." Evidently EPP had also wondered why Hilda hadn't asked for more information about the murder. SH's answer also reveals her disapproval of Miriam and partial exoneration of Donatello, which the novel does not share: "Hilda, *having seen Miriam allow* Donatello to drop the monk over the Tarpeian rock, had no need to make enquiries about it" (italics mine). See SH to EPP [spring 1860], Berg.

325. "like a sharp steel sword": *The Marble Faun,* p. 906.

325. "a great horror": "ideal which": UH to EPP, Oct. 4, 1859, BY; SH to Anna Parsons, Sept. 26, 1854, Smith.

325. "if I had had": Feb. 7, 1858, p. 59, and May 1, 1858, *FIN,* p. 195.

325. "I am a daughter," "live and die": *The Marble Faun,* pp. 1153, 1157.

325. "whatever precepts": *The Marble Faun,* p. 1236.

325. "Hilda had a hopeful": *The Marble Faun,* p. 1238.

326. Perhaps to fill: See, for instance, Leslie Stephen, "Nathaniel Hawthorne," *Cornhill Magazine* 2 (Dec. 1872), p. 724.

326. The *Westminster Review:* "Contemporary Literature/Belles Lettres: *Transformation,*" *Westminster Review* 17 (Apr. 1860), p. 626.

326. Nonetheless, not even: The *Centenary* editors estimate each British printing at one thousand three-volume sets, and I've found nothing to contradict them, or to verify these numbers. See Claude M. Simpson, "Introduction" to *The Marble Faun, C* IV, p. xxix. Smith & Elder and Ticknor & Fields paid Hawthorne a royalty of 15 percent. Ticknor ordered eight thousand two-volume sets of the novel printed and advertised the number in several newspapers as if the sheer volume would increase sales, which it probably did. See also Rosemary Mims Fisk, " *The Marble Faun* and the English Copyright: The Smith, Elder Contract," *Studies in the American Renaissance,* 1995, pp. 263–75.

326. Pretty soon sightseers: See, for example, Susan Williams, "Manufacturing Intellectual Equipment: The Tauchnitz Edition of *The Marble Faun,*" in Michele Moylan and Lane Stiles, ed., *Reading Books: Essays on the Material Text and Literature in America* (Amherst: Univ. of Massachusetts Press, 1996), pp.

117–50. Published in England on February 28, 1860, *Transformation* appeared in three volumes and sold for slightly over three pounds. *The Marble Faun* appeared a week later in America with two volumes selling for $1.50.

326. Sophia curtly rapped: SH to Henry Fothergill Chorley, Mar. 5, 1860, *C*XVIII, pp. 238–39. For the *Times* review, "*The Marble Faun*, or *The Romance of Monte Bene*," *New York Times*, Mar. 24, 1850, p. 3. The other reviews mentioned are cited in *Nathaniel Hawthorne: The Contemporary Reviews*, pp. 247–48.

326. "a want of finish": [Henry Bright], "Transformation," *Examiner*, Mar. 31, 1860, p. 197, quoted in *Nathaniel Hawthorne: The Contemporary Reviews*, p. 250.

326. Who was the man . . . Do they marry: SH to EPP, transcription and fragment, [1860], Berg.

326. "How easy it is": NH to Henry Bright, Apr. 4, 1860, *C*XVIII, p. 259.

326. "was one of its essential": NH to Francis Bennoch, Mar. 24, 1860, *C*XVIII, p. 251.

326. "not satisfactory"; "the actual experience": "The Ancestral Footstep," in *American Claimant Manuscripts*, p. 11; *The Marble Faun*, p. 1232.

326. "The charm lay": *The Marble Faun*, p. 968.

327. "The very dust": *The Marble Faun*, p. 937.

327. "In weaving": *The Marble Faun*, p. 929.

327. "I really put": NH to JTF, Apr. 26, 1860, *C*XVIII, p. 271.

CHAPTER TWENTY-FOUR: BETWEEN TWO COUNTRIES

328. "The sweetest thing": NH to WDT, Feb. 10, 1860, *C*XVIII, p. 227.

328. "where there is no shadow": *The Marble Faun*, p. 854.

328. "How could he say": MM to SH, [Mar.] 1860, Antioch. Among the many fine books about the American political situation during Hawthorne's years abroad, I have found particularly helpful David Herbert Donald, *Charles Sumner and the Coming of the Civil War* (New York: Alfred A. Knopf, 1960); David Herbert Donald, *Lincoln* (New York: Simon & Schuster, 1995); Eric Foner, *Free Soil, Free Labor, Free Men* (New York: Oxford Univ. Press, 1995); Wood Gray, *The Hidden Civil War: The Story of the Copperheads* (New York: Viking, 1942); Eric L. McKitrick, *Slavery Defended: The Views of the Old South* (Englewood Cliffs, N.J.: Prentice-Hall, 1963); Henry Mayer, *All on Fire: William Lloyd Garrison and the Abolition of Slavery* (New York: St. Martin's Press, 1998); Allan Nevins, *The War for the Union*, vol. 1, *The Improvised War, 1861–1862* (New York: Charles Scribner's Sons, 1959); Larry E. Tise, *Proslavery: A History of the Defense of Slavery in America* (Athens: Univ. of Georgia Press, 1987); Albert J. von Frank, *The Trials of Anthony Burns: Freedom and Slavery in Emerson's Boston* (Cambridge, Mass.: Harvard Univ. Press, 1998); and David M. Potter, *The Impending Crisis, 1848–1861*, ed. Don E. Fehrenbacher (New York: Harper & Row, 1976).

329. "I wholly and utterly": SH to EPP, June 4, 1857, Berg.

329. "Because I suggested": SH to MM, Sept. [between Sept. 20 and Sept. 26] 1857, Berg.

329. "no purpose": Abraham Lincoln, *Speeches and Writings, 1832–1858* (New York: Library of America, 1989), p. 521.

329. "You surely must know": SH to EPP, June 4, 1857, Berg.
330. "You always speak"; "My husband": SH to MM, Sept. [between Sept. 20 and Sept. 26] 1857, Berg; SH to EPP, [1857], Berg.
331. "I have read": SH to EPP, [1859–60], Berg.
331. "No doubt it seems": NH to EPP, Aug. 13, 1857, *C*XVIII, p. 89.
331. "We go all wrong": *The Marble Faun,* p. 1050.
331. "Vengeance and beneficence": NH to EPP, Oct. 8, 1857, *C*XVIII, p. 116.
331. "The good of others": NH to EPP, Oct. 8, 1857, *C*XXIII, p. 465.
332. "We human beings": SH to EPP, [1859–60], Berg.
332. "a transcendentalist above all": Henry David Thoreau, *Reform Papers,* ed. Wendell Glick (Princeton, N.J.: Princeton Univ. Press, 1973), p. 115. In 1862 Thoreau sent an essay called "The Higher Law" to James Fields for publication in the *Atlantic Monthly.* Understanding its political import, Fields suggested the title be changed to "Life Without Principle"; Thoreau complied. Particularly fine on Thoreau is Robert D. Richardson Jr., *Henry Thoreau: A Life of the Mind* (Berkeley: Univ. of California Press, 1986). For an excellent account of abolitionism's debt to transcendentalism, see Albert J. Von Frank, *The Trials of Anthony Burns.*
332. "I think him equal": May 8, 1859, *The Journals of Bronson Alcott,* ed. Odell Shepard (Boston: Little, Brown, 1938), p. 316.
333. "will make the gallows": Ralph L. Rusk, *The Life of Ralph Waldo Emerson* (New York: Charles Scribner's Sons, 1949), p. 402.
333. "Nobody was ever": "Chiefly About War Matters," in *Miscellaneous Prose and Verse, C*XXIII, p. 427. Actually, the essay makes clear that "nobody was ever more justly hanged. He won his martyrdom fairly, and took it firmly" (pp. 427–28).
333. There, he'd write: HWL, Oct. 27, 1860, journal, MS Am 1340(209), Houghton.
333. "I should like to sail": *Yesterdays,* p. 92. They disembarked from Liverpool, where the Hawthornes had again taken lodgings at Mrs. Blodget's. Prior to departure they'd been stopping at Bath, partly for SH's health and partly so that Hawthorne could avail himself of London social life and of Bennoch one last time.
333. "I fear I have lost": NH to WDT, Jan. 26, 1860, *C*XVIII, p. 217.
333. "I am really": NH to JTF, Feb. 3, 1859, *C*XVIII, p. 95.
333. "I feared his depression": SH to AF, Dec. 8, 1861, Berg.
334. "Surely, the bright": Feb. 18, 1860, *EN,* vol. 2, p. 463; see SH to Elizabeth Hoar, Apr. 15, 1860, Antioch.
334. "It is the school-boy's": See HWL, journal, June 30, 1860, MS Am 1340(209), Houghton.
334. "It is an excellent": NH to Henry Bright, Dec. 17, 1869, *C*XVIII, p. 355.
334. "even if a Democrat": quoted in Edward W. Emerson, *The Early Years of the Saturday Club,* p. 215.
334. "He has the look": Henry James, *Notes of a Son and Brother* (New York: Charles Scribner's Sons, 1914), p. 208.
334. "Beyond a general dislike": NH to Horatio Woodman, Nov. 5, 1860, *C*XVIII, p. 336.

334. "He is used": James Russell Lowell to Grace Norton, misdated June 12, 1860, in *The Letters of James Russell Lowell,* vol. 1, p. 303.

335. Hawthorne responded: When James Roberts Gilmore solicited a story for the *Knickerbocker Magazine,* Hawthorne resorted to his standard excuse, that his stories were too monotonous for serialization. He added that he needed the income from English copyrights that would be denied him should he publish serially in an American magazine. See NH to James Roberts Gilmore, Oct. 16, 1860, *C*XVIII, p. 331.

335. "I am very anxious": JTF to SH, Nov. 25, 1859, Berg. On Fields's encouragement of female writers, see, for instance, Elizabeth Stuart Phelps, *Chapters from a Life* (Boston: Houghton Mifflin, 1896), pp. 146–47.

335. "You forget": SH to JTF, Nov. 28, 1859, BPL.

335. "Perhaps I may"; "I don't know": NH to JTF, Nov. 28, 1859, and NH to Francis Bennoch, Nov. 29, 1859, *C*XVIII, pp. 203–4.

335. Bronson Alcott raced over: See UH to MM, [Aug.] 1860, Antioch; Bronson Alcott, journals, Sat., [late July] 1860, *59M-308(30), Houghton.

336. "doing exactly": MM to Miss Rawlins Pickman, July 10, 1860, Antioch.

336. "Mrs. H is as sentimental": Quoted in Marjorie Worthington, *Miss Alcott of Concord* (Garden City, N.Y.: Doubleday, 1958), pp. 109–10.

336. When the cook: MM to Miss Rawlins Pickman, July 10, 1860, Antioch.

336. "Una is a stout": Quoted in Worthington, *Miss Alcott of Concord,* pp. 109–10.

336. "bad for her darling son": Franklin B. Sanborn to Eleanor R. Larrison, Mar. 29, 1907, Autograph File, Houghton.

336. Emerson asked: See SH to EPP, [1861], Berg.

337. "Her Byronic papa": *The Selected Letters of Louisa May Alcott,* ed. Joel Myerson and Daniel Shealy (Boston: Little, Brown, 1987), p. 57. Eventually NH's friend George Bradford was hired to instruct Una, and Rose, at the age of ten, was sent to Concord's East Quarter Public School. See UH to EH, June 5, 1861, BY.

337. And she'd be in Salem: UH to Richard Manning, July 20, 1860, PE.

337. Poor Una, screaming: SH to unknown recipient [AF?], [1860], Berg.

337. "His spirits": SH to unknown recipient [AF?], [1860], Berg; SH to EPP, [early 1861], Berg.

337. Mrs. Rollins attributed: NH to FP, Oct. 9, 1860, *C*XVIII, p. 327.

337. "I lose England": NH to Francis Bennoch, Dec. 17, 1860, *C*XVIII, p. 352.

337. Defeated, Una attended: Sanborn, *Recollections of Seventy Years,* vol. 2, p. 524.

338. Weekdays, she mended: AF, diary, July 31, 1863, MHS.

339. Sophia recorded: See SH, diary, 1861, Bancroft.

339. "as if he feared": Bronson Alcott, diary, Feb. 2, 1861, Houghton, quoted in *The Journals of Bronson Alcott,* ed. Odell Shepard (Boston: Little, Brown, 1938), p. 335.

339. "He seems not at home": Bronson Alcott, diary, Feb. 2, 1861, Houghton, quoted in *The Journals of Bronson Alcott,* p. 335.

339. "unconquerable interest": "Etherege," in *American Claimant Manuscripts,* p. 124. As the *Centenary* editors make clear, there are two sets of unfinished manuscripts dealing with the American claimant, likely composed during late 1860/early 1861, when Hawthorne took occupancy of his tower. For identifica-

tion purposes, the first manuscript, concentrating mostly on the English chapters of the romance, is called "Etherege," after the main character. The second manuscript, called "Grimshawe," seems to me a reworking of the earlier manuscript. See also "Historical Introduction" to *American Claimant Manuscripts,* pp. 491–506. Moreover, since the *Centenary* editors have pieced together the various fragments in ways I find reliable, I will advert to their volume, with the caveat that the textual evidence does not make clear what Hawthorne composed when. However, I do find that the references in "Grimshawe" to war and politics reflect the events of the winter and spring of 1861. See also Edward H. Davidson, *Hawthorne's Last Phase* (New Haven, Conn.: Yale Univ. Press, 1949), pp. 1–71.

339. "hereditary connections": "Etherege," in *American Claimant Manuscripts,* p. 136.

339. "Oh home, my home": The rightful heir of the estate is an old pensioner who dwells in the hospital where Etherege is taken after the lord of Braithwaite Hall attempts to murder him.

339. "Is there going to be": NH to WDT, Dec. 7, 1860, *C* XVIII, p. 342.

340. "Secession of the North": HWL, journal, Dec. 3, 1860, MS Am 1340(209), Houghton.

340. "this wicked & crazy": John O'Sullivan to FP, Feb. 7, 1861, LC.

340. "It was the imbecility": *New York Herald,* Apr. 30, 1861, p. 1.

340. "how little I care": NH to Henry Bright, Dec. 17, 1860, *C* XVIII, p. 355.

340. "How can you feel": "Etherege," in *American Claimant Manuscripts,* p. 162.

340. "There is still a want": "Etherege," in *American Claimant Manuscripts,* pp. 115, 198–99, 219, 265.

341. And both of them are Hawthorne: NH mentions the story of Wakefield as he puzzles out one of his characters, the doctor's confidential servant, who intends to do mischief to the Braithwaite family. See "Etherege," in *American Claimant Manuscripts,* p. 327.

341. "I want you to be": Grimshawe," in *American Claimant Manuscripts,* p. 476. This version of his story seems, at the outset, more polished than earlier ones. It reads far more smoothly than "Etherege," and though Hawthorne makes notations to himself, he does not break the narrative to do so. Rather, he reminds himself where to fill out his story, as if planning to copy this draft of it into another and perhaps final one, with certain descriptions added.

341. "quiet recess": "Grimshawe," in *American Claimant Manuscripts,* p. 470.

342. On Saturday, April 13: SH, diary, Apr. 13, 1861, Berg.

CHAPTER TWENTY-FIVE: THE SMELL OF GUNPOWDER

343. "My literary success": NH to JTF, Feb. 27, 1861, *C* XVIII, p. 365.

343. "the example par excellence": Poe, "Tale-Writing: Nathaniel Hawthorne," p. 252.

343. "I am sensible": NH to JTF, Jan. 30, 1863, *C* XVIII, p. 533.

344. "He always, I believe": Ellery Channing to Ellen Channing, Oct. 30, 1851, MHS.

344. "The war continues": NH to WDT, May 16, 1861, *C* XVIII, p. 379.

344. "what we are fighting": NH to HB, May 26, 1861, *C* XVIII, p. 381.

344. "We seem to have little": NH to Francis Bennoch, [circa July 1861], *C* XVIII, p. 388.

344. "I wish they would": NH to WDT, May 26, 1861, *C* XVIII, p. 382.

344. "all we ought": NH to HB, Oct. 12, 1861, *C* XVIII, p. 412.

344. "Every man of you": NH to Henry Bright, Nov. 14, 1861, *C* XVIII, p. 421.

344. "If this is the literary tone": See *The Life of Lord Houghton,* ed. T. Wemyss Reid (New York: Cassell, 1891), vol. 2, p. 76.

345. Hawthorne sent him: "Near Oxford" appeared in the October 1861 *Atlantic* 8, pp. 385–97, and his "Pilgrimage to Old Boston" appeared in the January 1862 *Atlantic* 9, pp. 88–101; JTF to NH, July 24, 1862, in Austin, *Fields of the Atlantic Monthly,* p. 220.

345. "He allowed the photographer": SH to JTF, Jan. 1, 1862, BPL.

347. "I have no features": SH to AF, Dec. 8, 1861, BPL.

347. "He says this": Caroline Ticknor, *Hawthorne and His Publisher* (Boston: Houghton Mifflin, 1913), p. 262.

348. "take an antagonist": "Chiefly About War Matters," in *Miscellaneous Prose and Verse, C* XXIII, pp. 412–13.

348. Next day, Hawthorne: See Caroline Ticknor, *Hawthorne and His Publisher,* pp. 258–82; N. P. Willis, (New York) *Home Journal,* Mar. 29 and Apr. 12, 1862.

349. "Set men face to face": "Chiefly About War Matters," in *Miscellaneous Prose and Verse, C* XXIII, p. 421. Hawthorne kept a travel journal, drawing on it for "Chiefly About War Matters" and "Northern Volunteers: From a Journal." See, for example, UH to EH, Mar. 16, 1862, Rosary Hill, where Una Hawthorne mentions her father's journal. Doubtless it was later destroyed, probably by him; in any event, I unfortunately have found no trace of it. Meantime, after years of neglect, his "Chiefly About War Matters" essay has sparked some response; see, for instance, Patrick Brancaccio, " 'Chiefly About War-matters': Hawthorne's Reluctant Prophecy," in *Essex Institute Historical Collections,* 118 (Jan. 1982), pp. 59–66; Thomas R. Moore. "Hawthorne as Essayist in 'Chiefly About War Matters,' " *American Transcendental Quarterly* 6 (1992), pp. 263–78; Grace Smith, " 'Chiefly About War Matters': Hawthorne's Swift Judgment of Lincoln," *American Transcendental Quarterly* 15 (June 2001), pp. 149–52; or Nancy Bentley's proleptic, wide-ranging discussion in *The Ethnography of Manners: Hawthorne, James, Wharton* (New York: Cambridge Univ. Press, 1995), pp. 36–45. Hawthorne's racism is the focus of Jean Fagan Yellin's censorious "Hawthorne and the American National Sin," in Daniel Peck, ed., *The Green American Tradition* (Baton Rouge: Louisiana State Univ. Press, 1989), pp. 75–97, but she does not address "Chiefly About War Matters" here or in her subsequent revisions of the essay, published in Larry J. Reynolds, *A Historical Guide to Nathaniel Hawthorne* (New York: Oxford Univ. Press, 2000). Thus, Daniel Aaron remains the best interpreter of Hawthorne and the Civil War. See Daniel Aaron, *The Unwritten War: American Writers and the Civil War* (New York: Alfred A. Knopf, 1973), chap. 3.

349. "It was as if General McClellan": "Chiefly About War Matters" in *Miscellaneous Prose and Verse, C* XXIII, pp. 408, 407.

349. "As a general rule": "Chiefly About War Matters," in *Miscellaneous Prose and Verse, C* XXIII, p. 433.

349. "sacrificing good institutions": "Chiefly About War Matters," in *Miscellaneous Prose and Verse, C* XXIII, p. 419.

349. "Man's accidents": "Chiefly About War Matters," in *Miscellaneous Prose and Verse, C* XXIII, p. 431.

349. "Whosoever may be benefited": "Chiefly About War Matters," in *Miscellaneous Prose and Verse, C* XXIII, p. 420.

350. America is conceived: The best brief discussion of the image can be found in Larzer Ziff, "The Artist and Puritanism," in *Hawthorne Centenary Essays,* ed. Roy Harvey Pearce (Columbus: Ohio State Univ. Press, 1964), pp. 246–49.

350. "our brethren": "Chiefly About War Matters," in *Miscellaneous Prose and Verse, C* XXIII, p. 420.

350. "This is somewhat" . . . "I think the political": NH to WDT, May 17, 1862, *C* XVIII, p. 456.

350. "it will be politic": JTF to NH, May 21, 1862, in Austin, *Fields of the Atlantic Monthly,* p. 218.

350. "What a terrible": NH to JTF, May 23, 1862, *C* XVIII, p. 461.

351. "the stupidest looking": "Chiefly About War Matters," holograph manuscript, UVA.

351. "I shall insert it": NH to JTF, May 23, 1862, *C* XVIII, p. 461.

351. "we are compelled": "Chiefly About War Matters," in NH, *Miscellanies* (Boston: Houghton Mifflin, 1900), p. 378.

351. "Can it be": "Chiefly About War Matters," in *Miscellaneous Prose and Verse, C* XXIII p. 427.

351. "What an extraordinary": Charles Eliot Norton to George William Curtis, June 26, 1862, bMS Am 1124(195), Houghton.

351. " 'A fig' ": "The Thorn that Bears Haws," *Liberator,* June 27, 1862, p. 102.

351. Hawthorne dashed off . . . He contrasted: See Edward Dicey, *Spectator of America,* ed. Herbert Mitgang (Chicago: Quadrangle Books, 1971), p. 278. The reports were doubtless exaggerated, if at all true, but taken up by northern propagandists.

352. "If ever a man": Edward Dicey, "Nathaniel Hawthorne," *Macmillan's Magazine* 10 (July 1864), p. 242.

352. "It was impossible": Dicey, "Nathaniel Hawthorne," pp. 242–43.

352. " 'We cannot see' ": Rebecca Harding Davis, *Bits of Gossip* (Boston: Houghton Mifflin, 1904), pp. 34–35.

352. Whenever Hawthorne went: Henry James, "Mr. and Mrs. James T. Fields," in *Literary Criticism,* vol. 1, p. 166.

353. "the handsomest Yankee": JTF to NH, [Sept. 18, 1861], Huntington.

353. Annie Fields bore: See "148 Charles Street," in Willa Cather, *Not Under Forty* (New York: Alfred A. Knopf, 1936), pp. 52–75.

354. Cloistered within his tower: See SH to UH, Dec. 11, 1862, Berg.

354. "I love you with": SH to AF, Nov. 8 [1863], BPL. Readers interested in same-sex relationships and their cultural context in the early nineteenth century, before they had been labeled or criminalized, will find illuminating discus-

sions, for example, in the work of Caleb Crain, *American Sympathy: Men, Friendship, and Literature in the New Nation* (New Haven, Conn.: Yale Univ. Press, 2001); Martin Duberman et al., *Hidden from History: Reclaiming the Gay and Lesbian Past* (Markham, Ontario: New American Library, 1989); Lillian Federman, *Surpassing the Love of Men: Romantic Friendship and Love Between Women from the Renaissance to the Present* (New York: William Morrow, 1981); David Leverenz, *Manhood and the American Renaissance* (Ithaca, N.Y.: Cornell Univ. Press, 1989); and Carroll Smith-Rosenberg, *Disorderly Conduct: Visions of Gender in Victorian America* (New York: Alfred A. Knopf, 1985).

354. "I *will* say just": SH to AF, Aug. 2, 1863, BPL.

354. "that grief": AF, "To S.H.," [Sept. 1871], Fields addenda, Huntington.

354. On the iron-cold day: AF, Dec. 6, 1863, diary, MHS.

355. Hawthorne's reminiscence . . . In 1863: NH to WDT, Dec. 28, 1860, *C*XVIII, p. 358; NH to WDT, Jan. 30, 1861, *C*XVIII, p. 361; NH to HB, May 26, 1861, *C*XVIII, p. 380; NH to JTF, Oct. 6, 1861, *C*XVIII, p. 408. See Scott Derks, ed., *The Value of a Dollar, 1860–1989* (Detroit: A. Manly, 1994).

355. "Have you not almost": JTF to NH, Dec. 4, 1862, in Austin, *Fields of the Atlantic Monthly,* pp. 222–23.

355. Though Hawthorne was . . . And he composed: AF, Mar. 3, 1863, miscellaneous papers, Huntington; NH to JTF, Apr. 30, 1863, *C*XVIII, p. 560; AF, Feb. 2[8] 1863, "Fragrant Memories," Huntington. "A London Suburb," sent in January, published in March, *Atlantic Monthly* 11, pp. 306–21; "Up the Thames," sent in February, published in May, *Atlantic Monthly* 11, 598–614; and "Outside Glimpses of English Poverty," sent by mid-April, published in June, *Atlantic Monthly* 12, pp. 36–51; the essay on Dr. Johnson, earlier published in *The Keepsake* (London, 1857), pp. 108–13, was also reprinted in *Harper's New Monthly Magazine* 14 (Apr. 1857), pp. 639–41. He completed this revision mid-May and sent "Civic Banquets" to the *Atlantic* (finished in early June, published in the August issue of *Atlantic* 12, pp. 195–212). On May 30, 1863, he completed the introductory essay, "Consular Experiences." The twelve sketches that made up *Our Old Home* thus included, in the order in which they appeared in the volume: "Consular Experiences," "Leamington Spa," "About Warwick," "Recollections of a Gifted Woman" (a reminiscence of Delia Bacon published in the *Atlantic* 11, January 1863, pp. 43–58), "Lichfield and Uttoxeter," "Pilgrimage to Old Boston," "Near Oxford," "Some of the Haunts of Burns," "A London Suburb," "Up the Thames," and "Civic Banquets." With twelve essays in place, Fields sold the English rights to the volume to Smith & Elder for 150 pounds.

355. "to my life-long affection": NH to JTF, May 3, 1863, *C* XVIII, p. 567. Hawthorne also considered dedicating the volume to Francis Bennoch "to show him that I am thoroughly mindful of all his hospitality and kindness," but eventually decided in favor of Pierce, possibly because of the stir it might cause. One may suspect that Fields greeted NH's suggestion with dismay, to say the least.

355. In the words of Pierce's: See Nichols, *Franklin Pierce,* pp. 522–23; see also "The Voice of the Charmer," *Harper's Weekly,* Aug. 15, 1863, p. 515.

355. "He will not relent": AF, diary, July 31, 1863, MHS.

355. "Such adherence": AF, diary, July 26, 1863, MHS.

356. "The negroes suffer in NY": Franklin Sanborn to Moncure Conway, July 24 [1863], Moncure Conway Papers, Butler.

356. "Higginson is only slightly": Franklin Sanborn to Moncure Conway, July 24 [1863], Moncure Conway Papers, Butler.

356. "He is in despair": *An Englishman in the American Civil War: The Dairies of Henry Yates Thompson, 1863,* ed. Christopher Chancellor (New York: New York Univ. Press, 1971), pp. 46, 52.

356. Devoted to him: See EPP to HB, June 4, 1887, Bowdoin.

356. "There is a certain steadfastness": NH to EPP, July 20, 1863, *C* XVIII, p. 589. According to Peabody, this letter was one of the few from Hawthorne she did not destroy: "I promised not to dishonor his letters & every now & then he insisted on a mutual exchange of letters to be sure that they were destroyed," she wrote circa 1887. "The only one I kept was the one he wrote me on the dedication of his 'Old Home' to Franklin Pierce from which I desired to dissuade him." See EPP to Mrs. Lothrop, Sept. [1877], PE.

356. He added . . . "and never know they": NH to EPP, July 20, 1863, *C* XVIII, pp. 589–91. See also NH to Henry Bright, Mar. 8, 1863, *C* XVII, p. 543. Sophia, however, retained a virulent hatred for the abolitionists, which she freely confided to her husband. When she heard more details about the defeat of the Massachusetts Fifty-fourth, she wrote NH, then visiting his sister, that she'd heard an eyewitness say "he saw thousands of them in a drove like cattle, urged on against their will, and that's when many of the organized regiments were killed, the vacancies were filled up by some of these thousands in reserve. So much for Northern abolition accounts of the nigers [*sic*]" (SH to NH, [Aug./Sept. 1863], Morgan). To General Ethan Allen Hitchcock, a new friend, she wrote, "I was glad to find that you believe that God's law would without fail have removed slavery without this dreadful convulsive action. It always seems to me that Man is very arrogant in taking such violent measures to *help God* who needs no help. . . . For he can touch the body alone of his slave, while the slave's soul may remain intact and becomes purified by endurance. The white man loses more than the black man, as the victim of wrong always is in a superior attitude to the inflictor of wrong, I suppose. I find no one in Concord or hardly in Boston to whom I can utter such sentiments without exciting fiery indignation. My sisters cannot hear me speak a word. They believe alone in instant vengeance on the slave owner and instant release of the slave, and I cannot hold any sweet counsel with them about it. Negro worship seems to cloud the vision of the mind and love for him shuts off love for mankind. To my husband only I can speak. He is very all-sided and can look serenely on opposing forces and do justice to each." See SH to General Hitchcock, Aug. 9, 1863, LC.

357. "It would be a piece": NH to JTF, July 18, 1863, *C* XVIII, pp. 586–87.

357. "Can it be": "To a Friend: The Dedication to Pierce," dated the Wayside, July 2, 1863, Fields papers, Huntington.

357. Before its publication . . . "bravely": JTF to NH, [Sept. 1863], Huntington;

JTF to NH, Oct. 28, 1863, in Austin, *Fields of the Atlantic Monthly,* p. 233. Thirty-five hundred copies were printed July 22, 1863, and two thousand more in September. The book sold at $1.25 and gave NH a 12 percent royalty. A third printing in March ran a thousand copies. The numbers then dramatically drop.

358. "I have never believed": "Ex-President Pierce's Letter to Jeff. Davis," *New York Evening Post,* Sept. 19, 1863, p. 2; EPP to HB, June 4, 1887, Bowdoin.

358. "Pierce's infamy": See "Hawthorne's Letter to Pierce," *Harper's Weekly,* Oct. 3, 1863, p. 627.

358. "I was very sorry": George William Curtis to Richard C. Manning, Oct. 2, 1863, PE.

358. "That one of the most gifted": [George William Curtis], "Literary," *Harper's Weekly* 7 (Nov. 21, 1863), p. 739.

358. "His perception": [Franklin B. Sanborn or Moncure Conway], "A Review of Hawthorne's *Our Old Home,*" *Commonwealth,* Sept. 25, 1863.

358. "images reflected": "Critical Notices," *North American Review* 97 (Oct. 1863), p. 588.

358. "What was he to Liverpool": See [Henry Bright], "Our Old Home," *Examiner,* Oct. 17, 1863, pp. 662–63.

359. "reads like the bitterest": Charles Norton to George William Curtis, Sept. 21 [1863, misdated 1862], bMS Am 1088.2, box 2, Houghton.

359. "I never read the preface": Harriet Beecher Stowe to JTF, Nov. 3, 1863, Huntington.

359. Calling the book pellucid: AF, diary, Sept. 25, 1863, MHS.

359. Bright too was offended: Henry Bright to NH, Oct. 20, 1863, Berg; see [Bright], "Our Old Home," pp. 662–63; "Leamington Spa" in *OOH,* p. 48.

360. "Whether it be": "Hawthorne on England," *Blackwood's Magazine* 92:577 (Nov. 1863), pp. 610–23, quoted in *Nathaniel Hawthorne: Critical Assessments,* ed. Brian Harding (New York: Helm, 1990), vol. 2, p. 23. However, this reviewer also singled out for praise some of Hawthorne's most chilling observations, especially in "Outside Glimpses of English Poverty": "I come to the conclusion that those ugly lineaments which startled Adam and Eve, as they looked backward to the closed gate of Paradise, were not fiends from the pit, but the more terrible foreshadowings of what so many of their descendants were to be." See *OOH,* p. 287.

360. "Can any created woman": "A Handful of Hawthorn," *Punch* 45 (Oct. 17, 1863), p. 161.

360. It must seem; Sophia wondered: UH to EH, Nov. 22, 1863, Rosary Hill; SH to AF, Nov. 29, 1863, BPL.

360. "But they do me": NH to JTF, Nov. 8, 1863, *C* XVIII, p. 613.

360. "It is impossible": NH to Francis Bennoch, Oct. 12, 1862, *C* XVIII, p. 501.

360. "I feel as if": NH to Francis Bennoch, Oct. 12, 1862, *C* XVIII, p. 501.

361. "Mr. Hawthorne cannot read": SH to AF, May 3, 1863, BPL.

CHAPTER TWENTY-SIX: A HANDFUL OF MOMENTS

362. "He himself felt": "Septimius Felton," in *Elixir of Life,* pp. 22–23.

362. Six years after: See preface to *Passages from the English Notebooks,* vol. 1.

363. "charm lay partly": *The Marble Faun*, p. 968.
363. "Septimius" opens: Hawthorne obviously took some of his material from the earlier "Grimshawe" manuscript, moving the date backward in time in order to deal with issues of civil strife.
363. "believing nothing": "Septimius Felton," in *Elixir of Life*, p. 13.
364. He'd written of the latter: See NH to George William Curtis, July 14, 1852, *C*XVI, p. 568, and NH's notes to himself regarding his projected preface to an early version of the story: "Then come to the annals of the house," he instructed himself, "and introduce Thoreau's legend of the man who would not die" (in *Elixir of Life*, p. 504). In addition to its obvious connections to earlier stories like "Dr. Heidegger's Experiment" and "Rappaccini's Daughter," see also "The Haunted Quack," in *Tales*, p. 56: "This I dubbed in high flowing terms, 'The Antidote to Death, or the Eternal Elixir of Longevity.' "
364. "an internal one": "Septimius Felton," in *Elixir of Life*, p. 15.
364. "We are the playthings": "Septimius Felton," in *Elixir of Life*, p. 79.
364. "the mud of his own making": NH to JTF, Feb. 25, 1864, *C*XVIII, p. 641.
364. "A man no sooner": "Septimius Norton," in *Elixir of Life*, p. 293.
365. "You are deluding": "Septimius Norton," in *Elixir of Life*, p. 416.
365. Revising the first draft: Septimius Felton becomes Septimius Norton; by the end of the second draft, Hawthorne changed Septimius's name to Hilliard Veren, sometimes called Hillard Veren. Also, Hawthorne changed the name of Septimius's aunt and made the character identified as Rose Garfield into Septimius's half sister. Septimius may refer to the seventh circle of Dante's *Inferno,* its first ring of tyrants or warmongers, its second with the despair of suicides, and its third filled with blasphemers, usurers, and sodomites. In the case of the third ring, moreover, Dante finds his former spiritual father, Latini, who had first inspired Dante to the "way man makes himself eternal," via fame. The irony of Dante's still limited perspective with Latini, whom he admires, would not have been lost on Hawthorne. See *The Inferno of Dante,* trans. Robert Pinsky (Farrar, Straus & Giroux, 1994), p. 155. In addition, the other topics of this canto—the desire for a father figure, suppressed homosexuality, and earthly fame—must have resonated with Hawthorne, who, admiring Dante, reckoned with these subjects in one way or another. For the additional significance of names and naming in Hawthorne's "Septimius" manuscripts, see "Historical Commentary" on *Elixir of Life,* pp. 567–69, and Klaus P. Stich, "The Saturday Club as Intertext in Hawthorne's *The Elixir of Life Manuscripts,*" *Nathaniel Hawthorne Review* 20:2 (fall 1994), pp. 11–20. Veren is an anagram for "never," and although Hilliard Veren presumably refers to a seventeenth-century Salem customs official, Hilliard is written interchangeably with Hillard, Hawthorne's friend and lawyer and the administrator of his estate.
365. "We are all linked": "Septimius Norton," in *Elixir of Life*, p. 432.
365. "dark as a prophetic flight": *Memories*, p. 422.
365. "He did not write": MM to Horace Mann Jr., [May–June 1864], in Arlin Turner, "Hawthorne's Final Illness and Death: Additional Reports," *ESQ* 19 (1973), p. 125.

365. "just as real": NH to JTF, Feb. 11, 1860, *C* XVIII, p. 229.

365. "In short, it was a moment": "Septimius Felton," in *Elixir of Life*, p. 101. Hawthorne rewrites this passage in "Septimius Norton," making it seem less personal and asserting, at the end of the section, "And he is either a very wise man, or a very dull one, who can answer one way or the other for the reality of the very breath he draws, and steadfastly say 'Yes!' or 'No!' " See "Septimius Norton," in *Elixir of Life*, p. 354.

366. "They make themselves at home": "Septimius Norton," in *Elixir of Life*, p. 446.

366. "*This path*": *The Journals and Miscellaneous Notebooks of Ralph Waldo Emerson*, vol. 15, p. 60.

366. "a hope while": SH, diary, Jan. 14, 1862, Morgan.

366. When Hawthorne confided: JTF to NH, [Sept. 1861], Huntington.

367. "I don't mean to let": NH to JTF, Oct. 6, 1861, *C* XVIII, p. 408.

367. "Yes," he said: Davis, *Bits of Gossip*, p. 63.

367. "It is a pain": SH to EPP, [winter or fall 1863], OSU.

367. "I expect to outlive": "No, no": NH to WDT, July 27, 1863, *C* XVIII, p. 597; AF, diary, July 24, 1866, MHS.

367. "I do not know": SH to AF, July 1863, BPL.

367. "It is a new": "Septimius Norton," in *Elixir of Life*, p. 295.

367. "Life, which seems": "Septimius Norton," in *Elixir of Life*, p. 330.

367. "The Present, the Immediate": "To a Friend," in *OOH*, p. 4. However, compare this rationalization to the observation in the chapter from *The Marble Faun*, "Fragmentary Sentences": "In weaving these mystic utterances into a continuous scene, we undertake a task resembling, in its perplexity, that of gathering up and piecing together the fragments of a letter, which has been torn and scattered to the winds. Many words of deep significance—many entire sentences, and those possibly the most important ones—have flown too far, on the winged breeze, to be recovered." See *The Marble Faun*, p. 929. Hawthorne's outlook hadn't changed, but his mood had.

368. "negative," "I am afraid": SH to AF, Oct. 11, 1863, BPL.

368. "Una thinks": MM to Horace Mann Jr., May 15, 1864, Antioch.

368. "He thus had no": Conway, *Life of Hawthorne*, p. 206.

368. "How Thoreau would scorn": NH to JTF, Oct. 24, 1863, *C* XVIII, p. 605.

368. But as Fields pressed . . . Let's just call: See JTF to NH, Oct. 28, 1863, in Austin, *Fields of the Atlantic Monthly*, p. 232; NH to JTF, Dec. 9, 1863, *C* XVIII, p. 619.

368. Sophia guessed . . . "bedevilment": SH to AF, Nov. 29, 1863, BPL.

368. "I am amazed": SH to UH, Dec. 19, 1863, Berg.

369. "He cannot bear": SH to UH, Dec. 19, 1863, Berg.

369. "He is not a very manageable": SH to HB, Apr. 5, 1864, BY.

369. "amid the sloth of age": "The Dolliver Romance," in *Elixir of Life*, p. 460.

369. "virgin bloom"; "forlorn widow": Silsbee, *A Half-Century in Salem*, p. 37; "The Dolliver Romance," in *Elixir of Life*, p. 457. In another example of correspondence, Dolliver's great-granddaughter, Pansie, is likely named for Posy Loring, daughter of Dr. George B. Loring; later in the manuscript, Hawthorne calls her Posie. Moreover, that Dolliver's grandson was a devoted horticulturist

reminds the Hawthorne reader of his uncle Robert Manning; that Dolliver is a man of medicine, or tries to be, recalls Nathaniel Peabody, SH's father.

369. So old Dolliver: Why does Dolliver persist in drinking his elixir? Hawthorne wasn't sure, although he seems to have intended another satire of reform: his hero, in trying to eradicate poverty or slavery or war, "would have destroyed the whole economy of the world." Or, Hawthorne continues, perhaps he just wanted to "see how the American Union was going to succeed." See "The Dolliver Romance," in *Elixir of Life,* "Study 2," p. 532; "Study 5," p. 537. The *Centenary* editors have approximated the date of composition of these fragments; "Study 2" can be internally dated July 22, 1863, or later, by the fragment in the Huntington Library.

369. "I wish, with all": SH to HB, Apr. 5, 1864, BY.

370. "I am tired"; And what avails: NH to Donald Grant Mitchell, Jan. 16, 1864, *C* XVIII, p. 632; NH to HWL, Jan. 2, 1864, *C* XVIII, p. 626.

370. "two jovial Publishers": HWL to JTF, in *The Letters of Henry Wadsworth Longfellow,* ed. Andrew Hilen (Cambridge, Mass.: Harvard Univ. Press, 1972), vol. 4, p. 380.

370. Hawthorne sat gazing: AF, diary, Jan. 9, 1864, MHS.

370. "I cannot help thinking": MM to Horace Mann Jr., [Mar. 1864], Antioch.

371. "This mode of death": *The House of the Seven Gables,* p. 613.

371. "Say to the Public": NH to JTF, Feb. 25, 1864, *C* XVIII, p. 640.

371. Hawthorne was too weak: Conway, *Life of Hawthorne,* p. 210. See also UH to EH, Mar. 20, 1864, Rosary Hill.

371. "I think we could bear": MM to Horace Mann Jr., June 6, 1864, UVA; *Yesterdays,* p. 117.

371. He was wraithlike; At night: MM to Horace Mann Jr., June 6, 1864, UVA; AF, diary, Mar. 28, 1864, MHS, quoted in M. A. De Wolfe Howe, *Memories of a Hostess: A Chronicle of Eminent Friendships Drawn Chiefly from the Diaries of Mrs. James T. Fields* (New York: Arno Press, 1974), p. 63; see also *Yesterdays,* p. 117; AF, diary, Mar. 28, 1864, MHS.

371. Hawthorne, however, felt better: NH to RH, Apr. 3, 1864, Rosary Hill.

372. Later he conveyed: See James C. Derby, *Fifty Years Among Authors, Books, and Publishers* (New York: G. W. Carleton, 1884), pp. 345–46; Howe, *Memories of a Hostess,* p. 64; Caroline Ticknor, *Hawthorne and His Publisher,* pp. 312–31.

372. The gleam had gone: SH to AF, [Apr. 18, 1864], BPL.

372. Yet he managed . . . stipulated: After Hawthorne's death, Sophia Hawthorne discovered the bequest. See SH to FP, [June 1864], NHHS. See also SH to EH, Feb. 9, 1869, PE.

372. Years later, Rose: *Memories,* p. 477.

372. This pleased Sophia; But Sophia naively: See *The Journals of Bronson Alcott,* p. 362; SH to AF, [Apr. 19, 1864], BPL.

372. "He has become": MM to Horace Mann Jr., May 15, 1864, Antioch.

373. "If sometimes it impels": "Septimius Norton," in *Elixir of Life,* p. 241.

373. "He had the choice": "The Dolliver Romance," in *Elixir of Life,* p. 241.

373. "Think of the delight": AF, Mar. 28, 1864, MHS; Howe, *Memories of a Hostess,* p. 63.

373. "Men die, finally": "Septimius Norton," in *Elixir of Life,* p. 322.

373. "His death was a mystery": Franklin B. Sanborn, ms. dated Aug. 28, 1901, Concord Free Public Library.

373. "A man's days": Annie Sawyer Downs, "Mr. Hawthorne, Mr. Thoreau, Miss Alcott, Mr. Emerson, and Me," ed. Walter Harding, *American Heritage* 30:1 (Dec. 1978), p. 99.

373. The morning of Hawthorne's funeral: EPP to [Mary Pickman Loring], May 23, 1864, courtesy Kent Bicknell.

373. "like a snow image": *Memories,* p. 478.

373. "My father did not": *Memories,* pp. 480, 478.

373. They stopped by Charles Street: *Yesterdays,* p. 122.

374. In private, he said: See SH to JTF, May 21, 1864, BPL: "Will you be kind enough to refrain from saying a word to my sisters about what Mr. Hawthorne said of fear of not becoming able to—of not being himself as before because on any such suggestion I fear my sister would *talk* of it to others and inevitably exaggerate. . . . And you know his mind had not yet a shadow—Oh I wish Dr. Holmes would not say he feared it. Why not leave him intact as he is."

374. But the shark's tooth: Oliver Wendell Holmes, "Hawthorne," *Atlantic Monthly* 14 (July 1864), pp. 98–101. AF, diary, May 11, 1864, MHS.

374. Pierce signed: From a photograph of the register, courtesy Kent Bicknell.

374. "Happy the man": *The Blithedale Romance,* p. 667.

374. It would be a boon . . . "Not in my day": To Horatio Bridge, Pierce confided that Hawthorne had grown so weak he decided he'd call Sophia and Una to come to Plymouth (*Personal Recollections,* p. 178), but he told Sarah Webster that "I was much impressed with the idea that his journey of life might terminate nearer the sea, which he so much loved, than Dixville Notch," which suggests he knew Hawthorne was dying. See FP to Sarah Webster, Mar. 18, 1868, UVA.

374. After Hawthorne's death: See FP to Sarah Webster, Mar. 18, 1868, UVA; see also SH to Anne O'Gara, Sept. 4, 1864, Bancroft; *Yesterdays,* p. 123; *Personal Recollections,* pp. 176–79: my account of Hawthorne's last days is taken from these.

375. Later that day, May 19: Nichols, *Franklin Pierce* p. 525. I have not discovered Nichols's source or found further corroboration of the story, but despite his scant notes, Nichols is reliable in all other instances and is likely reliable here.

375. "I need not tell you": *Personal Recollections,* p. 179.

EPILOGUE: THE PAINTED VEIL

377. "He peacefully closed": The foregoing depends on MM to Horace Mann Jr., May 22, 1864, UVA; SH to Anne O'Gara, Sept. 4, 1864, Bancroft; EPP to Elizabeth Curson Hoxie in *The Letters of Elizabeth Palmer Peabody,* p. 455; SH to Thomas Wentworth Higginson, May 19, 1867, Berg.

377. "Trifling details stood out": JH, *The Memoirs of Julian Hawthorne,* ed. Edith Garrigues Hawthorne (New York: Macmillan, 1938), pp. 156–57.

378. "Sophia does not wish": MM to Horace Mann Jr., May 22, 1864, UVA.

378. "cannot bear to think": UH to James Freeman Clarke, [May 1864], MHS.

378. Sophia asked . . . Annie got: UH to AF, [May 1864], BPL.

378. "It looked like": *The Journals and Miscellaneous Notebooks of Ralph Waldo Emerson,* vol. 15, p. 59.

378. "We shall be alone": [May 21, 1864], quoted in *The Letters of Henry Wadsworth Longfellow,* p. 412.

378. Ebe Hawthorne was also: Sophia Hawthorne's letter to EPP, May 25, 1864, Berg, has wrongly been interpreted to indicate that EPP did not attend the funeral; however, shortly after the funeral, SH described it to various persons in attendance, as if to offer them further consolation, which she clearly aims to do in the case of EPP. Moreover, in EPP to Samuel Foster Haven Jr., Elizabeth Peabody writes that she thought the funeral service lovely, adding that Emerson said "it did not sufficiently recognize the tragedy of his loss to our literature" (n.d., Haven Papers, AAS). Also EPP to Mary Loring, May 23, 1864, courtesy Kent Bicknell, makes her intention to attend the funeral clear.

378. He was the friend: MM to Horace Mann Jr., May 24, 1864, UVA.

378. Julian, his hand cold: SH to EPP, May 23, 1864, Berg.

379. Afterwards Sophia said: Louisa Alcott, diary, n.d., Houghton.

379. He died with one hundred twenty: Nathaniel Hawthorne, probate record 33844, Archives and Records, Supreme Judicial Court, Boston, Mass.

379. "I thought I could": *Memories,* p. 456. The original letter contains slight variations. See RWE to SH, July 11 [1864], Morgan.

379. "tragic element": *The Journals and Miscellaneous Notebooks of Ralph Waldo Emerson,* vol. 15, pp. 59–60.

379. "I don't think people": James Russell Lowell to JTF, Sept. 7, 1868, Huntington.

379. "It was pleasant": Conway, *Autobiography, Memories, and Experiences,* vol. 1, p. 386.

380. "We are always finding": William Dean Howells, *Literary Friends and Acquaintances,* ed. David Hiatt and Edwin Cady (Bloomington: Indiana Univ. Press, 1968), p. 52.

380. "I never dared": SH to unknown, [June? 1864?], Berg.

380. But not everyone: Charles King Newcomb, *The Journals of Charles King Newcomb,* ed. Judith Kennedy Johnson (Providence, R.I.: Brown Univ. Press, 1946), p. 151; Caroline Healey Dall, diary, June 3, 1864, MHS; Charles Eliot Norton to George William Curtis, Sept. 6, 1864, bMS Am 1088.2, box 2, Houghton; *The Selected Letters of Louisa Alcott,* p. 321.

380. "There can be companionship": George S. Hillard, "The English Note-books of Nathaniel Hawthorne," *Atlantic Monthly* 26:155 (Sept. 1870), p. 266.

380. "He was a man": MM to Horace Mann Jr., May 22, 1864, UVA.

381. "Nobody would think": NH to SH, Jan. 1, 1840, *C* XV, p. 395.

381. James T. Fields swiftly: Today Fields's skill at making Hawthorne a "canonical" author is the subject of debate and concern, beginning with Jane Tompkins's fine essay in *Sensational Designs;* see also Richard Brodhead, *Cultures of Letters: Scenes of Reading and Writing in Nineteenth-Century America* (Chicago: Univ. of Chicago Press, 1993). Partly as a consequence of Hawthorne's undiminished popularity—his work has never suffered the eclipses that have occasionally shadowed Melville or James or Wharton—Hawthorne has become the canoni-

cal dead white male author that critics, particularly academic ones, love to hate, for his continuous popularity suggests, among other things, that his work confirms and constructs even while it undermines the "dominant ideologies" that presumably guarantee popularity.

381. "Is he human?": Curtis, "Nathaniel Hawthorne," p. 354.

382. "What other man": Curtis, "Nathaniel Hawthorne," p. 354.

382. "I said probably": George William Curtis to Richard C. Manning, June 18, 1864, PE.

382. "His genius continually": Charles Eliot Norton to George William Curtis, Sept. 6, 1864, bMS Am 1088.2, box 2, Houghton.

Selected Bibliography

(Excluding archival or primary material and reviews listed in the Notes)

Aaron, Daniel. *The Unwritten War: American Writers and the Civil War.* New York: Alfred A. Knopf, 1973.

Adams, Richard P. "Hawthorne's *Provincial Tales.*" *New England Quarterly* 30 (1957): 39–57.

Adkins, Nelson F. "The Early Projected Works of Nathaniel Hawthorne." *Papers of the Bibliographical Society of America* 39 (1945): 119–55.

———. "Notes on the Hawthorne Canon." *Papers of the Bibliographical Society of America* 60 (1966): 364–65.

Alcott, Bronson. *The Journals of Bronson Alcott.* Ed. Odell Shephard. Boston: Little Brown, 1938.

Alcott, Louisa May. *Selected Letters of Louisa May Alcott.* Eds. Joel Myerson and Daniel Shealy. Boston: Little, Brown, 1987.

Armstrong, Margaret. *Fanny Kemble: A Passionate Pilgrim.* New York: Macmillan, 1938.

Arvin, Newton. *Hawthorne.* Boston: Little, Brown, 1929.

Austin, James C. *Fields of "The Atlantic Monthly": Letters to an Editor, 1861–1870.* San Marino, Calif.: Huntington Library, 1953.

Bacon, Theodore. *Delia Bacon.* Boston: Houghton Mifflin, 1888.

Baker, Jean H. *Affairs of Party: The Political Culture of Northern Democrats in the Mid-Nineteenth Century.* Ithaca, N.Y.: Cornell University Press, 1983.

Baker, Paul R. *The Fortunate Pilgrims: Americans in Italy, 1800–1864.* Cambridge: Harvard University Press, 1964.

Bartlett, David W. *The Life of General Franklin Pierce, of New-Hampshire, the Democratic President of the United States.* Buffalo, N.Y.: G.H. Derby and Co., 1852.

Batchelor, George. "The Salem of Hawthorne's Time." *Salem Gazette,* March 11 and 18, 1887. Reprinted in *Essex Institute Historical Collections* 84 (January 1948): 64–9.

Baym, Nina. "Hawthorne and His Mother: A Biographical Speculation." *American Literature* 54 (1982): 1–27.

———. *The Shape of Hawthorne's Career.* Ithaca, N.Y.: Cornell University Press, 1976.

Bell, Millicent. *Hawthorne's View of the Artist.* Albany, N.Y.: State University, 1962.

———. "*The Marble Faun* and the Waste of History." *Southern Review* 35 (spring 1999): 354–70.

Bennoch, Francis. *Poems, Lyrics, Songs and Sonnets.* London: Hardwicke and Bogue, 1877.

———. "A Week's Vagabondage with Nathaniel Hawthorne," with introduction by T. A. J. Burnett. In *The Nathaniel Hawthorne Journal 1971,* ed. C. E. Frazer Clark, Jr. Englewood, Colo.: Microcard Editions, 1971.

Bensick, Carole Marie. *La Nouvelle Beatrice: Renaissance and Romance in "Rappaccini's Daughter."* New Brunswick, N.J.: Rutgers University Press, 1985.

Bentley, Nancy. *The Ethnography of Manners: Hawthorne, James, Wharton.* New York: Cambridge University Press, 1995.

Bentley, William. *The Diary of William Bentley, D.D., 1784–1819.* 4 vols. 1905. Reprint, Gloucester, Mass.: Peter Smith, 1962.

Bercovitch, Sacvan. *The Office of "The Scarlet Letter."* Baltimore: Johns Hopkins University Press, 1991.

Berlant, Lauren. *The Anatomy of National Fantasy: Hawthorne, Utopia, and Everyday Life.* Chicago: University of Chicago Press, 1991.

Bonham, Valerie. *A Joyous Service: The Clewer Sisters & Their Work.* Windsor, England: Valerie Bonham and the Community of St. John the Baptist, 1989.

Brancaccio, Patrick. "'The Black Man's Paradise': Hawthorne's Editing of the *Journal of an African Cruiser.*" *New England Quarterly* 53 (1980): 23–41.

———. "'Chiefly About War-matters': Hawthorne's Reluctant Prophecy." *Essex Institute Historical Collections* 118 (January 1982): 59–66.

Braude, Ann. *Radical Spirits: Spiritualism and Women's Rights in Nineteenth Century America.* Boston: Beacon Press, 1989.

Bremer, Frederika. *The Homes of the New World; Impressions of America.* Trans. Mary Howitt. 2 vols. 1853. Reprint, New York: Negro Universities Press, 1968.

Bridge, Horatio. *Journal of an African Cruiser.* Ed. Nathaniel Hawthorne. New York: Wiley and Putnam, 1845.

Bright, Henry. *Happy Country This America: The Travel Diary of Henry Arthur Bright.* Ed. Anne Ehrenpreis. Columbus: Ohio State University Press, 1978.

Brodhead, Richard. *Cultures of Letters: Scenes of Reading and Writing in Nineteenth-Century America.* Chicago: University of Chicago, 1993.

———. *The School of Hawthorne.* New York: Oxford University Press, 1986.

Brooks, Van Wyck. *The Dream of Arcadia: American Writers and Artists in Italy.* New York: E.P. Dutton, 1958.

Buell, Lawrence. *Literary Transcendentalism: Style and Vision in the American Renaissance.* Ithaca, N.Y.: Cornell University Press, 1973.

Cameron, Kenneth, ed. *Hawthorne among His Contemporaries*. Hartford, Conn.: Transcendental, 1968.

Cameron, Sharon. *The Corporeal Self: Allegories of the Body in Melville and Hawthorne*. Baltimore: Johns Hopkins University Press, 1981.

Capper, Charles. *Margaret Fuller: An American Romantic Life*. New York: Oxford University Press, 1992.

Carton, Evan. *Hawthorne's Transformations*. New York: Twayne, 1992.

———. *The Rhetoric of American Romance: Dialectic and Identity in Emerson, Dickinson, Poe, and Hawthorne*. Baltimore: Johns Hopkins University Press, 1985.

Caspar, Scott. "The Two Lives of Franklin Pierce." *American Literary History* 5 (summer 1993): 203–30.

Cather, Willa. *Not under Forty*. New York: Alfred A. Knopf, 1936.

Channing, William Ellery. *Thoreau, the Poet-Naturalist*. Boston: Charles Goodspeed, 1902.

Channing, William Henry. "*Mosses from an Old Manse*." *Harbinger* 3 (June 27, 1846): 43–4.

Charvat, William. *The Profession of Authorship in America*. Ed. Matthew Bruccoli. Columbus: Ohio State University, 1968.

Clark, C. E. Frazer, Jr. " 'The Interrupted Nuptials,' A Question of Attribution." In *The Nathaniel Hawthorne Journal 1971*, ed. C. E. Frazer, Jr. Englewood, Colo.: Microcard Editions, 1971.

———. *Nathaniel Hawthorne: A Descriptive Bibliography*. Pittsburgh: University of Pittsburgh Press, 1978.

———, ed. *Hawthorne at Auction, 1894–1971*. Detroit: Gale Research Company, 1972.

Cleaveland, Nehemiah, and Alpheus Spring Packard. *History of Bowdoin College*. Boston: Osgood and Company, 1882.

Coale, Samuel Chase. *Mesmerism and Hawthorne*. Tuscaloosa: University of Alabama Press, 1998.

Cohen, Bernard B., ed. *The Recognition of Nathaniel Hawthorne*. Ann Arbor: University of Michigan Press, 1969.

Colacurcio, Michael. *The Province of Piety*. Durham, N.C.: Duke University Press, 1995.

Conway, Moncure. *Autobiography, Memories, and Experiences*. Boston: Houghton Mifflin, 1904.

———. *Life of Nathaniel Hawthorne*. London: Walter Scott, 1890.

Crain, Caleb. *American Sympathy: Men, Friendship, and Literature in the New Nation*. New Haven: Yale University Press, 2001.

Crain, Patricia. *The Story of "A."* Palo Alto, Calif.: Stanford University Press, 2000.

Crews, Frederick C. *The Sins of the Fathers: Hawthorne's Psychological Themes*. New York: Oxford University Press, 1966.

Curtis, George. "Nathaniel Hawthorne." In *Essays from the "North American Review,"* ed. Allen Thorndike Rice. New York: D. Appleton and Co., 1879.

Davidson, Edward H. *Hawthorne's Last Phase*. New Haven: Yale University Press, 1949.

Davis, Rebecca Harding. *Bits of Gossip*. Boston: Houghton Mifflin, 1904.

Derks, Scott, ed. *The Value of a Dollar, 1860–1989.* Detroit: A. Manly, 1994.

Dicey, Edward. "Nathaniel Hawthorne." *Macmillan's Magazine* 10 (July 1864): 241–6.

———. *Spectator of America.* Ed. Herbert Mitgang. 1863. Reprint, Chicago: Quadrangle, 1971.

Donald, David Herbert. *Charles Summer and the Coming of the Civil War.* New York: Knopf, 1960.

———. *Lincoln.* New York: Simon and Schuster, 1995.

Downs, Annie Sawyer. "Mr. Hawthorne, Mr. Thoreau, Miss Alcott, Mr. Emerson, and Me," ed. Walter Harding. *American Heritage* 30 (December 1978): 94–105.

Duberman, Martin, et al. *Hidden from History: Reclaiming the Gay and Lesbian Past.* Markham, Ontario: New American Library, 1989.

Duyckinck, Evert. "Nathaniel Hawthorne." *Democratic Review* 16 (April 1845): 376–84.

Emerson, Edward W. *The Early Years of the Saturday Club.* Boston: Houghton Mifflin, 1918.

Emerson, Ralph Waldo. *Emerson in His Journals.* Ed. Joel Porte. Cambridge: Harvard University Press, 1982.

———. *The Journals and Miscellaneous Notebooks of Ralph Waldo Emerson, 1860–1866.* Eds. Linda Allandt, David Hill, et al. 16 vols. Cambridge: Harvard University Press, 1982.

———. *The Letters of Ralph Waldo Emerson.* Ed. Ralph Rusk. 6 vols. New York: Columbia University Press, 1939.

———. *The Letters of Ralph Waldo Emerson.* Ed. Eleanor M. Tilton. Vol. 8. New York: Columbia University Press, 1991.

Emerson, Ralph Waldo, William H. Channing, and James Freeman Clarke, eds. *Memoirs of Margaret Fuller Ossoli.* 2 vols. London: Richard Bentley, 1852.

Erlich, Gloria. *Family Themes and Hawthorne's Fiction: The Tenacious Web.* New Brunswick, N.J.: Rutgers University Press, 1984.

Federman, Lillian. *Surpassing the Love of Men: Romantic Friendship and Love between Women from the Renaissance to the Present.* New York: William Morrow and Co., 1981.

Felt, Joseph B. *Annals of Salem.* Salem, Mass.: W. and S. B. Ives, 1827.

Field, Maunsell B. *Memories of Men and of Some Women.* New York: Harper & Brothers, 1874.

Fisk, Rosemary Mims. "*The Marble Faun* and the English Copyright: The Smith, Elder Contract." *Studies in the American Renaissance* (1995): 263–75.

Foner, Eric. *Free Soil, Free Labor, Free Men.* New York: Oxford University Press, 1995.

Frederickson, George. *The Inner Civil War.* New York: Harper & Row, 1965.

Fuller, Margaret. "The Great Lawsuit." In *The Essential Margaret Fuller,* ed. Jeffrey Steele. New Brunswick, N.J.: Rutgers University Press, 1992.

———. "The Impulses of Human Nature: Margaret Fuller's Journal from June through October 1844," ed. Martha L. Berg and Alice De V. Perry. *Proceedings of the Massachusetts Historical Society* 102 (1990): 38–126.

———. *The Letters of Margaret Fuller.* Ed. Robert N. Hudspeth. 6 vols. Ithaca, N.Y.: Cornell University Press, 1983–8.

———. "Margaret Fuller's 1842 Journal: At Concord with the Emersons," ed. Joel Myerson. *Harvard Library Bulletin* 21 (July 1973): 320–40.

Gallup, Donald C. "On Hawthorne's Authorship of 'The Battle-Omen.'" *New England Quarterly* (December 1936): 690–99.

Gara, Larry. *The Presidency of Franklin Pierce.* Lawrence: University Press of Kansas, 1991.

Gilkes, Lillian B. "Hawthorne, Park Benjamin, and S. G. Goodrich: A Three-Cornered Imbroglio." *Nathaniel Hawthorne Journal 1971,* ed. C. E. Frazer Clark Jr. Englewood, Colo.: Microcard Editions, 1971.

Gilmore, Michael T. *American Romanticism and the Marketplace.* Chicago: University of Chicago Press, 1985.

Gollin, Rita. *Portraits of Nathaniel Hawthorne: An Iconography.* De Kalb: Northern Illinois University Press, 1983.

Goodrich, Samuel G. *Recollections of a Lifetime.* 2 vols. New York: Miller, Orton and Mulligan, 1856.

Gray, Wood. *The Hidden Civil War: The Story of the Copperheads.* New York: Viking, 1942.

Greene, Graham. *A Sort of Life.* New York: Simon and Schuster, 1971.

Greylock, Godfrey, and Joseph E. A. Smith. *Taghconic; or Letters and Legends about our Summer Home.* Boston: Redding and Co., 1852.

Guarneri, Carl J. *The Utopian Alternative: Fourierism in Nineteenth-Century America.* Ithaca, N.Y.: Cornell University Press, 1991.

Haraszti, Zoltán. *The Idyll of Brook Farm as Revealed by Unpublished Letters.* Boston: Boston Public Library, 1937.

Harwell, Richard. *Hawthorne and Longfellow: A Guide to an Exhibit.* Brunswick, Maine: Bowdoin College, 1966.

Hatch, Louis C. *The History of Bowdoin College.* Portland, Maine: Loring, Short and Harmon, 1927.

Hawthorne, Hildegarde. *Romantic Rebel.* New York: Appleton-Century-Crofts, 1932.

Hawthorne, Julian. "A Daughter of Hawthorne." *Atlantic Monthly* 142 (September 1928): 372–7.

———. *Hawthorne and His Circle.* New York: Harper Brothers, 1903.

———. *The Subterranean Brotherhood.* New York: McBride, Nast & Company, 1914.

Hawthorne, Manning. "A Glimpse of Hawthorne's Boyhood." *Essex Institute Historical Collections* 83 (1947): 178–84.

———. "Hawthorne and 'The Man of God.'" *Colophon* 2 (winter 1937): 262–82.

———. "Maria Louise Hawthorne." *Essex Institute Historical Collections* 75 (1939): 103–34.

———. "Nathaniel Hawthorne at Bowdoin." *New England Quarterly* 13, no. 1 (1940): 246–79.

Hawthorne, Sophia. *Notes in England and Italy.* New York: Putnam and Sons, 1869.

———. "A Sophia Hawthorne Journal, 1843–1844," ed. John McDonald. *Nathaniel Hawthorne Review 1974:* 1–30.

Headly, J. T. "Berkshire Scenery." *New York Observer,* September 14, 1850: 145.

Hedrick, Joan D. *Harriet Beecher Stowe: A Life.* New York: Oxford University Press, 1994.

Herbert, T. Walter. *Dearest Beloved: The Hawthornes and the Making of the Middle-Class Family.* Berkeley: University of California Press, 1993.

———. "Doing Cultural Work: 'My Kinsman, Major Molineux' and the Construction of the Self-Made Man." *Studies in the Novel* 23 (spring 1991): 20–27.

Higginson, Thomas Wentworth. *Part of a Man's Life.* Boston: Houghton Mifflin, 1905.

———. "Wedded Isolation." *The Woman's Journal* (December 20, 1884): 407.

Hoeltje, Hubert H. "Captain Nathaniel Hathorne, Father of the Salem Novelist." *Essex Institute Historical Collections* 89 (October 1953): 329–56.

Holden, George Henry. "Hawthorne Among his Friends." *Harper's Monthly* 63 (1881): 262–7.

[Holmes, Oliver Wendell.] "Hawthorne." *The Atlantic Monthly* 12 (July 1864): 98–101.

Homer, Bryan. *An American Liaison: Leamington Spa and the Hawthornes, 1855–1864.* Rutherford, N.J.: Fairleigh Dickinson University Press, 1997.

Honour, Hugh. *Neo-Classicism.* New York: Viking Penguin, 1987.

Hopkins, Vivian. *Prodigal Puritan: A Life of Delia Bacon.* Cambridge: Harvard University Press, 1959.

Hosmer, Harriet. *Letters and Memories.* Ed. Cornelia Carr. New York: Moffat, Yard and Co., 1912.

Howe, Mark DeWolfe. *The Later Years of the Saturday Club, 1870–1920.* Boston: Houghton Mifflin, 1927.

———. *Memories of a Hostess: A Chronicle of Eminent Friendships Drawn Chiefly from the Diaries of Mrs. James T. Fields.* 1922. Reprint, New York: Arno Press, 1974.

Howells, William Dean. *Literary Friends and Acquaintances.* Eds. David Hiatt and Edwin Cady. Bloomington: Indiana University Press, 1968.

Hudson, Gertrude Reese, ed. *Browning to His American Friends.* New York: Barnes and Noble, 1965.

Hull, Raymona E. *Nathaniel Hawthorne: The English Experience, 1853–1964.* Pittsburgh: University of Pittsburgh Press, 1980.

Idol, John L., Jr., and Sterling Eisminger. "Hawthorne Sits for a Bust by Maria Louisa Lander." *Essex Institute Historical Collections* 114 (1978): 207–12.

Idol, John L., Jr., and Buford Jones, eds. *Nathaniel Hawthorne: The Contemporary Reviews.* Cambridge: Cambridge University Press, 1994.

Idol, John L., Jr., and Melinda M. Ponder, eds. *Hawthorne and Women.* Amherst: University of Massachusetts Press, 1999.

Ilchman, Warren. *Professional Diplomacy in the United States.* Chicago: University of Chicago Press, 1961.

James, Henry. *The Bostonians.* New York: Library of America, 1985.

———. *Literary Criticism: Essays on Literature, American Writers, English Writers.* Ed. Leon Edel. New York: Library of America, 1984.

————. *Notes of a Son and Brother.* New York: Charles Scribner's Sons, 1914.

————. *William Wetmore Story and His Friends.* Vol. 1. Boston: Houghton Mifflin, 1903.

Jones, Wayne Allen. "The Hawthorne-Goodrich Relationship." *Nathaniel Hawthorne Journal 1975.* Ed. C. E. Frazer Clark Jr. Englewood, Colo.: Microcard Editions, 1975.

————. "Hawthorne's Slender Means." *Nathaniel Hawthorne Journal 1977.* Ed. C. E. Frazer Clark Jr. Detroit: Bruccoli Clark, 1977.

Kasson, Joy S. *Marble Queens and Captives: Women in Nineteenth-Century American Sculpture.* New Haven: Yale University Press, 1990.

Kendall, Phebe Mitchall, ed. *Maria Mitchell: Life, Letters, and Journals.* Boston: Lee & Shepard, 1896.

Kerr, Howard. *Mediums, Spirit-Rappers, and Roaring Radicals: Spiritualism in American Literature.* Urbana: University of Illinois Press, 1972.

Kesserling, Marion L. "Hawthorne's Reading, 1828–1850: A Transcription and Identification of Titles Recorded in the Charge-Books of the Salem Athenaeum." *Bulletin of the New York Public Library* 53 (1949): 55–71, 121–38, 173–94.

Knight, Ernest. *The Origin and History of Raymondtown.* Norway, Maine: Oxford Hills Press, 1974.

Kraitsir, Charles. *Significance of the Alphabet.* Boston: E. P. Peabody, 1846.

Lathrop, George Parsons. *A Study of Hawthorne.* 1876. Reprint, New York: AMS Press, 1969.

Lease, Benjamin. *That Wild Fellow John Neal and the American Literary Revolution.* Chicago: University of Chicago Press, 1972.

Leverenz, David. *Manhood and the American Renaissance.* Ithaca, N.Y.: Cornell University Press, 1989.

Levin, David, ed. *Emerson: Prophecy, Metamorphosis, and Influence.* New York: Columbia University Press, 1975.

Levine, Robert S. "Antebellum Rome in *The Marble Faun.*" *American Literary History* 2, no. 1 (spring 1990): 19–38.

Leyda, Jay. *The Melville Log: A Documentary Life of Herman Melville 1819–1891.* 2 vols. 1951. Reprint, New York: Harcourt Brace, 1969.

Lincoln, Abraham. *Speeches and Writings, 1832–1858.* New York: Library of America, 1989.

Loggins, Vernon. *The Hawthornes.* New York: Columbia University Press, 1951.

Longfellow, Fanny. *Mrs. Longfellow: Selected Letters and Journals of Fanny Appleton Longfellow.* Ed. Edward Wagenecht. New York: Longmans, Green, & Co., 1956.

Longfellow, Henry Wadsworth. *The Letters of Henry Wadsworth Longfellow.* Ed. Andrew Hilen. 6 vols. Cambridge: Harvard University Press, 1972.

Loring, George B. "Nathaniel Hawthorne." In *Papyrus Leaves,* ed. William Fearing Gill. Chicago: Belford, Clarke, & Co., 1884.

Lowell, James Russell. *The Letters of James Russell Lowell.* Ed. Charles Norton. Vol. 1. New York: Harper & Brothers, 1894.

Luedtke, Luther S. *Nathaniel Hawthorne and the Romance of the Orient.* Bloomington: Indiana University Press, 1989.

MacPherson, Gordon, ed. *Black's Medical Dictionary.* London: A. and C. Black, 1992.

Manning, Elizabeth. "The Boyhood of Hawthorne." *Wide Awake* 33 (November 1891): 500–518.

Manning, Robert. *The Book of Fruits.* Salem, Mass.: Ives & Jewett, 1838.

Manning, William H. *The Manning Families of New England.* Salem, Mass.: Salem Press, 1902.

Martin, Robert K. "Hester Prynne, C'est moi: Nathaniel Hawthorne and the Anxieties of Gender." In *Engendering Men,* eds. Joseph Boone and Michael Cudder. New York: Routledge, 1990.

Martin, Robert K., and Leland S. Person, eds. *Roman Holidays: American Writers and Artists in Nineteenth-Century Italy.* Iowa City: University of Iowa, 2002.

Matthews, Cornelius. "Several Days in Berkshire." *Literary World* 7 (August 24, 31, and September 7, 1850): 145–7, 166, 185–6.

Matthiessen, F. O. *American Renaissance: Art and Expression in the Age of Emerson and Whitman.* New York: Oxford University Press, 1941.

Mayer, Henry. *All on Fire: William Lloyd Garrison and the Abolition of Slavery.* New York: St. Martin's, 1998.

Maynard, Theodore. *A Fire Was Lighted: The Life of Rose Hawthorne Lathrop.* Milwaukee: Bruce Publishing Co., 1948.

McCall, Dan. *Citizens of Somewhere Else: Nathaniel Hawthorne and Henry James.* Ithaca, N.Y.: Cornell University Press, 1999.

McKitrick, Eric L., ed. *Slavery Defended: The Views of the Old South.* Englewood Cliffs, N.J.: Prentice-Hall, 1963.

McWilliams, John. "The Politics of Isolation." *Nathaniel Hawthorne Review* 15 (spring 1989): 3–7.

———. " 'Thorough-going Democrat' and 'Modern Tory': Hawthorne and the Puritan Revolution of 1776." *Studies in Romanticism* 15 (1976): 549–71.

Mellow, James. *Nathaniel Hawthorne in His Times.* Boston: Houghton Mifflin, 1980.

Melville, Herman. *Correspondence.* Eds. Harrison Hayford and Lynn Horth. Chicago: Northwestern University Press and Newberry Library, 1993.

Menand, Louis. *The Metaphysical Club: A Story of Ideas in America.* New York: Farrar, Straus & Giroux, 2001.

Metzdorf, Robert F. "Hawthorne's Suit against Ripley and Dana." *American Literature* 12 (1940): 235–41.

Michaels, Walter Benn. "Romance and Real Estate." *Raritan* 2 (winter 1983): 66–87.

Miller, Edwin Haviland. *Salem Is My Dwelling Place.* Iowa City: University of Iowa, 1991.

Miller, J. Hillis. *Hawthorne and History.* Cambridge, Mass.: Basil Blackwell, 1991.

Millington, Richard H. *Practicing Romance: Narrative Form and Cultural Engagement in Hawthorne's Fiction.* Princeton, N.J.: Princeton University Press, 1992.

Mitchell, Thomas. *Hawthorne's Fuller Mystery.* Amherst: University of Massachusetts Press, 1998.

Mitchell, Wilmot Brookings. *A Remarkable Bowdoin Decade.* Brunswick, Maine: Bowdoin College, 1952.

Mitford, Mary Russell. *The Correspondence of Mary Russell Mitford with Charles Boner and John Ruskin.* Ed. Elizabeth Lee. London: T. Fisher Unwin, 1914.

Moore, Margaret B. *The Salem World of Nathaniel Hawthorne.* Columbia: University of Missouri Press, 1998.

Moore, Thomas R. "Hawthorne as Essayist in 'Chiefly About War Matters.' " *American Transcendental Quarterly* 6 (1992): 263–78.

Morison, Samuel Eliot. *The Maritime History of Massachusetts.* Boston: Houghton Mifflin, 1921.

Murray, John. *Murray's Handbook of Rome and its Environs* 1858. London: John Murray, 1858.

Myerson, Joel. "James Burrill Curtis and Brook Farm." *New England Quarterly* (September 1978): 396–423.

———. "Two Unpublished Reminiscences of Brook Farm." *New England Quarterly* 48 (June 1975): 253–60.

———. "An Ungathered Sanborn Lecture on Brook Farm." *Atlantic Transcendental Quarterly* 26 (spring 1975): 1–10.

Naples, Diane. " 'Roger Malvin's Burial'—A Parable for Historians?" *American Transcendental Quarterly* 13 (1972): 45–48.

National Park Service, the Peabody Museum, and the Essex Institute. *Salem: Maritime Salem in the Age of Sail.* Salem, Mass.: National Park Service Handbook 126, 1987.

Neussendorfer, Margaret. "Elizabeth Peabody to William Wordsworth: Eight Letters, 1825–1845." *Studies in the American Renaissance* (1984): 181–211.

Nevins, Allan. *The Ordeal of the Union.* 2 vols. New York: Charles Scribner's Sons, 1947.

———. *The War for the Union.* 4 vols. New York: Charles Scribner's Sons, 1959–71.

Newberry, Frederick. *Hawthorne's Divided Loyalties.* Rutherford, N.J.: Fairleigh Dickinson University Press, 1987.

Newcomb, Charles King. *The Journals of Charles King Newcomb.* Ed. Judith Kennedy Johnson. Providence, R.I.: Brown University Press, 1946.

Newman, Lea Bertani Vozar. "One Hundred Fifty Years of 'The Minister's Black Veil.' " *Nathaniel Hawthorne Review* 13 (fall 1987): 5–12.

Nichols, Roy Franklin. *The Disruption of American Democracy.* New York: Macmillan, 1948.

———. *Franklin Pierce: Young Hickory of the Granite Hills.* Philadelphia: University of Pennsylvania Press, 1931.

Nissenbaum, Stephen. "The Firing of Nathaniel Hawthorne." *Essex Institute Historical Collections* 114 (April 1978): 57–86.

O'Connor, Flannery. *Mystery and Manners.* New York: Farrar, Straus & Giroux, 1969.

O'Sullivan, John Louis. "Annexation." *Democratic Review* 17 (July–August 1845): 2–10.

———. "The Course of Civilization." *Democratic Review* 6 (September 1839): 208–17.

———. "Dr. Channing's Recent Writings." *Democratic Review* 9 (October 1841): 315–26.

———. "The Martyrdom of Cilley." *Democratic Review* 1 (March 1838): 493–508.

———. "Wives and Slaves: A Bone for Abolitionists to Pick." *Democratic Review* 17 (October 1845): 264–72.

Packard, George Thomas. "Bowdoin College." *Scribner's Monthly* 12 (1876): 47–61.

Packer, Barbara L. "The Transcendentalists." In *The Cambridge History of American Literature,* ed. Sacvan Bercovitch. New York: Cambridge University Press, 1995.

Parker, Hershel. *Herman Melville, A Biography, 1819–1851.* Vol. 1. Baltimore: Johns Hopkins University Press, 1996.

———. *Herman Melville, A Biography, 1851–1891.* Vol. 2. Baltimore: John Hopkins University Press, 2002.

[Peabody, Elizabeth Palmer.] "The Genius of Hawthorne." *Atlantic Monthly* 25 (September 1868): 359–74.

———. *The Letters of Elizabeth Palmer Peabody.* Ed. Bruce Ronda. Middletown, Conn.: Wesleyan University Press, 1984.

Peabody, Elizabeth Palmer [Mrs.]. *Holiness; or The Legend of St. George: A Tale from Spenser's "Faerie Queene."* Boston: E.R. Broaders, 1836.

Pearce, Roy Harvey. "Robin Molineux of the Analyst's Couch: A Note on the Limits of Psychoanalytic Criticism. *Criticism* 1 (1959): 83–90.

Pearson, Norman Holmes. "Elizabeth Peabody on Hawthorne." *Essex Institute Historical Collections* 94 (July 1958): 256–76.

———. "A Good Thing for Hawthorne." *Essex Institute Historical Collections* 100 (October 1964): 300–305.

———. "Hawthorne's Duel." *Essex Institute Historical Collections* 94 (1958): 229–42.

———. *Hawthorne's Two "Engagements."* Northampton, Mass.: Smith College, 1963.

Pease, William, and Jane Pease. *Web of Progress. Private Values and Public Styles in Boston and Charleston, 1828–1843.* New York: Oxford University Press, 1985.

Perley, Sidney, *A History of Salem, Massachusetts.* 3 vols. Salem, Mass.: Sidney Perley, 1928.

Pfister, Joel. *The Production of Personal Life.* Stanford, Calif.: Stanford University Press, 1991.

Phelps, Elizabeth Stuart. *Chapters from a Life.* Boston: Houghton Mifflin, 1896.

Phillips, James Duncan. *Salem and the Indies: The Story of the Great Commercial Era of the City.* Boston: Houghton Mifflin, 1947.

Pickard, Samuel T. *Hawthorne's First Diary, With an Account of its Discovery and Loss.* Boston: Houghton Mifflin, 1897.

Pinsky, Robert, trans. *The Inferno of Dante.* New York: Farrar, Straus and Giroux, 1994.

Pope-Hennessy, James. *Monckton Milnes: The Years of Promise.* New York: Farrar, Straus, and Cudahy, 1955.

Potter, David M. *The Impending Crisis, 1848–1861.* Completed and edited by Don E. Fehrenbacher. New York: HarperPerennial, 1976.

Prince, Paul E., and Mollie Keller. *The U.S. Customs Service: A Bicentennial History.* Washington, D.C.: Department of the Treasury, 1989.

Putnam, Eleanor. *Chronicles of Old Salem.* Ed. Arlo Bates. Boston: Houghton Mifflin, 1899.

Rantoul, Robert S. "Some Notes on Old Modes of Travel." *Essex Institute Historical Collections* 11 (1871): 19–73.

Ratner, Lorman. *Powder Keg: Northern Opposition to the Antislavery Movement, 1831–1840.* New York: Basic Books, 1968.

"The Removal of Mr. Hawthorne." *Salem Register* (June 20, 1849): 1.

Reynolds, David. *Beneath the American Renaissance.* Cambridge: Harvard University Press, 1989.

Reynolds, Larry J. "Hawthorne and Emerson in 'The Old Manse.' " *Studies in the Novel* 23 (spring 1991): 60–81.

———. "*The Scarlet Letter* and Revolutions Abroad." *American Literature* 57 (1985): 44–67.

Richards, Leonard L. *Gentlemen of Property and Standing.* New York: Oxford University Press, 1970.

Richardson, Robert D., Jr. *Henry Thoreau: A Life of the Mind.* Berkeley: University of California Press, 1986.

Riddel, Joseph. *Purloined Letters: Originality and Repetition in American Literature.* Ed. Mark Bauerlein. Baton Rouge: Louisiana State University Press, 1995.

Robertson-Lorant, Laurie. *Melville.* New York: Clarkson Potter, 1996.

Robinson, David. "The Political Odyssey of William Henry Channing." *American Quarterly* 34 (summer 1982): 165–84.

Romero, Lora. *Home Fronts: Domesticity and Its Critics in the Antebellum United States.* Durham, N.C.: Duke University Press, 1997.

Ronda, Bruce A. *Elizabeth Palmer Peabody: Reformer on Her Own Terms.* Cambridge: Harvard University Press, 1999.

———. *The Letters of Elizabeth Palmer Peabody.* Middletown, Conn.: Wesleyan University Press, 1984.

Rose, Anne C. *Transcendentalism as a Social Movement, 1830–1850.* New Haven: Yale University Press, 1981.

Rusk, Ralph L. *The Life of Ralph Waldo Emerson.* New York: Charles Scribner's Sons, 1949.

Russell, Amelia. "Home Life on the Brook Farm Association." *Atlantic Monthly* 42 (October–November 1878): 458–563.

Sams, Henry. *Autobiography of Brook Farm.* Englewood Cliffs, N.J.: Prentice-Hall, 1958.

Samuels, Shirley, ed. *The Culture of Sentiment: Race, Gender, and Sentimentality in Nineteenth-Century America.* New York: Oxford University Press, 1992.

Sanborn, Franklin. *Recollection of Seven Years.* Vol. 2. Boston: Richard G. Badger, 1909.

Scharnhorst, Gary, ed. *The Critical Response to Nathaniel Hawthorne's "The Scarlet Letter."* Westport, Conn.: Greenwood Press, 1992.

Schlesinger, Arthur M., Jr. *The Age of Jackson.* Boston: Little, Brown, 1945.

Sears, John Van Der Zee. *My Friends at Brook Farm.* New York: Desmond FitzGerald, 1912.

Sedgwick, Ora Gannett. "A Girl of Sixteen at Brook Farm." *Essex Institute Historical Collections* 85 (1949): 394–404.

Shaw, Peter. *American Patriots and the Rituals of Revolution.* Cambridge: Harvard University Press, 1981.

Sherwood, Dolly. *Harriet Hosmer, American Sculptor.* St. Louis: University of Missouri Press, 1991.

Silsbee, M. C. D. *A Half-Century in Salem.* Boston: Houghton Mifflin, 1887.

Silverman, Kenneth. *Cotton Mather and His Times.* New York: Harper and Row, 1984.

Slater, Joseph, ed. *The Correspondence of Emerson and Carlyle.* New York: Columbia University Press, 1964.

Smith, Grace. " 'Chiefly About War Matters': Hawthorne's Swift Judgement of Lincoln." *American Transcendental Quarterly* 15, no. 2 (June 2001): 149–61.

Smith-Rosenberg, Carroll. *Disorderly Conduct: Visions of Gender in Victorian America.* New York: Alfred A. Knopf, 1985.

Sparks, Mary Crowninshield. *Hymns, Home, Harvard.* Boston: A. Williams and Company, 1883.

Stebbins, Theodore E., Jr., ed. *The Lure of Italy: American Artists and the Italian Experience: 1760–1914.* Boston: Museum of Fine Arts, 1992.

Stitch, Klaus P. "The Saturday Club as Intertext in Hawthorne's *The Elixir of Life Manuscripts.*" *Nathaniel Hawthorne Review* 20 (fall 1994): 11–20.

Stoddard, Richard Henry. "Nathaniel Hawthorne." *National Magazine* 2 (1853): 17–24.

———. *Recollections Personal and Literary.* 1903. Reprint, New York: A. S. Barnes, 1971.

Stuart, Graham. *The Department of State.* New York: Macmillan, 1949.

Swann, Charles. *Nathaniel Hawthorne: Tradition and Revolution.* New York: Cambridge University Press, 1991.

Swift, Lindsay. *Brook Farm.* 1900. Reprint, New York: Corinth Books, 1961.

Taymond, Meredith B., and Mary Rose Sullivan, eds. *The Letters of Elizabeth Barrett Browning to Mary Russell Mitford, 1836–1854.* Vol. 3. Kansas: Wedgestone Press, 1983.

Tharp, Louise Hall. *The Peabody Sisters of Salem.* Boston: Little, Brown, 1950.

Thompson, Lawrence. *Young Longfellow.* New York: Macmillan, 1938.

Thomson, Henry Yates. *An Englishman in the American Civil War: The Diaries of Henry Yates Thomson.* Ed. Christopher Chancellor. 1863. Reprint, New York: New York University Press, 1971.

Thoreau, Henry David. *The Correspondence of Henry David Thoreau.* Eds. Walter Harding and Carl Bode. New York: New York University Press, 1958.

———. *Reform Papers.* Ed. Wendell Glick. Princeton, N.J.: Princeton University Press, 1973.

Ticknor, Caroline. *Hawthorne and His Publisher.* Boston: Houghton Mifflin, 1913.

Tise, Larry E. *Proslavery: A History of the Defense of Slavery in America.* Athens: University of Georgia, 1987.

Tompkins, Jane. *Sensational Designs: The Cultural Work of American Fiction, 1790–1860.* New York: Oxford University Press, 1985.

Traubel, Horace. *With Walt Whitman in Camden.* 5 vols. Boston: Small, Maynard & Co., 1906–14.

Trow, Charles E. *The Old Shipmasters of Salem.* New York: G.P. Putnam, 1905.

Tryon, Thomas. *Parnassus Corner: A Life of James T. Fields.* Boston: Houghton Mifflin, 1963.

Tryon, Warren S., and William Charvat, eds. *The Cost Books of Ticknor and Fields, 1832–1858.* New York: Bibliographical Society of America, 1949.

Tuckerman, Henry T. "Nathaniel Hawthorne." *Lippincott's Magazine* 5 (May 1870): 498–507.

Turner, Arlin. *Hawthorne as Editor.* University: Louisiana State University Press, 1941.

———. "Hawthorne's Final Illness and Death: Additional Reports." *ESQ* 19 (1973): 124–7.

———. *Nathaniel Hawthorne.* New York: Oxford University Press, 1980.

Upham, Thomas C. *American Sketches.* New York: David Longworth, 1819.

Valenti, Patricia. "Sophia Hawthorne's American Notebooks." In *Studies in the American Renaissance 1996,* ed. Joel Myerson. Charlottesville: University Press of Virginia, 1996.

———. *To Myself a Stranger: A Biography of Rose Hawthorne Lathrop.* Baton Rouge: Louisiana State University Press, 1991.

Vance, William. *America's Rome.* New Haven: Yale University Press, 1989.

Von Frank, Albert. *The Trials of Anthony Burns: Freedom and Slavery in Emerson's Boston.* Cambridge: Harvard University Press, 1998.

Warren, Robert Penn. "Hawthorne Revisited: Some Remarks on Hellfiredness." *Sewanee Review* 81 (1973): 75–111.

Waters, Joseph E. "A Biographical Sketch of the Reverend William Bentley." *Essex Institute Historical Collections* 41 (1905): 237–50.

Webber, C. H., and W. S. Nevins. *Old Naumkeag.* Salem, Mass.: A.A. Smith and Co., 1877.

Whipple, Edwin P. *Character and Characteristic Men.* Boston: Ticknor & Fields, 1867.

Whitehill, Walter Muir. *The East India, Marine Society and the Peabody Museum of Salem: A Sesquicentennial History.* Salem, Mass.: Peabody Museum, 1949.

Whiting, Lilian. *Boston Days.* Boston: Little, Brown, 1902.

Widmer, Edward L. *Young America: The Flowering of Democracy in New York City.* New York: Oxford University Press, 1999.

Williams, Susan. "Manufacturing Intellectual Equipment: The Tauchnitz Edition of *The Marble Faun.*" In *Reading Books: Essays on Material Text and Literature in America,* eds. Michele Moylan and Lane Stiles. Amherst: University of Massachusetts Press, 1996.

Wilson, Carroll A. *Thirteen Author Collections of the Nineteenth Century and Five Centuries of Familiar Quotations.* New York: Charles Scribner's Sons, 1950.

Wineapple, Brenda. "The Biographical Imperative: Or, Hawthorne Family Values." In *Biography and Source Studies,* vol. 6, ed. Frederick R. Karl. New York: AMS Press, 1998.

———. "Hawthorne and Melville; or, The Ambiguities." *Emerson Society Quarterly* 46 (2000): 75–98.

Worthington, Marjorie. *Miss Alcott of Concord.* Garden City, N.Y.: Doubleday, 1958.

Wright, Nathalia. *American Novelists in Italy: The Discoverers: Allston to James.* Philadelphia: University of Pennsylvania Press, 1965.

———. "Hawthorne and the Praslin Murder." *New England Quarterly* 15 (1942): 5–14.

Yellin, Jean Fagan. "Hawthorne and the American National Sin." In *The Green American Tradition,* ed. Daniel Peck. Baton Rouge: Louisiana State University Press, 1989.

Ziff, Larzer. "The Artist and Puritanism." In *Hawthorne Centenary Essays,* ed. Roy Harvey Pearce. Columbus: Ohio State University Press, 1964.

Acknowledgments

For permission to quote from various archival material, for their assistance and their good cheer, I am grateful to the following people as well as to the collections they so ably represent: Thomas Knoles, Curator of Manuscripts, at the American Antiquarian Association; to William A. Wheeler; Daria D'Arienzo, Head of Archives and Special Collections at the Amherst College Library; Nina Myatt at Antiochiana, the Antioch College Library Archives; Susan Snyder at the Bancroft Library, University of California, Berkeley; Richard H. F. Lindemann, Director of the Bowdoin College Library, as well as Ian Graham, Dianne Gutscher, Susan Ravdin, and Carolyn Moseley; and at the Bowdoin College Museum of Art, Laura J. Latman, Registrar; my dear friend Patricia C. Willis, Curator of the Yale Collection of American Literature, at the Beinecke Rare Book and Manuscript Library, and Stephen Jones; Rodney Philips, Stephen Crook, Philip Milito, and, more recently, Diana Burnham and Isaac Gewitz, curator, all of the Henry W. and Albert A. Berg Collection of English and American Literature, New York Public Library; Roberta Zonghi, Keeper of Rare Books and Manuscripts at the Boston Public Library; the staff at Trinity College Library, Cambridge University; Jean Ashton, Director, Rare Book and Manuscript Library, Columbia University; Leslie P. Wilson, Curator, Special Collections, at the Concord Free Public Library; and Frederick Peña of the Grolier Club. I'm also very grateful to Leslie A. Morris, Curator of Manuscripts at the Houghton Library, Harvard University, and to Jenny Rathbun and the entire staff; to Leah Owens and other members of the staff as well as Sara S. Hodson, Curator of Literary Manuscripts at the Huntington Library; to Mary M. Wolfskill, Head, Reference and Reader Service Section, Manuscript Division, Library of Congress, and to the research staff in prints and reproductions; to Nicholas Noyes, Head of Library Services, and Bill Barry of the Maine Historical Society; to Nicholas Graham of the Massachusetts Historical Society; the staff at the Minnesota Historical Society; to Christine Nelson, Curator of American Literary Manuscripts at the J. Pierpont Morgan Library; to the helpful staff at the

National Archives; to David Smolen, Special Collections Librarian, and Wayne L. Gallup of the New Hampshire Historical Society; to Wayne Furman as well as the staff of the New York Public Library, Manuscripts and Archives Division, the Laura Johnson Papers and the Duyckinck Family Papers; to the staff at the Notre Dame Archives; to Geoffrey D. Smith, head of Rare Books and Manuscripts at the Ohio State University Library; to Carolle Morini, Heather Shanks, Christine Michelini, and Marc Teatum at the photographic division of the Phillips Library, Peabody Essex Museum; as well as Jane Ward, former curator, and Irene V. Axelrod, Head Manuscript Librarian, and the entire staff at the Phillips Library, Peabody Essex Museum; to the Historical Society of Pennsylvania; to Barbara Thorpe, Raymond Village Library, Raymond, Maine; to Kathleen Banks Nutter and the staff at the Sophia Smith Collection, Smith College; to Roberto G. Trujillo, Head of Special Collections, and John E. Mustain, Green Library, Stanford University; the staff at the Clifton Waller Barrett Library of American Literature, Alderman Library, University of Virginia; Michele Ostrow, Alex Rogers, and Tara Wenger at the Harry Ransom Humanities Research Center, University of Texas at Austin; to Robert N. Matuozzi, Manuscripts Librarian, Manuscripts, Archives, and Special Collections, Holland Library, Washington State University; and to the staff at Special Collections, University of Wisconsin, Madison.

I am also obliged to various members of the Hawthorne family: Gail Gardner, Rosemary Hawthorne, the late Randolf Hawthorne, Imogen Howe, Joan Ensor, Sylvia Smyth, Deborah Strong, and, with much pleasure, the remarkable Olcott Deming. I'm grateful to Evelyn Hamby for opening her trunkful of manuscripts to me, to say nothing of her kitchen and living room, and my meals with Alison Hawthorne Deming were a delight I'll never forget.

I'm also indebted to the late Merton M. Sealts, Jr., a dear friend whom I miss. Rallying his troops to my side, Mert sat through many of my Hawthorne talks and invited me to lecture in 1997 at the University of Wisconsin and at the Oakwood Retirement Community, where he introduced me to the inestimable Hawthorne descendant, Phillis Hawthorne, and to Emily Dodge. I thank them too for their loving friendship—and for showing me Louisa Hawthorne's sampler as well as many other Hawthorne family items. Mert also introduced me to another unusual man, Kent Bicknell, a collector of rare discernment and generosity. To him, I owe a debt of gratitude for his willingness to share treasures, even allowing me to cart away a box of special papers; to him and Karen Bicknell, many thanks for allowing me to camp out in their house while I furiously copied manuscripts.

Thanks, as well, to Mother Marie Edward and Sister DePaul at the Rosary Hill Home; to Eve Anderson, president, Thomaston Historical Society and her husband Olaf; to a founding father of Hawthorne studies, the late C. E. Frazer Clark Jr.; to the psychoanalysts, Dr. Louise Kaplan and Dr. Stuart Feder, for lunches and dinners of Hawthorne; to Scott Marshall and Stephanie Copeland, of the Edith Wharton Restoration, The Mount, for their Berkshire support; to Mary Cahill, for her unflagging assistance at Union College's Interlibrary Loan desk and, what's more, for sending me unsolicited squibs on Hawthorne and his family.

I am grateful to the American Council of Learned Societies and the National Endowment for the Humanities for full fellowships that released me from my teaching duties for years at a time. I'm similarly grateful to the Hertog Fellows Program at Columbia University's School of the Arts, administered by Patty O'Toole, and for the assistance of Fionn Meade, my own Hertog fellow, in the fall of 1998, and to the Dana Scholarship Fund at Union College, administered by Peter Tobiessen, and to Dana Scholars Jean Rho and Gregory Fox; also, I'm grateful to the ongoing support of Union College's Humanities Faculty Development Fund. Thanks also to Joshua Perry, for his assistance with permissions, and to the tireless Michelle Tardif, a former student, who spent some of her summer in England in 2001 trying to determine the cause of Una Hawthorne's death. Actually, I'm obliged to all my students in the Hawthorne seminars I've taught over the years at Union College and New York University.

To David Robinson, whom I've admired for more years than we'd both like to count, I am grateful for recommending I write the "Hawthorne" chapter in *American Literary Scholarship* as a boon to my book, which it was. I'm also beholden to the far-flung members of the Hawthorne scholarly community and over the years have appreciated the ready assistance of Thomas Woodson, editor of the *Centenary Edition of The Writings of Nathaniel Hawthorne*. I have also received kind offers of assistance from many others, like T. Walter Herbert and Megan Marshall. The former president of the Nathaniel Hawthorne Society, Larry J. Reynolds, first ushered me into its ranks in 1996 with the largesse for which he's known. More recently, its indefatigable and talented president, Millicent Bell, has consistently offered graceful support—enthusiasm, in fact—for my writing, and I thank her. I also thank her for inviting me to read a paper on Hawthorne at the Nathaniel Hawthorne Society meeting in Boston, Massachusetts, in 2000. I enjoyed a similar boon in 1997 after joining Frederick Newberry, editor of the *Nathaniel Hawthorne Review,* and his panel at the American Literature Association: it provided me with Fred's witty e-mails ever after. Robert Milder insisted I participate in the Melville/Hawthorne panel at the American Literature Association meeting in May 2000, and from this event comes the special issue of *ESQ* on Hawthorne and Melville. At the recommendation of Benita Eisler, I spoke at the New York Society Library on Hawthorne in 2001, and in 2003 at Bard at the suggestion of Elizabeth Frank. Thanks to them, to all connected with these institutions, and to the folks at the House of the Seven Gables and at C-SPAN, who allowed me to speak on live television about Hawthorne for two hours one icy day in May 2001.

Fortunate in friends, I'd like to thank the remarkable Sybille Bedford, a true inspiration; the extraordinary Richard Howard, for matters more important than literature; the late Kenneth S. Lynn, Honor Moore, Catharine R. Stimpson, and Larry Ziff for their heartening (and often written) support these many years; Kennth Silverman, a special friend whose talent, advice, and commiseration I value—and exploit. Thanks, also, to the ever-spry Ann Thorne, for putting me in touch with Higginsons and Channings and a great deal else. I've also imposed on a number of other friends, who read portions of the manuscript: novelist Christopher Bram, who read all of it with perceptive eye, offering both suggestions and succor; my former editor and longtime friend, the writer Frances Kiernan, who looked at the last chapter with the attention she inevitably shows to language; novelist Ben Taylor, who read the first and last chapters with ebullient wit; and the perspicacious editor/poet/

essayist, Ben Downing, who scoured the first four chapters with his usual clear-eyed precision. Ditto Anna Jardine, still copy editor supreme, on whose conscientiousness and downright smarts I continue to depend.

More than I can say, I'm touched by the many other good friends, colleagues, and acquaintances who've given of themselves in ways too numerous to mention: David Alexander, Frederick Brown, Mary Ann Caws, Ed Cifelli, Lisa Cohen, Benita Eisler, Wendy Gimbel, Rosemarie and Peter Heinegg, Don Hymans, Tamar Jacoby, Frederick Karl, the late Carole Klein, Bobbie Bristol Kinnell, the late R. W. B. Lewis, Herbert Leibowitz, Jane Mallison, Marion Meade, the late James Mellow, Hugh Rawson, Robert D. Richardson, Jr., Margo Viscusi, Lois Wallace, Patricia Willis, Susan Yankowitz, and Donald Yannella.

For their love, spunk, and continuous support, especially during my many research visits to Massachusetts (our native state), particularly to Haverhill (my mother's birthplace) and, of course, to Salem (my father's), I thank my parents.

I'm deeply indebted to my incomparable agent, Lynn Nesbit, and to her wonderful staff, as well as to the production and design staffs at Knopf, particularly Amy Robbins. But nothing is possible without the considerable skills of my editor, Victoria Wilson, whose kindness is as broad as her intelligence is deep. Thanks, too, to Lydia Grunstra, editorial assistant, for dependability—along with the convincing pretense she didn't mind my innumerable calls.

Finally, there's my husband, last because not least. This book is dedicated with love to him. Besides, he's the very best reader—of all things—I know. And then some.

Index

A NOTE ON THE TYPE

This book was set in Adobe Garamond. Designed for the Adobe Corporation by Robert Slimbach, the fonts are based on types first cut by Claude Garamond (c. 1480–1561). Garamond was a pupil of Geoffroy Tory and is believed to have followed the Venetian models, although he introduced a number of important differences, and it is to him that we owe the letter we now know as "old style." He gave to his letters a certain elegance and feeling of movement that won their creator an immediate reputation and the patronage of Francis I of France.

Composed by North Market Street Graphics, Lancaster, Pennsylvania
Printed and bound by Berryville Graphics, Berryville, Virginia
Designed by Robert C. Olsson